Early Education Curriculum

Custom Edition

Hilda L. Jackman
Gary D. Borich | James M. Cooper, Editor

CENGAGE
Learning·

Australia • Brazil • Japan • Korea • Mexico • Singapore • Spain • United Kingdom • United States

**Early Education Curriculum
Custom Edition**

Senior Project Development Manager:
Linda deStefano

Market Development Manager:
Heather Kramer

Senior Production/Manufacturing Manager:
Donna M. Brown

Production Editorial Manager:
Kim Fry

Sr. Rights Acquisition Account Manager:
Todd Osborne

EARLY EDUCATION CURRICULUM: A CHILD'S CONNECTION TO THE WORLD, FIFTH EDITION
Jackman
© 2012, 2009 Cengage Learning. All rights reserved.

AN EDUCATOR'S GUIDE TO FIELD-BASED CLASSROOM OBSERVATION
Borich | Cooper, editor

© 2004 Cengage Learning. All rights reserved.

For product information and technology assistance, contact us at
Cengage Learning Customer & Sales Support, 1-800-354-9706
For permission to use material from this text or product,
submit all requests online at **cengage.com/permissions**
Further permissions questions can be emailed to
permissionrequest@cengage.com

This book contains select works from existing Cengage Learning resources and was produced by Cengage Learning Custom Solutions for collegiate use. As such, those adopting and/or contributing to this work are responsible for editorial content accuracy, continuity and completeness.

Compilation © 2013 Cengage Learning
ISBN-13: 978-1-285-54956-9

ISBN-10: 1-285-54956-2

Cengage Learning
5191 Natorp Boulevard
Mason, Ohio 45040
USA
Cengage Learning is a leading provider of customized learning solutions with office locations around the globe, including Singapore, the United Kingdom, Australia, Mexico, Brazil, and Japan. Locate your local office at:
international.cengage.com/region.

Cengage Learning products are represented in Canada by Nelson Education, Ltd.
For your lifelong learning solutions, visit **www.cengage.com/custom.**
Visit our corporate website at **www.cengage.com.**

Printed in the United States of America

EARLY EDUCATION CURRICULUM
A CHILD'S CONNECTION TO THE WORLD

EARLY EDUCATION CURRICULUM

A CHILD'S CONNECTION TO THE WORLD

FIFTH EDITION

Hilda L. Jackman

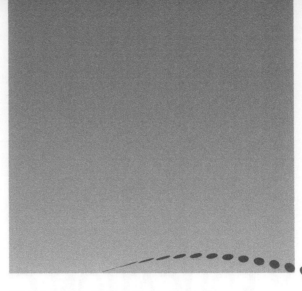

This book is lovingly dedicated

to my granddaughters Cambria and Rachel

and to the men in my life:

my husband, Phil, my sons,

Stephen and Larry,

my brother, Rick . . .

and, as always, to my nephew Jared.

Brief Contents

Contents

PART TWO
Discovering and Expanding the Early Education Curriculum

Preface

Research confirms the value of early education for young children. Our early childhood profession continues to guide us with effective teaching applications, position statements, and developmentally appropriate practices. With this in mind, we must help our students and developing professionals to make informed decisions about curriculum content. We should listen to the children and concentrate our efforts on their development, needs, abilities, interests, and cultural and linguistic diversity as we plan our early childhood curriculum. With this fifth edition of *Early Education Curriculum: A Child's Connection to the World*, my focus remains the same: *the children* and the dedicated early childhood professionals who contribute daily to improve the lives of children everywhere.

Philosophies of This Book

In response to the needs of our students, the early childhood profession is dedicated to discovering new knowledge through research and new professional positions, and to establish inclusiveness, equity, quality, and diversity through developmentally appropriate practices. It is the role of early education curriculum to integrate these insights into each classroom, from infancy through the early primary years.

In this fifth edition, these interconnecting philosophies are underscored.

- The first advocates that curriculum be *child centered and child initiated*, that it is sensitive to, and supportive of, the development of young children, individually and in a group, emphasizing acceptance of all children. This includes acceptance of diversity, individual differences, and special needs.
- The second focus is on the *curriculum* itself, which provides for all of a child's development by planning developmentally appropriate experiences that build upon what children already know and are able to do. New findings inform us even more about early cognitive, physical, social, and emotional development. These facts help us to make connections as to how we teach and how children learn.
- The third philosophy of this text is to encourage children to *learn by doing*. This encourages experimentation, self-control, and the building of a positive self-image ("I can do it myself!").
- The fourth recognizes the importance of *cultural context* in the development and learning of young children. Growing up as members of families and communities, children come to us with rich backgrounds of cultural experiences. Now, more than ever, the curriculum should promote opportunities to support a child's cultural and linguistic diversity.
- The fifth belief advocates developing a learning environment that invites *creativity*. This provides opportunities for unevaluated discovery and activity, while promoting acceptance and respect for one another's creations. This also helps one to develop an awareness that the process of creative thinking is complex.
- The sixth concept involves reciprocal *relationships between teachers and families*. Positive communication between home and school is crucial to providing a consistent and beneficial experience for young children.

- The seventh philosophy recommends that curriculum facilitate *physical activity and play* by integrating movement within activities throughout the day. Each of these philosophies allows children to make choices and is nourished by play. With less time and opportunity for children to play, it is critical for us to encourage and support play in all our early childhood programs.

Intended Audience

This book is designed for a beginning student as well as an experienced teacher looking for current early childhood philosophies, research, curriculum resources and activities, fresh ideas, and insights. It can be used by those in two-year college or four-year university early education curriculum courses, graduate classes, mini/fast-track courses, distance learning, and workshop/seminar courses for continuing education of teachers. It is also applicable for students working toward the Council for Professional Recognition (CDA) credential or any professional working with children and families.

Text Organization

The text is divided into two parts. Part One, "Creating the Environment That Supports Curriculum and Connects Children," presents the elements of the foundation of early education curriculum.

- Chapter 1, "Starting the Process," presents early childhood historical information, learning, and developmental theories of early childhood education; strategies for organizing instruction, with emphasis on developmentally, individually, culturally, and creatively appropriate practices; the importance of play in the lives of children; the planning process; ways to include diverse ages, groupings, and individual differences; and communication with parents.
- Chapter 2, "Creating Curriculum," offers examples of curriculum models and programs; explains the process of curriculum development, including multicultural, anti-bias, and special needs considerations; presents developmentally appropriate early learning environments, indoor and outdoor; develops concepts and skills, themes, specific lesson and activity plans, guidance guidelines, and a plan of observation, assessment and evaluation based on different ages and individual differences. These two chapters form the foundation for the remaining chapters.

Part Two, "Discovering and Expanding the Early Education Curriculum," explores each curriculum area in depth, taking into consideration the individual child, group of children, the process of setting up appropriate environments, special subject content, and integration of all curricula. Each chapter presents developmentally appropriate activities for each age group and encourages self-esteem and creativity development.

- Chapter 3 "Language and Literacy"
- Chapter 4 "Literature"
- Chapter 5 "Math"
- Chapter 6 "Science"
- Chapter 7 "Social Studies"
- Chapter 8 "Art"
- Chapter 9 "Sensory Centers"
- Chapter 10 "Music and Movement"
- Chapter 11 "Puppets"
- Chapter 12 "Dramatic Play"

All chapters of the text are separate and complete, while at the same time connecting to other chapters to form curriculum as a whole for children from infancy to age eight. This allows each instructor to use the chapters in any sequence. This approach is helpful in meeting the individual needs of the teacher, the student, and ultimately the children.

New to This Edition

FULL COLOR EDITION

For the first time, the text is printed in full color throughout to offer a more visual presentation and to help students understand the concepts presented in this book. This fifth edition also offers multicultural photographs taken on location at diverse early childhood settings (centers and schools), new color illustrations, and an attractive and professional design that says to students "This book is for you!"

UPDATED NATIONAL STANDARDS

National standards in literacy, mathematics, science, social studies, and music are included as they relate to specific standards. Essential recommendations and position papers of the National Association for the Education of Young Children (NAEYC) and Association of Childhood Education International (ACEI) are included as well. In particular, NAEYC's Code of Ethical Conduct defines core values that are deeply rooted in the field of early childhood care and education.

NEW NAEYC PROFESSIONAL STANDARDS

A correlation chart to the latest NAEYC Standards for Early Childhood Professional Preparation is found on the inside covers of this book. The chart identifies how the content in this text aligns with these standards.

UPDATED AND REVISED COVERAGE

Building upon the foundations of previous editions, this text has been thoroughly updated and revised with several chapters reorganized for better comprehension. New coverage of key topics include:

- **Guidance Guidelines:** Renewed emphasis has been placed on guidance techniques, both verbal and nonverbal. A new discussion on bullying, which is currently affecting young children, is included in Chapter 2. There are helpful "Tips for Teachers" throughout the text.
- **Technology:** New information of developmentally appropriate ways to use different types of technology as part of the early childhood curriculum are included throughout this edition.
- **Nutrition and Obesity Prevention:** New coverage of this increasingly important topic is provided in Chapters 6 and 9.
- **The Importance of Play, Green Playscapes, and Outdoor Activities:** Coverage of these topics is found in Chapters 1, 2, 6, 7, and 12.
- **Setting Up the Writing Environment:** Increased attention to writing, and the teaching of reading and writing together appears in Chapters 3 and 4.
- **Cultural and Linguistic Diversity:** Expanded emphasis on the importance of culturally relevant curriculum appears throughout this book.

NEW AND IMPROVED CHAPTER PEDAGOGY

Chapter-opening objectives have been rewritten to provide a clear road map of the major topics in each chapter. New Reflective Review Questions appear at the end of each chapter and can be used for homework activities and to give students opportunities for reflective thinking.

MORE FEATURES TO LOOK FOR

Focus on families that will reinforce the collaborative efforts of families and teachers is stressed in all the chapters. Current and improved children's book lists are included in chapters throughout the text. Expanded information is provided on themes, projects, webs, and developmentally appropriate activities. All of the features in this fifth edition are created to provide a resource of ideas, methods, suggested practices, and guidance goals that will give teachers and students guidelines to create and enrich their own curriculum.

Special Learning Features

This book is designed to help students build knowledge with each chapter. Concepts are introduced in a specific chapter and then reviewed for elaboration and application throughout the text. Topics are approached developmentally and placed appropriately within the curriculum area where students can benefit from their content. Each topic becomes a part of the entire curriculum.

Numerous learning aids appear in the text to help student comprehension. They include:

- **Objectives** at the beginning of each chapter help students focus on key issues and areas of learning.
- **Chapter Overviews** help direct the student's attention to what the chapters encompass.
- **DAP marginal icons** visually highlight concentrated coverage that relates to developmentally appropriate practice.
- **"Why I Teach Young Children" boxes** offer first-hand stories from early childhood educators.
- **Children's Book Lists** give readers a head start at building their book libraries and ideas for building curriculum.
- **Observation, Assessment Strategies, and Evaluation** guidelines, forms and suggestions provide effective tools to be used throughout the early childhood curriculum.
- **Activity Plan Worksheets** provide detailed lesson plans with guidance tips and assessment strategies.
- **Afterview** sections sum up the chapter concepts.
- New **Reflective Review Questions** stimulate reflective thinking and analysis of chapter content.
- **Key Terms** are listed at the end of each chapter and defined in an end-of-text Glossary.
- **Explorations** activities suggest opportunities for field observations and out-of-class projects.
- **Additional Resources and References,** including print and website resources, aid students in obtaining additional information on chapter topics.
- Updated **Appendixes** are designed to give teachers practical information that can be used across the curriculum. New Appendix A, "My Self," is an integrated curriculum theme with developmentally appropriate activities. Appendix B, "Resources for Teachers," and Appendix C, "Professional Organizations," include updated and new useful resources.

Ancillaries

The following ancillary materials are available to accompany the fifth edition of *Early Education Curriculum: A Child's Connection to the World.* Many thanks to Jennifer E. Berke, Ph.D., Director of the Early Childhood Program, Mercyhurst North East, for preparing the Instructor's Manual, Test Bank, PowerPoint® lecture slides, and website materials for the fifth edition.

INSTRUCTOR'S MANUAL AND TEST BANK

The updated Instructor's Manual provides chapter summaries, chapter competencies, extensive topics for class discussions, additional student exploration activities, selected websites, and activity sheets or checklists. It also includes guidelines for student observation of and participation with children. The addition of corresponding NAEYC standards for each chapter is new to the Instructor's Manual.

The updated test bank includes true/false, multiple-choice, matching, short-answer, and essay questions for each chapter.

POWERLECTURE W/EXAMVIEW CD

This one-stop digital library and presentation tool includes preassembled Microsoft® PowerPoint® lecture slides that can be used with this book. In addition to a full Instructor's Manual and Test Bank, PowerLecture also includes ExamView® testing software with all the test items from the Test Bank in electronic format, enabling you to create customized tests in print or online, and media resources in one place including an image library with graphics from the book itself and TeachSource Video Cases.

WEBTUTOR TOOLBOX™

WebTutor™ Toolbox for WebCT™ or Blackboard® provides access to all the content of this text's rich Book Companion Website from within your course management system. Robust communication tools—such as course calendar, asynchronous discussion, real-time chat, a whiteboard, and an integrated e-mail system—make it easy for your students to stay connected to the course.

EDUCATION COURSEMATE

Cengage Learning's Education CourseMate brings course concepts to life with interactive learning, study, and exam preparation tools that support the printed textbook. Access an integrated eBook, learning tools including flashcards and practice quizzes, additional forms, room diagrams, activity plans, puppet patterns, and sample lesson plans, plus Web activities and exercises, weblinks, videos including the TeachSource Video Cases, and more in your Education CourseMate, through www.CengageBrain.com. The accompanying instructor website offers access to password-protected resources such as an electronic version of the Instructor's Manual and PowerPoint® slides. Instructors can access the CourseMate website by visiting cengage.com/login.

Acknowledgments

My sincere and heartfelt appreciation is extended to the very special friends and colleagues who, throughout the years, have inspired me through friendship, devotion to children, and commitment to students and the community. These generous friends, who have spent their professional lives pursuing all that is best for children and who are most willing to share their expertise, are **Janet Galantay, Jo Eklof, Bea Wolf, Bonnie Rubinstein, Nita Mae Tannebaum, Salwa Sinnokrot, Kathy Burks, Judy Goodman, Beverly Carpenter, Barbara Batista,** and **Marie Basalone;** the early childhood teachers at Temple Shalom Preschool in Dallas, who welcomed me into their classrooms to observe and record the developmentally appropriate activities occurring daily with their delightful children and who shared their personal experiences for "Why I Teach Young Children." A big thank you goes to the teachers at the Collin College Child Development Lab School in Plano, who also contributed their personal experiences for "Why I Teach Young Children." I'd also like to thank **Carmen Osbahr ("Rosita")** and **Caroll Spinney ("Big Bird"** and **"Oscar the Grouch")** of *Sesame Street,* who contributed to Chapter 11 and who are unique individuals who bring exceptional joy to children every day. THANK YOU!

Special recognition must go to my son, **Laurent Linn,** for his illustrations throughout all five editions, which demonstrate his love and understanding of children and give depth and meaning to what I have tried to communicate in words.

My most special gratitude, love, and respect go to my husband, **Phil Jackman,** my "in-house editor" for his love, patience, encouragement, and participation in this project. As always, without him, this book would not have been possible.

To my son, **Stephen Linn,** who is always there with much-needed additional support and reassurance, a heartfelt "thank you."

With deep appreciation and many thanks to professors, students, and colleagues who continue to use *Early Education Curriculum* in their classes.

To **Lisa Mafrici,** Senior Development Editor extraordinaire, for encouragement and guidance and to **Chris Shortt, Linda Stewart,** the rest of the team at Cengage Learning, and **Kristin Jobe** of Elm Street Publishing Services, a huge THANK YOU.

And finally, I appreciate the time, effort, and contributions that the following reviewers have given me:

Gayle Bortnem, Northern State University

Susan Eliason, Anna Maria College

Maureen Gerard, Arizona State University, Tempe

Sherry Granberry, Wayne Community College

Jennifer Koel, Carroll University

Hadiyah Miller, Portland Community College

Alan Weber, Suffolk County Community College, Selden

Carrie Whaley, Union University

About the Author

Hilda Jackman brings to her authorship a background rich in experience and achievement as it relates to the education of young children. Long before she became professor emerita with the Dallas County Community College District and Professor-Coordinator of the Brookhaven Child Development/Early Childhood program, she pioneered children's television programming in the Dallas–Fort Worth area as a writer, producer, and puppeteer.

She went on to earn a master of science degree in Early Childhood Education at The University of North Texas and for many years was a teacher of young children (infants through kindergarten) and director of several Child Development programs. During her twenty years at Brookhaven, besides writing curriculum and teaching, she helped establish the first Certificate Program in Texas to train nannies, developed multicultural/anti-bias curriculum courses, and consulted with business and industry on child care. Since retiring from college teaching, Hilda continues to act as a mentor, presents workshops and staff development seminars, consults, and stays active in professional organizations. She is also the author of *Sing Me a Story! Tell Me a Song! Creative Thematic Activities for Teachers of Young Children* (2005), also published by Cengage Learning.

© Cengage Learning

Hilda is the proud mother of two adult sons and the very proud grandmother of twin granddaughters, shown with her in this photo.

To the Student

WELCOME to the world of early education. I am glad you are here. Our profession needs caring, committed individuals to encourage and support children through their early years.

Each of you has a different reason for wanting to be in an early childhood classroom. Some of you are just beginning. Others are experienced teachers. No matter what type of program or what age group you work with, it is important that you understand the development of young children, help them connect with the changing world of their families, and promote developmentally appropriate practices in early education environments and curriculum.

This text is designed to be a practical guide to help you develop a curriculum appropriate for young children. By learning about theory and developmentally appropriate activities found in this text, you can develop your own curriculum.

Use the resources on the Education CourseMate website which includes a demo of Inspiration® 8 software to get started creating curriculum webs. Write lesson and activity plans using the forms on the website as well. I hope these resources will help you develop appropriate curriculum for young children. Your experiences with young children are most important to your academic and professional development. I encourage you to use this curriculum text to stimulate your own creativity and knowledge of children. Mix and match, add to, and redesign the ideas and activities presented. Take the time to enjoy the uniqueness of each individual child, as well as the group of children, as they explore and interact with the curriculum.

It is also important to remember that professional ethics and confidentiality are concerns that are inseparable from all observation, assessment, and participation activities. It is crucial that you deal with each child and/or adult without prejudice or partiality and refrain from imposing your own views or values upon children or adults.

I hope this text will prove helpful to you as you strive to make a difference in the lives of young children and their families. We are all in this profession together, and, like the children, we too are growing and developing.

—HILDA L. JACKMAN

PART ONE

Creating the Environment That Supports Curriculum and Connects Children

I stand outside the classroom, teacher,
At the doorstep to the world.
I want to see it all,
To hear and feel and taste it all.
I stand here, teacher,
With eager eyes and heart and mind.
Will you open the door?

—Janet Galantay
Reprinted with permission

chapter
1

Starting the Process

Objectives

After Studying This Chapter, You Should Be Able To:

- Discuss why historical information is important to early childhood education.

- Define and outline the theories of Erik Erikson, Jean Piaget, Lev Vygotsky, and Howard Gardner.

- Identify developmentally appropriate practice, including child development and learning, individual strengths, interests, and needs.

- Explain why prekindergarten and kindergarten programs are considered an important foundation for four- and five-year-olds today.

- Recognize the importance of social and cultural identity in the development of young children.

- Discuss the importance of play in the lives of young children and describe the developmental stages of play.

- Explain the process of planning and implementing a developmentally appropriate environment for young children, including communicating with parents.

Overview

Please think of the children first. If you ever have anything to do with their entertainment, their food, their toys, their custody, their day or night care, their health care, their education—listen to the children, learn about them, learn from them. *Think of the children first.*

These words of Fred Rogers (2003) are meaningful to us as students and teachers. Children must be at the center of all we do. As adults who genuinely care about them, we should honor the uniqueness of each child and the child's family. Give them teachers with commitment, training, experience, and knowledge about child development and how children learn. "Children come into the world eager to learn. . . .There can be no question that the environment in which a child grows up has a powerful impact on how the child develops and what the child learns" (Bowman, Donovan, & Burns, 2000). Research is showing in early and elementary education that "all children can and will learn when educational communities are ready for them. . . .This requires a commitment that makes explicit the responsibility of education professionals to broaden their repertoires and hone their skills to create classrooms in which all children maximize their potential" (New, Palsha, & Ritchie, 2009).

As you read this chapter, its focus on making the environment and the curriculum child-centered will be apparent. This chapter extends this philosophy by studying historical aspects of early education, learning and developmental theories, developmentally appropriate practices (DAP), social and cultural contexts, importance of play for young children, curriculum planning, early childhood schedules and routines, and communicating with parents. Also included are ideas to enhance instruction and activities that respect a child's culture, language, and learning style. Additionally, in-depth attention should be paid to language development, cognition, physical development, and social and emotional competence.

Children's eagerness to learn about the world and their place in it should be nurtured by a supportive environment and teachers who understand their development.

Early Childhood Education

The field of early care and education has changed profoundly in the last decade. In some ways many longtime early childhood educators find it nearly unrecognizable. Standards and guidelines abound. Increasing numbers of early childhood programs are required to address state early learning standards (or guidelines) that will soon include three-year-olds and next, perhaps, even infants and toddlers. (Freeman & Feeney, 2006)

With this in mind it's important to look back at our profession to see how changes produced new ways to help children and families. Historical information gives us an opportunity to see how past generations viewed children and their acquisition of knowledge, based on religious, ethnic, political, and economic pressures of the times. Almy (cited in Greenberg, 2000) believes that "it's most important not to leave behind everything we already know about children as we go on learning new things. . . . New knowledge should build on prior knowledge, not erase and replace it."

Exploring the storied history and philosophy of early childhood education presents us with significant individuals and far-reaching developments that have impacted and influenced our thinking. "The history of early childhood education is like a tapestry—woven of many influences. . . . The ingredients that early childhood educators consider essential today—that care and education are inseparable, that teaching practices are developmentally appropriate, and that adequate funding is critical for success—all stem from historical events and people" (Gordon & Browne, 2011). Figure 1–1 is a timeline of historical highlights of early childhood education.

The professional organizations mentioned in the timeline are all striving to improve the field of early childhood education. Their efforts emphasize the importance of **advocacy**, an attitude that encourages professionals, parents, and other caring adults to work together on behalf of young children.

> Advocacy takes place at many different levels—from families who approach their child's teacher or program director to ask for an arts program, to teachers who approach the school board to request additional funding for books to help their students meet rigorous academic standards, to groups of business leaders who form coalitions with early childhood caregivers, to professional associations who create opportunities to educate policymakers about a particular problem that young children face. At all levels of advocacy, caring adults take a stand on behalf of children. (Robinson & Stark, 2002)

It is also essential for teachers to use every resource available to them, such as having membership in local, state, and national professional organizations. Attending meetings, workshops, and conferences offers opportunities for networking with other teachers. Reading professional journals keeps one up-to-date with current information as well. (See Appendix C for a comprehensive listing of professional organizations and their websites.)

LEARNING AND DEVELOPMENTAL THEORIES OF EARLY CHILDHOOD EDUCATION

As we continue to consider the influences that have contributed to the field of early childhood education, it is beneficial to review the **developmental theories** that examine children's growth, behavior, and process of learning. A **theory** refers to a systematic statement of principles and beliefs created to explain a phenomenon or group of facts that have been repeatedly tested or are widely accepted. "The foundation for all curricula is developmental theory or beliefs about how children develop and learn. These beliefs guide our view of teaching and supporting children as learners" (Catron & Allen, 2008).

Following are a few of the most influential theories and information about the individuals who developed them.

PSYCHOSOCIAL THEORY.   *Erik Erikson* (1902–1994), over five decades, made significant contributions to psychoanalysis, personality theory, education practice, and social anthropology.

Erikson recognized growth and development to be continuous throughout an individual's life. His eight **psychosocial** stages describe the interaction between an individual's social-emotional condition and the interpersonal environment. His stages of development help us understand the importance of allowing children to play out their feelings in an environment of acceptance. The first four stages are relevant to early childhood educators.

1. *Basic Trust vs. Mistrust* (birth to one year). This developmental stage is important to an infant's learning that people can be depended upon and that the child can depend upon himself. Love and acceptance are important for the child to learn that the world is a safe place in which to live. This foundation of trust will be developed if the infant's needs are met. This is observable when the infant babbles, coos, laughs, crawls, pulls up, and is comfortable with the environment.
2. *Autonomy vs. Shame and Doubt* (second year). This stage helps a child develop a basic sense of self-control and independence. The child is growing rapidly. It is significant during this stage that the toddler has opportunities to do things for himself.

---

advocacy An attitude that encourages professionals, parents, and other caring adults to work together on behalf of young children.

developmental theories Principles that examine children's growth, behavior, and process of learning.

theory A systematic statement of principles and beliefs that is created to explain a group of facts that have been repeatedly tested or widely accepted.

psychosocial Erikson's eight stages that describe the interaction between an individual's social-emotional condition and the interpersonal environment.

FIGURE 1–1   Timeline of Early Education Historical Highlights

1900s	In the early 1900s Patty Smith Hill created a curriculum that provided the foundation for kindergartens in the United States. She also founded the laboratory school at Columbia University Teachers College, which became the model for training early childhood educators, and began organizing a professional organization of early childhood educators (Isbell & Raines, 2007).
1910s	The development of the nursery school was conceived by two sisters, Margaret and Rachel McMillan, who first introduced their philosophy to America in 1910 and watched as their "nurture schools" grew. During the 1930s and 1940s nursery schools continued to spread throughout the United States reflecting the principles of a child-centered approach (Gordon & Browne, 2011; Spodek & Saracho, 1994).
1920s	During the 1920s more than one-half the households in the United States had at least one other adult living there besides the two parents, such as an aunt, uncle, or grandparent. At the same time, nursery schools linked to child development and psychology were available, while day nurseries focused on meeting the needs of poor and immigrant families (NAEYC, 2001).
1930s	The Depression of the 1930s produced an economic and social crisis in the United States. Out of this came the Works Progress Administration (WPA) nurseries. These child care facilities were designed "to develop physical and mental well-being of preschool children in needy unemployed families or neglected or underprivileged homes.... Almost two thousand WPA nursery schools were in operation by 1935" (NAEYC, 2001).
1940s	In response to World War II in the 1940s, the Lanham Act was passed by Congress to allow public funds to be used for child care. Nursery schools and day care centers were opened as millions of women went to work for the war effort. All families, regardless of income level, were eligible. Between 1943 and 1945, Kaiser Shipyards used Lanham Act funds to open child care centers for its employees. These became the largest centers in the country and functioned 24 hours a day all year long, offering quality care and comprehensive services to families. Once the war ended, however, the workers left and the centers closed (Gordon & Browne, 2011; NAEYC, 2001; Spodek & Saracho, 1994).
1960s	The rest of the twentieth century represents an active time in the formation of early childhood education (Essa, 2011). In the early 1960s the High/Scope Perry Preschool Project began. This program was originally designed to serve at-risk children from impoverished neighborhoods. It has developed into a landmark long-term study of the effects of high quality early care and education on low-income three- and four-year-olds (Wiekart & Schweinhart, 2007). (More information on this can be found in Chapter 2 of this text.)
1964	NANE, the National Committee on Nursery Schools (established in 1929), became the National Association for the Education of Young Children (NAEYC). NAEYC membership has grown to over 100,000 and continues to grow.
1965	As part of the Economic Opportunity Act's "War on Poverty," Project Head Start was funded to counteract the effects of poverty among children. (More information on this can be found in Chapter 2 of this text.)

(continued)

FIGURE 1–1   (continued)

1970	The National Black Child Development Institute (NBCDI) in Washington, DC, was created. This nonprofit organization has continued to provide and support programs, workshops, and resources for African-American children, their parents, and communities (NBCDI, 2002).
1971	The Child Development Associate (CDA) was created as part of the U.S. Department of Health, Education, and Welfare. In 1985 NAEYC became the administrator of the CDA Credential. Then, in 1989, the Council for Professional Recognition, as a separate organization, assumed the responsibility for the CDA Credential (NAEYC, 2001).
1973	The Children's Defense Fund in Washington, DC, was founded by Marian Wright Edelman. Currently, this organization's website gives early childhood professionals, advocates, families, and every member of our society essential information that can make a difference in children's lives (Children's Defense Fund, 2007).
1975	The Education for All Handicapped Children Act was passed by Congress. In 1997, this Act was reauthorized and strengthened to include early childhood services. It is now known as the Individuals with Disabilities Education Act (IDEA). (More information on this act can be found in Chapter 2 of this text.)
1982	The National Association for Family Day Care was established. As the profession of family child care changed, so did the focus of this organization. In 1994, it became the National Association of Family Child Care (NAFCC), with the goal of providing assistance for developing leadership, professionalism, and quality for family child care providers. NAFCC has published Quality Standards for NAFCC Accreditation. (NAFCC, 2002).
1984	NAEYC published its first position statement defining and describing developmentally appropriate practice in early childhood programs serving young children. In 1986 the statement was expanded and released in book form. This was revised in 1996 and 2009 in response to new knowledge and the rapidly changing context in which early childhood programs operate (Copple & Bredekamp, 2009). More information on DAP can be found throughout this text.
1992	The Association of Childhood Education International (ACEI) celebrated its centennial, having begun as the International Kindergarten Union in 1892 in Saratoga Springs, NY. ACEI is now the oldest professional association of its type in the United States with members in over 40 countries (ACEI, 2002).
2000s	In the last part of the twentieth century Reggio Emilia, an educational approach established in Italy in 1946, has influenced early childhood thinking around the world (Essa, 2011; Gordon & Browne, 2011). (More information about this curriculum model can be found in Chapter 2 of this text.)
2001	The No Child Left Behind Act of 2001, signed into law on January 8, 2002, has placed far more emphasis than ever before on program accountability and assessment. At the core of the NCLB Act are a number of measures designed to drive broad gains in student achievement and to hold states and schools more accountable for student progress in grades 3–8 (Essa, 2011; United States Department of Education, 2001).

This is observable when a toddler feeds and dresses himself, and generally has an "I can do it myself" attitude that is accepted and reinforced by the adults in his life.

3. *Initiative vs. Guilt* (three to five years). During this stage of life, children are becoming interested in exploring and are ready to learn. Children need to express their natural curiosity and creativity through opportunities in the environment. This stage of development is observable by watching how children demonstrate body control and motor skills while riding a tricycle and running. Initiative is reinforced when children are given freedom to engage in fantasy and other dramatic play activities. Social roles in dramatic play continue to show children identifying with adult roles. They enjoy making adult situations conform to their notion of the ways things are. Roles can be reversed and new roles can be tried out.

4. *Industry vs. Inferiority* (6 to 11 years). At this stage of life, the child is ready for challenges of new and exciting ideas. The child needs opportunities for accomplishment in physical, intellectual, and social development. This is observable by watching older children during creative dramatics activities. They improvise their own dialogue, play the scenes, and evaluate the results. This is informal and demonstrates individual and group imagination, problem solving, critical thinking, and cooperation with others.

The last four of Erikson's (1963) psychosocial stages follow the individual from the teenage years through the rest of the life span.

5. *Identity vs. Role Diffusion* (12 to 18 years).
6. *Intimacy vs. Isolation* (young adulthood).
7. *Generative vs. Stagnation* (adult middle years).
8. *Ego Integrity vs. Despair* (older years).

> Erik Erikson's work and wisdom have profoundly shaped the field of child development. What comes through most strongly in Erikson's work is his empathy and respect for children—and for their parents and the societies in which they live....Erikson's work has more than withstood the test of time; it continues to inform and inspire the fields of child development, life-span studies, anthropology, history, sociology, and others. (Stott, 1994)

COGNITIVE DEVELOPMENT THEORY.   **Cognitive development** is described as the intellectual acquisition of information, facts, or data and includes reasoning, understanding, problem solving, and language acquisition. Much of what is known about cognitive development has come from the work of *Jean Piaget* (1896–1980). He introduced the study of children's thinking and was the first to describe how each child creates his own mental image of the world, based on his encounters with the environment. "Piaget suggested that a child's system of thought develops through a series of stages common to all children of all cultures" (Spodek & Saracho, 1994).

A careful consideration of Piaget's concepts, along with close observation of children, helps teachers provide appropriate environments and experiences. Piaget believed that **learning**, or change in behavior, occurs as children construct knowledge through active *exploration* and *discovery* in their physical and social environments. He also asserted that learning happens through the dual process of assimilation and accommodation.

Assimilation is a process that occurs when a child handles, sees, or otherwise experiences something. (See Figure 1–2.) He adds this information to existing schemata.

A **schema** (plural, *schemata*) is an integrated way of thinking or of forming mental images. "We constantly create, refine, change, modify, organize, and reorganize our schemata" (Essa, 2011).

Accommodation occurs when a schema is modified as a result of experience. (See Figure 1–3.)

Equilibrium happens when there is a balance between assimilation and accommodation. According to Piaget, this continues until new information causes the process to begin again (Piaget, 1926).

cognitive development The mental process that focuses on how children's intelligence, thinking abilities, and language acquisition emerge through distinct ages; Piaget's study of children's thinking, involving creating their own mental images of the world, based on encounters with the environment.

learning Change in behavior or cognition that occurs as children construct knowledge through active exploration and discovery in their physical and social environments.

assimilation Piaget's process of cognitive development, which occurs when a child handles, sees, or otherwise experiences something.

schema An integrated way of thinking or of forming mental images.

accommodation Piaget's theory of modification of existing cognitive information. Cognitive schemes are changed to accommodate new experiences or information.

equilibrium A balance of one's cognitive schemes and information gathered from the environment; assimilation and accommodation.

Assimilation

FIGURE 1–2
Example of Piaget's concept
of assimilation.

A child has a concept for "ball" that fits all the balls the child has seen so far.

This child sees a football for the first time.

The football matches the "ball" concept, so the child adds it to the concept of ball.

Accommodation

FIGURE 1–3
Example of Piaget's concept
of accommodation

A child has a concept for "dog" that includes all animals with four legs.

This child sees a cat for the first time and calls it a "dog." When the child realizes the cat does not fit "dog," he may create a new category for "cat."

As the child matures, the process of accommodation will enable him to create a super-concept, or a broader category, which would include both the cat and the dog—such as "animal."

Cognitive development is divided into four stages by Piaget:

1. *Sensorimotor stage* (birth to about two years). During this time children grow from helpless newborns to children who are able to walk and talk. Infants begin learning through the use of their sensory system and reflexes. Gradually these reflex behaviors are changed and new behaviors develop. Babies enjoy repeating behaviors. Often something unexpected happens during repetitions and a new behavior is discovered. They then try to repeat the new behavior. Throughout the sensorimotor stage, infants are developing the concept of **object permanence**. According to Piaget's theory, a baby thinks that objects, including people, cease to exist the moment he stops seeing them. For example, if an object that has left returns, the infant considers it a new, though identical, object. As he develops, however, he begins to search for the missing object or person.

2. *Preoperational stage* (about two to seven years). Piaget believed that children's thinking during this stage is **egocentric**, that is, they think about the world only in relation to themselves. Along with this, the preoperational period is characterized by **symbolic thinking**. Symbols or mental representations are formed, allowing children to solve problems by thinking before acting. They begin to enjoy pretend play. As thinking emerges as verbal expression, language acquisition proceeds rapidly. Intellectual and language development blend together. The more a child uses all his senses and broadens his experiences, the more he has to think and talk about.

3. *Concrete Operations stage* (about 7 to 12 years). During this stage children are developing concepts of numbers, relationships, and processes, as well as thinking problems through mentally. Logical thought requires actual physical objects or events. Piaget explains,

> Manipulation of materials is crucial. In order to think, children in the concrete stage need to have objects in front of them that are easy to handle, or else be able to visualize objects that have been handled and that are easily imagined without any real effort.
>
> Teachers should select materials that make the child become conscious of a problem and look for the solution himself. And, if he generalizes too broadly, then provide additional materials where counter-examples will guide him to see where he must refine his solution. It's the materials he should learn from. (Piaget, 1961)

4. *Formal Operations stage* (12 years through adulthood). The individual reasons logically and moves from concrete manipulations to abstract thinking. The ability to hypothesize and think about what might be rather than what is usually occurs during this stage.

Each of these stages involves a period of formation and a period of attainment. Each builds on the development of the preceding stage. Teachers and parents should provide appropriate environments and ask appropriate questions, moving from simple to complex and from concrete to abstract.

For exploration of other Piagetian concepts, see the section on play in this chapter and Chapter 5, "Math."

SOCIOCULTURAL THEORY.   Over the past decade, the educational theories of Russian developmental psychologist *Lev Vygotsky* (1896–1934) have been translated and made available in the United States. Vygotsky asserted that a child's learning development is affected by his culture, including the culture of family environment. He focused on the whole child and incorporated ideas of culture and values into child development, particularly the development of language and self-identity. "Because Vygotsky regarded language as a critical bridge between the sociocultural world and individual mental functioning, he viewed the acquisition of language as the most significant milestone in children's cognitive development" (Berk & Winsler, 1995). It is from language that the child constructs reality.

object permanence A mature state of perceptual development. According to Piaget's theory, a baby thinks that objects, including people, cease to exist the moment he stops seeing them. An older child starts to search for the missing object or person.

egocentric A stage when individuals think about the world only in relation to themselves.

symbolic thinking The formation of symbols or mental representations, allowing children to solve problems by thinking before acting.

Much of what a child learns comes from the culture around him. In addition, interactions with teachers, parents, and more experienced peers contribute significantly to a child's intellectual development. Vygotsky believed that a difference exists between what a child can do on his own and what he can do with help. Vygotsky called this difference the **zone of proximal development**. In other words, the "zone" is the range of potential each child has for learning, with that learning being shaped by the social environment in which it takes place. This potential ability is greater than the actual ability of the individual when the learning is facilitated by someone with greater expertise (Wertsch, 1991).

According to Vygotsky (1978), "children first develop lower mental functions such as simple perceptions, associative learning, and involuntary attention. Through social interactions with more knowledgeable others, such as more advanced peers and adults, children eventually develop higher mental functions such as language, logic, problem-solving skills, moral reasoning, and memory schemas."

For teachers of young children, the zone of proximal development may be used to provide a theoretical base from which to understand cooperative learning. In the culture of the classroom, this can translate into small-group instruction in which students work together to solve problems. This approach encourages children to *construct* their own knowledge while engaging in activities that build and rebuild, or construct, ideas based on previous experiences. In addition, the role of the teacher "includes both designing an educative environment and collaborating with children by scaffolding their efforts to master new skills. From this perspective, Vygotsky-based teaching is *activity centered*, since it emphasizes creating opportunities for children to engage in culturally meaningful opportunities with the guidance of teachers and peers" (Berk & Winsler, 1995). This kind of teaching emphasizes **scaffolding**, which occurs as the teacher (adult) continually adjusts the level of help offered in response to the child's level of performance. Scaffolding can help instill the skills necessary for independent problem solving in the future. "To facilitate scaffolding experiences, Vygotsky, like Piaget, believed that teachers need to become expert observers of children, understand their level of learning, and consider what steps to take given children's individual needs" (Dodge, Colker, & Heroman, 2008).

For exploration of another major Vygotskian concept, see the section on play in this chapter.

MULTIPLE INTELLIGENCES THEORY. *Howard Gardner* (1943–), a psychologist and professor at Harvard Graduate School of Education, is also a researcher who has studied the mind and brain with particular reference to learning and education. He has challenged the view that something called "intelligence" can be objectively measured and reduced to a single number or "IQ" score. In fact, Gardner's definition of intelligence is multifaceted. His ongoing research, Project Zero, at Harvard suggests that an individual is not born with all of the intelligence he will ever have. Rather, intelligence can be learned and improved upon throughout a lifetime.

Gardner identifies his cross-cultural exploration of the ways individuals are intelligent as **multiple intelligences**. His philosophy also proposes that one form of intelligence is not better than another; all are equally valuable and viable. Gardner's theory also suggests that "it is important for teachers to take the individual differences in children very seriously.... Understanding of the intelligences should be linked with a curriculum focused on understanding where children are able to apply what they have learned in new situations" (Wortham, 2010).

The following explanations of Gardner's Multiple Intelligences are adapted from Gardner (1983, 1993), Hine (1996), Nicholson-Nelson (1998), and Wilkins (1996).

1. *Verbal-Linguistic Intelligence:* From the babbling of infancy to the toddler's simple sentences, the ability to use language and words continues to grow throughout early childhood. Whether written or spoken, it develops with sensitivity to the order

zone of proximal development The range of potential each child has for learning, with that learning being shaped by the social environment in which it takes place.

scaffolding The adjustable support the teacher offers in response to the child's level of performance.

multiple intelligences Gardner's theory, which proposes that one form of intelligence is not better than another; all eight are equally valuable and viable.

and rhythm of words. The learning environment should include a language and print-rich classroom with opportunities for reading, writing, speaking, and creative writing. Children who are accomplished in verbal-linguistic abilities enjoy reading, writing, telling stories, playing word games, and communicating effectively.

2. *Logical-Mathematical Intelligence:* Starting with babies inspecting their world and continuing on to toddlers recognizing similar characteristics of objects, the ability to categorize and to use numbers, patterns, sequencing, and cause and effect to solve problems develops and grows throughout early childhood. The learning environment should offer opportunities to relate math and science to real-life situations while providing activities that make math and problem solving fun, relevant, and challenging. Children who are adept in logical-mathematical abilities learn through asking questions in a logical manner, making connections between pieces of information, exploring, and developing strong problem-solving and reasoning skills.

3. *Musical-Rhythmic Intelligence:* Starting with the prenatal awareness of noises and rhythms and, later, imitations of sounds and pitches, a child soon develops the ability to produce and recognize simple and then complex songs and to perceive pitch, tone, and rhythmic pattern. He becomes immersed in the music and sounds of the world. The learning environment should provide opportunities for singing, listening, movement activities, sound awareness, and musical instrument appreciation and practice, while emphasizing cultural awareness through music. Children who are strong in musical-rhythmic abilities think in rhythms and melodies; enjoy listening to music, singing, dancing, humming, and playing musical instruments; and exhibit a sensitivity to environmental sounds.

4. *Visual-Spatial Intelligence:* From the infant's ability to discriminate among the faces around him to the toddler's first steps, the facility to perceive the visual world with a great deal of understanding continues throughout early childhood. Creating visual images with shape, color, and form opens up new understanding. The learning environment should be a graphic-rich classroom that encourages opportunities for visual processing as well as thinking and planning in three dimensions. Children who are highly capable in visual-spatial abilities think in images and pictures; like to draw, design, and create things; and often see things from different points of view.

Creating visual images with shape, color, and form opens up new understanding for young children.

A child's interest in seeing, smelling, and touching a flower demonstrates the ability to recognize important distinctions in the natural world.

5. *Bodily-Kinesthetic Intelligence:* From an infant's looking for and grasping different objects to the strength and coordination of an older child, the ability to use the body for self-expression develops through information gained from muscles, sensations, reflexes, coordination, and movement. The learning environment should reflect opportunities for physical challenges throughout the day, not just outdoors but indoors as well. The classroom should facilitate tactile experiences and the use of manipulatives in math, science, and language arts. Children who are resourceful in bodily-kinesthetic abilities learn through moving, doing, and touching. They enjoy physical activities, such as those involving hand-eye coordination and hands-on experiments.

6. *Interpersonal Intelligence:* From an infant's bonding with his parents to the meaningful relationships with others outside the family, the ability to understand other people and their actions, moods, and feelings develops as young children deal with person-to-person relationships and communication. The learning environment should provide opportunities for children to relate to others by cooperatively participating, sharing, negotiating, and communicating in groups or with individuals. Children who show interpersonal abilities learn through listening, cooperating in shared projects, demonstrating leadership skills, seeing things from other perspectives, and organizing and negotiating group activities.

7. *Intrapersonal Intelligence:* Starting with a baby's realization that he is a separate person from his mother, his ability to understand himself grows throughout early childhood and at the same time helps him to identify his feelings, moods, strengths, and weaknesses. The learning environment provides plenty of space and time for self-reflection and working alone in a safe environment that encourages appropriate risk taking. Children who are accomplished in intrapersonal abilities learn through understanding their role in relationship to others, have a strong sense of self, and enjoy setting goals, planning, and working on self-paced projects, all of which involve having choices.

8. *Naturalist Intelligence:* A child's interest in seeing, smelling, and touching a flower, reacting to the sound of a bird, or playing with the family pet demonstrates his ability to recognize important distinctions in the natural world. The learning environment should offer opportunities for exploring outdoors and bringing the outdoors inside by providing field trips, books, visuals, objects, and materials relating to the natural world. Children who show naturalist abilities learn through observing nature, being sensitive to all features of the natural world, and enjoying books, visuals, and objects related to the world around them.

The Multiple Intelligences theory is a useful model for developing a systematic approach to nurturing and teaching children and honoring their individual needs and strengths within a classroom setting. As teachers of young children, "we should help students to understand the world around them—the physical world, the biological world, the social world, the world of personal experiences" (Gardner, 2001).

The concept of multiple intelligences does not require discarding previous ideas. Teachers can supplement current appropriate activities with new ideas that will reach even more of their students. In fact, Gardner contends that teachers need to guide students into using their combination of intelligences to help them learn whatever they want to learn, as well as what teachers and society believe they have to learn.

The multiple intelligences approach provides a framework for us to identify how children learn to build on their strongest assets, to help them become more intelligent by exposing them to a variety of ways of learning, to better individualize for their interests and needs, and to use teaching strategies that make learning more appropriate, successful, and enjoyable for all children. Examples of using Gardner's Multiple Intelligences theory in the classroom can be found in the curriculum content chapters of this book. For further application of this and other theories, see the curriculum models and programs in Chapter 2.

Developmentally Appropriate Practice

Developmentally appropriate practice (DAP), introduced more than 20 years ago by the National Association for the Education of Young Children (NAEYC), defines and describes what is developmentally appropriate for young children in childhood programs serving children and families, birth through age eight. NAEYC's current position statement "reflects both continuity and change in the early childhood field.... DAP requires both meeting children where they are—which means that teachers must get to know them well—and enabling them to reach goals that are both challenging and achievable" (Copple & Bredekamp, 2009).

Developmentally appropriate early education recognizes the social nature of learning, and it values cultural and linguistic diversity. Also included is the understanding that children need an environment that allows them to interact at their own level of development with a minimum amount of adult direction. A strong emphasis is placed on children learning to think critically, work together cooperatively, and solve problems. Because developmentally appropriate classrooms are not only age/stage appropriate but also individually appropriate, they will not all look alike. In order to enhance the quality of educational experiences for young children, developmentally appropriate practice is a framework for continuing to meet the diverse needs of all the children in our care. Kostelnik, Soderman, and Whirin (1999) explain, "The essence of developmental appropriateness is not simply what we do, but how we think—how we think about children and programs; what we value children doing and learning; how we define effectiveness and success." Throughout this book, developmentally appropriate practice will be discussed in relation to chapter content.

developmentally appropriate practice The curriculum planning philosophy expressed by NAEYC defines and describes what is developmentally appropriate for young children in childhood programs serving children and families, birth through age eight.

CHILD DEVELOPMENT AND LEARNING

First, let us focus on what is developmentally occurring with young children, the variations in their development, and their developmental process for learning. **Development**, in relationship to early childhood education, can be defined as systematic and adaptive changes in the body and mind based on sequence and patterns

development Systematic and adaptive changes in the body and mind.

In a developmentally appropriate environment, teachers develop relationships with children that are consistent and supportive.

Infants are actively involved with their world.

of growth and maturity (Charlesworth, 2011; Swim & Watson 2011). "Developmental trends occur in a similar fashion for all children. This does not, however, imply uniformity. On the contrary, individual differences due to genetic and experiential variations and differing cultural and social contexts have strong influences on development" (Bowman, Donovan, & Burns, 2000).

As we think about development and learning, it's important to remember that the areas of physical, intellectual, emotional, and social growth may overlap, even as age groups may. "Children's development and learning in one domain influence and are influenced by what takes place in other domains" (Copple & Bredekamp, 2009).

INFANTS. The early months of infancy are crucial in creating a foundation for all areas of development. Infants are actively involved with their world. They explore with all their senses (seeing, hearing, tasting, smelling, and feeling) and are acutely aware of their environment. Infants and the significant adults in their lives establish very special relationships that involve getting to know each other and adjusting to each other. What adults do can modify how infants behave (Swim & Watson, 2011).

Infants learn about their surroundings by physically moving around, through sensory exploration, and by social interaction. Gallagher (2005) continues this thought, "A typically developing child needs frequent opportunities for movement and interactions with people and objects. Fixed pieces of equipment such as playpens, high chairs, and bouncy seats provide little opportunities for varied and active experiences." As they are learning, the sight of the adult who feeds, holds, and comforts the infant is reinforced when that adult shows pleasure in caring for the infant. Emotional attachment develops as the child learns to expect that special person to make him feel good. The infant then seeks more contact with that adult. Even after crawling and walking have begun, the child frequently asks to be held. Honig (2002) explains further, "Research and clinical findings over the past decades confirm the connection to later emotional well-being of a secure attachment between each baby or young child and a warm, stable adult."

A happy moment between baby and caregiver — just look at those faces!

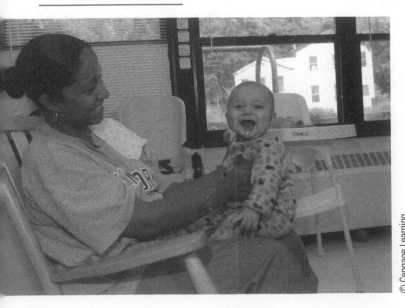

As teachers of the youngest children, we have a significant responsibility to the infants in our care. "Like dancers, the infant care teacher and infant synchronize their interactions, each responding to and influencing the other. The challenge is doing this with three, four, or five infants at once" (Zero to Three, cited in Copple & Bredekamp, 2009).

As families and infants enter child care it is most important that a solid relationship is built between each of them and the teachers. "Infant care teachers need to observe and learn from the experiences, knowledge, culture, and childrearing beliefs of family members" (Zero to Three, cited in Copple & Bredekamp, 2009). Daily communication between teachers and families is crucial. It fosters involvement and support and offers a culturally sensitive approach to dealing with caregiver/family member conflicts.

Decades of research by neuroscientists and others have found what we in early childhood education have been saying for years, namely, that a child's foundation for behavior and learning for the rest of his life is laid in the early years. The better the child's early nurturing, the better are his prospects for future development (Gabbard & Rodrigues, 2002).

Although it has been known for many years that most of a child's brain *cells* are formed in the prenatal stage, the brain is not completely developed at birth. Research indicates that important *neural (nerve) connections,* transferring information from one part of the body to another, occur and strengthen after birth. "To a certain extent, formation of the connections depends on exposure to our environment—through relationships and experiences" (Zero to Three, 2009). Research continues to refine scientists' insight into brain development, such as "understanding of developmental periods of dramatic brain growth, information about regions of brain growth, and details on brain functions. We know that the brain has growth spurts during certain times of development, such as early childhood and adolescence" (Schore, cited in Gallagher, 2005). By using new research techniques, scientists are discovering that babies are very aware of the world around them—more so than adults.

An important aspect of a young child's continued mental development is **self-regulation**, his growing natural ability to exercise control over physical and emotional needs in the face of changing circumstances. Shankoff and Phillips (cited in Gillespie & Seibel, 2006) believe that "the growth of self-regulation is a cornerstone of early childhood development and is visible in all areas of behavior." For example, by using consistent routines with infants, you are helping young children learn to self-regulate within the structure of a nurturing environment.

All of this, along with new and continuing exploration of brain function, from birth through the first 10 years of life, helps us understand more about the relationship between *nature* and *nurture.* "How humans develop and learn depends critically and continually on the interplay between nature (an individual's genetic endowment) and nurture (the nutrition, surroundings, care, stimulation, and teaching that are provided or withheld). Both are crucial" (Shore, 1997).

self-regulation A child's natural ability to exercise control over physical and emotional behavior in the face of changing circumstances.

self-help skills In early childhood, a child's ability to care for himself, such as dressing, feeding, and toileting.

TODDLERS. Children ages 16 to 36 months grow and learn rapidly. "The toddler is a dynamo full of unlimited energy, enthusiasm, and curiosity.... The toddler begins this period with the limited abilities of an infant and ends with the relatively sophisticated skills of a young child" (Allen & Marotz, 2010). This is a time for development in mobility, autonomy, and **self-help skills**, the child learning what can be done for himself by his own effort or ability, such as washing and drying hands, and feeding or dressing himself. "Perhaps one of the best ways to nurture good feelings about self is to encourage toddlers' already strong interest in doing things for themselves" (Gestwicki, 2011). They try many tasks that are often too difficult for them. At this time, the safety of the environment is critical. As a teacher, you should expect this newfound independence and allow for trial and error. Children love to repeat and use these new skills over and over again (Essa, 2011).

Toddlers are fascinated by words. As these active children become more independent, "their speech is limited, but their understanding of communication is beyond their speech.... Toddlers learn a great deal through imitation and especially from observing demonstrations accompanied by a verbal explanation" (Charlesworth, 2011). Chapter 3 emphasizes language and literacy development.

© Cengage Learning

This is a time for rapid development as a toddler learns self-help skills.

Young toddlers are busy exploring the world from their new, upright vantage point.... Once toddlers master walking, their motor skills grow by leaps and bounds. They learn to jump, tiptoe, march, throw and kick a ball, and make a riding toy go by pushing with their feet or perhaps even by pedaling. (Copple & Bredekamp, 2009)

Young children are full of
enthusiasm and high energy.

Appropriate teaching techniques require the building of trust between the children and the teacher, and between the children and their environment. This can develop only if there are safe, consistent, and child-centered surroundings that encourage success for both children and teachers. There is more information on developmentally appropriate learning environments in Chapter 2.

THREE- AND FOUR-YEAR-OLDS. The preschool years are special. "Now the preschool year or years before kindergarten are recognized as a vitally important period of learning and development in their own right, not merely as a time for growth in anticipation of the 'real learning' that will begin in school" (Copple & Bredekamp, 2009). Three-year-olds have a distinct period of development with added skills and challenges. They are anxious to try new things but get frustrated when they cannot do what they set out to do. With an enlarged vocabulary, they engage in more extensive conversations; and although they can play along with other children, they often find it difficult to cooperate in a game. The three-year-old enjoys fantasy and imaginative play, although the difference between fantasy and reality is not always clear.

Generally, the child's interest has become more sustained, but repetition is still important. He begins to enjoy looking at picture and story books, and has a better understanding of verbal cues. There is a continued need for exploration and experimentation. Teachers of three-year-olds need to respect their growing skills and competencies without forgetting just how recently they were acquired.

Four-year-olds are full of enthusiasm and high energy. The ability to do more things without help, along with increased large and small muscle control, allows the children to develop a greater self-confidence. Children of this age enjoy learning to do new things and like to have an adult's attention. At the same time, because they are so eager to learn and learn so fast, they can use a higher level of language (more and bigger words) than they really understand.

The four-year-old has broader and more diverse interests. He begins to understand his environment and benefits from field trips. His interest in others prompts him to ask searching questions about people and their relationships with others. He is interested in the letter carrier, the firefighter, the police officer, and everyone around him who performs various services.

The child is conscious of make-believe and begins to "be" other people or animals. He gradually builds a background for imaginative play. Essa (2011) explains, "Peers are becoming important. Play is a social activity more often than not, although fours enjoy solitary activities at times as well." As a teacher, when you interact with these active children, you will be bombarded with questions. Sometimes they will insist on trying to do things that are too difficult for them. Help them find many things that they *can do*. Observe the children and set up the environment to match their skills. More information on play is provided later in this chapter.

Prekindergarten programs that support effective teaching practices and opportunities for four-year-olds are available in approximately 40 states. Many school buildings have been created specifically for eligible preschoolers, which fills an expanding need for low-income children with disabilities (NIEER, 2009).

Teachers are encouraged to take a developmental perspective in implementing the Prekindergarten Guidelines. Teachers should "meet children where they are" and provide information and activities at a level that children can readily understand and engage with. This will mean building children's skills over time, working toward the school readiness outcomes step by step as children demonstrate mastery of beginning level skills. Teachers should have the outcome skills in mind, but will need to prepare children to meet these goals through scaffolding experiences and activities that are appropriate for individual children's current developmental levels and capabilities. (University of Texas System & Texas Education Agency, 2008)

FIVE-YEAR-OLDS. Five-year-olds are becoming more social; they have best friends and also enjoy playing with small groups of children. Their use of language, especially vocabulary, continues to grow along with the understanding that words can have several meanings. Experimentation with language is evident at this age.

Fives are more self-controlled, but family and teacher have the most influence on how they behave. They take responsibility very seriously and can accept suggestions and initiate action. With the increase of large and small muscle abilities, five-year-olds can run, jump, catch, throw, and use scissors, crayons, and markers easily.

Exploration of the environment is important to these children. They are learning about the world and their place in it. They act on their own and construct their own meaning. Each of their actions and interpretations is unique to them. They are developing an understanding of rules, limits, and cause and effect.

"Kindergarten children are undergoing profound transformations—in their capacity to think rationally, persist in the face of challenge, use language, adeptly suppress impulse, regulate emotion, respond sympathetically to others' distress, and cooperate with peers" (Berk, cited in Gullo, 2006). Children of this age also believe in their own abilities to master new skills.

The number of children attending child care and preschool programs continues to grow. Standards, guidelines, and academic demands continue to increase as well. These factors "have greatly transformed the role of kindergarten. More than a preparatory year—about 95 percent of kindergarten age children in America are enrolled in some type of kindergarten program" (NCES, 2008). Kindergarten is now generally considered the first year of school (Tomlinson, cited in Copple & Bredekamp, 2009). The teacher's role is to create the appropriate environment, encourage curiosity, and learn along with the children. Kindergarten has to be a place for *every* child to grow and learn, in every dimension of development (Graue, cited in Gullo, 2006).

© Cengage Learning

Young children playing outside can practice their newly discovered physical skills in a safe environment.

SIX-, SEVEN-, AND EIGHT-YEAR-OLDS. "The primary grades are a time for children to shine. They gain increasing mastery in every area of their development and learning. They explore, read, and reason, problem solve, communicate through conversations and writing, and develop lasting friendships" (Tomlinson, cited in Copple & Bredekamp, 2009). The body growth of six-to-eight-year-olds is slower but steadier, and physical strength and ability are important to them. Their motor coordination begins to improve, and playing games that require eye-hand coordination, such as baseball, becomes easier at this age. These children are able to think and learn in more complicated ways, both logically and systematically. They are developing the ability to concentrate their attention for longer periods of time.

The language and communication development in these primary-grade children is dramatic. They move from oral self-expression to written self-expression. They are becoming more independent and have strong feelings about what they eat, wear, and do. The six-to-eights are extremely curious about their world, and they actively look for new things to do, see, and explore. They are making new friends, and these peers play a significant role in their lives as they take into consideration the viewpoints and needs of others. "In order to make friends, certain skills are necessary: the ability to understand that others have different points of view, the ability to recognize that others have separate identities, and the ability to understand that each encounter is part of a relationship" (Click & Parker, 2009).

Seefeldt and Barbour (1998) extend this thought, "They're developing the ability to see things from another perspective and are able to be more empathetic. At the same time, they're very sensitive and their feelings get hurt easily." As these primary-age children try out their new independence, they need teachers' and parents' guidance, affection, encouragement, and protection as much as, if not more than, ever.

Including families in the program will encourage their support and provide you more insight into their children. Communication with family members is discussed throughout this book. Suggestions on how teachers can work in partnership with families and communities are discussed later in this chapter.

NOTE: The additional readings, resources, websites, and references listed at the end of this chapter offer additional in-depth information on the developmental process.

INDIVIDUAL STRENGTHS, INTERESTS, AND NEEDS

 Now let us examine individual appropriateness, which involves adapting an early childhood environment to meet a child's cultural and linguistic needs, as well as his individual strengths and interests. This includes providing each child with the time, opportunities, and resources to achieve individual goals of early education. The teacher should support a positive sense of self-identity in each child. It is important for a teacher to provide many opportunities for teacher-child interaction. However, individual appropriateness should not result in the lowering of expectations.

Individual appropriateness requires the teacher/adult to try to put herself in the place of the child in the classroom. It means asking questions, such as:

● What would make the environment comfortable for infants, toddlers, preschoolers, kindergarteners, early school-age children, or children with ability differences?
● What kind of adult support would be appropriate?
● What is planned to encourage parent participation?
● What is being done to develop a child's sense of trust, sense of self, and feeling of control over the environment?
● What should be happening to encourage positive self-concept development?
● What would I see if I were at the child's level?
● What kind of activities, supplies, and materials should be available?
● What is occurring to support a child's need for privacy or "alone time"?

In answering these questions, take into account what is known about how young children develop and learn, and match that to the content and strategies they encounter in early education programs. Being reflective and carefully listening to what children have to say is also important. As we continue through this book, the activities discussed in all curriculum areas will be developmentally appropriate, with an emphasis on meeting the needs of *all* children.

It is important to include opportunities for interacting with the child's family as well. Communication between home and school offers consistent and beneficial experiences for young children and their families.

Gestwicki (2011) says it clearly:

Developmentally appropriate practice does not approach children as if they were equal members of an age grouping, but as unique individuals....This knowledge [of specific uniqueness] primarily comes through relating and interacting with children and also their parents, who are important resources of knowledge about their children. Developmentally appropriate practice is based on parents' active involvement both as resources of knowledge and as decision makers about what is developmentally appropriate for their children.

By observing young children, gathering data about who they are, and developing awareness of their strengths, interests, and needs, you are starting to build a child-centered curriculum. You will discover that children benefit from being treated as individuals while being part of a class community. For curriculum and environments to be developmentally appropriate, they must be individually appropriate. We will study observation, assessment strategies, and evaluation of curriculum and environments in the ensuing chapters of this book.

SOCIAL AND CULTURAL CONTEXTS

Early childhood educators recognize the importance of cultural context in the development and learning of young children. Growing up as members of a family and community, children learn the rules of their culture—explicitly through direct teaching and implicitly through the behavior of those around them (Copple & Bredekamp, 2009). "Rules of development are the same for all children, but social contexts shape children's development into different configurations" (Bowman, 1994). To affirm these differences and similarities, an early education environment should encourage the exploration of gender, racial, and cultural identity, developmental abilities, and disabilities.

> Culturally appropriate practice is the ability to go beyond one's own sociocultural background to ensure equal and fair teaching and learning experiences for all. This concept developed by Hyun, expands DAP to address cultural influences that emphasize the adult's ability to develop a multiple/multiethnic perspective. (Hyun, cited in Gordon & Browne, 2011)

To eliminate **bias**—any attitude, belief, or feeling that results in unfair treatment of an individual or group of individuals—and to create an **anti-bias** atmosphere, you need to actively challenge prejudice and stereotyping. **Prejudice** is an attitude, opinion, or idea that is preconceived or decided, usually unfavorably. **Stereotype** is an oversimplified generalization about a particular group, race, or sex, often with negative implications (Derman-Sparks & A.B.C. Task Force, 1989). Literature by de Melendez & Beck (2010) explains further: "The Derman-Sparks antibias model presents and addresses cultural diversity content with an emphasis on promoting fairness and equality. It also refrains from using a tourist-like approach curriculum where the child 'visits' a culture and usually learns about its more exotic details. Such curricula only offer glimpses of cultures contributing little to development of awareness and knowledge about the daily life and problems people face in other cultures." (See Figure 1.4 for anti-bias curriculum goals.)

Early education classrooms today include children with learning, behavioral, or physical disabilities as well as those with multiple and diverse linguistic and cultural backgrounds. Each child *needs* to be appreciated by the teacher and other significant adults. He *needs* to experience an environment that reflects back to the child an awareness of and appreciation for his individual and cultural differences. The results of these positive influences will stay with the child for a lifetime. (Multicultural/anti-bias and special needs considerations are discussed more fully in Chapter 2.)

bias Any attitude, belief, or feeling that results in unfair treatment of an individual or group of individuals.

anti-bias An attitude that actively challenges prejudice, stereotyping, and unfair treatment of an individual or group of individuals.

prejudice An attitude, opinion, or idea that is preconceived or decided, usually unfavorably.

stereotype An oversimplified generalization about a particular group, race, or sex, often with negative implications.

play A behavior that is self-motivated, freely chosen, process-oriented, and enjoyable.

Importance of Play

Play is at the core of developmentally appropriate practice. **Play**—a behavior that is self-motivated, freely chosen, process oriented, and enjoyable—is a natural activity for children. It allows them the opportunity to create, invent, discover, and learn about their world. It provides children joy and understanding of themselves and others.

Every child will be able to

- construct a knowledgeable, confident self-identity.
- develop comfortable, empathetic, and just interaction with diversity.
- develop critical thinking skills.
- develop the skills for standing up for oneself and others in the face of injustice.

FIGURE 1–4
Curriculum goals of the anti-bias approach. Source: Derman-Sparks & the A.B.C. Task Force (1989), cited in de Melendez & Beck (2010), *Teaching Young Children in Multicultural Classrooms* (3rd ed.)

In exuberant outdoor play, there's a lot of learning going on!

Free, spontaneous, and self-initiated play was once the norm for young children. This is no longer the case.…Both parents and early childhood educators, who once encouraged young children to choose their own activities, are being pressured to replace them with adult-directed games, sports, and academic instruction.…*When children have the opportunity to engage in true play, they are learning to consider options and make choices (Elkind, 2002). Why in the world are we trying to teach the elementary curriculum at the early childhood level? (Elkind, 2009)*

Children coming to early childhood programs and schools today typically have very little time or opportunity to engage in informal play. Jambor in 2000 stated that "[t]his situation is the result of concerns of neighborhood violence, changing family structures, elimination of recess due to academic pressures, increased vehicle traffic, squeezed residential play space, unsafe and unchallenging playgrounds, and an increase in sedentary lifestyle brought on by TV, videos, and, most recently, computers." Now we can add video games, iPods, cell phones, and other new devices to the mix.

With less time and opportunity for children to play, it is crucial for those of us in early childhood education to keep focused on what we can do to encourage and support play in our daily programs. As with all aspects of early childhood growth and development, young children go through a series of stages in the development of play. Each new experience offers opportunities for play exploration. Some types of play are characteristic of children at identifiable stages, but children can use many of these stages in varying degrees of sophistication as they get older.

DEVELOPMENTAL STAGES OF PLAY

Children's observable behaviors that reflect social development and participation in play were first identified by Mildred Parten in 1932. She provided this landmark study that is still considered valid today (Essa, 2011; Gestwicki, 2011; Miller & Almon, 2009; Sluss, 2005). These stages of social play are described as follows.

Unoccupied behavior usually occurs during infancy and early toddlerhood. A child occupies himself by watching anything of momentary interest. Sometimes the child may not appear to be playing at all.

Onlooker play is sometimes observed in young toddlers or in children introduced to new situations. This play focuses on the activity rather than the environment. Onlookers place themselves within speaking distance of the activity. Although passive, they are very alert to the action around them.

Solitary play surfaces first for a toddler. The child actually engages in play activity alone at home but is within "earshot" of mother or another adult. In an early education setting, the child plays independently without regard to what other children are doing.

Parallel play can be observed in the older toddler and young three-year-old. A child this age is playing for the sake of playing. This child is within "earshot" and sight of another child and can be playing with the same toy but in a different way. Parallel play is the early stage of peer interaction, but the focus is on the object rather than another child.

Associative play finds the three- and four-year-old playing with other children in a group, but he drops in and out of play with minimal organization of activity. Two or three children use the same equipment and participate in the same activity, but each in his own way.

unoccupied behavior Refers to a child (infant or toddler) who occupies himself by watching anything of momentary interest.

onlooker play The play of young children introduced to new situations that focuses on an activity rather than the environment.

solitary play Independent play behavior of a child without regard to what other children or adults are doing.

parallel play Observable play in the older toddler and young three-year-old that emphasizes being near another child while playing with an object rather than playing with a child.

associative play An activity of a three- or four-year-old child playing with other children in a group; the child drops in and out of play with minimal organization of activity.

Cooperative play is organized for some purpose by the four-year-old and older child. This type of play requires group membership and reflects a child's growing capacity to accept and respond to ideas and actions not originally his own. Group play (social play) is the basis for ongoing relationships with people and requires sharing of things and ideas, organizing games and activities, and making friends. Another aspect of cooperative play is the emphasis on peers and moving away from the importance of adults in the life of a child. The six- to eight-year-old extends cooperative and symbolic play to include detailed planning and rule making. Leadership roles begin to emerge as play becomes serious.

According to Maxim (1997),

> The patterns of play enjoyed in infancy develop into new patterns as children grow older and participate in play experiences. But the earlier patterns do not disappear as new behaviors emerge, and the new patterns are not just enhancements of the earlier ones. They bring maturity to children's play as new experiences are encountered.

THEORISTS AND PLAY. Erik Erikson (1963) emphasized the importance of play in helping children to develop cooperative relationships and gain mutual trust. He believed that children develop their "self-esteem and sense of empowerment by allowing them mastery of objects" (Tsao, 2002). Hughes (1999) explains further that Erikson thought "play can also have an ego-building function since it brings about the development of physical and social skills that enhance a child's self-esteem."

© Cengage Learning

Introduce activities and materials appropriate for each child's age and stage of development.

According to the theory of Jean Piaget (1961), play provides opportunities for many types of learning in young children, with emphasis on developing representational language and thought. Piaget calls play during the first two years of life **practice play or sensorimotor play**, the stage in cognitive development during which the young child learns through repetitive sensory and motor play activities (Smilansky [1968] also calls this type of play *functional.*). In the beginning of Piaget's preoperational stage around the ages of two to four or five, **symbolic play** or **dramatic play** become observable in a young child by the way he spontaneously uses objects, images, and language. The use of the environment represents what is important to the child at that moment. This type of imaginative play allows the child to imitate realities of people, places, and events within his experiences, such as pretending to sleep while patting the baby doll to sleep, drinking "coffee" from an empty cup, and talking to imaginary friends. These imaginary friends allow children to work through anxieties in times of stress or change. In addition, symbolic play and language give children an outlet to practice new physical and mental activities for dealing with the world, such as practicing acceptable behaviors that they see around them so that they can act appropriately in different situations (Krissansen, 2002; Tsao, 2002). Superhero fantasy play is considered a type of symbolic play for a child. (Chapter 12 discusses dramatic play for young children in greater depth.)

Piaget's third stage of play, ages 5 to 11, is characterized by games with rules. The roles of the children are clearly defined, the rules of the game are clear-cut, and behavior imitates reality (Sluss, 2005). With increased maturity, children arrive at a complete understanding of rules both in behavior and thought.

Lev Vygotsky's theory (1978) states that social experiences shape children's way of thinking and that social play offers children a way to interpret the world by focusing on rules that underlie all play activities and social interactions. "Even the simplest imaginative situations created by very young children always proceed in accord with

cooperative play A type of play organized for some purpose by the four-year-old and older child. It requires group membership and reflects a child's growing capacity to accept and respond to ideas and actions not originally his own.

practice play or sensorimotor play The stage in cognitive development during which the young child learns through repetitive sensory and motor play activities.

symbolic play A type of play that allows the child to transfer objects into symbols (things that represent something else) and images into people, places, and events within his experiences. Symbolic play occurs during Piaget's preoperational stage (two to seven years). Superhero fantasy play is considered a type of symbolic play for a young child.

social rules, although these rules are not laid down in advance" (Berk & Winsler, 1995). Vygotsky further states that supportive guidance from adults can "create a scaffold for children's learning, essential for moving children to higher levels of cognitive development" (Isbell & Raines, 2007). Play provides children with important insights into themselves and the communities in which they live.

WHY PLAY IS IMPORTANT

Play	inspires	Imagination
Imagination	inspires	Creativity
Creativity	inspires	Exploration
Exploration	inspires	Discovery
Discovery	inspires	Solving Problems
Solving Problems	inspires	New Skills
New Skills	inspires	Self-confidence
Self-confidence	inspires	Sense of Security
Sense of Security	inspires	More Play

Tips for Teachers

Teachers have a responsibility to help children develop in their use of play. Play, particularly in preschool and kindergarten, needs to be an integral part of the educational process. Play is neurologically important. "Scientific studies of the brain have shown that essential neurological pathways occur in an environment free of stress, fatigue, and anxiety....All of the processes involved in play, such as repeating actions, making connections, extending skills, combining materials, and taking risks, provide the essential electrical impulses to help make connections and interconnections between neural networks, thus extending children's capabilities as learners, thinkers, and communicators" (Miller & Almon, 2009). Also, we should convey to parents the importance of play in the lives of young children. Play can be a valuable means of gauging a child's developmental progress. This information, in turn, can be communicated to parents. Other teacher responsibilities are to:

● Be aware of current research and resources that validate the importance of play.
● Create a positive and safe place for play.
● Provide open-ended play materials.
● Respect and encourage individual differences in play abilities.
● Have patience with children and give them time to learn new play skills.
● Introduce activities and materials appropriate for each child's age and stage of development.
● Take a sincere interest in learning discoveries.
● Provide a play environment that reflects attitudes and values of the surrounding culture.

© Cengage Learning

Observe how each child plays, what each child plays with, and what each child can do.

- Offer appropriate props from a child's culture that will help him make connections as he plays.
- Make available culturally diverse materials for all the children to enjoy and learn from as they play.
- Encourage cooperation.
- Allow children time without scheduled or *externally focused* activity. This offers an opportunity for children to be *internally focused* so that imagination and creativity can take over.
- Take time to listen to children as they play and to observe how each child plays, what he plays with, who he plays with, and what the child *can* do.

The Association for Childhood Education International's (ACEI) position paper, "Play: Essential for All Children," sounds "A Call to Action" (2002). (See Figure 1–5.)

Childhood play has a key role in the development of self and identity. Understanding this, you can help the children in your care develop to their fullest potential. As you continue through the chapters of this text, you will find specific examples of how curriculum planning and implementation influence and strengthen childhood play.

Elkind (cited in Koralek, 2004) explains further:

As teachers of young children, we need to resist the pressures to transform play into work—into academic instruction. We encourage true play by making certain that we offer materials that leave room for the imagination—blocks, paints, paper to be cut and pasted—and that children have sufficient time to innovate with these materials. When we read to young children, we can ask them to make up their own stories or to give a different ending to the story they are hearing. Most of all we need to adopt a playful attitude that will encourage our children to do the same.

A Call to Action

ACEI believes that all educators, parents, and policymakers must take the lead in articulating the need for play experiences in children's lives, including the curriculum. To assume strong advocacy roles, it is imperative that all educators, parents, and policymakers who work with or for children from infancy through adolescence fully understand play and its diverse forms. Equally important is the ability to use that knowledge to achieve what is best for children in all settings. This paper has argued strongly for legitimizing play as an appropriate activity in schools and other educational settings. Therefore, educators, families, and policymakers can and should:

Optimize brain functions by providing rich experiences that include a variety of learning materials, feedback, appropriate levels of challenge, and enough time to process information
Rethink and transform the nature of relationships and communication between adults and children
Make play a fundamental part of every school curriculum
Recognize, respect, and accept play in all its variations as worthwhile and valuable
Balance work and play to ensure that children reap the benefits of intrinsic motivation and experience sheer joy in their endeavors
Balance encouragement and opportunity to fulfill children's natural tendency and need to play; children will find the means to play if the environment affords an opportunity to do so
Create a climate of acceptance by respecting children's play choices, recognizing the cultural context in which play occurs, and providing many play options.

FIGURE 1–5
Reprinted with permission of J. P. Isenberg, N. Quisenberry, and the Association for Childhood Education International. Copyright 2002, Fall, by the Association.

Process of Planning

"There is an old cliché that states, 'If you want something to happen, you must plan for it to happen.' Furthermore, you can add, 'if you want something wonderful to happen with the children in your classroom, then you must make wonderful plans'" (Beaty, 2009).

Planning and scheduling are important in early education classrooms, including those with infants and toddlers. Detailed information about this process will follow in Chapter 2, but it is important to explore several guidelines at this point.

As teachers of young children, consider the following:

goals The general overall aims or overview of an early childhood program.

objectives The specific purposes or teaching techniques that interpret the goals of planning, schedules, and routines. These objectives are designed to meet the physical, intellectual, social, emotional, and creative development of young children.

- Long-range planning includes setting up goals and objectives. **Goals** help describe the general overall aims of the program. **Objectives** are more specific and relate to curriculum planning, schedules, and routines. Seefeldt and Barbour (1998) suggest, "The goals you select will be based on the nature of the children you teach, the values and goals of the community in which the children live, and your own values."
- Goals and objectives should involve developmentally, individually, culturally, and creatively appropriate practices. They should consider the physical, intellectual, social, and emotional development of the children you are teaching.
- The center or school in which you teach can offer a long-range plan that will help you see where you and the children fit into the total program.

SCHEDULES AND ROUTINES

The schedule and routine components of planning can help create a framework of security for young children. "Children who are provided with a predictable schedule and secure environment are more likely to feel confident about exploring their world....Through these explorations, children strengthen their connections to the people and environment around them" (Klein, 2002). The format becomes familiar to them, and they welcome the periods of self-selected activities, group time, outdoor play, resting, eating, and toileting. The establishment of trust that grows between teacher and parent is based on consistent daily contact and the well-being of the children.

schedule The basic daily timeline of an early childhood program.

routines The events that fit into the daily time frame of an early childhood program.

All early childhood programs include basic timelines, curricula, and activities that form the framework of the daily **schedule**. The events that fit into this time frame are the **routines**. The secret of classroom management is getting the children used to routines.

- *Arrival* provides interaction time for the teacher, parent, and child. It also offers a smooth transition from home. This early morning ritual reinforces the trust, friendship, and consistency necessary to young children and their families.
- *Departure* at the end of the day should also offer a relaxed transition for the child and family. This is another time for sharing positive feedback with the parents and provides a consistent routine for the child.
- *Mealtimes and snacks* are some of the nicest moments of the day when teachers and children sit down and eat together. "Snacks and meals are pleasant when they are orderly enough to focus on eating and casual enough to be a social experience" (Feeney, Moravcik, Nolte, & Christensen, 2010). Self-help skills are developed as well when children pour their own juice and milk and help themselves family-style during meals. If children bring food from home, teachers need to give the parents culturally sensitive and nutritionally sound guidance concerning what food is appropriate for the children to bring.
- *Diapering and toileting* are routines that are ongoing throughout the day as needed. The development of toileting skills and handwashing occurs as the young child matures. Adult handwashing and disinfecting diapering surfaces to prevent disease are other important daily routines.

- *Rest or naptime* runs smoothly if teachers make the environment restful, soothing, and stress free. Consistency in how this routine is handled each day provides security to the children. The use of soft music, dim lights, and personal books or blankets encourages children to rest or sleep on their mats or cots. Older children need a short rest-time too. Sitting quietly with a book offers a quiet period during the day.
- *Transitions,* such as cleanup, prepare the environment for the next activity. These times are part of your lesson plan and should be based on the developmental needs of the children. (A complete discussion of transition activities is included in Chapter 2.)
- *Activity time* offers children a large block of time for them to self-select from a variety of activities. "A wide variety of well-planned activities should reinforce the objectives and theme of the curriculum. Each day's activities should also provide multiple opportunities for development of fine and gross motor, cognitive, creative, social, and language skills" (Essa, 2011). In addition, appropriate times for solitary moments, small and large group activities, indoor and outdoor play, along with a balance of active and quiet activities, should be provided.
- *Outdoor activities* offer children many opportunities for growth and learning. To be developmentally appropriate, outdoor play requires the same planning, observation, and evaluation as indoor activities (Brewer, 2001). Large blocks of outdoor time should be scheduled and planned daily.

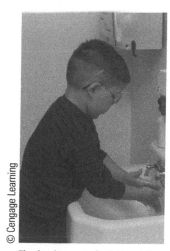

The development of toileting skills and handwashing occurs as the young child matures.

Figures 1–6 and 1–7 are examples of infant and toddler schedules and routines appropriate for early education programs.

Communication with Parents

As previously discussed in this chapter, it is the teacher's responsibility to keep the lines of communication open to families. It is the family's responsibility to be involved with their child's teacher and child care center or school. The following guidelines for developmentally appropriate practice, which offer suggestions on how teachers can work in partnership with families and communities, are adapted from Copple and Bredekamp (2009), and Gestwicki (2011).

1. Success in the education of young children must be built on a foundation of teamwork involving both teachers and families. It is not the teacher telling the parent what needs to be accomplished. It is both teachers and parents cooperatively sharing knowledge and beliefs about educating children and developing common goals. "Partnerships enrich both teachers' and families' relationships with children and bring together their mutual expertise for the benefit of the child" (Keyser, 2006).
2. Families are the primary educators of their own children. It is imperative that teachers respect that crucial role by maintaining open communication with parents, learning from them, and involving them in the education process.
3. There is a learning process that teachers and parents always face in the educational experience. The teacher is learning from the children and

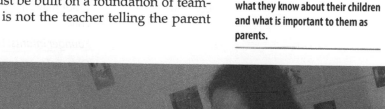

Encourage parents to share with you what they know about their children and what is important to them as parents.

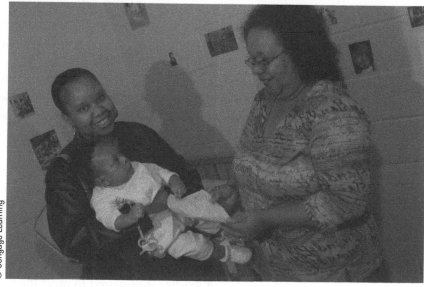

Infants

FIGURE 1–6

Example of a daily flexible schedule and routines for a group of infants.

(3–18 months)
Very Flexible Schedule and Routines

7:00	Morning arrival
	Greet parents and infants
	Put away bottles, food, and diaper supplies
	Spend individual time holding and talking to each child
8:00–9:00	Snack
	Younger infants: Individual cereal, fruit, formula, or juice. Younger infants have individual schedules that include feeding, diapering, and sleeping
	Older infants: Snack, cleanup, diapering, and looking at books
9:00–11:00	*Younger infants*: Individual play on floor, movement exercise, outdoor play, or take a walk in stroller
	Individual formula, juice, or water
	Talk to each child throughout the day
	Child sleeps when tired
	Older infants: Individual or group play, visit toddler playground, walk around center, or play in indoor playroom, read books, dramatic play, manipulatives, art, music and movement, and finger plays
11:00	*Older infants*: Lunch with formula, milk, juice, or water
	Talk to each child
11:30–12:30	Cleanup and prepare for naps: Lights dimmed, soft music, quiet play
12:30–2:00	Naptime
	Talk to and play quietly with infants who are awake
2:00–3:30	Quiet play with books and toys, individual exercises with each child
	Younger infants: Individual formula, juice, or water; soft snacks
	Older infants: snack
3:30–4:30	Individual play, group activities, outdoor play, walks
4:30–5:30	Prepare for going home read books, play on floor, and so on
	Talk to each parent

Diaper changes: As needed after snacks, after lunch, before and after naps, before departure, and changing of soiled diapers anytime during the day.

Note: All times are suggested ones. Times are sensitive to the needs of the children.

their families about the children's world apart from the early childhood setting, while family members are developing knowledge about the principles and techniques of early childhood education. Both are necessary and important. With increased communication, mutual respect emerges.

4. Assessing the child's needs and progress must take into account the child's culture and environment. A teacher's failure to do so is likely to create a breakdown in the educational process.

5. A teacher is prepared to meet the special needs of individual children, including those with disabilities.

Toddlers

(18 months–3 years)
Flexible Schedule and Routines

FIGURE 1–7
Example of a daily flexible schedule and routines for a group of toddlers.

7:00	Morning arrival Greet children and parents, free play (children choose activities)
8:00–8:50	Center activities (art, manipulatives, blocks, dramatic play), spend individual time with each child or small group activity
8:50–9:00	Cleanup with song or poem or special individual time
9:00–9:30	Bathroom time (wash hands, change diapers, toileting, etc.), talk to each child Snack and time for washing hands and face
9:30–10:30	Outdoor play
10:30–10:40	Bathroom time (wash hands, change diapers, toileting), talk to each child
10:40–11:15	Center activities Guided exploration Large group activity of a story, finger plays, language activities, or music
11:10–11:30	Bathroom time, wash hands for lunch, and change diapers if needed
11:30–Noon	Lunch
Noon–12:30	Bathroom time, brush teeth, and change diapers if needed
12:30–2:30	Quiet time with books and music while children finish in bathroom and get on their cots for naptime or rest
2:30–3:00	Wake-up time (put away cots and blankets , toileting, diaper change, washing, put on shoes), free play
3:00–3:15	Snack and clean up
3:15–3:30	Group time with story, song, flannelboard, or other language activity
3:30–4:30	Outdoor play, individual time with each child
4:30–4:45	Bathroom time
4:45–6:00	Quiet activities (books, puzzles, music), individual time with each child, playing games, singing, talking; prepare to go home

Note: This daily schedule is flexible, depending on the needs of the children and the weather.

Times are suggested ones and are compatible with the needs of the children

6. The early childhood teacher is in a unique position to be an advocate by recognizing the special circumstances of a child and his family and to help link up with whatever community resources are available and appropriate for helping them.

Positive communication between home and school is crucial to providing a consistent and beneficial experience for young children. "Just as the teacher deals with each child as a unique individual by employing a variety of teaching guidance methods, so must a flexible approach be maintained in communicating with families to meet their individual requirements" (Essa, 2011).

Prior and Gerard (2007) continue with this thought, "Family involvement has been shown to lead to an increase in children's positive attitudes about school, improved attendance, and better homework habits. Children tend to see a connection between their homes and school when their parents are involved." In the busy and complex lives of parents and teachers alike, this connection between home and school is more important today than ever before.

Teachers and other staff members in early childhood settings should be responsive to cultural and language differences of the children and their families. Affirming and supporting diversity includes being perceptive about differences in caregiving, feeding, and other practices (Wortham, 2010).

Here are some additional suggestions for active communication with parents.

● Provide an infant daily report (Figure 1–8).
● Provide a toddler daily or weekly report (Figure 1–9).
● Create bulletin boards with information regarding health and safety issues, family meetings, guest speakers, community resources and referrals, and tips for parents.

Infant Daily Report

FIGURE 1–8

Example of an infant daily report.

(Morning input from parents to teachers.)

My Name: _____ Date: _____

When I last ate: _____ Food: _____ Formula/Milk: _____

Time I woke up today: _____ Time I went to bed last night: _____ Hours slept: _____

Last diaper change: _____ Medication: Yes _____ No _____ (must sign in)

How I feel today: (circle one)   Great! OK Fussy Not well Feverish Upset tummy
                                     Teething   Diaper rash

Today, my teachers should know: _____

(Teachers, input to parents at end of infant's day)

Feedings: (Time & Description/Amount)	Naps: (Time Slept) (Time)	Changes: (My Diaper D W BM)
_____	_____	_____
_____	_____	_____
_____	_____	_____
_____	_____	_____
_____	_____	_____
_____	_____	_____

My day at school:

Supply needs: (circle one) Clothes Diapers Formula Food Wipes Other:

COMMENTS:

Toddler Daily Report

Child's Name: _____ Date: _____ Teacher: _____

Morning Input from parents to teachers:

(Note: Weekly menu is posted on parent bulletin board.)

MORNING SNACK: Child Ate: well ( ) fair ( )

LUNCH: Child Ate: well ( ) fair ( )

AFTERNOON SNACK: Child Ate: well ( ) fair ( )

NAP: _____

DIAPER CHANGES: TOILET USE:

ACTIVITIES:

ITEMS NEEDED FROM HOME:

COMMENTS:

FIGURE 1–9
Example of a toddler daily report.

- Provide parent letters discussing the goals, objectives, themes, and classroom activities. Offer suggestions for activities parents can do with children at home to extend or emphasize classroom experience.
- Encourage parents to share with you what they know about their children and what is important to them as parents.
- Encourage families to visit the classroom. They should be as welcome as their child.
- Conduct parent-teacher conferences that focus on the accomplishments and needs of the individual child and that ensure privacy and confidentiality for the family.
- Provide multilingual written communications as needed.
- Provide opportunities for parents to volunteer.

Afterview

Many influences, such as historical aspects of early childhood education, developmental theories, insightful educators, developmentally appropriate practices, and ongoing research have impacted and continue to impact our understanding of what is appropriate for the young children in our care. From them we learn that an early childhood program should be based on fulfilling the developmental needs of all children. It should be planned to meet each child's physical, intellectual, social, and emotional growth. Understanding the interrelationships among development, learning, and experiences is essential to providing the highest quality care and education for young children.

The program should be founded on the assumption that growth is a sequential process, that children pass through stages of development, and that children learn and grow through their play and by actively participating in the learning experiences offered. It should adapt to the developmental, individual, and cultural differences of the children.

As teachers, we need to offer age, individually, and creatively appropriate experiences and activities for each child. We should assist each child in growing to his fullest potential by recognizing each stage of development; by providing an environment that encourages the success of each child; by respecting the culture, language, and special needs of each child; and by welcoming family participation in the program.

As we plan for children and their families, we are saying: Welcome! This environment is safe and appropriate. We care, we will listen, we will share, and we will nurture you and recognize your uniqueness.

Reflective Review Questions

1. If you are going to explain what you do in a classroom to families, colleagues, and administrators, then you need to have knowledge about the contributions of early childhood education history and theorists to the profession. Think about how this information gives you the confidence to express that what you know is based on hundreds of years of experience and research.
2. Why is the term *developmentally appropriate practice* a key concept that every person involved in early childhood should learn about, and how would you explain the concept to someone outside the early education field?
3. What are the distinguishing characteristics of Erik Erikson's *psychosocial theory*, Jean Piaget's *cognitive development theory*, Lev Vygotsky's *sociocultural theory*, and Howard Gardner's *multiple intelligences theory*?
4. David Elkind said, "Free, spontaneous, and self initiated play was once the norm for young children. This is no longer the case...." Think back to your childhood. How did you play as a young child? Why was playing important to you? Using the ideas from your reflective thinking about your childhood and the information from this chapter, do you think the nature of play and the opportunity for play has changed? In what way or ways has it changed? If you think play has changed, what might be some explanations for those changes?

Key Terms

accommodation	equilibrium	scaffolding
advocacy	goals	schedule
anti-bias	learning	schema
assimilation	multiple intelligences	self-help skills
associative play	object permanence	self-regulation
bias	objectives	solitary play
cognitive development	onlooker play	stereotype
cooperative play	parallel play	symbolic play
development	play	symbolic thinking
developmental theories	practice play or sensorimotor play	theory
developmentally appropriate practice	prejudice	unoccupied behavior
dramatic play	psychosocial	zone of proximal development
egocentric	routines	

Explorations

1. The number of early childhood programs has increased in response to the growing need for out-of-home care and education during the early years. Identify and discuss the indicators of the current need for child care and education, including

changing lifestyles and family patterns. How is your local community responding to these needs of young children and their families? Give specific examples.

2. Describe what is meant by developmentally appropriate practice. Then, identify and describe at least three specific examples from your experiences and observations of young children that illustrate DAP. In addition, it is important for you to read through NAEYC's updated *Developmentally Appropriate Practice*, 3rd ed. by Copple & Bredekamp (2009), to note the major areas discussed. Share this assignment with your classmates.

3. It is common to hear a comment about a young child such as, "Oh, he's just playing." The implication is that what he's doing is not very important. From what you have learned about the developmental stages of play and from Parten's, Erikson's, and Piaget's theories about the function of play for children, what is incorrect about this type of comment? Why do you think people tend to undervalue play?

4. Select a group of toddlers or kindergarten children. Observe them at play in their classroom and in their outdoor environment. Using the information on *play* in this chapter, describe what activities the children were involved in and what developmental stages of play you observed. How did the teacher plan for the children's play activities? Was it child-directed or teacher-directed play? Would you change anything if you were the teacher? Explain.

5. Visit an early childhood program. Select a classroom and look at its daily schedule and the routines within the schedule. Obtain a copy, if possible. Are the schedule and routines developmentally appropriate? Do they consider the needs of all the children? Explain your answers. Did the teacher follow the posted schedule and routines? What was changed and why? Would you change anything? Why or why not?

Additional Readings and Resources

Carlisle, A. (2001, November). Using the multiple intelligences theory to assess early childhood curricula. *Young Children, 56*(6), 77–83.

Chen, D., Battin-Sacks, P., Prieto, R., & Prieto, C. (2008, May). Rethinking developmentally appropriate practice in a classroom routine. *Young Children, 63*(3), 44–51.

Christian, L. G. (2006, January). Understanding families. *Young Children, 61*(1), 12–20.

Copple, C. (Ed.). (2003). *A world of difference*. Washington, DC: NAEYC.

Dombro, A. L., & Lerner, C. (2006, January). Sharing the care of infants and toddlers. *Young Children, 61*(1), 29–33.

Drew, W. F., Christie, J., Johnson, J. E., Meckly, A. M., & Nell, M. L. (2008, July). Constructive play: A value-added strategy for meeting early learning standards. *Young Children, 63*(4), 38–44.

Edwards, C. P., & Raikes, H. (2002, July). Extending the dance: Relationship-based approaches to infant/toddler care and education. *Young Children, 57*(4), 10–17.

Fromberg, D. P. (2006). Kindergarten education and early childhood teacher education in the United States: Status at the start of the 21st century. *Journal of Early Childhood Teacher Education, 27*(1), 65–85.

Gestwicki, C. (2009). *Home, school and community relations* (7th ed.). Clifton Park, NY: Wadsworth Cengage Learning.

Gonzales-Mena, J. (2005). *Foundations of early childhood education: Teaching children in a diverse society* (3rd ed.). Boston, MA: McGraw Hill.

Gronlund, G. (2006). *Make early learning standards come alive*. St. Paul, MN: Redleaf Press & Washington, DC: NAEYC.

Kersey, K. C., & Masterson, M. L. (2009, September). Teachers connecting with families—In the best interest of children. *Young Children, 64*(5), 34–38.

NAEYC. (2005). *NAEYC early childhood program standards and accreditation criteria: The mark of quality in early childhood education*. Washington, DC: Author.

NAEYC. (2005, March). Why we care about the K in K–12. *Young Children, 60*(2), 54–56.

New, R., & Beneke, M. (2008). Negotiating diversity in early childhood education. In S. Feeney, A. Galper, & C. Seefeldt (Eds.), *Continuing issues in early childhood education* (pp. 303–323). Colombus, OH: Merrill.

Raikes, H. H., & Edwards, C. P. (2009). *Extending the dance in infant and toddler caregiving*. Baltimore, MD: Paul H. Brookes & Washington DC: NAEYC.

United States Department of Education. (2008). *Effects of preschool curriculum programs on school readiness: Report from the preschool curriculum evaluation research initiative*. Washington DC: Author.

Washington, V., & Andrews, J. D. (Eds.). (2010). *Children of 2020:Creating a better tomorrow*. Washington, DC: Council for Professional Recognition & Washington, DC: NAEYC.

Helpful Web Connections

Alliance for Childhood
    http://www.allianceforchildhood.org
Association for Childhood Education International
    http://www.acei.org
Children's Defense Fund
    http://www.childrensdefense.org
National Association for the Education of Young Children
    http://www.naeyc.org
National Association for Family Child Care
    http://www.nafcc.org

National Black Child Development Institute
    http://www.nbcdi.org
National Institute for Early Education Research
    http://www.nieer.org
Southern Poverty Law Center
    http://www.teachingtolerance.org
United States Department of Education
    http://www.ed.gov

References

Allen, K. E., & Marotz, L. R. (2010). *Developmental profiles: Pre-birth through twelve* (6th ed.). Clifton Park, NY: Wadsworth Cengage Learning.

Association of Childhood Education International (ACEI). (2002). On-line at: *http://www.acei.org*

Beaty, J. J. (2009). *Preschool appropriate practices* (3rd ed.). Clifton Park, NY: Wadsworth Cengage Learning.

Berk, L. E., & Winsler, A. (1995). *Scaffolding children's learning: Vygotsky and early childhood education*. Washington, DC: NAEYC.

Bowman, B. (1994). The challenge of diversity. *Phi Delta Kappan, 76*(3), 218–225.

Bowman, B., Donovan, M. S., & Burns, M. S. (Eds.). (2000). *Eager to learn: Educating our preschoolers*. Washington, DC: National Academy Press.

Brewer, J. (2001). *Introduction to early childhood education* (4th ed.). Boston, MA: Allyn & Bacon.

Catron, C., & Allen, J. (2008). *Early childhood curriculum* (4th ed.). Upper Saddle River, NJ: Merrill Prentice Hall.

Charlesworth, R. (2011). *Understanding child development* (8th ed.). Clifton Park, NY: Wadsworth Cengage Learning.

Children's Defense Fund. (2007). On-line at: *http://www.childrensdefense.org*

Click, P. M., & Parker, J. (2009). *Caring for school-age children* (5th ed.). Clifton Park, NY: Wadsworth Cengage Learning.

Copple, C., & Bredekamp, S. (Eds.). (2009). *Developmentally appropriate practice* (3rd ed.). Washington, DC: NAEYC.

de Melendez, W. R., & Beck, V. (2010). *Teaching young children in multicultural classrooms* (3rd ed.). Clifton Park, NY: Wadsworth Cengage Learning.

Derman-Sparks, L., & A.B.C. Task Force. (1989). *Anti-bias curriculum: Tools for empowering young children*. Washington, DC: NAEYC.

Dodge, D. T., Colker, L. J., & Heroman, C. (2008). *The creative curriculum for preschool* (College Edition). Washington DC: Teaching Strategies.

Elkind, D. (2002, November–December). The connection between play and character. *Child Care Information Exchange, 148*, 41–42.

Elkind, D. (2009). *Crisis in the kindergarten*. Online at: *http://www.nkateach.org*

Erikson, E. (1963). *Childhood and society* (2nd ed.). New York: Norton.

Essa, E. L. (2011). *Introduction to early childhood education* (6th ed.). Clifton Park, NY: Wadsworth Cengage Learning.

Feeney, S., Moravcik, E., Nolte, S, & Christensen, D. (2010). *Who am I in the lives of children?* (8th ed.). Upper Saddle River, NJ: Merrill.

Freeman, N. K., & Feeney, S. (2006, September). The new face of early care and education. *Young Children, 61*(5), 10–16.

Gabbard, C., & Rodrigues, L. (2002, May/June). Optimizing early brain and motor development through movement. *Early Childhood News, 14*(3), 32–38.

Gallagher, K. C. (2005, July). Brain research and early childhood development: A primer for developmentally appropriate practice. *Young Children, 60*(4), 12–20.

Gardner, H. (1983). *Frames of mind: The theory of multiple intelligences*. New York: Basic Books.

Gardner, H. (1993). *Multiple intelligences: The theory in practice*. New York: Basic Books.

Gardner, H. (2001). *An education for the future*. Online at: http://www.pz.harvard.edu/

Gestwicki, C. (2011). *Developmentally appropriate practice: Curriculum and development in early education* (4th ed.). Clifton Park, NY: Wadsworth Cengage Learning.

Gillespie, L. G., & Seibel, N. L. (2006, July). Self-regulation, a cornerstone of early childhood development. *Young Children, 61*(4), 34–39.

Gordon, A. M., & Browne, K. W. (2011). *Beginnings and beyond* (8th ed.). Clifton Park, NY: Wadsworth Cengage Learning.

Greenberg, P. (2000, January). What wisdom should we take with us as we enter the new century?—An interview with Millie Almy. *Young Children, 55*(1), 6–10.

Gullo, D. F. (Ed.). (2006). *K today: Teaching and learning in the kindergarten year.* Washington, DC: NAEYC.

Hine, C. (1996, November–December). Developing multiple intelligences in young children. *Early Childhood News, 8*(6), 23–29.

Honig, A. S. (2002*). Secure relationships: Nurturing infant/toddler attachment in early care settings.* Washington, DC: NAEYC.

Hughes, F. P. (1999). *Children, play, and development* (3rd ed.). Boston, MA: Allyn & Bacon.

Isbell, R. T., & Raines, S. (2007). *Creativity and the arts with young children* (2nd ed.). Clifton Park, NY: Delmar Cengage Learning.

Jambor, T. (2000, Fall). Informal, real-life play: Building children's brain connections. *Dimensions of Early Childhood, 28*(4), 3–8.

Keyser, J. (2006). *From parents to partners.* St. Paul, MN: Redleaf Press & Washington, DC: NAEYC.

Klein, A. S. (2002, Spring). Infant & toddler care that recognized their competence. *Dimensions of Early Childhood, 30*(2), 11–17.

Koralek, D. (Ed.). (2004). *Spotlight on young children and play.* Washington, DC: NAEYC.

Kostelnik, M., Soderman, A., & Whirin, A. P. (1999). *Developmentally appropriate programs in early childhood education* (2nd ed.). Upper Saddle River, NJ: Merrill.

Krissansen, D. (2002, November–December). Getting along with imaginary friends. *Child Care Information Exchange, 148,* 51–53.

Maxim, G. W. (1997). *The very young* (5th ed.). Upper Saddle River, NJ: Merrill.

Miller, E., & Almon, J. (2009). *Childhood: A time for play!* Online at: National Kindergarten Alliance: *http://www.nkateach.org*

National Association for the Education of Young Children (NAEYC). (2001). *NAEYC at 75, 1926–2001.* Washington, DC: Author.

National Association for the Education of Young Children (NAEYC). (2002, January). Our promise for children. *Young Children, 57*(1), 56.

National Association of Family Child Care (NAFCC). (2002). On-line at: *http://www.nafcc.org*

National Black Child Development Institute (NBCDI). (2002). On-line at: *http://www.nbcdi.org*

National Center for Education Statistics (NCES). (2008). Online at: *http://www.nces.ed.gov*

National Institute for Early Education Research (NIEER). (2009). Online at: *http://www.nieer.org*

New, R., Palsha, S., & Ritchie. (2009). *Issues in preK–3rd education: A FirstSchool framework for curriculum and instruction.* (#7). Chapel Hill, NC: The University of North Carolina at Chapel Hill, FPG Child Development Institute, FirstSchool.

Nicholson-Nelson, K. (1998). *Developing students' multiple intelligences.* New York: Scholastic Professional Books.

Piaget, J. (1926). *The language and thought of the child.* New York: Harcourt Brace.

Piaget, J. (1961). *Play, dreams and imagination in childhood.* New York: Norton.

Prior, J., & Gerard, M. R. (2007). *Family involvement in early childhood education.* Clifton Park, NY: Delmar Cengage Learning.

Robinson, A., & Stark, D. R. (2002). *Advocates in action.* Washington, DC: NAEYC.

Rogers, F. (2003). *The world according to Mister Rogers: Important things to remember.* New York: Hyperion.

Seefeldt, C., & Barbour, N. (1998). *Early childhood education* (4th ed.). Upper Saddle River, NJ: Merrill Prentice Hall.

Shore, R. (1997). *Rethinking the brain: New insights into early development.* New York: Families and Work Institute.

Sluss, D. J. (2005). *Supporting play: Birth through age eight.* Clifton Park, NY: Delmar Cengage Learning.

Smilansky, S. (1968). *The effects of sociodramatic play on disadvantaged children.* New York: John Wiley & Sons.

Spodek, B., & Saracho, O. N. (1994). *Right from the start: Teaching children ages three to eight.* Boston, MA: Allyn & Bacon.

Stott, F. (1994, September). In memoriam: Erik H. Erikson. *Young Children, 49*(6), 43.

Swim, T. J., & Watson, L. (2011). *Infants and toddlers* (7th ed.). Clifton Park, NY: Wadsworth Cengage Learning.

Tsao, L. L. (2002, Summer). How much do we know about the importance of play in child development? *Childhood Education, 78*(4), 230–233.

United States Department of Education. *No Child Left Behind Act of 2001.* On-line at: *http://www.highscope.org*

University of Texas System & Texas Education Agency. (2008). *Texas pre-k guidelines* (Revised ed.). Austin, TX: Author.

Vygotsky, L. S. (1978). *Mind in society.* Cambridge, MA: Harvard University Press.

Weikart, D. P., & Schweinhart, L. J. (2007). *Perry Preschool project.* On-line at: *http://www.highscope.org*

Wertsch, J. V. (1991). *Voices of the mind.* Cambridge, MA: Harvard University Press.

Wilkins, D. (1996). *Multiple intelligences activities.* Huntington, CA: Teacher Created Materials, Inc.

Wortham, S. C. (2010). *Early childhood curriculum* (5th ed.). Upper Saddle River, NJ: Merrill Prentice Hall.

Zero to Three (2009*). Prenatal development.* On-line at: *http://www.zerotothree.org*

chapter

2

Creating Curriculum

Objectives

After Studying This Chapter, You Should Be Able To:

- Define curriculum and discuss the process of curriculum development.

- Identify and describe early childhood curriculum models and theories.

- Develop awareness of, and sensitivity to, cultural and linguistic diversity and provide a multicultural/anti-bias and inclusive educational environment in which all children can succeed.

- Understand how to guide children from inappropriate behavior to appropriate behavior through the use of developmentally appropriate guidance techniques.

- Observe, plan, and evaluate developmentally appropriate early childhood learning environments, indoors and outdoors, including equipment, materials, and supplies selection.

- Identify the importance of using themes, units, projects, and webs in curriculum development and specify curriculum areas appropriate for early education programs.

- Select and describe ways to use observation, assessment strategies, and evaluation as part of the curriculum development process.

Overview

As we progress through this chapter, focusing on how to create a curriculum appropriate for young children, we once again emphasize the interconnecting philosophies of this text:

1. *Curriculum* is *child-centered* or *child-initiated* while being sensitive to, and supportive of, the development, age, and experiences of young children, individually and in a classroom community.
2. *Curriculum* provides for all of a *child's development* by planning experiences that build upon what children already know and are able to do.
3. *Curriculum* encourages children to *learn by doing* through experimentation, exploration, and discovery while building self-control and a positive self-image.
4. *Curriculum* includes appropriate supports and services for children with *special needs* in an inclusive environment.
5. *Curriculum* promotes opportunities to support each child's diverse cultural and linguistic heritage.
6. *Curriculum* invites *creativity* by providing opportunities for unevaluated discovery and activity while promoting tolerance and respect for each other's creation.
7. *Curriculum* facilitates *physical activity and play* by integrating movement within activities throughout the day.
8. *Curriculum* involves reciprocal *relationships between teachers and families.* Positive communication between home and school is crucial to providing a consistent and beneficial experience for young children.

This chapter illustrates how we develop an early education curriculum and all it encompasses, including classroom management techniques, appropriate practices for inclusion, arrangement of indoor and outdoor space, and selection of equipment and materials. The plan of observation, assessment strategies, and evaluation discussed at the end of this chapter will help determine if developmentally appropriate curriculum goals and content have been achieved.

Curriculum is a multilevel process that encompasses what happens in an early education classroom each day, reflecting the philosophy, goals, and objectives of the early childhood program. In an early education program, the **philosophy** expresses the basic principles, attitudes, and beliefs of the child care center, school, or individual teacher.

Goals are general overviews of what children are expected to gain from the program. Administrators and teachers consider what children should know, understand, and be able to do developmentally across the disciplines, including language, literacy, mathematics, social studies, science, art, music, physical education, and health (Copple & Bredekamp, 2009).

Objectives are specific teaching techniques or interpretations of the goals and meaningful descriptions of what children are expected to learn. They are designed to meet the physical, intellectual, cultural, social, emotional, and creative development of each child.

> In DAP [developmentally appropriate practices], the curriculum helps young children achieve goals that are developmentally and educationally significant. The curriculum does this through learning experiences (including play, small group, large group, interest centers, and routines) that reflect what is known about young children in general and about these children in particular, as well as about the sequences in which children acquire specific concepts, skills and abilities, building on prior experiences. (Copple & Bredekamp, 2009)

As we continue focusing on the process of curriculum development, let us remember that whatever we do, say, plan, or assess must concentrate on developing a child's

curriculum A multileveled process that encompasses what happens in an early education classroom each day, reflecting the philosophy, goals, and objectives of the early childhood program.

philosophy In an early childhood program, expresses the basic principles, attitudes, and beliefs of the center, school, or individual teacher.

goals The general overall aims or overview of an early childhood program that consider what children should know and be able to do developmentally across the disciplines.

objectives The specific purposes or teaching techniques that interpret the goals of planning, schedules, and routines, as well as meaningful descriptions of what children are expected to learn. These objectives are designed to meet the physical, intellectual, social, emotional, and creative development of young children.

NAEYC Ethical core values

As teachers of young children, we face many daily decisions that have moral and ethical implications. NAEYC's position paper, *Code of Ethical Conduct and Statement of Commitment*, (2005), defines core values that are deeply rooted in the field of early childhood care and education. The following are NAEYC's ethical core values:

● Appreciate childhood as a unique and valuable stage of the human life cycle.
● Base our work on knowledge of how children develop and learn.
● Appreciate and support the bond between the child and family.
● Recognize that children are best understood and supported in the context of family, culture, community, and society.
● Respect the dignity, worth, and uniqueness of each individual (child, family member, and colleague).
● Respect diversity in children, families, and colleagues.
● Recognize that children and adults achieve their full potential in the context of relationships that are based on trust and respect.

positive self-esteem. Valuing each child's cultural background, experiences, interests, and abilities is critical. The "I can do it!" feelings of competence strongly influence learning ability. This is true for all children, from the youngest infant to the preschooler or the eight-year-old. (See Figure 2–1.)

Process of Curriculum Development

The *process* of curriculum development is *ongoing*. It is both planned and impromptu, written or unwritten. "Creating a good curriculum for young children is not simply a matter of practicing curriculum planning. It is a matter of understanding the process: how children interact with people and materials to learn" (Gordon & Browne, 2007). The selection of themes, projects, integrated curriculum areas, equipment, and materials is based on sound *child development* theories reinforcing the child's current stage of development and challenging her to move toward the next stage. As you begin this process of curriculum development, the first step is to set goals for learning based on the philosophy of the center/school and on the knowledge of the individual children in your classroom. Throughout this chapter and all the other chapters, we will be discussing the ongoing process of curriculum development, culminating in the selection of topics and activities, writing of objectives, and planning for observation, assessment strategies, and evaluation.

The use of the terms *inclusive* curriculum, *integrated* curriculum, and *emergent* curriculum in early childhood education explain further what is appropriate in developing curriculum for young children. **Inclusive curriculum** underscores the importance of individual differences, special needs, and cultural and linguistic diversity among young children, allowing for children to learn at their own pace and style. **Integrated curriculum** encourages young children to transfer knowledge and skills from one subject to another while using all aspects of their development. Gestwicki (2011) explains that "integrated curriculum helps children build meaningful connections when presented with new information, allows children to use knowledge and skills from one area to explore other subject areas, and allows teachers to negotiate the tricky balance between standards and developmentally appropriate practice." **Emergent curriculum** emerges out of the interests and experiences of the children. "In traditional teaching, teachers give instructions to children about what to do, and the children

inclusive curriculum Underscores the importance of individual differences, special needs, and cultural and linguistic diversity among young children.

integrated curriculum Encourages young children to transfer knowledge and skills from one subject to another while using all aspects of their development.

emergent curriculum A curriculum that emerges out of the interests and experiences of the children.

(preferably) do it. In emergent curriculum, teachers and children together decide what to do and teachers participate in learning alongside children, asking their own questions and conducting their own quest" (Wien, 2008).

EXAMPLES OF CURRICULUM MODELS AND PROGRAMS

A curriculum model is a structure or organizational framework that is used to make decisions about everything from policies and priorities to teaching methods and assessment procedures. (Crosser, 2005)

As a teacher of young children, you will find many early childhood curriculum models and theories available today. It is important to identify curriculum approaches and resources that are based on the developmental and cultural needs and interests of the children in your classroom. Curriculum models are helpful to point out guidelines for planning and organizing experiences. However, keep in mind that no single model addresses all the developmental and cultural priorities, such as anti-bias, inclusion, emergent curriculum, and the project approach. The following is an overview of curriculum model examples that were chosen because they continue to be identified by the early childhood profession, have been implemented in multiple locations, and "are accompanied by an extensive literature describing their educational objectives, content and structure, and assessment procedures" (Goffin, 2001). As teachers, we should continue to investigate other models and programs as well, looking for additional insights into early education curriculum.

Children learn best in a child-sized environment that is stimulating and inviting.

MONTESSORI (1870–1952). Montessori programs are based on Dr. Maria Montessori's original ideas, materials, and methods, which were designed to meet the needs of impoverished children in Italy. The Montessori method is the second curriculum model created expressly for early education (Goffin, 2001). (The first model was created by Friedrich Froebel in Germany, who began the kindergarten, or "garden for children," in the mid-1800s). In the United States today there exist wide variations and interpretations of the Montessori principles. According to Dr. Montessori's philosophy, children learn best in a child-sized environment that is stimulating and inviting for their *absorbent minds*—an environment that offers beauty and order. The arrangement of the room offers low open shelves holding many carefully arranged materials. Placed in that environment, the child may choose her own work—activities that have meaning and purpose for her. For example, to teach her students how to write, Montessori cut out large sandpaper letters and had the children trace them with their fingers, and later with pencil or chalk. Soon, the four-year-olds were able to write letters and then words by themselves. The Montessori classroom was one of the first to emphasize a warm and comfortable environment based on independent learning. "Many of [Montessori's] once radical ideas—including the notions that children learn through hands-on activity, that the preschool years are a time of critical brain development, and that parents should be partners in their children's education—are now accepted wisdom" (Schute, 2002).

Another important aspect of Montessori classrooms is an attitude of cooperation rather than competition in completing work. Students complete work independently and then check responses with the "control" material or ask other children for help. Here students are not perceiving the teacher as the sole source of information in the room....Therefore, the teacher's job is not to artificially "teach in" what the child lacks but rather to be a careful observer of each child's development. (Torrence and Chattin-McNichols, cited in Roopnarine & Johnson, 2009)

After the child is introduced to the Montessori materials by a guide (teacher), she is free to use them whenever she likes, for as long as she wishes, undisturbed by others. The materials are *self-correcting*. If the child makes a mistake, she can see it for herself, without the need for an adult to point out her errors. Montessori materials are also *didactic*, designed to teach a specific lesson; focused on *daily living practical tasks* to promote self-help and environmental care skills; *sensorial*, planned to encourage children to learn through using their senses; and *conceptual*, or involving academic materials designed to develop the foundations of reading, writing, and math. Some examples of Montessori-type materials found in many early childhood classrooms today are:

puzzles—self-correcting

nesting or stacking cups, rings, or blocks—self-correcting

rough and smooth boards and fabrics—didactic and sensorial

containers and tops—self-correcting and practical life task

setting a table—practical life task

washing dishes—practical life task

sound or scent bottles—sensorial

sandpaper letters and numbers—sensorial and conceptual

measuring materials—conceptual

HEAD START.   Head Start programs are the largest publicly funded educational programs for infants and toddlers (Early Head Start) and preschool children. They include health and medical screening and treatment, required parent participation and involvement, and comprehensive services to families. "Today there are Head Start programs in every state and territory, in rural and urban sectors, on American Indian reservations, and in migrant areas" (Essa, 2011). From its inception in 1965, Head Start has sought to provide classroom-based and, most recently, home-based comprehensive developmental services for children from low-income families. Head Start's experience has shown that the needs of children vary from community to community and that to serve these needs most effectively, programs should be individualized, thus meeting the need of the community served and its ethnic and cultural characteristics (Head Start, 2003).

Developing a curriculum that continuously meets the needs of children is an important task for any Head Start program. The Head Start program performance standards define curriculum as a written plan that includes:

Younger children enjoy having snacks outdoors.

© Cengage Learning

- goals for children's development and learning
- experiences through which they will achieve the goals
- roles for staff and parents to help children achieve these goals
- materials needed to support the implementation of a curriculum
- support for children's first language while they acquire English
- creation of a respectful and culturally sensitive environment (U.S. Department of Health and Human Services, 2005).

Head Start programs have a low child–staff ratio, with 10 percent of the enrollment in each state available for children with special needs. Head Start provides staff at all levels and in all program areas with training and opportunities, such as the Child Development Associate (CDA) credential and related subjects at colleges and universities.

An essential part of every Head Start program is the involvement of parents in parent education, program planning, and operating activities. Head Start also addresses families' unmet needs (housing, job training, health care, emotional support, and family counseling) that may stand in the way of a child's full and healthy development.

> Many different programs have been developed and evaluated as part of Head Start, and much research in early childhood education has been undertaken in Head Start programs. Thus, Head Start has been beneficial not only to the millions of children who have attended programs but also to the profession of early childhood education. (Brewer, 2001)

The original vision of Head Start has been improved and expanded for the new century as a model that challenges the effects of poverty and promotes physically and mentally healthy families. In 1994, Early Head Start was created to promote healthy prenatal outcomes, enhance the development of infants and toddlers, and encourage healthy family functioning while responding to the unique strengths and needs of each individual child and family. "Among model early childhood programs in this country, Head Start has perhaps the most comprehensive and detailed set of provisions for working with families" (Powell, cited in Roopnarine & Johnson, 2009).

Early Head Start fulfilled a growing need that developed during this same period. Research on brain development revealed how crucial the first years of a child's life are to healthy development, how the lack of infant and toddler care was desperately affecting most communities, and how welfare reform was creating new child care needs. As Early Head Start continues to serve diverse families across the United States, with both center-based and home-based support, it is strengthening developmentally appropriate and culturally sensitive services for infants and toddlers (Essa, 2011; Head Start Bureau, 2005).

© Cengage Learning

A developmentally appropriate environment encourages young children to develop self-help skills.

The U.S. Congress continues to address the ongoing needs and funding requirements of Head Start. As advocates for young children and their families, we should continuously stay abreast of new developments.

BANK STREET. Founded in 1916 by Lucy Sprague Mitchell, this program continues to be an important model of early childhood education in the United States. Mitchell envisioned a new type of educational experience for all children, which essentially shifted the focus to *child-centered learning*, emphasizing individual children and how they learn. "These ideas have carried Bank Street through growth and change over nearly ninety years of influencing the lives of children and the educational system" (Stavisky, 2002). Bank Street's *developmental interaction* method is dedicated to fostering all aspects of a child's development, the whole child, and not simply promoting specific learning. It also emphasizes the interaction between the child and the environment, as well as the interaction between the cognitive and affective areas of the child's development, thus underscoring that thinking and emotion are not separate but truly interactive. Children are creators of meaning. They work to understand the world they inhabit. The creation of meaning is the central task of childhood; if this task is fostered by the adults who care for them, children will become learners for life (Bank Street School for Children, 2002). At Bank Street School for Children, teachers arrange the classroom environment into distinct learning centers such as math, science, art, dramatic play, and music. These centers, along with a variety of materials and experiences, relate to the ages and interests of the children in the group to encourage integrating the curriculum, making choices, taking risks, and accepting help.

Children learn best through active experiences with people, materials, and ideas.

© Cengage Learning

"The school provides consistent opportunities for children to experience democratic living…. The allocation of space provides ample room for dramatic play, block building, and group meetings as well as space to work alone or in a small group. Flexibility in the schedule provides extended periods of time for children to actively explore the potential of materials, to take trips, to become involved in expanding ideas and interests, and to work together" (Cuffaro & Nager, cited in Roopnarine & Johnson, 2009). Teachers and children alike learn from and teach one another by building on shared experiences to develop meaningful relationships. This sharing extends to the families and communities.

> The Bank Street approach is considered synonymous with open education, a term encompassing programs that operate on the premise that children, provided a well-conceived environment, are capable of selecting and learning from appropriate activities. The program does not aim to teach children a lot of new concepts, but rather to help them understand what they already know in more depth. (Essa, 2011)

HIGH/SCOPE.   Under the leadership of David Weikert, this educational approach began over 30 years ago as an intervention program for low-income, at-risk children. The High/Scope Perry Preschool Study is a landmark long-term study of the effects of high-quality early care and education on low-income three- and four-year-olds that followed the children to 40-year-old adults (High/Scope, 2003). Today the High/Scope program serves a full range of children—infant, toddler, preschool, elementary, and early adolescent—adapting to the special needs and conditions of their group, their setting, and their community. The High/Scope program has been successfully implemented in both urban and rural settings in the United States and around the world.

Active learning, High/Scope's central principle for all age levels, emphasizes that children learn best through active experiences with people, materials, events, and ideas. Influenced by Jean Piaget's and Lev Vygotsky's theories of cognition and social interaction, this cognitively oriented model assists children in constructing their own knowledge from meaningful experiences. Materials are organized in each activity area so that children can get them out easily and put them away independently. In this kind of environment, children naturally engage in *key experiences*—activities that foster developmentally important skills and abilities (Hohmann, Banet, & Weikert, 1995).

A pioneer in conducting research and developing programs for young children, High/Scope implemented its first home visiting program for parents of infants over 40 years ago. It continues to focus on the development and needs of infants, toddlers, and families, while creating infant and toddler key experiences for teachers of this young age group (High/Scope Educational Research Foundation, 2003).

Teachers in a High/Scope program give children a sense of control over the events of the day by planning a consistent routine that allows children to anticipate what happens next. Central to this curriculum is the daily *plan-do-review* sequence in which the children, with the help of teachers, make a plan, carry it out, and then recall and reflect on the results of their chosen activities. Plan-do-review was developed to help *play* become more meaningful. Planning allows children to consider the what, where, when, how, and why of what they will be doing for the next time period. Doing means action, such as working with materials, interacting with other children, choosing, creating, and sharing, thus stimulating the children's thinking abilities through the application of skills to problem-solving tasks. Reviewing involves putting what one has done into words or pictures and sharing the representation with other children, teachers, or parents. Daily schedules provide for both large and small group interaction, a time for outside play, and time for the plan-do-review sequence of student-selected activities (Hohmann, Banet, & Weikert, 1995).

In addition to *plan-do-review,* the High/Scope approach emphasizes *key experiences* in which the children have plenty of time for active exploration in the classroom and accentuates the High/Scope *Child Observation Record* compiled from the daily recorded observations of the teacher. All of these are unique components of the High/Scope framework.

REGGIO EMILIA.   Reggio Emilia, a small city in industrial northern Italy, established what is now called "the Reggio Emilia approach" shortly after World War II, when working parents helped to build new schools for their young children (New, 2000). Founded by Loris Malaguzzi, the early childhood schools of Reggio Emilia, Italy, have captured the attention of educators from all over the world. Inspired by John Dewey's progressive education movement, Lev Vygotsky's belief in the connection between culture and development, and Jean Piaget's theory of cognitive development, Malaguzzi developed his theory and philosophy of early childhood education from direct practice in schools for infants, toddlers, and preschoolers.

The teachers in Reggio Emilia are partners and collaborators in learning with the children and parents. The teachers become skilled observers of children in order to plan *in response to the children*. Each group of children is assigned co-teachers. There is no lead teacher or director of the school. A *pedigogista*, a person trained in early childhood education, meets with the teachers weekly. Every school has an *atelierista*, who is trained in the visual arts, working closely with teachers and children. *The hundred languages of children* is the term teachers use in referring to the process of children depicting their understanding through one of many symbolic languages, including drawing, sculpture, dramatic play, and writing. Teachers and children work together to solve any problems that arise. Children stay with the same teacher and group of children for three years (Albrecht, 1996; Gandini, 1993; New, 2000).

In 1987, The National Association for the Education of Young Children (NAEYC) introduced the first presentation on Reggio Emilia at the annual conference. Since then, inspired by the exhibition "The Hundred Languages of Children" and supported by delegations of educators who have seen the city and its early childhood classrooms firsthand, American interest in Reggio Emilia has grown at a remarkable pace (New, 2000). The Reggio Emilia approach is currently being adapted in early childhood classrooms throughout the United States, including many Head Start programs.

Bredekamp (1993) concludes that "[t]he approach of Reggio Emilia educators is both old and new. Fundamentally the principles of Reggio Emilia schools are congruent with the principles of developmentally appropriate practice as described by NAEYC, presumably because both sets of principles share some of the same philosophical origins." See Figure 2–2 for concepts of the Reggio Emilia approach. Throughout this book you will find suggestions for incorporating Reggio Emilia principles into the curriculum.

Multicultural/Anti-Bias Considerations

By 2050, Hispanic and African American children under age five will outnumber non-Hispanic whites in the United States (NAEYC, 2007). "Spanish accounts for almost 80 percent of the non-English languages, but more than 460 languages are spoken by English language learners nationwide. The dramatic rise in ethnic and linguistic diversity in the United States means more and more children in kindergarten and other early childhood programs speak a language other than English as their first language" (Copple & Bredekamp, 2009).

You are, and will continue to be, an important person in the lives of these children. Your ability to understand and address their individual needs will help determine whether they have the knowledge and skills to succeed in school (Colbert, 2007). Each time you set up an appropriate, warm, supportive environment for young children, much of what you do is very familiar to you. At the same time, if you are exploring

Guiding Principles of the Reggio Emilia Approach

FIGURE 2-2
Concepts of the Reggio Emilia Approach. (Source: Fraser & Gestwicki, 2002, p. 11)

The following are some of the concepts of the Reggio Emilia Approach:

● the image of the child—the cornerstone of Reggio Emilia experiences conceptualizes an image of the child as competent, strong, inventive, and full of ideas with rights instead of needs

● environment as a third teacher—preparing an environment that acts as a third teacher carefully designed to facilitate the social constructions of understanding, and to document the life within the space

● relationships—seeing the importance of relationships physically in the way objects are displayed in the classroom; socially and emotionally in the interactions of the people in the environment; and intellectually in the approach to learning that is always seen in context and depends on co-construction of knowledge

● collaboration—working together at every level through collaboration among teachers, children and teachers, children and children, children and parents, and the larger community

● documentation—providing a verbal and visual trace of the children's experiences and work, and opportunities to revisit, reflect, and interpret

● *progettazione*—this difficult to translate Italian word means making flexible plans for the further investigation of ideas, and devising the means for carrying them out in collaboration with the children, parents, and, at times, the larger community

● provocation—listening closely to the children and devising a means for provoking further thought and action

● one hundred languages of children—encouraging children to make symbolic representations of their ideas and providing them with many different kinds of media for representing those ideas

● transparency—creating transparency through the light that infuses every space and in the mirrors, light tables, and glass jars that catch and reflect the light around the classroom; and metaphorically in the openness to ideas and theories from other parts of the world, and in the availability of information for parents and visitors

new ways to encompass each child's uniqueness, you may find many things that are unfamiliar to you. Exploring gender, culture, race/ethnicity, and different-abledness offers opportunities to develop new insights about yourself and the children in your care. You may feel comfortable and uncomfortable at the same time. It is important to understand that exploring and implementing a multicultural/anti-bias curriculum becomes a continuous journey of growth and change. As a teacher of young children, you should take, as one of the first steps in your exploration of multicultural education, the task of *discovering your own cultural uniqueness*. By reflecting on the culture and race/ethnicity of your family, you learn about yourself and about the culture of others as well.

Exploring your feelings about individuals who differ from you culturally or racially or individuals with special needs or disabilities is another step in the anti-bias curriculum development process. Discovering and coming to terms with your own feelings and attitudes will help you when these children join your group. Thus, **anti-bias** is an attitude that actively challenges prejudice, stereotyping, and unfair treatment of an individual or group of individuals. The inclusion of all children, whether they are differently abled or not, is a supporting principle of the anti-bias rationale. Ask yourself the following questions and then evaluate yourself: Which of these issues have surfaced? What have I already accomplished? On what areas do I need to work?

anti-bias An attitude that actively challenges prejudice, stereotyping, and unfair treatment of an individual or group of individuals.

- What differences among people or children make me feel uncomfortable?
- Do I have strong reactions to children from certain economic backgrounds, cultures, or races?
- How do I feel when children do not conform to my expectations about appropriate or acceptable behavior?
- Do I generally tend to prefer children of one sex?
- How do I react to families who have lifestyles that are very different from my own, and do these reactions influence my relationships or feelings about their children?
- When have I experienced or witnessed bias in my life, and how did I respond?
- How did I become aware of the various aspects of my identity and culture?

At the center of each program is the child, and at the center of each child is culture.

The *Anti-Bias Curriculum*, developed by Derman-Sparks and the A.B.C. Task Force (1989), is a comprehensive curriculum that offers helpful guidelines, activities, and materials that create an early education environment rich in possibilities for valuing differences and similarities. "Through anti-bias curriculum, teachers enable every child to achieve the ultimate goal of early childhood education: the development of each child to her or his fullest potential."

Cech (1991) explains, "At the center of each program is the child, and at the center of each child is culture." We must be sensitive to and respectful of the cultural background of each family member. The home and the center or school should develop a partnership to enable children to make an easy transition from known to unknown. We must support and retain the language and culture of the family as we add the language and culture of the early education program to each child's experiences.

Many children today are bicultural and bilingual. "The number of multiracial babies born since the 1970s has increased more than 260 percent compared to a 15 percent increase of single-race babies....More than one million first generation biracial babies were born since 1989" (Wardle, 2001). West (2001) explains further, "Third culture children whose lives span two cultures, so-called for the third culture created within them, may hold two citizenships or hold citizenship in only one country but be born of parents representing two different races or ethnic groups." Increasing diversity means that as teachers and caregivers we must become more observant of individual children.

As teachers we must also be aware that some cultures emphasize a child's relationship to her group with group problem solving, rather than independence, individualism, and competition. In addition, some cultures value learning by active participation, while others encourage learning by observing and listening. "A simple but sometimes problematic cultural difference involves personal space. In cultures where people are often in crowded groups, children may sit and stand very close, touch a lot, and bump up against each other. This behavior may feel aggressive to children who aren't used to so much closeness and may require some guidance from the teacher.... It takes real sensitivity on the part of teachers and providers to decide how to handle behavior that is acceptable to one child within his family but considered aggressive by other children or by a teacher" (Gonzalez-Mena & Shareef, 2005). Therefore, we must give young children time to develop independence and accept responsibility within their own cultural framework. As teachers we should recognize our own defensiveness, continue to work on understanding, appreciating, and respecting differences, and developing patience with ourselves and the children. "The diversity of life is astounding, and the world is more complex than ever before. Our children will experience more new ideas, people, and change than any other generation in history" (Perry, 2002).

CULTURE IS LEARNED

No one is born acculturated. You must learn the beliefs of your culture. Anthropologists and educators consider culture to be something that is learned and transmitted from

Each child and each teacher adds their culture and their uniqueness to the group.

© Cengage Learning

generation to generation. Another dimension is the concept that culture is something that members of a group share in common. You are born to a group with rules. However, groups borrow and share with other groups. As a result, culture is ever-changing rather than static and fixed.

> Culture is a glass prism through which we look at life. Like a prism, culture has many facets. Early childhood educators need to be cognizant and aware of these various angles that help explain the behavior, reactions, and manners of children in the classroom. (de Melendez & Beck, 2010)

culture The sum total of a child's or family's ways of living: their values or beliefs, language, patterns of thinking, appearance, and behavior. These are passed or learned from one generation to the next.

Culture, then, is the sum total of a child's or family's ways of living: their values or beliefs, language, patterns of thinking, appearance, and behavior. It includes the set of rules that govern a family's behavior and that are passed or learned from one generation to the next. However, as we learn about cultures other than our own, we should be careful not to assume that just because children or families are from a specific ethnic or racial group that they necessarily share a common cultural experience. Recognize differences *within cultures* and *within families* (Marshall, 2001).

A multicultural/anti-bias curriculum is one that actively challenges prejudice and stereotyping and represents an opportunity for the development of mutual respect, mutual sharing, and mutual understanding. It is crucial to establish an early education environment that enables children to make connections to their own reality as well as to the larger world, to develop positive self-esteem, and to receive approval, recognition, and success.

Irvine (2009) believes "[a] culturally relevant pedagogy builds on the premise that learning may differ across cultures and teachers can enhance students' success by acquiring knowledge of their cultural background and translating this knowledge into instructional practice." Therefore, as teachers we need to utilize the strengths that our children bring to the classroom—a rich language, a strong culture, and a remarkable history.

As you continue to study curriculum development in this book, you will understand how the anti-bias approach can flow through every element of the early childhood curriculum. Expanding learning experiences to include others helps young children develop values, respect, and a cultural sense of belonging. Suggestions for

Guidelines for a Multicultural Anti-Bias Environment

The following guidelines can help you provide a developmentally appropriate, multicultural/anti-bias environment for young children.

- Be sensitive to, and respectful of, each child's cultural learning style without stereotyping. Include content about ethnic groups in all areas of the curriculum.
- Use differences in language and culture as a foundation for learning. Identify staff members or other adults from the community to serve as role models to help develop language learning and cultural activities.
- Communicate with parents to clarify home and school values about socialization and children's cultural and racial identities.
- Involve parents in the planning and implementation of activities.
- Model acceptance and appreciation of all cultures.
- Adapt curriculum materials to make them more relevant to all your children, and offer accurate information about different cultural groups in contemporary society.
- Ensure that the environment contains abundant images that reflect diverse abilities and current racial, ethnic, gender, and economic diversity.
- Make the necessary instructional and environmental adaptations (when possible) to meet the needs of children with special needs.
- Discuss cultural, racial, physical, and language differences *and* similarities honestly with children. Children are aware of differences in color, language, gender, and physical ability at a very young age.
- Provide opportunities for children to reinforce and validate their own racial and ethnic identities. Help children develop pride in their language and in their skin, hair, and eye color. Place value on the uniqueness of each individual.
- Help children find alternative ways or words to deal with racism and racial stereotypes.
- Focus curriculum material about cultures on similarities *and* differences, such as food, clothing, shelters, celebrations, and music. Global awareness of similarities and differences builds understanding and respect.
- Provide opportunities to ask children questions about the activities/materials to assess their knowledge and help them to construct new knowledge. Allow time for children to practice changing perspectives.

FIGURE 2–3
Guidelines for a multicultural anti-bias environment. (Adapted from Essa, 2011; Derman-Sparks & A.B.C. Task Force, 1989; Feng, 1994; Gonzalez-Mena, 2001; Marshall, 2001; Spodek & Saracho, 1994; York, 2003).

integrating multicultural/anti-bias content and materials into specific curriculum areas can be found in Chapters 3 through 12. (See Figure 2–3 for guidelines for a multicultural anti-bias environment.)

SPECIAL NEEDS CONSIDERATIONS

Increasing numbers of young children with special needs are being cared for in early childhood settings in their community (Watson & McCathren, 2009). Children with learning, behavioral, or physical disabilities are now included in early childhood classrooms. **Inclusion** efforts reflect the blending of practices from both early childhood education and early childhood *special* education. Willis (2009) explains that "the combining of practices that are referred to as blending practices can be used to address the needs of all children in inclusive settings. This term usually means that regular early childhood practices and early childhood special education practices are blended in such a way that all children learn and participate in classroom activities."

inclusion Reflective of the blending of practices from early childhood education and early childhood special education.

Inclusion is not about a place, or an instructional strategy or a curriculum; inclusion is about belonging, being valued, and having choices. Inclusion is about accepting and valuing human diversity and providing the necessary support so that all children and their families can participate successfully in the program of their choice. (Allen & Schwartz, 2005)

According to Public Law 94–142, 1975 (amended to PL 99–457 1986, and further amended in PL 102–119, 1991, and reauthorized in 1997 to PL–105–17), children with disabilities should be placed in the *least restrictive environment* (Deiner, 2010). This means an environment that is as close as possible to the environment designed for nondisabled children, while remaining appropriate for their special needs (Gordon & Browne, 2011; Spodek & Saracho, 1994).

To agree with the Individuals with Disabilities Education Act (IDEA) public law, a written *individualized family services plan* (IFSP) that identifies the needs and goals of young children and their families must be developed for children ages birth to three in an early childhood setting.

This law, later renamed the Individuals with Disabilities Education Improvement Act of 2004 (PL-108-446), ensures early intervention, special education, and related services for more than 6.5 million infants, toddlers, children, and youths with special needs (U. S. Department of Education 2009, cited in Ray, Pewitt-Kinder, & George, 2009).

Klein, Cook, Richardson-Gibbs (2001) and Gargiulo and Kilgo (2000) identify several key activities that are expected to occur in the IFSP process. These include the following:

● In accordance with each individual state's criteria, *eligibility* must be determined for each child. This involves sharing, gathering, and exchanging information between families and staff.
● To assist families in making choices, *assessment* of the family's resources, priorities, and concerns, as well as the child's strengths, is made. A statement of the infant's or toddler's present levels of physical, cognitive, communication, social or emotional, and adaptive development should also be included.
● The initial IFSP document is developed at a meeting, conducted in the native language of the family. At this point, a service coordinator is designated.

Wide pathways help all children move comfortably around the classroom.

- To *Implement* and *monitor* the IFSP document, the service coordinator is responsible for coordinating, facilitating, and monitoring the timely delivery of early intervention services, with a review of the IFSP every six months and a full evaluation annually.
- Steps are identified to *support* the *transition* of the toddler with a disability to services provided under Part B (preschool).

An *individualized education plan* (IEP) is the legal document that must be written with input from the child's teacher and parents, outlining the educational goals for the child during a given period (usually one academic year). The IEP must also include how the goals will be met and what services will be provided to the child to help meet these goals (Willis, 2009). The federal guidelines, as in the original law, still require children who will receive any special education services to be seen for a diagnostic study by members of a multidisciplinary team before services can begin (Klein, Cook, & Richardson-Gibbs, 2001; Willis, 2009). How much help professionals in special education or related services should provide depends on the needs of the children and on state and local resources. These specialists, together with the family and the early childhood teacher, function as a team.

Klein, Cook, and Richardson-Gibbs (2001) and Gargiulo and Kilgo (2000) expand on what the written IEP must include:

- A statement of the child's present levels of educational performance
- A statement of annual goals and related short-term behavioral objectives
- A statement of the specific special education and related services to be provided to the child
- The extent to which the child will be able to participate in regular education programs
- The supporting services needed within the regular program
- The projected dates and duration of services
- The objective criteria and evaluation procedures, as well as how progress toward annual goals will be measured and a statement of how the student's parents (guardians) will be regularly informed of such progress

© Cengage Learning

Teacher-family interaction creates a consistent and beneficial experience for young children.

It is crucial to be aware of the special needs that families of children with disabilities have and determine how the early childhood program can help meet these needs. As a teacher, you need to be sensitive to the various reactions that parents may experience, such as grief, guilt, anger, and even disregard of their child's special needs. It is important to acknowledge and accept their reactions by listening, providing practical advice, and offering information on community resources that can be of help (Essa, 2011). Services to families must be individualized with regard for their cultures, strengths, values, skills, expectations, and needs.

INCLUSIVE ENVIRONMENT.   Establishing an inclusive environment in an early childhood program should reflect and be sensitive to the cultural and linguistic diversity of all the children and their families. Each child, whether with special needs or not, should be viewed as an individual with unique characteristics, strengths, and needs.

> Be a teammate with families, and do not try to work alone in educating their child. Together, you and the family can help their child reach his or her full potential. Finally, don't fear or worry about having a child with special needs in your classroom, center, or school. See the whole child, not just the hearing impairment, the cerebral palsy, or the autism. Remember, they are just kids! (Ray, Pewitt-Kinder, & George, 2009)

NOTE: Refer to the Checklist for Room Arrangement, Figure 2–9 and on this text's website to help you, as a teacher, determine what you have done and what you need to do to create a developmentally appropriate early childhood environment, one that includes multicultural/anti-bias and special needs considerations. Adaptations and modifications of the classroom environment and curriculum will be discussed in each of the ensuing chapters of this book, Chapters 3–12.

MANAGING THE ENVIRONMENT WITH APPROPRIATE GUIDANCE TECHNIQUES

Management in early education, including infant and toddler programs, is a direct result of understanding child development, establishing a philosophy, determining goals and objectives, and applying appropriate guidance techniques. This includes the personal philosophy of the teacher and the overall philosophy of the early education program. Inclusion of both indoor and outdoor environments is involved. The **environment** represents all the conditions and surroundings affecting the children and adults in an early childhood setting. "The environment is the stage on which children play out the themes of childhood: their interests, triumphs, problems, and concerns" (Gordon & Browne, 2011).

The arrangement of indoor and outdoor space requires *planning* for each individual child and group of children, *understanding prior experiences and development* of the children, and supporting the formation of trust, independence, and creativity in the children. If the children feel they belong and their needs are being met, appropriate behavior usually follows.

Set clear, consistent, and fair limits for classroom and playground behavior; guide younger children toward appropriate ways to relate to others and to function in a group environment; and help older children set their own limits. Setting limits means security for young children. It is appropriate to remind children of the rules and listen when they express their feelings and frustrations. The National Association for the Education of Young Children, in the brochure *Helping Children Learn Self-Control* (2000), suggests, "The rules should be kept simple, few in number, clear, truly necessary, and reasonable for the age of the child." Whenever possible, explain the reason for the rule. For example, "The water stays in the water table so the floor will not be wet. Someone could fall on the wet floor." Remember, too, that as a teacher, you should model good behavior. You must follow the rules you expect the children to follow.

Miller (2010) suggests that, we can use the following guidelines to determine the appropriateness of children's day-to-day behaviors and help them learn the difference between right and wrong:

● Behavior must not infringe on the rights of others. (Be kind! Wait for your turn.)
● Behavior must not present a clear risk of harm to oneself or others. (Be safe! Go down the slide feet first.)
● Behavior must not unreasonably damage the environment, animals, objects, or materials in the environment. (Be neat! Put your paper towel in the trash can.)

Many times children experience intense and dramatic emotions. A part of early education management is to help children deal effectively with the outward expression of their feelings. Help the individual child identify what she is feeling, place a limit on her behavior, and give the child an appropriate outlet for that feeling. For example, "I know you are angry with Jared, but I cannot let you hit him. You may hit the play dough instead." "Use your words to tell Maria how you feel."

Try to explain a child's behavior to another child. "I think Larry wants to play with you." "I think Stephen needs to play by himself for a while." Also, try to use suggestion or redirection rather than the word *don't*. It is helpful to say, "Sand stays in the sandbox!" rather than "Don't throw the sand!" Tell children what you expect them to do in a positive manner. (See Figure 2–4.)

environment In an early childhood setting, the conditions and surroundings affecting children and adults.

Appropriate Verbal Guidance with Young Children

Practice saying "DO," not "DON'T." Focus on the positive. Use clear, short, meaningful phrases that encourage and offer positive suggestions to the child.

Say This:	Instead of Saying:
"Thank you for sitting down when you slide."	"Don't stand up when you slide."
"Please keep the puzzle on the table."	"Don't dump the puzzle pieces on the floor."
"Please turn the book pages carefully."	"Don't tear the book!"
"Thank you for talking in a quiet voice."	"Don't shout!"
"Please wipe your brush on the side of the paint cup."	"Don't drip paint on the floor."
"It's time to go inside. I have something to show you."	"Shall we go inside?"
"You need to turn off the faucet after you wash your hands."	"Don't waste the water."
"Please give me the ball to hold while you're climbing."	"Don't climb with that ball."

FIGURE 2–4
Appropriate verbal guidance can help young children develop self-confidence and respect for others.

Handle spills and mishaps as a natural part of a child's day. By saying, "Juanita, please get some paper towels to clean up the milk," and "I'll help you clean that up," you preserve a child's self-concept while allowing her responsibility for herself. See Figure 2–5 for suggestions on how to develop responsibility and independence.

The following guidance techniques are additional suggestions to think about as we deal with challenging behaviors of children in our classrooms:

- Remember to address the behavior, not the child, when a behavior occurs that is not appropriate. Our goal should be to help guide the child from inappropriate behavior to appropriate behavior. Redirection, getting them interested in something else, is a nonthreatening way to achieve this.

- It's important to identify and stop *bullying behavior* immediately. Lipman (cited in Riley & Boyce, 2007) explains that "[b]ullying is not an occasional unkind act. Bullying is distinguished by repeated acts of aggression and unequal power between bully and victim." Make sure the children in your class know that any type of bullying is *never* acceptable. Help the children learn to manage their own behavior; help them to learn how to cope with difficulties; and limit aggressive behavior firmly and consistently. Also, "children may use their improved cognitive and language skills as tools to intentionally hurt others' feelings. (*'You can't come to my birthday party,' 'Your hair is ugly.'*) This relational bullying, as well as physical bullying, may be seen toward the end of the preschool years having potentially negative effects on both the bully and the bullied child" (Hanish, cited in Copple & Bredekamp, 2009).

- "Teachers, parents, and child care providers quite often are trapped by the idea that if something does not work the first time, then it will never work. Children eventually change a behavior when they finally comprehend and remember that the action will quickly and consistently be stopped or redirected" (Miller, 2010). As teachers, we should remind ourselves that in order for children to behave appropriately, there must be *consistency* in both our expectations and our applications of rules.

Guidance Guidelines for Developing Responsibility and Independence

FIGURE 2–5
Suggested guidance guidelines for young children.

- Arrange the environment to allow children access to age-appropriate toys, materials, supplies, learning centers, the restroom, etc.
- Expect children to do things for themselves, while understanding what their capabilities are. Do not expect more of them than they can give. Be patient and give the children time.
- Encourage self-help skills such as self-feeding and toileting, while planning opportunities for learning new skills, especially first attempts by children to do things for themselves. Keep in mind cultural values of independence versus interdependence.
- Give positive reinforcement for children's independent behaviors. It is the effort that counts—not the outcome.
- Offer simple yet consistent guidelines for the group and the individual child. Be sure your expectations are in line with the children's abilities and cultural expectations.
- Offer choices, and then respect the child's preference and wishes. Suggest an easier or better way to do something when necessary, but leave the final decision up to the child.
- Allow and encourage children to participate in planning. Sometimes a child will come up with a better idea than the adult does.
- Allow children the privilege of learning through their mistakes without feeling guilty for having made a mistake. Be sensitive enough to know when not to help.
- Show each child that you trust and have confidence in her.
- Help each child change inappropriate behavior to appropriate behavior by using consistent, positive guidance techniques.
- Model appropriate behaviors for children so that they can be guided to attain the same behaviors.
- Avoid using words that would shame the children or cause them to doubt their competence.
- Support children when they feel frustrated and need security as they strive for independence.

- Shidler (2009) reminds us to be mindful of what we intend to teach:

  > It is evident from my observations in more than 100 classrooms over the last 15 years that children's behaviors are influenced by their teacher's behavior and use of language....When we choose how we will interact with children, we choose what we will teach them.

- Remember to communicate with parents. Teacher-family interaction creates a consistent and beneficial experience for young children. Our cultural values profoundly influence our perceptions about what guidance practices are most appropriate for children. Parents oftentimes assume that other parents naturally share the same underlying beliefs about how children should be disciplined (Miller, 2010). It is important that you, as the teacher, clarify what appropriate behavior is expected of the children in your care. If a child's behavior creates problems, open discussions between home and school are important.
- *Model* expected behavior and demonstrate *self-control*. Name feelings. Teach acceptable ways to express feelings. All of these actions can further show children how to be kind to and considerate of others.
- As a teacher, you need to develop a support system for yourself. Create a teaching team whose members can help each other when children have crises or long-term needs.

Look for additional guidance suggestions throughout this book.

Setting limits, anticipating, and preparing for behavior difficulties are only part of a teacher's responsibility. Ensuring safety and preventing accidents in the environment for young children must also be considered at all times and in everything we do with and for young children. "Health and safety are not external patches or optional aspects of programs. Regardless of the limits imposed by funding, staffing, physical or curricular constraints, the health component should be an integrated part of the daily program activity" (Aronson, 2002). Indoor and outdoor safety is essential for all children. Preparation and prevention are critical to child safety. Catron and Allen (2008) remind us, "Only when safety is ensured, needs are met, and problems are prevented or diminished can the staff turn their full attention to implementing the program goals and objectives for enhancing children's growth and development."

ARRANGEMENT OF THE EARLY CHILDHOOD LEARNING ENVIRONMENT

The indoor environment should invite you to "come on in." If you do not feel a positive welcoming, it is a signal that something probably needs changing. "It is important to remember, however, not to change everything at once. When making changes, think about what will appeal to you and the children and see where it takes you. Also think about the various areas and materials in the classroom and the type of behaviors and activities you wish to foster. If something is not functional or attractive, be brave enough to let it go" (Klein, 2007).

© Cengage Learning

Arranging appropriate indoor and outdoor areas in an early education program is significant to curriculum development. This is an extension of classroom management and part of a teacher's strategy to accomplish the learning goals and objectives. Organization of the outdoor environment, like the indoor classroom, should set limits with reasonable, appropriate rules that are consistently reinforced to promote appropriate behavior. Teachers and children spend many hours in the classroom and on the playground. The extra time you spend to organize, plan for the needs of the children, and plan effective and efficient use of space will aid you in creating a developmentally appropriate learning environment.

Selection of appropriate materials and efficient use of space stimulates children's interest and learning.

INDOOR LEARNING ENVIRONMENT.

> Although we talk about the environment in terms of the materials, equipment, and enhancements that create it, what we are trying to create is less tangible than the pieces we use to create it. It is the way a room feels in its entirety, the way it looks but also the way it smells and sounds, the way the air moves through it, whether it is warm or cold, whether it invites us to linger or encourages us to pass quickly through....The environment sets the stage for children's living at school, as the primary aesthetic experience. (Wurm, 2005)

Children need to feel that they belong. The environment should tell the children "we care about you." For example, have a personal space or "cubbie" for each child with her name or photo. In a shared space, each child needs to know there is one place that belongs to her. Display children's art, special projects, pictures, and bulletin boards at their eye level. These wall areas should be a visual extension of what is happening in the classroom. Ideas suggested by the children and their involvement in the final product should be part of the creative process of assembling the bulletin board. Reflect the interests of the children in all that you do.

Think about how you use color in the classroom. Try to express an anti-bias atmosphere. Primary colors and colors of the rainbow are used most often, but you should be sure to include brown and black as well. Many times we send a message that these colors are not aesthetically equal to other colors (Thomson, 1993).

A characteristic of a responsive, organized classroom is the presence of a variety of well-defined **learning centers**, sometimes called interest centers, zones, clusters, or activity centers, where materials and supplies are combined around special groupings and common activities. These centers support children's learning and enable them to explore, experiment, and interact with the environment at their own rate of development.

Arranging and organizing the space for preschool, prekindergarten, kindergarten, and primary classes becomes more specific and complex. The following learning centers are suggested for early education classrooms and outdoor areas (many of these can be combined or expanded):

- Books, language, literacy, listening, and writing center
- Dramatic play, home living area, or puppet center
- Art center
- Sensory activities with manipulatives; woodworking; cooking; water, sand, and mud play
- Blocks
- Music and movement
- Science, discovery, and nature
- Math and manipulatives
- Social studies/multicultural
- Computers/technology center

The learning centers involve hands-on experiences with a variety of materials. These materials and supplies have a direct correlation to a particular objective, theme, lesson plan, or concept being introduced. Well-planned, continuous introduction and rotation of new materials stimulate interest. The learning centers make possible individual and small group instruction while providing an opportunity for the children to make choices in many different areas. The placement of the centers is important for balancing the number of noisy and quiet activities. How many of the areas are used at the same time depends on what is happening in relationship to the schedule, routines, and lesson plans. Sometimes specific learning centers may be closed to allow for expansion of other centers, for reasons relating to guidance and discipline, or because the size of the room necessitates rotation of activities. Also, the ages of the children and regulatory requirements will affect the numbers and types of learning centers available in an early education setting. Chapters 3 through 12 offer specific curriculum activities and a rationale for each learning center.

The clearly arranged spaces and classroom design assist children in setting their own pace and making choices that will help them to be more self-directed, which in turn will improve their self-control. (See Figures 2–6, 2–7, 2–8, and 2–9 for suggested room arrangements for infants, toddlers, and preschoolers and a room arrangement checklist. Additional room arrangement diagrams can be found on the premium website.)

The environment tells children how to act and respond. Children are more likely to follow classroom rules when the environment reinforces these. For instance, if it is important for reasons of safety that children not run inside, classroom furnishings should be arranged in a way that makes walking, rather than running, natural (Essa, 2011; Isbell, 2007).

For children with special needs, additional environmental conditions should be considered. Allen and Schwartz (2005) explain that "effective early education is based on the principle that children are children, regardless of their abilities. All children have the same needs, though the needs may be more pronounced in some. For example:

- Moving about safely—in an environment free from clutter, slippery floors, or rumpled rugs—contributes to the safety and security of every child. For children with limited vision or physical problems, an environment free of obstacles protects against serious injury.
- Minimizing clutter and confusion enhances the ability of all young children to concentrate on the tasks at hand. For children with attention or learning disorders, reducing distractions may be the best way to promote learning."

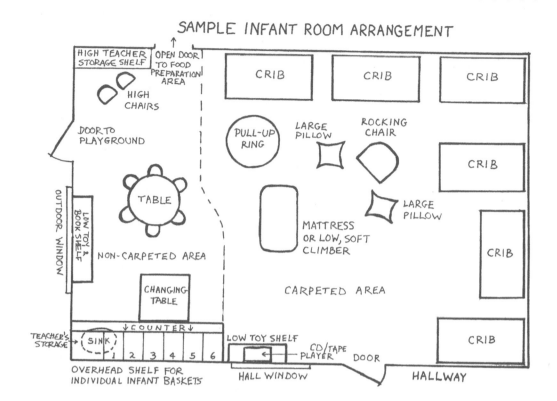

SAMPLE INFANT ROOM ARRANGEMENT

FIGURE 2–6
A suggested room arrangement diagram for infants.

SAMPLE TODDLER ROOM ARRANGEMENT

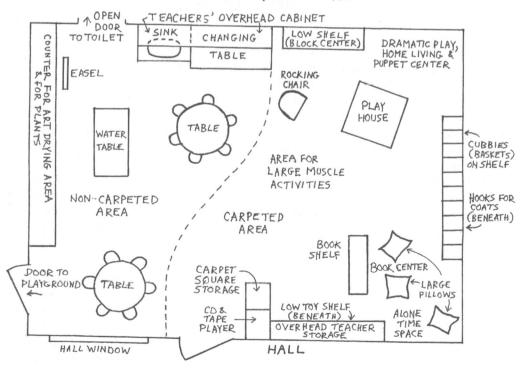

FIGURE 2–7
A suggested room arrangement diagram for toddlers.

FIGURE 2–8

A suggested room arrangement diagram for preschoolers.

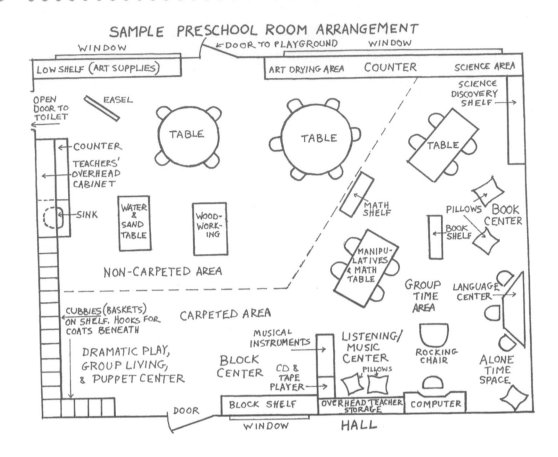

Exploring their physical environment comprises a great deal of the curriculum for mobile infants and toddlers. For them, a safe and healthy environment offers major activity areas designed for eating, sleeping, diapering, and playing. Caring for and playing with a few infants or toddlers at a time are the focuses of these areas. Rocking chairs or gliders are a must. Babies enjoy rocking while being fed or comforted. If possible, sleeping should be in a separate room or quiet place away from active areas. These young children explore and interact with their environment through their senses; therefore, opportunities for open-ended exploration, visible and accessible materials, and safe possibilities for grasping, reaching, pushing, and pulling should be available. Mirrors add enjoyment for children during diapering and washing time.

Developmentally appropriate toddler programs are not a scaled down version of appropriate preschool programs. For toddlers, the addition of a toileting area is necessary. Their play areas can be more specific, for example, featuring blocks, books, and large and small muscle activities. They also need space where they can play alone or be onlookers as others play.

OUTDOOR LEARNING ENVIRONMENT. The outdoor environment should invite you to "come on out." Open the door to outside play and learning. Planning includes a process for developing curriculum for the outdoors in a way that parallels what teachers do indoors.

Planning a balanced and varied outdoor environment, according to Catron and Allen (2008), "involves understanding children's perceptual motor development, incorporating outdoor activities into lesson plans, and regularly altering the outdoor

A Checklist for Room Arrangement

___ Does your arrangement support the goals and objectives you have set up for your indoor environment and outdoor area?

___ Are the learning centers well defined? Can they be restructured for special needs?

___ Is there enough space for the activity to take place, but not too much open space to encourage running?

___ Is each center located in the best possible place in the room? Are windows used for appropriate centers?

___ Are water play and art centers located near water sources? Do you have hooks near your art table for children to hang up paint smocks?

___ Are noisy and quiet centers separated?

___ Is protection from "traffic" given to centers that need it so that traffic flow does not interrupt children's play?

___ Can both children and teacher move about freely?

___ Are there wide pathways available for children with wheelchairs?

___ Is the room uncluttered but still warm and inviting?

___ Is there clear visibility so you can see all the children?

___ Are equipment and furniture movable and is the arrangement flexible according to changing needs? When you convert your room for lunch or nap, do you do it the same way every day to encourage your children to feel comfortable and secure?

___ Is the furniture appropriate for the physical size of the children? To promote independence, are hooks, washbasins, toilets, and drinking facilities easily reached by the children? Can they all be child-operated?

___ Is the environment flexible to accommodate children with special needs?

___ Are bathroom facilities convenient?

___ Are electrical outlets available in the right place? Are they covered when not in use?

___ Is lighting adequate? Is the temperature of the classroom comfortable for the children?

___ Are the materials and supplies for each center visible to and available for use by the children? Are directions clear and age appropriate? Do the materials stimulate a child's natural curiosity?

___ Is the number of children per center controlled? Does the arrangement or a visual clue suggest the desired number of children?

___ Are materials limited in each center to offer choices that are not overwhelming but still offer enough materials for all?

___ Does each center offer visual clues for placement of materials and equipment while encouraging cleanup? Are storage containers labeled with objects, pictures, photographs, or outlines of the contents? Are labels written in languages other than English?

___ Are the learning centers organized and attractive and appropriate for young children? Do they reflect cultural diversity free of stereotyping? Do the cultures represented visually reflect the multicultural reality of the world rather than your classroom reality?

___ Does the arrangement within the learning center promote social skills while encouraging cooperative group learning or individual learning?

___ Is there a space for a child to have some alone time?

___ Are pictures and bulletin boards placed at the eye level of children? Do they display the children's projects appropriately and attractively?

___ Does each child have individual space for storage (cubbie)?

___ Is the environment welcoming to parents as they enter the classroom?

FIGURE 2–9

A checklist for room arrangement in an early childhood environment that includes developmentally appropriate and special needs considerations.

environment to enhance opportunities for skill development." Many outdoor activities can also encourage independence and socialization.

> Simple experiences with nature can be very powerful opportunities for teaching and learning with very young children. Observing and talking about the many sensory aspects of nature—the sounds and smells of wind and rain, changing colors of the seasons, the tastes of fruits, vegetables, and herbs—inspire interest and appreciation of the beauty of nature. (Torquati & Barber, 2005)

An outdoor space for infants can be as simple as placing a blanket or mat in an unused section of a larger playground, or it can be an area with appropriate infant-sized equipment. It is important that infants have access to the outdoors where they can experience the change in temperature, color, smell, sounds, and textures (Reynolds, 2002).

As a part of learning, children explore and test the environments, and so the playground, like the indoor classroom, must have limits. Fences, mandated by licensing requirements, set the parameters, and the teacher sets reasonable and appropriate rules that are consistently enforced. For example, "We sit on the slides and come down feet first."

Safety is the first priority. At least two adults should be supervising the playground at all times. McCracken (2000) advises, "Outdoor time requires adults who are playful, have sharp senses and quick reactions, and who will closely observe children. Save reading, resting, parent conferences, team meetings, and even casual conversations with other adults for more appropriate occasions. Your attentive eyes can prevent an injury." (In Figure 2-10, Marotz offers a safety checklist for indoor and outdoor environments.)

Outdoor play is an essential part of the overall early childhood curriculum.

© Cengage Learning

Outdoor play is an essential part of the overall primary grade curriculum. Play reflects and enhances all areas of children's development, yet today outdoor recess is in jeopardy in many schools. Recess is increasingly viewed as the most useless of activities. Nonetheless, the available research suggests that recess can play an essential role in the learning, social development, and health of elementary school children. Recess may be the only opportunity for some children to engage in social interactions with other children. According to Louv (2008), "One U. S. researcher suggests a generation of children is not only being raised indoors, but is being confined to even smaller spaces.... [T]hey spend more and more time in car seats, high chairs, and even baby seats for watching TV. When small children do go outside, they're often placed in containers—strollers—and pushed by walking or jogging parents."

As you continue to plan outdoor spaces for play and learning, think back to when you were a child. What were your favorite outdoor play settings? They probably included dirt, water, flowers, trees, places to be alone, places to climb, places to hide, places to build, and plenty of unstructured playing time with your friends. As teachers, we have the opportunity to give the children in our care these same activities in safe, creative, stimulating, and developmentally appropriate play environments. Chapter 10 also suggests other activities for outdoors.

CRITERIA FOR EQUIPMENT, MATERIALS, AND SUPPLIES SELECTION

The selection of indoor equipment (furniture and other large and expensive equipment), materials (smaller items such as puzzles, books, toys), and supplies (consumables such as paint, paper, glue) should be developmentally appropriate for the

Indoor Areas Safety Checklist

1. A minimum of 35 square feet of usable space is available per child
2. Room temperature is between 68°–85°F (20°–29.4°C)
3. Rooms have good ventilation
   a. windows and doors have screens
   b. mechanical ventilation systems are in working order
4. There are two exits in all rooms occupied by children
5. Carpets and draperies are fire-retardant
6. Rooms are well lighted
7. Glass doors and low windows are constructed of safety glass
8. Walls and floors of classrooms, bathrooms, and kitchen appear clean; floors are swept daily, bathroom fixtures are scrubbed at least every other day
9. Tables and chairs are child sized
10. Electrical outlets are covered with safety caps
11. Smoke detectors are located in appropriate places and in working order
12. Furniture, activities, and equipment are set up so that doorways and pathways are kept clear
13. Play equipment and materials are stored in designated areas; they are inspected frequently and are safe for children's use
14. Large pieces of equipment (e.g., lockers, piano, bookshelves) are firmly anchored to the floor or wall
15. Cleaners, chemicals, and other poisonous substances are locked up
16. If stairways are used
    a. handrail is placed at children's height
    b. stairs are free of toys and clutter
    c. stairs are well lighted
    d. stairs are covered with a nonslip surface
17. Bathroom areas:
    a. toilets and washbasins are in working order
    b. one toilet and washbasin is available for every—10–12 children; potty chairs are provided for children in toilet training
    c. water temperature is no higher than 120°F (48.8°C)
    d. powdered or liquid soap is used for handwashing
    e. individual or paper towels are used for each child
    f. diapering tables or mats are cleaned after each use
18. At least one fire extinguisher is available and located in a convenient place; extinguisher is checked annually by fire-testing specialists
19. Premises are free from rodents and/or undesirable insects
20. Food preparation areas are maintained according to strict sanitary standards
21. At least one individual on the premises is trained in emergency first aid and CPR; first aid supplies are readily available
22. All medications are stored in a locked cabinet or box
23. Fire and storm/disaster drills are conducted on a monthly basis
24. Security measures (plans, vigilant staff, key pads, locked doors, video cameras) are in place to protect children from unauthorized visitors.

FIGURE 2–10

A safety checklist for early childhood indoor and outdoor environments. (Source: Marotz. [2009]. 7th ed., pp. 203–204.)

Outdoor Areas Safety Checklist

1. Play areas are located away from heavy traffic, loud noises, and sources of chemical contamination
2. Play areas are located adjacent to premises or within safe walking distance
3. Play areas are well drained
4. Bathroom facilities and drinking fountain are easily accessible
5. A variety of play surfaces (e.g., grass, concrete, sand) are available; there is a balance of sunny areas and shady areas

(continued)

FIGURE 2–10
(continued)

6. Play equipment is in good condition (e.g., no broken or rusty parts, missing pieces, splinters, sharp edges, frayed rope)
7. Selection of play equipment is appropriate for children's ages
8. Soft ground covers are present in sufficient amounts under large, climbing equipment; area is free of sharp debris
9. Large pieces of equipment are stable and anchored in the ground
10. Equipment is placed sufficiently far apart to allow a smooth flow of traffic and adequate supervision

11. Play areas are enclosed by a fence at least four feet high, with a gate and a workable lock for children's security and safety
12. There are no poisonous plants, shrubs, or trees in the area
13. Chemicals, insecticides, paints, and gasoline products are stored in a locked cabinet
14. Grounds are maintained on a regular basis and are free of debris; grass is mowed; broken equipment is removed
15. Wading or swimming pools are always supervised; water is drained when not in use

children in each classroom. Items must be child-size, nontoxic, aesthetically appealing, sturdy with rounded corners and edges, easy to maintain, and not easily broken. Many activities can be done on the floor, so the floor covering must be "child-proof" and made of linoleum, tile, or carpeting that can take spills and hard wear. Tables can serve as art, manipulative, and eating places. Boys and girls need experiences with the same kinds and variety of learning materials. Soft toys, big and comfy pillows, and furnishings that fit the children's size, abilities, and interests should also be included.

Arrange the environment to allow children access to materials, supplies, and learning centers. Labels, signs, and other kinds of print around the room offer visual guidance for children.

The Bank Street College of Education (1992) emphasizes the importance of including sensory materials in the selection for young children, especially toddlers. The use of "tactile materials (things you can feel) is a full-body experience for toddlers—they will be up to their armpits in shaving cream or finger paint and will often want to paint with their hands instead of brushes."

In the outdoor area, play structures are lower and wider for those young children who need time to climb up or down. The design, according to Frost (1992), "should 1) allow a wide range of movement; 2) stimulate the senses; 3) offer novelty, variety, and challenge; and 4) be safe and comfortable."

The selection of outdoor equipment and materials emphasizes safety, durability, and age appropriateness for all children. The outdoor space should contribute to physical, intellectual, creative, emotional, and social development and offer a variety of stimulation for play and exploration. The design should also offer ramps and tracks that accommodate wheelchairs and adapted vehicles, giving proper attention to slope, width, types of surface, and direct and safe accessibility to play and structures (Frost, 1992). The surfaces should offer various textures and colors, such as a hard-surfaced area for games and wheeled toys, a large soft grassy area with trees, a garden area, organic loose material such as play bark/wood chips and pine bark mulch, inorganic loose material such as sand and pea gravel, and rubber or foam mats.

The following are suggestions for equipment selection:

● permanent climbers
● take-apart climbers for older children to rearrange
● sturdy wooden crates and barrels

- tire swings with holes punched in several places for drainage (steel belted tires are not appropriate)
- slides
- balance beam
- tricycles, wagons, other wheeled toys
- plastic hoops
- balls of various sizes
- mounted steering wheel
- sturdy cardboard boxes
- equipment and materials that eliminate head entrapment points

With recess in many public schools still being reduced or eliminated, it is more important than ever that we, as teachers of young children, plan additional activities outdoors. Also, sharing activity ideas with parents will help ensure that children get more opportunities to experience the world of nature. Louv (2008) emphasizes why children *need* to spend time outdoors with access to nature.

© Cengage Learning

Children need to spend more time outdoors with access to nature.

As the nature deficit grows, another emerging body of scientific evidence indicates that direct exposure to nature is essential for physical and emotional health. For example, new studies suggest that exposure to nature may reduce the symptoms of Attention Deficit Hyperactivity Disorder (ADHD) and that it can improve all children's cognitive abilities and resistance to negative stresses and depression.

Themes, Units, Projects, and Webs

You will find that the core of curriculum development is your capability, as a teacher of young children, to integrate the children's needs, interests, and abilities with your conceptual plan for implementing goals and objectives. As discussed earlier in this chapter, emergent curriculum themes actually *emerge* from the interests of the children and adults in the program with no specific time frame for the learning to unfold (Essa, 2011; Jones & Nimmo, 1994). Themes, units, projects, and curriculum webs will aid you in developing a child-centered, emergent curriculum approach.

THEMES AND UNITS

Thematic curriculum is curriculum that focuses on one topic or theme at a time. This is a process for managing curriculum while achieving developmental appropriateness. Integrated curriculum is intertwined with the thematic approach and enables the teacher to tie in the observations, interests, and abilities of the children to major content areas of language and literacy, dramatic play, art, sensory centers, music and movement, math, science, and social studies with curriculum direction and expansion initiated by the children.

Many educators use the terms *theme* and *unit* interchangeably. This book presents a **theme** as a broad concept or topic, such as "Magnificent Me," "Seasons," "My Community," "Friendship," and "The Environment." This approach can be used to introduce children to activities that require active exploration, problem solving, and acquisition of a specific concept or skill. A **unit** is a section of the curriculum that you determine to be important for the children to know more about and is based on the unifying theme around which activities are planned. This is often offered as an activity planned for a particular learning center.

theme A broad concept or topic that enables the development of a lesson plan and the activities that fit within this curriculum plan.

unit A section of the curriculum based on the unifying theme around which activities are planned.

Developing a list of themes is usually the first phase. This is useful as you move toward developing a lesson plan and the activities that fit within this plan. Remember to remain flexible and responsive to the children, including being adaptable to the varying developmental stages, special needs, and experiences within the group. Your theme planning should merge play with child-directed and teacher-initiated experiences.

Here are some examples of themes that have proven to be favorites. These can be modified to fit any age group:

● Magnificent Me
● My Family and Me
● My Community
● Families
● Friendship
● Caring and Sharing
● The Seasons
● Weather
● My Five Senses
● Colors and Shapes in Our World
● Textures
● Things That Grow
● The Environment
● Plants and Gardening
● Animals
● Pets
● Cars, Trucks, and Buses
● Airplanes, Trains, and Tracks

BASIC CONCEPTS FOR DEVELOPING THEMATIC CURRICULUM

1. Themes and activities should reflect the philosophy suggested by the National Association for the Education of Young Children (NAEYC) for Developmentally Appropriate Practice (DAP) in Early Childhood Programs, such as: the critical role of teachers in understanding and supporting children's development and learning; the concept of classrooms or groups of children as communities of learners; the importance of each child in the group; and the significant role of families in early childhood education.
2. Themes and activities should take into consideration the age, stage of development, and experiences of young children.
3. Themes and activities should emphasize and integrate different aspects of development and learning.
4. Themes and activities should be developmentally appropriate and underscore the importance of individual differences and cultural and linguistic diversity among young children. This allows children to learn at their own pace and style.
5. Themes and activities should encourage the development of positive self-esteem and a sense of "I can do it" in young children.
6. Activities should be easily adaptable to large group, small group, or individual instruction.

See Appendix A for an example of an integrated curriculum theme with activities: *My Self*.

PROJECTS

project An in-depth investigation of a topic.

A **project** is an in-depth investigation of a topic worth learning more about. This is usually undertaken by a small group of children within a class, sometimes by an entire class, or individually by an older child. This approach involves children applying skills, asking questions, making decisions and choices, and assuming responsibility. Projects may last for a few days or for extended periods of time. It's important to remember that "[t]he less first hand experience the children have in relation to the topic, the more dependent they are on the teacher for the ideas, information, questions, hypotheses, and so forth that constitute the essence of good project work" (Katz & Chard, cited in Roopnarine & Johnson. 2009).

Some examples of project work include:

> drawing, writing, reading, recording observations, and interviewing experts. The information gathered is summarized and represented in the form of graphs, charts, diagrams, paintings and drawings, murals, models and other constructions, and reports to peers and parents. In the early years, an important component of a project is dramatic play, in which new understanding is expressed and new vocabulary is used. (Katz, 1994)

The *first phase* in beginning the project process is to choose a topic, such as pets, cars, flowers, or the grocery store. Sometimes children have ideas for a topic, and sometimes a teacher chooses a theme based on the children's experiences (Gandini, 1993). The teacher uses these personal experiences and recollections to review their actual knowledge of the topic. The teacher can also develop a topic web as a visual approach to the project. This web can also provide assistance for documenting the progress of the project (see Figure 2–11). The topic should allow the integration of a range of subject areas, including social studies, science, and language arts, as well as literacy and math skills (Katz, 1994).

Chard (2001) suggests the following criteria be used "to discriminate among different possible topics of study that depend on how children learn best, the basic social values we expect children to live by, and what we understand the role of the school to be in educating children." These criteria can be expressed in the form of questions about the value of studying any given topic. For example, how can study of this topic

- build on what children already know?
- help children to make better sense of the world they live in?
- help children to understand one another better?

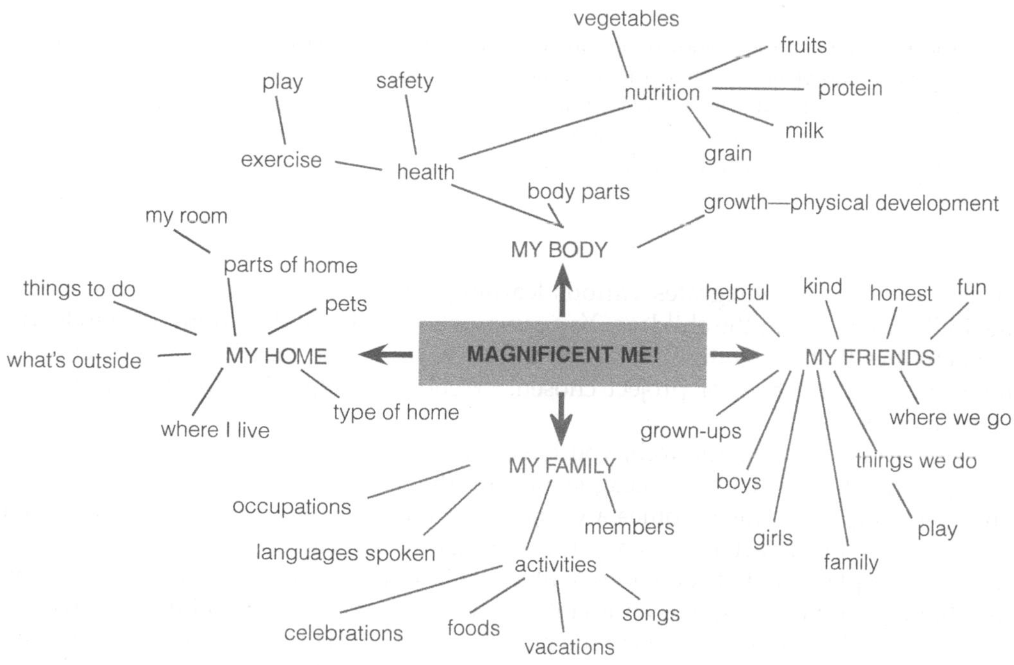

FIGURE 2–11
An example of a thematic web.

● enable children to understand the value of literacy and numeracy in real life contexts?
● encourage children to seek sources of information outside school?
● facilitate communication with parents? (Chard, 2001)

Progressing to the *second phase* involves gaining new information, especially by means of first-hand, direct, real-world experience. The children develop and expand the topic by their investigation and exploration of objects or events of the project while collecting data, making observations on field trips, making models, and using Internet resources. (Refer to Chapter 7, "Social Studies," for information on planning and experiencing field trips.)

In the *third phase* of the project process, as interest reaches its maximum point, end the project by reviewing what you and the children have learned and participate in a culminating group activity. Throughout the project process, families act as partners in the children's learning. With you as their guide, everyone takes part in an exciting exploration together.

Helm and Katz's (2001) use of the project approach explores how early childhood professionals can apply project work to meet the challenges they encounter in their classrooms. They offer these comments:

● Projects provide contexts in which children's curiosity can be expressed purposefully, and that enable them to experience the joy of self-motivated learning.
● Teachers and children embark on these learning adventures together.
● Parents also become involved and interested in the children's projects.
● The use of technology by teachers and children during the project is beneficial.
● Projects are helpful to children who are learning English and native-English-speaking children who are learning second languages. Children get meaning from hands-on experiences, demonstrations, and role-playing as well as from language.
● Projects can be done in classrooms where children have special needs, both in self-contained classrooms and others with full inclusion. Teachers determine interests through observation, encourage verbalization from children who are not verbal, and support children by offering a multitude of ways to investigate.

Finally, Katz and Chard (cited in Roopnarine & Johnson, 2009) extend our understanding of the project approach further:

The inclusion of project work in the curriculum for young children addresses the four major learning goals of all education: the construction and acquisition of worthwhile knowledge; development of a wide variety of basic intellectual, academic, motor, and social skills; strengthening of desirable dispositions [organizational skills]; and engendering of positive feelings about self as a learner and participant in group endeavors.

WEBS

A **curriculum web** integrates various learning activities. This visual process offers flexibility for you and the children. You can move in different directions, design learning activities that integrate various curriculum areas in special ways, and extend the thematic planning and/or project chosen. "Webbing" helps develop the scope and content of the theme.

curriculum web A visual illustration or process that integrates various learning activities and curriculum areas.

To produce a thematic web, you have the choice of brainstorming a single idea or topic by yourself, with a colleague, or with the children. Then record the ideas in an expanding web. This becomes a visual illustration of what could be included in a theme or unit or project approach to the curriculum. You can then put the elements of the web into planned daily activities, with the children actively investigating, initiating, questioning, and creating. For an infant, toddler, or child with special needs, have the individual child be the center of the theme (web) in order to plan activities for that child.

Buell and Sutton (2008) explain their approach to emergent curriculum planning for young preschoolers by using the child-centered webbing:

- Write each child's name in the center of a separate sheet of paper.
- Circle each child's name.
- Observe each child during play.
- Record interests observed on the right side of each child's web.
- Record developmental needs observed on the left side of each child's web.

Then, review each child's interests and create activities for the children that focus on the identified needs/goals.

To make the program inclusive, Buell and Sutton found this child-centered approach meets the Individualized Education Plan (IEP) and the Individualized Family Services Plan (IFSP) goals.

Figure 2–11 is an example of a curriculum planning web. Other examples of a thematic web can be found in Chapter 9, "Sensory Centers," Appendix A, and online in this text's premium website.

Lesson Plans

The **lesson plan** is an outgrowth of theme selection, brainstorming/webbing, and selection of projects and activities. This involves making a series of choices based on the developmental stages, learning styles, and interests of the children; the goals and objectives of the program; and the availability of materials, supplies, and resources.

As you plan for the weekly, biweekly, or monthly period, think about the following:

- A classroom that is well planned, attractive, and organized provides an environment that facilitates learning and becomes a part of the learning program itself.
- It is helpful to schedule a specific teacher planning time during each week. This allows you time to reflect on your observations of the children, what is working, what needs to be changed, and what additional materials and supplies are needed.
- It is helpful to develop a planning form, such as a written lesson plan worksheet. This will clarify your thinking and aid you in articulating your rationale for what you plan to do. It can also be posted for parents, teacher-assistants, and substitute teachers to see and refer to. (See Figures 2–12, 2–13, and 2–14 for lesson plans of infants, toddlers, and preschool children. The activities included in these plans are in Chapters 3–12.) Blank lesson plan worksheets can be found online on this text's premium website along with additional lesson plans. There are also examples of lesson plans for individual children.
- The lesson plan allows for planning the emergent curriculum theme or unit, concepts to be explored, skills to be developed, individual activities and large or small group activity times to be created, integration of the learning centers and curriculum areas, and preparation for special activities or field trips.
- It is helpful for you to develop a "things to remember" form for writing down items or materials to prepare or gather before the children arrive. It also allows you to write down ideas that come to mind to be used at another time. You will find that many new or remembered ideas come to mind during this special planning time.

lesson plan An outgrowth of theme selection, brainstorming/webbing, and selection of projects and activities. Involves making a series of choices based on the developmental stages, learning styles, and interests of the children; the goals and objectives of the program; and the availability of materials, supplies, and resources.

The lesson plan offers opportunities for small group activity times.

© Cengage Learning

FIGURE 2–12   An infant lesson plan worksheet.

SAMPLE **INFANT LESSON PLAN** (12–18 MONTHS)

TEACHER(S): ___   DATES: ___   THEME: Magnificent Me!

CENTERS & ACTIVITIES	MONDAY	TUESDAY	WEDNESDAY	THURSDAY	FRIDAY
SENSORY: ART, MUSIC, TACTILE ACTIVITIES	Scribble with multicultural crayons. Make banana/raisin snack.	Sing "Name Song." Use large soft blocks.	Sing "If You're Happy and You Know it" with jingle bells.	Watch or chase bubbles floating to music. Play with play dough.	Cover table with white sheet & use non-toxic markers.
COGNITIVE & LANGUAGE ACTIVITIES	Sing "I Have Two Ears" and read **Yellow Ball.**	Show and talk about family pictures. Read **My Family**	Play "Pat-a-Cake" with jingle bells. Read the book **Pat-a-Cake**	Play "Peek-A-Boo" and read the book **Peek-A-Boo.**	Play "Where's ___? There s/he is!"
SMALL MUSCLE & LARGE MUSCLE ACTIVITIES	Push & pull toys	Roll ball back & forth, crawl on soft rug	Drop (wooden) clothespins into a container one at a time	Crawl up soft foam incline	Stack bean bags
SELF-AWARENESS, SELF-HELP ACTIVITIES	Make faces into a mirror	Play Peek-A-Boo in mirror	"Jack Frost", fingerplay naming parts of body	Sing "Rock-a-Bye Baby" with soft babydolls.	"This is the Way We Wash Our Hands"
SPECIAL ACTIVITIES	Take stroller walk	Play on a quilt outdoors	Hang wind chimes near window or vent and listen to them.	Sing or chant "Roll the ball to ___. Roll it back to me.	Visit from grandparents (if possible)
BOOKS OF THE WEEK	**Peek-a-Boo** (Ahlberg), **Pat-a-Cake** (Kemp), **Yellow Ball** (Bang), **I Hear** (Isadora), **I See** (Isadora), **I Touch** (Oxenbury), **My Family** (Ostarch), **Baby Says** (Steptoe)				
SPECIAL NOTES	Dramatic play with soft multicultural baby dolls and blankets. Multicultural music and song tapes.				

FIGURE 2–13   A toddler lesson plan worksheet.

SAMPLE TODDLER LESSON PLAN

TEACHER(S):

DATES: **THEME:** Magnificent Me!

CONCEPTS: I am special & wonderful! I'm learning to do many things.

SKILLS: Self-Help, Language, Social

DAY	LARGE GROUP ACTIVITIES	SMALL GROUP ACTIVITIES
MONDAY	Sing "I'm a Special Person and So Are You"	Practice dressing with dress-up clothes
TUESDAY	Read **A Baby Just Like Me** while sitting on a cozy quilt	Bathe baby dolls in warm soapy water (use no-tear baby shampoo), pat dry
WEDNESDAY	Read **My Feet** Wiggle toes together	Take off and sort shoes, then put your own back on
THURSDAY	Read **Caps For Sale** while wearing caps from dramatic play	Add caps to the pile of shoes, sort, put on, then look in the mirror
FRIDAY	Read together "Una Casita Roja (A Little Red House)"	Use small, unbreakable hand mirror "_____, who do you see?"

SENSORY ACTIVITIES	DRAMATIC PLAY / HOME LIVING & PUPPETS	MOVEMENT / OUTDOOR ACTIVITIES
Sand box toys Colored water in water table Play dough in various skin colors	Play kitchen with dishes, aprons, dress-up clothes include hats, full-length mirror, family puppets	Chase bubbles Push and pull toys, trikes Climbing structure

MUSIC ACTIVITIES	SELF-AWARENESS, SELF-ESTEEM, SELF-HELP ACTIVITIES	SMALL MUSCLE / MANIPULATIVE ACTIVITIES
Sing "Rock-a-Bye Baby" to dolls Sing "If You're Happy & You Know It..." Listen to multicultural music & dance.	Dress self, put on shoes and caps Serve and pour at meals	Cut & tear paper in tactile table Puzzles of babies & families Small figures & doll house

ART ACTIVITIES	LANGUAGE ACTIVITIES	TRANSITIONS
Scribble on sheet-covered table Put torn paper on sticky-backed paper Foot & hand prints with paint	"Humpty Dumpty" finger play Discuss torn paper: color, feel, sizes Flannel board "Una Casita Roja"	"If your name is _____, then go to _____. (the door, etc.)" "Name Song"

BOOKS OF THE WEEK:

Here Are My Hands, To Baby With Love, Making Friends, Where's the Baby? On Mother's Lap, The Napping House

ACTIVITIES / NOTES:

Take a walk in the neighborhood

Visit from grandparents (if possible)

Cut up apples and eat.

FIGURE 2–14   A preschool lesson plan worksheet

SAMPLE PRESCHOOL LESSON PLAN

TEACHER(S):

DATES: **THEME:** Magnificent Me!

CONCEPTS: I am unique, special, and part of a family

SKILLS: Prewriting, writing, measuring, graphing, problem-solving, and awareness of similarities/differences

CENTERS & ACTIVITIES	MONDAY	TUESDAY	WEDNESDAY	THURSDAY	FRIDAY
MORNING GROUP ACTIVITY	Sing "Good Morning." Introduce "My Body."	Take individual instant photos. Introduce "My friends."	Read On the Day You Were Born. Introduce "My Family."	Make breadsticks formed initials. Introduce "My Home."	Healthy snack chart: finish & discuss.
AFTERNOON GROUP ACTIVITY	Identify body parts and what they do.	Animal friends: share stuffed animals and/or pets	Chart birthdays of the children and family members.	Read How My Parents Learned to Eat.	Bring and share something about yourself.
LANGUAGE & LITERACY	Begin "All About Me" books.	Write about photo and put into "Me" book with photo.	Add family photo to book. Write or draw about photo.	Write class story about field trip experience.	Finish "All About Me" books and share. Finish class story.
ART	Make life-sized self-portraits.	Make thumbprint and footprint pictures.	Make puppet papercup family pop-ups.	Make kitchen gadget puppets.	Mix playdough to match skin color.
MUSIC & MOVEMENT	"Name Song" Body parts move to music.	Sing "I'm A Special Person and So Are You" and "Friends Go Marching."	Beanbag toss and Kitchen marching band	Sing "So Many Ways to Say Good Morning" and dance.	Dance in hats with streamers to music.
DRAMATIC PLAY HOME LIVING	Home living center with a full mirror and baby pictures of children.	Add phones, paper, and pencils for message-taking.	Bathe baby dolls in warm sudsy water. Add stuffed animals to area.	Add a Wok and other cookware to center.	Add hats to dress-up clothes.
MATH MANIPULATIVE	Measure and record height of each child.	Graph the children's heights.	Use puzzles of family celebrations.	Gather items from home and play "What's missing?"	Estimate number of pennies in a jar; then count them.
SCIENCE & DISCOVERY	Listen to heart with stethoscope. Examine picture or model of skeleton.	Magnifying glasses to see thumbprints. Exploring shadows.	Food colors, eye droppers, and ice trays	Weigh on scales for "Me" book. "What's That Sound?"	Magnets and what sinks, what floats?

BLOCKS
Add: people figures, animal figures, boxes, houses, cars

OUTDOOR/LARGE MUSCLE
Nature walk: obstacle course on playground Hop, run, skip, jump

TRANSITIONS
Puppet helper of the day Variations on "Name Song"

SENSORY CENTERS
Water table with warm, soapy water Multicultural skin colored playdough. Healthy snacks "Tasting Tray"

SOCIAL STUDIES
Invite family members to visit. Field Trip to grocery store. We are all alike. We are all different.

BOOKS OF THE WEEK
My Five Senses, **Big Friend, Little Friend, Mommy's Office, William's Doll**

SPECIAL ACTIVITIES & NOTES
Field trip to grocery store. Children decide which healthy snacks to buy. Explain decisions.
Week-long project: Make chart or diagram re: food groups. Prepare and eat snacks. Write class story.

- Remember to plan for "a rainy day." Unexpected events, such as bad weather, can require you to have on hand materials and supplies for new activities to be implemented at a moment's notice. A new puppet, a book, a game, a flannelboard story, a song, and an art activity are examples of items you can put in a special box to use for such an occasion.
- As you plan, develop a checklist for yourself that includes the following questions:

  What do the children already know? How can I build on that? What have they thought of ?

  Is the theme or activity appropriate for the age and stage of development of the children?

  Are the selections too general or too broad?

  Are there too many or too few activities?

  Are multicultural and anti-bias activities included?

  Is the lesson plan flexible enough to allow for unexpected events or spontaneous moments?

  Is there a wide selection of books, songs, finger plays, and so on?

  Are the units of instruction open-ended, allowing for exploration and learning opportunities to occur?

As the children learn at their own pace about the world around them, they are organizing, manipulating, experimenting, communicating, and trying out different roles. To help children initiate their activities, trust the value of play experiences and spontaneous moments. If all of this is happening in your early childhood environment, then independent thinking and creative responding will happen.

ACTIVITY PLANS

Using an activity plan format as you set up learning centers will help you focus on clearly describing the activity, objectives, concepts, skills, space and materials needed, step-by-step procedure, guidance and limits for expected behavior, and assessment strategies and follow-up.

The presentation of an activity works on many levels. Fortson and Reiff (1995), in their discussion of continuous goals for teaching and learning, help us understand that "[t]he way we present materials, lead activities, and guide discussions makes an enormous difference in whether children use independent thinking and exercise powers of thought, feeling, and expression." We hope each activity will encourage children to solve problems, complete a project, and develop an eagerness to learn more.

When writing measurable objectives for an activity, "describe the precise quality of change in knowledge, behavior, attitude, or value that can be expected from the learner upon completion of the learning experiences" (Marotz, 2009). For example, the child will be able to demonstrate math concepts such as one-to-one-correspondence, counting, and measuring. The key word in this objective is *demonstrate*.

Other examples of measurable terms are:

- compare
- describe
- explain
- identify
- list
- match
- recognize
- write

The activity plan worksheet (Figure 2–15) is a suggested format that can be used to help you plan activities. Multiple activity plan examples are included in Chapters 3 through 12 and online at this text's premium website.

FIGURE 2–15
An activity plan worksheet.

ACTIVITY PLAN WORKSHEET

Date of activity:_____

Children's age group:_____

Number of children in this group (large group, small group, or individual activity):_____

Learning center to be used:_____

NAME OF ACTIVITY AND BRIEF DESCRIPTION

PURPOSE/OBJECTIVES OF ACTIVITY

(Concepts, skills, awareness, or attitudes you have designed the activity to teach or develop. Describe in measurable objectives.)

SPACE AND MATERIALS NEEDED

PROCEDURE

(Step-by-step description of the activity. Tips for getting started: describe what you will say or do to get the children interested in the activity, and let them know what they will be doing. Describe the activity in the sequential order you will use with the children. Where will this activity take place? Plan for ending the activity. How will you help the children make a smooth transition to the next activity?)

GUIDANCE

Establish necessary limits for behavior and boundaries of activity. Anticipate problems that may develop during this activity and consider ways to handle them.

ASSESSMENT AND FOLLOW-UP

What was the children's response? What worked well? What didn't work? How could this activity be changed to make it effective or more appropriate? List possible activities that would extend or give practice to the objectives of this activity.

Transitions

transitions Activities or learning experiences that move children from one activity to another.

Transitions are activities/learning experiences that move children from one activity to another. They are also teaching and guidance techniques. A sensitive teacher determines in advance the transition times in the daily program so that the children avoid lining up or waiting their turn, and the change of pace will not be jarring or interruptive to them.

There will be times when transitions do not seem to be working. Think about *why* the children are engaging in some form of challenging behavior. "Challenging behavior is more likely to occur when there are too many transitions, when all the children transition at the same time in the same way, when transitions are too long, and when there are not clear instructions....Perhaps it is the child's first experience in a group setting or the classroom rules and routines are different than at home" (Hemmeter, Ostrosky, Artman, & Kinder, 2009).

Children need time to adjust to change; therefore, as a teacher you should use a transition activity to direct children from

● a self-initiated to a teacher-directed activity.
● an active to a quiet activity or from quiet to active play.

- cleanup and toileting to snack time
- lunch to naptime.
- outside to inside or inside to outside play.

In addition, for the younger child, transitions can be used to help them adjust to arriving and then separating from mommy or daddy, learning to listen, sitting down, and joining in a small group activity for a brief time. For older children, transition activities can be used for getting attention, giving directions, gathering the group, and helping them understand the sequence of events or when events change without warning.

When the children get used to the schedule and routines of the day, the number of transitions used can be reduced. Children who are free to choose their play and activities will develop their own natural transitions as their interests and curiosity direct.

EXAMPLES OF TRANSITION ACTIVITIES

- Use a CD, or sing a song such as "The Hokey Pokey," where children can join the group as they finish with cleanup.
- Provide opportunities for supporting social skills and emotional competencies. Encourage children to work together ("Look at all of you cleaning up!" "Cambria, can you help Rachel get her coat on?").
- After group time, ask all children who are wearing red to stand up. Continue calling various colors until all the children are standing. Then give directions for the next activity.
- Prepare a set of flannel circles with each child's name on one. Place them name side down on flannelboard, and take them off one at a time while saying each child's name. When a child's name is called she chooses a song, finger play, or activity for the group to do.
- Use rhythm instruments to accompany a song you are singing. Let the children take turns using these instruments. As each child finishes her turn, she chooses a learning center to go to.
- Children gather quickly when you play the autoharp, guitar, or other instrument. Let a few children strum the instrument while you are waiting for others to gather.
- Pretend that one child is the engine on a train. As that child "chugs" around the room, other children join the train by putting their hands on the shoulders of the child ahead. When all children are part of the train, then "chug" along outdoors.
- Play "Simon Says." On the last direction, Simon says, "Sit down." You are now ready for a story or other quiet activity.
- Play directional games such as "Touch your nose, turn around, sit down." Start with simple directions and get more complicated as the children are able to follow through on two and three directions.
- Gently remind children when it is time to begin to complete their activities. A simple blinking of the overhead lights will let them know it is time to clean up.
- Help children move toward closure of the daily activities. Put things away and gradually close down the centers. Then read or tell a story until all the children have been picked up.

Plan of Observation, Assessment, and Evaluation

The process of curriculum development is one of continuous planning, implementing, observing, assessing, and evaluating. A curriculum is planned to meet the needs of the individual children in the group by defining philosophy, goals, and measurable, meaningful objectives.

Observation is the process for taking in information and objectively interpreting it for meaning. Ahola and Kovacik (2007) explain that "...watching children is not the same as observing them, and that only by observing the developing child can we truly understand him.... Why observe? The answer to this is very basic. We observe a child in order to understand the true nature of the child."

observation The process of observation is taking in information and objectively interpreting it for meaning.

Bentzen (2009) describes observation this way: "Observation entails the noting and recording of 'facts.' We refine this meaning to include the idea of looking for something in a *controlled, structured* way. 'Controlled' means that your observations are not random or haphazard. You know beforehand *what* you want to observe, *where* you want to observe, and essentially *how* you want to observe."

In this age of technology, video cameras are sometimes being used in the observation of young children. In doing so, as a teacher of young children, you should be aware that video cameras often change the very behavior you want to observe. Children begin to "act" for the camera instead of continuing with whatever activity they were doing. It is difficult to observe just one child when all the children want to be part of the action. If possible, it would be helpful to have the video camera out of sight and operated by someone else who is knowledgeable in what you want recorded for later observation. Additionally, remember that *permission* from the family to videotape each child is required.

Bentzen (2009) further clarifies, "...we *believe* that under most circumstances in the professional lives of child care providers and early childhood educators, persistent and extensive use of a video camera would be unfeasible....However, we recognize that some of you will want to use the video camera regardless of its disadvantages, real or imagined. In that event, we can recommend only that you use it judiciously and in combination with sound basic observational recording skills."

(See Figure 2–16 for Observing Young Children Guidelines.)

The following methods for observing and recording are often used in the assessment and evaluation process:

Anecdotal record: A brief, informal narrative account describing an incident of a child's behavior that is important to the observer. It may apply to a specific child or to a group of children. Anecdotes describe the beginning and ending times of the observation, an objective, and a factual account of what occurred (telling how it happened, when and where it happened, and what was said and done). Anecdotal records come only from direct observation, and are written down promptly and accurately (Essa, 2011). "The anecdotal record allows us to view the child's behavior within the contexts in which it is happening" (Ahola & Kovacik, 2007).

Checklist: A record of direct observation that involves selecting from a previously prepared list the statement that best describes the behavior observed, the conditions present, growth and development, or the equipment, supplies, and materials available. "They are intended to reflect common activities and expectations in classrooms that are structured around developmentally appropriate activities and are based on national, state, and local standards" Meisels, (2000). Checklists are easy to use and helpful in planning for individual or group needs. They eliminate the need to record all details of behavior.

Reflective Log or Diary: A teacher's or administrator's record of the most significant happenings, usually made at the end of the day or during an uninterrupted block of time. This includes what stood out as important facts to remember for the day, written in as much detail as possible, and extends over a long period of time. The diary description is an informal method of observation and it is considered the oldest method in child development (Wright, cited in Bentzen, 2009).

Case study: A way of collecting and organizing all of the information gathered from various sources, including observations of and interviews with the child, to provide insights into the behavior of the individual child studied. Interpretations and recommendations are included. The main purposes for this detailed observational record are to discover causes and effects of behavior, child development research, and to plan for the individual child.

Portfolio assessment: This method is based on a systematic collection of information about a child's ongoing development and the child's work gathered by both the child and teacher over time from all available sources. A portfolio is a collection of child-produced material, such as "works-in-progress," creative drawings, paintings,

anecdotal record A brief, informal narrative account describing an incident of a child's behavior that is important to the observer.

checklist A record of direct observation that involves selecting from a previously prepared list the statement that best describes the behavior observed, the conditions present, or the equipment, supplies, and materials available.

reflective log or diary A teacher or administrator's record of the most significant happenings, usually made at the end of the day or during an uninterrupted block of time.

case study A way of collecting and organizing all of the information gathered from various sources to provide insights into the behavior of the child studied.

portfolio assessment An evaluation method based on a systematic collection of information about a child and the child's work, gathered by both the child and teacher over time from all available sources.

Observing Young Children Guidelines

Reasons for observing children:

- To gain knowledge of age-appropriate behaviors
- To gain knowledge of individual differences
- To become aware of the total environment and influences on children
- To identify specific strengths and difficult areas for individual children
- To gather data to plan for individual children
- To gain understanding of children—the stages of physical, intellectual, emotional, social, and language development
- To gain an appreciation of young children—their abilities, interests, perceptions, and personalities
- To gain knowledge of how children learn
- To identify how individual children react/relate to a group situation
- To become aware of positive (pro-social) and negative (anti-social) behaviors of young children

Guidelines for recording the behavior of young children:

- Remember that all information is confidential
- Observe quietly with little or no interaction with the child (children) being observed
- Record objective observations in a clear, precise, and useful manner
- Think of the child and respect her as she is, not as you think she should be
- Be familiar as possible with the age group before beginning to observe
- Use the speaker's exact words when recording conversation

Guidelines for interpreting the behavior of a young child:

- To identify consistent patterns of behavior for a particular child over a specific period of time
- To document patterns of behavior with specific examples of such behavior
- To identify areas of difficulty and developmental delays as well as age-appropriate and accelerated development
- To remember not to make assumptions about the child's family life as the cause of her behavior at school/center
- To remember not to make assumptions about the child's behavior away from the school/center

FIGURE 2–16
Guidelines for observing young children.

and dictated stories; lists of books and stories read; product samples showing a child's strengths and skills; samples of a child's self-initiated "work"; photographs, audio and video tapes; teacher objectives for the child, observations and anecdotal records, developmental checklists; and family interviews and comments. Teacher comments on each portfolio sample can help document what the child knows, can do, and how she does it. Portfolios can be a file folder or an accordion-type folder for each child (Batzle, 1992; Hendrick; 2003). Portfolio information helps the teacher "construct a well-rounded and authentic picture of each child so you are better able to plan your program, to build on individualized strengths, and to support each child's growth.... Because you want portfolios to be integrated into your daily program, they need to be within children's easy reach. Children enjoy looking back through their work, and browsing and reflection are important parts of this process" (Cohen, 1999). Harris (2009) adds, "Portfolios can foster continuous reflection and richer, deeper communication among all the members of the learning community—children, teachers, caregivers, administrators, and families."

NOTE: A sample portfolio assessment checklist and multiple observation forms are available online at this text's premium website.

assessment refers to the collection of information for the purpose of making educational decisions about children or groups of children or to evaluate a program's effectiveness. The National Association for the Education of Young Children (NAEYC) and National Association of Early Childhood Specialists in State Departments of Education (NAECS/SDE) in 2003 updated their 1991 joint position statement on Curriculum, Assessment, and Program Evaluation. This statement is still valid today. Concerning assessment they stated:

> Make ethical, appropriate, valid and reliable assessment a central part of all early childhood programs. To assess young children's strengths, progress, and needs, use assessment methods that are developmentally appropriate, culturally and linguistically responsive, tied to children's daily activities, supported by professional development, inclusive of families, and connected to specific, beneficial purposes: (1) making sound decisions about teaching and learning, (2) identifying significant concerns that may require focused intervention for individual children, and (3) helping programs improve their educational and developmental interventions.

In most states early childhood educators are finding that state standards are guiding assessment. This has prompted early childhood educators to find better ways to assess children, particularly those with special needs. One way that has been shown to be very valuable is called *play-based* assessment (Ahola & Kovacik, 2007). Zero to Three (2005) defines play-based assessment as:

> A form of developmental assessment that involves observation of how a child plays alone, with peers, or with parents or other familiar caregivers, in free play or in special games.
> This type of assessment can be helpful because play is a natural way for children to show what they can do, how they feel, how they learn new things, and how they behave with familiar people.

Developmentally appropriate practice emphasizes that "the experiences and the assessment are linked (the experiences are developing what is being assessed, and vice versa); both are aligned with the program's desired outcomes or goals for children.... In addition to this assessment by teachers, input from families as well as children's own evaluations of their work are part of the program's overall assessment strategies" (Copple & Bredekamp, 2009).

Evaluation is the process of determining whether the philosophy, goals, and objectives of the program have been met. Interpretations and decisions are made based on the collected information. Assessment and evaluation are closely related and can happen simultaneously. Gordon and Browne (2011) explain further: "Evaluation is a continuous process. It is at once a definition, an assessment, and a plan....In its simplest form, evaluation is a process of appraisal." Informal and formal evaluation of a program should include the indoor and outdoor environments, schedule, routines, the curriculum as a whole, themes, lesson plans, activities, performances of the children, and the teacher's role. Ongoing evaluation is part of the curriculum process. Evaluation provides feedback concerning the effectiveness of the program, the goals and objectives, the teaching approach, the observation cycle, and once again the evaluation process.

You will find suggestions for observation, assessment strategies, and evaluation in each of the following chapters of this book. Hopefully, this will help you link observation, assessment strategies, and evaluation with planning and curriculum.

Afterview
● ●

A child-centered early education environment focuses on children playing and learning. As we know, young children develop and learn in a variety of ways. As teachers we have the responsibility to understand the cultural influences and developmental characteristics of young children, to extend and support children's ideas and interests, and to provide appropriate learning activities and guidance techniques to meet their needs. The children acquire the skills, concepts, and knowledge of the curriculum through rich and varied interaction with peers, teachers, and materials. As a teacher, you prepare and organize a developmentally, individually, and culturally appropriate classroom to provide children with a range of high-quality learning experiences. This is based on curricular goals and objectives, age-appropriate practices, children's interests and instructional needs, and appropriate observation, assessment, and evaluation.

Young children entering our programs are naturally curious about their environment and are eager to explore and learn about their world. Classroom arrangements and materials directly affect children's learning and self-esteem. A developmentally appropriate classroom should give children the opportunity to select activities from a variety of centers that are interesting and meaningful. The learning centers allow the children to create situations using both the real world and their fantasy world to solve problems and express creative ideas. The selection of open-ended materials for these centers encourage children to freely explore, experiment, and create.

Effective early education classrooms involve children in multisensory and multicultural experiences in a variety of settings, including independent activities, small group activities, and large group projects. Children are encouraged to talk about and share their experiences with their peers and adults. An early education environment is truly an active one when children are engaged in learning and play.

Reflective Review Questions
● ●

1. If curriculum is inclusive, integrated, emergent, child-centered, and child-directed, then what is your responsibility in planning curriculum? Explain your answer in a written format.

2. Many Americans take the position that this country is a *melting pot*, and that immigrants should quickly assimilate with the culture of the United States. Is this position consistent with a multicultural/anti-bias curriculum in an early childhood setting? Why or why not?

3. In a short paragraph, summarize the history and background of each curriculum model you were introduced to in this chapter, including significant individuals who were involved in the creation of the model. Can you identify some similarities and differences as you compare them? If you had a choice, which curriculum model would you choose to implement in your own classroom, and why?

4. Careful observation and assessment of children is essential to planning appropriate learning experiences for them. However, isn't this just wishful thinking? How can teachers with a myriad of tasks to do every day possibly squeeze in observation and assessment of children? How will you accomplish (or do you accomplish) this when you are responsible for a classroom of children?

Key Terms

anecdotal record	environment	observation
anti-bias	evaluation	philosophy
assessment	goals	portfolio assessment
case study	inclusion	project
checklist	inclusive curriculum	reflective log or diary
culture	integrated curriculum	theme
curriculum	learning centers	transitions
curriculum web	lesson plan	unit
emergent curriculum	objectives	

Explorations

1. Research the Individuals with Disabilities Education Improvement Act of 2004. Study the IFSP and the IEP, which are requirements of this law. Share your findings with your classmates.

2. Interview a teacher from one of the model programs discussed in this chapter, such as Montessori or Head Start. Ask the teacher to describe the philosophy of the school; how she develops curriculum to meet the abilities, interests, and needs of the children in her class; and how she assesses or evaluates the development of the children and the program itself.

3. Keep a journal or notebook for one week on multicultural/anti-bias and inclusion activities you observed or culturally related activities that you personally experienced. List the date, event, and what you learned or experienced for each entry. Your listings can report your observations in an early education classroom; present a synopsis of articles you read in newspapers, magazines, or journals; or describe ethnic events you attended, new ethnic foods you ate, or a multicultural resource center or museum you visited in your community. Turn in your journal or notebook to your instructor, and discuss your findings with your classmates or colleagues.

4. Based on the information from this chapter and from observing in an early education classroom (infant, toddler, preschool, prekindergarten, kindergarten, or primary), generate a list of the guidance techniques you have observed teachers using with a group of young children. Were any of the children you observed children with special needs? Did any of the children display challenging behaviors? Share the list with your classmates and decide whether each guidance technique was developmentally appropriate?

5. Based on the information from this chapter and from observing an early education classroom, create a diagram of a room arrangement for a classroom of preschool children. Include doors, windows, furniture, sources of electricity, water, and so on. Label each learning center. Use "A Checklist for Room Arrangement" (Figure 2–9) to test the validity of your diagram. Explain how your room arrangement will impact the behavior of the children in this room.

Additional Readings and Resources

Cohen, L. E. (2009, May) Exploring cultural heritage in a kindergarten classroom. *Young Children, 64*(3), 72–77.

Copple, C. (Ed) (2003). *A world of difference.* Washington, DC: NAEYC.

Cowles, M. (2006, Fall). Creating emotionally safe and supportive environments for children. *Dimensions of Early Childhood, 34*(3), 36–38.

Debord, L. L., Heseness, R. C., Moore, N., Cosco, N., & McGinnis, J. R. (2002, May). Paying attention to the outdoor environment is as important as preparing the indoor environment, *Young Children, 57*(3), 32–35.

Division for Early Childhood (DEC) and National Association for the Education of Young Children (NAEYC). (2009). *Early childhood inclusion: A joint position statement of DEC & NAEYC.* Online at: *http://www.naeyc.org*

Edwards, C. P., Gandini, L., & Forman, G. E. (Eds.). (1998). *The hundred languages of children: The Reggio Emilia approach—Advanced reflections* (2nd ed.). Greenwich, CT: Ablex Publishing.

Evans, B. (2007). *"I know what's next!" Preschool transitions without tears or turmoil.* Ypsilante, MI: High/Scope Press.

Fenton, A. (2005, March). Collaborative steps: Paving the way to kindergarten for young children with disabilities. *Young Children, 60*(2), 32–37.

Friedman, S., & Soltero, M. F. (2006, July). Following a child's lead. Emergent curriculum for infants and toddlers. *Beyond the Journal.* On-line at: *http://www.naeyc.org*

Gartrell, D., & Gartrell, J. J. (2008, May). Guidance matters: Understand bullying. *Young Children, 63*(3), 54–55.

Helm, J. (2006). Projects that power young minds: Why child-initiated projects should be central in the early grades. *Educational Leadership, 62*(1), 59–62.

Helm, J. H., & Beneke, S. (Eds.). (2003). *The power of projects.* New York: Teachers College Press, Washington, DC: NAEYC.

Jackson, C. (2007). The ABC's of bullying. *Teaching Tolerance, Classroom Activities* (January). Online at: *http://www. tolerance.org/teach/activities*

Koralek, D. (Ed.). (2007). *Spotlight on young children and families.* Washington, DC: NAEYC.

Lee, R., Ramsey, P. G., & Sweeney, B. (2008, November). Engaging young children in activities and conversations about race and social class. *Young Children, 63*(6), 68–76.

Malenfont, N. (2006). *Routines and transition: A guide for early childhood professionals.* St. Paul, MN: Redleaf Press.

Matthews, H., & Ewen, D. (2006). *Reaching all children: Understanding early care and education participation among immigrant families.* Washington, DC: Center for Law and Social Policy.

Mindess, M., Chen, M., & Breener, R. (2008, November). Social-emotional learning in the primary curriculum. *Young Children, 63*(6), 56–59.

Scruggs, A. E. (2009, Fall). *Color blindness: The new racism.* Online at: *http://www.tolerance.org/magazine/number-36-fall-2009*

Sorrels, B., Norris, D., & Sheeran, L. (2005, Spring/Summer). Curriculum is a verb, not a noun. *Dimensions of Early Childhood, 33*(2), 3–10.

Helpful Web Connections

American Academy of Pediatrics
http://www.aap.org (Put an End to Bullying)

American Montessori Internationale
http://www.montessori-ami.org

American Montessori Society
http://www.amshq.org

Bank Street College of Education
http://www.bankstreet.edu

Circle of Inclusion
http://www.circleofinclusion.org

Council for Exceptional Children, Division for Early Childhood   http://www.dec-sped.org

Head Start Resource—Early Childhood Learning & Knowledge Center   http://eclkc.ohs.acf.hhs.gov/hslc

High/Scope
http://www.highscope.org

Project Approach
http://www.projectapproach.org

Teaching Tolerance
http://www.tolerance.org

References

Ahola, D., & Kovacik, A. (2007). *Observing and understanding child development: A child study manual.* Clifton Park, NY: Delmar Cengage Learning.

Albrecht, K. (1996, Fall). Reggio Emilia: Four key ideas. *Texas Child Care, 20*(2), 2–8.

Allen, K. E., & Schwartz, I. S. (2005). *The exceptional child: Inclusion in early childhood education* (4th ed.). Clifton Park, NY: Delmar Cengage Learning.

Aronson, S. S. (Ed.). (2002). *Healthy young children* (4th ed.). Washington, DC: NAEYC.

Bank Street College of Education (1992). *Exploration with young children.* Mt. Rainier, MD: Gryphon House.

Bank Street School for Children. (2002). *Bank Street School for Children's Parent Handbook.* New York: Author.

Batzle, J. (1992). *Portfolio assessment and evaluation.* Cypress, CA: Creative Teaching Press.

Bentzen, W. R. (2009). *Seeing young children* (6th ed.). Clifton Park, NY: Wadsworth Cengage Learning.

Bredekamp, S. (1993, November). Reflections on Reggio Emilia. *Young Children, 49*(1), 13–17.

Brewer, J. (2001). *Introduction to early childhood education* (4th ed.). Boston, MA: Allyn & Bacon.

Buell, M. J., & Sutton, T. M. (2008, July). Weaving a web with children at the center. *Young Children, 63*(4), 100–105.

Catron, C. E., & Allen, J. (2008). *Early childhood curriculum* (4th ed.). Upper Saddle River, NJ: Merrill.

Cech, M. (1991). *Globalchild: Multicultural resources for young children.* Menlo Park, CA: Addison-Wesley.

Chard, S. (2001). *Project approach.* On-line at: *http://www. projectapproach.com*

Cohen, L. (1999, February). The power of portfolios. *Early Childhood Today, 13*(5), 31–33.

Colbert, J. (2007). *Bridging differences with understanding: Helping immigrant children be more ready to learn.* Online at: *http://www. earlychildhoodnews.com*

Copple, C., & Bredekamp, S. (Eds.) (2009). *Developmentally appropriate practice* (3rd ed.). Washington, DC: NAEYC.

Crosser, S. (2005). *What do we know about early childhood education? Research based practice.* Clifton Park, NY: Delmar Cengage Learning.

de Melendez, W. R., & Beck, V. (2010). *Teaching young children in multicultural classrooms.* Clifton Park, NY: Wadsworth Cengage Learning.

Derman-Sparks, L., & A.B.C. Task Force (1989). *Anti-bias curriculum: Tools for empowering young children.* Washington, DC: NAEYC.

Essa, E. L. (2011). *Introduction to early childhood education* (6th ed.). Clifton Park, NY: Wadsworth Cengage Learning.

Feng. (1994). Adapted from Essa, 2011; Derman-Sparks & A.B.C. Task Force, 1989; Feng, 1994; Gonzalez-Mena, 2001; Marshall, 2001; Spodek & Saracho, 1994; York, 2003

Fortson, L. R., & Reiff, J. C. (1995). *Early childhood curriculum.* Boston, MA: Allyn & Bacon.

Fraser S., & Gestwicki, C. (2002). *Authentic childhood: Reggio Emilia in the classroom.* Clifton Park, NY: Wadsworth Cengage Learning.

Frost, J. L. (1992). *Play and playscapes.* Clifton Park, NY: Delmar Cengage Learning.

Gandini, L. (1993, November). Fundamentals of the Reggio Emilia approach to early childhood education. *Young Children, 49*(1), 4–8.

Gargiulo, R., & Kilgo, J. L. (2000). Young children with special needs: An introduction to early childhood special education. Clifton Park, NY: Delmar Cengage Learning.

Gestwicki, C. (2011). *Developmentally appropriate practice: Curriculum and development in early education* (4th ed.). Clifton Park, NY: Wadsworth Cengage Learning.

Goffin, S. G. (2001). *Curriculum models and early childhood education* (2nd ed.). Upper Saddle River, NJ: Merrill.

Gonzalez-Mena, J. (2001). *Multicultural issues in child care.* (3rd ed.). New York: McGraw Hill.

Gonzalez-Mena, J., & Shareef, I. (2005, November). Discussing diverse perspectives on guidance. *Young Children, 60*(6), 34–38.

Gordon, A. M., & Browne, K. W. (2007). *Beginning essentials in early childhood education.* Clifton Park, NY: Delmar Cengage Learning.

Gordon, A. M., & Browne, K. W. (2011). *Beginnings and beyond* (8th ed.). Clifton Park, NY: Wadsworth Cengage Learning.

Harris, M. E. (2009, May). Implementing portfolio assessment. *Young Children, 64*(3), 82–85.

Head Start (2003). *Head Start: A child development program* [Brochure]. Washington, DC: U.S. Department of Health and Human Services.

Head Start Bureau. (2005). *Head Start Facts.* Washington, DC: U. S. Department of Health and Human Services.

Helm, J. H., & Katz, L. (2001). *Young investigators: The project approach in the early years.* New York: Teachers College Press, Washington, DC: NAEYC.

Hemmeter, M. L., Ostrosky, M. M., Artman, K. M., & Kinder, K. A. (2009, May). Planning transitions to prevent challenging behavior. *Young Children, 63*(3), 18–25.

Hendrick, J. (2003). *Total learning* (6th ed.). Upper Saddle River, NJ: Merrill Prentice Hall.

High/Scope Educational Research Foundation. (2003). *Professional development programs.* Ypsilanti, MI: Author.

Hohmann, M., Banet, B., & Weikert, D. P. (1995). *Young children in action: A manual for preschool educators* (2nd ed.). Ypsilanti, MI: The High/Scope Press.

Irvine, J. J. (2009, Fall). *Relevant beyond the basics.* Online at: *http://www.tolerance.org/magazine/ number-36-fall-2009*

Isbell, R. (2007). *An environment that positively impacts young children.* On-line at: *http://www.earlychildhoodnews. com*

Jones, E., & Nimmo, J. (1994). *Emergent curriculum.* Washington, DC: NAEYC.

Katz, L. G. (1994). The project approach (Report No. EDO-PS94-6). *ERIC Digest.* Urbana, IL: ERIC Clearinghouse on Elementary and Early Childhood Education.

Klein, A. S. (2007). *Creating peaceful environmental designs for the classroom.* On-line at: *http://www.earlychildhoodnews. com*

Klein, M. D., Cook, R. E., & Richardson-Gibbs, A. M. (2001). *Strategies for including children with special needs in early childcare settings.* Clifton Park, NY: Delmar Cengage Learning.

Louv, R. (2008). *Last child in the woods.* Chapel Hill, NC: Algonquin Books.

Marotz, L. R. (2009). *Health, safety, and nutrition for the young child* (7th ed.). Clifton Park, NY: Wadsworth Cengage Learning.

Marshall, H. H. (2001, November). Cultural influences on the development of self-concept. *Young Children, 56*(6), 19–25.

McCracken, J. B. (2000). *Playgrounds safe and sound* [Brochure]. Washington, DC: NAEYC.

Meisels, S. J. (2000). Performance assessment in early childhood education. Urbana, IL: ERIC.

Miller, D. F. (2010). *Positive child guidance* (6th ed.). Clifton Park, NY: Wadsworth Cengage Learning.

National Association for the Education of Young Children (NAEYC). (2005). *Code of ethical conduct and statement of commitment.* Online at: *http://www.naeyc.org*

National Association for the Education of Young Children (NAEYC). (2007). *Where we stand. Many languages, many cultures. Respecting and responding to diversity.* Online at: *http://www.naeyc.org*

National Association for the Education of Young Children (NAEYC) & National Association of Early Childhood Specialists in State Departments of Education (NAECS/SDE). (2003). Joint Position Statement. Early childhood curriculum, assessment, and program evaluation: Building an effective, accountable system in programs for children birth through age 8. Online at: *http://www.naeyc.org*

New, R. S. (2000). Reggio Emilia: Catalyst for change and conversation (Report No. EDO-PS-00-15). *ERIC Digest.* Urbana, IL: ERIC Clearinghouse on Elementary and Early Childhood Education.

Perry, B. D. (2002, November–December). A different world. *Parent and Child, 10*(3), 47–49.

Ray, J. A., Pewitt-Kinder, J., & George, S. (2009, September). Partnering with families of children with special needs. *Young Children, 64*(5), 16–22.

Reynolds, E. (2002). *Infant environments.* Online at: *http://www.earlychildhood.com*

Riley, J. G., & Boyce, J. S. (2007, Winter). Buddying or bullying? A school-wide decision. *Dimensions of Early Childhood, 35*(1), 3–11.

Roopnarine, J. L., & Johnson, J. E. (2009). *Approaches to early childhood education.* Upper Saddle River, NJ: Merrill.

Schute, N. (2002, September). Madam Montessori. *Smithsonian, 33*(6), 70–74.

Shidler, L. (2009, September). Teaching children what we want them to learn. *Young Children, 64*(5), 88–91.

Spodek, B., & Saracho, O. N. (1994). *Right from the start: Teaching ages three to eight.* Boston, MA: Allyn & Bacon.

Stavisky, K. (2002, Fall). A richness of purpose in teacher education: A Bank Street tradition. *Street Scenes, Bank Street College of Education, 10*(1), 1.

Thomson, B. J. (1993). *Words can hurt you: The beginning of anti-bias education.* Menlo Park, CA: Addison Wesley.

Torquati, J., & Barber. J. (2005, May). Dancing with trees: Infants and toddlers in the garden. *Young Children, 60*(3), 40–46.

U. S. Department of Health and Human Services. (2005). On-line at: *http://eclkc.ohs.acf.hhs.gov*

Wardle, F. (2001, November). Supporting multiracial and multiethnic children and their families. *Young Children, 56*(6), 38–39.

Watson, A., & McCathren, L. (2009, March). Including children with special needs. *Young Children, 64*(2), 20–26.

West, M. M. (2001, November). Teaching the third culture child. *Young Children, 56*(6), 27–32.

Wien, C. A. (Ed.). (2008). *Emergent curriculum in the primary classroom.* New York: Teachers College Press, & Washington, DC: NAEYC.

Willis, C. (2009). *Creating inclusive learning environments for young children.* Thousand Oaks, CA: Corwin Press.

Wurm, J. P. (2005). *Working in the Reggio way.* St. Paul, MN: Redleaf Press & Washington, DC: NAEYC.

York, S. (2003). *Roots and wings.* (Revised ed.). St. Paul, MN: Redleaf Press.

Zero to Three. National Center for Infants, Toddlers and Families. (2005). Online at: *http://www.zerotothree.com*

 Additional information and resources on early childhood curriculum can be found on the Education CourseMate website for this book. Go to **www.CengageBrain.com** to register your access code.

PART TWO
Discovering and Expanding the Early Education Curriculum

A child is sunshine,
Sparkling in every step she takes.
A child is laughter,
Filling the air with sounds he makes.
A child sees beauty,
Wonder, and excitement everywhere
And freely offers
A vision of joy, to treasure, to share.

—Hilda Jackman
Reprinted with permission

Astrid Dininno/Getty Images

chapter

3

Language and Literacy

Objectives

After Studying This Chapter, You Should Be Able To:

● Discuss language development in young children and relate stages of child development to literacy development.

● Define and give examples of developmentally appropriate ways to support emergent literacy at home and in an early education program.

● State why it is extremely important to respect and meet the needs of bilingual and bicultural young children.

● Describe reading and writing development as well as organizing and planning for integrated language and literacy experiences.

● Understand how to use observation and assessment to support literacy learning in an early childhood classroom.

● Design a developmentally appropriate language arts center that includes the use of technology to enrich the literacy experience.

● Create and present literacy activities appropriate for young children, including flannelboard, group time, and other activities.

© Cengage Learning

Overview

As human beings, we have the desire to communicate with others. We do this in many ways. A smile communicates a friendly feeling; a clenched fist transmits anger; tears show happiness or sorrow. From the first days of life, a baby expresses pain or hunger by cries or actions. Gradually, the infant adds expressions of pleasure and smiles when a familiar person comes near. Then, the little one begins to reach out to be picked up.

A baby eventually learns the words of his parents. If the parents speak English, the baby will learn to speak English. If the baby spends a lot of time around significant adults who speak Spanish, Japanese, Hebrew, or any other language, the infant will learn the language of the people around him.

The process of learning a language is important. It is one of the most important skills a child develops. The development of oral language is a natural accomplishment. Usually, a child learns the rules of language at an early age without formal instruction. A child learns language by listening and speaking. He learns language by using it. Learning to talk, like learning to walk, requires time for development and practice in everyday situations. During the first few years of life, listening and speaking constitute a large part of a child's experience with language.

According to recent brain research, we now understand that "even in the womb, the infant is turning towards the melody of the mother's voice. The brain is setting up the circuitry needed to understand and reproduce language" (Zero to Three, 2009). There are "windows of opportunity" or critical periods in a young child's life when he can "easily acquire a new language because the brain cells that process language are in the process of being wired, and are therefore especially responsive to experience. . . . How a brain develops hinges on a complex interplay between the genes you're born with and the experiences you have. . . . By the time children reach age three, their brains are twice as active as those of adults" (Shore, 1997).

Fleming (2002) explains, "Each child has more than 50,000 nerve pathways that can carry sounds of the human voice from the ears to the brain. The brain encodes the words and actually rearranges its brain cells into connections or networks to produce language." Therefore, infants and toddlers need experiences with caring adults "who offer many one-on-one, face to face interactions with them to support their oral language development and lay the foundation for later literacy learning" (Neuman, Copple, & Bredekamp, 2000).

Tomlinson (cited in Copple & Bredekamp, 2009) adds, "The first five to seven years of life are a sensitive period for brain development. . . . The brain is more malleable than it will be later, making kindergarten an optimum time for learning and effective intervention with all children." Vygotsky's (1978) theory extends the thought: "The changes in brain structure processes are important not only in and of themselves but also because they influence how children interact with the environment—and how people in the environment interact with children."

Emergent literacy in young children is a process of developing awareness about reading and writing before they can actually read or write. Their emergent literacy skills are the building blocks for later reading, writing, and communicating.

Helping you, the teacher, promote appropriate language and literacy environments is the intent of this chapter. Understanding language and literacy development

© Cengage Learning

Reading books with a friend is rewarding at any age.

emergent literacy A process of developing awareness about reading and writing before young children can read or write.

in young children, encouraging family support, and setting up a developmentally appropriate environment to strengthen and extend this development will also be examined. (Chapter 4, "Literature," is a continuation of the language arts program introduced in this chapter.)

Early Language and Literacy Development

language Human speech, the written symbols for speech, or any means of communicating.

language development Developmental process of a predictable sequence that includes both sending and receiving information. It is related, but not tied, to chronological age.

literacy The ability to read and write, which gives one the command of a native language for the purpose of communicating.

Language can be defined as human speech, the written symbols for speech, or any means of communicating. Genishi and Dyson (2009) point out that "language is a cultural means of expression, that like a culture itself, has multiple facets and uses." **Language development** follows a predictable sequence. It is related, but not tied, to chronological age. This developmental process includes both sending and receiving information. *It is important to remember that language is learned through use.*

Literacy, the ability to read and write, gives one the command of a native language for the purpose of communicating. This involves skills in listening, speaking, reading, and writing. The excitement of learning to read and write, we hope, will be as rewarding as a child's first words and first steps.

Long before babies can speak, they listen to sounds and words. They hear differences in voices and sounds. Infants will turn their heads in the direction of a particular sound. Friendly verbal interaction with and encouragement from nurturing adults help a baby form his first words out of randomly babbled sounds. An infant learns quickly that communicating is worthwhile because it results in reactions on the part of others.

Gestwicki (2011) develops this idea further when she states, "In reality it is through the same social relationships that introduce infants to the emotions of love and trust, and to the behavior of people in their environment, that babies learn language as part of the complex system of communication they will use throughout their lives."

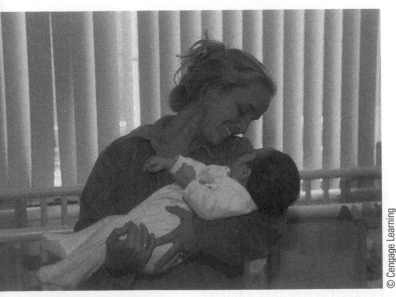

An infant and a caring adult need time to develop their own way of communicating.

LANGUAGE DEVELOPMENT OF YOUNG CHILDREN

Children learn language through predictable stages of development. As with many other aspects of child development, individual differences are apparent in the development and use of language.

Baby's cry: This form of communication varies in pitch and intensity and relates to stimuli such as hunger, discomfort, or fear. Just as adults respond differently to a baby's cry (some touch, some talk), the baby's response varies as well. An infant can stop crying and then smile or laugh in reaction to an adult's facial expression, to words spoken, or to being held.

Cooing: These are the sounds made when an infant's basic needs are met and he is relaxed, content, or stimulated by what is seen or heard. A baby derives a great deal of pleasure from practicing and listening to his own gurgling and cooing.

Smiling and laughing: Babies seem to be smiling when they are only a few days old. Some smile in their sleep, possibly through inner motivations. Adult facial, auditory, or motor stimuli can also be sources of smiles. "An infant's early laughter is usually full of squeals, howls, hoots, giggles, and grins" (Machado, 2010).

Babbling: These early random sounds made by an infant are a repetition of sequences of clear, alternating consonant and vowel sounds. This vocalization will eventually be combined into words, such as *baba* for bottle and *wawa* for water.

Association: A baby begins to get some idea of the meaning of a few words at about six to nine months. An association between the sounds an infant makes and the meanings of these sounds starts to become clear. When an adult begins to recognize and interpret these sounds, another level of communication has been reached. Playing "peek-a-boo" and "pat-a-cake" are fun to do and help the child develop an association between sounds and meanings.

Fields and Spangler (2000) explain further:

Before the first year is over, babies have narrowed their utterances from all the possible sounds to those significant in their environment. Babies in Mexico will trill the r sound, while babies in Germany will practice guttural sounds they hear, and English speaking babies will learn neither. Before long, they all begin to make the sounds of their language in combinations that mean something specific. As soon as they acquire this ability to communicate with words, they begin to string them together for even greater results.

© Cengage Learning

A child is developing an awareness of reading and writing before he can actually read or write.

One-word usage: Many first words are completely original, private words of the child. They may be sequences of sounds or intonations used on a consistent basis. "The physical organs need to function in a delicate unison, and the child must reach a certain level of mental maturity. At around the age of 12 months, the speech centers of the brain are poised to produce what is perhaps the most magical moment of childhood: the first word which marks the flowering of language" (Machado, 2010). In the early stages of language development, a word, such as *hot* or *no*, often stands for a whole object or an experience. The one-word stage also uses a word to get something or some action from others, such as *go, down,* or *mine.* Getting the appropriate response, approval, and smiles from adults encourages the child to make the sounds again and again. Language is a two-way process. Reaction is an important feedback to action. Although a child can speak only in "one-word sentences," he can understand more complex sentences and can react to what others are saying. From this point on, the child has progressed from receptive language, that is listening and understanding, to the period of expressive language, that is speaking.

Recall: A child's ability to remember an object named even when the object is not visible is helped by the touching, grasping, and tasting of the object. Responding to his name, identifying family members, and watching, pointing to, and naming an object usually occur toward the end of the first year. Recall is sometimes called "sign-language" communication, such as when a child holds up his arms to be picked up.

Telegraphic speech: The two-word sentence is the next step in the development of language of the young child. This speech helps a child express wishes and feelings, and ask questions. "Many words are omitted because of the child's limited ability to express and remember large segments of information" (Machado, 2010). The child repeats words over and over, such as *all gone, drink milk,* or *throw ball.* It is important to talk and listen to a toddler. This is a critical language-growth period, because the young child is processing, testing, and remembering language. See Figure 3–1 for toddler language characteristics.

Toddler Language Characteristics

FIGURE 3–1
Toddler language characteristics.
(Source: Machado, 2010)

- Uses two- to five-word sentences.
  "Baby down."
  "Baby boom boom."
  "No like."
  "No like kitty."
  "Me dink all gone."
  "See me dink all gone."
- Uses verbs.
  "Dolly cry."
  "Me going."
  "Wanna cookie."
- Uses prepositions.
  "In car."
  "Up me go."
- Adds plurals.
  "Birdies sing."
  "Gotta big doggies."
  "Bears in dat."
- Uses pronouns.
  "Me big boy."
  "He bad."
- Uses articles.
  "The ball gone."
  "Gimme a candy."
- Uses conjunctions.
  "Me and gamma."
- Uses negatives.
  "Don't wanna."
  "He no go."
- Runs words together.
  "Allgone," "gotta," "gimme," "lookee."
- Asks questions.
  "Wa dat?"
  "Why she sleep?"
- Does not use letter sounds or mispronounces spoken words.
  "Iceam," "choo" (for shoe), "member" (for remember), "canny" (for candy).
- Sings songs.
- Tells simple stories.
- Repeats words and phrases.
- Enjoys word and movement activities.

Multiword speech: When a young child reaches the stage of adult-like speech with longer sentences and almost all of the words present, he asks questions and understands the answers. The child can express feelings and tell others what he wants. At the same time, the child can understand the words of other people and absorb new knowledge. The child's vocabulary increases, and the repetition of songs, stories, and poems comes more easily. Words become important tools of learning, and they help a young child grow socially. Children talk together, and friendships grow. Thus, it becomes obvious that oral language is the foundation of early literacy.

Allen and Schwartz (2005) remind us that our knowledge of the language acquisition and development of young children will help us understand that speech and language irregularities come and go and appear to be self-correcting unless the child is pressured. We also need to be aware of early warning signs that a child could be having some difficulty.

> By late preschool and kindergarten, reading and writing emerge as children become aware of language as an entity itself and of the written word as a way of documenting what is spoken. Awareness of print and emerging literacy are the outgrowth of this last stage of [language] development. (Gordon & Browne, 2011)

LITERACY DEVELOPMENT OF YOUNG CHILDREN

literacy development
A lifelong process that begins at birth and includes listening, speaking, reading, and writing.

As previously indicated, **literacy development**, a lifelong process that begins at birth, includes listening, speaking, reading, and writing. Listening is a prerequisite to speaking. Learning to speak is an important step toward learning to read.

Bank Street College (2009) helps us understand even more about literacy development:

> Literacy learning is circular; learners may move forward in some areas and seem to step back as they consolidate understanding in others. Thus, reading and writing may not develop evenly. A child may be fluent in one area and emergent in another. Ultimately, however, whatever the timetable or path, the goals are the same for all:
>
> - To become fluent and efficient readers and writers who can make sense of and convey meaning in written language;
> - To become thinkers and communicators who are actively reviewing and analyzing information;
> - To enjoy reading and writing; and
> - To feel successful as users of literacy for a variety of purposes.

Researchers also believe children learn about reading and writing through *play*. As a teacher of young children, you see this happening every day. You have observed children learning to talk, read, or write when they are playing "peek-a-boo," engaging in nonsense speech play, listening to and singing familiar jingles and rhymes, scribbling, pretending, and using objects as symbols. Because literacy is a continuous process, children are working on all aspects of oral and written language at the same time.

> Because the brain uses the innate language pathway to learn to read, the development of language is an essential precursor to reading. . . . Speaking is a natural development, reading is not. Reading is an acquired skill. (Nevills & Wolfe, 2009)

Understanding what is developmentally appropriate for young children can help you recognize what is important in the development of oral and written language. Here are the skills identified by the National Institute for Literacy (2009) as most important for children's development of literacy:

- Knowing the names of printed letters
- Knowing the sounds associated with printed letters
- Manipulating the sounds of spoken language
- Rapidly naming a sequence of letters, numbers, objects, or colors
- Writing one's own name or even isolated letters
- Remembering the content of spoken language for a short time

The following terms help us understand language and literacy development:

Phonics is the relationship between the letters of written language and the sounds of spoken language. Phonics emphasizes the sound-symbol relationship through "sounding out" unfamiliar syllables and words.

As teachers you can emphasize the sounds of language by providing opportunities for children to practice with the **phonemes**, the smallest unit of speech, as well as helping them write the letter-sound relationships they know by using them in words, sentences, messages, and their own stories.

When children sing nursery rhymes, jingles, and songs, they are playing with and exploring the sounds of language. **Rhyming** is the ability to hear two words that end the same way, a beginning concept of **phonological or phonemic awareness**, which is the awareness and the ability to hear and identify individual sounds and spoken words, and the development of listening skills.

In addition, Neuman and colleagues (2000) inform us that

> phonological awareness refers to the whole spectrum from primitive awareness of speech sounds and rhythms to rhyme awareness and sound similarities, and at the highest level,

phonics The relationship between the letters of written language and the sounds of spoken language.

phonemes The smallest units of speech.

rhyming The ability to auditorily distinguish two words that end the same way.

phonological or phonemic awareness The ability to hear and identify individual sounds and spoken words.

Shared reading experiences give young children opportunities to develop literacy skills.

vocabulary This refers to the words we must know to communicate.

awareness of syllables and phonemes. Phonemes are the smallest units in speech, for instance, the /b/, /a/, and /t/ sounds that make up the word bat. Becoming attentive to the sound structure of language—becoming phonologically or phonemically aware—is an "ear" skill, unlike phonics, which is the relation between letters and sounds in written words.

Another important aspect of language development is **vocabulary**. This refers to the words we must know to communicate. Tomlinson and Hyson remind us that teachers recognize "the value of expanding children's vocabulary in the course of studying topics of interest. For example, when children study transportation, they learn words such as *vehicle, enormous, haul*, and *propeller*" (cited in Copple & Bredekamp, 2009).

Through shared reading experiences, writing their names, and playing games related to their letter discoveries, they are developing literacy skills at their own pace. You are building on what children already know and can do, while creating a developmentally appropriate language and literacy environment, when you:

● Talk to children, even while diapering or feeding them.
● Talk to children in standard spoken language—not baby talk. Speak clearly and give simple explanations.
● Reinforce a child's native language. Understand that every child's language or dialect is worthy of respect as a valid system for communication.
● Speak in a voice that helps children listen—not too fast or too soft.
● Encourage children to talk to you.
● Enable children to use language to communicate their thoughts about ideas and problems that are real and important to them.
● Listen when children talk to you. Give children your full attention when they speak. Be on their level and make eye contact. Use nonverbal communication, such as eye-to-eye contact, smiling, and holding a child's finger or hand to reinforce that you are listening. Be patient.
● Use children's names frequently.
● Allow time and opportunity for children to listen and talk freely without interruption.
● Play music for children to listen to. Provide different types of music in the environment, such as tapes or CDs of lullabies, songs from many cultures, and classical music.
● Sing songs. Make up songs with the children.
● Play finger plays, which offer a combination of stories, poems, directions, songs, and hand movements. Finger plays also offer a transition into a story or activity.
● Help children remember spoken information by giving simple multi-step directions for activities (National Institute for Literacy, 2009).
● Read or tell stories to children. "Reading to children helps to build the brain structures they will need in order to read" (Nevills & Wolfe, 2009). Make a wide selection of books available to children. Be sure there are books in a variety of languages, including Braille and sign language. (Chapter 4, "Literature" offers detailed information.)
● Read books that expose children to a varied and rich vocabulary.
● Enhance children's concept of and exposure to print. "Some teachers use Big Books to help children distinguish many print features, including the fact that print (rather than pictures) carries the meaning of the story, that the strings of letters between spaces are words and in print correspond to the oral version, and that reading progresses from left to right and top to bottom" (IRA & NAEYC, 1999).

- Take walks and listen to the sounds of the environment. Talk about what you see and hear. Write down what the children say and then put their words in a classroom book or on a large sheet of paper posted on an easel or a wall.
- Play listening games to develop sound awareness, such as clapping hands in a fast or slow tempo; then have children repeat the clapping as they heard it. Audio tape the games, and then play them back to the children to see if they can associate the taped claps with the ones they did.

"Literacy experiences should be prevalent in every primary classroom, incorporated into every area of the curriculum. Learning to read and write must be viewed as a developmental process, not a set of skills to be mastered" (Miels, 2001).

The more children read, the better they get at reading—and the more they want to read. During the primary grades, children must master conventional reading—a task that requires a lot of hard work. (Tomlinson cited in Copple & Bredekamp, 2009)

Additional and specific examples of language and literary developmental activities are presented later in this chapter. As stated earlier, in a developmentally appropriate setting, speaking, listening, reading, and writing are integrated into or combined with other curriculum areas. You will find examples of this throughout the chapters of this book.

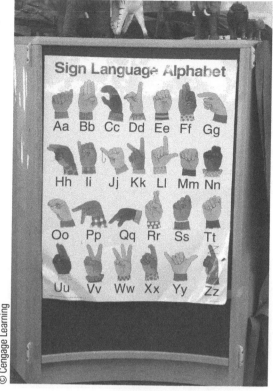

© Cengage Learning

Sign Language poster, Copyright School Specialty Publishing, used with permission.

Sharing Literacy: Encouraging Family Support

As previously stated, family members are a child's primary teachers of language. They are the first people a child hears speak, the first adults spoken to, and the most important people a child will communicate with throughout his life. Awareness of the importance of parents and other significant family members to a child's language and literacy development is one of the first steps in working with parents. It is also helpful to let family members know how valued their efforts are. Express to them how much you appreciate their interactions with you. Let them know what you are doing in the early childhood program. Point out ways they can contribute to or extend language and literacy development at home with their child.

- Developmentally appropriate early childhood programs establish and maintain collaborative relationships with each child's family to foster children's development in all settings. "These relationships are sensitive to family composition, language, and culture. To support children's optimal learning and development, programs need to establish relationships with families based on mutual trust and respect, involve families in their children's educational growth, and encourage families to fully participate in the program" (NAEYC, 2009). For example, welcome and encourage all families to be involved in every aspect of the program.
- Talk with families about their family structure and their views on child rearing and use that information to adapt the curriculum and teaching methods to the families served.
- Use a variety of strategies to communicate with families, including family conferences, new family orientations, individual conversations, telephone calls, and emails.
- Provide program information—including policies and operating procedures—in a language that families can understand. (NAEYC, 2009)

© Cengage Learning

Reading a book with daddy is a favorite language activity for a young child.

In addition, some teachers find it helpful to send notes or emails home periodically. Here are some suggestions for "Language Links" from you to the parents:

1. Read to your child. Read books, stories, magazines, comic strips, and poems. Have children's books around the house for your children. Some can be purchased and some can be checked out from the library. Read them often, and add to them regularly. These are the books we are reading in class this week. (You could list several books with the author's and illustrator's names, such as *Family Pictures, Cuadros de Familia*, by Carmen Lomas Garza; *Grandma Calls Me Beautiful*, by Barbara Joosse, illustrated by Barbara Lavalles; *I Love My Family*, by Wade Hudson; *On Mother's Lap*, by Ann Herbert Scott, illustrated by Glo Coalson; *Papa and Me*, by Arthur Dorros; *Friday Night Is Papa Night*, by Ruth A. Sonneborn, illustrated by Emily A. McCully; and *The Day of Ahmed's Secret*, by Florence P. Heide and Judith H. Gilliland, illustrated by Ted Lewin.)

2. Talk about the illustrator or photographer. Look at the pictures in the book you are sharing with your child. Can "Larry" think or guess what the story will be about? If it is a picture book, let your child tell you about the pictures or photographs. You will help him use pictures or other clues for reading comprehension. (You might then tell the parent something such as, "We are looking at Lois Ehlert this week. Her colorful collage illustrations are in these books: *Dia de Mercado, Market Day: A Story Told with Folk Art; Oodles of Animals; Growing Vegetable Soup*; and *In My World*."

3. Have a regular story time before or after meals or at bedtime. It will help both you and your child relax and share some private time together. Look at the book cover together. Use the words *front cover, back cover, title, author, illustrator, top, bottom, left, right*. This exposes your child to reading vocabulary.

4. Read all kinds of signs, labels, restaurant menus, and calendars to your child. Point out print on home equipment and products, and items of print used in your daily life. Point out signs when you are out riding together.

5. Let your child see you reading newspapers, magazines, books, and letters. Reading together and sharing stories is a family affair. Enjoy it and do it often!

6. Do activities together and then talk about them. This includes routine shopping, worship services, the zoo, museums, movies, television viewing, and sports activities.

7. Surround your child with opportunities to play with words. Provide a variety of things to write with: chalk, crayons, pencils, markers, and all kinds of paper. Encourage your child to draw. Besides clarifying thoughts and ideas, drawing tells stories and expresses feelings. It also reinforces the motor skills your child needs for writing.

8. Tell family stories. Encourage your child to ask questions. Let him tell a family story of his own.

9. How's the "art gallery" coming along? Post your child's scribbles and drawings on the refrigerator or the wall in his room. This gives all the family members a chance to look at his efforts. It is fun to add your own drawings.

10. Write to your child. Put notes in lunchboxes, in book bags, under pillows, in pockets, on the refrigerator. Your child will look forward to "being surprised." Let your child see you write. When you write a letter, let him write a letter, too. When you send a birthday card, let him add some scribbles. (These suggestions are adapted from Machado, 2010; U.S. Department of Education, 2009; and personal experiences and conversations with early education teachers.)

Respecting a Child's Bilingual, Bicultural World

You may now have or eventually will have young children in your classroom who speak languages other than English and whose country of origin is not the United States.

> The United States has always been a nation of many languages. Now, in the 21st century, new waves of immigration, as well as migration within the country, mean that early childhood programs are serving increasing numbers of children whose home language is not English. . . . An anti-bias approach includes finding ways to support children's home language as an essential component of respecting and integrating home cultures into early childhood programs. (Derman-Sparks & Edwards, 2010)

The following stages of second language learning are adapted from Bank Street (2009); Hernandez (1995); Ramsey (1987); Hickman-Davis (2002); and Espiritu, Meier, Villazana-Price, & Wong (2002):

● *The Preproduction or Silent Stage:* A child's initial response to a new language is to listen to or "take in" the language rather than to speak it. He is trying to make sense of what goes on around him. Many times the child will imitate what other children do in the class, pretending that he understands. The length of this particular stage will vary from child to child. During this period, music, movement, dramatic play, and art activities are appropriate. Reading books aloud to the child can offer a one-on-one experience with a teacher as well. Do not rush children through this nonverbal period.

● *Early Production Stage:* At this stage, children have limited verbalization and growing comprehension. Occasionally asking questions that require a "yes" or "no" answer from the child will give a teacher an informal assessment of what the child is understanding. Speech can also be encouraged by asking questions that request the labeling of familiar objects ("What is this?") or finishing a statement ("We are eating . . ."; "The color of this crayon is . . ."). This can be accomplished easily in informal conversations with the child. Group time, classroom games, outdoor play, and one-on-one activities will provide ample opportunities in which you can guide children through this stage. At the beginning, English language learners will have to mentally translate the question into their native language, formulate a response, and then mentally translate the response back into English. This takes time.

● *Expansion of Production Stage:* This is the speech emergence and expansion stage. With this comes increased comprehension and the ability to speak in simple sentences. Encourage the child to talk about his family and friends. Motivate him to describe, using his words, what he is experiencing with his five senses. The child may experiment more with a new language when he is with peers than with adults. Observe your students interacting with other children. This will give you information about the extent of his vocabulary and fluency. Finger plays, songs, and rhymes are useful in stimulating the child toward using his new language.

In acquiring a new language, "it is important to keep in mind that different children may enter school at different stages, and that all children may not pass through all stages at the same rate or even in the same sequence" (Bank Street, 2009). You should appreciate the countless ways in which children learn and do not rely on a set curriculum for teaching oral language or literacy. Instead, "learn from the children and adopt their curricula to allow for group preferences and individual variations" (Genishi, 2002).

Throughout the history of education many different terms have been used to describe or characterize children whose second language is English. Here are some examples:

● students with Limited English Proficiency (LEPs)
● students for whom English is a Second Language (ESLs)
● Second Language Learners (SLLs)

Currently educators refer to these children as:

● English Language Learners (ELLs),
● Dual Language Learners (DLLs), or
● Emergent Bilinguals (EBs).

(Bank Street, 2009; NAEYC (2009); and Genishi & Dyson, 2009).

It is essential that teachers see second language learners as children with prior knowledge and experience about language learning.

Be sensitive and encourage each child to communicate in his own way during social interaction with other children. Emphasize the child's strengths, and help to build his positive self-concept. Provide consistent and continual modeling of English, and whenever possible allow the child to speak his primary language as well as English.

It is important to understand that accepting a child's language is part of accepting a child. The children in the classroom will model your behavior. Children can be very accepting and caring of each other. They communicate by gestures or by taking a child's hand and leading him to an activity, many times without your guidance.

Children will feel more successful if you involve their parents in activities and understand the different learning styles each child may have. Create an atmosphere in which sharing cultures is valued. The celebrations of many cultural holidays at the school that include the family members of *all* the children in your class offer positive reinforcement. Invite them to visit the classroom and share their language with the children. Maintain personal contact with the child's family throughout the year. "Once families feel comfortable and understand how important they are to their child's success, a strong relationship begins. The partnership strengthens as school and teacher become a source for positive information" (Kersey & Masterson, 2009).

Parents can help you identify some basic words used in the child's language, especially those that are important to the child. *Be sure to use the child's correct name and not an "Americanized" one. Use the name often and pronounce it correctly.* (Listen carefully to the parents' pronunciation and imitate it.)

At first, if possible, have a family member or someone who speaks the child's native language available to help the child learn the routines and expectations, as well as the new language. If another child in the class speaks the language, interaction between the two should be encouraged (Essa, 2011).

See Figure 3–2 for additional suggestions to guide you in respecting each child's bilingual and bicultural world in the classroom environment.

Organizing and Planning for an Integrated Language and Literacy Environment

To focus on reading alone disregards the importance of children's experiences with writing. Reading and writing skills develop simultaneously and are interconnected. Progress in one fuels development of the other. (Mayer, cited in Essa & Burnham, 2009)

As previously discussed, throughout a child's life listening, speaking, reading, and writing are a prominent part of a child's world. As the significant adults in a child's life, we should ensure that the environment surrounding each child be the very best it can be—developmentally, individually, and creatively. When this occurs, children use and expand their language in almost every activity and curriculum area in which they participate.

Tips for Teachers

Derman-Sparks & Edwards (2010) and Nemeth (2009) offer suggestions to help you support the home languages of children in your class. These ideas will get you started until you add new ones of your own.

1. Have labels, children's books, signs, and authentic pictures in the diverse languages of the children.
2. Use words for common objects, numbers, days of the week, and so on, in the languages of the children.
3. Place authentic items from each child's culture and language in all learning centers. For example, have parents share empty food containers, menus, games, dolls, musical instruments, clothing and art supplies from their home countries.
4. Create a family shelf for families to take turns displaying objects they use in daily life and on special days.
5. Read children's books about families that are reflective of the ethnic/cultural groups in your class. Ask for parent volunteers to read books written in the home languages of the children.
6. Encourage families to share snacks and meals from their home culture. Cooking and preparing food activities provide ways to build pre-literacy and pre-math skills, to emphasize healthy eating, and to infuse anti-bias education into the program. Family members can help with recipes and ideas for places to get ingredients.

FIGURE 3–2
Tips for teachers.

As you plan the physical space for the language and literacy activities, you should keep in mind that how you design this area will affect the choices children make in their selection of activities. This part of the environment, sometimes called the language arts center, should be arranged so children can use this area independently or in small groups.

We should remember, too, that the physical classroom space should allow children to move from center to center, from large group to small group, and from small group to individual choice activities as well (Bobys, 2000). All of this is carefully orchestrated by the teacher, with selection of language and literacy activities by the children being the ultimate goal.

As with everything in an early childhood environment, the organization and focus is on creating a child-centered space. For infants and toddlers, the surroundings should be sensory-rich—bright colors everywhere, the air full of soft music, words from around the world being spoken, songs being sung, books being read, drawings being scribbled, and textures within reach.

You will find the language arts center is most effective when it

- is set in a part of the room that is quiet with little traffic, but is accessible from any other center.
- invites the children to use every inch of table, floor, and wall space.
- displays things at the children's eye level.
- attracts them to listen, look, think, write, draw, and read.
- includes materials, supplies, and equipment that offer explorative and developmentally appropriate hands-on experiences for young children.

The language arts center should be an environment that is soft. This can be accomplished by having a carpet, rug, or carpet squares on the floor; by adding large pillows

© Cengage Learning

In a developmentally appropriate language and literacy environment, writing is an important part of a child's literacy development.

When you plan the physical space for language and literacy activities, how you design this area will affect the choices children make in their selection of activities.

and beanbag chairs; and by adding some "creative spaces," such as enormous stuffed animals with large laps for children to sit on or an old-fashioned bathtub filled with pillows of all sizes and colors for an individual child to spend some alone time in reading a book or listening to a CD.

The center also should have good lighting and easy access to child-size tables, chairs, and bookcases that are arranged for group or individual use. Include both "stand-up" (chalkboard, easels, murals, window, clipboards) and "sit-down" (tables, lap desks, floor) writing places.

SETTING UP THE WRITING ENVIRONMENT

Children should have access to listening, reading, and writing materials in every learning center. Many of the items usually placed in the language arts center can be duplicated in other centers. When children want to write, copy, or draw, the "tools" should be available. Offer pressure-free experimentation with writing, and encourage children to write often. "The process of using written language begins by playing with it before it is used to communicate" (Wortham, 2010). Remember that children's first writing attempts appear as scribbling. Help them when you feel they need it. For example, "This is how I write your name. How do you write your name?"

> Emergent writing means that children begin to understand that writing is a form of communication, and their marks on paper convey a message. Emergent forms of writing include drawing, scribbling from left to right, creating letter-like forms, or creating random strings of letters, all used—sometimes even simultaneously—in the child's attempt to communicate an idea through print. (Mayer, cited in Essa & Burnham, 2009)

Encourage children to learn written language in the same energetic and interactive ways they learn oral language. Invite children to experiment with language in any way they choose, and accept whatever the child "writes," such as lists, creative calendars, children's dictation, posters, signs, labels, songs, and "creative" spelling. Materials should be available at all times for children to use for writing. They should be separated into appropriate, brightly colored containers to make it easy for children to choose what they need. The use and care of the materials should be discussed each time something new is added to the learning center. The classroom should also be print-rich. Identification of words in the environment appears to be one of the first steps in learning to read. Signs, logos, and labels can be used as valuable literacy learning tools. Include environmental print in children's home language as well as English. Young children are aware of logos/trademarks of their favorite fast food restaurants, the products they eat or use, and the signs around their neighborhoods. "It is suggested that environmental print can be used as the springboard for learning other factors inherent in being able to read such as phonics and phonemic awareness" (Charlesworth, 2011). (See Figure 3–3.)

Early writing experiences should introduce and reinforce meaningful and authentic opportunities for the children in your classroom. The following activities provide a wide range of writing activities:

© Cengage Learning

Offer pressure-free experimentation with writing and encourage children to write often.

- *Writing with Water:* Take a bucket of water and several large and small paintbrushes outside. The children can "write" on or "paint" the sidewalk, the building walls, the tricycles, the wagons, and the fence. This activity helps develop large muscle control, and at the same time provides the beginnings of literacy development. It is easy and fun, too.
- *Labeling:* Encourage the children to label things in the classroom as well as outdoors. Start the labeling yourself and let the children help. Listen to the children and let them label what they think needs labeling. This will help them "read the room." (The children love to use Post-its to label things and they can change them whenever *they* want to.) It is also fun to make floor signs, such as traffic signs, that say "enter," "exit," "stop," and "go."

Planning a Print-Rich Literacy Environment

A print-rich literacy environment includes the following:

- examples of signs, labels, and logos from product packaging (e.g., cereal boxes, toothpaste boxes, fast food containers, store bags, magazines, or newspapers)
- photographic images taken around the school's neighborhood, such as street signs
- all types of books that are displayed attractively and within easy access of the children, including big books placed on story easels or on laundry drying racks
- books and journals made and written by individual children
- class collaborative projects that offer language-experience stories
- magazines and newspapers appropriate for young children
- recorded stories
- message boards
- calendars
- rebus and symbol charts and graphs
- story props for retelling stories
- alphabet charts and vocabulary posters
- a wide variety of pictures depicting life around the world
- labels on materials, on supplies, on equipment, and in learning centers throughout the room and outdoors
- lists of all kinds
- children's names displayed
- child dictation or writing and drawings displayed

FIGURE 3–3
Planning a print-rich literacy environment.

● *Writing to Others:* Have the children write thank-you letters or notes to community members who visit the class and to those they have visited during field trips.
● *Story Starters:* Have the children tell you a story about when they were babies, or what happens when the wind blows, or what sounds they hear and sights they see. Use a tape or video recorder to capture their storytelling. Older children can write and illustrate their own big book based on the story.
● *Birthday Celebration:* Create a birthday celebration center once a month that lasts a week. Stock it with paper to make birthday cards; markers and crayons; old birthday card fronts; and scraps of lace, yarn, fabric, stickers, and birthday words. Use *happy birthday* in other languages, such as, *joyeux anniversaire* (French) and *feliz cumpleaños* (Spanish). Children can make cards for family members and classmates. This is a wonderful way to promote thoughtfulness, socialization, language, writing, reading, and creativity. Extend this activity by making a "Birthday Book" of the class. (If a child's family does not celebrate birthdays, the child does not have to visit this particular learning center.)
● *Journal Writing:* Motivate the children to write about their day, record things they want to remember, jot down words from the world wall, or copy the words of the titles of books, songs, finger plays, and recipes in their journals. These journals can be used in any learning center in the classroom.
● *Dictionaries:* Promote opportunities for the children to go for "word walks" around the classroom and copy words from labels, books, and so on. They learn name recognition by writing their classmates' names in their dictionary. This helps the children to become more aware of print and identifies early alphabetizing or sequencing. Also have actual dictionaries around (Bobys, 2000).

Observation and Assessment to Support Literacy Learning

Use assessment to support learning in the early childhood classroom. Select useful information about children's knowledge, skills, and progress by observing, documenting, and reviewing children's language and literacy work over time. "The most powerful outcome of ongoing assessment is the positive relationship teachers can build with each child. Every child is different, but the one thing every child needs is to feel accepted and appreciated. . . . A system of ongoing assessment also helps the teachers build a relationship with each child's family" (Dodge, Heroman, Charles, & Maiorca, 2004).

Neuman and colleagues (2000) emphasize that

> assessment should support children's development and literacy learning. Good assessment helps to identify children's strengths, needs, and progress toward specific learning goals. . . . Good assessment uses a variety of tools, including collection of children's work (drawings, paintings, writings), and records of conversation and interviews with children. . . . The core of assessment is daily observation. Watching children's ongoing life in the classroom enables teachers to capture children's performance in real activities rather than those contrived to isolate specific skills.

Here are some suggestions for assessment collection of children's language and literacy activities and projects:

● written language as collected in captions on drawings, labels, or child-made books
● items that indicate a child's learning style and interests
● spoken language as collected in anecdotal notes or on audio and videotapes
● musical expressions such as made-up songs and dances
● webs, lists of words, or other records of vocabulary

● multiple examples of how a child expresses ideas
● multiple examples of a child's self-portrait, even if it shows scribbling
● multiple examples of anecdotal records of language and literacy skill development

(Adapted from Helm, Beneke, & Steinheimer, 2007; Gober, 2002; Santos, 2004; and conversations with early education teachers.)

See Figure 3–4 for an example of an appropriate assessment checklist for recording young children's reading and writing development.

Refer to Chapter 2 for an explanation of other appropriate assessment tools in early childhood education, as well as online at this textbook's website.

Child _____ Age _____ Grade _____
School _____ Teacher _____

What Child Can Do	Assessment Dates	Comments
Goals for Preschool: Awareness and Exploration		
● Enjoys listening to and discussing storybooks		
● Understands that print carries a message		
● Engages in reading and writing attempts		
● Identifies labels and signs in the environment		
● Participates in rhyming games		
● Identifies some letters and makes some letter-sound connections		
● Uses known letters or approximations of letters to represents written language		
Goals for Kindergarten: Experimental Reading and Writing		
● Enjoys being read to and retells simple narrative stories or informational texts		
● Uses descriptive language to explain and explore		
● Recognizes letters and most letter-sound connections		
● Shows familiarity with rhyming and with beginning sounds		
● Understands basic concepts of print, such as left-to-right orientation and starting at the top of the page		
● Understands that spoken words can match written words		
● Begins to write letters of the alphabet and some high frequency words, such as own name, family names, or words such as *cat*, *dog*, and so on		
Goals for First Grade: Early Reading and Writing		
● Reads and retells familiar stories		
● When comprehension breaks down, uses a variety of strategies, such as rereading, predicting, questioning, and contextualizing		

(continued)

FIGURE 3–4
This checklist is not exhaustive, and any individual child may be at different levels of development in different areas. (Source: Charlesworth, 2011.)

FIGURE 3–4
(continued)

What Child Can Do	Assessment Dates	Comments
● Initiates using writing and reading for his or her own purposes		
● Can read orally with reasonable fluency		
● Identifies new words through letter-sound associations, word parts, and context		
● Identifies an increasing number of words by sight		
● Can sound out and represent all the major sounds in a spelling word		
● Writes about personally meaningful topics		
● Attempts to use some punctuation and capitalization		
Goals for Second Grade: Transitional Reading and Writing		
● Reads with greater fluency		
● When comprehension breaks down, uses strategies more efficiently		
● Uses strategies more efficiently to decode new words		
● Sight vocabulary increases		
● Writes about an increasing range of topics to fit different audiences		
● Uses common letter patterns and critical features to spell words		
● Punctuates simple sentences correctly and proofreads own work		
● Spends time each day reading		
● Uses reading to research topics		
Goals for Third Grade: Independent and Productive Reading and Writing		
● Reads fluently and enjoys reading		
● Uses a range of strategies when drawing meaning from the text		
● When encounters unknown words, uses word identification strategies appropriately and automatically		
● Recognizes and discusses elements of different text structures		
● Makes critical connections between texts		
● Writes expressively in different forms, such as stories, poems, and reports		
● Uses a rich variety of vocabulary that is appropriate to different text forms		
● Can revise and edit own writing during and after composing		
● Spells word correctly in final written drafts		

Literacy and Learning with Technology

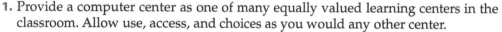

Technology has now found its place in the early education environment along with books, flannelboards, finger paints, markers, play dough, and other media. As a result, the use of technology in an early childhood setting requires that each of us, as early childhood educators, continue to learn as much as we can about technology issues and trends.

Computers, along with developmentally appropriate software, whiteboards, inexpensive cameras, digital cameras, mini-cams, age-appropriate/nonviolent video games, interactive CDs, DVDs, and cassette tape audio recorders, can make a unique contribution to the education of young children. As with any learning resource available, *how* technology is used is more important than *if* technology is used at all.

Technology, especially computers, can bring different learning opportunities to the language and literacy curriculum. "If children come from families in which there is little technology in the home, they will need to develop these skills at school" (Deiner, 2010).

The following guidelines for using and selecting technology are adapted from Buckleitner, 2009; Deiner, 2010; and Wardle, 2007.

© Cengage Learning

Technology, especially computers, can bring learning experiences to the language and literacy curriculum.

1. Provide a computer center as one of many equally valued learning centers in the classroom. Allow use, access, and choices as you would any other center.
2. Link technology activities with hands-on classroom materials.
3. Encourage children to work on the computer in pairs. Place two chairs by each computer. If your child care center or school offers wireless laptop computers, it is even easier to bring Web-based experiences to children in the context of their play or project activities.
4. Allow children lots of time to explore how to use a computer: what can or cannot occur, and simple exploration of the medium or literacy software/websites.
5. Young children need interactive programs they can gain control over. They need to learn cause-and-effect reasoning and that they can cause the computer to do something.
6. Don't try to formally "teach" technology skills and competencies. Instead, set the stage for successful experimentation by providing the materials, introducing them, and offering support.
7. Do carefully evaluate all software, both for developmental appropriateness and for nonsexist, nonracist, nonstereotypical and nonviolent material. Do not accept software brought from home without a similar evaluation.
8. New software is being developed daily. Many school districts have qualified individuals to assist teachers with this evaluation process. Many times funds are limited; this is another reason to select your language and literacy software carefully. You will be able to use the software longer if each selection meets the curriculum goals you have set.
9. Provide ways for children with special needs to use computers; encourage Individual Education Plans (IEPs) that use technology to address specific learning disabilities.
10. Encourage children to use digital cameras to expand their language and literacy activities.

Look for additional information on teaching with technology in all of the following chapters of this book.

Tips and Activities

Figure 3–5 is a suggested list of what to place in the language arts center, including things to write with, to write on, and to write in.

There are many techniques you can use to place items promoting language and literacy around the room. Some we have already discussed in this chapter. The following suggested activities are additional ones that teachers of young children have found to be developmentally and multiculturally appropriate, as well as lots of fun to do.

FLANNELBOARD ACTIVITIES

flannelboard Used as a prop to tell or extend a story effectively.

Often teachers hear a child say, "Tell it again." One of the ways to tell or extend a story effectively is with the use of a **flannelboard**.

> As children use flannelboard activities to retell a new or familiar story they represent oral and written language in picture form, thereby gaining structures for later abstract thinking. Young children's symbolic play signals the development of representational thought (Piaget) and has been recognized as critical in the development of abstract thought (Vygotsky). . . . Using flannelboards with primary grade children provides a natural connection to process writing. Students enjoy writing and rehearsing their own scripts. (Short, Harris, & Fairchild, 2001)

A good flannelboard activity:

● attracts attention.
● stimulates interest.
● is flexible in use.

FIGURE 3–5
A list of language arts center materials and supplies.

- Pencils, pens, and chalk of various sizes and colors
- Crayons of various sizes, colors, and thicknesses
- Markers of various colors, fine-tipped, thick-tipped, washable, permanent, and scented
- Magnetic letters and numbers
- Typewriter
- Computer
- Toy or nonworking telephone
- Toy microphone
- Paper of various sizes, colors, and textures; lined and unlined paper; drawing paper; construction paper; and scraps
- Cardboard and posterboard
- Stationery
- Journals
- Note pads
- Index cards
- Envelopes
- Graph paper
- Post-its

- Order forms
- Business forms
- Large and individual chalkboards, dry erase boards, and magic slates
- Carbon paper
- Finger paints
- Pencil sharpener
- Rulers
- Tape
- Glue
- Scissors
- Stapler
- Stickers
- Date stamp and pad
- Other donated office stamps and pads
- Paper clips
- Hole punch
- Brads
- Maps and globes
- Pictionaries and dictionaries
- Message board
- Folders and notebooks
- Old newspapers and magazines

- frees a teacher's hands.
- adds texture to the activity.
- is a visual prop for a story, song, or poem that does not have illustrations.
- improves communication.
- dramatizes concepts.
- is easily made and easily stored.

Other important aspects of this type of activity are as follows:

- The children can help the teacher tell the story by placing the pieces on the board at the appropriate time in the story.
- After the teacher tells the story, the flannelboard and character pieces can be placed in any activity center or curriculum area.
- The children or individual child can then tell the story to each other or make up another story to relate to the flannelboard pieces.
- Flannelboard figures can be touched, held, and moved, forming a bridge between the real and the abstract.

You can purchase a commercial flannelboard or you can make your own. Select plywood, masonite, or any wood-based board for durability. Styrofoam board, heavy cardboard, display board, and prestretched artist's canvas are more lightweight and easier to carry but not as durable. The board may be freestanding or placed on an easel, on a chalkboard tray, or on a chair. Smaller, individual boards can be placed in the language arts center for children to use by themselves or with a friend.

Flannel cloth is usually the best material to use for covering the base. It has excellent adhering qualities and is lightweight and colorful. Felt cloth also can be used with good results, as can most fuzzy textured material. Velour (material used for making

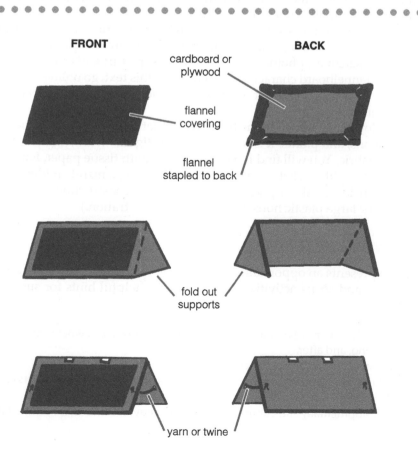

FRONT   BACK

cardboard or plywood

flannel covering

flannel stapled to back

fold out supports

yarn or twine

WHY I TEACH YOUNG CHILDREN

As an early childhood educator of many years, certain memories never leave. The memories help me remember how literal children are. This also helps me remember how to speak to children so that they understand what I am saying. For example, I was introducing a three-year-old class to community helpers. One of the activities relating to mail carriers was to learn our home address. Each child made a crayon picture on manila paper that we folded in thirds. I sat with each child individually to write out his or her *address*. We mailed the letters and I said that in a few days they would receive it as a present, since their address was on the drawing.

After a few days had passed, one of the parents came to tell me that I had made her daughter very angry. She said that when the mail came, her daughter had ripped open the paper and then in an angry voice said, "Where is my red dress? Mrs. Rubinstein told me she was sending me a *red dress.*"

—BONNIE RUBINSTEIN

house robes and blankets) stretches slightly to cover the board, maintains its texture, and is available in an assortment of colors. (See illustration.)

An almost unlimited variety of materials to use with flannelboard characters and activities are easily available and inexpensive. The most commonly used items are nonwoven interfacing material from the fabric store, felt, and heavy flannel. When selecting materials to be used for flannelboard activities, it is important to be sure the adhesive quality of the material is great enough to support its own weight or the weight of the item to which it will be attached.

Some of the resources for finding flannelboard poems, stories, and figures are: teachers of young children, commercial activity sets, and shapes and figures traced from books, magazines, photographs, illustrations, pictures, and drawings. (For puppet and flannelboard characters introduced in this text, go online to this textbook's website and Appendix B for a listing of teacher resources.) Be creative and draw some yourself.

Color can be added to the flannelboard set pieces with permanent felt markers, crayons, and paints. It is fun to accent the figures with wiggly eyes and imitation fur fabric. You will find it helpful to trace with tissue paper. For easy storage, use a folder with pockets, a large mailing envelope, a manila folder with the story stapled inside (make a pocket of tag board or construction paper to hold the pieces), or large plastic household bags. (See illustration.)

GROUP TIME ACTIVITIES

Group time presents an opportunity for listening, speaking, vocabulary development, and cognitive and social activities. Here are a few helpful hints for successful group time activities:

- Organize activities ahead of time, plan carefully, and think about what is going to happen before, during, and after.
- Have realistic expectations of the children and be flexible.
- Select a time and place where a few children can be involved or where others can join in when they finish cleaning up. Be able to accommodate the entire group.
- Select developmentally and culturally appropriate activities that relate to the children's experiences.

Group time offers an opportunity for quality interaction time among children and adults.

- Guide children in and out of group time with appropriate transitions.
- Change the pace often and include a variety of activities.
- Encourage listening and discussing skills. Respond to a child's meaning even if his words are not correct words. Model the appropriate words when you clarify what he has said.
- Anticipate problems and take steps to avoid them by explaining expected behaviors to the children.
- Acknowledge and reinforce *appropriate* behavior.
- Give clear, simple directions.
- Respond to each individual child as well as to the group.
- Maintain physical and emotional closeness.
- Anticipate a "good" stopping point, or stop before the children lose interest.
- Be prepared with an extra activity in case what you have planned does not work or the activity time needs to be extended.
- Evaluate and make needed changes for next time.
- Enjoy the children.

Appropriate group time activities are finger plays, poetry, songs, stories, flannel-board activities, and sensory activities. These should be developmentally appropriate and reflect multicultural/anti-bias content.

The activity "HOP-HOP!" (see box) illustrates a musical finger play activity that toddlers and preschoolers enjoy doing.

The story of *A Little Red House (Una Casita Roja)* is an example of another appropriate group activity. It can be told in group time, then repeated by using flannelboard pieces (online at this text's premium website). Follow-up activities can be: Put the flannelboard pieces and the written story in the language arts center, have a special cooking center set up so children can find their own "little red house," and then make applesauce.

Putting the applesauce recipe on a **rebus chart** (Figure 3–6) is another way to integrate literacy into the curriculum. The rebus chart offers visual picture signs and directions to help children make sense of any activity, that is, read left to right, top to bottom, and recognize letters and symbols. This helps put children in charge of their own learning. For older children, placing the rebus chart in a learning center helps them work independently without teacher direction.

rebus chart Visual pictures, such as signs, illustrations, and directions, to help children make sense of any activity.

HOP-HOP!
(FINGER PLAY ACTIVITY WITH SONG)
(Suitable for Ages Toddler- Three)

Teacher:	Let's tell a story together. Our hands can help. First, make a fist, like this: *(Teacher makes a fist and continues to model for the children all the actions that follow.)* Now, hold up two fingers *(index and middle fingers).* See, we have a bunny! These are his ears. *(Wiggle fingers.)* Wiggle, wiggle, wiggle, it's Robby Rabbit! Can he hop? *(Make hopping motions.)* Up and down, up and down—good! Now, make another bunny with your other hand. This is Reba Rabbit. Wiggle her ears—wiggle, wiggle, wiggle. Now we have two bunnies. Can they both hop? Good! Let them hop behind your back and hide. Now we can begin our story. Everyone sing softly: "Ta-dah!"
Children:	Ta-dah!
Teacher:	*(Bringing one hand forward with hopping motion)* Here comes Robby Rabbit—wiggle, wiggle, wiggle! And here comes Reba Rabbit! (Other hand) Wiggle, wiggle, wiggle! *(Bunnies face one another. When they speak, their ears wiggle. Reba's voice should be pitched higher than Robby's.)*
Teacher:	Robby Rabbit says, "Hello!"
Reba:	Hello Robby! How are you?
Robby:	I'm fine. *(Both bunnies gasp and begin to tremble.)*
Teacher:	Now they're both so scared that they hop behind you and hide. Do you want to see them again? Sing, "Ta-dah!" *(Repeat the whole procedure through Robby's line, "I'm fine!" This time, only Reba begins to tremble.)*
Teacher:	Reba is so scared, she hops behind you to hide again. But Robby Rabbit is not scared. He sings this song: *(Robby hops and sings:)*

Refer to the online textbook website for additional suggestions for activity plan worksheets, curriculum web examples, and interactive curriculum webs.

SONG TO ACCOMPANY HOP-HOP!*

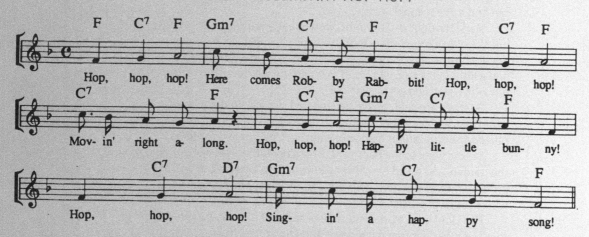

Hop, hop, hop! Here comes Rob- by Rab- bit! Hop, hop, hop!

Mov- in' right a- long. Hop, hop, hop! Hap- py lit- tle bun- ny!

Hop, hop, hop! Sing- in' a hap- py song!

TEACHER: Like this -- bring out Reba Rabbit --- hop, hop, hop!

Now we have two bunnies again. Let them hop and sing together:

Spring's a love- ly time of year, full of joy, full of cheer!

Spring- time flow- ers all are here, and so are al- ler- gies!

*Reproduced by permission of B. Wolf
Copyright B. Wolf - 1993

A LITTLE RED HOUSE
(Una Casita Roja)

Once upon a time, there was a little girl named Maria. Maria had her favorite toys, and she had a big backyard with a garden where she liked to play. One day, she was tired of doing the things she usually did, and she wanted to do something different.

So, Maria went to her mother and asked, "Mamá, what can I do?"

Maria's mother thought for a minute, and then she said, "I know what you can do. You can try to find a little red house, *una casita roja*, with no windows and no doors, but with a star, *una estrella*, inside."

"Mamá, is there really such a thing as a little red house, *una casita roja*, with no windows and no doors, but with a star, *una estrella*, inside? How can I find something like that?" asked Maria.

(continued)

"Yes, *sí*, Maria, there is," answered her mother, "and I know that you can find it, if you look."

Maria thought and thought about what her mother had said, but she didn't know where to find a house like that. So, she went to her big brother, Paco, and asked him, "Paco, do you know where I can find a little red house, *una casita roja*, with no windows and no doors, but with a star, *una estrella*, inside?"

"Maria," Paco said, "I have never heard of a little red house, *una casita roja*, with no windows and no doors, but with a star, *una estrella*, inside. I cannot help you. Why don't you go and ask Papá?"

So, she went to the back yard, where her father was working in the garden, and asked him, "Papá, do you know where I can find a little red house, *una casita roja*, with no windows and no doors, but with a star, *una estrella*, inside?"

Papá looked at Maria, and smiled, and said, "Our house is red, *roja*, but it has doors and windows, and I don't think there is a star, *una estrella*, inside. I'm afraid I can't help you, Maria."

Maria was getting a little tired of looking by now, so she sat down in her favorite back yard spot, under the apple tree, to rest and to think. Her cat, Chica, came and sat in her lap. Maria stroked Chica's soft fur and asked, "Chica, do you know where I can find a little red house, *una casita roja*, with no windows and no doors, but with a star, *una estrella*, inside?" Chica didn't answer. She just went on purring her soft purr.

Maria thought to herself, "I'm not having much luck. I might as well ask the wind." So she did. "Señor Wind, can you help me? I am looking for a little red house, *una casita roja*, with no windows and no doors, but with a star, *una estrella*, inside." Just then, the wind began to blow gently, and down from the tree fell a bright, shiny red apple. Maria picked up the apple, and went to find her mother to tell her that she just could not find the little red house, *una casita roja*.

When Maria's mother saw her walking in the door with the apple, she said, "Maria, I see you found the little red house, *una casita roja*, with no windows and no doors, but with a star, *una estrella*, inside." Maria was puzzled, but followed her mother into the kitchen, where she took out a knife, and cut the apple in half, and . . .

THERE WAS THE STAR! *(UNA ESTRELLA!)**

(Cut the apple through the center perpendicular to the core.)

una—oo' na	*casita*—cas ee' ta	*roja*—ro' ha
estrella—ess tray' ya	*señor*—seen yore'	*Sí*—see

By Janet Galantay
Reprinted with permission

FIGURE 3–6
Rebus chart of applesauce recipe.

Here is the recipe for applesauce:

Applesauce
6 apples
1/2 cup water
1 teaspoon lemon juice
sugar, to taste
1/8 teaspoon cinnamon
Peel apples. Remove core. Cut up apples. Add water, lemon juice, and sugar.
Cook until tender. Add cinnamon. Press through a colander. Then eat!

APPLE SAUCE

Peel six apples 🍎🍎🍎🍎🍎.

Remove cores and cut them up.

Add ½ cup water,

Sugar to taste and

One teaspoon lemon juice.

Cook until tender.

Add ⅛ teaspoon cinnamon.

Press through a colander. THEN EAT!

Afterview

Through language and literacy, a child

- develops listening skills.
- develops the concept of print.
- recognizes that print is talk on paper.
- acquires verbal comprehension and association skills.
- develops letter recognition skills.
- practices scribbling; drawing; and making letters, numbers, and words.
- recognizes and differentiates between shapes, sizes, signs, and sounds.
- experiments with word formation.
- learns left-to-right progression.
- uses new vocabulary in everyday communication.
- strengthens visual memory.
- interprets pictures.
- recognizes sequencing of pictures and illustrations.
- practices storytelling and dictation of stories, while imagining events and situations.
- develops the ability to recall stories and experiences.
- practices writing and illustrating an original story or book.
- learns about other cultures and broadens concepts and experiences about life.
- acquires the ability to use technology with language and written activities.

Reflective Review Questions

1. Describe language development in young children. How does this relate to literacy development?
2. How does an early childhood teacher show that a child's bilingual and bicultural world is respected?
3. A new student to a classroom of four-year-olds recently arrived from Honduras and speaks virtually no English. Although he listens to and watches everything going on around him, he says nothing for days. Is this fairly normal behavior for a child in his situation? What strategies should his teacher pursue in helping him?
4. You've been asked to set up a language and literacy (language arts) center in a pre-k classroom. Using paper and colored pens, pencils, or markers, design the learning center. What criteria will you use? Think about how this center will relate to the other learning centers in the classroom. How does this language arts center support the emergent reading and writing development of the children?

Key Terms

emergent literacy	literacy	phonological or phonemic awareness
flannelboard	literacy development	rebus chart
language	phonemes	rhyming
language development	phonics	vocabulary

Explorations

1. Select an early education classroom and observe for at least one hour. Describe, in writing, six language and literacy activities the children were involved in at the time of your observation. What did you learn from this observation?

2. Select and plan a language activity for young children. Specify which age group this activity is planned for: infants, toddlers, preschoolers, or primary-age children. In writing, list objectives, materials needed, step-by-step procedures for presenting this activity, follow-up activities, and evaluation guidelines. (Use the activity plan worksheet in Chapter 2.) Prepare this activity and demonstrate it during class or with a group of children.

3. Visit an early childhood classroom where there are children who speak more than one language. Describe, in writing, the following:

   - How did the teacher interact with the children?
   - Which stage or stages of language acquisition did you observe?
   - What social interaction between the children did you observe?
   - What activities of the children did you observe?
   - What languages were evident in written materials in the classroom?
   - What languages were spoken by the adults in the classroom?
   - What was done in the classroom to support the language and literacy development of a multilingual group of children? Explain.
   - What did you learn from this observation?

4. Select a classmate or colleague as a partner. Share ideas on games and activities to extend a child's vocabulary. Discuss ways to use or adapt these games to extend the vocabulary of children who speak other languages or dialects. Then, develop one activity that helps a child learn new words and appropriate language usage. If possible, share your activity with a group of young children. Evaluate its appropriateness and effectiveness. Did it accomplish your objectives? Explain.

5. Based on the information in this chapter and on your observations of early education environments, design a language and literacy learning center. Sketch a floor plan showing where materials, supplies, and equipment are placed.

Additional Readings and Resources

Ada, A. F. (2003). *A magical encounter: Latino children's literature in the classroom*. Boston, MA: Allyn & Bacon.

Baker, C. (2007). *A parent's and teacher's guide to bilingualism* (2nd ed). Buffalo, NY: Multilingual Matters Ltd.

Dickinson, D. K., & Tabors, P. O. (2002, March). Fostering language and literacy in classrooms and homes. *Young Children, 57*(2), 10–18.

Howes, C. (2009). *Culture and child development in early childhood programs: Practices for quality education and care*. New York: Teachers College Press.

Hughes, E., & Wineman, K. (2009, Spring/Summer). Learning language: Listening and writing with diverse children. *Dimensions of Early Childhood, 37*(2), 3–9.

Love, A., Burns, M. S., & Buell, M. J. (2007, January). Writing empowering literacy. *Young Children, 62*(1), 12–19.

Macrina, M., Hoover, D., & Becker, C. (2009, March). The challenge of working with dual language learners. *Young Children, 64*(2), 27–34.

Martin, L. E., & Thacker, S. (2009, July). Teaching the writing process in primary grades. *Young Children, 64*(4), 30–35.

Ordonez-Jasis, R., & Ortiz, R. W. (2007). Reading their worlds: Working with diverse families to enhance children's early literacy development. In D. Koralek (Ed.), *Spotlight on young children and their families* (pp. 44–49). Washington, DC: NAEYC.

Pattnaik, J. (2003, Fall). Multicultural literacy starts at home. *Childhood Education, 80*(1), 18–14.

Raikes, H. H., & Edwards, C. P. (2009, September). Supporting relationships with families. *Young Children, 64*(5), 50–55.

Tabors, P. O. (2008). *One child, two languages: A guide for early childhood educators of children learning English as a second language* (2nd ed.). Baltimore, MD: Paul H. Brookes.

Helpful Web Connections

Get Ready to Read
> http://www.getreadytoread.org

Harvard Family Research Project
> http://www.hfrp.org/family-involvement

National Institute for Literacy
> http://www.nifl.gov

PBS KIDS Island for Parents and Teachers
> http://www.pbskids.org

Reading Is Fundamental
> http://www.rif.org

Reading Rockets
> http://www.readingrockets.org

Teachers and Families
> http://www.teachersandfamilies.com

Word World for Preschoolers
> http://www.pbskids.org

Zero to Three
> http://www.zerotothree.org

References

Allen, K. E., & Schwartz, I. S. (2005). *The exceptional child: Inclusion in early childhood education* (4th ed.). Clifton Park, NY: Delmar Cengage Learning.

Bank Street College. (2009). *Early literacy development*. On-line at: *http://www.bankstreet.edu/literacyguide*

Bobys, A. R. (2000, July). What does emerging literacy look like? *Young Children, 55*(4), 20–22.

Buckleitner, W. (2009, April). What should a preschooler know about technology? *Early Childhood Today*. Online at: *http://www.scholastic.com*

Charlesworth, R. (2011). *Understanding child development* (8th ed.) Clifton Park, NY: Wadsworth Cengage Learning.

Copple, C., & Bredekamp, S. (Eds.). (2009). *Developmentally appropriate practice in early childhood programs* (3rd ed.). Washington, DC: NAEYC.

Deiner, P. L. (2010). *Inclusive early childhood education* (5th ed.). Clifton Park, NY: Wadsworth Cengage Learning.

Derman-Sparks, L., & Edwards, J. O. (2010). *Anti-Bias education for young children and ourselves*. Washington, DC: NAEYC.

Dodge, D. T., Heroman, C., Charles, J., & Maiorca, J. (2004, January). Beyond outcomes: How ongoing assessment supports children's learning, and leads to meaningful curriculum. *Young Children, 59*(1), 21–28.

Espiritu, E., Meier, D., Villazana-Price, N., & Wong, M. K. (2002, September). A collaborative project on language and literacy learning. *Young Children, 57*(5), 71–78.

Essa, E. L. (2011). *Introduction to early childhood education* (6th ed.). Clifton Park, NY: Wadsworth Cengage Learning.

Essa, E. L., & Burnham, M. M. (Eds.). (2009). *Informing our practice: Useful research on young children's development*. Washington, DC: NAEYC.

Fields, M. V., & Spangler, K. L. (2000). *Let's begin reading right: Developmentally appropriate literacy* (4th ed.). Upper Saddle River, NJ: Merrill.

Fleming, B. (2002). *Brain keys language development*. On-line at: *http://www.nncc.org/release/brain.language.html*

Genishi, C. (2002, July). Young English language learners—Resourceful in the classroom. *Young Children, 57*(4), 66–72.

Genishi, C., & Dyson, A. H. (2009). *Children, language, and literacy: Diverse learners in diverse times*. New York: Teachers College Press & Washington, DC: NAEYC.

Gestwicki, C. (2011). *Developmentally appropriate practice: Curriculum and development in early education* (4th ed.). Clifton Park, NY: Wadsworth Cengage Learning.

Gober, S. Y. (2002). *Six simple ways to assess young children*. Clifton Park, NY: Delmar Cengage Learning.

Gordon, A. M., & Browne, K. W. (2011). *Beginnings & beyond: Foundations in early childhood education* (8th ed.). Wadsworth Cengage Learning.

Helm, J., Beneke, S., & Steinheimer, K. (2007). *Windows on learning: Documenting young children's work* (2nd ed.). New York: Teachers College Press.

Hernandez, A. (1995, July–August). Language acquisition: What to expect. *Instructor, 105*(1), 56–57.

Hickman-Davis, P. (2002, Spring). "Cuando no hablan Inglés": Helping young children learn English as a second language. *Dimensions of Early Childhood, 30*(2), 3–10.

International Reading Association (IRA) & National Association for the Education of Young Children (NAEYC). (1999). *A joint position paper: Learning to read and write, developmentally appropriate practice for young children*. [Booklet]. Washington, DC: NAEYC.

Kersey, K. C. & Masterson, M. L. (2009, September). Teachers connecting with parents: In the best interest of children. *Young Children, 64*(5), 34–38.

Machado, J. M. (2010). *Early childhood experiences in language arts* (9th ed.). Clifton Park, NY: Wadsworth Cengage Learning.

Miels, J. C. (2001, March). Abby Bear deserves to be heard: Setting early writers free. *Young Children, 56*(2), 36–41.

National Association for the Education of Young Children (NAEYC). (2009). Online at: *http://www.naeyc.org*

National Institute for Literacy. (2009). On-line at: *http://www.nifl.gov*

Nemeth, K. (2009, March). Meeting the home language mandate. *Young Children, 64*(2), 36–42.

Neuman, S. B., Copple, C., & Bredekamp, S. (2000). *Learning to read and write*. Washington, DC: NAEYC.

Nevills, P., & Wolfe, P. (2009). *Building the reading brain* (2nd ed.). Thousand Oaks, CA: Corwin Press.

Ramsey, P. G. (1987). *Teaching and learning in a diverse world: Multicultural education for young children*. New York: Teachers College Press.

Santos, R. M. (2004, January). Ensuring culturally and linguistically appropriate assessment of young children. *Young Children, 59*(1), 48–50.

Shore, R. (1997). *Rethinking the brain*. New York: Families & Work Institute.

Short, R. A., Harris, T. T., & Fairchild, S. H. (2001, Spring). "Once upon a time": Telling stories with flannelboards. *Dimensions of Early Childhood, 29*(2), 3–9.

United States Department of Education. (2009). *Helping your child become a reader: No child left behind*. Washington, DC: Author.

Vygotsky, L. (1978). *Mind in society*. Cambridge, MA: Harvard University Press.

Wardle, F. (2007). The role of technology in early childhood programs. *Early Childhood News*. Online at: *http://www.earlychildhoodnews.com*

Wortham, S. C. (2010). *Early Childhood Curriculum* (5th ed.). Upper Saddle River, NJ: Merrill.

Zero to Three. (2009). Online at: *http://www.zerotothree.org*

• •

Additional information and resources on early childhood curriculum can be found on the Education CourseMate website for this book. Go to **www.CengageBrain.com** to register your access code.

chapter 4

Literature

Objectives

After Studying This Chapter, You Should Be Able To:

● Discuss children's literature in relationship to literacy development.

● Explore the purposes and values of children's books.

● Identify types and genres of books for children and discuss children's book awards.

● Develop criteria for selecting appropriate books for infants, toddlers, preschoolers, and primary-grade children.

● Describe the process of integrating literature into other curriculum areas.

● Select and share appropriate literature with young children and their families.

● Expand skills as a storyteller and observe, plan, present, and evaluate developmentally appropriate children's literature activities.

Overview

Each story changes with the voice that tells it, each picture with the eyes that see it.
(Thomas, 1998)

Children's literature is a wondrous and exciting part of early education curriculum. Most of us can still recall favorite childhood stories that were read or told to us by a loving adult. Books have a way of connecting us to others. They put us in a different time and place and capture our imaginations and our hearts. That is the thrust of this chapter: connecting children to literature by developing ideas and ways of making literature an integral and stimulating part of the early education curriculum.

Where you place the book center, whether it is for two children or a special, private place for one child, indicates how much importance you place on a child's interacting with books and stories. When and how often you read a book to the group or an individual child points this out as well. Is it always at the same time each day or in the same location? Are you spontaneous? Sometimes do you just *feel* like telling a story, reading a book, or developing an activity? Being flexible and creating on-the-spot activities with children's suggestions are just as important and worthwhile as having planned activities.

These interactions with children through books help us enfold literature into language and literacy development. The language of literature provides the child with vivid, imaginative, well-ordered words—words to think about, to listen to, and to try out and make her own. Oral language relates to reading and writing. It is a part of the development of both. The child who hears stories all through childhood learns language and structure and develops attitudes and concepts about the printed word (Morrow, 1989).

Early education emphasizes reading and writing opportunities *across the curriculum.* Sawyer (2009) explains further, "Integrating each of the content areas with literature brings a cohesiveness to the program and the classroom. It also lends stability, an important component of early childhood education. Yet, integration of content areas still allows wonderful things to happen in the classroom." (See Chapter 3, "Language and Literacy," for additional information.)

In support of children, the International Reading Association (IRA) and the National Council of Teachers of English (NCTE) have developed and updated their 12 Standards for the English Language Arts in 2007.

> These standards assume that literacy growth begins before children enter school as they experience and experiment with literacy activities—reading and writing, and associating spoken words with their graphic representations. Recognizing this fact, these standards encourage the development of curriculum and instruction that make productive use of the emerging literacy abilities that children bring to school.

In 2009, the National Council of Teachers of English (NCTE) redefined literacy for the twenty-first century by making it clear that further evolution of curriculum, assessment, and the teaching practice itself is necessary.

Throughout a child's discovery of literature, there should be encouragement by significant adults.

Literacy has always been a collection of cultural and communicative practices shared among members of particular groups. As society and technology change, so does literacy. Because

© Cengage Learning

technology has increased the intensity and complexity of literate environments, the twenty-first century demands that a literate person possess a wide range of abilities and competencies, many literacies.

Applied to students of English language arts, the literacy demands of the twenty-first century have implications for how teachers plan, support, and assess student learning.

Beginning in infancy and continuing throughout the early childhood years, literature can reflect the joy, pleasure, sadness, and expectations that are experienced in a child's life. Throughout a child's discovery of literature in all its forms, there should be encouragement by the significant adults the child encounters. A lifelong love of literature will be the result.

Children's Literature and Literacy Development

Our cultural history is tied to literature. (Arnoff, 2003)

literature All the writings (prose and verse) of a people, country, or period, including those written especially for children.

Literature, in its simplest sense, is all the writings (prose and verse) of a people, country, or period, including those written especially for children.

Children's literature can be defined in many ways. By looking at purposes, values, types, and genres of books for early education, we can define what literature is for young children. The material comes from many sources in both language and illustrated materials.

> Using literature to foster the development of understanding requires that we focus our use of books on more than just teaching children to read. We must also use books as tools for helping children learn about the world. Through books, children can explore science, social studies and math concepts, develop multicultural understandings, learn how to do and make things, and learn more about topics of personal interest. (Owocki, 2001)

Young children develop visual literacy skills even before they can read. As teachers we can encourage this by helping them to use illustrations to decode meaning from the text and to challenge them to describe, compare, and value both visual and written communication. Furthermore, by starting with the literal and concrete, children begin to think about what they see in an illustration and, in turn, describe what they think will happen next in the book they are reading. Aesthetics can be emphasized to young children when teachers focus on line, color, and shape, as well as evaluate the illustrations for strength, mood, and feeling.

According to Strickland (2002), today's informed early childhood educator should understand and be able to build upon the following principles in order to support young children's literacy development:

● Children's language and culture have a direct influence on their learning.
● Learning to read and write is a complex process.
● Language and literacy development are interdependent and interactive. What children know about communication through talk is used to build understandings about reading and writing.
● Children learn best when teachers understand and address the variability among them.
● Children learn best when teachers understand the developmental continuum of reading and writing, are skilled in a variety of strategies to help children achieve, and know how to monitor children's learning in terms of challenging but achievable goals.

Literacy development also can be encouraged by using Vygotsky's (1986) theory of *scaffolding*. This occurs as the teacher (adult) continually adjusts the level of help offered in response to the child's level of performance. For example:

Shared work—the teacher, in a leadership role, selects and shares a book with the children.

Guided work—the teacher guides and encourages the students on an as-needed basis as they explore children's literature, such as helping them to draw illustrations of stories read to them.

Independent work—by this time children are embarking on their own responses to literature that interests them, the teacher being only minimally supportive, such as five-year-olds doing a puppet version of a favorite story (adapted from Bickler, cited in Jalongo, 2004).

Purposes and Values of Children's Books

As we explore the many purposes of including children's books in early childhood classrooms and homes, it is crucial to understand their fundamental role in the learning experience. Because learning is basically the process of associating that which is new with that which is already known, stories can be a powerful tool to accomplish it. A book introduces a child to something new, which can give her greater understanding of the world and create an excitement to know more.

In addition, Sawyer (2009); Huck, Hepler, & Hickman (1993); and Owocki (2001) have suggested the following purposes and values of children's books:

© Cengage Learning

Children's eagerness to learn about the world and their place in it should be nurtured by a supportive environment and teachers who understand their development.

- provide sheer enjoyment for a child
- help develop a child's imagination
- help a child find meaning in life
- offer a child time to reflect on experiences that relate to real life
- help a child reinforce discoveries about the world
- give a child opportunities to reread parts enjoyed or not understood
- introduce a child to many kinds of learning through the enjoyment of books
- help a child develop processes and skills
- help a child focus on predicting outcomes, drawing conclusions, and solving problems
- encourage a child to develop a curiosity about learning and life
- help a child build a foundation for learning to read
- give a child exciting experiences with books and with language
- provide a means for a child to listen to others
- give a child an awareness of and sensitivity to others
- help a child appreciate the writing and illustrations in books
- enable a child to build a foundation for the use and care of books

It is important for teachers and parents of young children to share with each other what they think the purposes are of creating an environment filled with books as part of a child's life. Open communication can offer a partnership to enrich relationships for everyone.

Types and Genres of Books for Children

Before a teacher, parent, or other significant adult selects books for children, understanding about the many *types* and *genres* of books available is essential. **Genre** is a category used to classify literary works, usually by form, technique, or content.

genre Category used to classify literary works, usually by form, technique, or content.

format The overall arrangement of the way a book is put together, such as size, shape, paper quality, colors, and content of each page.

A book's **format** is the overall arrangement, or the way the book is put together, involving factors such as size, shape, paper quality, colors, and content of each page. Isbell and Raines (2007), Machado (2010), and many other children's literature professionals believe that teachers and parents should select books from a wide variety of genres and types. This is fairly easy when you are working with adult literature, which falls into familiar categories, such as fiction, nonfiction, poetry, and prose. But with children's literature in all of its many varieties, the labeling is much more difficult.

Although several systems are used to group children's books, educators do not always agree on how a given book might be labeled or placed. Many books do not neatly fit any category, or they may fit more than one. Nevertheless, most books relating to children's literature fall into the categories that follow. The types of literature are listed with specific characteristics that identify each kind of book. For clarity and organization, the types or categories of children's books are arranged in alphabetical order.

ALPHABET BOOKS

alphabet books Simple stories based on the alphabet that present letter identification and one-object picture association.

Alphabet books are books based on the alphabet that

- offer simple stories.
- present letter identification and one-object picture association.
- offer paired words and objects with matching illustrations.
- have a consistent theme.
- present opportunities to discover names and association of alphabet letters that are easily identified.
- provide emergent readers with opportunities for oral and written language development.

An example of an alphabet book:

> Pearle, I. (2008). *A child's day: An alphabet of play.* Orlando, FL: Harcourt.

BEGINNING-TO-READ BOOKS

beginning-to-read books Predictable books that are easy to read and present words that are simple and repetitive.

Beginning-to-read books may also be referred to as easy-to-read books. These books

- present words that are simple and repetitive.
- have short sentences.
- are usually predictable.
- are designed to be read by the emergent reader.

An example of a beginning-to-read book:

> Rylant, C. (2008). *Annie and snowball and the pink surprise.* Illustrated by S. Stevenson. New York: Simon & Schuster Books for Young Readers.

BIG BOOKS

big books Oversized books that present extra-large text and illustrations.

Big books may also be called oversized, giant, or jumbo books. Big books

- present extra-large text and illustrations.
- allow teachers to share books with a group of children easily.
- are mass published, so many popular titles are available in this format.

An example of a big book:

> Wood, Audrey. (1984). *The napping house.* Illustrated by Don Wood. Orlando, FL: Harcourt Big Books.

BOARD BOOKS

Board books are usually the first books for infants and toddlers because they are made of heavy cardboard and are laminated. Board books

- offer ease of page turning for children learning to handle books.
- are sometimes referred to as minibooks because they are small and can easily be picked up by a young child.
- have simple illustrations.

An example of a board book:

> Hamm, D. J. (2008). *Rock-a-bye-farm*. Illustrated by S. A. Natchev. New York: Little Simon.

board books First books for infants and toddlers made of laminated heavy cardboard.

CONCEPT BOOKS

Concept books have been identified as a young child's first informational book. These books

- present themes, ideas, or concepts with specific examples.
- identify and clarify abstractions, such as color or shape.
- help with vocabulary development.
- include alphabet and counting books as favorite types of concept books.

An example of a concept book:

> Gibbons, G. (2007). *The vegetables we eat*. New York: Holiday House.

concept books Books that present themes, ideas, or concepts with specific examples. They also identify and clarify abstractions, such as color or shape, and help with vocabulary development.

COUNTING BOOKS

Counting books are books based on counting and numeral recognition. These books

- describe simple numeral and picture association.
- often tell a story.
- offer one-to-one correspondence illustrations.
- show representations of numbers in more than one format.
- vary from simple to complex.
- present illustrations that are consistent in adding to understanding for young children.

An example of a counting book:

> Seeger, L.V. (2008). *One boy*. New York: Roaring Brook Books.

counting books Books that describe simple numeral and picture associations, and often tell a story. They show representations of numbers in more than one format and vary from simple to complex.

FOLK LITERATURE

Folk literature may also be called folk tales, fairy tales, fables, tall tales, myths, and legends. These tales

- come from the oral tradition of storytelling.
- appeal to the child's sense of fantasy.
- teach value systems.
- offer language that is appealing to children and create strong visual images.
- are available in picture book format.
- connect with other cultures and countries because they retell traditional stories that are shared from generation to generation. (Some specific examples include: Hans Christian Andersen's original and adapted stories, which are modern fairy tales; fables, which

folk literature Tales that come from the oral tradition of storytelling that appeal to the child's sense of fantasy.

present explicit morals with animals speaking as humans; myths, which describe the creation of the world and nature; and legends, which are based on the actions of a single hero. Story collectors, such as the Grimm brothers, wrote down stories from the oral tradition.)

An example of folk literature:

Wolff, F., & Savitz, H. M. (2008). *The story blanket*. Illustrated by E. Odriozola. Atlanta: Peachtree.

INFORMATIONAL BOOKS

informational books Books that offer nonfiction for emergent readers by providing accurate facts about people and subject matter.

Informational books offer nonfiction for emergent readers. They also

● explore new ideas.
● answer "why" and "how."
● stimulate and expand individual or group interest.
● give accurate facts about people (biographies) and subject matter.

An example of an informational book:

DK Children. (2007). *See how it's made.* New York: DK Publishers.

INTERACTION BOOKS

interaction books Books used to stimulate imagination by using some device for involving young readers, such as pop-ups, fold-outs, scratch and sniff, pasting, puzzle pictures, humor, and riddles.

Interaction books are sometimes called novelty, toy, or participation books. These books

● use some device for involving young readers, such as pop-ups, foldouts, scratch and sniff, pasting, puzzle pictures, humor, and riddles.
● provide audiocassettes or CDs.
● stimulate imagination.
● can be designed in different sizes and shapes for exploring and touching.

An example of an interaction book:

Johnson, T. (2009). *My little red fire truck.* New York: Simon & Schuster Books for Young Readers.

MOTHER GOOSE AND NURSERY RHYMES

Mother Goose and nursery rhyme books Books passed from generation to generation and known by children all over the world. These are often a child's first introduction to literature.

Mother Goose and nursery rhyme books are often a child's first introduction to literature. These books

● are known by children all over the world.
● are passed from generation to generation.
● offer varied illustrations of the rhymes.
● appeal to infants and toddlers.

An example of a Mother Goose and nursery rhyme book:

Ross, T. (2009). *Three little kittens.* New York: Henry Holt.

MULTICULTURAL BOOKS

multicultural books Books that develop awareness of and sensitivity to other cultures. They also help to increase positive attitudes toward similarities and differences in people.

Multicultural books are also referred to as cross-cultural or culturally diverse books. These books

● develop awareness of and sensitivity to other cultures.
● increase positive attitudes toward similarities and differences in people.
● offer accurate portrayals and rich details of individual and group heritage.

● can extend to seasonal and holiday books (a separate listing of *anti-bias literature* that promotes gender equity and the importance of the inclusion of children with special needs may include multicultural books as well).

An example of a multicultural book:

> Brown, M. (2007). *Butterflies on Carmen Street/Mariposas en la calle de Carmen Street.* New York: Piñata Books.

PICTURE BOOKS OR PICTURE STORY BOOKS

Picture books are often referred to as the most popular type of children's literature. These books

● are written in a direct style that tells a simple story.
● offer varied illustrations that complement and associate closely with the text.
● are written especially for adults to share with children.
● are uniquely appropriate for the young child.

An example of a picture book:

> Yolen, J. (2009). *The scarecrow's dance.* Illustrated by B. Ibatoulline. New York: Simon & Schuster Books for Young Readers.

picture books Books written in a direct style that tell a simple story with illustrations complementing the text.

POETRY

Poetry is overlooked many times as part of children's literature. Poetry

● can be one book, one poem, or a collection of poems.
● contributes imaginative rhyme, rhythm, and sound.
● is another way to present culture, country, and language.
● stimulates imagery and feelings.
● is pleasing and can relate to life in terms that children can understand.

An example of a poetry book:

> Yolen, J. (2007). *Here's a little poem.* Cambridge, MA: Candlewick Press.

poetry A form of literature that contributes imaginative rhyme, rhythm, and sound.

PREDICTABLE BOOKS

Predictable books contain familiar and repetitive sequences. These books

● describe events that are repeated or added to as the story continues.
● permit successful guessing of what happens next.
● supply opportunities for children to read along.
● build self-confidence.
● encourage children to read naturally.

An example of a predictable book:

> Barton, B. (1993). *The little red hen.* New York: HarperCollins.

predictable books Books that contain familiar and repetitive sequences.

REALISTIC LITERATURE

Sometimes called bibliotherapy or therapeutic literature, **realistic literature** deals with real-life issues. These books

● help children cope with common, actual experiences.
● offer positive solutions and insights.

realistic literature A form of literature that helps children cope with common, actual experiences by offering positive solutions and insights.

- encourage talking about a child's feelings.
- are often tied in with anti-bias literature that relates to children with special needs.

An example of realistic literature:

> Heelan, J. R. (2000). *Rolling along: The story of Taylor and his wheelchair.* Illustrated by N. Simmonds. Atlanta, GA: Peachtree.

REFERENCE BOOKS

reference books Books that emphasize individualized learning through special topic books, picture dictionaries, and encyclopedias.

Reference books emphasize individualized learning through special topic books, picture dictionaries, and encyclopedias. They also encourage older children to find a resource that answers questions.

An example of a reference book:

> Ajmera, M. (2008). *Children of the U. S. A.* Watertown, MA: Charlesbridge.

SERIES BOOKS

series books Books written for primary-grade children and built around a single character or group of characters.

Series books are often written for primary-grade children. These books

- are built around a single character or group of characters.
- can introduce the concept of books written in chapter form.
- can be related to television characters that are familiar to children.

Examples of series books:

> *Amelia Bedelia* books. New York: Greenwillow.
>
> *The Magic Treehouse* books. New York: Random House Books for Young Readers.

TEACHER- AND CHILD-MADE BOOKS

teacher- and child- made books Books made by the teacher and child that encourage self-esteem, creativity, and the sharing of ideas. They also encourage children to articulate experiences.

Teacher- and child-made books are a part of developmentally appropriate early education classrooms. These books

- encourage self-esteem, creativity, and sharing ideas with others.
- reinforce group learning.
- develop children's understanding of authorship by seeing their names in print.
- encourage children to articulate experiences.
- invite children to use their imagination.
- include parents in the process of reading and writing with their children.

Examples of subjects for individual or class-made books:

> *My Family*
>
> *My Friends*
>
> *My Community*
>
> *My Favorite Things To Do*

WORDLESS PICTURE BOOKS

wordless picture books Books that tell a story with visually appealing illustrations. These books promote creativity by encouraging a child to talk about experiences and use his or her imagination.

A young child develops language, reading skills, and meaning through the illustrations with **wordless picture books**, sometimes called stories without words. These books

WHY I TEACH YOUNG CHILDREN

I teach to see the faces of the children who are so engrossed in an activity that one can physically see how much learning is taking place. This happens when the children can relate to the topic either through their own experiences or the experiences of their friends and/or teacher.

As an example, our pre-k class has been very involved learning about ocean life. I had just returned from a trip to the east coast of Florida where I saw a manatee slowly meandering through the water, very close to shore. It was eating seaweed as it swam along and almost seemed to turn its head to smile at the many observers on the beach. I took a digital photo of the manatee and, as a librarian, was most eager to share my picture and experience with the children.

I showed the picture while telling my story but did not name the animal. No child could identify the picture, so I told them, and then read a book about manatees. The children did not make a sound. Their eyes were wide, their jaws were dropped, and there was no movement as I read. Afterwards, I asked them what they learned about manatees and wrote down what they said. They shared so much information that I am sure they will remember.

This was an example of how children learn through many types of experiences. They related to my story and it made the manatee seem real to them. It made me also realize that we are not just teachers while in our classrooms. We are teachers wherever life takes us and we can never pass up the opportunity to capture the moment.

—BONNIE RUBINSTEIN

- help develop building blocks of language.
- offer visually appealing illustrations.
- aid in developing eye coordination.
- present sequential action from page to page.
- promote creativity by encouraging a child to talk about experiences.
- use imagination.
- invite older children to write a story about what is seen, with character descriptions and dialogue.

An example of a wordless picture book:

Lee, S. (2008). *Wave.* San Francisco, CA: Chronicle.

Children's Book Awards

An understanding of who gives awards for outstanding children's literature and the nature of each award provides a guide to choosing books.

In 1938, Frederick G. Melcher, editor of *Publisher's Weekly,* established the Caldecott Award. This medal is awarded annually to the artist of "the most distinguished picture book for children" printed in the United States and published during the preceding year. It is named in honor of the English illustrator Randolph Caldecott (1846–1886),

© Cengage Learning

Select books that appeal to children and relate to their experiences.

Many developmentally appropriate books are available for young children. They should be placed in a comfortable and inviting area in the classroom.

a nineteenth-century pioneer in the field of children's books. The selection is made by a committee, the members of which are either elected or appointed from the ranks of children's and school librarians who are members of the Association for Library Services to Children, a part of the American Library Association.

The Caldecott Award is presented at the same time as the Newbery Award. Named for John Newbery (1713–1767), the first English publisher of children's books, and established in 1922, the Newbery Award is for "the most distinguished contribution to American literature for children" published the preceding year. It honors the quality of the author's writing and is usually a book appropriate for older children who are more mature readers. Both the Caldecott and Newbery Awards are presented at the annual conference of the American Library Association.

The Hans Christian Andersen Medal, established in 1956, is given by the International Board on Books for Young People. This award is presented every two years to a living author and an illustrator in recognition of their entire body of work.

The International Reading Association Children's Book Award is given to new authors.

The Coretta Scott King Awards are presented to an African-American author and illustrator for "outstanding inspirational and educational contributions to literature for children." In addition, the National Jewish Book Awards and the Catholic Book Awards add to the list of over 100 awards made annually to recognize authors and illustrators of literature for children (Isbell & Raines, 2007; Huck, Hepler, & Hickman, 1993).

In 2004, the American Library Association established the Theodor Seuss Geisel Award, named in honor of "Dr. Seuss." This is given annually (beginning in 2006) to the author(s) and illustrator(s) of the most distinguished contribution to the body of American children's literature known as beginning reader books published in the United States during the preceding year (American Library Association, 2009).

Use award books as a starting point for selecting literature. Personal evaluation and knowledge of individual children, their interests, and their needs should also be criteria for selection.

> We can, through employment of picture books, bring a second and third teacher into the classroom. Authors and illustrators have done half our planning for us—and high-quality planning it is too—and we can piggyback on their talent and industry and use their books to jumpstart our own imaginations. (Graham, 2000)

Selection of Books for Young Children

Walters (cited in Brinson, 2009) stresses, "For children, to have experiences with literature that provide windows to the world and a view of other peoples is even more important today. Lifelong experiences with literature help us mirror those who are like us and those who are loved or admired." This expresses why it is so important for us, as teachers and parents, to be most vigilant when we select the books to share with young children.

Many developmentally appropriate books are available for use in early education. The following criteria should be considered when making selections for young children:

- Select books for enjoyment.
- Select books that encourage a child's capacity for laughter.
- Choose durable books. Books are to be handled and used by children.
- Select books with different styles of illustrations.
- Consider the length of the story. Books should be age and developmentally appropriate.
- Pick books that appeal to children and relate to their experiences.
- Choose books that have an appealing story and style. Children like sound, rhythm, and repetition in their stories.
- Avoid overly frightening, confusing stories.
- Offer children a variety of writing styles and languages, especially those spoken by children, families and staff in the child care program or school.
- Choose books that appeal to a young child's senses. Especially enjoyable are books with descriptive words that make children taste, smell, and feel, as well as see and hear.
- Use literature as a stimulus for activities that require children to use their senses in discovery or exploration.
- Pick books that help children develop positive self-esteem by emphasizing the capabilities children have.
- Share books that promote feelings of security.
- Choose books that show characters seeing themselves positively.
- Select books in which characters show emotions common to young children.
- Read several books on the same topic to provide more than one perspective.
- Introduce books that will expand vocabulary.
- Present books that reinforce concepts already being acquired.
- Select books that may help clarify misconceptions.
- Select stories that have a plot in which there is action; for example, stories that tell what people did and what they said.
- Enrich a child's experiences with literature by providing poetry selections and books of poems.

Multicultural books for children should introduce a variety of family compositions, including single parents, grandparents who play key roles in nurturing children, and extended families who share a home and each other's lives (Reading Is Fundamental, 2009). Marshall (cited in Brinson, 2009) encourages teachers of young children to use multicultural literature to discuss issues of diversity, to talk about differences, and to discuss why recognizing and celebrating differences is important.

- Include a wide variety of multicultural/anti-bias books. There are many that present the uniqueness of a present-day culture as seen through the eyes of a child.
- Select books that do not stereotype people according to gender, ethnic background, culture, age, or types of work. Choose books that present accurate images and information with no overt or covert stereotypes (Derman-Sparks & Edwards, 2010).
- Minority characters should be shown as independent thinkers who can face challenges and solve problems. Select books with well-developed characters that show a range of occupations and income levels (that support and supplement the diversity present in the center or school) (Derman-Sparks & Edwards, 2010).
- Illustrations should not use stereotypical caricatures of a group's physical features.
- Look for accuracy in stories.
- Share literature from other countries to expand children's global awareness.
- Select books that challenge unfairness and prejudice.

(See Figure 4–1 for a list of suggested multicultural/anti-bias books for young children.)

FIGURE 4-1
Suggested multicultural/anti-bias books for young children.

- Addasi, M. (2009). *The white nights of Ramadan*. Illustrated by N. Gannon. New York: Boyds Mills.
- Adoff, A. (2002). *Black is brown is tan*. New York: HarperCollins.
- Aston D. H. (2009). *The moon over star*. Illustrated by J. Pickney. New York: Dial Books for Young Children.
- Cheltenham Elementary School Kindergarten. (1991). *We are all alike . . . We are all different*. New York: Scholastic.
- Cumpiano, I. (2008). *Quinito, day and night/Quinito, día y noche*. Illustrated by J. Ramirez. San Francisco: Children's Book Press.
- Ichikawa, S. (2009). *My father's shop*. New York: Kane/Miller.
- Isadora, R. (2008). *Uh-oh!* Orlando, FL: Harcourt.
- Joosse, B, M. (2008). *Grandma calls me beautiful*. Illustrated by B. Lavallee. San Francisco: Chronicle.
- Jules, J. (2009). *Duck for turkey day*. Illustrated by K. Mitteer. Morton Grove, IL: Albert Whitman.
- Katz, K. (2004). *The color of us*. New York: Henry Holt.
- Murphy, M. (2008). *I like it when. . . Me gusta cuando. . . .* Translated by F. I. Campoy & A. F. Ada. Orlando, FL: Harcourt.

The Reading Is Fundamental (RIF) organization (2009) suggests the following guidelines in the selection of books that include children with special needs:

- Choose books that show differently-abled people in active and interactive roles. Be sure that some books have a person with special needs as the main character.
- Read those books that regard children with disabilities as children first. Pick those that approach special needs children as being more like other children than different.
- Make positive reading experiences a priority for children with disabilities. Read books to children which have characters with disabilities similar to theirs.
- Make use of technology by individualizing instruction for each student and match programming to student learning styles.
- Partner with families on reading strategies.

Select books with well-developed characters that support and supplement the diversity present in the center or school.

Recommended Books

The examples of representative books have been divided into two lists: One suggests books for age and developmental appropriateness, and the other is a thematic list of children's books. There is some overlap between the two listings. These are books that were suggested over and over again by teachers of young children, are used as examples of quality literature by educators in the field, or have been selected as personal favorites and current discoveries. (You can add favorites of your own to these. Ask colleagues, librarians, and parents to suggest additional titles and authors.)

© Cengage Learning

AGE AND DEVELOPMENTALLY APPROPRIATE CHILDREN'S BOOKS

> Books are particularly important story tools for introducing children to the power, pleasure, rhythm, and richness of language in print and pictures. . . . [Story experiences] introduce children to the rhythms, rhymes, and beauty of language. They can encourage children to use their imaginations, to giggle and laugh, and to ask questions. Stories can help them see that they are part of a world in which other people face the same daily challenges they do. (Birckmayer, Kennedy, & Stonehouse, 2008)

INFANTS. When you hold an infant in your lap and share a special story or book, you are making a difference in that child's life. When you set up the special places in the infant room for reading or telling a story or for singing a nursery rhyme, include pillows, stuffed animals, quilts, and mats. Sawyer (2009) points out that "babies sit on laps, crawl about, and listen in various positions and in various places." It is important for infants to interact with the books. For them, that means chewing on the pages, touching and looking at them in unique ways, and making them a part of their "personal turf."

See Figure 4–2 for suggested books for infants.

TODDLERS. The special place for story time in the toddler room should be surrounded with colorful pillows, carpet squares, and other comfortable spots available for these young children to listen to, participate with, and enjoy books. Small groupings offer the children a chance to turn the pages, point, and identify things, while sharing their choice of books with the teacher and each other. For those toddlers who enjoy one-on-one time with a teacher and a favorite book, sitting in a rocking chair fulfills this need in a special way.

Story time outdoors on a big quilt, under a tree, and surrounded by grass can be exciting and appropriate for toddlers, too. Copple and Bredekamp (2009) explain, "Two-year-olds are learning to produce language rapidly. They need simple books, pictures, puzzles, music, and time and space for active play such as jumping, running,

© Cengage Learning

Choose durable books. Books are to be handled and used by children.

- Brett, J. (1999). *Gingerbread baby.* New York: Putnam.
- Brown, M. W. (1991, First Board Book Edition). *Goodnight moon.* Illustrated by C. Hurd. New York: HarperCollins.
- Carle, E. (2007). *Baby bear, baby bear, what do you see?* New York: Henry Holt.
- Fox, M. (2008). *Ten little fingers and ten little toes.* Illustrated by H. Oxenbury. Orlando, FL: Harcourt.
- Katz, K. (2008, Board Book). *Where is baby's belly button?* New York: Simon and Schuster Books for Young Readers.
- Kubler, A. (2002, Board Book). *Head, shoulders, knees, and toes.* New York: Child's Play International.
- McBratney, S. (2008, Board Book). *How much I love you.* Illustrated by A. Jeram. Cambridge, MA: Candlewick Press.
- Rescek, S. (2006, Padded Board Book). *Twinkle, twinkle little star and other favorite nursery rhymes.* New York: Tiger Tales.
- Shaw, C. G. (1993, First Board Book Edition). *It looked like spilt milk.* New York: HarperCollins.
- Steckel, Dr. R., & Steckel, M. (2007). *My teeth.* Photographs by Dr. R. Steckel. Berkeley, CA: Tricycle Press.

FIGURE 4–2

Suggested books for infants.

FIGURE 4–3
Suggested books for toddlers.

- Baker, K. (2008). *Potato Joe*. Orlando, FL: Harcourt.
- Boynton, S. (2004, Lap-size Board Book). *The going to bed book*. New York: Little Simon.
- Emberly, R. (2000). *My colors/Mis colores*. Boston: Little, Brown & Company.
- Henkes, K. (2008). *Old bear*. New York: Greenwillow.
- Isadora, R. (2008). *Peekaboo bedtime*. New York: Penguin Young Readers.
- Krensky, S. (2008). *Chaucer's first winter*. Illustrated by H. Cole. New York: Simon & Schuster Books for Young Readers.
- Raposo, J. (2001). *Imagination song*. Illustrated by L. Linn. New York: Random House.
- Smith, C. R., Jr. (2008). *Dance with me*. Illustrated by N. Z. Jones. Cambridge, MA: Candlewick Press.
- Thompson, L. (2008). *Wee little lamb*. Illustrated by J. Butler. New York: Simon & Schuster Books for Young Readers.
- Wood, A. (2000, Board Book Edition). *The napping house*. Illustrated by D. Wood. New York: Red Wagon Books.

© Cengage Learning

Young children enjoy alone time with a book of their choice.

and dancing." Physically enjoying the story is important for these children. See Figure 4–3 for suggested books for toddlers.

THREE-, FOUR-, AND FIVE-YEAR-OLDS.   The story center, library, or book center should be one of the most inviting and exciting learning centers or curriculum areas in a classroom for these children, with many comfortable reading spaces provided, such as a soft rug; a big, empty "refrigerator-size" box with pillows to sit on and "windows" cut in the box to look out of; and child-size tables and chairs set up with a variety of books, magazines, catalogs, newspapers, books with CDs, blank paper, and writing instruments.

As teachers, you should read aloud to your three-, four-, and five-year-olds every day. Plan activities that integrate listening, speaking, reading, and writing. It is also important for you to continue to read to individual children if they ask you to, because the children still need this special time with a significant adult. For example, they will benefit from hearing predictable books. These books help children practice decoding words. Seefeldt and Wood (cited in Copple & Bredekamp, 2009) explain further, "[Children of this age] begin to develop the concept of story structure and even come up with their own theme story with classmates."

The magic of book reading is amplified when children are on a lap.... Children become active participants when they point to specific things in pictures, turn the pages, ask questions, and make comments. The lap reading experience is vital for children to acquire "book language," "story sense," and a host of other early reading knowledge.... Although instruction is helpful, what children most need in order to learn how to ride horseback, is to get up in the saddle and ride. To learn how to skate, they must lace up their skates and give skating a try. To learn to read, children need exposure to a lot of good books and a mentor who can read with them and coach them along the way. (Lamme, 2002)

(Review Chapter 3 for suggestions of physical space arrangement and activity plans for setting up the library, literature center, or literacy center.) See Figure 4–4 for suggested books for three-, four-, and five-year-olds.

SIX-, SEVEN-, AND EIGHT-YEAR-OLDS.   Computers, cell phones, movies, television shows, video games, and music videos pose a challenge to teachers, librarians, and parents trying to capture the reading attention of six-, seven-, and eight-year-olds. As a result, literature for this age reflects the addition of topics grounded in real-life issues. Illustrations are more complex and artistic, and a greater diversity is available.

As a teacher, you should provide many opportunities and motivations for reading and writing in the primary classroom. "During the primary grades, most children become

● Cote, N. (2008). *Jackson's blanket.* New York: Putnam.
● Emberly, R., & Emberly, E. (2009). *Chicken little.* New York: Roaring Brooks.
● Gravett, E. (2009). *The odd egg.* New York: Simon & Schuster Books for Young Readers.
● Heap, S. (2009). *Danny's drawing book.* Cambridge, MA: Candlewick Press.
● Katz, K. (2007). *The colors of us.* New York: Henry Holt.
● Martin, B., Jr., & Archambault, J. (1988). *Listen to the rain.* Illustrated by J. Endicott. New York: Henry Holt.
● McKissack, P. (2008). *Stitchin' and pullin': A Gee's Bend quilt.* Illustrated by C. A. Cabera. New York: Random House Books for Young Readers.
● Van Fleet, M. (2009). *Cat.* Photographed by B. Sutton. New York: Simon & Schuster Books for Young Readers.
● Williams, M. (2008). *Knuffle bunny too: A case of mistaken identity.* New York: Hyperion.

FIGURE 4–4
Suggested books for three-, four-, and five-year-olds.

real readers. And perhaps most important, many children across these years come to thoroughly enjoy reading and seek out reading activities voluntarily" (Tomlinson, cited in Copple & Bredekamp, 2009).

The more emphasis you place on the importance of books in the lives of six-, seven-, and eight-year-olds, the more important literature will be to the children. As with all ages, *read aloud* to them as often as you can. Let them tell you and others about what they have read, and encourage open-ended questioning by everyone. Encourage parents to continue reading aloud to their children, too.

Special time should be regularly set aside for children to choose and read books on their own. Also, when visitors come to your classroom, have them tell a story or read to the children. Inviting parents, grandparents, community volunteers, other teachers, or staff to read provides another dimension. Keep a well-stocked reading corner that is regularly infused with new books. See Figure 4–5 for suggested books for six-, seven-, and eight-year-olds.

THEMATIC SELECTION OF CHILDREN'S BOOKS

Many teachers find that using a thematic approach to literature selection gives them more individuality in curriculum development. The thematic strategy leads children to activities that suggest active exploration, problem solving, and the acquisition of specific concepts or skills. You can introduce new themes weekly, biweekly, or monthly. Select the theme that relates to the children in your class according to their experiences and their age and stage of development. (Review Chapter 2 for specific explanations

© Cengage Learning

There should be plenty of time to share a book with a friend.

FIGURE 4–5
Suggested books for six-, seven-, and eight-year olds

- Addasi, M. (2008). *The white nights of Ramadan*. Illustrated by N. Gannon. New York: Boyds Mills Press.
- Beil, K. M. (2008). *Jack's house*. Illustrated by M. Wohnouthka. New York: Holiday House.
- Bruchac, J. (2009). *Buffalo song*. New York: Lee & Low Books.
- Giovanni, N. (2005). *Rosa*. Illustrated by B. Collier. New York: Holt.
- Larson, K., & Nethery, M. (2008). *Two Bobbies: A true story of Hurricane Katrina friendship and survival*. Illustrated by J. Cassels. New York: Walker.
- Muñoz, R. P. (2002). *When Marian sang: The true recital of Marian Anderson*. Illustrated by B. Selznick. New York: Scholastic.
- Naylor, P. R. (2008). *Eating enchiladas*. Illustrated by M. Ramsey. New York: Cavendish.
- Paratore, C. M. (2008). *Catching the sun*. Illustrated by P. Catalanotto. Watertown, MA: Charlesbridge.
- Williams, V. B. (2009). *A chair for always*. New York: HarperCollins.
- Zemach, K. (2008). *Ms. McCaw learns to draw*. New York: Arthur A. Levine.

FIGURE 4–6
Suggested books for the theme of "natural environment."

- Appelt, K. (2005). *Miss Ladybird's wildflowers: How a First Lady changed America*. Illustrated by J. F. Hein. New York: HarperCollins.
- Aronsky J. (2008). *A guide to nature's footprints*. New York: Sterling.
- Callery, S. (2009). *I wonder why there's a hole in the sky and other questions about the environment*. New York: Kingfisher.
- Donald, R. L. (2002). *Water pollution*. New York: Children's Press.
- George, J. C. (2008). *The wolves are back*. Paintings by W. Minor. New York: Dutton.
- Hiscock, B. (2008). *Ookpik: The travels of a snowy owl*. New York: Boyds Mills Press.
- Leavell, C., & Cravotta, N. (2005). *The tree farmer*. New York: VSP Books.
- Martin, B., Jr., & Sampson, M. R. (2006). *I love our earth*. Watertown, MA: Charlesbridge.
- Swanson, S. M. (2008). *To be like the sun*. Illustrated by M. Chodos-Irvine. Orlando, FL: Harcourt.
- Walsh, M. (2008). *10 things I can do to help my world*. Cambridge, MA: Candlewick Press.

of themes, units, projects, and webs.) Then, select the literature that will emphasize, explain, and extend the theme. For suggestions, see Figure 4–6 for books about the natural environment. Glazer (2000) suggests that:

> Books with characteristics in common can be grouped together into units that focus on a single item, describe similar content or represent literature of a particular genre or by a particular author or illustrator.... [C]onsider a variety of titles, but narrow the selection to those books which best fit your purposes, and include only those which you actually plan to use.

Integrating Literature into Other Curriculum Areas

The connection between literature and the other curriculum areas, as Machado (2010) explains, "includes reading aloud to children, making use of informational books, and encouraging children's response to books using drama, art, and child-dictated writing." Sawyer (2009) describes literature-integrated units as being "taught around a general theme or a key idea....One may wish to develop a theme around a single book. . . . The focus may also be in a content area such as science, social studies, basic concepts, or holidays."

Nelsen and Nelsen-Parish (2002) suggest other ways of connecting books to areas of the curriculum.

> Reproductions and retellings are children's responses to literature through art, music, and drama, using their own language. In a reproduction, children make language come to life as they interact with the original text. A retelling is a summary of a story in the children's words. It is an effective tool for teaching children to recognize and organize story elements.

Glazer (2000) presents another way of looking at integrating curriculum:

> Children should be guided to perceive literature as a body of work rather than as separate and unrelated stories and poems. If you group books for presentation, you set the stage for children to see the relationships among books, to notice the recurring structural patterns of literature.

"Putting literature around the room" can be done realistically by creatively decorating containers for books with bright contact paper, wallpaper, or children's drawings and by placing baskets of books in every learning activity center. For example, books relating to houses and buildings can be put in the block center; those dealing with shapes and colors can be put in the art center; and books concerning gardening, fish, and turtles can be near the sand and water table.

TECHNOLOGY AND THE LITERACY CURRICULUM

Primary-age children are adding digital and media technology to the literacy curriculum. "[These children] are drawn to technology. They also love a good story. Combining the two can be a powerful educational tool" (Adams, 2009). One way to support this literacy experience is to supply the tools to make a *digital story*—using a computer, a digital camera, a scanner, a printer, and software. A digital story mixes still images (photos or artwork), voice narration, and music to tell a story. As teachers, we should have the learning experiences with the technology first. This will enable us to become enthusiastic and ready to share digital storytelling with the children. It is also important to remember that the *story* is the starting point and the finishing goal. For this activity to be successful, all aspects must be developmentally appropriate for the children in the classroom.

See Figure 4–7 for suggested children's literature Internet websites.

ACTIVITIES THAT ENCOURAGE CHILDREN TO BECOME AUTHORS AND ILLUSTRATORS

One of the most stimulating child-centered activities a teacher can use is having the children write original books or one-page stories. "In a collaborative classroom project, each child contributes a unique individual piece to the collaborative process—especially the collaborative bookmaking process—in your classroom" (Spann, 1997). You can help the youngest children put their artwork together in the form of a book, using string or rings to do so; for older children, pair them as "book buddies" or "book partners" to write and illustrate their own books. Some teacher preparation or assistance may be needed or requested. Machado (2010) presents the values of books authored by children or their teachers:

- They promote interest in the classroom book collection.
- They help children see connections between spoken and written words.

FIGURE 4–7
Suggested children's literature websites.

- Alma Flor Ada website—http://almaflorada.com
- American Library Association—http://www.ala.org
- Carol Hurst's Children's Literature—http://www.carolhurst.com
- Children's Book Council—http://www.cbcbooks.org
- Denise Fleming website—http://www.denisefleming.com
- Eric Carle website—http://www.eric-carle.com
- Gail Gibbons website—http://www.gailgibbons.com
- Jan Brett website—http://www.janbrett.com
- Laura Numeroff website—http://www.lauranumeroff.com

Internet Resources for the Children to Explore:

- The Children's Digital Library—pages full of stories and activities, including a Spanish version—http://www.storyplace.org
- KIDS—illustrate a story, poetry in pictures, meet the illustrators—http://www.rif.org
- KidsClick—Web search for kids by librarians—http://www.kidsclick.org
- Kids Storytelling Club—join the fun and become a storyteller http://www.storycraft.com
- PBS Kids—coloring, games, videos, music and all PBS children's shows—http://www.pbskids.org
- Poetry—poetry playground—http://www.poetry4kids.com
- Scholastic website for children—http://www.scholastic.com

- The material is based on the interests of both the children and the teacher.
- They personalize book reading.
- They prompt self-expression.
- They stimulate creativity.
- They build feelings of competence and self-worth.

You can encourage children's (and teachers') roles as authors and illustrators in many ways. Having children make book covers for their books can affirm the importance of all books. In the writing or art center, provide paper, wallpaper, or contact paper that will cover a child's favorite book. The child can decorate the cover and write the title, author, and illustrator as well.

How about a "Let's Pretend Book"? In the dramatic play area, have a camera (digital, video, or disposable type) ready for children to take pictures of what is going on in the grocery store, pet shop, post office, or whatever the area represents for that week. You can then place these images on sheets of paper to be made into a book together. The children can tell or dictate the story of who they were pretending to be. Visually and concretely, this helps children understand that their words and actions make stories and books.

Reading Is Fundamental (RIF) (2009) suggests that looking at and understanding both words and pictures demands a higher cognitive level than merely seeing that words and pictures are there.

© Cengage Learning

Encourage children to write and illustrate their own books.

Teachers should develop many opportunities for children to become illustrators, such as:

● Have children author a book without illustrations and then author the same story, including illustrations.
● Have children develop a traditional storybook in which the text and illustrations are mutually supportive.
● Encourage children to try their hand at authoring and illustrating a wordless picture book.
● Help children see the relationship between a book's meaning and its art.

As with any child-directed activity, the teacher prepares materials and space in advance and is available to offer assistance. Suggestions for putting the book together can come from the teacher as well, with the children putting the book together with yarn, staples, masking tape, metal rings, or brads. The size and shape of the cover and pages of the book can be another creative element, such as books shaped to match the current curriculum theme or children's interests. For example, books can be in the shape of a bird, butterfly, car, bus, animal, fish, vegetable, and so on.

Keep in mind that however and whenever you mix and match literature with other curriculum areas, all activities should benefit the children developmentally, individually, and creatively. (There are specific examples at the end of this chapter. See Developmentally Appropriate Activities for Young Children.)

Family involvement in children's learning is also important in promoting children's love of literature. One way to encourage a family to contribute is to give each child a chance to take home one of the books she made individually or with a classmate. Many times the family does not know that their child is the author and illustrator of a book.

Encourage family members to participate in the process by asking them to extend the story that their child began in school. Send the book home in a bag with index cards so family members can write the next part of the story. To make this a family activity, suggest that family members use the children's words when continuing the story. Primary-age children can write the words of the story on the cards themselves.

When the child brings the book back to the class, all the children can enjoy the story. This literacy project can go on until the child or the family decides to stop. (See Figure 4–8 for information about the Eric Carle Museum of Picture Book Art.)

TEACHERS AS STORYTELLERS

"Throughout the world, in every culture, people have told stories," says Jimmy Neil Smith, executive director of the National Association for the Preservation and Perpetuation of Storytelling. The oral tradition was once the primary method for passing history and culture from one generation to the next. Eventually it became unpopular. "This may have been due," he continues, "to books and print media, radio, television and computerization. They fill us with images that were once the province of the oral tradition," concludes Mr. Smith (cited online at Community Arts Reading Room, 2009). Sawyer (2009) agrees. "At one time, storytelling was the dominant method for sharing a culture's heritage with the next generation."

A story is one of the means by which children make sense of their world and organize events, experiences, and facts. A teacher *telling* a story without a book and using changes in pitch, tone, and dramatic flair; using puppets, props, toys, songs, flannelboard pictures, and finger plays; or drawing a story while it is being told can captivate and entertain a small or large group of children. This unique way of presenting children's literature encourages children to tell their own stories or retell the stories back to the teachers.

"Storytelling is perhaps the most powerful way that human beings organize experience" (Engel, 1996/1997). Im, Parlakian, and Osborn (2007) tell us, "Adults can tell stories through language, but infants and toddlers tell their stories with a flick of their eyes, the point of a finger, or a coo.... Remember that much of infant and toddler

The Eric Carle Museum of Picture Book Art

FIGURE 4–8

By sharing a book, an adult shows a child, "I have time for you, I care for you—therefore I read to you. By reading together, we also give children an early taste of beauty. We clothe children, we feed children—and we read to children. It's part of growing up. It's culture, the human spirit" (Carle quoted in Brozowsky, 2002).

● The Eric Carle Museum of Picture Book Art, which celebrates the art of the picture book, opened to the public November 22, 2002, in Amherst, Massachusetts.
● Conceived by Carle, the museum is 44,000 square feet, situated in a 7.5 acre apple orchard next to the Hampshire College campus.
● The museum collection includes picture book art from around the world and has at its core the work of Eric Carle.
● It is designed to do what picture books always have done: create intimate moments between adults and children as they talk with each other about what they see and feel. Museum Director Nick Clark (quoted in Brozowsky, 2002) explains, "With the great books, there is a pace and a magic. But it's not just the book. You remember that you were snuggling with somebody."
● You can visit the museum on-line at: *http://www.picturebookart.org*

communication is nonverbal. Very young children need patient and willing listeners who can accurately read their cues…and respond appropriately."

It is helpful for the teacher to select stories with simple plots and small numbers of characters for the younger children. Older children like the challenge of remembering a complex plot with multiple characters.

POETRY

Teachers should read poetry to children often. Kindergarten and primary children can memorize a few poems of their choosing. Not only is this an enjoyable activity, it is also a valuable way to develop phonemic awareness and cognitive skills. Appreciation for poetry develops slowly, but the time and place for poetry is any time, any place. See Figure 4–9 for suggested poetry books for young children.

FIGURE 4–9
Suggested poetry books for young children.

● Baker, K. (2009). *Just how long can a long string be?!* New York: Scholastic.
● Barrett, J., & Moreton, D. (2003). *I knew two who said moo: A counting and rhyming book.* New York: Aladdin.
● de Paola, T. (2004, Board Book). *Tomie's little book of poems.* New York: Putnam.
● Howe, A. (2008). *Come and play: Children of our world having fun with poems by children.* New York: Bloomsbury.
● Lujan, J. (2008). *Colors! Colores!* Illustrated by P. Grobler. New York: Groundwood.
● Prelutsky, J. (2002). *The frog wore red suspenders: Rhymes.* Illustrated by P. Mathers. New York: Greenwillow.
● Scieszka, J. (2009). *Truckery rhymes.* Illustrated by D. Shannon, L. Long, & D. Gordon. New York: Simon & Schuster Books for Young Readers.
● Wells, R. (2003, Board Book). *Read to your bunny.* New York: Cartwheel.
● Williams, S. (2006). *Round and round the garden: Play rhymes for young children.* Illustrated by I. Beck. New York: Oxford University Press.
● Yolen, J. (2007). *Here's a little poem.* Cambridge. MA: Candlewick Press.

Tongue Twisters for Young Children

Busy buzzing bumble bees.
Papa, papa picked a pot of peas.

A flea and a fly flew up in a flue.
Said the flea, "Let us fly!"
Said the fly, "Let us flee!"
So they flew through a flaw in the flue.

                          —Author Unknown

She sells sea shells by the seashore.
He sells shells at the sea shell store.

Which wristwatch is a Swiss wristwatch?

Mama, mama mashes marshmallows.
Mama, mama mashes marshmallows.
Mama, mama mashes marshmallows.
    MMMMM!

FIGURE 4–10
Tongue twisters for young children.

Have snack time become a "poetry break time." Start by reading a poem to the children during their snack. Then, on following days, let the children read or tell a poem to each other and the teacher after snack time. Adding a musical background, recorded or live, offers a different dimension to poetry reading.

Other activities can be to act out a poem, draw an illustration for a poem, include poetry at group time, pick a theme and make an illustrated booklet or exhibit of poems that relate to the theme, and create a "Poetry Line" (clothesline or thick yarn) stretched across the back of the room with poems attached.

The following examples of poems are appropriate to share with young children. Figure 4–10, "Tongue Twisters for Young Children," is a different kind of poem. Children learn about language with this fun activity.

Sharing Literature: Family-School Connection

Make reading to your child a part of every day. You can help parents understand that when reading books is a regular part of family life, they send their children a message that books are important, enjoyable, and full of new things to learn.

WHY I TEACH YOUNG CHILDREN

I recall a time when I was teaching a young toddler class. My co-workers and I had a mother's day tea party. We wanted to do a special literacy activity that would be meaningful, as well as model to the parents. We decided to read the book *Love You Forever* by Robert Munsch. Once we had our refreshments, we requested that everyone sit down, make a circle and listen to a very special story. I introduced the book to everyone and explained that it was a story that celebrated the bond of mother and child. I read the book page by page. As I read, I heard sniffles from the crowd and saw babies and toddlers kissed and cuddled with so much affection that I began to sniffle myself. I tried to get through the book without crying, but the room was filled with so much emotion I could not keep from being a part of it. When the story was over, the group clapped. I witnessed a magical moment that children's literature brought to a group of mothers and their young children.

                  —Barbara Batista

SPRING SHOWERS

The sunlight is shining down through the trees.
The flowers stir and sway in the breeze.
Then here come the clouds—crowds of clouds—
hurrying, scurrying, covering the sun.
The lightning flashes!
The thunder crashes!!
The flowers are happy, for now the rain has begun.
Listen!

Raindrops falling, Raindrops falling,

Rain falls with a lovely sound.
Rain is very fine, I think!
Rain falls on the thirsty ground, giving all the plants a drink.

Raindrops falling, Raindrops falling, down

And now the clouds all blow away—
leaving a bright, sunshiny day.
And all the flower faces glow;
and all the plants begin to grow,

s-t-r-e-t-c-h-i-n-g … r-e-a-c-h-i-n-g …

up … so … high …

to … touch … the … sky!

t-r-y-i-n-g, … t-r-y-i-n-g …

Now rainbows are sparkling over the trees.
The flowers stir and sway in the breeze.

Reproduced by permission of B. Wolf—1995
Copyright B. Wolf—1993

"WHAT A SPLASH!"

If all the lakes were one lake,
What a great lake that would be!
And if all the oceans were one ocean,
What a great sea that would be!
And if all the people were one person,
What a great person that would be!
And if the great person took a great jump
And jumped as high as could be,
And jumped into the great ocean
What a great splash that would be!

Philip Jackman
(Reprinted with permission)

LOOKING AT THE WORLD

When I wake up
What do I do?
I open my eyes
Just like you.
  When I get up
  What do I see?
  I see my bedroom.
  It's all around me.
I go to the window
And look outside.
I see the world
So big and wide.
  It's filled with wonderful
  Things to see.
  Like the sun and flowers,
  Like grass and trees.
Like cars on the street,
Like clouds in the sky.
I love to watch
The world with my eyes.

Philip Jackman
(Reprinted with permission)

MOUSE

I am a *little* mouse,

a teeny, tiny mouse.

I live in someone's house in a *tiny* hole in the wall.

That's where I find it best to build my cozy nest, so the people in the
house won't know I'm there at all.

I eat my *tiny, little* breakfast, and then a snack I munch;

and then, before I know it, I'm sitting down to lunch,

after which I take a *little* nap, before I have my tea.

And just when tea is over, it's dinner time, you see.

What a treat for me!

Oh, what fun it is to be a *teeny, tiny mouse*—

the smallest little mouse,

and live in someone's house in a *tiny* hole in the wall.

That's where I find it best to build my cozy nest

so the people in the house won't know I'm there at all.

in *my tiny hole in the wall.*

Reproduced by permission of B. Wolf—1995
Copyright B. Wolf—1993

Part of a teacher's responsibility in early education is to effectively inform parents of this basic fact and to answer questions about ways for parents and their children to become involved with books. The following suggestions have been successful for some teachers of young children:

- Find opportunities to suggest titles and authors of books for the child and the parents.
- Give parents addresses of local libraries and list the story times.
- Suggest local or online bookstores that specialize in or offer a large selection of children's literature.
- Send home a list of the books that are going to be or have been read to the children. Personalize the information with a special note to each family about a book their child especially enjoyed.
- Set up a parent-lending library at your school. Supply a bright-colored folder or large envelope in which the borrowed book can be returned.
- Encourage parents to read a story to their child at the end of the day before going home from the child care setting. This helps both parent and child make a relaxed transition.
- For older children, ask parents to allow a block of time in the evening to have their child read to them; encourage parents to read aloud to the child as well.
- Ask parents to be role models by letting their child see that they read books. Suggest that they talk about what they read and what the child reads.
- Suggest that a special place for the children's books be provided at home.
- Have parents provide children's reading material in their family's home language and encourage them to read to their child in that language.
- Encourage parents to give books as gifts to let their child know that they think books are important and special.

- Read more than books. Use grocery shopping to encourage reading. Read whatever is close at hand—anything and everything: magazines, cards, newspapers, milk cartons, cereal boxes, street signs, and signs in stores.
- Encourage parents to limit television time, watch less television on school nights, read about things they see together that interest their child, and view children's books on video.
- Promote cooking with their child, reading recipes, and making a family cookbook of favorite recipes.

The more a teacher includes the child's parents or caregivers in the literature experience, the more a child can see how books are related to everyday life. Children enjoy the connection of parent and teacher.

Tips for Teachers

A common teacher misconception is that sharing picture books is a separate activity to be reserved for a storytime of a few minutes a day. Actually, teachers who are successful in promoting literacy infuse picture books into their entire program by making their classrooms and centers places where books are shared, recommended, connected with all curricular areas, and supportive of the goals of diversity. (Jalongo, 2004)

Select age-appropriate stories and read to the children whenever they show an interest.

When reading aloud to a group of children:

- Start the process by selecting an appropriate piece of literature for your age group.
- Read through the story several times before reading aloud to the children. Practice your presentation.
- Plan the appropriate time, place, and purpose for the story time. Alternate small group and large group activities.
- Make sure everyone is comfortable.
- Show the cover and read the title, author, and illustrator of the book.
- Suggest things the children can look for or listen for during the story.
- Try to maintain as much eye contact with the children as possible while you share the story.
- Sit on the floor with the children or on a low chair.
- Hold the book so that everyone in the group will be able to see the page. The use of big books can be effective.
- Use different voices for different characters. The children will enjoy your involvement with the story, and these "voices" help children to distinguish between characters.
- Ask children to make predictions about the plot, the characters, and the setting.
- Allow children to ask questions or make comments during the story.
- Ask questions about the story after you read it. Give all the children time to answer your questions and then to ask some of their own.

WORD WALLS

In early childhood classrooms, a **word wall** is a tool children can use to discover new words while practicing and expanding their language skills. "It is an interactive ongoing display of words and/or parts of words used to teach spelling, reading and writing

word wall An alphabetically arranged display or chart of words that children have experienced throughout the school year.

strategies, letter-sound correspondence, and more" (Wagstaff, 2005).The word wall is an alphabetically arranged display or chart of words that children have experienced. These words should be reviewed daily to help the children internalize them. As teachers we should collaboratively build word walls with the children. They choose words from meaningful contexts such as shared reading materials and oral language experiences, thereby reinforcing their growing vocabulary and special interests they have explored in each previous unit of study (Houle & Krogness, 2001).

Neuman, Copple, and Bredekamp (2000) emphasize, "To read, children must be able to distinguish the letters of the alphabet and to connect letters and letter clusters with sounds. To become proficient readers they need to be able to recognize many familiar words at a glance as well as decode words they don't know by sight."

The following are a few tips for teachers from Houle and Krogness (2001):

● Create the wall at the children's eye level in an accessible and highly visible area.
● Keep the wall simple and uncluttered for easy reference.
● Make sure there is ample room to add new words.
● Encourage children to help build the wall with words they wish to spell and/or words they know and want to add.
● Make your word walls interactive by attaching key words with Velcro strips, sticky tack, or pockets. This allows the children to go to the wall, remove a word, use it, and return it.
● For younger children, add pictures describing each word.

GUIDANCE GUIDELINES

The following guidance techniques can be helpful to use during story time:

● When a child wants to leave the group during story time, gently encourage the child to stay, but do not insist. Sometimes a reassuring arm around the child will help.
● Young children are easily distracted. Listening as part of a group is a skill they must learn. Begin with books that have only a few pages.
● Asking a child a question about what might happen next will help direct her attention back to the story.
● While telling the story, whatever has to be said or done to handle a problem should be as brief an interruption of the story as possible. (Sometimes interruptions can be an important part of the literature experience, if they offer focused discussion of the story or book.)
● Be sure that the children have elbow and knee room. Be sure that everyone can see. For the habitual nudger or distracter, catching her attention might be achieved by inserting her name as part of the story.
● It is helpful to include the children in the process by having them retell the story using their own words, joining in to repeat lines, or letting them add the flannelboard pieces as you tell the story. Using a puppet is effective in guiding the children through the story.

ACTIVITY PLANS

As suggested in Chapter 2, using an activity plan worksheet will help you clearly describe the activity, objectives, concepts, skills, space and materials needed, step-by-step procedure, guidance and limits for expected behavior, and assessment and follow-up strategies. The following activity plan worksheets are examples for developmentally appropriate activities for infants, toddlers, three-, four-, and five-year-olds, and kindergarten children.

ACTIVITY PLAN WORKSHEET

DEVELOPMENTALLY APPROPRIATE ACTIVITIES FOR YOUNG CHILDREN

Children's age group: Infants (3 to18 months)

NAME OF ACTIVITY AND BRIEF DESCRIPTION

Sharing nursery rhyme books with individual children
These are the books we will share:

Hoberman, M. A. (2003, Sing Along Stories). *Mary had a little lamb*. Illustrated by N. B. Westcott. New York: Little Brown Young Readers.

Fox, M. (2008). *Ten little fingers and ten little toes*. Illustrated by H. Oxenbury. Orlando, FL: Harcourt.

Wells, R. (2001, Board Book). *Twinkle, twinkle little star*. New York: Scholastic.

PURPOSE/OBJECTIVES OF ACTIVITY

- to listen to a short story for the development of listening skills
- to look at books and rhymes
- to recognize and point out objects and familiar animals
- to turn pages
- to say words and sing rhymes

SPACE AND MATERIALS NEEDED

Rocking chair, floor, pillows, and books

PROCEDURE

The following activities are mainly inside ones, carried on next to the bookshelf while the child sits on the adult's lap, on the floor, or in a rocking chair. These activities can also be taken outside and done while you are sitting on a blanket.

1. Let the child choose a book from the low shelf.
2. Read the book to the child. Point to what is going on in the pictures. See if the child will try to say a word or part of a word with you.
3. Do the finger plays for the rhymes, such as "Twinkle, Twinkle Little Star."
4. Repeat these finger plays or songs often during transition times.

GUIDANCE

Usually this is a one-on-one activity, but other children in the group are welcomed to look at the pictures and encouraged to do the finger plays, too. If other children want a book read to them at the same time, have enough books on the shelf or nearby so they can look at them. Keep the stories short.

ASSESSMENT AND FOLLOW-UP STRATEGIES

These nursery rhyme books are popular with the infants, and so are the follow-up activities. Sing the nursery songs and do the rhymes often to encourage language and motor development. Play dough makes a great "Pat-a-Cake." Have a tea party for "Polly Put the Kettle On." Use cotton balls to make "Mary Had a Little Lamb." Eat muffins to relate to "Muffin Man," and do exercises (sit, stand up, and fall down) with "Humpty Dumpty." To achieve effectiveness in this activity, keep the stories short and do not mind when a child turns the page before you finish the rhyme. However, be sure there are plenty of books available, because a child this age does not share easily.

ACTIVITY PLAN WORKSHEET

DEVELOPMENTALLY APPROPRIATE ACTIVITIES FOR YOUNG CHILDREN

Children's age group: Toddlers (18 months–3 years)

NAME OF ACTIVITY AND BRIEF DESCRIPTION

Group time story and art activity
Here are the books we will share:

DK Preschool. (2005, Board Book). *Lift the flap: Things that go*. New York: DK Publishing.

Priddy, R. (2002, Big Board Book). *My big truck book*. New York: Priddy Books.

Ziefert, H., & Baruffi, A. (1992). *Where is Mommy's truck?* New York: HarperCollins.

Reading a book about trucks or things that go offers a large format that brings images to life. Teacher and children can spend a few minutes together talking about the people who drive cars and trucks, big and small. Sometimes mommy and daddy drive a truck to work. Mommies and daddies go to many different kinds of jobs. By asking open-ended, short questions, toddlers can spend time one-on-one with the teacher and the book. After reading the book, the teacher will explain the art activity: car and truck painting. This activity will be available for any child to do with minimal assistance from the teacher, if needed. The children should direct the process.

PURPOSE/OBJECTIVES OF ACTIVITY

- to practice small muscle skills
- to practice hand-eye coordination
- to demonstrate cause and effect
- to practice color recognition

SPACE AND MATERIALS NEEDED

Indoor (or outdoor) table with or without chairs, individual sheets of paper, washable paint on a tray, and small cars and trucks

PROCEDURE

1. Place cars and trucks on a tray with paint.

2. One child at a time (wearing a painting smock) rolls the cars and trucks through the paint and then "car paints" on his sheet of paper. (If possible, have several places set up for this activity.)

3. The teacher talks to the child and asks questions throughout this activity, such as: "Can you drive the car and make some tracks?" "Show me how you can drive on the paper." "Does your car make some sounds?" "What color is your car or truck or the road you're making?"

4. At the end of the activity for each child, the teacher can say: "Your paper is full of roads and tracks." "Show me how you can wash your hands and hang your smock up." "Thank you."

Some children will participate in this activity in their own way. That is all right. It is the process that is important, not the product.

GUIDANCE

Anticipating what a toddler might do, the teacher can easily use her words to guide the child. This encourages the child to "use her words." Examples: "Your car drives on the tray or on the paper." "Show me how you can sit on your bottom on the chair." "Your paper is so full of roads, now it is another friend's turn." "Would you like another piece of paper?"

It is helpful to have another teacher or teacher assistant guiding the other children into activity centers while the teacher at the art table works one-on-one with a child.

ASSESSMENT AND FOLLOW-UP STRATEGIES

Were all the objectives met? When an older toddler is participating in the art activity, the teacher can suggest placement of the car on the tray or paper, such as back-and-forth or up-and-down. And at this point, other paint colors on additional trays can be added. This helps a child see how one road can cross another. To further extend the activity, add puzzles of cars and trucks to the manipulative center. Sing songs such as "Little Red Wagon" or "The Wheels on the Bus."

ACTIVITY PLAN WORKSHEET

DEVELOPMENTALLY APPROPRIATE ACTIVITIES FOR YOUNG CHILDREN

Children's age group: three-, four-, and five-year-olds

NAME OF ACTIVITY AND BRIEF DESCRIPTION

Group time story and cooking activity

These are the books we will share:

Heloua, L. *Tangerine and Kiwi visit the bread baker.* (2007). Illustrated by N. LaPierre. New York: Owlkids Books.

Levenson, G. (2008). *Bread comes to life: A garden of wheat and a loaf to eat.* Photographed by S. Thaler. Berkeley, CA: Tricycle Press.

Morris, A. (1989). *Bread, bread, bread.* Photographs by Ken Heyman. New York: Lothrop, Lee & Shepard.

Paulsen, G. (1998, reprint edition). *The tortilla factory.* New York: Voyager.

Reiser, L. (2008). *Tortillas and lullabies/Tortillas y cancioncitas.* Illustrated by C. Valientes. New York: Greenwillow Books.

Share the books with the children. (Place the ones you do not read to them in a basket in the home living area.) After reading one of the books, invite the children to go to the snack table. The teacher has provided a "tasting party" of different types of bread. Blunt table knives for spreading butter or margarine and jam or jelly are available for the children.

The teacher (with her teacher assistant) explains how she plans to let any child who wants to help with the cooking activity.

PURPOSE/OBJECTIVES OF ACTIVITY

- to introduce the concepts that people all over the world eat bread and that bread comes in many different shapes, sizes, and colors
- to recognize that some families serve bread for various festivities and ceremonies
- to ask open-ended questions about the type of bread each child eats at home, such as: "Which is your favorite type of bread?" "Have you ever eaten corn bread?"
- to introduce children to different ingredients
- to provide opportunities for measuring, pouring, sifting, stirring, and baking
- to practice a cooking activity and to involve children in the process of doing, thinking, talking, and asking

SPACE AND MATERIALS NEEDED

Large low table, small chairs, mixing bowls, ingredients, measuring cup, measuring spoons, large spoon for stirring, muffin pan, paper muffin cup liners, oven tray, blunt plastic knives, butter or margarine, jam or jelly, variety of breads to taste, recipe, and book to introduce activity

PROCEDURE

1. At group time, read either *Bread, Bread, Bread* or *Bread Comes to Life.*
2. Ask open-ended questions about the families shown in the photographs in the book, the children's families, what kind of bread they eat at home, and which is their favorite.
3. Children go to the large table for snack time. They taste all kinds of bread, margarine, and jam.
4. The teacher explains the activity choices for the day. Making corn bread muffins is one of the activities. Three children and the teacher will make the first batch. Later the teacher will make some more corn bread with another three children. The corn bread muffins will be the afternoon snack.
5. The children and the teacher wash their hands and the table, put on smocks, put out the cooking utensils and ingredients, and read the recipe together. (The teacher has printed the recipe on a large poster with both illustrations and words.)

Corn Bread

(1) 1 cup flour	(5) 1/2 teaspoon salt
(2) 1 cup cornmeal	(6) 1 egg
(3) 1/4 cup sugar	(7) 1 cup milk
(4) 4 teaspoons baking powder	(8) 1/4 cup cooking oil

Sift together #1, 2, 3, 4, and 5. Add #6, 7, and 8. Beat until smooth. Pour into a greased pan and bake for 20 minutes at 425 degrees.

GUIDANCE

Anticipating what could occur, the teachers prepare to help children understand why they cannot taste the ingredients that are measured to go into the corn bread. There will be time when the muffins are cooking for them to taste the ingredients. (Put some ingredients aside for small tastes. Exclude the raw egg. Then, talk about pre- and post-baking.) Remind the children of safety factors when using utensils. Supervise closely.

(continued)

Provide sponges and soap and water for cleanup and child-size brooms for sweeping.

ASSESSMENT AND FOLLOW-UP STRATEGIES

After this specific activity, the children participate with open-ended questions.

Other extended activities might include:

● Read other books about bread.
● Take a field trip to a bakery or bagel shop.
● Relate bread to nutrition and the food groups.
● Bake other breads, such as *tortillas*.

CORN BREAD

Sift together:

One cup flour, one cup cornmeal,

¼ cup sugar, 4 teaspoons baking powder, and ½ teaspoon salt.

Add one egg, one cup milk and

¼ cup cooking oil. Beat until smooth.

Pour into a greased pan and bake for 20 minutes at 425 degrees.

(continued)

Tortillas
2 cups masa
1 cup water
Mix together. Roll into 1-inch balls. Press very flat, using waxed paper to keep from sticking. Cook in a greased electric skillet at 350 degrees. Turn when you can "slip" a spatula under, and cook on the other side until done.

Tortillas
Mix these ingredients in a bowl:

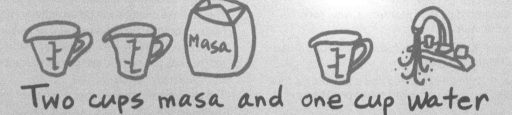

Two cups masa and one cup water

Roll into 1 inch balls.

Press flat using waxed paper to keep from sticking.

Fry in a greased electric skillet at 350 degrees.

Turn when you can "slip" a spatula under and cook on the other side until done.

ACTIVITY PLAN WORKSHEET

DEVELOPMENTALLY APPROPRIATE ACTIVITIES FOR YOUNG CHILDREN

Children's age group: Kindergarten

NAME OF ACTIVITY AND BRIEF DESCRIPTION

Group time story, writing invitations, and making no-bake cookies

These are the books we will share:

Carmi, G. (2006). *A circle of friends*. New York: Star Bright Books.

de Regniers, B. S. (1999) *May I bring a friend?* Illustrated by Beni Montresor. New York: Atheneum.

Hallinan, P. K. *A rainbow of friends*. New York: Ideals Children's Books.

Wilson, S. (2008). *Friends and pals and brothers, too.* Illustrated by L. Landry. New York: Henry Holt.

This is an introduction for the theme "Friends and Families." After reading one of the books, continue discussing friends, the ones in the book as well as the friends in the class.

The teacher explains how during the week each child can write an invitation to her friend in the classroom to come to the party on Friday during afternoon snack time. Another activity will be to make cookies to share with their friends at the party.

PURPOSE/OBJECTIVES OF ACTIVITY

● to introduce concepts that friends can be people or animals, and that friends are kind to each other
● to recognize that everyone can *be* a friend and *have* a friend at the same time
● to provide opportunities for cooperation, sharing, and kindness
● to practice math skill development: counting, measuring, number value, and quantity

SPACE AND MATERIALS NEEDED

Book to introduce the activity; various colored and textured papers; markers and crayons; pencils; scissors; paste; tape; rulers; large, low table; small chairs; mixing bowls; small plastic bags; rolling pins; cookie ingredients; recipe

PROCEDURE

1. At group time, read one of the books.
2. Ask open-ended questions about the book.
3. Explain the activity choices for the day. Making invitations for the "friend party" on Friday is one of the activities, and this center will be open for two children at a time until Thursday afternoon.
4. On Friday morning, the children give the invitations to their friends. (The teacher has asked each child to make just one invitation without a name on it.) The teacher then puts all of the invitations in a sack, and the children close their eyes and reach in to select one. Part of the fun is to see if the children get their own invitation or one that someone else made.
5. The no-bake cookies will be an activity choice for Friday morning. Two children at a time will make no-bake cookies until everyone has made some. (The teacher has printed the recipe on a large poster with both illustrations and words.)
6. The children and the teacher wash their hands and the table, put on smocks, put out the cooking utensils and ingredients, and read the recipe together.

Graham Cracker No-Bake Cookies
    1/2 cup raisins
    1/2 cup chopped dates
    2 tablespoons honey
    graham crackers
Let the children pour raisins, dates, and honey into a mixing bowl. Place several graham crackers in a plastic bag. Children can crush these with a rolling pin. Add to honey-fruit mixture. Mix until dry enough to roll into balls. Eat at snack time!

GUIDANCE

By limiting the number of children at the writing table and having fewer at a time participating in the cookie making, the teacher has limited many of the problems that could occur. This is a time when the teacher can talk about sharing and taking turns with friends.

As with all cooking activities, provide sponges, soap, and water for cleanup. It is helpful to have the teacher assistant moving around the room to supervise the other learning activities. This will give the teacher an opportunity to have some special one-on-one time with the children involved in the cookie making activity.

(continued)

ACTIVITY PLAN WORKSHEET (Continued)

ASSESSMENT AND FOLLOW-UP STRATEGIES

Were all the objectives met? Extended activities might include:

● Place the recipe poster in the writing center. This gives the children an opportunity to write out the recipe to take home.

● Make fingerprint paintings. Children can look at their own and those of their friends. Use the magnifying glass to look at the fingerprints. Are they alike? Are they different? How?

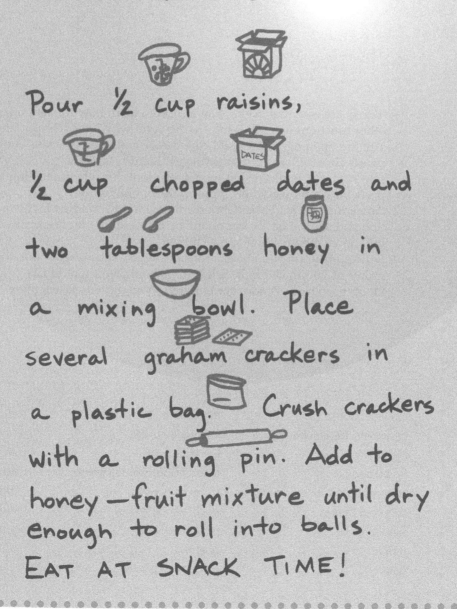

GRAHAM CRACKER NO-BAKE COOKIES

Pour ½ cup raisins, ½ cup chopped dates and two tablespoons honey in a mixing bowl. Place several graham crackers in a plastic bag. Crush crackers with a rolling pin. Add to honey—fruit mixture until dry enough to roll into balls. EAT AT SNACK TIME!

Afterview

Through books, a child

● learns to listen to stories.
● develops imagination and creativity.
● gets new ideas and develops interests in many things.
● adds to previous experiences.
● learns more about the world and the people in it.
● increases attention span.
● attempts to read and write independently.
● increases vocabulary and language skills.
● develops the concept of print and the written word.
● begins to take responsibility for the care of books.
● enjoys quiet moments alone with her thoughts.
● develops a lifelong interest in literature and reading.

Reflective Review Questions

1. Books are essential in enabling a child to learn how to read, but they serve many other functions as well. What are they, and why is each important?
2. You are opening a new child care center and need to order books to go in classrooms for children of different ages. Identify specific sources you would use to select quality books. What would you look for when deciding whether or not a particular book would be appropriate for children?
3. Any adult can read aloud, but reading aloud to children involves special preparation and skills. List six important guidelines that you might advise a new teacher to follow when reading to the children.
4. Reflect on what you should consider when choosing a book to read aloud to a group of young children. Select three books you would like to read to a class of kindergarten or primary age children. Why did you select these specifically?

Key Terms

alphabet books
beginning-to-read books
big books
board books
concept books
counting books
folk literature
format
genre

informational books
interaction books
literature
Mother Goose and nursery
  rhyme books
multicultural books
picture books
poetry
predictable books

realistic literature
reference books
series books
teacher- and child-made
  books
word wall
wordless picture books

Explorations

1. Bring to class a selection of children's books that represent the types and genres of books described in this chapter. Discuss with other students which books are appropriate for infants, toddlers, preschoolers, and primary-grade children and why they are suitable. Read one book aloud and describe ways of extending this book for a class of young children.

2. Select one of the books listed in this chapter and make a flannelboard story out of it. Share it with a child or a group of young children. What worked well? What would you change? Was it easier or more difficult than you expected?

3. Create a book for young children. Complete an Activity Plan Worksheet, such as the one in this chapter; then read the book to a small group of young children. Observe their responses. What age group did you select? Was your book developmentally appropriate for that age group? Explain your answers and your assessment and follow-up activities.

4. Visit a library or an early childhood classroom and observe during the time books or stories are being read or told to a group of children. Do the children focus visually on the storyteller? What questions do the children ask? Do they seem to understand the story? How can you tell? Does the story seem appropriate in content and vocabulary for young children? What kinds of things distract the children? What guidance techniques does the storyteller use in relating to inappropriate behavior?

5. How would you answer a parent who asked, "Of what possible value could a book be to an infant? She can't read or even understand what the pictures are about. Shouldn't you wait to expose her to books when she is older?" How would you go about explaining to the parent why infants should be exposed or introduced to books? How would you encourage the parent to do the same?

Additional Readings and Resources

Ada, A. F. (2003). *A magical encounter: Latino children's literature in the classroom.* Boston, MA: Allyn & Bacon.

Children's Book Committee of Bank Street College of Education. (2009). *Celebrating 100 years: The best children's books of the year.* New York: Bank Street Children's Book Committee & Teachers College Press.

Courtney, A. M., & Montano, M. (2006, March). Teaching comprehension from the start: One first grade classroom. *Young Children, 61*(2), 68–74.

Creech, N., & Bhavnagri, N. (2002, Summer). Teaching elements of story through drama to 1st graders: Child development frameworks. *Childhood Education, 78*(4), 219–223.

Greenman, J. (2009, September). Meet the author: Karen Beaumont. *Young Children, 64*(5), 92–94.

Isbell, R. T. (2002, March). Telling and retelling stories: Learning language and literacy. *Young Children, 57*(2), 26–30.

Isbell, R. T., & Raines, S. (2007). *Creativity and the arts with young children* (2nd ed.). Clifton Park, NY: Delmar Cengage Learning.

Jones, C. G. (2003, Winter). Choosing good books for toddlers. *Dimensions of Early Childhood, 3*(1), 29–36.

Kara-Soteriou, J. (2008, July). Using children's literature to teach positive character traits. *Young Children, 63*(4), 30–36.

Maderazo, C. (2009, May). Responsive reading: Caring for Chicken Little. *Young Children, 64*(3), 86–90.

Mazzeo, D. A., & M. R. Jones. (2002, Summer). Children's literature that encourages the identity development of interracial children. *Dimensions of Early Childhood, 30*(3), 13–20.

Ortiz, R.W., & Ordoñez-Jasis, R. (2005). Leyendo juntos—Reading together: New directions for Latino parent early literacy involvement. *Reading Teacher, 59*(2), 110–121.

Sackes, M., Trundle, K. C., & Flevares, L. M. (2009, November). Using children's books to teach inquiry skills. *Young Children, 64*(6), 24–26.

Swanson, M., & Ros-Voseles, D. (2009, Spring/Summer). Dispositions: Encourage young children to become lifelong readers. *Dimension of Early Childhood, 37*(2), 30–37.

Swope, S. (2005). *I am a pencil: A teacher, his kids, and their world of stories.* New York: Henry Holt.

Helpful Web Connections

American Library Association
   http://www.ala.org
Bank Street Children's Book Committee
   http://www.bankstreet.edu
Children's Book Council
   http://www.cbcbooks.org
International Children's Digital Library
   http://en.childrenslibrary.org
National Association for the Education of Young Children
   http://www.naeyc.org

Read, Write, and Think
   http://www.readwritethink.org
Reading Is Fundamental
   http://www.rif.org
Reading Rockets
   http://www.readingrockets.org
Society of Children's Book Writers and Illustrators
   http://www.scbwi.org

References

Adams, C. (2009). *Digital storytelling.* Online at: *http://www. scholastic.com*

American Library Association. (2009). Online at: *http://www. ala.org*

Arnoff, I. (2003). Reflection on children's literature. Working paper, New York University. In M. R. Jalongo, *Young Children and Picture Books.* Washington, DC: NAEYC.

Birckmayer, J., Kennedy, A., & Stonehouse, A. (2008). *From lullabies to literature.* Washington, DC: NAEYC.

Brinson, S. A. (2009, January). Behold the power of African American female characters! *Young Children, 64*(1), 26–31.

Brozowsky, S. (2002, September 22). Why we love picture books. *Parade Magazine,* 12–13.

Copple, C., & Bredekamp, S. (Eds.) (2009). *Developmentally appropriate practice in early childhood programs* (3rd ed.). Washington, DC: National Association for the Education of Young Children.

Derman-Sparks, L., & Edwards, J. O. (2010). *Anti-bias education for young children and ourselves.* Washington, DC: NAEYC.

Engel, S. (1996/1997). The guy who went up the steep nicken: The emergence of storytelling during the first three years. *Zero to Three, 17*(3), 1, 3–9. Online at: *http://www.zerotothree.org*

Glazer, J. I. (2000). *Literature for young children* (4th ed.). Upper Saddle River, NJ: Merrill.

Graham, J. (2000, July). Creativity and picture books. *Reading, 34,* 61–69.

Houle, A., & Krogness, A. (2001, September). The wonder of word walls. *Young Children, 56*(5), 92–93.

Huck, C. S., Hepler, S., & Hickman, J. (1993). *Children's literature in the elementary school* (5th ed.). New York: Harcourt.

Im, J., Parlakian, R., & Osborn, C. A. (2007, January). Stories: Their powerful role in early language and literacy. *Young Children, 61*(1), 52–53.

Isbell, R. T., & Raines, S. C. (2007). *Creativity and the arts with young children* (2nd ed.). Clifton Park, NY: Wadsworth Cengage Learning.

International Reading Association. (2007). Online at: *http:// www. ira.org*

Jalongo, M. R. (2004). *Young children and picture books* (2nd ed.). Washington, DC: NAEYC.

Lamme, L. L. (2002, Fall). Reading good books: Priming the pump for literacy development. *Dimensions of Early Childhood, 30*(4), 17–21.

Machado, J. M. (2010). *Early childhood language arts* (9th ed.). Clifton Park, NY: Wadsworth Cengage Learning.

Morrow, L. M. (1989). *Literacy development in the early years.* Upper Saddle River, NJ: Prentice Hall.

National Association for the Preservation and Perpetuation of Storytelling. (2009). Online at: *http://www.communityarts. net/readingroom*

National Council of Teachers of English. (2009). Online at: *http://www.ncte.org*

Nelsen, M., & Nelsen-Parish, J. (2002). *Peak with books: An early childhood resource for balanced literacy* (3rd ed.). Clifton Park, NY: Delmar Cengage Learning.

Neuman, S. B., Copple, C., & Bredekamp, S. (2000). *Learning to read and write: Developmentally appropriate practices for young children.* Washington, DC: NAEYC.

Owocki, G. (2001). *Make way for literacy! Teaching the way young children learn.* Portsmouth, NH: Heineman; Washington, DC: NAEYC.

Reading Is Fundamental (RIF). (2009). Online at: *http://www. rif.org*

Sawyer, W. E. (2009). *Growing up with literature* (5th ed.). Clifton Park, NY: Delmar Cengage Learning.

Spann, M. B. (1997) 30 Collaborative books for your class to make and share. New York: Scholastic.

Strickland, D. S. (2002). Bridging the gap for African American children. In B. Bowman (Ed.), *Love to read: Essays in developing and enhancing early literacy skills of African American children.* Washington, DC: National Black Child Development Institute, Inc.

Thomas, M. (1998). *Free to be you and me.* New York: McGraw Hill.

Vygotsky, L. S. (1986). *Thought and language.* Cambridge, MA: MIT Press.

Wagstaff, J. (2005, March). Word walls that work. *Instructor.* Online at: *http://content.scholastic.com/browse/article.jsp? id=4380*

● ●

 Additional information and resources on early childhood curriculum can be found on the Education CourseMate website for this book. Go to **www.CengageBrain.com** to register your access code.

chapter 5

Math

Objectives

After Studying This Chapter, You Should Be Able To:

- Discuss math concept development in young children.

- Describe math language and processes based on the National Council of Teachers of Mathematics (NCTM) Standards and the research of early childhood educators.

- Discuss ways to integrate math experiences with other curriculum areas.

- Specify materials for developing math concepts.

- Describe how technology helps young children gain mathematical skills.

- State why assessing the mathematical knowledge of young children is important and explain procedures for assessment.

- List ways to encourage a child's family to become involved with math activities at home.

- Identify developmentally appropriate math activities for young children.

Overview

Mathematics is everywhere! We are involved with math concepts from infancy onward. Much of what we do as part of our everyday lives relates to mathematics: telling time with clocks and watches, cooking and eating, getting dressed, watching a basketball game, and planning our lives by the calendar (electronic or otherwise). Daily activities involve problem solving, one-to-one correspondence, classifying, measuring, and sequencing. This is true for children, too.

As you progress through this chapter, the approach to setting up the developmentally appropriate math environment will parallel the approach to, and interconnect with, all the content areas in this book. The math-rich environment is built on basic math concepts, the children's developmental level (individually and collectively), and their interests.

"In today's high-tech, increasingly connected world, it is important that young children build confidence in their ability to do mathematics" (Furner & Berman, 2003). The National Research Council (2009) states, "Early childhood mathematics is vitally important for young children's past and future educational success. Research has demonstrated that virtually all young children have the capability to learn and become competent in mathematics." Providing hands-on, developmentally appropriate math experiences in a safe and trustworthy environment gives children opportunities to develop math awareness and understanding. "The best way to teach children is in a purposeful manner—in a context that has a purpose to the child" (Baroody, 2000). This is very different from the rote learning, rigid rules, workbooks, and flash cards many of us grew up with. The goal for children today is to focus on conceptual math, not pencil-and-paper figuring.

The new view of math is that it should be relaxed and comfortable for the teacher and the children.

Children need to acquire basic skills and concepts *first* to live in our world, which is exploding with information and continuously changing.

> Young children continually construct mathematical ideas based on their experiences with their environment, their interactions with adults and other children, and their daily observations. These constructed ideas are unique to each child and vary greatly among children the same age. (Copley, 2000)

It is also important to understand that the *acquisition of math skills and concepts occurs in stages over time,* as with all growth and development in young children. Teachers should recognize that early math instruction and experiences are not limited to a specific period or time of day. Instead, these math opportunities are a natural part of the learning environment (Texas Education Agency and University of Texas System, 2008). When a child builds with blocks, counts the number of buttons on his shirt, recognizes how many butterflies are on the page, gives each child a napkin at snack time, or claps a rhythmic pattern, he is learning math.

Repetition is meaningful during this process. Children need to rethink and practice what they know as they continue to add new skills and concepts. Making the environment, both indoors and outdoors, available for young children to experience the world and their place in it will encourage them to understand that mathematics is everywhere!

© Cengage Learning

Young children continually construct mathematical ideas based on their experiences with their environment.

Concept Development in Young Children

> Early childhood is a period when children actively engage in acquiring fundamental concepts and learning fundamental skills. Concepts are the building blocks of knowledge; they allow people to organize and categorize information.... Concepts can be applied to the solution of new problems that are met in everyday experience. (Charlesworth & Lind, 2010)

early mathematics Refers to exposure to and interaction with materials that contribute to the acquisition of knowledge about the underlying concepts of mathematics.

physical knowledge Learning about objects in the environment and their characteristics, such as color, weight, and size.

logico-mathematical knowledge Includes relationships constructed in order to make sense out of the world and to organize information, such as counting and classification.

concept development The construction of knowledge through solving problems and experiencing the results, while being actively involved with the environment.

The term **early mathematics** refers to exposure to and interaction with materials that contribute to the acquisition of knowledge about the underlying concepts of math (National Association for the Education of Young Children [NAEYC] & National Council of Teachers of Mathematics [NCTM], 2002). When child development and mathematics are mentioned together, Jean Piaget and Lev Vygotsky come to mind.

Jean Piaget pioneered the study of children's thinking (cognitive growth and development) and described how each child creates his own mental image or knowledge of the world, based on his encounters with the environment. Piaget called this **physical knowledge** or learning about objects in the environment and their characteristics, such as color, weight, and size. Piaget's **logico-mathematical knowledge** is the type that includes relationships each individual constructs in order to make sense out of the world and to organize information, such as classification, counting, and comparing (Charlesworth & Lind, 2010).

Like Piaget, Lev Vygotsky also studied children's thinking. He contributed significant insight into the way we learn from those around us, especially those who have more skill. He believed that we develop ways of cooperating and communicating, as well as exhibiting new capacities to plan and to think ahead (Charlesworth & Lind, 2010). "Vygotsky was intrigued not only by the skills and understanding that children possess, but also by the skills and understanding they're on the verge of possessing, also known as the zone of proximal development" (Bank Street, 2002). Refer to Chapter 1 for additional information.

Howard Gardner includes logical/mathematical thinking in his research relating to multiple intelligences, sometimes referred to as "different ways of knowing." Children strong in this form of intelligence think conceptually in logical and numerical patterns, making connections between pieces of information. Young children who excel in Logico-Mathematical intelligence have strong problem-solving and reasoning skills and ask questions in a logical manner. They thrive in logical and consistent sequencing of daily schedules and routines (Gardner, 1993; Nicholson-Nelson, 1998). Review Chapter 1 for information on all of Gardner's multiple intelligences.

When you observe children, you become aware of how they think (problem solve) and talk (communicate) about what they are discovering. **Concept development** is fostered by *solving problems* or figuring things out. Constructing knowledge by making mistakes is part of this process as well.

A curriculum that accommodates a variety of developmental levels as well as individual differences in young children sets the stage for problem-solving opportunities (Copple & Bredekamp, 2009). This, too, is a process. Beginning with the needs and interests of the children; developing themes, lesson plans, and webs; and providing time, space, and materials, encourages problem solving.

A young child needs to rethink and practice what she knows as she continues to add new skills and concepts.

Tell me mathematics, and I will forget;
Show me mathematics and I may remember;
Involve me … and I will understand mathematics.

(Williams quoted in Furner & Berman, 2003)

Math Language of Early Childhood

Young children understand math in relationship to how it affects them. The infant discovers the shape of the object by putting it in his mouth and holding on to it. The toddler can let you know he is two years old by trying to show you two fingers. The three-year-old likes to sing a number song, while the four-year-old counts "one twothreefourfivesix." The five-year-old shows you how tall his block building is, and the school-age child wants to win at the board game he is playing. All these children are using *math language*. See Figure 5–1 for examples of math language used by the National Council of Teachers of Mathematics.

In the beginning, children can say the names of numbers in order. They remember the *words*, but they do not understand the *meaning* of what they are saying. This number sense evolves during the first eight years of a child's life. How you set up the early education environment will determine how often the child has opportunities to develop number sense and logical ways of thinking about time, space, and other mathematical ideas.

For young children, infants and toddlers especially, the schedules and routines of the day become a consistent sequence of events. This regular predictable pattern helps put order to things, which is part of the process of math learning. When you frequently sing number songs and finger plays, read number books, share number flannelboard stories, and repeat numerals, you are placing math in the environment and making it part of the day's routine.

"All decisions regarding mathematics curriculum and teaching practices should be grounded in knowledge of children's development and learning across all inter-related areas—cognitive, linguistic, physical, and social-emotional" (NAEYC and NCTM, 2002). With this in mind, as teachers you should plan environments that build on children's curiosity and enthusiasm and encourage them to discover math concepts in the process of play. "Long before children encounter school mathematics, they have had significant mathematical experiences in their play....For young children, playful activity is simply the means to learning" (Eisenhauer & Feikes, 2009).

"Teachers need to find or devise worthwhile tasks that create a real need for young children to learn and practice mathematics; for example, incorporating mathematics into everyday situations, children's questions, games and children's literature" (Baroody & Li, cited in Essa & Burnham, 2009). The following discussions of math concepts, processes, and skills are based on recommendations from NCTM's *Principles and Standards for School Mathematics* (2000).

Examples of Math Language

1. *Numbers and Operations* includes counting, one-to-one correspondence, classifying and sorting, part-whole relationships, comparison, recognizing and writing numerals, and place value.
2. *Patterns, Functions, and Algebra* includes use of symbols and order.
3. *Geometry and Spatial Sense* includes analyzing, exploring, and investigating shapes and structures.
4. *Measurement* includes recognizing and comparing attributes of length, volume, weight, and time.
5. *Data Analysis and Probability* includes collecting and organizing data about individuals and the environment.
6. *Problem Solving* includes reasoning, communication, connections, and representation.

FIGURE 5–1
Examples of math language used by the National Council of Teachers of Mathematics (NCTM) Curriculum Standards Goals, 2000.

NUMBERS AND OPERATIONS

Young children use numbers to solve everyday problems by constructing number meanings through real-world experiences and the use of physical materials. The following concepts, skills, and processes are fundamental to early mathematics.

number sense A concept that develops over time as children think about, explore, and discuss mathematical ideas.

1. **Number sense** is a concept and *counting* is a skill that children use often in their everyday activities. "Number sense develops over time as children engage in activities that encourage them to think about, explore, and discuss mathematical ideas. Teachers and the classroom environments they create are fundamental in developing children's number sense" (White, 2002).

   Because the development of number concepts does not occur in one lesson, one theme, or even one year, we should understand that it is a continuous process that provides the foundation for much more of what is taught in mathematics for young children (Copley, 2000; Texas Education Agency & University of Texas System, 2008). The most effective and developmentally appropriate way to work toward number sense and all the NCTM standards is to *begin wherever the child is.* "Any other strategy simply wastes the child's time and prevents the development of the essential foundational understandings and skills needed for future success" (Richardson, 2000).

one-to-one correspondence The pairing of one object to another object or one group of objects to another group of equal number.

2. **One-to-one correspondence** is based on the premise that each object has the value of one. It is the foundation for relating one object to one counting number. This is the most fundamental component of numbers (Charlesworth & Lind, 2010). One-to-one correspondence is also a focal point for numbers and operations at the prekindergarten level (NCTM, 2000). One-to-one correspondence is established when one object is paired with one other object or a group of objects is paired with another group of equal number. The assigning of a number name (one, two, three, etc.) to each object helps children place the objects in a one-to-one correspondence. Children show an awareness of this relationship daily.

   The following are examples of this awareness:

   ● Language is important to toddlers, so a teacher touching and counting aloud (one child, one book, one block, one doll) is expressing one-to-one correspondence. A child is learning self-help skills and one-to-one correspondence when he puts one arm into a coat sleeve.
   ● For preschoolers and older children, activities such as putting one peg in one hole, setting the table with one napkin for each child, or putting one sock on one foot is one-to-one correspondence. Giving a child four pennies and asking him to put one penny in each of four cups also demonstrates one-to-one correspondence.

rote counting The ability to recite names of numerals in order.

rational counting Requires matching each numeral name, in order, to an object in a group.

3. Count anything and everything! Count real things to help children use their own experience with objects to better understand numbers. "Counting is a powerful tool for extending young children's nonverbal numerical and arithmetical competencies. Teachers should provide abundant opportunities for children to learn and practice counting skills and should praise the counting solutions" (Baroody & Li, cited in Essa & Burnham, 2009). Throughout the day sing number songs, repeat finger plays and rhymes, share number flannelboard stories, and read books that include counting. Counting with young children starts with **rote counting**, the ability to recite names of numerals in order. **Rational counting** requires children to match each numeral name, in order, to an object in a group.

   A basic understanding of accurate rote counting and one-to-one correspondence is the foundation of rational counting. The ability of rational counting assists children in understanding the concept of number by enabling them to check their labeling of quantities as being a specific amount. It also helps them to compare equal quantities of different things—such as two apples, two children, and two chairs—and to realize that the quantity two is two, regardless of what makes up a group. (Charlesworth & Lind, 2010)

4. Children grouping objects by a common *attribute* or characteristic, such as size, shape, or color, are **classifying and sorting**. These children are interacting with the environment, using visual discrimination, and manipulating real objects.

classifying and sorting Grouping objects by a common characteristic, such as size, shape, or color.

Sorting activities allow teachers to naturally introduce the language of mathematics with words such as more, few, many, most, least, and none to describe children's collections. Once children complete a sorting activity, they are often interested in how groups relate to each other. Children may be overheard saying, "This group has more" or "This group is bigger." (White, 2002)

As a teacher, your role is to extend the children's concepts about the material's attributes.

The following are some examples:

- Infants learn about shapes through using their hands, mouth, and eyes. They are discovering that some toys are easier to hold, while others roll better.
- During late infancy, babies grasp an important developmental concept— object permanence. "This realization is key for learning and is especially important for developing thinking and number skills. Once toddlers grasp object constancy, sorting by size and color is within reach" (Poole, 1998).
- Toddlers begin noticing alike and different when they sort colored blocks into blues and reds or big and little ones. It is important to remember to keep concepts simple and consistent for toddlers. For example, have all the blue and red blocks they are sorting be the same size and shape so the children are dealing only with the concept of color. Simple puzzles also help toddlers begin to develop classification skills.
- Preschool children begin by sorting objects with one characteristic or quality. They enjoy sorting buttons, plastic animals, wooden beads, and shells. Provide a muffin tin (see Figure 5–2), plastic cups, or an empty, clean egg carton for the sorted objects. For older preschoolers, classifying becomes more involved by isolating a set from a collection, such as counting children and sorting them into boys and girls, and then observing which children are wearing stripes and which are not.
- Primary-grade children use more complex concepts by sorting sets into subsets and looking at what materials objects are made of (wood, plastic, metal) or what function they have (forks, knives, spoons), or which piece of string is longer (or shorter, or thicker) than the other two. Older children can explain to you their rule for making the sorting decision. This process involves comparing, beginning measurement, as well as one-to-one correspondence, counting, and classifying skills.

FIGURE 5–2
Classifying and sorting objects by a common characteristic.

Patterning is another way for children to see order in their world.

© Cengage Learning

PATTERNS, FUNCTIONS, AND ALGEBRA

pattern A sequence of colors, objects, sounds, stories, or movements that repeats in the same order over and over again.

Patterning is another way for children to see order in their world. A **pattern** is a sequence of numbers, colors, objects, sounds, shapes, or movements that repeat, in the same order or arrangement, over and over again. "Patterns serve as the cornerstone of algebraic thinking....Recognizing, describing, extending, and translating patterns encourage children to think in terms of algebraic problem solving (Taylor-Cox, 2003).

Copley (2000) explains, "Mathematics is the science and language of patterns. Thinking about patterns helps children make sense of mathematics." Some examples follow:

● For infants, patterning is recognizing the human face with eyes, nose, and mouth in a specific place. For older infants, looking in a mirror helps them place their face in the same pattern.
● Toddlers asking for the same book to be read again and again soon begin to "read" the story along with the teacher. They are placing the events of the story in a sequencing pattern.
● For preschoolers and older children, stringing beads or putting pegs in a pegboard in a specific pattern, such as blue, red, green, and yellow, is visual patterning. The younger children can duplicate the pattern and the older children can duplicate and extend it.

Auditory patterning is repeating or singing sounds (such as soft, loud, soft, loud, soft) over and over again and then having the children repeat the sequence. You can do this with tactile patterning by creating a texture board with articles that are smooth, rough, smooth, rough, smooth.

● Instead of talking about a pattern, the teacher "reads" the pattern using simple vocabulary: *circle, square, circle, square, circle, square* or *a, b, a, b, a, b*. Create a pattern physically: *jump, jump, clap, clap, jump, jump, clap, clap* (Copley, 2000).
● See Figure 5–3 for a shape pattern flannelboard activity.
● With linking cubes the plus-one pattern can be visually shared with children.

> Not only do young children need many experiences with repeating patterns, they also can work with growing patterns that increase (or decrease) by a constant amount. The simplest of all growing patterns increases by one and begins with a small number. For example, 1, 2, 3, 4, 5, 6...is a growing pattern based on a constant change of plus one. This is best understood by young children through concrete representation. (Taylor-Cox, 2003)

seriation Seriation or ordering of objects is based on the ability to place them in logical sequence, such as smallest to largest or shortest to tallest.

SERIATION. Teachers should provide opportunities for children to recognize, extend, and create a wide variety of patterns. **Seriation** is a concept underlying patterning. Seriation or ordering of objects is based on the ability to place them in logical sequence, such as smallest to largest. "Simple seriation involves concrete objects; for instance, arranging objects from longest to shortest or widest to narrowest. Sensory seriation can include ordering sounds from loudest to softest, tastes from sweetest to sourest, or colors from darkest to lightest. Seriation can also relate to time sequences; for example, what happened first, second, third, and so forth" (Essa, 2011).

According to Kennedy, Tipps, and Johnson (2011), "Comparative vocabulary develops with seriation: good, better, best; big, medium, small; lightest, light, heavy, heaviest; lightest, light, dark, darkest."

EARLY GEOMETRY AND SPATIAL SENSE

geometry The area of mathematics that involves shape, size, space, position, direction, and movement.

Geometry is the area of mathematics that involves shape, size, space, position, direction, and movement, and describes and classifies the physical world we live in. See Figure 5–3.

> Geometry offers students an aspect of mathematical thinking that is different from, but connected to, the world of numbers. As students become familiar with shape, structure, location, and transformations and as they develop spatial reasoning, they lay the foundation for understanding not only their spatial world but also other topics in mathematics and in art, science, and social studies. (NCTM, 2000)

Shape Patterns

●   ● ● ● ● ● ● ● ● ● ●

- This is a small group activity.
- Put a large flannelboard and shapes of many sizes and colors in the math center. You can also have small individual flannelboards, chalkboards, and chalk there as well.
- Ask the children to choose partners. The pairs of children will take turns with other pairs at the large flannelboard.
- On a large card set up a simple pattern. Ask the children to arrange the same pattern on the flannelboard. For example, place a circle, square, another circle, and a triangle.
- Continue holding up patterns for the children to duplicate. Increase the difficulty of each pattern. (A square, two circles, a star, two triangles, a rectangle, an oval, and two more rectangles.)
- For older children, add colors and sizes to the shape patterns. Add new shapes, such as the pentagon, hexagon, and octagon.
- Leave the flannelboard(s) and shapes in the math center for the children to create patterns by themselves.

FIGURE 5–3

Real objects and abstract shapes have one-, two-, or three-dimensional features that can be examined and compared.

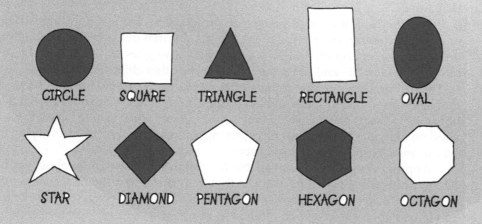

CIRCLE SQUARE TRIANGLE RECTANGLE OVAL

STAR DIAMOND PENTAGON HEXAGON OCTAGON

Spatial sense is a child's awareness of himself in relation to the people and objects around him. Games and movement activities can be the keys to spatial relationship awareness, such as location/position (on/off, over/under), direction/movement (up/down, forward/backward, in/out, in front of/in back of, around/through), and distance (near/far, close/far from). Figure 5–4 illustrates this with children and large boxes.

Manipulating shapes in space introduces children to vocabulary words. In addition, "distinguishing between letters of the alphabet involves attention to shape and position. In art, spatial relationships and geometric forms are critical elements in both two-dimensional and three-dimensional creations" (Copley, 2000). Other examples are filling and emptying, such as playing in the sandbox; fitting things together and taking them apart, such as Legos and boxes with lids; and setting things in motion, such as things that roll and spin (High/Scope, 2003).

"Imagine, for example, the wealth of concepts relating to *space, position, time, sound, rhythm, body parts,* and *body control* a child might grasp through a group activity involving music and rhythmic movement" (Fortson & Reiff, 1995). Toddlers and young preschoolers enjoy moving streamers in time with the music. You can help increase spatial awareness by saying, "Move your streamer over your head or in

spatial sense Comparisons that help children develop an awareness of themselves in relation to people and objects in space, such as exploration using blocks and boxes.

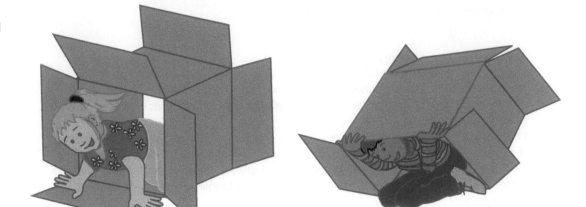

FIGURE 5–4
Helping children understand spatial relationships.

An early childhood manipulative area should offer a quiet place for an individual child to practice using his small muscles with materials especially designed for him.

measurement Finding the length, height, and weight of an object using units like inches, feet, and pounds.

front of you." You are encouraging them to change the arrangement of space they are in.

Play the "hide an object" game with preschoolers. For example, hide a block or a beanbag somewhere in the room. Let the children guess if you have hidden it over, under, on top of, and so on. The child who guesses where the object is hidden becomes "it" and hides the object for the other children to guess where it is. The children are thinking in images and pictures. They are finding the object that has been placed in space and out of sight. Older children extend spatial relationships to board games, where they count squares and move forward or backward on the game board. They are exploring a new spatial layout and varying the arrangement of the game pieces in space.

Appropriate software is available for children to learn more about spatial relationships using the computer, but first it is critical that they understand the basic math concepts used in the relationships. Math language of early childhood overlaps, interconnects, and involves all the senses. No matter what terminology they use, children are counting, classifying, thinking, reasoning, comparing, measuring, problem solving, and learning about math naturally as they play.

MEASUREMENT

According to NCTM's Standards (2000), "Measurement is one of the most widely used applications of mathematics. It bridges two main areas of school mathematics—geometry and number." **Measurement** is finding the length, height, and weight of an object using units like inches, feet, and pounds. Offer children activities to identify and compare attributes of length (longer, shorter), capacity (holds more, holds less), weight (heavier, lighter), and temperature (colder, warmer). Time is measured using hours, minutes, and seconds by reading time on both digital and analog clocks.

Measurement is an important way for young children to look for relationships in the real world. Through playing, imitating, and learning to use standard units of measurements, young children explore and discover measurement. By practicing measurement, they will learn how big or little things are and how to figure that out.

Many daily activities involve measurement. Here are a few examples: cooking, matching objects, comparing sizes of containers at the sand and water table, measuring the number of steps it takes to get somewhere, comparing and ordering objects according to their length using terms such as longer and shorter, estimating and measuring length to the nearest inch and foot, and linking cubes to find objects that are shorter or longer than ten linking cubes.

DATA ANALYSIS AND PROBABILITY

As teachers plan to integrate data analysis into their classroom curriculum, they must first take into account their students' levels of readiness. Prerequisite skills such as understanding number concepts, number recognition, counting, and one-to-one correspondence are all necessary precursors to performing many data analysis tasks. (Andrews & Thornton, 2008)

Questions that cannot be answered by direct observation can often be assessed by gathering data. Data can be organized, represented, and summarized in a variety of ways. Using graphs and charts, children can discover how to organize and interpret information and see relationships. Graphing and charting offer children a way to show and see information and can make it easier to make predictions about related events. The data findings can be represented through the use of a vertical or horizontal bar graph, a pie graph, a line graph, or a circle graph. Ask the children questions that require collection and organization of data, and then display relevant data to answer the questions (NCTM, 2000). Examples of this are: (1) children asking questions about their environment and then gathering data about themselves and their surroundings, and (2) sorting and classifying objects according to their attributes and organizing data about the objects (Charlesworth & Lind, 2010).

Figure 5–5 offers a variety of suggestions for getting children to think and talk about math.

Many daily activities involve estimating, weighing, and measurement.

PROBLEM SOLVING

Teachers provide an environment that encourages problem solving and verbalize children's methods as they solve problems. Problem solving is critical to being able to do all other aspects of mathematics. Children learn that there are many different ways to solve a problem and that more than one answer is possible.

Many early childhood educators and researchers emphasize the importance of problem solving in helping children clarify and strengthen their math understandings:

Problem solving means engaging in a task for which the solution method is not known in advance. To find a solution, students must draw on their knowledge, and through this process, they will often develop new mathematical understandings. Solving problems is not only a goal of learning mathematics but also a major means of doing so. (NCTM, 2000)

The development of problem-solving skills is a long-term activity; it is not learned in one lesson. It must be focused on the process of problem-solving, not just the answer. Therefore, you must provide children with problem-solving situations and observe how they meet them....Behavior noted can be recorded with anecdotal records or checklist. (Charlesworth & Lind, 2010)

Problem solving and reasoning are the heart of mathematics....While content represents the what of early childhood mathematics education, the processes—problem solving, reasoning, communication, connections, and representation—make it possible for children to acquire content knowledge....Children's development and use of these processes are among the most long-lasting and important achievements of mathematics education. (NAEYC and NCTM, 2002)

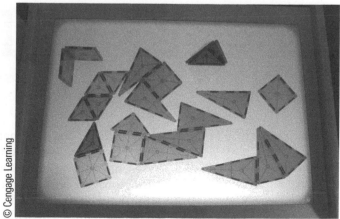

The math-rich environment is built on basic math concepts including the attributes of shape and pattern and applying them to problem-solving.

Math Questions Teachers Should Ask

FIGURE 5–5
Math questions teachers should ask.

After asking questions, listen to the child's answers. This will give you insight into what each child knows and does not know. The following questions help young children to visualize math as well as thinking and talking about math.

How can we make 7 feet? How can we make 5 elbows? How can we make 12 fingers? How many *X*s go in the empty square?

| X | XX | XXX | X | XX | XXX | X | XX | |

What numbers should go in the empty squares?

| 5 | 6 | 5 | 6 | 5 | | 5 | 6 | | 6 |

Which circle has 3 dots?

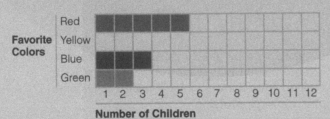

Does this bar graph tell you which color is the class's favorite color?

How can we make this shape pattern longer? Shorter?

In 2006, The National Council of Teachers of Mathematics introduced *Curriculum Focal Points*, an extension of their *Principles and Standards Goals (2000)*. "*Focal points* present a way to bring focus to the teaching, learning, and assessing of mathematics. They provide a framework for designing and organizing curricular expectations and assessments. Collectively, they describe an approach that can be used in developing a mathematics curriculum for prekindergarten through grade 8" (NCTM, 2006). Discussion of focal points can be found online at: http://www.nctm.org.

In addition, the focal points are intended as a first step toward a national discussion on how to bring consistency and coherence to the mathematics curricula used in the United States (NCTM Press Release, September, 2006).

Integrating Math Experiences with Other Curriculum Areas

Math concepts are better understood when they are a part of the daily activities. Other curriculum areas can include math easily and successfully. In addition, according to NAEYC and NCTM (2002):

> Young children do not perceive their world as if it were divided into separate cubbyholes such as "mathematics" or "literacy." Likewise, effective practice does not limit mathematics to one specified period or time of day. Rather, early childhood teachers help children develop mathematical knowledge throughout the day and across the curriculum. The classroom environment is organized so that children can investigate mathematics through many types of hands-on experiences.

MATH AND OUTDOOR ACTIVITIES

Math awareness continues outdoors, too. Applications for math concepts are everywhere. The following examples offer a variety of ideas to help you provide these math experiences:

© Cengage Learning

Math awareness continues outside. It is fun to experience the math concept of a circle when you can crawl through it.

- Toddlers enjoy play structures that are lower and wider and allow them opportunities to climb up and down. The wheels on the tricycles are round and the sandpile is a square.
- Preschool children can look for rough and smooth objects to compare and count. They like to weave crepe paper or ribbon through a chain link fence to create a pattern and count how many times they toss a beanbag back and forth to each other.
- Older children can take chalk and make a giant hopscotch area with numerals from 0 to 20 as well as measure and record rainfall using a clear container with 1/4-in., 1/2-in., and 1-in. markings.
- You can help the children collect boxes, small to large, and set up an outdoor obstacle course for them to crawl through, around, over, and under.
- Line up two rows of small, smooth stones with each row having six stones. Space the stones farther apart in one row. Ask the children if one row has more or less than the other. Most preschoolers will answer that the longer row has more rocks than the other. When children reach the developmental stage of knowing that both rows have the same amount of stones, no matter how they are spaced, they are also practicing the concept of conservation or "the ability to retain the original picture in the mind when material has been changed in its arrangement in space" (Charlesworth & Lind, 2010).
- Ask open-ended questions to learn more about children's thinking, such as, "Which of the cups do you think will hold the most sand?"; "How many circles can you find in our room?"; "How many circles do you see outside?"; "How many steps do you think it will take to go from the tricycle to the sandbox?"; or "What can we use to measure the length of the art table?" You will get a lot of answers that will lead to more mathematical discoveries.

MATH AND SCIENCE

Math and science are like a two-piece puzzle. They fit together to make a whole, but each piece is important by itself. That is why these two curriculum areas are separate chapters in this book. Chapter 6, "Objectives," covers the science curriculum in early childhood. Here are several suggestions on how to use math concepts and relate them to the science center and theme.

- Sort collections of shells, magnets, leaves, seeds, and rocks. Classify them according to size.
- Use a thermometer and ask open-ended questions, such as, "What happens when you put the thermometer into hot water?" or "What happens when you put it in cold water?" Guide the children to find the answers themselves.
- Older children can graph the daily temperature. This can extend the daily calendar activity of marking the day of the week and month of the year.
- Have children count the number of legs on insects. Use both pictures and real insects, if possible.
- Plants offer opportunities for children to keep a chart or graph of the days or times plants should be watered and how much they have grown.
- Children's literature can create strategies to integrate math and science concepts in the curriculum. "Nearly any topic of interest can be developed using books, real-life artifacts, and related hands-on learning experiences" (Benson & Downing, 1999).
- *Planting a Rainbow* (1988) and *Growing Vegetable Soup* (1987), both by Lois Ehlert, are two books that integrate math and science in an exciting way. "Gardens in all their colors, shapes, and sizes offer linkages with many books that support a wide variety of activities, and of course more thinking, problem solving, and questioning" (Hinnant, 1999).

MATH AND COOKING

One of the most delightful ways to invite children into the world of math is through cooking. Ask a young child playing in the dramatic play area to explain the ingredients of the imaginary cake he is baking, and the answer will probably be something like this: "I put in 20 cups of sugar, a bunch of flour, two eggs (one for each hand), and mix 'em all up and put it in the stove for ten minutes." Even though his numbers may be inaccurate, this shows that he is aware of quantities in recipes.

Invite children into the world of math through cooking.

Extend both the dramatic play and math. Let the children bake an actual cake. Just think about the ways you can help children clarify math concepts through experiences with cooking. You are involving children with counting, one-to-one correspondence, fractions, time, temperature, weight, shapes, sizes, amounts, measurements, reading a recipe, and following a sequence.

Here's an easy cake recipe, and all you do is "dump" everything together: Put 1 can of fruit, including juice, into a buttered cake pan. Dump 1 box of cake mix over the fruit. Chop up 1 stick of butter or margarine. Dump these pieces on the top of the cake mix. Bake at 350 degrees for 30 to 40 minutes. Then divide into servings, one for each child, and eat!

You can also make *pretzels* and *cheese* shapes. Children really enjoy making these. You will need:

14-ounce block of cheddar cheese

package of stick pretzels

1. Wash hands.
2. Cut cheese into various shapes.
3. Put ends of pretzels into the cheese shapes.
4. Eat and talk about the shapes the children are eating.

For a time, rumors circulated that Howard Gardner was going to add cooking to his list of multiple intelligences. Although I was disappointed that this addition never came to pass, I will continue always to describe cooking ability as a type of intelligence. It is an area in which children can shine and excel. It is also a domain that teachers can use to teach socioemotional, cognitive, physical and literacy skills as well as to foster children's creativity and self-expression. My firm belief is that cooking—like block building, reading, and the arts—should be an integral part of every preschool and kindergarten program. (Colker, 2005)

WHY I TEACH YOUNG CHILDREN

I will always remember a little girl I observed several years ago. She was learning about subtraction in her second grade class. The teacher, knowing that we all learn better with concrete examples, brought in donuts. The children had set up a "donut bakery" in the classroom. The girl was "buying" the donuts and was supposed to figure out how much change she should get from her $1 bill. Instead, she told the "baker" to "keep the change." She took her donuts and left. (The teacher also learned a lesson that day.)

The above observation came to my mind yesterday, when four-year-old Dylan was telling me all about his mommy and daddy's anniversary. I asked him how long his mom and dad had been married. His answer was, "*Forever.*" Young children do tell us exactly where they are, mathematically.

—Bonnie Rubinstein

MATH AND ART

The arts help children grow cognitively. Arts activities invite counting, sorting, and classifying. Through questioning, children involved in arts activities can become aware of number concepts. They can count the number of flowers they have drawn. They can graph the shapes in their collages, and sort the leftover paper scraps by color. They can represent the rhythm of a song with symbols, or map the patterns in the steps to a dance. (Koster, 2009)

Children need to relate math to themselves, and adding art projects to the math activities will help them do this. For example, make an "All About Me" book, poster, or chart. Include the child's weight, height, and shoe size or foot outline at the beginning of the year, at various times during the year, and at the end of the year. This offers a child a concrete way to compare his stages of growth. This is also another way to do assessment.

Another art and math activity, one that has been part of the preschool curriculum for many years, is to draw an outline around a child's body on a large piece of white butcher paper or brown wrapping paper. The younger child will need you to do it, but the older child can select a partner to do it. Each child can then weigh himself on a scale in the classroom, measure different parts of his body, and record the results on the drawing. Next, the child can add finishing art to the drawing by adding facial features, hair, clothing, and shoes.

MATH AND LANGUAGE, LITERACY, AND LITERATURE

Teachers and parents have begun to realize that mathematics truly is everywhere. As, more and more, we consciously include critical thinking, problem solving, and communication as important goals within the mathematics curriculum, so we have become aware that children's literature holds countless creative opportunities for working towards these goals. (Wright, 2002)

For language, literacy, and literature development, select math books of all types and genres to read to the children, or have the children read and discuss during group time. "These books also feature rich vocabulary important for both captivating young children's imaginations and building their language skills" (Schickedanz, 2008). Here are a few to get you started:

- Ayers, K. (2008). *Up, down, and around.* Illustrated by N. B. Westcott. New York: Candlewick.
- Diehl, D. (2007, Board Book). *A circle here, a square there: My shape book.* New York: Lark Books.
- Falconer, I. (2002). *Olivia counts.* New York: Atheneum.
- Hoban, T. (2000). *Cubes, cones, cylinders, and spheres.* New York: Greenwillow.

● Pallotta, J. (2003). *Apple fractions*. Illustrated by R. Bolster. New York: Cartwheel Books.
● Tang, G. (2005). *Math for all seasons*. Illustrated by H. Briggs. New York: Scholastic.
● Williams, R. L. (2001). *The coin counting book*. Watertown, MA: Charlesbridge Publishing.
● Wood, A. (2004). *Ten little fish*. Illustrated by B. Wood. New York: Blue Sky Press.

(See Chapter 10 for Math and Music Activities.)

Materials for Developing Math Concepts

As we know, young children are interested in math. Their natural curiosity is evident in their everyday play and activities. The role of teachers and parents is to provide children with the appropriate words, materials, and resources to explore their interests and scaffold new levels of understanding (Epstein, 2003).

The following materials offer children many ways to develop their understanding of math concepts:

● balances, weights, scales
● bingo cards
● blocks—Legos, wooden table blocks, parquetry blocks, and pattern blocks
● board games
● counters—Unifix cubes, base-10 blocks, plastic animal shapes, popsicle sticks, straws, and beads in various colors and sizes
● calendar
● calculators
● cans or egg cartons, with numbers on them to put a matching number of objects into
● children's socks, shoes, mittens, and gloves, to match in pairs
● clocks with numbers (*not* digital)
● computer software that allows children to interact with math concepts
● geometric boards (geoboards): to manipulate rubber bands or elastic loopers to form shapes or designs
● magnetic boards with plastic numerals
● measuring cups, spoons, and pitchers
● milk cartons to demonstrate liquid measures and relationships between half-pints, pints, quarts, and gallons
● number strips and counting boards
● objects to count, sort, and classify, such as buttons, paper clips, pennies, colored cubes, bottle caps, aluminum washers, colored plastic clothespins, empty spools, shells, Popsicle or craft sticks, keys, bread tags, and nuts and bolts
● puzzles
● rulers, yardsticks, and measuring tapes
● sandpaper numerals
● self-help skill forms (buttoning, zipping, and tying)
● shape puzzles and flannelboard characters, such as circle, square, rectangle, triangle, cone, sphere, cube, cylinder, oval, diamond, star, and heart
● stacking, nesting, and sorting boxes/blocks
● storage containers in graduated sizes
● table games, such as parquetry blocks, pattern blocks, card games, and dominos
● telephones
● thermometers (outside)
● timer
● unit, hollow, shape, and table blocks, which offer opportunities to learn about balance, measurement and estimation, width, height, length and dimensionality, size relationships, and how shapes fit into space
● wooden pegboard and pegs

WHY I TEACH YOUNG CHILDREN

I had been talking about shapes with the children in my preschool class. We had explored and counted squares, circles, triangles, and even some three-dimensional shapes, such as cones, cubes, and spheres. The children had really enjoyed pointing out the different shapes throughout the day, and even commented on the shapes of the foods they had for lunch. During naptime, I sat in the quiet classroom and reflected on the events of the day. I got out a pad of paper and a pen and began walking quietly around the room, making a list of the areas that I felt needed to be changed the next day. One little girl, Avery, was not yet asleep and quietly watched me from her cot. When I got to her side of the room, she looked up at me and quietly asked, "Ms. Janet, what are you doing?" I whispered back to her, "Well, Avery, we are having a work day tomorrow, and I just wanted to see what shape this room was in." She looked at me with an expression on her face that told me she thought I'd said something completely ridiculous and said, "Can't you see it's a square!" I struggled to keep a straight face when I told her she was right and didn't she feel good about knowing her shapes so well. Those are the moments that make teaching young children special.

—JANET GALANTAY

Tips for Teachers

As you plan, facilitate, observe, and evaluate the math activities in your early education classroom, think about the following:

- Let the children know it is acceptable not to have an immediate answer to the math activity on which they are working. Let them know that there may be more than one way to solve a problem or complete a task.
- Let the children make mistakes and correct them themselves.
- Hand pieces of a manipulative toy one by one to a child who is easily distracted when playing or completing a task. For example, start with objects to count or a puzzle.
- Break down a cooking project into its parts when a child is overwhelmed. Describe the steps in clear terms: first we do this, then we do that. Use rebus charts to help with the explanation.
- Encourage collective or cooperative problem solving, which builds positive self-esteem.
- Allow time for trying out new ideas and taking risks.
- Guide the children to develop math skills needed for the new, changing information age of sophisticated machines, technology, computers, and calculators.
- Allow math materials to be moved to other curriculum centers. Spontaneity and creativity are exciting and important!

© Cengage Learning

Technology use that is connected to what children already know and can build upon leads to greater motivation and self-direction.

Technology in the Mathematics Program

Calculators and computers are part of a young child's world. They are now a given resource in learning mathematics (Wortham, 2010). Kostelnik, Soderman, and Whiren (2007) suggest, "Although young children need to learn to estimate and calculate problems mentally (mental math), they must eventually learn to do paper-and-pencil math and to use a calculator. Each of them should have access to a calculator, and the calculators they are given should have easy-to-read numbers found directly on the keys, and easy-to-depress keys." Teachers must also learn to use the calculator appropriately with children.

Computers provide games and simulation that aid problem solving and skill building for young children when they practice with developmentally appropriate software. Software for teaching math is being developed at a rapid rate. Educators should review and evaluate software carefully before using it with young children. NCTM (2000) proposed, "Technology is essential in teaching and learning mathematics; it influences the mathematics that is taught and enhances students' learning."

> Certainly the computer is not a cure-all for every problem in education, especially mathematics. It is not enough to place a few computers in a classroom and expect improvement. Improvement will not come even if every child has her or his own computer. Along with the technology must come appropriate use of the computer, effective programs that take advantage of the computers and proper training and knowledge by teachers who will use the computers in the classroom. (Kennedy, Tipps, & Johnson, 2011)

Technology use that is connected to what children already know and can build upon leads to greater motivation and self-direction. Loss of creativity can be a problem if children use drill-and-practice software. Open-ended software—software that provides opportunities to discover, make choices, and find out the impact of decisions—encourages exploration, imagination, and problem solving (Northwest Regional Educational Laboratory, 2001). In addition,

> Children working at the computer solve problems together, talk about what they are doing, help and teach friends, and create rules for cooperation. In fact, they prefer working on the computer with a friend to doing it alone. (Epstein, 2007)

Early childhood teachers guide children's mathematical learning through the use of manipulatives—pattern blocks, Unifix cubes, Cuisenaire rods, and so on. Rosen and Hoffman (2009) have observed, "In the past few years, online resources for virtual versions of these common manipulatives have become available."

The emergence of **virtual manipulatives**, interactive, web-based computer-generated images of objects that children can manipulate on the computer screen, can be especially beneficial to students with special needs or those who speak English as a second language. Many websites offer virtual manipulatives. One, for example, is the Utah State University National Library of Virtual Manipulatives, online at: http://nlvm.usu.edu (Kennedy, Tipps, & Johnson, 2011; Rosen & Hoffman, 2009).

Through early exposure to computer-based math activities, young children enjoy experiences that can link successfully to their ongoing concrete experiences with math materials.

virtual manipulatives Refers to interactive, web-based computer-generated images of objects that children can manipulate on the computer screen.

Observation, Assessment, and Evaluation

Support children's learning by thoughtfully and continually assessing all children's mathematical knowledge, skills, and strategies. Assessment data on young children should be through observations, interviews, and anecdotal records as children are actively involved in hands-on math problem solving and investigation. Assessment is an ongoing process to determine a child's strengths and needs. Support teacher planning by using the information and insights you gain to evaluate your teaching techniques and curriculum.

> Assessment is crucial to effective teaching....Child observation, documentation of children's talk, interviews, collections of children's work over time, the use of open-ended questions, and appropriate performance assessments to illuminate children's thinking are positive approaches to assessing mathematical strength and needs. Careful assessment is especially important when planning for ethnically, culturally, and linguistically diverse young children and for children with special needs or disabilities. (NAEYC & NCTM, 2002)

One form of assessment that can be used often and successfully is the *anecdotal record*. This will provide a helpful description of what a child does during an observational period. It is an attempt to record a specific episode that is of particular interest or concern. Gober (2002) comments, "Anecdotal records (notes) work well alone or with other assessment methods such as documentation for checklists and parent interviews....Children of all ages should be observed for anecdotal records. Be sure to keep anecdotal records on *all* children....When you keep these notes over an entire year, they provide an objective picture of how that child has grown or changed." Charlesworth and Lind (2010) explain further, "Recording observations can become a habit and provides an additional tool in assessing children's learning and your teaching strategies. Anecdotes are also invaluable resources for parent conferences."

Using Figure 5–6, the "Anecdotal Record Worksheet," offers one way to take notes on what you observe. This should be done first without including your opinions. You can separate your subjective thoughts and include them in a separate column. The more you observe, the better an observer you will become. Information gained from this observation should be used to support the development of the child. Also, think about how to use your observations to effect changes in the classroom and the curriculum. (The online premium website for this text offers additional anecdotal record/observation forms.)

Anecdotal Record Worksheet

Date of observation	Observation (factual/objective)	Comments (opinion/subjective)	FIGURE 5–6
Beginning time:	(Suggestions of what to include: Date of observation. Description of the situation or activity. What is happening? Description of what the child is doing. Location of the child? Who else is near the child? Description of the child's body movements. What is the child, children, or adult saying? What changes occur between the beginning and the end of the observation?)	(Suggestions of what to include: your interpretations, opinions, and conclusions of what you observe. How interested is the child in what he is doing? Is the child really being included in what is happening? What do you think the child is feeling? Was any guidance, positive or negative, offered? Describe.)	This anecdotal record worksheet will help with observations that are part of the assessment process.
Ending time of observation:			

Sharing Math: Encouraging Family Support

"As teachers, we must communicate to parents how much they have already participated in their children's mathematical knowledge merely by living life with them and serving as examples. Research, of course, also supports parent interests and involvement in children's acquisition of math concepts" (Prior & Gerard, 2007).

Young children enjoy assisting Mom or Dad in the kitchen or helping to sort the laundry. You can help the parents understand that these experiences offer their children math activities. Parents become very interested in supporting their children's mathematical learning once you provide them with activities for doing so.

Following are a few ways to explain this to family members. Hopefully, this will get parents started in asking you questions about what else they can do at home. They may even start observing the schedule, routines, and activities that are occurring daily in their child's classroom.

● LEARNING MATH AT HOME

● Your child will learn to sort and classify objects by helping you with the clean laundry. He could start with sorting clothes by color. He could help put all the white clothes in one pile and the dark clothes in another pile. He can learn to sort and classify items by types, putting the shirts in one pile, the sheets in another pile, and the towels in another pile. Start simply, and then go to the complex sorting. For example, sorting socks gives practice in pairing by color, size, and design. Putting rough jeans in one pile and soft bedclothes in another pile offers sorting and classifying of items by texture.

● Your child can also learn math concepts in the kitchen. He can learn number concepts when helping you to set the table. How many people will be at breakfast or dinner? How many knives will you need? How many forks? How many spoons?

● Your child can also learn spatial concepts by setting the table. The fork goes next to the plate on the left. The knife goes next to the plate on the right. He learns about the sequence of your mealtime. First, you set the table. Next, you eat your dinner. Last, you wash the dishes. Keep the steps to three at first, and gradually add more steps. This sequencing helps your child recognize the pattern or sequence of events in the world around him.

Children learning these basic concepts in early childhood will be able to understand and adjust to the growing technology that is and will be a part of their lives. They will likely be the ones who will one day help explain to us how to successfully use the latest technology.

Additional Activities

The following activity plan worksheets and songs offer opportunities for developmentally appropriate activities teachers can do along with other math projects. The songs suggest flannelboard activities, finger plays, music, and movement learning experiences.

ACTIVITY PLAN WORKSHEET

DEVELOPMENTALLY APPROPRIATE AND MULTICULTURAL/ANTI-BIAS ACTIVITIES

Children's age group: appropriate for two- and three-year-olds

NAME OF ACTIVITY AND BRIEF DESCRIPTION

The flannelboard shape game is designed to help young children become aware of shapes, begin to identify them by name, and look for shapes in their environment.

PURPOSE/OBJECTIVES OF ACTIVITY

- develop shape awareness and recognition
- identify shapes
- enhance matching ability
- recognize equal amounts
- sort and classify objects by shapes and sizes
- develop fine motor skills
- offer tactile learning experience

SPACE AND MATERIALS NEEDED

This activity can be done on the floor during circle time or at a table during small group time with a flannelboard and felt pieces cut into shapes (circles, squares, triangles, and rectangles) of various colors and sizes. These shape pieces should be sizes that two- and three-year-olds can manipulate. Also, cut a large version of each shape from cardboard, construction paper, or felt.

PROCEDURE

1. Introduce the activity by placing one shape at a time on the flannelboard. Ask the children if they can name the shape. Discuss the properties of each shape with the children; for example, the triangle has three sides and three corners. Say, "count with me" before you point to each side.

2. Continue placing shapes on the flannelboard and repeating the above procedure until all the small shapes are displayed.
3. Below the flannelboard, place the large shapes that you cut out.
4. Ask the children to match the shape by taking a small shape from the flannelboard and placing it on the larger piece that it matches. Help the younger children take just one shape at a time from the flannelboard and guide them to place it on the proper large shape.
5. Encourage them to continue matching shapes until *they* decide the activity is over, usually by wandering off to another center.

GUIDANCE

Anticipating the sometimes short attention span of the children in the group, the teacher should be fully prepared before beginning the activity. If the majority of the children are not interested in the activity, give them a choice of going to another center while you interact with the children who are interested. If one child takes two or three shapes at a time, give the other children two shapes as well. Then guide the children to take turns with their two shapes and make this a positive, not confrontational, time.

ASSESSMENT AND FOLLOW-UP STRATEGIES

Were all the objectives met? Did the activity hold the children's attention? Were they able to do the activity? What will you change if you do it again?

Extend the activity by leaving the flannelboard and shapes out for the children to use throughout the day. Also, take a shape walk around the room and around the center/school. Point out the shapes they see every day. See how many shapes the children recognize.

Make shape cookies with the children using shape cookie cutters. Later the children can use the cookie cutters to make shapes with play-dough. Read children's books relating to math, such as *Shapes, shapes, shapes* by Tana Hoban (1986). New York: Greenwillow.

ACTIVITY PLAN WORKSHEET

DEVELOPMENTALLY APPROPRIATE AND MULTICULTURAL/ANTI-BIAS ACTIVITIES

Children's age group: appropriate for prekindergarten and kindergarten children

NAME OF ACTIVITY AND BRIEF DESCRIPTION

The Name Game is designed for the children to find opportunities to measure, count, and have fun with their names.

PURPOSE/OBJECTIVES OF ACTIVITY

- build math connections
- develop an awareness that math is everywhere
- develop math concepts, such as one-to-one correspondence, counting, and measuring
- encourage cooperative problem solving
- become aware of similarities and differences in names
- recognize the importance of names and learn names from other cultures
- increase listening skills and encourage language development

SPACE AND MATERIALS NEEDED

This activity can be done in the math center, the art center, on the floor, or anywhere that the children can use rulers, measuring tape, pencils, crayons, markers, and paper.

PROCEDURE

1. At group time introduce the activity. Briefly talk about names. Ask the children if they have ever thought about the number of letters in their names. Have they ever counted the letters? Have they ever measured their names?
2. Using your name as an example, you can demonstrate what you want them to do. Show your name printed on a piece of paper. Have the children count the number of letters in your name. Then place

a ruler along the bottom of your name and measure how many inches long your name is.
3. Explain that this is what you would like for them to do with their names. They can do it now, or they can do it another time. They get to choose. Count how many want to do it now and how many want to do it later. Add the two numbers together to figure out how many children are in class today.
4. Use a transitional activity, such as the child whose first name begins with the letter closest to A goes to a center of his choice or begins the name activity. Continue through the alphabet until all the children have selected what they want to do.
5. You can then observe who needs assistance in getting started and who does not need any help.

GUIDANCE

In anticipating what the children might do, remember to guide them through this activity. Let them work together to problem solve. The children will probably discover for themselves that some names are shorter than others and compare the shortest name with the longest one. You may need to facilitate, especially with the younger children.

Some children may not want to participate in this activity. That is acceptable. Guide them into another activity center.

ASSESSMENT AND FOLLOW-UP STRATEGIES

Were all the objectives met? Did the younger children participate for a short or long period of time? How much did the children discover? Did they share and problem solve together? What would you leave the same and what would you change the next time you did this activity with the children?

Extend this activity by having children assign a color to each letter. When they use crayons and markers to "decorate" their names, they are adding another dimension to the activity. The next day at group time have the children rhyme their name with another word. Then go around the circle and have the children try to say all the rhymes together.

COUNTING IS FUN

Words and Music by Jo Eklof

From *Bringing Out the Best in Children Songbook #2*
Reprinted by permission of Miss Jo Publications
http://www.missjo.com

BIRDS ON THE ROOFTOP
Words and Music by B. Wolf

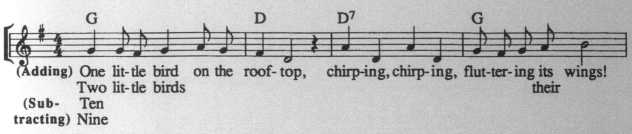

(Adding) One lit-tle bird on the roof-top, chirp-ing, chirp-ing, flut-ter-ing its wings!
Two lit-tle birds their
(Sub-   Ten
tracting) Nine

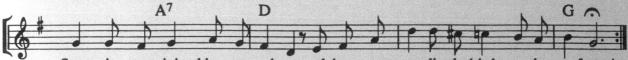

Soon it was joined by an-oth-er, and there were two lit-tle birds on the roof-top!
Soon they were   three (etc.)
One flew a-way to the for-est,   nine
One flew a-way to the corn-field,   eight (etc.)

Reproduced by B. Wolf—1995
Copyright © B. Wolf—1993

(Repeat as necessary to match number of birds desired.)

Afterview

Through math activities, a child

● relates life experiences to math.
● develops number concepts through concrete experiences.
● develops number sense.
● learns one-to-one correspondence.
● sorts and classifies objects by size, shape, color, and texture.
● identifies shapes and numerals.
● explores spatial relationships and develops math language.
● experiments with concepts of volume, weight, and measurement.
● recognizes patterns, a skill that develops into algebraic problem solving.
● learns how to interpret the calendar and the clock.
● has opportunities to make comparisons and to see relationships of concrete objects.
● develops problem-solving skills through experimentation.
● learns to cooperate with others.
● continues with language development by incorporating math vocabulary, such as less than, greater than, and equal to.
● interacts with math by technology exploration on the computer.

Reflective Review Questions

1. What is meant by the statement "*number sense* is a concept, and *counting* is a skill"? Which of these terms is more fundamental? Does that mean the other is unimportant?
2. Describe four group activities for young children that involve *patterning*. Two should involve vigorous physical activity, and two should involve the manipulation of objects.
3. Explain why cooking is an excellent activity to develop math skills in young children. Describe specific aspects typically found in cooking that utilize math.
4. Develop criteria for the selection of developmentally appropriate math activities for a specific age group of your choice. Create a list of the materials and supplies necessary to set up these math activities, including the cost of the equipment.

Key Terms

classifying and sorting	measurement	rational counting
concept development	number sense	rote counting
early mathematics	one-to-one correspondence	seriation
geometry	pattern	spatial sense
logico-mathematical knowledge	physical knowledge	virtual manipulatives

Explorations

1. What is the difference between a rote-learning, rule-based approach to learning math and a conceptual approach? Characterize each approach with examples. Do you think early childhood teachers have shifted the emphasis to the conceptual approach? Give examples that support your answer from your observations in early education classrooms.
2. Interview two teachers who teach kindergarten or primary-grade children. Have them explain what math skills and concepts are important for the age of children they teach. Have them describe their math program. If possible, observe the children in the classroom doing some of the math activities. How will you use the information gained from these interviews and observations?
3. After visiting a library and/or a bookstore, select five children's books that relate to math concepts for young children. Discuss your selections and explain how you would use each book with the children.
4. Select and plan a math activity for young children. Specify which age group this activity is planned for: infants, toddlers, preschoolers, or primary-age children. Write a list of objectives, materials needed, step-by-step procedures for presenting this activity, follow-up activities, and assessment guidelines. (Use the activity plan worksheet in Chapter 2.)
5. Based on the information in this chapter and on your observations of early education environments, describe how you would introduce one-to-one correspondence, classifying and sorting, patterns, spatial relationships, and other math concepts to a group of preschoolers. Put these descriptions in writing and share them with a classmate or colleague.

Additional Readings and Resources

Brenneman, K., Stevenson-Boyd, J., & Frede, E. C. (2009, March). *Math and science in preschool*. Online at: *http://www.nieer.org*

Cesarone, B. (2008). Learning stories and children's mathematics. *Childhood Education, 84*(3), 187–189.

Cutler, K. M., Gilkerson, D., Parrott, S., & Bowne, M. T. (2003, January). Developing math games based on children's literature. *Young Children, 58*(1), 22–27.

Geist, E. (2009, May). Infants and toddlers exploring mathematics. *Young Children, 64*(3), 39–41.

Guha, S. (2002, May). Integrating mathematics for young children through play. *Young Children, 57*(3), 90–92.

Kamii, C. (2003, September). Modifying a board game to foster kindergartners' Logico-Mathematical thinking. *Young Children, 58*(5), 20–26.

Kato, Y., Honda, M., & Kamii, C. (2006, July). Kindergartners play lining up the 5s: A card game to encourage Logico-Mathematical thinking. *Young Children, 61*(4), 82–88.

Murphy, M. S. (2009, May). Mathematics and social justice in grade 1. *Young Children, 64*(3), 12–17.

National Association for the Education of Young Children (NAEYC) and National Council of the Teachers of Mathematics (NCTM). (2002, July). Math experiences that count. *Young Children, 57*(4), 60–62.

Sarama, J., & Clements, D. H. (2009). Building blocks and cognitive building blocks: Playing to the world mathematically. *American Journal of Play, 1*(3), 313–337.

Sarama, J., & Clements, D. H. (2009, March). Teaching math in primary grades. *Young Children, 64*(2), 63–65.

Sloane, M. W. (September, 2007). First grade study groups deepen math learning. *Young Children, 62*(4), 78–82.

Trafton, P. R., & Andrews, A. (2002). *Little kids—Powerful problem solvers: Math stories from a kindergarten classroom*. Portsmouth, NH: Heinemann.

Whitin, D. J., & Piwko, M. (2008, March). Mathematics and poetry. *Young Children, 63*(2), 34–39.

Wolf, A. L., & Wimer, N. (2009, May). Shopping mathematics in consumer town. *Young Children, 64*(3), 34–38.

Worsley, M., Beneke, S., & Helm, J. H. (2003, January). The pizza project: Planning and integrating math standards in project work. *Young Children, 58*(1), 44–50.

Note: *The National Research Council (NRC)* is completing a 24-month project analyzing the past 20 years of research in early childhood mathematics. The goal of this study is to evaluate what we know about young children and mathematics from research and to disseminate best practices in mathematics to teachers, educators, policymakers, and researchers. Learn more about the study at the *National Academies* website online at: *http://www.nationalacademies.org/cp*. Click on "project title," then click on E, then select *EC math*.

Helpful Web Connections

National Association for the Education of Young Children
    http://www.naeyc.org
National Council of Teachers of Mathematics
    http://www.nctm/org
National Academies/National Research Council
    http://www.nationalacademies.org/cp

National Library of Virtual Manipulatives
    http://nlvm.usu.edu
PBS Kids
    http://www.pbskids.org
Scholastic
    http://www.scholastic.com

References

Andrews, N., & Thornton, J. (2008, Spring/Summer). Investigating the world around them. *Early Years Journal of TAEYC, 30*(1), 6–9.

Bank Street. (2002). *Mathematics*. Online at: *http://www.bankstreetcorner.com/develop_practices.shtml*

Baroody, A. J. (2000, July). Does mathematics instruction for three-to five-year-olds really make sense?—Research in review. *Young Children, 55*(4), 61–67.

Benson, T. R., & Downing, J. E. (1999, Spring). Rejuvenate math and science—Revisit children's literature. *Dimensions of Early Childhood, 27*(2), 9–15.

Charlesworth, R., & Lind, K. K. (2010). *Math and science for young children* (6th ed.). Clifton Park, NY: Wadsworth Cengage Learning.

Colker, L. (2005). *The cooking book: Fostering young children's learning and delight*. Washington, DC: NAEYC.

Copley, J. V. (2000). *The young child and mathematics*. Washington, DC: NAEYC; Reston, VA: National Council of Teachers of Mathematics.

Copple, C., & Bredekamp, S. (Eds.). (2009). *Developmentally appropriate practices in early childhood programs* (3rd ed.). Washington, DC: NAEYC.

Eisenhauer, M. J., & Feikes, D. (2009, May). Dolls, blocks, and puzzles: Playing with mathematical understandings. *Young Children, 64*(3), 18–24.

Epstein, A. S. (2003, Summer). Early math: The next big thing. *High/Scope Resource. A Magazine for Educators,* 5–10.

Epstein, A. S. (2007). *The intentional teacher: Choosing the best strategies for young children's learning.* Washington, DC: NAEYC.

Essa, E. L. (2011). *Introduction to early childhood education* (6th ed.). Clifton Park, NY: Wadsworth Cengage Learning.

Essa, E. L., & Burnham, M. M. (Eds.). (2009). *Informing our practice: Useful research on young children's development.* Washington, DC: NAEYC.

Fortson, L. R., & Reiff, J. C. (1995). *Early childhood curriculum.* Boston, MA: Allyn & Bacon.

Furner, J. M., & Berman, B. T. (2003, Spring). Math anxiety: Overcoming a major obstacle to the improvement of student math performance. *Childhood Education, 79*(3), 170–174.

Gardner, H. (1993). *Multiple intelligences: The theory in practice.* New York: Basic Books.

Gober, S. (2002). *Six simple ways to assess young children.* Clifton Park, NY: Delmar Cengage Learning.

High/Scope. (2003). Online at: *http://www.highscope.com*

Hinnant, H. A. (1999, March). Growing gardens and mathematicians: More books and math for young children. *Young Children, 54*(2), 23–26.

Kennedy, L. M., Tipps, S., & Johnson, A. (2011). *Guiding children's learning of mathematics.* Clifton Park, NY: Wadsworth Cengage Learning.

Kostelnik, M. J., Soderman, A. K., & Whiren, A. P. (2007). *Developmentally Appropriate Curriculum* (4th ed.). Upper Saddle, NJ: Prentice Hall.

Koster, J. B. (2009). *Growing artists: Teaching the arts to young children* (4th ed.). Clifton Park, NY: Wadsworth Cengage Learning.

National Academies/National Research Council (NRC). (2009). Online at: *http://www.nationalacademies.org/cp*

National Association for the Education of Young Children (NAEYC) & National Council of Teachers of Mathematics (NCTM). (2002). *Joint position paper—Early childhood mathematics: Promoting good beginnings.* Washington, DC: NAEYC; Reston, VA: NCTM.

National Council of Teachers of Mathematics (NCTM). (2000). *Principles and standards for school mathematics.* Reston, VA: Author. Online at: *http://www.nctm.org*

National Council of Teachers of Mathematics. (2006). *Focal points.* Online at: *http://www.nctm.org*

Nicholson-Nelson, K. (1998). *Developing students' multiple intelligences.* New York: Scholastic.

Northwest Regional Educational Laboratory. (2001, June). *Technology in Early Childhood Education.* Online at: *http://www.nwrel.org*

Poole, C. (1998, January). The path to math. *Early Childhood Today, 12*(4), 13–14.

Prior, J., & Gerard, M. R. (2007). *Family involvement in early childhood education.* Clifton Park, NY: Delmar Cengage Learning.

Richardson, K. (2000). Mathematics standards for pre-kindergarten through grade 2. (Report EDO-PS-00-11) *Eric Digest.* Urbana, IL: ERIC Clearinghouse on Elementary and Early Childhood Education.

Rosen, D., & Hoffman, J. (2009, May). Integrating concrete and virtual manipulatives in early childhood mathematics. *Young Children, 64*(3), 26–33.

Schickedanz, J. A. (2008). *Increasing the power of instruction.* Washington, DC: NAEYC.

Taylor-Cox, J. (2003, January). Algebra in the early years? Yes! *Young Children, 58*(1), 14–21.

Texas Education Agency and University of Texas System. (2008, Revised). *Texas prekindergarten guidelines.* Austin, TX: Author.

White, D. Y. (2002, Summer). Developing number sense in prekindergarten and kindergarten children. *ACEI Focus on PreK and K Newsletter, 14*(4), 1–5.

Wortham, S. C. (2010). *Early childhood curriculum: Developmental bases for learning and teaching* (5th ed.). Upper Saddle, NJ: Prentice Hall.

Wright, C. (2002). *Integrating mathematics and literature.* Online at: *http://www.bankstreetcorner.com/mathematics_literature.shtml*

Additional information and resources on early childhood curriculum can be found on the Education CourseMate website for this book. Go to **www.CengageBrain.com** to register your access code.

chapter

6

Science

Objectives

After Studying This Chapter, You Should Be Able To:

● Identify and discuss scientific process skills and concepts for young children based on the National Science Education Standards.

● Describe ways to create a scientific environment for young children.

● Identify and give examples of ecology in the early education environment, including gardening with young children.

● List appropriate science materials and equipment to include in an early childhood classroom.

● Explain why the study of animals is part of science education for young children.

● Describe ways in which families and children can share science activities at home.

● Identify appropriate multicultural/anti-bias activities and other developmentally appropriate science activities.

● Explore anecdotal record observations to aid in assessing children's science learning.

Overview

The science curriculum in an early childhood environment should shout "Please touch! Please explore!" We must nourish young children's excitement about learning and encourage them to ask, "What would happen if...?" and then give them the materials to find out the answers. These active encounters help children define basic concepts and stimulate natural curiosity, exploration, and discovery.

As we discuss throughout this text, all children learn about the world around them through their senses. Infants and toddlers, as well as preschoolers and primary children, base their scientific knowledge on what they see, hear, taste, smell, and touch. A developmentally appropriate science curriculum expands on this basic fact of child growth and development by stimulating observation, inquiry, interest, and verbalization.

As a teacher, you will also observe, question, predict, experiment, and verify many scientific occurrences along with the children. That is what science in early childhood is all about: setting the environmental stage for finding out about the world. Encourage young children to want to know, "What's in *my* environment? What effect do *I* have? What changes can *I* make?" Attitudes are formed early. We should nurture young children's natural curiosity and their need to know *why,* which will, in turn, encourage future scientific exploration and enthusiasm.

As you brainstorm ways to make exploration and discovery take place, you will come to realize that "A good science program is skillfully integrated into the total life of the classroom" (Copple & Bredekamp, 2009). Part of this encouragement can be to spontaneously and creatively change the physical environment (indoor room arrangement) when the children initiate and motivate the changes, and to take advantage of what is happening in the outdoor environment. Materials that can be manipulated and reconstructed should be included. Plenty of time should be allowed so that questions can be asked, assumptions can be explored, and ideas can be expanded. This can provide the spark for a lifelong love of science.

Continue to display your own enthusiasm for science and discovery in our world. Ziemer (1987) offers us a stimulating way to do this:

> When you look up to the highest branches of an oak tree on an early summer morning, you may not be thinking of scientific principles operating to get nutrients from the soil, up the trunk, and out to every newly forming leaf and embryo acorn. But you have an awareness of it, and guiding your small students to be aware also is part of teaching science. Ask wondering questions: "I wonder what makes the leaves so green." "I wonder how long it took this tree to grow so tall." . . . *We may not be teaching facts, but we are teaching curiosity.*

© Cengage Learning

An early childhood science environment is everywhere.

Basic Scientific Process Skills and Concepts for Young Children

Science is a combination of both *process skills* (*how* children learn) and *content* (*what* children learn) (Dodge, Colker, & Heroman, 2000). **Process skills** allow children to process new information through concrete experiences. These build on and overlap each other (Charlesworth & Lind, 2010). These process skills are also known as *inquiry* skills. An **inquiry** is a questioning process that can be developed in young children. The opposite of rote learning, it encourages their natural curiosity and exploration.

process skills The abilities to process new information through concrete experiences.

inquiry A questioning process that encourages curiosity and exploration. The opposite of rote learning.

In 1996, the National Research Council published the *National Science Education Standards*, which were designed to support the development of a scientifically literate society.

> From the earliest grades, students should experience science in a form that engages them in the active construction of ideas and explanations that enhance their opportunities to develop abilities of doing science. Teaching science as inquiry provides teachers with the opportunity to develop student abilities and to enrich student understanding of science. Students should do science in ways that are within their developmental capabilities. . . . *Full inquiry involves asking a simple question, completing an investigation, answering the question, and presenting the results to others.* (National Research Council, 1996)

The science curriculum content for young children responds to their need to learn about the world around them. As teachers, you know that children learn by doing. Therefore, the best way to learn science is to do science. "The science curriculum can be predominantly child centered and child initiated because knowledge is acquired best through firsthand investigation and experimentation" (Wortham, 2010).

The core of all science is observation. From the starting point of observing, children continue their investigation by comparing, classifying, measuring, communicating, inferring, and predicting. As a teacher, you should teach less and experience more by observing how eagerly the children use their senses to discover, to think about their experiences, and to talk about what they have seen and done. You will be learning right along with the children as you reinforce their curiosity and natural interests. Children learn science "within the context of both past experiences and present environment. . . . Teaching strategies involve a cooperative atmosphere where children and teachers are co-inquirers in the problem-solving process" (Desouza & Staley, 2002).

Essa (2011) believes, "Science concepts need to be concrete and observable. A concept that is abstract and not within the realm of children's experiences is not appropriate." Wortham (2010) suggests, "Children learn science concepts in a social milieu. While observing and working with other children in learning centers, cooperative groups, and paired activities, children exchange ideas, engage in science projects, and discuss their findings." Accordingly, based on the National Research Council standards, the fundamental science concepts and knowledge should be determined by what the children see and do each day and their developmental growth. The suggested categories are:

science as inquiry Offers frequent opportunities to question, investigate, clarify, predict, and communicate with others.

life science The study of living things, people, plants, and animals.

physical science The sciences (physics, chemistry, meteorology, and astronomy) that relate to nonliving materials.

chemistry The science dealing with the composition and transformations of substances.

● **Science as inquiry**—offers frequent opportunities for children to question, investigate, classify, predict, and communicate with others. "Teachers modeling the use of 'I wonder . . .', 'What if . . . ?', and 'How can we find out?' introduces children to the basis of science inquiry. When children pose a question, we can introduce the process of observing, researching, creating, and testing hypotheses, and collaborating to find answers" (Bosse, Jacobs, & Anderson, 2009).

● **Life science**—the study of living people, plants, and animals, including the functions and parts of living organisms (a butterfly's transformation cycle, for example). "Life science investigations lend themselves to simple observations, explorations, and classifications" (Charlesworth & Lind, 2010).

● **Physical science**—the study of nonliving materials. It includes the study of matter (solids, liquids, and gases) and energy (light, heat, sound, electricity, motion, and magnetism) and their laws, such as gravity (an infant dropping a spoon from a high chair), balance (a child building an unbalanced block tower that falls), and **chemistry**, the science dealing with the composition and transformations of substances (such as those that occur in cooking).

> Young children enjoy pushing on levers, making bulbs light, working with magnets, using a string-and-can telephone, and changing matter. This is the study of physical science—forces, motion, energy, and machines. . . . Keep in mind that children are growing up in a technological world. They interact daily with technology. It is likely that future lifestyles and opportunities may depend on skills related to the realm of physical science. (Charlesworth & Lind, 2010)

- **Earth and space science**—the study of earth materials, objects in the sky, and changes in the earth and sky. It includes **geology**, the study of the earth, such as rocks and shells (for example, comparing a container of dirt from the playground with a container of dirt from a child's backyard); **meteorology**—the science of weather and atmosphere; and **astronomy**—the study of the universe beyond the earth's atmosphere, such as the sun, moon, planets, and stars.
- **Science in personal and social perspectives**—a developing understanding of personal health, changes in the environments, and ways to conserve and recycle (National Research Council, 1996). This includes ecology.
- **Ecology**—the relationship between living things and their environment and each other (caring for classroom plants and animals helps young children understand this concept).
- **Science and technology** focuses on establishing connections between natural and man-made items. Simple tools such as a kitchen timer, an apple peeler, a potato masher, and a flashlight invite children's hands-on investigations of how technical objects operate. "Opportunities for children to use developmentally appropriate software and digital cameras can be catalysts for curiosity and wonder" (Bosse, Jacobs, & Anderson, 2009).

METHODS OF DISCOVERY

[T]he visions of both state and national standards serve to validate our belief that science is an ongoing process that requires children to be able to construct their own knowledge. . . . Learning is not a race for information; it is a walk of discovery. (Buchanan & Rios, 2004)

Give children many open-ended opportunities to investigate, self-discover, and problem solve. Use the "hands-on, minds-on" approach that Grieshaber and Diezmann (2000) suggest. Find out what children know at the beginning of any scientific investigation. Ask the children questions and listen carefully to their answers. Work with the children to identify particular areas in which they want to further their understanding about the topic. Then, in small groups, the children decide how the investigation will proceed. Continue by actually investigating, exploring, and discovering. Examples of observation and exploration activities follow.

- Sensory exploration outdoors can include touching the bark of a tree or the grass, seeing the birds building nests or leaves blowing, hearing the sounds carried by the wind or the honking of a car horn nearby, smelling freshly cut grass or the fragrance of flowers, and tasting the vegetables grown in the school garden they helped to plant.
- Investigating the properties of items can be done using a magnifying glass to examine shells, rocks, feathers, or objects discovered on a nature walk.
- Children can problem solve while predicting or guessing which items will float or sink in a container filled with water.
- Using their naturalist intelligence, children can discriminate among living things (plants and animals) as well as develop sensitivity to the features of the natural world (clouds, rock configurations). "Some people from an early age are extremely good at recognizing and classifying artifacts. For example, we all know kids who, at age three or four, are better at recognizing dinosaurs than most adults" (Gardner, 1997).

Give children many open-ended opportunities to question, to compare similarities and differences, and to use trial-and-error to try out their theories. Experimentation, verification, and discovery activities follow.

- With a teacher's supervision, children can experiment with cooking and discover how certain foods change through the cooking process as well as what happens when foods are mixed together.
- Tasting different foods gives children a hands-on experience and at the same time enables them to discover the similarities and differences of ingredients such as flour, salt, and sugar.

earth and space science The study of earth materials, objects in the sky, and changes in the earth and sky.

geology The study of the earth, such as rocks and shells.

meteorology The science of weather and atmosphere.

astronomy The study of the universe beyond the earth's atmosphere, such as sun, moon, planets, and stars.

science in personal and social perspectives A developing understanding of personal health, changes in environments, and ways to conserve and recycle.

ecology The study of living things in relation to their environment and to each other.

science and technology The focus on establishing connections between natural and man-made items.

WHY I TEACH YOUNG CHILDREN

One morning, Sammi came bounding across the classroom to me calling, "Come and look!" I followed her across the room, where she pointed to the window. She was bursting with excitement. Expecting to see no less than an elephant on the playground or a hot air balloon caught in the tree, I looked out, and saw nothing different. A quick glance at Sammi told me that it was still there, and I looked again. I saw nothing. She must have realized my inability to share her excitement, and lifted a tiny finger to the window, and said, "There." Then I saw *it*. On the outside of the windowpane was the tiniest spider I'd ever seen. Thank you, Sammi, for reminding me about the little things in life.

—Janet Galantay

● Classifying leaves by comparing their color, type, and vein structure offers another way to distinguish the similarities and differences of nature.
● Investigate a varied assortment of magnets with the children. Supply enough for each child to have one. What happens when the children select a magnet and attempt to pick up items from a tray filled with toothpicks, plastic straws, marbles, pencils, crayons, pieces of paper, cloth, shells, hairpins, small screws, keys, scissors, buttons, brads, paperclips, and pebbles? Which items did the magnet pick up? Which ones did it not pick up? Sort them into two piles. Why did it pick up some and not others? What conclusions can the children draw from this experiment? (Magnets attract objects made of metal.) Was the horseshoe magnet stronger or weaker than the magnetic wand or other magnets? Add new items and ask the children to predict if a magnet will pick them up. Keep this activity in the science center for the children to continue with their investigation. (Adapted from Allen, 2007).

Give children many open-ended possibilities to concretely demonstrate their discoveries. Reproducing and reworking what they observe and remember helps the children and the teacher learn together. Recording and communicating activities follow.

● Children's drawings, paintings, charts, tape recordings, and/or discussions can record their scientific experiences.
● Children can mark off days on a calendar as they watch the silkworms go through their life cycles or predict how long it will take acorns that they planted to grow.
● The children can then reflect on what they might do next.
● Church (2006) clarifies why it is so important for children to experiment. "This is when children test out their predictions and try out their ideas. The key to this step is to provide plenty of different materials and TIME to explore. Provide materials for free exploration in your science area so children can visit and revisit them on their own—which is how children conduct their own version of an 'independent study.' For example, How can we test if light will shine through a leaf? How many different leaves can we test? What places can we put plants to see if they will grow?"

Creating a Scientific Environment

Fraser and Gestwicki (2002) remind us that we should prepare an environment that allows the child to be actively engaged in the process of learning. "Given this belief in the active exploration of young children, the space must encourage investigations and be open to change to respond to the demands of active learners."

Children notice everything in their world—icicles on the roof, the zigzag path of a ladybug, the dancing dust caught in the sunlight. As early childhood educators, we want to provide experiences that allow children to closely examine what interests them, although this often may mean rearranging instructional plans to take advantage of teachable moments. (Kupetz & Twiest, 2000)

The following areas of inquiry should get you and the children started.

INVESTIGATE WATER

Children learn by doing. Therefore, the best way to learn science is to do science.

● Indoors or outdoors, place water in the water table or a large plastic tub. Let the children select which color they want the water to be. Add several drops of food coloring to the water. Also be sure to have plastic pouring and measuring containers along with funnels and spray bottles.

● Later add boats, corks, sponges, rocks, pieces of wood, large marbles, keys, feathers, and pine cones. What sinks? What floats? Guide the children in making a chart of what items sink and what items float. Ask the children why they think some things stay above water and others settle to the bottom? For example, the air holes in a sponge make it float. When the children squeeze the sponge under the water they can see bubbles of air come out of the sponge. What happens when they let go of the squeezed sponge? What other items can the children add?

● What happens to the items that sink or float in water when you add sugar, salt, oil, or sand to the water?

● Place plain water and one or two eggbeaters in the water table or tub. What happens when the children "beat the water"? Have them add liquid dish detergent, and then beat the water. Now what happens? (The water can then be used to wash the doll dishes from the dramatic play area.)

● Fill a sink full of water and notice how, when you pull the plug, the water always swirls down the drain in the same *clockwise spiral*. (This is because of the rotation of the earth. South of the equator, it goes in the opposite direction.) This can be fascinating to young children. Follow up this activity by looking at a globe and demonstrating how the world turns.

● Introduce the children to absorption and evaporation by having them dampen cloth rags and paper towels with water; then hang them in the sun to dry. What happens to the water? Does the cloth or the paper dry faster? Why?

● Making and blowing bubbles are delightful additions to water investigation. They float on air, glimmer with color, change shape, and pop! Why do bubbles pop? To make bubbles, mix one part liquid dish detergent into five parts water in a shallow tub or pan. Plastic circles on a handle or circles made with pipe cleaners work fine for making bubbles. Let the children experiment with blowing bubbles or moving the bubble ring in any manner they can think of to make bubbles.

● See how water magnifies pebbles in a glass jar.

● Taste water, then add salt or sugar or both. Discuss what this tastes like. What else will the children want to add?

● Examine how water takes the shape of the container it is in.

● Boil water in a pan on a hot plate (with close teacher supervision). Discuss the steam that forms.

● Guide children on how to change a liquid into a solid, and then reverse the process. First, place the water in a small, sealable plastic bag, and then freeze it. Next, let the children watch the ice melt. Encourage them to predict how long they think it will take the water to freeze and then how long to melt. Actively discuss the changes in the water.

● Chapter 9 offers additional activities.

Look! Even snails have shadows!

© Cengage Learning

DISCOVER RAINBOWS

● Set the scene for activities relating to rainbows by introducing a prism (a triangular piece of glass that breaks up a ray of light into a colored spectrum). This can be purchased inexpensively. Glass beads can be used as well. (Parents may even have glass costume jewelry that can be used.) Whatever you choose, tape this "rainbow-making" glass onto a window of the classroom that faces the outdoors to catch the sunlight. Let the children locate the rainbow by themselves. This rainbow will mean more to them if they make the discovery. How many colors do they see? Have they seen a rainbow before? When? Do they remember how many colors it had? Encourage the children to draw the rainbow. What colors do they choose?

● Create other rainbows with the children by taking a shallow bowl of water out into bright sunshine. Place a drop or two of oil on the surface of the water. How many colors do the children see? Are they the same colors as the prism rainbow? If you stir the water with a stick, do the colors change?

● On a sunny day, you can help children find a rainbow by spraying water across the sun's rays with a garden hose or a spray bottle. The rays of the sun contain all the colors mixed together, but the water acts as a prism and separates the colors. Are they the same colors as the other rainbows the children discovered?

EXPLORE SHADOWS

● What is a shadow? It is fun to find out what the children will answer. Can they offer suggestions about how to produce a shadow? Try out their predictions. Are shadows created? If they have difficulty, you might guide them by suggesting that one child holds her hand in front of a bright light. (Shade is a dark place that light cannot reach. A shadow is the shape cast by whatever is in front of the light.) The shadow of an object gets bigger when you move the object closer to the light.

● Let the children experiment with different objects in the room to find out which ones cast shadows and which ones do not. They can make a chart of the items.

● Refer to Chapter 11 and have the children make shadow puppets and share them with each other.

● Extend "shadow play" into dramatic play or music and movement activities.

● The children can outline their shadows in chalk outside on the sidewalk. They can measure how long or how short their shadows are. Try this at different times during the day. Do the shadows change?

● Take the children on a nature walk and look for shadows that the plants, trees, buildings, or cars make. They can come back and create shadow drawings or write a story of what they discovered during their explorations.

● Here are some suggestions of books to read to the children and then place in the book center:

Asch, F. (2000). *Moonbear's shadow*. (Revised ed.). New York: Aladdin.

Berge, C. (2007). *Whose shadow is this?* New York: Picture Window Books.

Dodd, A.W. (1994). *Footprints and shadows*. New York: Scott Foresman.

Hoban, T. (1990). *Shadows and reflections*. New York: Greenwillow.

FOCUS ON NATURE

For teachers it is exciting to share the natural world with young children. The children are eager for active firsthand experiences.

> If teachers hope children will use their senses to explore the natural world, they need to encourage real contact with the world. From the feel of oozing mud or jagged tree bark to the smell of freshly cut hay or decaying leaves; from the visual experience of a hovering hummingbird to the repetitive sound of a calling cricket; from the taste of a crisp, sweet apple to the bitter bite of a sour grape—nothing offers the variety in sights, sounds, tastes, textures, and smells as well as nature. (Kupetz & Twiest, 2000)

AIR. Can the children taste or see air? Can they feel it? How? On the playground, guide the children to experience how the wind (moving air) can come from different directions. Children can experiment with wind streamers, windsocks, wind chimes, and bubbles. You might read the following book as an introduction or extension to other activities relating to air:

> Branley, F. (2006). *Air is all around you.* Illustrated by H. Keller (A Let's-Read-and-Find-Out Science series.). New York: Collins.

NATURE WALK. There are opportunities for many discoveries to take place during a walk around the children's natural environment. Before you go for a walk, encourage the children to make binoculars. Tape together two toilet paper rolls or a paper towel roll cut in two. Place holes in one end of the rolls and attach a piece of yarn or string to make a neck strap. Looking for bird nests and watching butterflies or birds fly are only samples of the many things the children can do with their binoculars (Figure 6–1).

Each child can also make an individual nature walk "collection bag" (see Figure 6–2). Construct it with folded construction paper or tagboard and lace it with yarn that is long enough to serve as a shoulder strap (Ziemer, 1987). Construct a classroom book with pages made out of sturdy cardboard and fastened together with rings. The children can glue or tape items that they find on the nature walk onto the pages. Then place it in the book center for the children to enjoy.

Humphryes (2000) adds a special word for teachers. "Children have a tendency to want to take home everything they find. Explain to them that the balance of nature is very delicate and that everything in nature has a purpose (for example, a seed pod holds the seeds for next year's plants, a piece of bark may be home to many insects). ... In general, *find, examine,* and *return.*" Fresh leaves can be pressed easily by placing them between sheets of newspaper, which are then sandwiched between two pieces of cardboard and secured tightly with rubber bands. After a week, the leaves can be removed and glued into a scrapbook (see Figure 6–2) or displayed in other ways in the classroom.

GROW GRASS. Go on a "science search" in which children look for different kinds of grass growing around their environment. In the classroom provide grass seeds for the children to plant. The quickest and easiest way to germinate the seeds is to place a damp sponge in a pie pan of water and sprinkle the seeds on the sponge. These seeds usually grow almost anywhere as long as they are watered regularly and have sunlight. (It is fun to cut the sponges into different shapes and watch the grass grow into a circle, triangle, or heart shape.) This is another way for children to observe nature firsthand. An alternative way to grow grass is to fill a plastic cup (which the children can decorate to look like a face) with dirt or potting soil. Sprinkle the grass seeds on the dirt, then water. The children really enjoy watching the "hair" grow.

© Cengage Learning

Children are eager to investigate what nature has to offer.

FIGURE 6–1
This illustrates childmade binoculars.

FIGURE 6–2
These are examples of a collection bag and nature book.

Ecology in the Early Education Environment

Plants in an early childhood environment give each child an opportunity to learn something about the growth and needs of plants.

Early involvement with the environment will help foster a sense of appreciation and caring in a generation of children who will then make a difference in how our future world is treated. Howard Gardner's theory of multiple intelligences includes his eighth intelligence, *naturalistic intelligence,* which emphasizes nature. Gardener (cited in Louv, 2008) explains, "The core of the naturalist intelligence is the human ability to recognize plants, animals, and other parts of the natural environment, like clouds or rocks."

To help our children extend this eighth intelligence and guide them to explore environmental education, we, as teachers, need to help them notice things in the environment that others might miss; heighten awareness of and concern for the environment and endangered species; recognize characteristics, names, and categories of objects and species found in the natural world; as well as create and keep collections, scrapbooks, photos, specimens, logs, or journals about natural objects (adapted from Wilson in Louv, 2008).

As defined earlier in this chapter, ecology is the study of living things in relation to their environment and to one another. The environment is everything that surrounds us. We human beings change the environment with our actions and reactions. In addition, everything in nature is constantly changing, and change in one area can cause changes in another.

There are several approaches you can take in your early childhood curriculum planning that will include the changing environment and what we can do to protect it. One suggestion is to select the theme "Things in Nature That Are Always Changing." Using the thematic method, you can introduce the children to changing seasons, specific weather changes, night changing into day, and the changes that take place with the individual child.

> We will serve our children well when we turn their attention to the stones, the grasses and flowers, the trees and animals by finding meaningful and creative ways to allow nature to enter our classrooms and play areas, and by bringing our children out into nature as much as possible. A loving relationship with nature will not only promote health for our planet but health for our children as well. (Petrash, 1992)

Some activities that focus on ecology are offered next.

PLANT AND GARDEN AT DIFFERENT TIMES OF THE YEAR.   In some places it is warm all year round, and plants there grow well at any time. In places where the ground freezes in winter, you will have to wait for warmer weather to garden outdoors, but indoor planting can work well. You can start plants in a collection of cans, grow a tree in a tub, or plant seeds in cracks in the concrete. Hachey & Butler (2009) suggest, "Hang plants from the ceiling, place them on shelves and window ledges; use them to fill empty spaces on tables and furniture. . . . Just about anything can be used to hold plants, but be sure to use containers (with holes for drainage) that are big enough to hold plenty of soil and water." Children can plant an indoor garden (flowers and/or vegetables) in the sand and water table or in a window box. If there is a protected space outdoors, they can plant a garden there. This activity is another way to encourage children to take responsibility for living things. As a result, they develop a sense of pride by nurturing a seed into a plant. Discover with the children which plants grow well in your area and when are the best times to plant and harvest them.

Gardening and nature-based play encourages children's desire to question and seek answers. In addition, "Teachers learn to trust children with gardening jobs, understanding and accepting that they can't do the job the same way or as long as adults can" (Nimmo & Hallett, 2008).

MAKE A COMPOST PILE. The children can place leaves, plant cuttings, and food scraps in a compost bin or pile, along with worms to help "mix-up" the compost. Then they can use the compost when they plant a garden in the spring. This can be a cooperative experience with one or two other classes. Children enjoy participating with other children in the center or school.

CATCH RAIN WATER IN A CONTAINER AND RECYCLE IT TO WATER THE PLANTS. Filter rain water through a fine sieve, such as a tea strainer. This will provide an opportunity for the children to see what pollutants rainwater collects, in addition to providing clean rain water to water the indoor plants and vegetables.

ADOPT-A-TREE OR PLANT-A-TREE. The children can select a tree on the playground or in a nearby park to "adopt" as their tree to take care of and to observe throughout the year. Sometimes children prefer to plant a tree of their own on the playground or in a tub. Whatever choice is made can lead to an environmental discussion when you ask the question, "What do you think the tree takes from the environment, and what does it give to the environment?"

It is helpful to invite a parent who knows a lot about trees or a professional gardener to visit the class to answer the children's questions and advise them in their selections. In addition, a field trip to a garden shop can motivate the children. Giving young children the responsibility of taking care of a tree can be a significant factor in encouraging them to take care of the environment.

After they select the tree and identify what kind it is, they can make drawings of it, take photos of their tree in different seasons, and compare it to other trees. They will also find it interesting to examine the bark, leaves, and bugs on the tree with a magnifying glass and observe and identify which birds like their tree. Children will enjoy hanging a bird house or a bird feeder in their tree and watching the activity it attracts.

RECYCLE AND CONSERVE MATERIALS AND NATURAL RESOURCES. The children can recycle newspapers, other types of paper, aluminum, glass, some plastics, and clothing. Find out about the recycling projects in your community and get the children and their families involved.

Try fixing broken items in the classroom instead of buying new things or throwing old things away. Encourage the children to stop wasting water. Have them turn off the water while brushing their teeth or washing their hands, instead of letting it run.

USE GROCERY SACKS AND NEWSPAPERS TO MAKE ART. Provide one or both, along with paints, for the children to paint on. To make newspaper logs for the block center, take a section of newspaper and roll into a tight roll. Use tape to hold the "logs." These can then be used to build towers, fences, and so forth.

STRESS THE IMPORTANCE OF NOT LITTERING. Trash should be placed in a trash container. Because littering can be dangerous and unhealthy, the children should be shown how to avoid littering and to participate in cleaning up instead.

EARTH DAY IS APRIL 22. Make party hats out of newspaper and grocery bags. Bake an Earth Day cake decorated to look like the planet earth. Cut out eco-cookies in natural shapes, such as birds, leaves, and trees. Celebrate with an environmental musical band. Provide recycled materials for the children to make instruments, and have a parade!

ASK THE CHILDREN OPEN-ENDED QUESTIONS ABOUT THE ENVIRONMENT. The following questions will help children think about why it is important to take care of our environment:

- What would happen if everyone threw trash on the ground?
- What do you think would happen if we poured polluted water into clean water?

FIGURE 6-3
Books on outdoor experiences help keep children's curiosity alive while extending their investigation of nature.

NATURE BOOKS FOR YOUNG CHILDREN

- Aguilar, D. A. (2008). *11 planets: A new view of the solar system*. New York: National Geographic.
- Brown, P. (2009). *The curious garden*. New York: Little, Brown.
- Brunelle, L. (2007). *Camp out: The ultimate kids' guide*. New York: Workman.
- Chin, J. (2009). *Redwoods*. New York: Flash Point.
- Hague, M. (2007). *Animal friends: A collection of poems for children*. New York: Henry Holt.
- Helman, A. (2008). *Hide and seek: Nature's best vanishing acts*. Photographed by G. Jecan. New York: Walker.
- Johnson, J. (2008). *Animal tracks and signs*. New York: National Geographic.
- Leslie, C. W., & Roth, C.E. (2003). *Keeping a nature journal: Discover a whole new way of seeing the world around you*. New York: Storey.
- Morgan, B. (2005). *Rock and fossil hunter*. New York: DK Publishing.
- Serafini, F. (2008). *Looking closely through the forest*. New York: Kids Can.
- Tait, N. *Insects and spiders*. (2008). New York: Simon & Schuster Books for Young Readers.
- Ward, J. (2008). *I love dirt!* New York: Trumpeter.

- Why do we recycle?
- What would happen if we cut down trees instead of planting them?
- Why do you think plants are important to us?
- What are ways we can help the environment at home?

> Virtually all outdoors is science. This is where children become part of the natural world.... *School yards, sidewalks, vacant lots, or any strip of ground can be an area for outdoor learning.* (Charlesworth & Lind, 2010)

See Figure 6–3 for some suggestions of books on nature to read to the children, and then place these in a basket in the science center as well as in the book center.

Suggested Science Materials and Equipment

Many materials in a science center can be donated and many can be recycled. Some equipment can be purchased inexpensively. Figure 6–4 lists suggested materials and equipment that are appropriate for early education science investigations.

It is important to examine how materials and equipment are constructed. What they are made of and how they are put together will determine their durability when used by very young children. Only some of the items will be appropriate for infants and toddlers, such as color paddles and measuring spoons and cups. You will need to be very cautious in what you select, and close supervision is required when these objects are in use.

Extended Science Activities

The following activities extend over a period of time. Participating in these will demonstrate to the children that many scientific investigations take time to evolve and that some are unpredictable. These experiments can also offer a concrete way to introduce the children to edible plant parts.

Aluminum foil pans	Pinecones	**FIGURE 6–4**
Aquarium with contents and supplies	Pipe cleaners	A list of science materials
Ant farm	Plants	and equipment.
Binoculars	Plastic bottles, jars, and trays	
Batteries, wires, bulbs	Prisms	
Birdhouse and bird feeders	Pulleys and levers	
Collection boxes and collecting net	Rain gauge	
Color paddles	Rock and seashell collections	
Compass	Rulers, tape measure, and yard stick	
Corks, plugs, and stoppers	Scales	
Digital camera	Seeds and seed catalogs	
Disposable cameras	Sieves, sifters, and funnels	
Dried plants, such as flowers	Shallow pans	
and grasses	Smelling jars and sound jars	
Eggbeaters and wire whip	Soil samples, such as clay, sand, and	
Eyedroppers	loam	
Feathers	Stethoscope	
Flashlights	Sundial	
Food coloring	Tape recorder and cassettes	
Fossils	Telescope	
Garden hose	Terrarium	
Keys and locks	Thermometers, both indoor and	
Kitchen timer	outdoor type	
Magnets, such as bar and horseshoe	Tongs and tweezers	
types	Watering cans	
Magnifying glasses and tripod magnifier	Waxed paper and foil	
stand, microscope, and slides	X-rays (parents who are doctors	
Observation sheets and science	or veterinarians often can give	
journals	teachers old ones)	

● Roots—Carrots, potatoes, turnips, radishes, and beets are the roots of plants.
● Stems—Celery and asparagus are examples of the stems of plants that connect the roots with the leaves.
● Leaves—Lettuce, spinach, cabbage, and parsley are the leaves of plants.
● Flowers—Broccoli and cauliflower are examples of the flowers of plants.
● Vegetables/fruits—Tomatoes and squash are examples of the "fruit" of plants.

Try the following activities:

CARROT TOP GARDEN.   After cutting the tops off of three or four carrots, the children can place them in a shallow pan or dish. The carrot tops should be sitting in 1/4 inch of water and be watered daily, a task that could be performed by the "plant helper" of the day. (A child can use a ruler to determine exactly how much ¼-inch is.)

The children can predict how many days it will take the carrot tops to sprout new green foliage. Guide them to make a chart or graph that shows them how correct their predictions were. If some of the tops do not sprout, ask the children *why* they think they did not.

ROOTING A SWEET POTATO.   This is another experiment children enjoy doing. Push toothpicks halfway into a sweet potato. Then place the potato in a glass or jar of water with the toothpicks resting on the top rim. Be sure the end of the potato is immersed in water. The plant helper can be responsible to see that the bottom of the potato is *always*

CARROT TOP GARDEN

SWEET POTATO
"EXPERIMENT"

● ● ● ● ● ● ● ● ● ● ●

FIGURE 6–5
This illustrates the rooting of a carrot garden and a sweet potato.

immersed in water. Place the potato where it will receive enough light. (Put another sweet potato in a dark spot of the room so the children can see what happens to the potato's growth without adequate light.) See Figure 6–5 for illustrations of a carrot top garden and a rooting sweet potato.

The children can create a group art activity by drawing the sweet potato and adding to it over the time it takes for roots to grow out of the sides and bottom of the potato and the leaves to grow out of the top. A "before and after" drawing is interesting, too.

THIRSTY CELERY.   This science experiment demonstrates how plants get their water. Fill two tall, clear plastic glasses with water. Let the children put a few drops of red food coloring in one glass and a few drops of blue food coloring in the other. Put a piece of celery into each of the glasses, being careful to make a fresh cut at the base of the celery stalks before you place them in the water. Ask the children to watch the celery and record what happens. They can do this with a drawing or verbally with a tape recorder. Over the next few days, the colored water should travel up the stalk and into the leaves. Ask the children what happened to the celery. Why do they think this happened?

MINI GREENHOUSE.   This indoor gardening activity can expand children's understanding of how things grow. The needed materials are: one egg carton per student, six cotton balls per student, and seeds—birdseed, radish seeds, or grass seeds. Guide the children to put the cotton balls in the carton. Place three seeds on top of each cotton ball. Saturate the cotton with water and close the lid. Set in a warm spot. Check daily and use an eyedropper to wet the cotton. When green leaves appear, keep the lid of the egg carton open. What has happened? What will happen next? What should be done to keep the plants alive? Provide blank books for children to use as observation logs, and encourage them to record plant growth through drawing. They can use the classroom camera to take photos to show what is happening day by day or week by week.

SEEDS.   Several weeks before you plan to introduce this activity, gather all kinds of seeds. Encourage the children to place the seeds in a line from the smallest to the largest. Discuss the texture of the seeds. Try to sprout some seeds in damp paper towels and some in dry ones to find out whether seeds need moisture to sprout. Ask children to guess what would grow from the seeds if they were planted? Make a rebus chart for planting seeds. (An example of a rebus chart is in Chapter 3.) Give each child a small planting pot. Then ask each child to fill it with the potting soil you have provided, and water it. Each child should put several seeds into her planting pot. Place a number on each pot for identification. During the next few weeks, the children will take care of the plants, as well as measure the growth of each one and make a graph showing the progress. During this time, you and the children can try to figure out what kind of plants you have planted. Look up the leaf structure on the computer or in a gardening book. To expand this project, have the children place their planted seeds in various lighting conditions to observe the differences between plants grown in sunlight and those left in the dark. Water some of the plants and leave some dry. Encourage children to examine the contrast between the plants grown under different conditions and discover for themselves that plants do need water and sunlight. This activity can be the starting point for a project approach (an in-depth investigation) of seeds by several children or an individual child.

Here is another activity that can extend the focus on seeds. Set up a tray with different fruits and vegetables, such as apples, cucumbers,

© Cengage Learning

Children develop responsibility when they take care of their plants.

oranges, plums, and green peppers. Allow the students to manipulate the items on the tray. Cut open one fruit and one vegetable. Ask the children what is inside these that is the same? (Seeds) Cut open the rest of the fruits and vegetables. Place each fruit and each vegetable seed on a separate paper plate labeled with a picture of each. Give the children a small taste of each fruit and each vegetable. Have they tasted any of them before? In what ways are seeds of each different? Both you and the children will continue asking and answering questions. Days later, the children may think of something else they want to know. You are actually planting "seeds" of interest and inquiry with all of these explorations.

ORANGE JUICE.   To reinforce the science of nutrition, have the children make their own orange juice. This helps the youngest ones connect the actual fruit with the juice. Many children think that orange juice always comes in a carton or bottle at the grocery store. Ask each child to place one-half of an orange in a resealable bag. Zip the seal closed. Have the children squeeze the orange. (You may have to help.) This will produce juice. Then, they can open the bag and take out the half, being careful not to spill the juice. Close the bag, leaving only enough of an opening for the child to insert a straw into the bag. Then, she can drink and enjoy the juice! (Chapter 9, "Sensory Centers," offers more activities that relate to nutrition and cooking.)

© Cengage Learning

Help the children develop respect for animals by learning how to take care of classroom animals.

Animals in the Early Education Classroom

The world of animals inspires wonder and curiosity in young children. You can guide the children into drawing pictures of their experiences with animals, moths, butterflies, and ants. Extend this by making puppets of the animals they draw.

For language development, the children can bring in their favorite stuffed animals and talk about them during group time. Play music and have a parade of stuffed animals. Read books aloud, and place those that relate to animals, moths, butterflies, and ants in the book center.

● THE ANIMALS IN OUR WORLD

As an animal lover and a wildlife rehabilitator, I have come to the conclusion that there are two categories of animals—not good or bad, but rather, touchable and untouchable. Touchable are those we know and with whom we have a relationship. I have spent many wonderful hours with my very special domesticated animals. We have learned to love and trust each other. I have the responsibility to see that all their needs are met.

Untouchable animals are those we do not know, who will probably be frightened of us and will do whatever they need to do to protect themselves. These animals, which are not domesticated, are born to be free. It is not fair to put them in a cage. They deserve to live as nature intended them to live. Because they are not used to people, they will be frightened and potentially very dangerous. They can also have diseases that *you, the children,* or your pets can catch, such as distemper or rabies. Enjoy watching and listening to them, but LEAVE THEM ALONE!

Occasionally, one comes upon an animal that looks as though it needs help; either it is injured or in some

(continued)

● THE ANIMALS IN OUR WORLD (CONTINUED)

way unable to care for itself. It is important to know when and when not to rescue it. As an added precaution, even domesticated animals that we do not know (such as dogs in the neighborhood) should be classified as untouchable also.

What Not to Do

- *Do not* "rescue" an animal that does not need help. Most "orphaned" animals are not orphaned at all. The parent is usually hiding nearby, afraid to attend to its offspring when people are present. If you can see a nest from which a baby has fallen, it is best to place the baby back in the nest. Despite myths to the contrary, the scent of human hands will not disturb the parents, and they will usually care for their returned offspring.
- *Do not* be tempted to raise an orphaned animal yourself. Federal and state laws prohibit the possession of most nondomesticated animals—and with good reason. These creatures need special care, far different from domestic animals. Wildlife rehabilitators are trained to provide that care.

What to Do

- *Do* rescue an animal if the parent is known to be dead and the baby is too young to survive on its own, or if the animal is injured or in obvious danger. Emergency care can be given if you have determined that the animal really needs care. Put on a pair of gloves before you touch it. For your safety and the animal's well-being, handle it as little as possible. Place it in a covered box with air holes for ventilation. The box should be just a little larger than the animal. Put the box in a dark, quiet room away from the children (and pets), and free from drafts.
- *Do* resist the urge to feed an animal or give it liquids. The wrong food or wrong feeding method can do more harm than good. These animals have special diets and, as babies, must be fed often. For example, some baby birds must be fed every 20 or 30 minutes during the day and some baby mammals must be fed during the night.
- *Do* contact a wildlife rehabilitator immediately. Wildlife babies need to learn from their parents what kind of animal they are and how to take care of themselves (just like human babies). You can find a rehabilitator through your state Parks and Wildlife Department or other private organizations in your community. Rehabilitators have been trained to care for wildlife orphans during the early stages of life and to reintroduce them to their natural environment.

We, as teachers of the future citizens of the world, have opportunities every day to instill in our children a love and respect for themselves and for all the people, animals, and plants with whom we share our world.

There are many interesting animal-related learning exhibits you can have in your classroom. While visiting classrooms, I have seen some wonderful science centers with plants and animals, but I have also been very saddened by sights of animals being poorly fed or improperly housed. Before you get any animal, be sure you understand and are prepared to meet its needs. Get answers to the following questions:

- What kind of enclosure should it have?
- What kind of food does it require?
- What temperature must it have?
- Is there any kind of special light it needs?
- Should it be kept with another animal?
- Is it safe for children to handle it?
- Does it need any special veterinary care?
- Does it meet your state licensing requirements? (Some states require documentation that shows that animals requiring vaccinations have been vaccinated according to state and local requirements. Some also require that parents must be advised when animals are present in the classroom or school.)

In addition to animals that are commonly found in centers that can be displayed safely and effectively (small rodents, such as gerbils and hamsters, frogs, fish, birds, and turtles), you might try some of the following:

- *Earthworms*—You'll need a large plastic or glass jar, sand or loose moist soil, cloth cover, damp leaves or grass, and a dozen or so earthworms. (You can look for earthworms after a spring rain or buy them from a local bait shop.)

Place a layer of pebbles in the jar; then fill it with sand or loose moist soil. Put in some earthworms. Keep the soil moist but not wet. The children can feed the worms damp leaves and grass clippings. Be sure to cover the container with a dark cloth to shield the worms from light, because they are used to being in the dark ground.

The children can observe how the worms burrow tunnels in the soil. They can also carefully place a worm on a table to watch its movements (with teacher supervision). Note the difference between its back and underside. Using a magnifying glass, count the rings on its body. Notice the worm's reaction to various stimuli: light, sound, types of food, and soil.

After viewing the worms for a while, the children can return them to their garden or playground. Earthworms are very important for healthy soil. They loosen it so that air and water can get to plant roots. They also fertilize the soil.

● THE ANIMALS IN OUR WORLD (CONTINUED)

● *Silkworms*—You will need a terrarium, mulberry leaves, and silkworm eggs or larvae. Many early childhood centers and schools store the eggs laid in one season in a small bottle in a refrigerator until the next season. When the mulberry leaves are on the trees, these eggs are placed in a terrarium with the leaves. (Network with other colleagues to get a supply of silkworm eggs or order a supply from Insect Lore Products, http://www.insectlore.com.)

The silkworm (like all other moths and butterflies) undergoes a complete metamorphosis. *There are four stages of development: egg, larva, pupa, and adult moth.* One female silkworm moth can lay from 300 to 400 eggs. In about 10 days, cream to light-green colored caterpillars hatch from the eggs and eat voraciously on mulberry leaves for about 30 days. Be sure you have access to mulberry leaves that have not been sprayed with insecticide. (Often, parents can help supply the mulberry leaves.)

Each silkworm will then construct a cocoon from a single fiber of silk, which could be up to a quarter mile long! It takes about three days to complete the cocoon. Inside the cocoon, the silkworm metamorphoses into a cream-colored moth, which will not eat, rarely flies, and lives only a few days. One ounce of silkworm eggs produces 30,000 larvae, which can spin approximately 100 pounds of silk! (As you can see, you need only a few eggs to get started.) Introducing children to silkworms offers a very special way to help them understand what a life cycle is.

● *Butterflies*—The following company will ship butterflies directly to your center or school. Butterfly Garden is available from Insect Lore Products (http://www.insectlore.com). Children can watch the metamorphosis of larva into chrysalides into butterflies and then have the fun of releasing the butterflies back into nature.

● *Ants*—Commercially sold ant farms are widely available in stores selling educational materials. It is fascinating to watch these little creatures dig tunnels, drag food, and interrelate with each other.

—By Jo Eklof (2003)

Jo is an educator, wildlife rehabilitator, songwriter, and performer. Many of her songs are shared with you throughout this book.

Sharing Science: Encouraging Family Support

Many of the activities in this chapter can be shared with parents so that science can become a family affair. Help families understand that children are *natural* scientists discovering their world. Send information and suggestions home. Begin with general ideas as to what parents can do with their children, and then show them specific activities that are ongoing in the classroom. For example, families also can grow a carrot-top garden or root a sweet potato at home. The following are some other specific suggestions to give families:

● Look at science experiences all around you. Observe plants, insects, animals, rocks, and sunsets with your child.
● Go for a walk in the park or in the woods and talk about the natural things you and your child see.
● Feel a tree. Talk about the parts of the tree.
● Collect all kinds of things—from shells to sticks to rocks. Talk about where they came from.
● Help your child use her senses—sight, smell, touch, hearing, and taste—to explore the world around her. Look at leaves, smell them, and run your fingers across their tops and undersides. Compare one kind of leaf with another, and look for changes over time.

© Cengage Learning

Opportunities occur every day for children to discover the beauty of butterflies.

WHY I TEACH YOUNG CHILDREN

While teaching a unit about our bodies to a group of three-year-olds, I decided to show them a small doll house. We looked at all of the different rooms. I told them that our hearts had different rooms, also called chambers. The next day, a mom came in and told me that her daughter had come home and told her, "I learned that I have a four bedroom heart!"

—BONNIE RUBINSTEIN

● As your child begins to talk about plants in her environment, she can observe their growth by taking care of plants at school and at home. Together, learn the names of plants, flowers, shrubs, fruits, vegetables, and trees.

● Explain what items you recycle. Share some of these with us at school: plastic containers, egg cartons, paper towel and bathroom tissue rolls, samples and end-cuts from wallpaper, fabric, floor tile, framing materials, and newspapers.

Tips for Teachers

Children are able to attune themselves to all kinds of learning if they have appropriate developmental experiences. (Louv, 2008)

● Provide hands-on experiences that make science a part of every child's day.

● Preserve and value a child's natural curiosity.

● Avoid "telling" children about a scientific activity that they themselves cannot observe or experiment with. Relying on teacher information *only* is not useful or appropriate for children, as we have discussed throughout this chapter.

● If you have difficulty with setting up a science environment, identify an individual interest or area of the real world you would like to know more about. Set up your early education classroom so that you can discover and learn things *along with the children*. Start with one of the science inquiries suggested in this chapter.

● Allow the children to control the time spent on experimenting with appropriate materials. Children need time to try out ideas, to discover, to make mistakes and learn from them, and to learn from one another.

● Some adaptations of materials may be necessary to help children with special needs, such as providing additional tactile cues for visually impaired children and helping those with hearing impairments experience sound by feeling the vibrations of tuning forks, guitar strings, or rubber bands stretched across a cigar box (Brewer, 2004).

● Ask open-ended questions, and give children plenty of time to answer questions. This helps children to observe carefully and encourages them to put their ideas into words. (What does a feather look like? How does the sky look when it is going to rain?)

● Allow for across-the-curriculum integration of activities.

Developmentally Appropriate and Multicultural/ Anti-Bias Activities

To introduce an awareness of the different environments in various parts of the world, read books to the children, display objects and artifacts from different cultures, show photographs, and explore websites of faraway places like the rainforests in Central and

South America, the deserts in the Middle East and Africa, and the rivers around the world. Keep a globe or a map of the world available for the children to find the areas discussed. Encourage them to draw or write about *their* world as *they* see it. Provide them with digital or disposable cameras to take photographs that illustrate what they see. This activity can also stimulate further investigations of the children's homes, backyards, neighborhoods, and school environments. Photographs are useful devices for developing diversity recognition and science teaching and learning. Children begin to see patterns and make connections between their own personal explorations and discoveries and what is outside in the world at large (Hoisington, 2002).

Brewer (2004) offers us another reminder: "Teachers should make sure they know enough about the cultures of children in their classrooms that they do not engage the students in activities that will be offensive. For example, some cultures would be disturbed by studies of plants or animals that have symbolic meaning in their particular cultures. The key is to understand the various communities of the children well enough that you can avoid offending them."

Visit agencies and organizations in your community that offer resources and information relating to various cultures. As you gather materials and facts, ask the parents of children in your class for specific examples of what would be inappropriate to their culture. Continue to be aware of, and sensitive to, the many elements in each child's world.

Poetry, flannelboard stories, dramatic play, music, and movement offer additional opportunities for young children to become more aware of the world around them and their place in it. The poem and songs in this chapter are creative ways for the children to share their appreciation of the world and each other. (Flannelboard characters for the poem "Seeds" can be found online at this textbook's premium website.)

Observation, Assessment, and Evaluation

> As children work on projects, you will find yourself interacting with them on an informal basis. Listen carefully to children's concepts, and watch them manipulate materials. You cannot help but assess how things are going. (Charlesworth & Lind, 2010)

As explained in Chapter 5, the anecdotal record process of assessment (observations written down in an organized way) is one of the developmentally appropriate ways teachers can evaluate a child's learning. Review the process of keeping anecdotal records described in Chapter 5. Use the Anecdotal Record/Observation Form, Figure 6–6, to record your observations. Make recording observations a habit. This is an additional tool for assessing children's learning and your teaching strategies (Charlesworth & Lind, 2010).

Chalufour and Worth (2004) offer the following key elements to assessment that are helpful to documenting children's inquiry skills and growing understanding of science concepts.

- Collecting data. Spend at least ten minutes three times a week collecting different kinds of data that capture children's level of engagement and their science understandings, including casual conversations, written observations, photographs, videotapes, audiotapes, and samples of their other work.
- Analyzing data regularly. Time spent reflecting on your collection of documents will help you understand the growing skills and understandings of each child in your class. The more kinds of documents you have, the fuller the picture you will have of each individual.
- Drawing conclusions and making decisions. Analysis of the documents you have collected will help you make the important connections between your teaching and the children's learning. Use your analysis of children's growth to consider what your next steps should be with individual children and the group.

Anecdotal Record/Observation Form

FIGURE 6–6
This form can be found online at this text's premium website along with additional observation forms.

CHILD'S NAME	LOCATION
DATE	TEACHER
TIME AT START OF OBSERVATION	DEVELOPMENTAL DOMAIN (circle or underline all that apply)
TIME AT END OF OBSERVATION	
OBSERVATION	COMMENTS

The following poem, "Seeds," and songs, "Let's Handle Our World with Care," "I'm So Glad That You Live in the World with Me," and "What A Lucky Day," have been written especially for this chapter.

SEEDS*

The little seeds are sleeping under their blanket made of earth.

They dream until the rainclouds cover the sky;

then all the little seeds begin to sigh,

"We are thirsty! We're thirsty!

We need some rain to drink!"
And now there are raindrops falling, raindrops falling,

and all the little seeds are busy drinking up all the
raindrops falling, raindrops falling, and soon ——

the little seeds begin to grow ———

s l o w l y ...s l o w l y - . - . - .

and some turn into flowers-.-.-.

and others turn into trees,

and many turn into good things to eat!

And all of them are beautiful;

they're very beautiful, reaching up so high

as they try to touch the sky!

*Reproduced by permission of B. Wolf—1995
Copyright B. Wolf—1993

LET'S HANDLE OUR WORLD WITH CARE
Words and Music by Jo Eklof

From *Bringing Out The Best in Children Songbook*
Reprinted by permission of Miss Jo Publications
http://www.missjo.com

I'M SO GLAD THAT YOU LIVE IN THE WORLD WITH ME
Words and Music by Jo Eklof

WHAT A LUCKY DAY
Words and Music by Jo Eklof

Additional verses

What a lucky day it was for me. Do you know that? Today is the day that I got to see a cat.
It meow-meowed here and it meow-meowed there as I went on my way.
Oh boy, it was a very very very lucky day.

What a lucky day it was for me. Please take my word. Today is the day that I got to see a bird.
It flapp-flapped here and it flap-flapped there as I went on my way.
Oh boy, it was a very very very lucky day.

What a lucky day it was for me. Make no mistake. Today is the day that I got to see a snake.
It wiggled here and it wiggled there as I went on my way.
Oh boy, it was a very very very lucky day.

Everyday is lucky. The world is a beautiful place. It's full of wonderful things that put smiles on my face.
I look and learn and listen and then go on my way.
Everyday is a very very very lucky day.

Afterview

Through science activities, a child

● enjoys sensory experiences and uses the senses to gain information about the world.
● becomes more aware of life and physical sciences; earth and space sciences; and ecology.
● sharpens her curiosity, formulates and evaluates predictions, gathers simple data, and draws conclusions.
● observes nature and develops an appreciation of natural beauty.
● learns to garden and care for plants.
● learns to care for animals and develops sympathy and tenderness through association with pets.
● learns that the earth is very special.
● realizes that the earth is our home and that we need to take care of it.
● understands that the earth belongs to all living creatures.
● learns that every living thing must have water to live.
● discovers how growing things enrich the environment.
● realizes that recycling is important to protecting our world.
● learns ways to help clean up litter.
● develops ways to preserve and conserve our natural resources.

Reflective Review Questions

1. Reflect on your past experiences with science concepts and activities in school. Which were the most exciting or boring? Why were they exciting or boring? Based on what you now know, what did your teacher do (or not do) to help these experiences stay with you?
2. What strategies would you use to integrate other curriculum areas into science? Give examples.
3. Think about an early childhood classroom and outside area. List the materials and equipment that encourage scientific investigation. Based on information from this chapter, discuss the developmentally appropriate approach to introducing these objects to the children and how you would promote methods of exploration and discovery to take place.
4. Reflect on the following statements from this chapter. In writing, discuss what each one means to you.

   (a) "A good science program is skillfully integrated into the total life of the classroom."
   (b) "Virtually all outdoors is science."
   (c) "We, as teachers, have opportunities to instill in our children a love and respect for themselves and for all the people, animals, and plants with whom we share our world."

Key Terms

astronomy	inquiry	process skills
chemistry	life science	science as inquiry
earth and space science	meteorology	science in personal and social perspectives
ecology	physical science	science and technology
geology		

Explorations

1. Select at least two early childhood classrooms. Observe for one hour in each. Describe objectively (factually) in writing how science activities were introduced to the children. Which methods of inquiry and process skills (as described in this chapter) were used? Explain by giving examples. Which science activities happened indoors and which ones occurred outdoors? Was there a science learning center as part of the room arrangement? Explain. Describe at least four activities you observed. What are your subjective (opinion) thoughts about early education science activities now that you have completed this assignment?

2. Find out what materials are collected in your community and how they are recycled. Then, using this information, plan a recycling program appropriate for a preschool classroom. What will you recycle? How will you collect the discarded materials? What are your objectives? What projects can you and the children do to reuse the materials instead of discarding them? Share your plan with another classmate or colleague.

3. With another classmate, conduct a science activity with a group of prekindergarteners. For example, compare how sand and water flow through sieves. This helps children extend the concept of flow to dry as well as to wet. This also reinforces the scientific method of investigation. While one adult is involved with the children, the other should take photos of the activity and record what the children are doing and saying. For the children who are interested, follow up with further investigation on the Internet. Afterward, evaluate the activity. Were the children actively involved? What should stay the same? What should change? How would the activity change if planned for a group of toddlers?

4. Select two of the activities suggested in this chapter, such as the carrot-top garden, rooting a sweet potato, thirsty celery, or growing grass, and experiment with them at home. Then plan how you will arrange the environment, what transitions into the activities you will use, and what materials you will supply for the scientific investigations as you set up the activities for a group of young children.

5. Based on the information from this chapter, write a letter about science activities to give to the parents of the children in your class. Be creative. Explain what science projects you and the children are doing. Give suggestions for extended activities the parents can do with their children. Describe other ways to communicate with parents.

Additional Readings and Resources

Benson, J., & Miller, J. L. (2008, July). Experiences in nature: A pathway to standards. *Young Children, 63*(4), 22–28.

Blake, S. (2009, November). Engage, investigate, and report. *Young Children, 64*(6), 49–53.

Brenneman, K. (2009, November). Preschoolers as scientific explorers. *Young Children, 64*(6), 54–60.

Brown, J., & Izumi-Taylor, S. (Spring/Summer, 2009). Sciencing with young children: Moon journals. *Dimensions of Early Childhood, 37*(2), 24–29.

Conezio, K., & French, L. (2002, September). Science in the preschool classroom: Capitalizing on children's fascination with the everyday world to foster language and literacy development. *Young Children, 57*(5), 12–18.

Danoff-Burg, J. A. (2002, September). Be a bee and other approaches to introducing young children to entomology. *Young Children, 57*(5), 42–46.

Egertson, H. A. (2006, November). In praise of butterflies: Linking self-esteem and learning. *Young Children, 61*(6), 58–60.

Galizio, C., Stoll, J., & Hutchins, P. (2009, July). Exploring the possibilities for learning in natural spaces. *Young Children, 64*(4), 42–48.

Kemple, K. M., & Johnson, C. A. (2002, Summer). From the inside out: Nurturing aesthetic response to nature in the primary grades. *Childhood Education, 78*(4), 210–218.

Moriarty, R. F. (2002, September). Helping teachers develop as facilitators of three- to five-year-olds' science inquiry. *Young Children, 57*(5), 20–24.

National Arbor Day Foundation. (2007). *Learning with nature idea book: Creating nurturing outdoor spaces for children.* Lincoln, NE: Author.

Spangler, S. (2009, July). Beyond the fizz. *Young Children, 64*(4), 62–64.

Worth, K., & Grollman, S. (2003). *Worms, shadows, and whirlpools: Science in the early childhood classroom.* Portsmouth, NH: Heinemann; Newton, MA: EDC; and Washington, DC: NAEYC.

Helpful Web Connections

Arbor Day and Earth Day—The Arbor Day Foundation's Nature Explore Program
http://www.arborday.org/explore
Children and Nature Network
http://www.cnature.org
Council for Environmental Education (CEE)
http://www.councilforee.org
Green Teacher
http://www.greenteacher.com
Insect Lore Activities and more
http://www.insectlore.com

National Environmental Education and Training Foundation's Classroom Earth
http://www.classroomearth.org
Natural Learning Initiative
http://www.naturallearning.org
Project Learning Tree
http://www.plt.org
Try Science
http://tryscience.org

References

Allen, M. (2007). Look, think, discover: Adding the wonder of science to the early childhood classroom. Online at: *http://www.earlychildhoodnews.com*

Bosse, S., & Jacobs, G., & Anderson, T. L. (2009, November). Science in the air. *Young Children, 64*(6), 10–15.

Brewer, J. A. (2004). *Introduction to early childhood education* (4th ed.). Boston, MA: Allyn & Bacon.

Buchanan, B. L., & Rios, J. M. (2004, May). Teaching science to kindergartners. *Young Children, 59*(3), 82–87.

Chalufour, I. & Worth, K. (2004). *Building structures with young children: The young scientist series.* St. Paul, MN: Redleaf Press & Washington, DC: NAEYC.

Charlesworth, R., & Lind, K. K. (2010). *Math and science for young children* (6th ed.). Clifton Park, NY: Wadsworth Cengage Learning.

Church, E. B. (2006). Scientific thinking: Step by step. Online at: *http://www.scholastic.com*

Copple, C., & Bredekamp, S. (Eds.). (2009). *Developmentally appropriate practice in early childhood programs* (3rd ed.). Washington, DC: NAEYC.

Desouza, J. M., & Staley, L. M. (2002, Winter). The Reggio Emilia philosophy inspires scientific inquiry. *Dimensions of Early Childhood, 30*(1), 3–8.

Dodge, D. T., Colker, L. J., & Heroman, C. (2000). *Creative curriculum for early childhood: Connecting content, teaching, and learning* (3rd ed.). Washington, DC: Teaching Strategies.

Eklof, J. (2003). *Animals in the classroom.* Dallas, TX: Miss Jo Publications.

Essa, E. (2011). *Introduction to early childhood education* (6th ed.). Clifton Park, NY: Wadsworth Cengage Learning.

Fraser, S., & Gestwicki, C. (2002). *Authentic childhood: Exploring Reggio Emilia in the classroom.* Clifton Park, NY: Delmar Cengage Learning.

Gardner, H. (1997). Teaching for multiple intelligences. *Educational Leadership, 55*(1), 9–12.

Grieshaber, S., & Diezmann, C. (2000). The challenge of teaching and learning science with young children. In N. J. Yelland (Ed.), *Promoting meaningful learning.* Washington, DC: NAEYC.

Hachey, A. C., & Butler, D. L. (2009, November). Science education through gardening and nature-based play. *Young Children, 64*(6), 42–28.

Hoisington, C. (2002, September). Using photographs to support children's science inquiry. *Young Children, 57*(5), 26–32.

Humphryes, J. (2000, March). Exploring nature with children. *Young Children, 55*(2), 6–13.

Kupetz, B. N., & Twiest, M. M. (2000, January). Nature, literature, and young children: A natural combination. *Young Children, 55*(1), 59–63.

Louv, R. (2008). *Last child in the woods: Saving our children from nature-deficit disorder.* Chapel Hill, NC: Algonquin Books.

National Research Council. (1996). *National Science Education Standards (NSES)*. Washington, DC: National Academy Press.

Nimmo, J., & Hallett, B. (2008, January). Childhood in the garden. *Young Children, 63*(1), 32–38.

Petrash, C. (1992). *Earthways*. Mt. Rainier, MD: Gryphon House.

Wortham, S. C. (2010). *Early childhood curriculum: Development bases for learning and teaching* (5th ed.). Upper Saddle River, NJ; Pearson Prentice Hall.

Ziemer, M. (1987, September). Science and the early childhood curriculum. *Young Children, 42*(6), 44–51.

● ●

 Additional information and resources on early childhood curriculum can be found on the Education CourseMate website for this book. Go to **www.CengageBrain.com** to register your access code.

chapter 7

Social Studies

Objectives

After Studying This Chapter, You Should Be Able To:

● Identify the core of social studies—the social sciences.

● Recognize Developmentally Appropriate Practice (DAP) and the National Council for the Social Studies (NCSS) Curriculum Standards and explain their importance in early education curriculum development.

● Outline the goals of early education social studies.

● Describe activities that support the goals.

● Discuss how to create partnerships with families and the community.

● Specify types of field trips and discuss how to plan for these.

● Identify developmentally appropriate and multicultural/anti-bias activities.

Overview

Social studies, like all the content chapters in this book, is a developmentally appropriate link in the early childhood curriculum chain. Social studies emphasizes ways to provide care and education for each child by focusing on the child, the child's family, the community, the nation, and the world. Young children are enthusiastic as they gain understanding of the many aspects of their cultural and environmental world.

Seefeldt, Castle, and Falconer (2010) emphasize:

> The field of social studies is uniquely suited to prepare children with the knowledge, skills, and attitudes they need to participate in, and contribute to, the small democracies of their homes, their preschool or primary groups, and their immediate neighborhoods today, as well as to become functioning citizens of society in general in the future.

Social studies, like math and science, needs to be experienced firsthand by the children. To have this happen, children need to be taken out into the world of people as well as have the world brought to them in the classroom (Feeney, Moravcik, Nolte, & Christensen, 2010). Through interactions with children's families and the community, you can assist children in learning about the core of social studies—the **social sciences**. Individually they are the following: **anthropology**, the study of the way people live, such as their beliefs and customs; **sociology**, the study of group living, cooperation, and responsibilities; **history**, the study of what has happened in the life of a country or people; **geography**, the study of the earth's surface, and resources, and the concepts of direction, location, and distance; **economics**, the study of the production, distribution, and consumption of goods and services; **psychology**, the study of the mind, emotions, and behavioral processes; and other areas of study such as environmental science, art, and current events. (Specific activities relating to the social sciences will be discussed as we continue through this chapter.)

Children today are aware at a very young age about aspects of all the social sciences. They are experiencing moving to and living in different places or knowing family members and friends who have. Many travel on a regular basis and have access to the Internet, television, video games, movies, books, and magazines that introduce them to an ever-changing world.

With all of this in mind, your role as an early childhood teacher continues to be nurturing, valuing, and accepting of the children and families in your care, both individually and as a group. Supportive adults in a supportive environment allow children to release their feelings, ask questions and expect appropriate answers, solve problems, and resolve conflicts. As you continue through this chapter, you will understand how social studies follows the path through the preschool years of a child's own life, to those of his family, school, neighborhood, then branching off during the primary years to his state, nation, and then the larger world or global community.

social sciences The core of social studies: anthropology, sociology, history, geography, economics, and psychology.

anthropology The study of the way people live, such as their beliefs and customs.

sociology The study of group living, cooperation, and responsibilities.

history The study of what has happened in the life of a country or people.

geography The study of the earth's surface, resources, and the concepts of direction, location, and distance.

economics The study of the production, distribution, and consumption of goods and services.

psychology The study of the mind, emotions, and behavioral processes.

© Cengage Learning

Children's everyday experiences are the foundation of their social studies learning.

Developmentally Appropriate Practice and the National Council for the Social Studies Curriculum Standards

Using a developmentally appropriate practice model (Copple & Bredekamp, 2009), teachers can develop a natural social studies curriculum, as suggested by Mindes (2005):

● Build on what children already know. Use children's familiar, everyday experiences as the foundation for their social studies learning.
● Integrate children's development of social skills with their knowledge of social studies.
● Develop concepts and processes of social studies rather than focusing on isolated facts. Integrate with other learning domains.
● Provide hands-on activities.
● Use relevant social studies throughout the year.
● Capitalize on child interest.
● Tap into primary grade children's experiences that extend to other parts of the country and even beyond (through travel, immigration, or technology).

Foster children's understanding of democratic processes and attitudes in concrete experiential ways that young children are able to understand, such as making and discussing rules, solving together the problems that arise in the classroom community, and learning to listen to others' ideas and perspectives. (Copple & Bredekamp, 2009)

Written in 1994 and currently under revision, The National Council for the Social Studies (NCSS) curriculum standards are organized into ten thematic strands based on the social sciences and designed to act as a framework for social studies curriculum while guiding the development of worthwhile learning experiences in early education. The following explanations of the ten themes are adapted from Kostelnik, Soderman, and Whiren (2007), Mindes (2005), Wallace (2006), and Wortham (2010).

● CULTURE—Through activities in the classroom, children develop knowledge of their own culture and the culture of others. A child's culture is a fundamental building block in the development of a child's identity. During the preschool years children explore the concepts of likenesses and differences to help them understand themselves and others.
● TIME, CONTINUITY, AND CHANGE—Important to the lives of young children is their personal history and that of their family. The social studies curriculum should include experiences that provide for the study of ways human beings view themselves in and over time.
● PEOPLE, PLACES, AND ENVIRONMENTS—Where things are in the children's near environment is important information for them to have as they move further from home. Younger children draw upon immediate personal experiences as a basis for exploring geographic concepts and skills. They are also concerned about the use and misuse of the environment.
● INDIVIDUAL DEVELOPMENT AND IDENTITY—The self, the family, and the community are most important to young children. A sense of belonging, and the ability to take care of themselves and their own needs impact children in the early years. For the youngest citizens, infants and toddlers, content focuses on self-development in the social world. In the preschool and primary years, social studies offer a structure for broad theme-based content.
● INDIVIDUALS, GROUPS, AND INSTITUTIONS—Children belong to many groups—family, class, after-school activity groups, congregations, and so forth. This NCSS standard is better suited to study by older children.
● POWER, AUTHORITY, AND GOVERNANCE— Children should be exposed to experiences that provide for the study of how people create and change structures of power, authority, and governance. This standard is also better suited for the older grades to investigate. The concepts are too abstract for young children.
● PRODUCTION, DISTRIBUTION, AND CONSUMPTION—Children can be made aware of the diverse kinds of work adults engage in by talking to them and observing them at work. Prekindergarten and kindergarten children can develop an understanding of how goods and services are produced, distributed, and consumed through social studies projects.
● SCIENCE, TECHNOLOGY, AND SOCIETY—Social studies for young children can introduce the concept that technology influences their lives and their families through household

appliances, television, video and audio tapes, digital cameras, computers, automobiles, trucks, railroads, airplanes, and ships. Activities that encourage further study can be accomplished individually or with small or large groups.

● GLOBAL CONNECTIONS—This NCSS curriculum standard is designed for older children to show the interconnectedness of the world. Global education is abstract, so it is less appropriate for young children. For primary grade children, Copple and Bredekamp (2009) emphasize, "As our society becomes ever more global, knowledge of the interconnected relations between groups of people as well as between nations becomes increasingly vital for our children's generation."

● CIVIC IDEALS AND PRACTICES—Children have opportunities to practice aspects of democratic living when they learn to understand the rules that govern the classroom and when they become involved in making some of the rules themselves.

© Cengage Learning

A sense of belonging and the ability to take care of themselves and their own needs impact children in the early years.

Goals of Early Education Social Studies

A curriculum is not an end in itself but a means, a tool for accomplishing educational goals. These goals are learner outcomes—the knowledge, skills, attitudes, values, and dispositions to action that one wishes to develop in students. (Brophy & Alleman, 2007)

The social studies curriculum emphasizes basic goals that encourage children to become self-reliant, contributing members of their society—namely, in their families, in the classroom, and in the community, while developing an awareness of being a part of the world. These goals encourage children to make choices, act independently, and develop a sense of responsibility and respect for themselves and others. In the *Curriculum Guidelines for Social Studies Teaching and Learning* (2008), the NCSS states, "The primary purpose of social studies is to help young people develop the ability to make informed and reasoned decisions for the public good as citizens of a culturally diverse, democratic society in an independent world."

The following goals help us focus on the core of the social studies curriculum. They are adapted from various sources (Mayesky, 2009; Seefeldt, Castle, & Falconer, 2010; Taylor, 2004) and from conversations with early education teachers.

● *To develop a child's positive self-concept:* A child's understanding and appreciation of himself must come first, before learning to appreciate and relate to others. From infancy on, a child is learning to adjust and accept himself in the family and the larger community. Curriculum activities to emphasize this goal should relate to a child's developing sense of autonomy and his place in the world.

● *To further an understanding of a child's role in the family:* As the child learns about himself, he is also learning about his family. Knowing about the family history, where family members lived before, and the family's values, attitudes, customs, celebrations, and occupations contributes to a child's sense of belonging. That, in turn, helps him to solidify a positive self-concept. Activities should offer opportunities for a child to talk about and identify things about himself and his family.

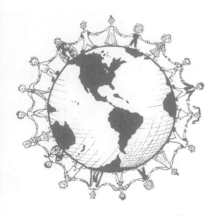

FIGURE 7–1

Social studies activities offer an understanding of people around the world.

● *To develop an awareness of a child's own cultural heritage as well as the traditions of others:* Continuing in the classroom what the child is experiencing in the home environment requires a teacher to communicate openly and often with the child's family. It also means that a teacher should start where the child is with his language, customs, traditions, and values and build on his growth toward self-understanding and acceptance.

● *To provide an inclusive, multicultural classroom environment:* This should reflect the lives and interests of the children, families, and teacher who live in the immediate environment, as well as foster a respect for people everywhere. Social studies activities should blend this diversity into themes, lesson plans, and daily activities *throughout the year.* An appreciation of different ideas, physical appearances, ways, and behaviors will result.

● *To understand the need for rules and laws:* Starting with the rules of the family, the child begins to understand the limits placed on him within his environment at a very young age. Conflicts often occur as the child's sense of independence clashes with the rules of the home and classroom. To minimize these encounters, the child should participate in setting the rules.

Social studies is connected to all learning centers in an early education environment.

© Cengage Learning

Howard Gardner's theory of *multiple intelligences* (tools for learning, problem solving, self-definition, human interaction, and creativity), Lev Vygotsky's *sociocultural theory* (influences and interactions from culture and social groups), and Jean Piaget's *cognitive development theory* (information and exploration gathered from the physical and social environment) can all assist teachers to guide young children into experiencing and building knowledge. (Review Chapter 1 for additional information on Piaget, Vygotsky, and Gardner.)

As teachers, we are daily role models for young children. By incorporating the goals for social studies into our activities, we can create a supportive environment for the children and their families. We can emphasize an anti-bias approach that influences children to respect and appreciate differences and similarities among people. Figure 7–1 illustrates this approach. (All chapters of this book extend this philosophy. Review Chapter 2 for additional multicultural/anti-bias considerations.)

WHY I TEACH YOUNG CHILDREN

I have been a teacher for more than 20 years. I have taught in three different countries and have worked with children of many nationalities. In all of the diversity I have seen and experienced among the children, one thing stays common: they can all be taught the love of learning. By reading to them, we give them the gift of love for reading and writing. By giving them opportunities to create, we help them become creative, and by modeling positive behaviors and interactions with others, we give them social tools to help them function in the world. With love and patience, we have the opportunity to enable the children we teach to have better lives as they grow into adults. What a pivotal role teachers play in touching the future of the world!

—Susy Mathews

Activities That Support the Goals

> As children interact with materials, ideas, peers, and adults, young children gain new and individualized insights about their realities. In the case of social studies, where children are in the process of developing knowledge about social phenomena, the optimal environment is a classroom that replicates society. In an active classroom environment, opportunities abound for children to look at reality through the classroom. (Robles de Melendez, Beck, & Fletcher, 2000)

The social studies curriculum is connected to all learning centers in an early education environment. Rather than create a separate center for social studies activities, the teacher needs to integrate these projects into all other learning centers. When using the project approach, children are building on what they know. At the same time, they are practicing cooperative learning; developing opportunities for observation, reading, writing, interviewing, and inquiry; and using multiple learning domains (Mindes, 2006). Many of the activities described in the other chapters can become part of the social studies curriculum. The following are some additional suggestions to get you started:

● Appropriate *themes* to encourage the development of authentic self-esteem are "Magnificent Me" or "All About Me." Extensions of this can be "Me and My Family," "Me and My Friends," or "Me and My Community." (See Appendix A for a complete thematic, integrated curriculum for "My Community.")

● Children can dictate stories about themselves to the teacher or create an "I Like" book from drawings and pictures they cut from magazines. These very meaningful activities can be introduced at group time and continued in the language and art centers.

● Plan for the social studies curriculum to include topics that relate specifically to children's families. For infants and toddlers, creating an atmosphere that makes them feel safe, secure, and special while they are away from home is most important. Activities for all children can include creating an individual or class scrapbook with photographs of family members and pets and magazine pictures depicting toys and home furnishings. Preschoolers can make craft stick puppets, coloring and designing one puppet for each family member. (Refer to Chapter 11.)

Social studies provides opportunities for children to learn about themselves and others.

Books About Diverse Families

FIGURE 7–2
List of books about diverse families.

● Carmen-Gallo, V. (2008). *We're three: A story about families and the only child.* Illustrated by C. Simcic. New York: Trafford Publishing.

● D'Aluisio, F. (2008). *What the world eats.* Photographed by P. Menzel. Berkeley, CA: Tricycle Press.

● Dooley, N. (2005). *Everybody brings noodles.* Illustrated by P. J. Thornton. Minneapolis, MN: Carolrhoda Books.

● Dooley, N. (1991). *Everybody cooks rice.* Illustrated by P. J. Thornton. Minneapolis, MN: Carolrhoda Books.

● Fearnley, J. (2008). *Martha in the middle.* Cambridge, MA: Candlewick Press.

● Isadora, R. (2008). *Peekaboo bedtime.* New York: Putnam.

● Joosse, B. M. (2008). *Grandma calls me beautiful.* Illustrated by B. Lavallee. New York: Chronicle.

● Kerly, B. (2005). *You and me together: Moms, dads, and kids around the world.* Washington, DC: National Geographic.

● Morris, A. (2000). *Families.* New York: Scholastic.

● Murphy, M. (2008). *I like it when…/Me gusta cuando….* Orlando, FL: Harcourt.

● Simon, N. (2003). *All families are special.* Illustrated by T. Flavin. New York: Albert Whitman & Co.

● Wilson, S. (2008). *Friends and pals and brothers, too.* Illustrated by L. Landry. New York: Henry Holt.

● It is important for children to feel good about themselves and their families. As you continue to prepare your classroom to reflect this attitude, consider the following: What members are in a child's family? How many family members (or others) live in a child's home? What ages are they? What are the roles of family members, both inside and outside the home? What do family members do together? What holidays or events do they celebrate? How are they celebrated? What is the family's history and ethnic background? What changes has the family experienced? Figure 7–2 suggests some books that offer appropriate topics about family diversity.

● An exciting social studies theme can be "Homes." Stretch your and the children's interest and creativity by investigating information about all kinds of shelters for humans and animals. What types of habitats do the following live in: birds, rabbits, turtles, dogs, horses, and cows? Think of all the residences people live in, such as apartments, houses, duplexes, trailers, hotels, and tents. What are they made of, besides wood, brick, and stone? Examine what climate and location have to do with determining how a house is built. Gather books, pictures, computers, and computer software to illustrate concretely what you are talking about. The children can even experiment with building models of some of these residences with blocks, pieces of fabric, scrap wood, boxes, and other materials.

● Taking a social studies viewpoint can become a process you can apply to most curriculum themes. Ramsey (2004) suggests a multicultural approach to learning about pets that could include the following activities and topics:

    ● Caring for pets: social responsibility
    ● Cooperative care of a classroom pet
    ● Similarities among all pets
    ● Diversity of pets
    ● Learning about pets belonging to people in the classroom

- Friendships, despite differences, between people and pets
- Names of animals in other languages
- Pets in other places
- Communicating with pets
- Animals communicating with each other
- Protecting the rights of pets
- Different ways that animals feed, clean, and care for their young
- Working to change conditions that are harmful to animals

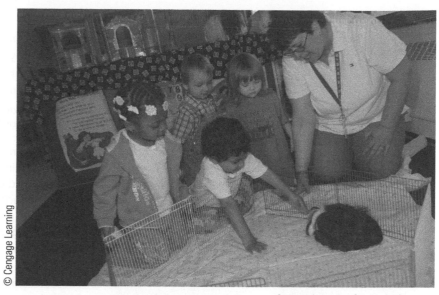

This social sciences/social studies approach can also be used with other topics, such as different ways of cooking and eating, types of clothing, kinds of occupations and work roles, weather conditions, and how people in the world are transported from one place to another.

Cooperative caring for pets in the classroom teaches children social responsibility.

- This social studies activity relates to maps or place awareness. The main objective is to introduce children to a map as a picture that shows places and things, where they are located, and how to get from one to another. Young children can usually understand this concept by working with puzzles or by drawing maps of their rooms at home, the classroom, or the playground. Map making is an abstract concept, so the activities should be fairly simple. Keep a globe and other types of maps available to provide visual answers to children's questions about places in the world. Children can use these also as props in their dramatic play activities. To introduce this mapping project share the following book and its illustrations with the children: Sweeney, J. (2000). *Me on the map.* Illustrated by A. Cable. New York: Dragonfly Books.
- Create an opportunity for the children to make a three-dimensional map (model) of the classroom, their bedroom (see Figure 7–3), or the playground. Clear a large space of classroom floor where the children can construct their map. Place a large piece of cardboard, such as the side of a large box, on the floor. Gather materials, such as pipe cleaners, Styrofoam pieces, small counting cubes, crayons, markers, glue, and various types and colors of paper. The children will let you know what other materials they need during the creative process. They can work cooperatively in small groups to make their map. This activity may take several days or weeks to complete. Let the children make the decision as to when it is time to stop working on and playing with this activity.
- Another type of mapping relates to children's literature. Wallace (2006) introduces the concept of *story mapping*. "The use of story maps is a great introduction to mapping skills with young children. As with most activities we do with young children, there are multiple purposes and outcomes of this activity.... [W]e are giving them strategies for increasing comprehension of a story, of understanding story elements,... of using multiple modalities to learn and show what they have learned, and frequently to work cooperatively with other students." Wallace suggests the following steps:

1. Begin with a book familiar to the children. Choose one you have read to them before.
2. Discuss and chart the different places the main character goes.
3. Have the children, either individually or in pairs or small groups, illustrate the locations.
4. Cut out and label each picture.
5. In sequential order of the locations, glue the illustrations on a large piece of paper. This becomes a very graphic way to introduce children to a map of the locations reached by the main character of the story.

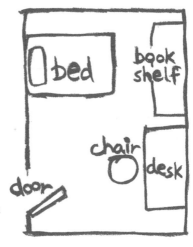

FIGURE 7–3

Map-making opportunities for children are an important part of early education social studies activities.

Here are a few book suggestions:

Caseley, J. J. (2002). *On the town: A community adventure.* New York: Greenwillow.

Gilliland, U. H. (1990). *The day of Ahmed's secret.* Illustrated by T. Lewin. New York: Lothrop, Lee & Shepard.

Gresko, M. S. (2000). *A ticket to Israel.* Minneapolis, MN: Carolrhoda Books.

Heiman, S. (2004). *Mexico ABC's: A book about the people and places of Mexico.* Illustrated by Todd, O. New York: Picture Window Books.

● "Timelines are used to represent data in chronological or sequential order. This technique offers visual aid for children by helping them begin to think in terms of sequence and chronology" (Wallace, 2006). Introduce primary-age children to personal time lines starting with the year they were born through the present. For each year the student will include at least one event that happened in the world or in his or her personal life (Seto, 1999). This can be an activity to be shared with families. The children can bring photographs from home relating to each year or ask their parents to write about what they remember from each year.

● Brophy and Alleman (2007) suggest "co-constructing learning resources, a strategy in which the teacher and students work together to construct interactive timelines.... Teaching about developments in transportation, for example, can be built around a timeline that begins with people traveling by foot and is structured around key inventions such as boats, wheeled vehicles, and engine powered vehicles." Use a large piece of paper and draw a line horizontally to make a timeline. Then, use cut-out pictures, drawings, and teacher sketches to help illustrate the transportation timeline. As the students continue, they can incorporate information and graphics from the Internet and social studies software available. This approach encourages the children to use what they have learned to create something new (Brophy & Alleman, 2007).

© Cengage Learning

Invite parents to visit and to participate in classroom activities with their child.

Sharing Social Studies: Creating Partnerships with Families and the Community

As you establish partnerships with families, it is important to continuously assess their needs and interests and use this knowledge to involve the parents as active partners in the lives of the children at the center or school. The families of today offer new challenges to early childhood educators. "The families with whom a teacher works may not resemble the teacher's own and may be quite unlike each other in their structure, family lifestyle and values, and relationships. As America grows increasingly diverse, teachers need to prepare themselves to recognize, appreciate, and work with such diversity" (Gestwicki, 2010).

Knowing this, we should relate to the families of our children with a commitment to accept their individual differences. We should acknowledge and respect children's home language and **culture** (National Association for the Education of Young Children [NAEYC] 2005). We should maintain positive interactions with them while communicating our goals of a child-centered, developmentally appropriate curriculum.

Get parental and family input as you plan activities and services. If the parents help to set the priorities and agenda, your planned activities will better meet their needs. "Teachers need to be prepared to build partnerships with several parents and family members who are active in a child's life in different configurations and are concerned about the child's development, education, and future" (Rockwell,

culture The sum total of a child's or family's ways of living: their values or beliefs, language, patterns of thinking, appearance, and behavior. These are passed or learned from one generation to the next.

Andre, & Hawley, 2010). The following are some examples of how to communicate with parents to maximize their involvement:

- "Parents are the most important people in their child's life. They know their child well, and their preferences and choices matter. Excellent teachers work hard to develop *reciprocal relationships* with families, with communication and respect in both directions" (Copple & Bredekamp, 2009).
- With parents of an infant or toddler, you will need to spend a lot of time making them feel comfortable in leaving their child with you. It is most important to build a sense of trust, and this takes time. Show them that you will communicate with them through daily notes and conversations. Let them know that there will be a period of adjustment for their child as well as for them. Explain that during this time, it might be helpful if their child brought a "security" toy or blanket. The parents can also call or visit during the day to check on how their child is doing, if this will help them feel more at ease. All these suggestions can open lines of communication between you and the family members.
- Place a parent bulletin board or information sheet on the door of your classroom. For family members who bring and pick up the child each day, this offers a consistent place to look for messages and items of interest. Change materials often.
- Post weekly lesson plans on the classroom door to keep the parents up-to-date on the curriculum. This sends a signal that you want the parents to be fully aware of the daily activities of their children.
- The weekly menu of lunch and snacks should also be posted for parents to see, as required by licensing regulations in most states.
- An email newsletter, in the family's language, is another way to get parents involved. Some enjoy receiving it, whereas others are interested in taking the responsibility for writing it or collecting information to be in the newsletter. The teacher can contribute facts about what is happening in the classroom, suggestions for children's books and videos, parenting articles, and children's art.
- The program's governing or advisory groups include family as members and active participants in the program.
- Have a family breakfast, potluck supper, or picnic on the playground. Food always adds to the welcoming environment of family-school activities.
- An open house or family meeting is a time for sharing with parents what their children are doing and what they are learning. This is an excellent opportunity to talk about the importance of play and other developmentally appropriate learning experiences. Be prepared to answer questions. Give family members an opportunity to take part in some of the activities the children have been doing. Set up materials and supplies in each learning center so that they can "learn by doing," the same as the children. Read a story to the parents or have them participate in a music and movement or social studies activity.
- Once or twice a year, plan individual parent-teacher conferences to discuss each child's developmental progress. Plan both day and evening conferences to accommodate the parents' work schedules.
- Invite family members to share their interests, talents, and occupations with the children in the class. This offers another way to make parent involvement special. Work together to plan events.

© Cengage Learning

Parents are the most important people in a child's life. Their preferences and choices matter.

> [W]hen teachers and families create real partnerships, their spheres of influence overlap and form a caring community around students. The Harvard Family Research Project refers to the need for complementary learning for children to be successful, an array of linked learning supports around them, including families, early childhood programs, health and social service agencies, businesses, libraries, museums, and other community resources. (Caspe, Lopez, & Wolos, cited in Gestwicki, 2010)

Creating partnerships with community members and resources can be helpful. One of the most important groups of individuals to invite into your classroom consists

WHY I TEACH YOUNG CHILDREN

Teaching in an early childhood program is truly a gift. As an infant teacher, I feel fortunate and privileged to be part of each infant's and family's life. I get the most enjoyment out of gently encouraging and providing a variety of enriching activities that enable infants to explore their environment and develop physically, cognitively, socially, and emotionally. In that way, I am committed to being there for families, especially working parents. It is truly a wonderful feeling to know that I and my colleagues are helping to provide the foundation for a life-long love of learning.

—SALWA SINNOKROT

of older members of the families of children in your class as well as senior adults in the community. Intergenerational programs offer many ways to connect young children with the history and family customs of their own or other cultures.

After the visit or visits, it is important to keep in touch with the older adults. The children can establish a pen pal relationship, send frequent drawings, or dictate/write stories to send to their new friends. Many times the children will receive replies that they can share with their classmates.

Field Trips as Concrete Experiences in Early Education

Another way of connecting the child to the community is through taking field trips with the children in your class. Such trips are an enriching part of early education curriculum that adds a special dimension to classroom learning by providing firsthand

Connect children to the community by taking enriching field trips.

© Cengage Learning

experience that books, pictures, or discussions alone cannot provide. Young children need to see, hear, feel, taste, and touch their world to connect words and ideas to locations and people within their community.

TYPES OF FIELD TRIPS

There are different types of field trips to consider. Leipzig (1993), Seefeldt, Castle, and Falconer (2010), and some early childhood classroom teachers suggest the following.

A WALKING TRIP AROUND A FAMILIAR ROOM.   This trip offers infants and toddlers an opportunity to notice and learn the names of everything in the room. It can then be extended to another room until the children feel comfortable exploring and noticing things in the entire building or house.

A WALKING TRIP AROUND THE NEIGHBORHOOD.   This is the natural extension of the room walk, and there are advantages to neighborhood field trips. They are free, and you do not have to arrange for cars or buses. They are short in duration and less tiring for the children. There is not a rush to meet schedules, so the children can make discoveries, their questions can be answered, and learning can occur. Repeated trips around the neighborhood offer chances to learn something new each time you visit the same places. (First take a walk without the children. Look at things from a child's point of view. Find connections that can be natural outgrowths of classroom activities.)

TAKING A SMALL GROUP OF CHILDREN AT ONE TIME ON A MINI-FIELD TRIP.   Once the children become used to taking turns, go on a mini-trip. There are frequent opportunities to do so. There usually is no difficulty in planning trips for a specific purpose with a small group of children.

SPECIFIC-PURPOSE FIELD TRIPS.   This type of field trip can be as simple as a neighborhood walk to go bird-watching or to record sounds around the neighborhood. It can be a short trip to the grocery store to get carrots and celery to go into the vegetable soup the children are making or down the block to see the new house being built.

MAJOR FIELD TRIPS.   These are often taken by the entire class to a community location. This type requires additional adults and travel arrangements for cars, a van, or a bus. (This type of field trip is discussed in more detail as you read through the rest of this chapter.)

PLANNING FOR A SUCCESSFUL FIELD TRIP

Many child care centers and schools are not taking as many field trips as they once did for reasons that include tightening of the budget and shortage of staff. For those of you who are still planning field trips, *careful* planning is most important.

Making decisions about what an appropriate field trip should provide, selecting the site, visiting the location, planning for the trip, taking the trip, preparing follow-up activities, and evaluating the trip are all parts of the *process*. Think about the following guidelines as you plan field trips for young children.

Appropriate field trips provide:

- opportunities to clarify misconceptions young children have about places and people in the community.
- concrete experiences for the children.
- sensory activities outside the classroom.
- occasions to discover firsthand examples of "real life" work settings.
- contact with adult work models.
- opportunities to gather information and observe multiple environments.
- reinforcement and extension of concepts already learned, while developing new concepts.
- a common core of experiences for play and problem-solving activities.

An appropriate site should:

- be safe for young children to visit.
- be fairly close by so that the children have only a short car trip or bus ride.
- not be too fatiguing for the children.
- not be too crowded or noisy.
- offer the children sensory experiences.
- offer genuine learning experiences through participation.

Before you step out of the classroom door with the children, you should:

- visit the field trip site *yourself*.
- talk to the contact person who will be there on the day you and the children visit and call that individual for verification the day before the field trip.
- explain how many children and adults will be coming and the ages of the children; arrange for a time when the site is not too crowded.
- explain the children's need to be able to explore, see, and touch.
- find out the site's rules and regulations.
- find out where the bathrooms are located.
- find out accommodations for children with special needs, if applicable.
- determine arrangements for lunch or snack.
- walk around the location and look for dangerous places.
- set up the length of the visit, date, and time.
- get brochures, posters, and any other information to share with the children during pretrip discussions.

Prepare the children for the trip by:

- giving them an idea of what to expect.
- reading books; showing videos, pictures, and posters; and talking about the planned trip.
- involving them in the planning of the trip.
- reminding them of the rules of expected behavior.
- reminding them that during the field trip they are not to talk to or go with anyone other than the people on the field trip.
- selecting a partner or buddy for each child and explaining how important it is to stay with their partner.
- telling them what to do if they get separated from the group.

Prepare the parents for the trip by:

- having the parent or guardian sign a walking field trip permission form at the beginning of the year, so that you can take the children on spontaneous walks around the neighborhood. (Figure 7–4 is an example of a walking trip permission form.)
- having the parent or guardian sign a field trip form for major types of field trips a week before the trip is to be taken. (Figure 7–5 is an example of a field trip permission form.)

FIGURE 7–4
Walking trip permission form

I give my permission for my child (child's name) to take part in any walking field trip around the neighborhood immediately surrounding the (center or school name). This permission is valid for the entire year (year date).

(signature of parent or guardian)

(date)

Dear Parent,

We will be going on a field trip to (name of site) on (day–date–time–return time). We will travel by (mode of transportation).

    If you give permission for your child to go on this field trip, please sign this form in the space provided below.

(Child's name)

(Signature of parent or guardian)

(date)

Cost (if any) to be paid to the center (or school) by (date) in the amount of (amount).

FIGURE 7–5
Field trip permission form.

- emailing or sending information home to parents explaining the field trip, its purpose, and other details.
- involving parent volunteers to accompany you and the children (one adult for every two or three children is advised. For older children, one adult for every five or six children seems to work well. You will need to decide what child-adult ratio is best for you and the children.)
- explaining the emergency procedures and assuring them that all of the adults going on the trip understand the procedures.
- explaining that arrangements have been made for any child who does not have permission to go on the trip to visit another class during the duration of the field trip.

TAKING THE FIELD TRIP

Consider the following guidelines when you and the children take the field trip:

- Take at least one fully charged cell phone with you.
- Be sure that the drivers of cars, vans, or buses have a map with simple, precise directions on how to get to the field trip location.
- Prepare a trip kit containing bottled water and paper cups, a basic first-aid kit, and several wet washcloths in individual, self-seal bags.
- Keep the most apprehensive children close to you.
- Take the time to see things along the way.
- Listen to the children to find out what they do and do not know. Talk to them; ask open-ended questions and answer their questions.
- Count "heads" often throughout the trip.
- It is helpful if the children wear T-shirts or name tags with the center's or school's name on them. It is best not to put the child's name where it is visible, because a stranger calling the child's name could pull him away from the group.
- Enjoy the field trip!

FOLLOW-UP TO AND ASSESSMENT OF THE FIELD TRIP

There should be many opportunities for follow-up activities. Here are a few suggestions:

- Have the children write thank-you notes or draw pictures to send to the parent volunteers and the field site guides or managers who helped make the field trip successful.

A field trip is all about discovery!

● Encourage group discussions with the children on what they liked best or what they remember about the trip.
● Expand lesson plans to include follow-up activities.
● Deepen the children's understanding and recall through follow-up activities: dictate or write stories, draw pictures, create songs and poems, make puppet characters, and draw maps. Add related props and materials to the dramatic play, block, and other learning centers.
● Clarify and build upon what the children have seen, heard, experienced, and shared.
● Get written evaluations from all of the adults participating in the trip. Did the activity fulfill the trip's goals and objectives? How could the activity be changed to make it effective or more appropriate?

SUGGESTED FIELD TRIPS

Children's museums provide a safe harbor in a scary, busy, and complicated world. They offer children the gift of playing freely in an inviting and complex environment and of playing with new things and people in time-tested ways. These positive play experiences are changing children's lives, not merely by what they learn during a museum visit, but by helping them believe in their own powers to learn, to succeed, to make their own choices, to get along with other people, to make their own discoveries, and to know that they are interesting people with good ideas. (Sinker & Russell, 2000)

David Elkind, a noted early childhood educator, observed in 2001 that "it is interesting that the number of children's museums has increased as the sociological, psychological and physical spaces for children have decreased." At the turn of the twentieth century (1899), the first museum for children opened in Brooklyn, New York. Now, in the twenty-first century, there are about 250 children's museums, with approximately 100 more in the planning stage. There are over 400 children's museums around the world.

The national goals of a children's museum work hand-in-hand with each local museum. A children's museum is a place dedicated to children, their families, and educators, where children learn to be proud of their own families and heritage and develop a better understanding of their classmates' and neighbors' cultures. It also serves as an extension of the classroom for educators and a place for parents to "get down on the floor" and play with their children while spending time together. See Appendix B for a suggested list of children's museums, with their websites.

● SUGGESTIONS OF PLACES TO VISIT

Aquarium	Farmer's market	Puppet show
Arboretum	Fire department	Science museum
Art museum	Library	Sports field or arena
Bird-watching site	Museum of natural history	Wildlife sanctuary
Children's museum	Newspaper	Zoo
Children's theater	Pet shop	
City Hall	Planetarium	

Name of Possible Site/Location

FIGURE 7–6
Index card site form.

Address: _____

Phone: _____

Contact: _____

Days and hours open: _____

Length of tour or presentation: _____

What the tour or presentation consists of: _____

_____

Size of group permitted: _____

Ages of children: _____

Adult/child ratio required: _____

How early do reservations need to be made: _____

Special notes: _____

The field trip sites listed on page 214 are only suggestions. You know your community best and can make the most appropriate selection of places to visit with the children. If you choose not to take any trips outside the center or school, it is possible that individuals connected to the organizations or institutions mentioned could visit, making presentations, bringing exhibits or animals, and interacting with the children.

Teachers will find that making a card file of possible field trip sites can be helpful. It is easy to add to or correct. Place the information on an index card, color coding each type of location. After you complete a visit to the site to see if it is appropriate for the children in your class, you can make notations on the card for easy reference. Figure 7–6 is a suggested index card form.

Tips for Teachers

It is helpful to have a checklist to complete on the day of the field trip. This should be filled out completely by you. Not only will this give you an opportunity to double-check all of your preparations, but it is also written documentation that you are in compliance with state and/or school requirements for taking children away from the center or school. (See Figure 7–7.)

FIGURE 7-7
Teacher checklist for field trip.

1. Notification of field trip was posted in a prominent place for the parents to see at least 48 hours before the planned trip. Name, address, and phone number of where we are going was clearly stated. Name of contact person was listed. Times of departure and return were clearly stated.

   Yes ___ No ___

2. Field trip permission forms, specifically for this trip, have been signed by each child's parent or guardian. These permission forms are on file in the director's or administrator's office.

   Yes ___ No ___

3. Only adults, 18 years of age or older, are counted as part of the child-adult ratio. Requirements have been met for the number of adults to accompany the children, including the teachers.

   Yes ___ No ___

4. The medical emergency consent form signed by the parent or guardian for each child is being taken on the field trip, as well as the emergency phone numbers for each child's family and a written list of children in the group taking the field trip. This information should be put in the vehicle transporting the child.

   Yes ___ No ___

5. An emergency first-aid kit is in each vehicle going on the trip.

   Yes ___ No ___

6. There is an adult trained in first aid and another adult trained in CPR going on the field trip.

   Yes ___ No ___

7. Arrangements for lunch or snack have been made. They are the following:

8. The driver(s) of the bus (van or cars) is/are:
   The driver's license number of each is:
   The license plate number of each vehicle is:

9. Names of adults going on trip:

10. Names of children going on trip:

11. Departure time: _____ Return time: _____

12. Additional information:

Developmentally Appropriate and Multicultural/Anti-Bias Activities

 Connect the social studies curriculum to the theme of "Self and Family" to assist children in learning the values, cultural traditions, and history of families.

FAMILY QUILTS

An effective way to accomplish this goal is to introduce children to quilts. Throughout the history of many countries, you will find quilting, an ancient craft. In American pioneer days, families and friends got together to make quilts for special occasions, such

SUGGESTED FAMILY QUILT BOOKS FOR CHILDREN

Bolton, J. (1994). *My grandmother's patchwork quilt. A book and pocketful of patchwork pieces.* New York: Doubleday Book for Young Readers.

Bourgeois, P. (2003). *Oma's Quilt.* Illustrated by S. Jorisch. New York: Kids Can Press.

Flournoy, V. (1985). *The patchwork quilt.* Illustrated by J. Pinkney. New York: Dial Books for Young Readers.

Franco, B. (1999). *Grandpa's quilt.* New York: Children's Press.

Hopkinson, D. (1993). *Sweet Clara and the freedom quilt.* Illustrated by J. Ransome. New York: Alfred A. Knopf.

Jonas, A. (1994). *The quilt.* New York: Greenwillow.

Polacco, P. (1988). *The keeping quilt.* New York: Simon and Schuster Books for Young Readers.

Ransom, C. F. (2002). *The promise quilt.* Illustrated by E. Beier. New York: Walker Books.

Root, P. (2003). *The name quilt.* Illustrated by M. Apple. New York: Farrar, Straus & Giroux.

Wallace, N. E. (2006). *The kindness quilt.* Tarrytown, NY: Cavendish.

Waterstone, R. (1999). *The too much loved quilt.* Clarksville, TN: First Story.

as weddings, births, and farewells to families moving West. This tradition continues today, and the act of quilting brings many adults together in friendship and sharing.

The term *quilt* "refers to a fabric sandwich made of a top, a bottom or backing, and a soft filler [batting] in between. The top consists of blocks arranged in a pattern. Each block may be a *patchwork,* that is—pieces of fabric cut in squares, rectangles, and other shapes and sewn together to form the block" (Parks, 1994).

Invite a quilter to visit your class. This individual can bring some handmade quilts and also show the children the three unfinished parts of a quilt—top, batting, and backing.

"The fascinating tradition of quilt-making can become an inclusive, engaging experience for children when the early childhood teacher considers a cross-curricular approach" (Helm, Huebner, & Long, 2000).

Your children may enjoy making a friendship quilt of single pieces of fabric or paper. To further illustrate this activity, there are several books that give information about family quilts. These selections offer opportunities for literature-based integrated curriculum. As you read one of the books during group time, pass a quilt around the circle of children. This is a tangible example of the abstract story you are reading. (Older children will be able to read the books by themselves or read them to younger children.)

These books, when shared with family members, stimulate the telling of family stories and, many times, the discovery of family quilts. The stories relate not only to families, but also to the multiple relationships within a family.

After you read the story, encourage the children to retell it by acting out the parts in small groups. You can extend the quilt to many learning centers. There are many projects that can promote the development of large and small muscle skills, as well as problem solving, socialization, cognitive development, language, and literacy abilities. The following are suggestions for these extended activities:

- Develop a story or sequencing chart that diagrams the story line of the book. This can be a way of developing how the story can be reenacted.
- Ask the children open-ended questions, such as, "Do you have a quilt at your house?" "Would you like to make a paper quilt in the art center?" "Do you want to write your story about a quilt in the writing center?" "Would you help me collect fabric to make new squares for our class quilt?" "How do you think we can find the fabric?" "Who should we ask to help us?" "Would you like to make a quilt for the doll bed?"

● Explore color in the science center. Children can mix colors, look through kaleidoscopes, or dye their own fabrics (Helm, Huebner, & Long, 2000).
● Place a "quilt box" in the manipulative area containing an assortment of fabric squares (all the same size) with snaps or Velcro on each corner (top and bottom). A child can snap pieces together to make his own quilt, or several children can do this activity together. Some of the squares should have different patterns and shapes on the fabric.
● Each child can design and paint a paper square for the classroom quilt. Patch the painted squares together with clear tape. Then place the completed quilt on the wall outside the classroom to share with the parents and other children.

Children enjoy creating buildings designed like those in the neighborhood.

● Put washable paint of skin-tone colors into individual shallow aluminum pans, and let each child make a single handprint on a piece of paper. Cut out each handprint and glue it onto a precut, individual square of construction paper. Let each child label his handprint with his name. Make holes in the corners of each square and use brightly colored yarn to lace the squares together. Hang this "quilt" in the classroom so that the children can daily enjoy seeing their art displayed.
● "Our Classroom Family Quilt" in the form of a bulletin board can be made by mounting photographs of the children on squares of fabric. Add the children's dictated comments to the squares. A variation of this bulletin board can be to make a "Family Tree," with the photographs added as leaves of a tree.
● During group time, discuss with the children activities that they enjoy doing with their families. They can draw pictures of what they like to do best.

MAKING THE CLASS INTO A NEIGHBORHOOD

Another, more complex social studies theme and series of activities is making the entire classroom into a neighborhood. This can be a creative follow-up to a walking trip around the neighborhood. It requires careful planning with the children to decide on how to do this, which will then indicate to the teacher what supplies, materials, and props will be needed for each area. Each learning activity center can be restructured into a part of the neighborhood, such as a home, construction site, fire station, grocery store, or other business establishment in the community. This all-encompassing plan benefits the physical, intellectual, social, emotional, and language development of all the children. The neighborhood concept connects children to their immediate world and brings about a feeling of community.

© Cengage Learning

Afterview

Through social studies activities, a child

● learns about his world and his place in it.
● identifies his family members and the multiple relationships within the family.
● develops an awareness of his own cultural heritage as well as the traditions of others.
● learns about other people who live in the world with him and the interconnectedness of the world.
● explores the geography, lifestyles, customs, and languages of other people.
● explores his neighborhood and community and the resources within them.
● participates in the democratic society of his classroom, school, and family.
● has opportunities to learn firsthand about differences and similarities of classmates and other people in his world.

- develops a positive self-concept and an acceptance of others.
- participates in field trips within his neighborhood and wider community to learn about people, places, occupations, and resources.

Reflective Review Questions

1. Explain why the use of high-quality children's literature can be appropriate for teaching social studies to young children.
2. What, from a social studies standpoint, is the value in making maps? How might this type of activity be integrated into other areas, such as art, science, or math?
3. List and discuss the ten thematic strands of the NCSS Curriculum Standards that are based on the social sciences.
4. Many state standards have been revised, updated, or perhaps created for social studies. Conduct an Internet search to find out whether your state has current standards for social studies. Print or save them so that you can use them in your activity planning for children, as well as for other assignments.

Key Terms

anthropology	geography	social sciences
culture	history	sociology
economics	psychology	

Explorations

1. Using the information in this chapter, survey the resources available in your community, and plan (on paper) an appropriate field trip for a group of preschoolers. Select a specific location, visit the site, and follow all the procedures of preparation as if you were actually going to take the children on the field trip. Share this information with your classmates or colleagues.
2. Invite a family member or other person from the community to share with your class his interests, occupations, talents, and other information about himself. If he is from another country, he can share his personal experiences, language(s), and traditions. If the person is from a community organization, museum, or service agency that would be interesting to visit, find out what arrangements need to be made to take a group of children to visit that person where he works.
3. Observe an early education classroom that is participating in an intergenerational program. Describe what activities the older adult and the children were involved in. Interview the adult and get first-hand information about how the program works, what he thinks about participating in the program with young children, and what personal goals he is fulfilling. Share this information with the class or colleagues.
4. Select an early education classroom and observe for at least one hour. List at least ten items in the environment that relate to social studies activities, and describe one social studies activity in which the children were actively involved. How did the

teacher introduce the activity, and what were his goals? If you are already teaching, evaluate your own classroom, list the items, and describe one social studies activity.

5. Choose a children's book that is familiar to the children in your practicum or classroom. Then, following Wallace's suggestions from the text, engage a small group of students in a story mapping activity. Share the results with your classmates and discuss the pros and cons of this technique. Would you do anything differently the next time you used this activity?

Additional Readings and Resources

Briody, J., & McGarry, K. (2005, September). Using social studies to ease children's transitions. *Young Children, 60*(5), 38–42.

D'Addesio, J., Grob, B., Furman, L., Hayes, K., & David, J. (2005, September). Learning about the world around us. *Young Children, 60*(5), 50–57.

Friedman, S. (2005, September). Social studies in action. *Young Children, 60*(5), 44–47.

Howes, C. (2009). *Culture and child development in early childhood programs.* New York: Teachers College Press.

Hyland, N. E. (2010, January). Social justice in early childhood classrooms. *Young Children, 65*(1), 82–87.

Hyson, M. (2008). *Enthusiastic and engaged learners.* New York: Teachers College Press, & Washington, DC: NAEYC.

Jacobs, G., & Crowley, K. (2010). *Reaching standards and beyond in kindergarten.* Thousand Oaks, CA: Corwin, & Washington, DC: NAEYC.

Maxim, G. W. (2003, Fall). Let the fun begin! Dynamic social studies for the elementary school classroom. *Childhood Education, 80*(1), 2–5.

McLennan, D.M. (2009, July). Ten ways to create a more democratic classroom. *Young Children, 64*(4), 100–101.

Randolph, B. (2008). *I didn't know there were cities in Africa.* Teaching Tolerance. Online at: *http://www.tolerance.org*

Scruggs, A. (2009). *Colorblindness: The new racism?* Teaching Tolerance. Online at: *http://www.tolerance.org*

Helpful Web Connections

Children's Museum of Boston
http://www.bostonkids.org
Children's Museum of Chicago
http://www.chichildrensmuseum.org
Children's Museum of Manhattan
http://www.cmom.org
National Council for the Social Studies
http://www.ncss.org

National Geographic Society
http://www.nationalgeographic.com
Project Approach
http://www.projectapproach.org
Teaching Tolerance
http://www.tolerance.org

References

Brophy, J., & Alleman, J. (2007). *Powerful social studies for elementary students.* Clifton Park, NY: Wadsworth Cengage Learning.

Copple, C., & Bredekamp, S. (Eds.). (2009). *Developmentally appropriate practice in early childhood programs* (3rd ed.). Washington, DC: NAEYC.

Elkind, D. (2001, Summer). A place for us: Children's museums in a child unfriendly world. *Hand to Hand: Newsletter of the Association of Children's Museums, 15*(2), 1–2, 6.

Feeney, S., Moravcik, E., Nolte, S., & Christensen, D. (2010). *Who am I in the lives of children?* (8th ed.). Upper Saddle River, NJ: Merrill.

Gestwicki, C. (2010). *Home, school, & community relations* (7th ed.). Clifton Park, NY: Wadsworth Cengage Learning.

Helm, J., Huebner, A., & Long, B. (2000, May). Quiltmaking: A perfect project for preschool and primary. *Young Children, 55*(3), 44–49.

Kostelnik, M. J., Soderman, A. K., & Whiren, A. P. (2007). *Developmentally appropriate curriculum: Best practices in early childhood education* (4th ed.). Upper Saddle River, NJ: Prentice Hall.

Leipzig, J. (1993, May–June). Community field trips. *Pre-K Today, 78*(8), 44–51.

Mayesky, M. (2009). *Creative activities for young children* (9th ed.). Clifton Park, NY: Wadsworth Cengage Learning.

Mindes G. (2005, September). Social studies in today's early childhood curricula. *Young Children, 60*(5), 12–18.

Mindes, G. (2006). Social studies in kindergarten. *K today: Teaching and learning in the kindergarten year*. Gullo, D. F. (Ed.). Washington, DC: NAEYC.

National Association for the Education of Young Children (NAEYC). (2005). *NAEYC position statement responding to linguistic and cultural diversity*. Online at: http://www.naeyc.org

National Council for the Social Studies. (1994). *Expectations for excellence: Social studies* (Bulletin 89). Washington, DC: Author. On-line at: http://www.socialstudies.org/standards

National Council for the Social Studies. (2008, May/June). *Curriculum guidelines for social studies teaching and learning* (Position Statement). Washington, DC: Author. Online at: http://www.socialstudies.org

Parks, I. (Ed.). (1994, Spring). Make a friendship quilt. *Texas Child Care, 17*(4), 22–28.

Ramsey, P. G. (2004). *Teaching and learning in a diverse world* (3rd ed.). New York: Teachers College Press.

Robles de Melendez, W., Beck, V., & Fletcher, M. (2000). *Teaching social studies in early education*. Clifton Park, NY: Delmar Cengage Learning.

Rockwell, R. E., Andre, L. C., & Hawley, M. K. (2010). *Families and educators as partners* (2nd ed.). Clifton Park, NY: Wadsworth Cengage Learning.

Seefeldt, C., Castle, S. P., & Falconer, R. (2010). *Social studies for the preschool–primary child* (8th ed.). Upper Saddle River, NJ: Merrill.

Seto, K. (1999). *Getting ready to teach second grade*. Torrance, CA: Frank Schaffer.

Sinker, M., & Russell, I. (2000, Summer). Describing for play. *Hand to Hand: Newsletter of the Association of Children's Museums, 14*(2), 3–4, 10.

Taylor, B. J. (2004). *A child goes forth* (10th ed.). Upper Saddle River, NJ: Merrill.

Wallace, M. (2006). *Social studies: All day, everyday in the early childhood classroom*. Clifton Park, NY: Delmar Cengage Learning.

Wortham, S. C. (2010). *Early childhood curriculum: Developmental bases for learning and teaching* (5th ed.). Upper Saddle River, NJ: Prentice Hall.

chapter

8

Objectives

After Studying This Chapter, You Should Be Able To:

- Identify how art contributes to physical, cognitive, social, emotional, perceptual, and language development.

- Discuss children's developmental stages in art.

- Describe how a teacher establishes an environment for creative expression and experimentation.

- Discuss the various forms of art in which children can be involved.

- Explain how art can be a stimulus for other curriculum areas.

- Describe how to encourage family support for the sharing of children's art.

- Explore adaptations for special needs and the use of technology in conjunction with art for young children.

- Identify and give examples of the forms of visual art that are developmentally appropriate for children in an early childhood classroom, including multicultural/anti-bias activities.

- Summarize how children's artistic growth can be assessed, with emphasis on portfolio authentic assessment.

Overview

The arts are creative works that express the history, culture, and soul of the peoples of the world, both past and present. (Koster, 2009)

As we begin this chapter, it is important to understand that a child's art—or artwork, as some educators call it—belongs to the child. Her awareness that she can produce something is critical to a child's development of a sense of self (Baghban, 2007). No adult interpretations or descriptions can, or should, describe what a child has created. This is part of the child's own process of communication and creativity.

Fortson and Reiff (1995) explain further:

When a young child brings to you, a teacher or parent, something made through desire, effort, and originality (a scribbled drawing, a bulky shape squeezed out of clay, or a splash of bold colors), this child is intuitively attempting to bring into being a type of relationship that lies at the very core of living. When bringing to you a "creation," however simple or strange, this child is unconsciously saying, "Here is a part of myself I am giving you."

The first time a child makes a mark with a crayon, dips a brush into paint, or glues colored circles onto paper is the birth of a *creative process*. A child's blank sheet of paper soon becomes a creation that never existed before. This sensory event involving paints, crayons, and glue enables the child to freely experience the sheer pleasure of getting to know herself in a new way—through self-expression, "a way of communicating nonverbally with others" (Libby, 2000).

Art is *fundamental* to the growth of a child and an integration of many skills and basic experiences that begin at home and are continued and expanded in early childhood programs. **Art** is *visual* communication through the elements of color, line, shape, and texture instead of words." Art is *developmental*, and its contributions can be seen in physical, cognitive, social, and emotional development.

Physical development involves children using large muscles (gross motor development) in activities such as easel painting or clay pounding; manipulating small muscles (fine motor development) in actions such as fingerpainting or cutting; developing eye-hand coordination (using eyes and hands at the same time) through involvement with all types of materials; and acquiring self-help skills (gaining control over what the body can do) by freely manipulating materials to create expressions in art.

Cognitive development relates to children making art forms that represent and clarify how they see the world; finding new ways to problem solve with art materials and supplies; experimenting with cause and effect by asking, "What happens if?"; comparing sizes and shapes; and predicting outcomes through their involvement with art activities. All of these projects actively stimulate cognitive development for young children.

Social and emotional development in art consists of children developing positive images of themselves; expressing personality and individualism; representing imagination and fantasy; establishing enjoyable relationships with others; and expressing feelings by using as their "vocabulary" paints, paper, pencils, chalk, clay, fabrics, and other media while participating in developmentally appropriate art activities.

Language development is included in cognitive and social development as children clarify color, size, shape, texture, and patterns while talking about their art and the art of others. For example, when a toddler picks out a piece of velvet from the art materials box and asks you to "'sof' it," in her stage of telegraphic speech she is saying to you, "Touch it and feel how soft it is!" Older children are introduced to new words when they pound the clay, make brush strokes, create a design, and make an arrangement of lines and patterns. Koster (2009) believes that "the arts are the child's first language. Through the arts children's minds can demonstrate their concepts of the world long before they can put their constructs into spoken and written words."

art Visual communication through the elements of color, line, shape, and texture instead of words.

physical development Type of development involving children using large muscles, manipulating small muscles, developing eye-hand coordination, and acquiring self-help skills.

cognitive development The mental process that focuses on how children's intelligence, thinking abilities, and language acquisition emerge through distinct ages; Piaget's study of children's thinking, involving creating their own mental image of the world, based on encounters with the environment.

social and emotional development Type of development consisting of children developing positive images of themselves, expressing personality and individualism, representing imagination and fantasy, establishing enjoyable relationships with others, and expressing feelings.

language development Developmental process of a predictable sequence that includes both sending and receiving information. It is related, but not tied, to chronological age.

perceptual development Type of development in which children use their senses to learn about the nature of objects, action, and events.

Perceptual development occurs when children use their senses to learn about the nature of objects, actions, and events. Perception refers to the ways a child knows what goes on outside her body. A child perceives through systems: touch, taste, smell, hearing, and sight (Charlesworth, 2011).

Teachers need to provide experiences that are sensually rich and varied, and which require children to use their perceptual abilities in many different ways. Observational and visual perception skills are heightened as children use their senses to study the patterns, colors, textures, and shapes found in nature and in the artwork of others. (Koster, 2009)

As we continue through this chapter, we will look at how the developmental stages relate to specific art activities for infants, toddlers, preschoolers, kindergarteners, and primary school children. Creating an environment that values artistic expression and encourages children's creativity and experimentation is the focus of your role as teacher, facilitator, and observer. As one child suggested, "Let's do some arting today!"

Make materials available where children can create in an undisturbed environment.

Children's Developmental Stages in Art

"Stages in artistic development do not have discrete beginnings and endings in the developmental sequence, but rather children exhibit a tendency to move back and forth between stages as they learn and grow" (Taunton & Colbert, 2000). This includes not only the physical, cognitive, social, emotional, perceptual, and language development of each child; it also accounts for "social, cultural, religious, individual and environmental factors in tracing the development of child art" (Schirrmacher & Fox, 2009).

A teacher can recognize characteristics that are identifiable to help in understanding the needs and interests of the children in an early childhood program. Understanding what has come before helps in knowing what to look for as the child matures.

[Howard] Gardner's writings [1983] have stimulated new interest in the arts and their importance in the development of children. The theory of multiple intelligence recognizes that children may be talented in specific areas and learn in different ways. For some children, art may be the way they learn the best; for others, it may be a new way to experience the world. (Isbell & Raines, 2007)

INFANTS AND TODDLERS

Art is a sensory experience for infants and toddlers. The child uses her entire body when interacting with the art materials. The enjoyment for the child comes from this exploration.

Think about safety and appropriateness when selecting supplies and materials for this age. Younger children may be overwhelmed or overstimulated at first by too many choices, so start slowly and add items a few at a time. Crayons, fingerpaints, paints, paper, play dough, and water play should be available. The child needs opportunities to poke, pat, pound, shake, taste, smell, and scribble.

Transitions into and out of art activities are very important. The younger the child, the more verbal and visual clues are needed to help her move from one activity to another.

Scribbling with crayons is more enjoyable with a friend.

© Cengage Learning

Flexibility, both inside and on the playground, is needed. This age child loves to water paint on the floor, table, brick wall, and sidewalk. Opportunities for experiencing color (add food coloring to the water or play dough), texture (art materials box or texture board), and temperature (warm water, cold play dough) can encourage a child to participate.

Scribbling begins around age two, but as with all developmental stages, it can begin earlier or later. The important thing is to supply the opportunity. "*Scribbles* are the building blocks of children's art. From the moment the child discovers what it looks like and feels like to put these lines down on paper, he has found something he will never lose, he has found art" (Kellogg & O'Dell, 1967).

Kohl (2003) observes,

Once or one is never enough for most toddlers. Repeat activities over and over and allow toddlers to make one or many art projects. The more they create the more they learn. If it won't work today, try it tomorrow. Being flexible, supportive and nurturing is the key to working with toddlers.

Expect an older infant and toddler to explore and manipulate art materials, but do not expect them to produce a finished art product (Copple & Bredekamp, 2009). See Figures 8–1, 8–2, 8–3, and 8–4 for infant and toddler drawings.

When using their fine motor skills to rub a crayon on paper or to make lines in sand or across a frosted window, toddlers learn that they can leave marks on these surfaces through their actions. Toddlers are pleased with their abilities and motivated to continue exploring scribbling. (Baghban, 2007)

PRESCHOOLERS, PREKINDERGARTENERS, AND KINDERGARTENERS

From her research of two million pieces of children's art from 30 countries (Baghban, 2007), Rhoda Kellogg found that these scribbles are meaningful to a child and believed that they should be valued by the adults in their environment (Kellogg, 1959). Kellogg's

FIGURE 8-1
Drawing made by a 14-month-old child.

FIGURE 8-2
Drawing made by an 18-month-old child.

● ● ● ● ● ● ● ● ● ● ● ● ● ● ● ● ● ● ● ●

FIGURE 8–3
Drawing made by a child 2 years, 6 months old.

● ● ● ● ● ● ● ● ● ● ● ● ● ● ● ● ● ● ● ●

FIGURE 8–4
Drawing made by a child 2 years, 6 months old.

"20 basic scribbles" (vertical, horizontal, diagonal, circular, curving, waving, zigzag lines, and dots) continue to be discovered by preschoolers. Their art also shows them passing through the Placement Stage (definite patterns of scribbles placed in the left half, right half, center, or all over the page), into the Shape and Design Stages (combinations of scribbles forming definite shapes and designs), and then into the Pictorial Stage (structured designs that begin to look like something adults have seen before) around ages four and five (Kellogg & O'Dell, 1967).

The child enjoys exploration and manipulation of materials. Watch for a younger preschool child to paint her hands, for example. An older child still enjoys sensory experiences but will demonstrate this by experimenting with the materials in new and unusual ways. It is important for the child to develop control over the process. A child may even tear up her work during the process.

Art represents feelings and perceptions of a child's world. A child draws pictures and writes to organize ideas and construct meaning from her experiences (Baghban, 2007). The child creates what is important to her. A child uses colors that please her, and these colors may bear little relation to the actual colors of the objects created. An older preschooler creates forms and shapes, chooses materials carefully, and looks at the materials in new ways.

> A respect for the personal nature of the child's artwork means the teacher does not direct the process, but allows the child to proceed and experiment in the ways she deems appropriate. The child is able to create and combine materials in ways that the teacher may have never imagined. (Isbell & Raines, 2007)

A child enjoys using her imagination. Copying a model changes the whole experience for her. A child who has used coloring books tends to lose the capacity to create naturally and individualistically.

See Figures 8–5 and 8–6 for children's drawings. See Figure 8–7 for Kellogg's 20 scribbles.

EARLY PRIMARY GRADE

The child at this stage becomes more serious and focused in the art process. The child's early concrete experimenting and learning-by-doing art activities become a

FIGURE 8–5
Drawing made by a child 4 years, 7 months old.

FIGURE 8–6
Drawing made by a child 4 years, 8 months old.

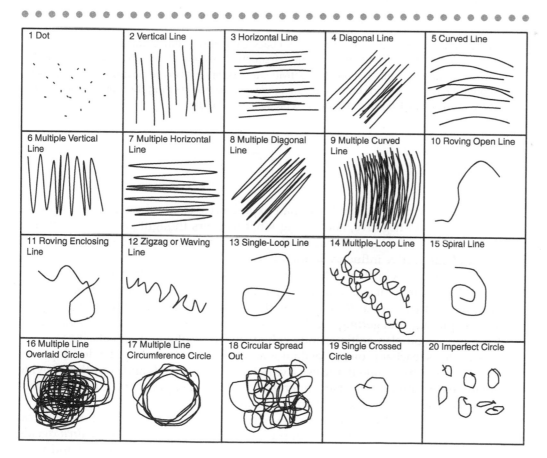

FIGURE 8–7
Representations of the 20 types of scribbles identified by Rhoda Kellogg. (Source: Isbell and Raines, 2007, p.110)

bridge to complex thinking. Realistic color and proportion are evident in the child's finished art. Careful planning is also becoming more apparent as part of the process. See Figures 8–8 and 8–9 for drawings by early-primary grade children.

FIGURE 8–8

Drawing made by a child 7 years, 5 months old.

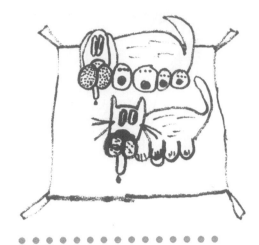

FIGURE 8–9

Drawing made by a child 8 years, 10 months old.

The opinion of the adult observer becomes important. The child feels her art must be recognizable in both content and subject matter to the viewer. Often the child offers critical evaluation about her own work.

> In the early primary grades, art often takes a backseat to other curriculum areas, such as math and literacy. However, children benefit from frequent art experiences both during specialized instruction and from integration of art activities and techniques in the classroom . . . . Teachers should involve children in complex, meaningful tasks, such as creating short picture books or storyboards for making videos. (Copple & Bredekamp, 2009)

Teacher as Facilitator and Observer

When you were young you probably had experiences, some of which were positive but some that were negative, concerning what teachers thought about *your* art. You should strive to be the kind of teacher the children in your care will remember as a positive and supportive influence in their lives.

In this chapter, as in all chapters of this book, you are asked to view what a child has created with different eyes than perhaps you have used before. Do not focus on the outcome or product: *Look at the process.* Is the child participating, interacting, experimenting, exploring, and getting involved "up to the elbows"? This is what you should be observing as you plan, initiate, and evaluate the art center and art activities.

Your role as teacher is one of facilitator and observer. You set up the developmentally appropriate environment, furnish a variety of safe materials and supplies, provide opportunities for child-directed art experiences, and offer support and encouragement to the children as you observe their unique creations.

Approaching children's art from the perspective of facilitator can take any real or imagined pressures off of you *and* the children. For example, let the *children* decide whether to talk about their art or not talk about it. If they freely describe it and want you to write down a description, do so—otherwise *don't*.

Many times we try to get some response from the children and ask them to "Tell me about your picture" or "Tell me a story about what you're painting." This puts stress on the child to say what he or she thinks you want to hear. I overheard one child emphatically tell a teacher, "This is not a story! This is a picture to look at!" (That answer certainly made the teacher reflect on what she had asked the child.)

Some suggestions of what you could say should describe what you observe. Talk about the children's actions: "I see you used different colors in your picture." "You're feeling the fingerpaint, aren't you?" "You have a lot of dots on your paper today." "I see you covered the whole page." These statements and others like them do not ask for the child to "come up with an answer." This type of response from you offers affirmation and encouragement and avoids vague and extremely judgmental types of praise. "This is 'ART TALK' that infers 'show me' instead of 'tell me'" (Aulthouse, Johnson, & Mitchell, 2003).

Another part of your responsibility as a facilitator is to make materials available where children can create in an undisturbed environment. As you decide which activities and materials are appropriate, try them out yourself before you put them out for the children. This will enable you to introduce new supplies or materials comfortably and show the children how to use them appropriately. Once this is accomplished, step back and allow the children to investigate, explore, and try out the materials for themselves.

© Cengage Learning

Introduce new supplies or materials, such as watercolor paints, and allow the children time to investigate, explore, and try out the materials.

Establishing an Environment for Creative Expression and Experimentation

Creativity is the process of doing, or bringing something new and imaginative into being. "Creativity is a combination of motivation, openness/flexibility, curiosity and autonomy as well as divergent thinking" (Mitchell, 2006). By encouraging creativity in children, we can help them become adults who can solve problems creatively. "In reality everyone is creative in one way or another. No one is uncreative" (Mayesky, 2009).

Isbell and Raines (2007) believe:

> In a rapidly changing world, we must develop programs for young children that include the competencies they will need now and in the future.... The creative arts provide an avenue for learning and experiencing that is uniquely different. Their inclusion, during the early years of children's lives, establishes a rich foundation that adapts to change, provides joy, and inspires involvement.

For those of us in early education, Gordon and Browne (2011) extend the point of view even further: "The roots of creativity reach into infancy, for it is every individual's unique and creative process to explore and understand the world, searching to answer larger questions 'Who am I?' 'What and where am I?' and 'Where am I going?'"

We should offer encouragement by providing opportunities for creativity to be expressed and by showing that we genuinely respect its expression. Children need to be in an inspiring environment, one that they help create and interact with. Creativity can be destroyed by a teacher who does not appreciate the creative act or the child who expresses the act.

Mayesky (2009) helps us understand that "[t]eachers who allow children to go at their own pace and be self-directed in a relaxed atmosphere are fostering creative development . . . . The learning environment must also welcome exploration by elimination of conditions providing stress, and too strict time limits."

We should value what the child is creating or attempting to create and provide many opportunities for her to do so. Setting up an appropriate art center is the first step in establishing this priority. "The simplest choices for teachers become major

creativity The process of doing or bringing something new and imaginative into being.

The art area should be close to a sink for easy cleanup.

decisionmaking opportunities for children. What color paper to choose, what color crayons or paint, what shape and size of paper, which way to hold the paper are all options the child should have" (Szyba, 1999).

The following are some additional thoughts that teachers should consider when establishing an art environment:

- Develop an awareness that the process of creative thinking is complex.
- Understand that there is no right or wrong way of doing things, only possibilities.
- Recognize that some children are more creative in one area than another.
- Recognize that creativity may reflect an ability to think divergently or seek multiple solutions rather than a single solution to problems.
- Arrange an appropriate classroom space for children to leave unfinished work to continue the next day.
- Encourage children to engage in creative processing as they manipulate and play with objects, while remembering that it may not result in a finished product.
- Help parents to appreciate their child's creative abilities, with or without a finished product.
- Offer encouragement for, and acceptance of, a certain amount of messiness, noise, and freedom.
- Continue to experiment and test alternatives to determine what is best for your children and your classroom situation.
- Understand that creative expression should flow through the entire curriculum.

(Adapted from Isbell & Raines, 2007; Mayesky, 2009; and Schirrmacher & Fox, 2009.)

GENERAL GUIDELINES FOR PROVIDING AN ART ENVIRONMENT

As you plan or redesign your visual art environment, provide *time, space,* and *materials* that allow children to work at their own pace without interference. The area should be large enough to accommodate the easels and art table. The art center should be a free-choice area. The National Art Education Association (NAEA) states, "We believe that children construct and reconstruct their own learning as they interact with their environment. This constructivist point of view places as much importance on *how* children think as on *what* children think" (quoted in Aulthouse, Johnson, & Mitchell, 2003).

In an integrated, open-ended arts program "there is no art corner or art project of the day. A wide variety of arts activities are available in many places in the room" (Koster, 2009).

- Clarify your goals and objectives for the art area or areas. Relate them to the theme and lesson plan when appropriate. (Review Chapter 2 for detailed information.)
- Establish rules with the children concerning the care of and use of art materials and limits within the art area. Guide them toward assuming responsibility for the use, care, and cleaning of materials and tools.
- The art area should be close to a sink for easy cleanup. If this is not possible, place a bucket or plastic tub with warm soapy water nearby. Change the water often.
- Encourage the children to participate in all phases of an art activity, including preparation and cleanup. Have sponges and paper towels handy for the children to use. Protect the environment and the children so they do not have to be concerned about making a mess. Have smocks or aprons available for the children to wear during art activities.
- Continue to keep safety in mind as you select exciting and appropriate supplies and materials for the children to use. Select only nontoxic materials.
- It is important to think about using recycled materials, but a word of caution: *Do not reuse Styrofoam trays that have had meat or poultry on them.* Even after washing they may contain bacteria from the raw meat or poultry. Use clean, unused Styrofoam trays, which many grocery stores will give you at very little or no cost.
- Add several drops of liquid dishwashing soap to tempera paint. It washes out of clothes more easily and also prevents paint from chipping off the children's art when dry.
- A place for finished art should be provided. If they need to dry, plan ahead of time for a special drying place or hanging rack.
- Place an art area near a window, if possible, so the children can see outside while they are creating. Extend freedom of movement and free expression by allowing children to stand or sit at the art table as well as use the floor to spread out large sheets of paper for art activities.
- Balance the activities: new with familiar, messy with clean, indoor with outdoor, large muscle and small muscle.
- Children are fascinated by color, texture, shape, and design. You can attract the children to the art area by including activities that promote each of these. For example, invite the children to make a collage (pasting objects together onto a surface) of varying yellow colors found in magazines. This activity encourages preschoolers to cut, glue, look for, and discover that any color can have many shades.
- Most of all, children need a teacher who will enable them to be successful.

© Cengage Learning

You can attract children to the art area by including activities that offer color, texture, shape, and design.

GUIDANCE GUIDELINES

When designing an environment in which young children can integrate visual art into all areas of the classroom, you should consider how the surroundings, organization, and storage will affect the children. Clarify your goals and objectives for the art area and each art activity. Relate them to the theme and lesson plan when appropriate. Establish rules with the children concerning the care and use of art materials and limits within the art area or areas. Guide them toward assuming responsibility for the use, care, and cleaning of materials and tools by showing them where they are kept, how the children are to take them, where to use them, and how they are to be returned.

Help children and their parents deal with being messy. Being messy is okay! Supply smocks or aprons. The children can be responsible for getting a smock, putting it on during an art activity, and putting it back when they have finished. Continue to repeat rules of the art areas when necessary.

As you introduce each new activity or group of materials or supplies, explain the appropriate ways to use them. Help all children learn to respect their own art and the art of others. Many times a cooperative art activity, such as painting a mural with each child having her own space on the paper, will demonstrate to a child how to focus on her own creation and to work together as a team with others.

The following are some additional ideas for teachers to consider:

● Bring order to the environment by setting up the structure of space, time, and materials to reflect your educational goals.
● Design well-thought-out space where children can discover, process, experiment, and explore.
● Arrange the materials and space so that the children can self-select if you want them to work independently.
● Store and label materials and tools so that children learn how to get what they need and put an item back and clean up by themselves.
● Be flexible. Adjust the arrangement of the easels, tables, chairs, and other furniture to suit the needs of individual children at specific times.

(Adapted from Koster, 2009; Mayesky, 2009; and Schirrmacher & Fox, 2009.)

USE OF FOOD IN ART PROJECTS

Using food in art activities with children is a continuing topic of discussion. Teachers and administrators are divided on this issue. I have found that not using food works better for the following reasons:

● It is difficult to justify using food when many parents are working long hours to put food on the table for their families. Food is expensive. Also, the casual use of food in art when many are homeless and hungry can be upsetting to some adults.
● The use of food in an art activity may offend some cultural groups who use that food item for religious or ethnic celebration (Schirrmacher & Fox, 2009).
● Many children are severely allergic to some food items, such as milk, wheat, soy, eggs, and peanuts.
● It is important *not* to use foods for art because toddlers are developing self-regulatory skills and must learn to distinguish between food and other objects that are not to be eaten (Copple & Bredekamp, 2009).
● Children become confused when they are told that they can eat one art material but not another one that seems similar (Koster, 2009).
● Using cornstarch, flour, salt, and food coloring is acceptable because these are used in small amounts as additives to make play dough and other recipes for art.
● There are other alternatives for art projects. For example, instead of using macaroni, string together paper shapes with a hole punched in the middle or paper straws cut in various lengths. Sand or buttons can be glued instead of rice. Use cotton balls, Styrofoam, or toothpicks instead of beans for collages and textured art. It is fun to come up with other creative choices.

You will need to decide for yourself whether you want to use food in art projects or not. Consider your own values, economic factors, and the policies of your center or school.

OUTDOOR ENVIRONMENT

Take it all outdoors! Children enjoy the space and freedom offered by outdoor art activities. Take the easels, a table, long sheets of butcher paper, paints, and cleanup buckets outdoors. Let the children use chalk on the sidewalk; explore rocks, shells, flowers, trees, birds, and butterflies; go for walks and look for colors, textures, and shapes; and gather leaves for making rubbings or prints or for using as materials on paintings and collages.

> Nature excursions also can inspire creativity in artwork. Children can draw or paint pictures about their experiences. Collections of natural materials (berries for dyes; dried weed stalks for tracing or relief rubbings; acorns, seeds, sticks, and pebbles for collages) can be used to create artistic masterpieces. You may even find real clay to dig up and sculpt. (Humphryes, 2000)

If your playground has a chain link fence, it can be used as a drying area. Clothespins easily attach the paintings or murals to the fence. A safe drying area can also be arranged inside a large cardboard box. Plan for cleanup with buckets, hoses, and lots of paper towels.

Chapter 9 offers additional ideas for outdoor activities with sand, water, and woodworking.

AESTHETIC ENVIRONMENT

Greenman (1987) captures the essence of environmental aesthetics in the following description:

> Imagine a room where there are bright splashes of color, often attached to moving bodies, and warm muted hues on carpet and walls. Sunshine catches the light of a prism in one corner, and there is a small patch of sunlight so bright you have to squint. There are soft indirect lights, shadows, and cool dark corners.
>
> There are hanging baskets of trailing green plants, flowers, pussy willows and cattails, angel hair and dried grasses. The beauty of life is captured by Monet and Wyeth and assorted four-year-olds.

We can actively create such an **aesthetic environment** for children, one that cultivates an appreciation for beauty and a feeling of wonder and excitement of the world in which we live. We can do this by:

aesthetic environment An environment that cultivates an appreciation for beauty and a feeling of wonder and excitement of the world in which we live.

- designing indoor and outdoor environments to emphasize beauty, attention to detail, color, shape, textures, lines, and patterns in carefully thought-out space and arrangements.
- allowing time for looking at and talking about all kinds of art.
- providing beautiful books with all types of illustrations.
- introducing children to fine art by displaying prints of paintings and sculptures in the classroom (the water gardens of Monet, the mothers and children of Cassatt, the ballerinas of Degas, and the splashed action paintings of Pollock) and by visiting local galleries and museums.
- encouraging the aesthetic display of children's art in a classroom "museum," which offers an opportunity for the children to take turns being the **curator**, the person who decides what art to display and how to display it (Fox & Diffily, 2001).
- hanging up objects that play with the light, including mobiles made of cellophane, papers, and children's art (Schirrmacher & Fox, 2009).
- including art, wall hangings, weavings, and tapestry from diverse cultures as part of the aesthetic room environment.
- exposing children to nature by allowing time to watch a spider spin a web or to look closely at a wildflower.
- supporting children's self-expression and creativity as they reflect the world around them.
- involving and informing parents how art production and appreciation are integrated into curriculum areas and inviting them to participate in museum trips.

curator The person who decides what art to display and how to display it.

Painting, in all its forms, provides opportunities for creative expression and developmental growth.

Additionally, Epstein (2001) emphasizes that:

> too often, early childhood practitioners limit art education to the making of art. But being artistic in the fullest sense also involves developing a sense of aesthetics. Enabling young children to appreciate art gives them another mode of learning through direct encounters with people (artists) and objects (the work they create).

Involving Children in all Forms of Art

Children involved with art develop sensory awareness, aesthetic appreciation, self-expression, and improve visual and motor coordination. The process of experimenting with and creating two- and three-dimensional projects from a variety of media connects children to another facet of their world.

We see, time and again, a young preschooler put one color of paint on the easel paper and then place another color exactly on top of the first, and then continue this process until the result is a mass of "indescribable" color. The color is beautiful to the child, and she has created it. This newfound ability to change color is important and exemplifies learning for the child. The older child paints masses of color next to each other and may surround the color with dots and shapes. Both exemplify the process of making art.

The emphasis throughout this chapter is on allowing appropriate time, space, and flexibility for creating; to give permission and responsibility to the children; and to nurture and value their creativity. This will provide children with many opportunities to move beyond investigation to using these materials in unique, imaginative, and individually creative ways.

TEARING, CUTTING, AND GLUING

Tearing, cutting, and gluing offer individual activities to young children and provide small muscle development and tactile experiences; offer opportunities for controlling scissors and direction of cutting for creative purposes; provide discovery of form,

WHY I TEACH YOUNG CHILDREN

It's natural instinct and craving for me to have young children in my life. Their laughter with each other keeps my days going and their curious natures keep me on my toes. Their expressions upon their new discoveries or a friend's hug, or solving the world's problems, like what color to make the play dough, remind me of the simple pleasures of life.

Their eyes let me see into their world. It's such a magical, exciting place to be. Teaching keeps what's important and real in my life.

—BEV SANDHEINRICH

shapes, colors, sizes, and textures; develop eye-hand coordination; and encourage verbal communication and sharing.

Let the children do the tearing, cutting, and gluing. Use white glue, school paste, flour and water paste, glue sticks, masking tape, and clear tape. Pour white glue into small plastic squeeze bottles or pour small, individual amounts of glue into jar lids, small bowls, or other containers. Children can use cotton swabs or their fingers to manipulate and spread the glue. Supply a wet paper towel for each child to have at her place, or moisten a sponge that several children can share to wipe their fingers.

Children can tear and cut tissue paper, construction paper, fabric scraps, old greeting cards, wallpaper samples, newspapers, and catalogs. Glue these materials to construction paper, corrugated paper, any sizes of paper plates, index cards, box lids, brown wrapping paper, foil, or gift wrapping paper.

During an art activity of tearing, cutting and gluing, children discover they are making a **collage**. "This art activity, making a picture containing glued-on objects or paper, is very popular with young children . . . . Children are extraordinarily free of restraints as they become immersed in the creative process of making a collage" (Koster, 2009).

> **collage** An art activity that involves making a picture containing glued-on objects on paper.

PAINTING

> Painting, like talking and writing, is a way of expressing ideas and feelings . . . . Instead of words you use lines, colors, shapes, and arrangements. You can find these in every painting in the world. (The Metropolitan Museum of Art, 1959)

Painting, in all its forms, provides sensory experiences, allows for coordinated use of many body muscles, encourages language development, helps with the judgment of spatial relationships, provides an opportunity for manipulation and experimentation, develops form perception, is often a two-handed experience, and develops skill in handling a brush and other art materials and tools.

© Cengage Learning

Easel painting is popular with young children.

Painting develops skills that are used in reading and writing. The curves, patterns, and lines that children make are similar to letters and words. The awareness of spatial relationship and configurations on the page relates to reading skills. Distinguishing painted forms, lines, and patterns from the background requires the same discrimination as reading. When you read, you separate, or "pull out," letters from the background.

Organizing the art environment for painting will help make the activities successful for children. When fingerpainting, children can use the paint directly on the table top, on a table that is covered with butcher paper, or on individual pieces of paper. For younger children, place a spoonful or two of fingerpaint into plastic bags. Close the bags carefully and seal with tape to prevent leaks. Each process offers a different experience for children. They have direct sensory contact with the material. They create changeable patterns, designs, and shapes in a short amount of time while maintaining their interest for a long time. To preserve a table-top painting, blot the fingerpainting with a piece of butcher paper to get the reverse design that the child can keep.

Fingerpaints in many colors are commercially available. Selecting skin-tone colors offers young children another way to develop self-esteem. They often choose paint that matches their skin colors. This reinforces the anti-bias approach that all colors are beautiful. Other items to use as fingerpaints are toothpaste, cold cream, hand lotion, or wet sand.

Easel painting is popular with young children. Easels can be placed indoors or outdoors. If several are set up, place them close together. This encourages interaction

Young children enjoy spontaneous expression when painting on a mural or extra large piece of paper.

© Cengage Learning

string painting A type of painting that involves moving string dipped in paint around on paper to make a design.

and conversation between the painters. Easels should be the correct height for young children, washable, and sturdy, and should have a tray for holding containers of paint. You could also tape the easel paper to a wall indoors or a fence outdoors.

Furnish large sheets of easel paper or paper cut into different shapes, brushes (one for each color being used) in a wide variety of sizes, and a choice of colors. For younger children, it is helpful to start with one color at a time. Have them use the primary colors of red, blue, and yellow; the secondary colors of orange, purple, and green (the colors obtained by blending pairs of primary colors); and black, brown, and white. Mixing black or white with primary colors teaches pastel tints and grayed tones. Children quickly discover for themselves what happens when colors are mixed together.

To thicken paint, add liquid starch or cornstarch (children will need large brushes to paint with thick paint). A teaspoon of alcohol added to each pint of paint or a drop or two of oil of wintergreen will prevent the paint from souring.

Before children start to paint, you may have to remind them to put on a smock or apron. After the children are through, let them wash the brushes with soap and water, shape them, and place them brush-end up in a container to dry. Additional tools that can be used as brushes are paint rollers, pot scrubbers, sponges, feathers, tooth-brushes, and fly swatters.

String painting is another art activity that young children enjoy doing. It involves moving a string dipped in paint around on paper to make a design. You might first attach a button to one end of the string so that the children can hold the button to manipulate the string more easily.

They can also dip short lengths of string or yarn into bowls of paint mixed with a small amount of white glue (holding the string with a clothespin can help those children who do not want to get their fingers in the paint). They then lay the yarn or string onto a piece of construction paper to form a design. Children can vary the lengths of yarn, string, or twine to add texture to the painting.

Children can fold a sheet of paper in half, then open it and place the paint-wet string on one side of the paper. Fold the other side of the paper over and hold it with one hand. Then gently pull the string through while holding the folded paper in place with the other hand. To complete this activity, younger children may need assistance from you or another child.

Children enjoy experimenting with *object or gadget painting*. Provide items such as kitchen utensils, forks, corks, sponges, pieces of wood, combs, and cookie cutters for dipping into paint or a paint pad (made by pouring thick tempera paint onto several layers of paper towels or a thin sponge). The children press the object down onto a piece of manila or colored construction paper. A unique print is the result.

Painting with feet offers another sensory experience for children. (This is an extension of hand painting.) Begin by covering the floor or outdoor sidewalk with newspaper, and then place long pieces of butcher paper or brown wrapping paper over the newspaper. Tape the corners so that the paper will stay in place. The children remove their shoes and socks and then stand at one end of the paper. Help them step into containers or tubs you have prepared with tempera paint. Paint is slippery, so you may need to assist some children as they walk on the paper. At the other end of the paper place a tub of warm, soapy water and some towels. After the children make their "feet design," they will end up by stepping into the tub of water (Figure 8–10). This project makes a wonderful mural. This is a fun activity to do with parents as well. (I still remember the first time I did feet painting, when my oldest child was in preschool. It was a parent-child activity during an open house. I have used it many times since with children, parents, and teachers.)

FIGURE 8-10
The feet painting process.

Other types of painting for young children are fingerprint painting (walking fingers dipped in paint across paper), sand mixed with paint (gritty paint), salt and paint (sparkle paint), flour and paint (lumpy paint), ball or marble painting (dipped items rolled over paper placed in a box), painting on rocks, and painting with watercolors.

DRAWING WITH CRAYONS, MARKERS, AND CHALK

According to Koster (2009), "Drawing is the most basic of all the visual arts. It is usually the first art experience young children have and is the first step toward literacy." Crayons and markers are familiar to most young children. They have used them at home and other places, such as at restaurants that welcome children to color on the paper table covering or on the children's menu. *Caution:* Young children should use only water-based markers because permanent markers may contain toxic solvents. Chalk provides another type of drawing experience. All these materials are ready-to-use, easy to store, and require very little cleanup.

When using crayons, markers, and chalk, children utilize different types of muscular coordination than those they use to control a paintbrush or a finger. They also encourage exploration of what colors can do, provide an excellent prewriting experience, develop hand-eye coordination, and stimulate the imagination.

© Cengage Learning

Chalk provides an interesting type of drawing experience for young children.

Scribbling, as discussed earlier in this chapter, is important to young children. Crayon scribbling is usually one of the first activities children enjoy doing over and over again. It's easier for children to control crayons when they are sitting down. They often use pressure to make marks on the paper, so having large, less breakable crayons available for younger children works well. Older children prefer the small crayons.

By starting with large sheets of paper, then moving on to all sizes, shapes, and textures of paper, you can extend the crayon scribbling and drawing activities. Using crayons on colored paper teaches children what happens when one color is applied to another.

Crayon rubbings can be introduced early in the year, then continued as the variety of objects to be rubbed changes throughout the year. To make a crayon rubbing of a texture, children place an object under newsprint or other type paper and rub with a crayon. (You might need to tape objects down on the table at first.) Rubbing the side of a peeled crayon across the paper usually works best. Suggestions of objects to be rubbed: cardboard squares, circles, rectangles, triangles, and ovals; coins and leaves of various sizes and shapes; different textures of wallpaper; and bricks, tree bark, and sandpaper. (Let the children discover these and others.)

A favorite art activity of toddlers and preschoolers is to "draw a child." For the young ones, you can draw around each child lying on a large piece of paper. Older children can choose partners, and they can draw around each other. Then each child can color herself. She can add a face, hair, clothes, and shoes with additional materials from the art materials scrap box.

Crayon resist is an interesting art activity for older children. They can draw a picture on paper with light-colored crayons, then cover the picture with watercolors or thin tempera paint. The paint will cover all but the crayon markings. A variation of this project is for the children to place waxed paper over a sheet of white paper and draw on it with a pencil, pressing wax lines and design into the bottom paper. They then remove the waxed paper and brush thin paint over the wax lines on the paper. A design of white lines will appear on the painted surface.

For a wet chalk project (wet chalk provides an interesting texture different from dry chalk), guide the children into dipping the chalk in a cup of water before writing on paper. Another way to do this is for the children to wet the paper, including paper plates, instead of the chalk. For big pictures and designs, sweep the sides of the chalk across the paper. Children soon discover that they can mix the colors together by blending them with their fingers or with a tissue.

THREE-DIMENSIONAL MATERIALS

The sensory experience of handling and shaping a variety of materials encourages young children to experiment, explore, and discover original ways to create three-dimensional art. These activities can help children release emotional tensions and frustrations, work with their hands, develop small muscles, and provide opportunities to manipulate, construct, and learn about spatial relationships.

Three-dimensional art (having depth as well as height and width) is demonstrated through the use of play dough, clay, and "goop." These materials should be used on a surface that is easily cleaned and is large enough for children to have plenty of "elbow room." These materials should be soft enough for the children to manipulate easily, neither too wet nor too dry. Placing individual amounts of these materials on a tray, linoleum square, or manila folder for each child helps the children identify limits and gives them personal space. It is helpful to provide a bucket of water for the children to wash their hands in when they are finished with the activity. This will keep the residue of the materials out of the sinks.

Play dough, clay, and goop are extremely valuable because the children are able to use the materials with their hands without having to learn how to manage a tool, such as a paintbrush. (Younger children do better with play dough because it is softer and easier to manipulate.) The children are concerned with managing the material and

crayon rubbings Duplicating an object of texture by placing it under paper and rubbing over it with a crayon.

crayon resist A type of art for older children that involves drawing a picture in light-colored crayons then covering the picture with watercolors or thin tempera paint. The paint will cover all but the crayon drawing.

three-dimensional art An art form that has three sides. Play dough and clay are examples of three-dimensional materials.

learning what they can do with it. You can add rolling pins, cookie cutters, or other accessories after the children have had a lot of time to handle and experience the feel of the clay or dough. Many classrooms have both commercially prepared clay and play dough. In others, the teachers prefer to make these materials themselves. You might want to supply both to the children.

The following are recipes for play dough (*do not eat*) and goop.

COOKED PLAY DOUGH

1 cup flour	1 tablespoon cooking oil
1/2 cup salt	2 teaspoons cream of tartar
1 cup water	

Mix the above ingredients. Heat and stir over low heat until the mixture forms a ball. Remove from heat and wrap in waxed paper to cool. Knead it well and store in an airtight container. The dough will last much longer if kept in the refrigerator. Add food coloring, if desired. You can make this first and then give it to the younger children. You and the older children can make it together so they can see the process. Some teachers put the food coloring in before cooking; others add color after cooking so the children can see the change from white, to marbled, to the final color. For more play dough, just double the recipe.

The following is the recipe for uncooked play dough (do not eat). For younger children, give it to them already made. Let the older children make it with your guidance.

UNCOOKED PLAY DOUGH

1 cup flour	food coloring (optional)
1/2 cup salt	1 tablespoon salad oil
1 cup water	

Mix flour and salt. Add oil. Slowly add water until the mixture sticks together but does not feel sticky. Add more water if too stiff, add more flour if too sticky. Knead it well and store in airtight container.

GOOP

1/2 box to 1 box of cornstarch
Water

Add water slowly to cornstarch until it is semifirm. Mix it with your hands or let the children do it. They can feel and see the changes in the texture. Store covered in the refrigerator. As it becomes dry from storage and handling, simply add more water.

Other three-dimensional works of art can be made into the form of sculptures by adding materials such as the following: toothpicks, Styrofoam, boxes, pieces of wood, egg cartons, paper towels and toilet paper rolls.

Art as a Stimulus for Other Curriculum Areas

When teachers facilitate young children's observations and conversations about paintings, sculpture, photography, ceramics, and other media, they encourage children to develop an understanding of the communicative power of visual art. (Eckhoff, 2010)

Try connecting art to everything you do. For example, children can listen to music and draw or paint in rhythm to the music. They can express in their creations how the music makes them feel. Verbal and nonverbal language is expressed through art. As pointed out earlier in this chapter, children learn to include an art vocabulary into their everyday conversations with other children and adults. They express and represent what they know through their art. "Looking, talking, and creating together turns an art activity into a social activity in which children can learn from each other" (Mulcahey, 2009). The art activities discussed in this chapter also give children an understanding of themselves and others. Their study of artists and their visits to art galleries and museums help them relate to their community and to the world. (See Figure 8–11.)

Koster (2009) and Williams (1995) suggest that math and art content can be combined on a regular basis. For example, the math concepts of problem solving, inventing patterns, measurement, sorting, and classifying relate to the art concepts of awareness of line and shape, decoration of line and pattern, and awareness of texture and changing shape.

Schirrmacher and Fox (2009) point out that children quantify art materials, equipment, and supplies by counting the number of brushes and jars of paint that are in use

FIGURE 8-11

Children's books featuring art, artists, and illustrators.

These books for young children encourage them to create their own illustrations using a variety of techniques, as demonstrated by the artists and illustrators in the following examples:

Adoff, A. (2000). *Touch the poem.* New York: Sky Press.

Carle, E. (2006). *The very busy spider.* New York: Putnam.

Carle, E. (2002). *The art of Eric Carle.* New York: Philomel.

Jenkins, S., & Page, R. (2003). *What do you do with a tail like this?* Boston: Houghton Mifflin.

Lee, S. (2008). *Wave.* San Francisco, CA: Chronicle.

Lionni, L. (2006). *A color of his own.* New York: Alfred A. Knopf.

Morrison, T., & Morrison, S. (2010). *Little cloud & lady wind.* Illustrated by S. Qualls. NY: Simon & Schuster Books for Young Readers.

Muhlberger, R. (1993). *What makes a Monet a Monet?* New York: The Metropolitan Museum of Art and Viking.

Muhlberger, R. (1993). *What makes a Van Gogh a Van Gogh?* New York: The Metropolitan Museum of Art and Viking.

Praeger, E. J. (2006). *Sand.* Washington, DC: National Geographic Children Books.

Reynolds, P. H. (2003). *The dot.* Cambridge, MA: Candlewick.

Sayre, H. S. (2004). *Cave paintings to Picasso: The inside scoop on 50 masterpieces.* San Francisco: Chronicle.

Scieszka, J., & Smith, L. (2005). *Seen Art?* New York: Viking.

Stone, T. L. (2008). *Sandy's circus: A story about Alexander Calder.* Illustrated by B. Kulikov. New York: Viking.

Venezia, M. (1990). Getting to know the world's greatest artists: Mary Cassatt. Chicago: Children's Press.

Weitzman, J. P., & Glasser, R. P. (2002). *You can't take a balloon into the Museum of Fine Arts.* New York: Dial Books.

Wood, A. (2000). *The Napping House.* (Board Book). Illustrator: Don Wood. New York: Harcourt.

Yolen, J. (2009). *The scarecrow's dance.* Illustrated by B. Ibatoulline. New York: Simon and Schuster Books for Young Readers.

and by deciding which brushes have longer handles, which crayons are fatter, and which geometric shapes are being used in their art creations.

Many scientific principles have already been discussed in this chapter, including:

- discovering what a specific material can do and what the child can do to control it
- observing what happens when colors are mixed together
- noticing what happens when flour and water are combined
- experimenting with thick paint and thin paint
- discovering what happens when you press down hard or lightly with a brush or crayon on paper
- observing what happens when paint is brushed over a crayon picture
- determining what occurs when different ingredients are mixed together
- setting up a "discovery table" with art materials such as paper of different shapes and colors, clay, and other art media that can be integrated into any subject that is being discussed in the classroom

> Art activities are one of the best ways to promote literacy and brain development in early childhood. Early childhood is an especially important time for hands-on, self-directed learning. Art engages children's senses in open-ended play; develops cognitive, social-emotional, and multisensory skills; and provides children with authentic self-expression. (Reyner, 2002)

Sharing a Child's Art: Encouraging Family Support

Another part of the teacher's role is to help parents understand that the many pages or examples of art the children bring home are the results of creative and imaginative processes—all of them from the children. If families understands *why* art is valued in the early childhood setting, they can more easily offer support to their child at home.

You can also guide the parents into setting up a special place at home for their child to continue experimenting and creating with art. Send home suggestions and lists of what materials and supplies are appropriate as well as explanations of what she has been doing in the classroom. *Interpret the child's developmental progress to the parents, not what the child's art is or is not.*

As you share the children's art and activities with the families, ask each family to share with you. Invite them to bring in any of the art their children create at home. Some may want to take photographs at home showing the child and family member involved with the activity. Start a "Family Art" section on your parent bulletin board.

SPECIAL NEEDS

It is important to explain to the family of a child with special needs how their child participates in art activities.

> Because of the open-ended nature of well-designed art activities, children with special needs can participate fully in most art programs, often without many modifications. If necessary, changes can be made in the tools and environment to allow active participation. The other children also need to be encouraged to accept and support those with special needs. (Koster, 2009)

For example, Koster (2009), Schirrmacher and Fox (2009), and special needs educators suggest the following:

- Put trays across wheelchairs.
- Provide wheelchair-height tables.

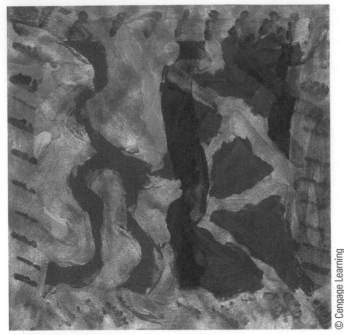

© Cengage Learning

Display all kinds of children's creations around the classroom, such as abstract paintings.

● Place a stool under the table so that a child sitting in a regular child-size chair who cannot reach the ground will be able to rest her feet on the stool and stabilize her body. This stability helps children more easily use their fine motor skills.
● Wrap art tools such as crayons, markers, pencils, and brushes in foam hair curlers to improve grip.
● Use scented crayons and markers.
● Provide many tactile materials.
● Tape papers to the table to keep them from wrinkling or moving when the children are using them.
● Use contact paper or other sticky paper as the backing for collages. The child only has to put things on paper. This eliminates the difficulty of gluing and pasting for some children.
● Lower the easel and give a child a chair if she has difficulty standing at an art easel.
● Ensure access to appropriate technology for children with special needs, for whom assistive technologies may be essential for successful inclusion.
● Use computer voice-text software that allows children to both receive and produce written communication, either with words or symbols.
● Use adaptive peripherals, usually special switches or hardware that plug into the computer. This can provide alternatives for children unable to use a mouse or keyboard.

TIPS FOR DISPLAYING CHILDREN'S ART

As you send the children's art home, remember to save some of the creations to place around the classroom—with the child's permission, of course. The early education environment should reflect the children, and a wonderful way to do this is to display their art. (This also actively creates an aesthetic environment, as previously discussed in this chapter.)

Displays show the parents what is happening in their child's classroom. Provide a place with wall and table displays outside the classroom in a hall or lobby for parents' enjoyment.

Art should be displayed at the child's eye level. Frame children's art attractively in a variety of ways using colored paper, wallpaper, or gift wrap as a background; rick-rack, fabric, or yarn to outline pictures; and a large group fingerpainting to serve as a mounting for individual art. Taking the time and effort to mat and frame the children's art is another way to show that you value what they have done.

Display all kinds of children's creations (clay models, Styrofoam structures, mobiles, wood sculpture, and collages). These kinds of art can be displayed on tables or shelves and arranged attractively on brightly colored paper. Change the art displays frequently. Let the children help decide when to change the selections and what to put up next. Arrange art in different kinds of groupings, such as several art items belonging to an individual child, several pictures that share the same colors, pictures with the same theme created from different media, and art connected to the theme or lesson plan of the week (see Figure 8–12).

● ● ● ● ● ● ● ● ● ●

FIGURE 8–12
A kiosk is a self-standing display with three or more sides.

An art kiosk is a workable solution to limited wall space. A kiosk is a self-standing display with three or more sides. It can be constructed of panels of sturdy cardboard, wood, or stacked cartons. It is space-efficient in that many pictures can be simultaneously displayed on a number of sides in a few feet of floor space. (Schirrmacher & Fox, 2009)

Technology

The use of technology in conjunction with art expands the classroom environment and creates new expressions for children's art. Aulthouse and colleagues (2003) suggest the following:

- *Overhead projector:* Children can place color paddles, colored tissue paper, or cellophane on the overhead projector to find out what happens to light and color.
- *Cameras:* Digital or inexpensive disposable cameras can immediately document children's art activities. Taking photographs is yet another way for children to explore their world. Computers, printers, and scanners streamline this process and allow for flexibility with image size. Jacobs and Crowley (2010) expand the use of cameras this way: "Children can take photographs, study them, and then try to recreate the image with paint, crayons, play dough or other media."
- *Photocopier:* Children and teachers can also enlarge photographs on a color copier to display the pictures taken of their art.
- *Videos:* Video of children's activities can show not only how children are engaged in art, but also how art can be integrated into all learning centers.
- *Computer technology:* Children can use computers for word processing as they write and illustrate books. When selecting computer tools to use with art, it is important to use software that allows a child to design the art and control the creation of the pictures or illustrations. There are paint programs available for young children. Schirrmacher and Fox (2009) suggest, "Try viewing computer art as one component of your art program rather than as a replacement of all hands-on art experiences in your classroom."

Isbell and Raines (2007) help us understand how to choose appropriate software for art, especially with many different computer programs available for children.

1. The child is able to determine what will be drawn.
2. Options are available for creating lines, forms, colors, and making changes.
3. Different drawing tools can be used to change the texture, size, and proportion of the drawing.
4. The child's name and title/description can be added.

Different types of software have different effects. Open-ended programs foster cooperation and collaboration, which in turn encourage children to be active participants. The pace should be set by the child and not the software program (Mayesky, 2009). Always preview a program before offering it to children. It is important for the software to be developmentally appropriate and meet your educational objectives.

Developmentally Appropriate Multicultural and Anti-Bias Activities

Art activities are developmentally appropriate for children when "teachers use a variety of strategies to increase children's awareness and appreciation of the arts in their own culture and local communities and beyond. These include bringing the arts into the classroom (e.g., displaying prints of fine art and books that include art reproductions); inviting community artists to visit or going to their studios; and taking field trips to galleries, museums, performances, and public art displays" (Copple & Bredekamp, 2009).

> Using reproductions of art in the curriculum is surprisingly easy and provides a broad range of benefits for children. Introducing artwork to young children allows them to construct their own knowledge, teaches appreciation of diversity, encourages storytelling, and fosters imaginative and critical thinking skills. (Mulcahey, 2009)

In our global society it is necessary that we encourage children to look at art from different cultures as a way to see the world. This requires us, as teachers, to choose carefully the art reproductions that our children will explore. Select from various forms of art, geographic locations, time periods, and cultures. This will give children a window into the diverse traditions of the art world (Eckhoff, 2010).

Multicultural art materials should always be available to young children. Just as each culture brings its own richness to our world, so do the projects and creations of each child bring richness and beauty to our classrooms and communities.

Guide children to discover projects that reflect both ancient and modern cultures. Ancient cultures produced some of the most beautiful art and exciting artifacts ever created. Many of these techniques have passed from generation to generation.

> When children see the art of their heritage displayed and honored, they feel valued as people. When they see the art of others treated with respect, they learn to value people who are different. (Koster, 2009)

The following example of an activity can get you started in introducing an appreciation of color in a fun and simple way. A book, first introduced in 1955, that is one of the most popular ones for both children and teachers is Crockett Johnson's *Harold and the Purple Crayon*. You can use this imaginative story as a springboard for many art activities related to multicultural and anti-bias curriculum in an early childhood program. For example:

● Read the book to the children at group time. Ask the children to think of other things Harold can do with his purple crayon. At the next group time introduce a flannelboard story that has Harold as the main character doing some of the things the children suggested.
● In the art center place only purple items, such as crayons, markers, and construction paper. This is a creative way to introduce children to all the different shades of purple. Let the children experiment with paints and problem solve which ones to mix together to make purple. Also have purple play dough available for creative play.
● For their snack you can serve purple grapes, or introduce the children to eggplant or other purple foods.
● The children will also suggest other purple things to do.

Observation and Assessment Strategies

Art assessment can be described as authentic assessment because it visually documents a child's growth and development over time, using the child's art and explanations of her art in her own words. Each picture or piece of artwork shows where the child started at the beginning of the school year and where she is at the end of the year.

A **portfolio**, which is a collection of work over time, can be a record of the child's process of learning—how she thinks, questions, analyzes, synthesizes, and creates (Gober, 2002). Portfolios come in many shapes and sizes, such as expanding, accordion-type files, file folders, cardboard boxes, scrapbooks, three-ring binders, or unused pizza boxes.

portfolio A collection of a child's work over time and a record of the child's process of learning.

Nilson (2011) clarifies how children's artistic growth can be assessed.

> Portfolios, collections of the child's work and written observations are becoming an accepted form of documenting the child's progress. Written observations which are thorough, objective, regular, and done in the natural classroom environment are accurate measures of a child's progress.

You need to work out a routine with the children as to how the selection process of what goes in the portfolio will work. Some suggestions include: (a) You can take one day per week, such as Friday, for the children to go through their weekly art and select one or two items they want to include. (b) You can also go through the art prior to or after the children have selected pieces to be included. (c) Art that is sent from home can be placed in each portfolio with date and explanation at any time. (d) It is important that children have an opportunity to choose and comment on each article of art, because it promotes self-evaluation and self-assessment. It is also good for the child's self-esteem for her to focus on all the things she knows she can do. (e) Keep in mind that each child's portfolio should be respected and confidential. (d) There is no right way to do portfolio saving. You have to try different ways and decide on which is right for you and the children in your class. (e) Write an end-of-the-year summary that you will keep, and make a memory book of each child's artwork to send home.

You will find a portfolio checklist, a portfolio sample form, and file folder labels for organizing an individual child's portfolio online at this textbook's premium website.

Afterview

Through art, a child

- heightens an awareness of and appreciation for an aesthetic environment.
- strengthens her self-expression, self-understanding, patience, and self-control.
- acquires visual, spatial, and tactile awareness.
- develops small and large muscles.
- develops eye-hand coordination and hand-hand coordination.
- experiments with color, line, form, shape, texture, size, balance, and configurations.
- increases creative problem solving, decision making, and abstract thinking abilities.
- experiments with different art media and recycled materials.
- communicates ideas nonverbally.
- releases emotional tensions and frustrations.
- grows in social relationships.
- increases vocabulary and language skills.
- develops respect for artistic expressions of others.
- increases awareness of the diversity of the world of art

Reflective Review Questions

1. We often hear an adult asking a child about a painting by saying such things as "What is this?" or "Tell me about your picture." True, the adult is giving attention to the child and the painting, but are these appropriate questions? What might the adult say that would be more appropriate? Why?

2. How would you counter a family member's criticism about the messy condition his/her preschool child is in at the end of the day?

3. Describe how a classroom's art environment and materials might be altered to make it more suitable for children with special needs.

4. What do outdoor arts activities mean to you? Why is it important to take art outdoors? What difference will it make to a group of young children? Are there ways of planning an arts activity for outdoors that differs from art done indoors? Explain.

Key Terms

aesthetic environment	crayon rubbings	physical development
art	creativity	portfolio
cognitive development	curator	social and emotional development
collage	language development	string painting
crayon resist	perceptual development	three-dimensional art

Explorations

1. Based on information in this chapter and your observations of early childhood environments, develop a list of appropriate materials and supplies to have available in the art area for young children. Are there materials that are new to you? Explain.

2. Collect at least ten examples of children's art (different ages, if possible). Determine what developmental stage each represents. What materials were used? Is it two- or three-dimensional art? Share these with others in your class. (Keep the children's names confidential.)

3. Select and plan an art activity for young children. Specify which age group this activity is planned for: infants, toddlers, preschoolers, or primary-age children. Write a list of objectives, materials needed, step-by-step procedures for presenting this activity, follow-up activities, and evaluation guidelines. (Use the activity plan worksheet in Chapter 2.) Prepare this activity and demonstrate it during class or with a group of children.

4. Select two early childhood classrooms and observe for at least one hour in each. Describe, in writing, six art activities you observed. Were these new to you? How did the teacher present the activities to the children? Which ones were child-directed? Were any of these teacher-directed? What transitions did the teacher use before and after the activities? What adaptations or modifications were made for special needs children? Will you use or have you used any of the six activities with children? Explain.

5. Paint a picture using an easel or by hanging a large sheet of paper on the wall. Concentrate on noticing the fine and gross motor movements required and record your observations. Then do a painting on a table top, once again recording your motor requirements. Compare and contrast the two activities. Think about the implication of large and small muscle development in children that is necessary for these art activities. Now consider cutting, pasting, tearing paper and other materials and creating sculptures. What other skills would need to be developed? After doing these activities yourself, will you approach art activities in an early childhood classroom differently? Explain.

Additional Readings and Resources

Armistead, M. E. (2007, November). Kaleidoscope: A creative arts program prepares children for kindergarten. *Young Children, 62*(6), 86–93.

Damian, B. (2005, March). Rated 5 for five-year-olds. *Young Children, 60*(2), 50–53.

Eckhoff, A. (2008). The importance of art viewing experiences in early childhood visual arts. *Early Childhood Education, 35*, 463–472.

Epstein, A. S., & Trimis, E. (2002). *Supporting young artists: The development of visual arts in young children.* Ypsilanti, MI: HighScope Educational Research Foundation.

Fox, J. E. (2000, Fall). Constructive play in the art center. *Dimensions in Early Childhood, 28*(4), 15–20.

Jalongo, M. R. (2003, Summer). The child's right to creative thought. *Childhood Education, 79*(4), 218–228.

Johnson, M. H. (2008, January). Developing verbal and visual literacy through experiences in the visual arts. *Young Children, 63*(1), 74–79.

Mulcahey, C. (2002, January). Take-home art appreciation kits for kindergartners and their families. *Young Children, 57*(1), 80–88.

Riccio, L. L., Morton, K. C., & Colker, L. J. (2005, July). The SAIL effect: An arts-based charter school buoys children's learning. *Young Children, 60*(4), 42–49.

Sidelnick, M. A., & Snoboda, M. L. (2000). The bridge between drawing and writing: Hannah's story. *The Reading Teacher, 54*, 174–184.

Wien, C. A., Keating, B., Coates, A., & Bigelow, B. (2008, July). Sculpture with three-to-five-year-olds. *Young Children, 63*(4), 78–86.

Zimmerman, E., & Zimmerman, L. (2000, November). Research in review—Art education and early childhood education: The young child as creator and meaning maker with a community context. *Young Children, 55*(6), 87–92.

Helpful Web Connections

Arts Education Partnership
    http://www.aep-arts.org
Crayola
    http://www.crayola.com
Creative Arts Curriculum
    http://www.artjunction.org
Global Children's Art Gallery
    http://www.naturalchild.com
Kennedy Center Artsedge
    http://www.artsedge.kennedy-center.org

Metropolitan Museum of Art (New York)—Explore Museum Kids
    http://www.metmuseum.org
National Art Education Association (NAEA)
    http://www.naea-reston.org
National Association for the Education of Young Children
    http://www.naeyc.org

References

Aulthouse, R., Johnson, M. H., & Mitchell, S. T. (2003). *The colors of learning: Integrating the visual arts into the early childhood curriculum.* New York: Teachers College Press; Washington, DC: NAEYC.

Baghban, M. (2007, January). Scribbles, labels, and stories: The role of drawing in the development of writing. *Young Children, 62*(1), 20–26.

Charlesworth, R. (2011). *Understanding child development* (8th ed.). Clifton Park, NY: Wadsworth Cengage Learning.

Copple, C., & Bredekamp, S. (Eds.). (2009). *Developmentally appropriate practice in early childhood programs* (3rd ed.). Washington, DC: NAEYC.

Eckhoff, A. (2010, January). Using games to explore visual art with young children. *Young Children, 65*(1), 18–22.

Epstein, A. S. (2001, May). Thinking about art: Encouraging art appreciation in early childhood settings. *Young Children, 56*(3), 38–43.

Fortson, L. R., & Reiff, J. C. (1995). *Early childhood curriculum.* Boston, MA: Allyn & Bacon.

Fox, J. E., & Diffily, D. (2001, Winter). Integrating the visual arts—Building young children's knowledge, skills, and confidence. *Dimensions of Early Childhood, 29*(1), 3–10.

Gardner, H. (1983). *Frames of mind: The theory of multiple intelligences.* New York: Basic Books.

Gober, S. Y. (2002). *Six simple ways to assess young children.* Clifton Park, NY: Delmar Cengage Learning.

Gordon, A. M., & Browne, K. W. (2011). *Beginnings & beyond: Foundations in early childhood education* (8th ed.). Clifton Park, NY: Wadsworth Cengage Learning.

Greenman, J. (1987, November). Thinking about the aesthetics of children's environments. *Child Care Information Exchange, 58*, 9–12.

Humphryes, J. (2000, March). Exploring nature with children. *Young Children, 55*(2), 16–20.

Isbell, R. T., & Raines, S. C. (2007). *Creativity and the arts with young children* (2nd ed.). Clifton Park, NY: Delmar Cengage Learning.

Jacobs, G., & Crowley, K. (2010). *Reaching standards & beyond in kindergarten.* Thousand Oaks, CA: Corwin Press, & Washington, DC: NAEYC.

Kellogg, R. (1959). *What children scribble and why.* Palo Alto, CA: National Press Books.

Kellogg, R., & O'Dell, S. (1967). *The psychology of children's art.* New York: Random House.

Kohl, M. A. (2003, Spring). Art with toddlers and twos? Face the fear! *Early Years, 25*(1), 2–3.

Koster, J. (2009). *Growing artists: Teaching art to young children* (4th ed.). Clifton Park, NY: Wadsworth Cengage Learning.

Libby, W. M. L. (2000). *Using art to make art: Creative activities using masterpieces.* Clifton Park, NY: Delmar Cengage Learning.

Mayesky, M. (2009). *Creative activities for young children* (9th ed.). Clifton Park, NY: Wadsworth Cengage Learning.

The Metropolitan Museum of Art. (1959). *How to look at paintings: A guide for children.* New York: Author.

Mitchell, A. (2006, November). From our president. *Young Children, 61*(6), 6.

Mulcahey, C. (2009, July). Providing rich art activities for young children. *Young Children, 64*(4), 107–112.

Nilson, B. (2011). *Week by Week* (5th ed.). Clifton Park, NY: Wadsworth Cengage Learning.

Reyner, A. (2002, November–December). Creative connections. *Early Childhood News, 14*(6), 12.

Schirrmacher, R., & Fox, J. E. (2009). *Art and creative development for young children* (6th ed.). Clifton Park, NY: Wadsworth Cengage Learning.

Szyba, C. M. (1999, January). Why do some teachers resist offering appropriate, open-ended art activities for young children? *Young Children, 54*(1), 16–20.

Taunton & Colbert. (2000). Art in the early childhood classroom. In N. J. Yelland (Ed.). *Promoting meaningful learning.* Washington, DC: NAEYC.

Williams, D. (1995). *Teaching mathematics through children's art.* Portsmouth, NH: Heinemann.

● ●

Additional information and resources on early childhood curriculum can be found on the Education CourseMate website for this book. Go to **www.CengageBrain.com** to register your access code.

chapter 9

Sensory Centers

Objectives

After Studying This Chapter, You Should Be Able To:

- Discuss the importance of providing young children with opportunities to use and develop their five senses.

- Describe water, sand, and mud play activities and outline the purposes and objectives of these sensory activities.

- Identify the appropriate types of blocks for young children and discuss the developmental stages of block building.

- List the appropriate equipment and materials to have in the woodworking center and provide the purposes and objectives of this sensory area.

- Discuss nutrition and developmentally appropriate cooking experiences in an early childhood classroom.

- Plan and implement sensory activities that address many curriculum areas.

Overview

● ●

We all learn about the world through our senses. Young children learn best through **sensory experiences** that offer them opportunities for free exploration in a variety of curriculum areas and through repeated explorations. The sensory area gives them multiple possibilities to do this. The importance of sensory activities for young children "cannot be emphasized enough. Such activities are crucial for brain development because it is through exploration with the body, and the senses that children's earliest learning takes place " (Essa, 2011).

As you read this chapter, focus on how children see, hear, feel, touch, and taste the world around them. Observe carefully how the children in an early education setting make choices and react to the environment. The quality of the environment also contributes to the sensory development of children. Ask yourself if the classroom is "their room." Is it set up so that they can claim ownership? Is it giving them hands-on knowledge about their world?

These children have the ability to take in and make sense of information obtained from their senses: *visual*—to see, *auditory*—to listen, *olfactory*—to smell, *tactile*—to touch, and *gustatory*—to taste. We have discussed this previously, and this chapter uses that information as a foundation on which to build additional developmentally appropriate experiences. The main *sensory centers* in the early childhood curriculum— water-sand-mud play, blocks, woodworking, and cooking experiences—can be indoors or outdoors, separate from or a part of other learning centers. These areas can be changed easily as the children's developmental needs change and the children's sensory involvement with their environment changes as well.

> Children and adults inhabit different sensory worlds. Imagine a young infant's world of touch and taste—a world where you see and hear more than you look and listen—where you, in effect, think with your body and actions, and your whole body is your only means of reacting. (Gestwicki, 2011)

Every day the early education classroom should be filled with sensory activities that are sticky, squishy, slippery, smooth, heavy, light, soft, loud, crunchy, colorful, aromatic, and flavorful. Sensory experiences are exciting because each child can use the materials differently while involving multiple senses. **Sensory awareness**, the use of the senses, promotes self-discovery. It is another way the body gives the mind information (Gordon & Browne, 2011). In addition, children learn to cooperate and work together around the sensory table, the sand box, the block area, the woodworking bench, the cooling table, and outdoors.

> Daily interactions with young children should be peppered with statements and questions that show the wonder and value of the sensory qualities of the environment. Adults cannot verbalize these qualities to the children if they do not experience them themselves. (Koster, 2009)

As you continue through this chapter, sharpen *your* sensory awareness and observe how the sensory centers interact and interconnect with the total curriculum.

sensory experiences Experiences that use the senses and offer opportunities for free exploration in a variety of curriculum areas.

sensory awareness The use of the senses.

© Cengage Learning

These children are learning about their world through the senses of sight, smell, and touch.

Water, Sand, and Mud Play

Water, sand, and mud play can be an individual or a small group activity. Projects can be done indoors and outdoors. There is no right or wrong way to play with these multisensory materials. They are used in many different ways by the children using them. Even very young children enjoy splashing, pouring, squishing, and mixing. Water, sand, and mud can relate to any theme, lesson plan, or curriculum web.

Water play can be lively and at the same time relaxing. Young children enjoy running through a sprinkler, playing at the water table, bathing dolls in a plastic tub, filling and emptying water containers, and watering plants. It is fun, and children are naturally drawn to water play.

Stephenson (2001) clarifies the importance of outdoor water play for toddlers:

> Looking through George's eyes revealed to me the wonder of this strange sloppy substance that uncontrollably slides through fingers and disappears irretrievably into sand. Babies spend many hours handling solid objects yet have relatively limited opportunities to experiment with liquids, so it is not surprising that water is such a deeply fascinating material.

Sand play is irresistible to young children. Starting with dry sand in the sandpile, sand tray, or sand table, children can spoon, pour, measure, dig, and shovel. They add props as they construct cities, farms, and airports, and they love to drive trucks through and over sandy roads.

Adding water to sand creates opportunities for additional sensory learning to take place. Combining props such as sunglasses, hats, towels, and an umbrella can turn the outdoor sand area into a beach. Have you tried adding live small crabs in a sand bucket to the "beach"? The children will be fascinated.

Mud play is a sensory activity like no other. After a rain, the playground takes on an added dimension. It is special. What you and the children do with the mud offers many possibilities. Try experimenting with a bucketful of mud. Make mud pies or "pizza," for example. Mix the mud to make paint. Brush the mud on different textures of paper. Dirt taken from different areas of the playground shows different pigmentations, which the children themselves will point out to you.

© Cengage Learning

Sand play is irresistible to young children. They can spoon, pour, measure, dig, and shovel this fascinating substance.

Nimmo and Hallett (2008) offer another suggestion for exploration with mud:

> Gardens by their very nature involve mud—a phenomenon that simultaneously inspires delight in young children and a wonderfully interesting reaction from adults. Mud inspires children to wonder about the transformation of passive dirt into an almost sinister substance. It resists muscles when a child is in the thick of it and speaks to the child's need to explore nature.

This child-centered activity of mud play offers children another way to experience their world. "When so much of our good earth is being covered with wall to wall concrete, it is imperative to save more than a spot of earth for growing children" (Hill, 1977). Jensen and Bullard (2002) reminisce

> about the pleasures of creating mud pies and mud sandwiches and holding tea parties with a variety of mud treats. We [remember] the deep sense of satisfaction in baking mud pies for the entire neighborhood .... Our children are affected by traffic, lack of space, and schedules that

allow little time for outdoor play . . . . [As a result,] the idea of a dramatic play mud center outdoors [at a child care center or school] emerges from the interests of both children and adults.

PURPOSES AND OBJECTIVES

When you plan opportunities for children to grow developmentally and practice skills in the water, sand, and mud learning centers, you are providing relevant meaningful learning experiences. Encourage children to do the following:

DEVELOP INQUIRY-BASED LEARNING.   Investigate to gather information about water, sand, mud, and rocks. Ask questions. How does water get into the faucets? What is mud? What is a rock? Why are some rocks big and others little? What makes sand? What makes sand gritty? According to Ogu and Schmidt (2009), "Because inquiry is such an intrinsic human learning strategy, it makes sense for teachers to use an inquiry-based approach in their curriculum."

PERFORM SIMPLE EXPERIMENTS.   Predict whether objects will sink or float in plain water—try rocks, marbles, Styrofoam, ping-pong balls, coins, corks, and sponges. Add salt to the water to see whether the objects will sink or float. Explore various types of sand with magnets by running the magnet through the sand to see whether any grains stick to the magnet, or search for hidden metal objects buried in the sand. Discover how long it takes for water to evaporate outside on a hot or a cold day. Examine dirt using magnifying glasses and sifters.

MEASURE, COMPARE, AND PROBLEM SOLVE.   Provide empty cardboard milk cartons, such as half-pint, pint, quart, and half-gallon containers, for children to pour from one carton to another to discover how much water each one holds. Measure equal amounts of wet and dry sand and put them on opposite sides of a balance scale to determine which is heavier. After a rain, ask the children to problem solve how to get the water out of a mud puddle.

PLAY CREATIVELY.   Provide soapy water, sponges, and washable toys for the children to clean. Experiment with sand molds and determine whether dry sand or wet sand works best. Have boat races with children, problem solving how to get their boats across the water-filled tub. (Hint: Children can either blow on the boats to make them move or pull them across with a string.) Make designs in the sand with sand combs made from pliable plastic containers such as clean bleach or detergent bottles. Put out buckets and sponges to scrub the playground equipment. Set up a "truck wash" for sand box construction toys. Build underwater cities with Legos.

DEVELOP NEW VOCABULARY. Introduce words such as *pour, fill, flow, spray, squirt, splatter, empty, full, shallow, deep, measure, absorb, droplets, sift, sink, float, evaporate, melt,* and *dissolve.*

DEMONSTRATE NEW CONCEPTS.   Demonstrate how gravity causes water to flow downhill through tubes and funnels, how water takes the shape of its container, and how the liquid form of water can change into a solid by freezing in ice trays, paper cups, or milk cartons. Offer indoor and outdoor water play often.

Give each child unstructured time to spend experimenting with sand.

Offer indoor and outdoor water play often.

THE TEACHER'S ROLE

The following suggestions should be helpful to you in defining the teacher's role in water, sand, and mud play:

Sand play offers children a unique sensory activity that lets them experience their world in a different way.

- Observe, ask open-ended questions, and make comments to show support and interest. "The children learn what it means to answer an open-ended question: there are no right or wrong answers, all ideas are accepted, valued, and appreciated and become part of the learning process" (Ogu & Schmidt, 2009).
- Encourage children to talk about what they are doing and what is happening.
- Support children's exploration by providing space for messy activities and materials that can be fully explored without concern about waste (Feeney, Moravcik, Nolte, & Christensen, 2010).
- Structure the centers so children have interesting and challenging materials to stimulate their water and sand play.
- Depending on the type and size of the area used for the water and sand activities, decide when and if you should limit the number of children playing at one time.
- Offer indoor and outdoor water play *often*. "The sensory table encourages children's development of skills through natural exploration and discovery. . . . Observing children play at the sensory table can give teachers more information about how individuals react to sensory stimulation" (Hunter, 2008).
- Take your cues from the children on what to change and when to change it.
- Have smocks, aprons, and changes of clothes available for the children—and the teacher too!
- Remember the safety and health rules of water, sand, and mud play: (1) Never leave children unattended around any type of water; (2) empty the water tub or table daily; (3) sanitize the water, wet sand toys, and tub each day with a fresh bleach solution of one tablespoon bleach to one quart of water in a spray bottle, and rinse with running water (Miller, 1994); and (4) check the sand and mud play areas each day for foreign objects, such as glass, that should be removed.
- Discuss with older children the importance of water and the shortages that will arise if we do not work to preserve this resource. Get the children's families involved, too.

PROPS AND MATERIALS

The following is a suggested list of props and materials to include in water, sand, and mud play. It is best to use dry, finely textured sand (available at toy stores and lumber, building, or garden supply stores). Use plastic props and containers, if possible, because metal will rust. "Take note of which materials the children seem to use most and start with just a few simple props, such as plastic bottles or dolls to wash. Gradually add props to introduce a range of new possibilities" (Dodge, Colker, & Heroman, 2008).

Suggested Props

Basters	Rotary eggbeaters
Eyedroppers	Spray bottles
Funnels	Cookie cutters
Measuring cups and spoons	Gelatin molds
Scoops	Salt shakers
Sieves	Scale

Colander
Straws
Slotted spoon
Buckets, pails, and tubs
Magnifying glass
Plastic tubing
Child-size brooms and dust
   pan

Sand timer
Sand combs
Spoons and shovels
Bowls and pitchers
Paintbrushes
Sponges
Pulleys
Bubbles

Suggested Containers

Sand and water table
Wading pool
Dishpan
Bathtub

Outdoor sandpile
Wash tubs
Boxes
Infant tub

Suggested Substitutes for Sand

Seashells
Washed gravel
Cork pieces

Styrofoam pieces
Birdseed

WHY I TEACH YOUNG CHILDREN

I can't imagine myself in any other profession. When you work with young children, you are reminded of their innocence and their unique outlook on life. You never know what you may say or do that will affect them for the rest of their lives. I never realized until Andrew, "the first-grader," stopped by for a visit. I had him in my class when he was three years old. I asked him if he remembered me. I really did not think he would because it had been over three years since I had seen him. He said he did remember me. He told me in such a sweet manner that I was still his favorite teacher ever! Andrew said I made him feel safe when his Mom was at work. He remembered that he could have his blanket anytime he needed it. At that moment, I was reminded how teachers leave lasting impressions no matter the age.

—Barbara Batista

Blocks

When you are setting up an early childhood environment, one of the first items you should purchase is blocks. Many teachers consider blocks to be the most used and the most useful materials in a program for young children. "They are the most versatile and open-ended of the nonconsumable materials in the early childhood setting, and well worth the investment of their price" (Petersen, 2003). Along with selecting blocks, you should plan carefully what type and quantity you choose, the way in which the blocks will be organized, and how you will arrange the physical environment to ensure developmentally appropriate activities with blocks.

Unit blocks are the most popular variety used in early education environments. Children continue to use them as they grow from infancy to primary age. Blocks were first introduced in an educational setting by Friedrich Froebel in 1837 (Tunks, 2009). The sturdy hardwood blocks used today were designed by Carolyn Pratt in the early 1890s. The individual unit block is 13⅛ inches by 2¾ inches by 5½ inches, and all other blocks are multiples or divisions of this basic size (see Figure 9–1).

The cylinders and curved blocks are of similar width and thickness. Pratt's blocks were of

smooth, natural-finish hardwood—free from details or color. In addition, she designed unpainted wooden people, 6 inches tall, in the form of family members and community workers, to be used with the unit blocks. She omitted painted details on any of her toys because she wanted children to apply their own imagination in their use of the materials. (Beaty, 2009)

Hollow blocks are also made of wood and are larger than unit blocks. "The basic square is 51.2 inches by 11 inches by 11 inches. There are five other pieces in a set: a half-square, a double square, two lengths of flat board, and a ramp. Hollow blocks are open on the sides so they can be carried more easily" (Dodge, Colker, & Heroman, 2008).

Playing with shaving cream is a fun sensory activity!

unit blocks Hardwood blocks used in early education environments, especially in block center play.

hollow blocks Wooden blocks larger than unit blocks and open on the sides.

FIGURE 9–1
Unit blocks.

SQUARE or HALF-UNIT   UNIT

DOUBLE-UNIT   QUADRUPLE-UNIT

PILLAR   CURVE

SMALL TRIANGLE   LARGE TRIANGLE

SMALL CYLINDER   LARGE CYLINDER

FIGURE 9–2
Hollow blocks.

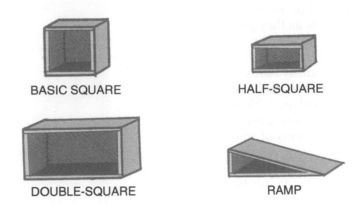

BASIC SQUARE   HALF-SQUARE

DOUBLE-SQUARE   RAMP

Hollow blocks require additional space both indoors and outdoors for optimal use by the children (see Figure 9–2).

Other types of blocks appropriate for young children's play are: shoe-box size cardboard blocks, some of which are designed to look like bricks; small, wooden, colored ones that can be used as table blocks; log-type building blocks; interlocking blocks, such as Legos® or Bristle Blocks®; and foam blocks and large brightly colored lightweight blocks for infants' and toddlers' first experiences with block play.

The unit blocks should be placed on low shelves according to shape and size for organization and storage. Label the shelves with the outlines of the shapes and sizes of the different types of blocks. This assists children with cleanup and emphasizes classification. Place blocks other than the unit or hollow blocks in plastic containers or boxes clearly labeled for identification (see Figure 9–3).

Block play is noisy, so the center should be placed next to other active areas, such as dramatic play. The block area should be clearly defined on three sides. This offers protection and security for the children's activities. An area rug or carpeting should be on the floor to absorb some of the noise as well as to offer comfort to the children playing (Dodge, Colker, & Heroman, 2008).

> If children are taught to build slightly away from the shelves, fighting and stress will be reduced as other youngsters also try to reach in for blocks. The construction area needs to be shielded from traffic to discourage children from delivering a kick at some treasured structure as they pass by. (Hendrick, 2003)

FIGURE 9–3
Visually label block shelves to show the children where and how to replace the blocks.

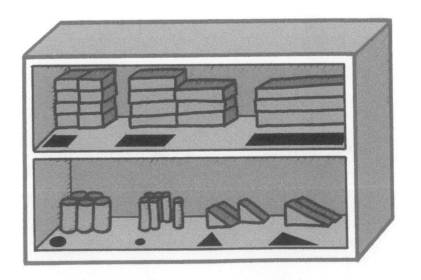

DEVELOPMENTAL STAGES OF BLOCK BUILDING

"Current interest in problem solving and brain research provides new support for integrating curriculum using blocks in both preschool and primary grades" (Starns, 2002). There are developmental stages in the way children use and play with blocks: First, infants and toddlers carry blocks from place to place. They are learning about how the blocks feel, how heavy they are, and how many they can carry at once (Nielsen, 2006). This may not look much like block building, but it is a necessary stage.

Next, the children pile blocks one on top of another. In the beginning there is an irregular pattern to the stacking, then the blocks begin to form a tower, which often falls when additional blocks are added. Repetition of this activity will help children know how many blocks they can add before the tower will fall (toddlers).

At the same time children are making block towers, they are also trying to make block rows. They lay blocks close together, side by side, or edge to edge (flat rows suggest roads, so adding small trucks and cars is appropriate). The children may also space the blocks, alternating the sizes as they place them in rows (toddlers and three-year-olds).

Each of these steps in developmental block building includes repetition (see Figure 9–4). Practicing their accomplishments over and over is important to young children as they get more comfortable with using blocks. The next stage for children

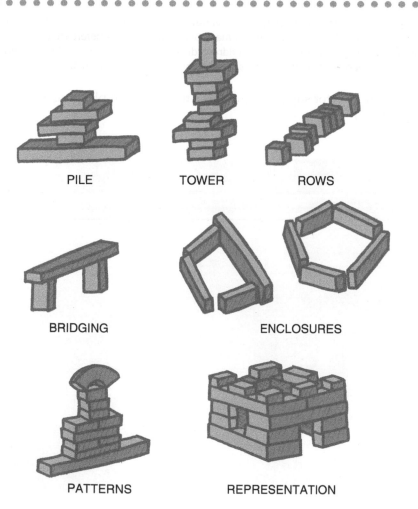

PILE   TOWER   ROWS

BRIDGING   ENCLOSURES

PATTERNS   REPRESENTATION

FIGURE 9–4

Examples of the developmental stages of block building.

is bridging. This is observable by watching children set up two blocks, leaving space between them, and roofing that space with another block. Through repetition, the structures increase in complexity and difficulty (three- and four-year-olds).

Enclosures made by children, sometimes done simultaneously with bridging, involve putting blocks together to enclose a space. Placing four blocks together so that a space is completely enclosed is not a simple task (two-, three-, and four-year-olds). Patterns and designs begin to appear when children feel comfortable enough with blocks to build balanced and decorative patterns (four-year-olds). Finally, representation occurs with the naming of block constructions and the combination of all elements of block building. Children (four-year-olds and older) demonstrate that they are aware of their world and their place in it with these structures (Hirsch, 1993).

The addition of miniature people representing various cultures, doll furniture, small animals, cars, trucks, boats, barges, canoes, sleds, airplanes, trains, and buses extends children's block play. For self-selection by the children, put each group of small items in clearly labeled (with pictures and words) plastic tubs or boxes near the unit blocks. This will also help with cleanup.

Books and pictures of different buildings from all around the world can stimulate children to build all kinds of structures. Older children create elaborate highways, bridges, and ramps. They add traffic signs, "Do Not Touch!" signs, and other kinds of labels.

The use of developmentally appropriate guidance is critical in the block center. It is difficult for young children to take turns or clean up blocks when they are absorbed in their vision for a specific block structure. This sensory experience involves the total child.

> We give subtle messages to children about how we expect them to behave by the surroundings we plan for them. We can prevent many behavior problems before they ever begin by careful planning, by understanding children's developmental needs, and by creating a perfect match between their needs and the settings around them. (Miller, 2010)

(See Figure 9–5 for suggested guidance techniques in planning a block center for young children.)

The teacher in this classroom has provided time, space, materials, and freedom for children to develop creative experiences with blocks.

© Cengage Learning

Suggested Guidance Techniques

- Supply an adequate number and enough different shapes of blocks and a variety of materials for the number of children using them.
- Provide ample space. Help prevent children from knocking over constructions made by other children. Mark off one to two feet of space away from the perimeter of the block shelves with colored masking tape. Explain that structures cannot be built between the shelves and the tape. This will help prevent conflicts.
- Use open shelves, not baskets or bins, for easy access to the blocks. This helps to show the children that the block center is a place with a purpose and a sense of order.
- Guide children to match the blocks to the shapes on the shelves to put them away.
- Help children understand that they should take down their *own* buildings using only their hands.
- Have children put blocks away before leaving the block center. Children need guidance and sometimes teacher's physical assistance in putting blocks and other classroom materials away.
- Preserve structures, if possible, from day to day if the children make a request to do so. This shows respect for their buildings and roadways.
- Have a camera available for photographs. Taking photographs and making sketches are important to preserve the children's block designs.
- Encourage the children to make signs for their structures.
- Approach each difficulty in the block area with a developmentally appropriate response.

FIGURE 9–5
Suggested guidance techniques. Source: Adapted from Tunks (2009), Alexander (2008), and Nielsen (2006).

PURPOSES AND OBJECTIVES

When you provide time, space, materials, and freedom for children to gain sensory and creative experiences with blocks, you will encourage children to

- strengthen such perceptions of space as under, below, in front of, behind, above, inside, and outside.
- develop concepts of big/little, more than/less than, equal to, and taller/shorter.
- develop concepts of shape, depth, width, height, length, fractions, and multiples.
- become aware of whole-part relationships.
- practice balancing, stabilizing, and matching skills.
- classify according to shapes, sizes, colors, textures, and types.
- develop symbolic representations as the blocks become whatever the children want them to be.
- experiment and problem solve through trial and error.
- create architectural forms by bridging and making tunnels, ramps, and grids.
- develop awareness of scientific principles such as gravity, levers, pulleys, and rollers.
- improve inquiry skills by asking questions and discovering answers.
- make use of imagery and recall by reproducing and recreating forms from past experiences.
- strengthen large and small muscle skills and eye-hand coordination.
- develop oral language skills.
- participate in cooperative block play with peers while combining ideas and solving problems.
- Release emotions in an acceptable way.

Young children participate in cooperative block play with peers while combining ideas and solving problems.

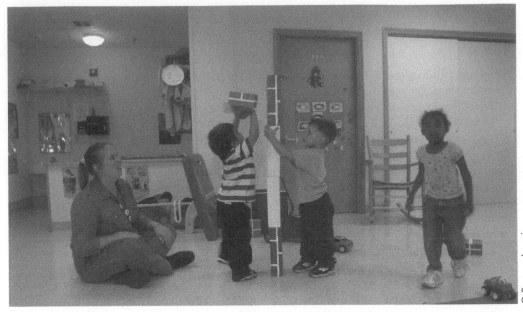

THE TEACHER'S ROLE

● Let the parents know what the children are accomplishing through their block play. Invite the parents to participate in the block center when they drop off or pick up their children. Provide opportunities for a family member who is in construction or architectural work to share his or her time and talent with the children.

● Observe developmental levels of the children. This knowledge will enable you to know when to introduce hollow blocks, other blocks, or accessories to the block center.

● Keep in mind the natural stages of block building as you support the children's efforts to gain confidence and to feel comfortable with blocks.

● Take photographs often of the block constructions. This offers an alternative to leaving the structures up for extra long periods of time if you do not have the space to do so. The children can have photos to remember their special buildings. This will also help the children understand that you value their efforts. The photos can lead to children dictating stories about their creations. Perhaps they will recreate them in the art center as well.

Take photographs or videos of children and their block constructions.

● Set limits on the number of children in the block center at one time, and clearly label the rule. Define a few other basic rules, such as blocks are not for throwing or hitting. If the building project continues to grow, expand the space to another center so more children can be involved. This will eliminate some difficulties before they start. For example, put hard hats in the block center to indicate how many children can be in the block center at one time.

● Guide children who never use the block center into developing a project that uses blocks.

● Help children plan cooperatively and recognize the problems they have encountered and solved. This will contribute to positive self-esteem development.

● Remember blocks are for all ages. The primary-grade children will often surprise you with their exploration of structural engineering by testing the stability of their buildings.

● Watch for **teachable** moments that provide an opportunity for scaffolding. Help the children develop new skills in block construction by building on their existing skills.

> During the years children are in the primary grades, their thinking abilities change considerably.... [D]evelopmental changes are reflected in primary age children's approach to constructive play and block-building activities.... Negotiation, problem-solving, and collaboration are characteristic of the social constructive play of primary-age children. (Wellhousen & Kieff, 2001)

Woodworking

The **woodworking center** in an early childhood environment has been a part of many early education classrooms for a number of years. This activity center provides young children with many different sensory and three-dimensional experiences.

Unfortunately, in some settings the woodworking center is often nonexistent or underused. Think about how and when you can successfully incorporate carpentry into your curriculum. Boys and girls alike can develop physical, cognitive, social, and language skills through woodworking activities (see Figure 9–6).

woodworking center An activity center providing many different sensory and three-dimensional experiences.

PURPOSES AND OBJECTIVES

When you include woodworking experiences in early education, you will encourage children to

● develop and coordinate large and small muscles.
● improve eye-hand coordination.
● use wood as a medium of creative expression.
● communicate, plan, and work cooperatively with others.
● use woodworking as an emotional release and means of nonverbal expression.
● focus on the process while mastering the skills of sanding, gluing, hammering, nailing, sawing, and drilling to gain a sense of self-esteem.
● sharpen their senses through the smells, textures, and sounds of woodworking.
● learn to sustain interest and overcome frustration successfully.
● extend concepts of experimenting, creating, investigating, and problem solving into other areas of the curriculum.

FIGURE 9–6
The woodworking center provides sensory experiences for young children.

> Woodworking provides children with opportunities to become aware of textures and forms. Senses are sharpened as children explore the field of construction. Fingers explore many textures, ears pick out the sounds of different tools, noses test the different smells of various woods, and eyes see the many hues of wood. (Mayesky, 2006)

Figure 9–7 illustrates how woodworking equipment can be stored.

THE TEACHER'S ROLE

The following guidelines can assist you through planning, setting up, and evaluating a woodworking center for young children.

● Before beginning carpentry with real tools, plan for the children to have many spontaneous play experiences with bits of wood used as building blocks, match tools to shapes in puzzles, and (in the math center) pair up photos of tools and supplies, such as hammer and nails and screwdriver and screws.
● Be sure to allow plenty of time to explore.
● If you have not worked with tools or wood before, practice *before* you supervise the children. Ask a colleague or parent to share knowledge with you and the children.

FIGURE 9–7
Children should properly replace
woodworking tools after using
them.

Practice using all the tools yourself until you are comfortable with them. If you are a female teacher competently using tools, you become a role model, especially for girls.

● When starting, be sure you (or another teacher) are available the entire time to closely supervise and observe the children. Limit the center to one child at a time. Add a second child later, when all children are comfortable with the tools.

   ● Place this center away from quiet centers. Many teachers like to take woodworking outdoors or into the hallway right outside the classroom door.

   ● Allow enough time for the children to explore the materials at their own pace.

   ● The woodworking center requires specific rules that are consistently reinforced:

      Goggles must be worn at all times.

      Tools must be kept at the workbench, and they are to be used only for the purpose for which they are designed. (Help the children learn to use tools properly.) Return the tools to the tool kit or rack when finished.

      Use only one tool at a time.

      When two children are working at the workbench, let one stand on each side with plenty of space between them. Safety is always the first consideration when children are using tools. They must learn where to put their hands when hammering and sawing.

A child should have plenty of time in the woodworking center to explore the materials at her own pace.

● Remember, it is the *process* that is important, not the result.

● To ensure success for children from the beginning, start with white glue and wood. Then gradually add hammers, roofing nails, soft wood, and a saw.

● If a child is using a hammer for the first time, you can pound several nails halfway into the wood to get him started. Roofing nails with large heads are the easiest for young children to use.

● Children may want to paint the projects they have made. Allow time for completion of this activity, too.

● Evaluate throughout each step of the process. Planning, initiating, and evaluating will help you and the children be successful in the woodworking center.

● Essa (2011) suggests additional guidelines:

   For very young children, wood can be replaced by thick Styrofoam packing material, which is much softer and easier to saw . . . . Older preschoolers who have gained proficiency in using the tools and purposefully made objects in wood will be interested in adding props. These should include round objects that suggest wheels, such as wooden spools, slices of large dowels, bottle caps, the metal ends from 6-ounce frozen juice containers, and a variety of other items.

EQUIPMENT AND MATERIALS

Use *real* tools. They are much safer than toy ones. You may have to remind children to put on *safety goggles* before they start working with wood. A list of suggested equipment and materials follows:

Workbench—sturdy in construction, with vise or C-clamps attached, approximately 24 inches high or as high as the children's waists; a sturdy table can also be used.

Hammers—small claw hammers weighing 8 to 12 ounces.

Nails—roofing nails and assorted other sizes. The nails can be set out in small foil pie plates to keep the sizes from getting mixed up. The pie plates can be nailed to a long board to prevent spilling (Mayesky, 2006).

Soft wood—white pine, cedar, spruce, and redwood are light in weight and take nails easily. Lumber companies and construction sites are sources for soft wood scraps.

Glue

Cross-cut saw—approximately 18 inches long

C-clamps or vise

Braces and bits

Sandpaper or sanding sponges

Ruler or square

Tape measures

Pencils and paper

Toolbox

Pegboard tool rack or tool cabinet to store items

Markers, crayons, and thinned tempera paint

Screws and screwdrivers are difficult for young children to use. Perhaps you can add these to activities for older children along with wood files, planes, levels, and an eggbeater-style hand drill with two or three different size bits.

Nutrition and Cooking Experiences in Early Education

A child can feel responsible, independent, and successful when involved in cooking activities.

Why do you think nutrition education in an early childhood classroom is necessary or important? Essa (2011) comments, "Because food is a basic human need and so often provides great pleasure, nutrition education and cooking experiences should be an integral part of the curriculum . . . . You will need to tailor nutrition concepts to the ages and ability levels of the children, your own knowledge about nutrition, and the depth in which you plan to approach the subject." Introducing nutrition concepts at an early age can influence a lifetime of food choices and balances.

nutrition The study of foods and how it is used in the body.

nutrients Substances found in foods that provide for the growth, development, maintenance, and repair of the body.

NUTRITION

Nutrition is the study of food and how it is used by the body. **Nutrients** are substances found in foods that provide for the growth, development, maintenance, and repair of the body (Robertson, 2010). The body has three main uses for nutrients: as sources of energy, as materials for the growth and maintenance of body tissue, and to regulate body processes.

Additionally, Marotz (2009) offers the following nutritional concepts relating to young children:

● Children should have food to grow and to have healthy bodies.
● Nutrients come from foods. It is these nutrients that allow children to grow and be healthy.
● A variety of foods should be eaten each day. No one food provides all of the needed nutrients.
● Foods should be carefully handled before they are eaten to ensure that they are healthful and safe.
● Snacks should contribute to the child's daily food needs and educational experiences.

obesity An excess percentage of bodyweight due to fat, which puts people at risk for health problems.

Children should be exposed to and encouraged to accept a variety of foods from each of the food groups suggested by the USDA Food Guide Pyramid. This pyramid was created by the U. S. Department of Agriculture (USDA) to help children improve their food intake choices and the amounts needed to help them meet nutritional guidelines. The USDA offers a wealth of information designed to introduce children to food and its impact on the body (see Figure 9–8). Visit the USDA website at http://www.mypyramid.gov.

The importance of good nutrition in the lives of young children has become a national issue. There has been a great deal in the news recently about how obesity is affecting many children.

> Obesity in young children cannot be ignored. Prevention is always the most effective method. However, promising results can also be obtained by taking action when a child is young and still in the process of establishing lifelong eating and activity habits. (Marotz, 2009)

What is **obesity?** The American Academy of Pediatrics (AAP) explains that obesity is an excess percentage of bodyweight due to fat, which puts people at risk for many health problems. In children older than two years of age, obesity is assessed by a measure called the body mass index (BMI). A pediatrician is the best source for information regarding BMI and its application. For more information, visit to the AAP website at: http://www.aap.org.

The USDA and the AAP guidelines recommend that children, teachers, and families find a balance between food intake and physical activity. They advise that older infants and toddlers should be provided with at least 30 minutes of play a day, though not all at once. Preschoolers and older children should have at least 60 minutes of active play each day.

Allowing time for physical activities and exercise is a necessary part of creating nutritional policies to protect children's health and well being (Robertson, 2010). (Chapter 10 offers physical/movement activities for children, parents, and teachers to do together.)

COOKING

© Cengage Learning

Time spent outdoors contributes to a young child's fitness and appropriate weight.

Cooking activities give children firsthand experiences that involve them in the process from planning to cleanup. A sense of accomplishment, the thrill of experimentation, and an awareness of taste, touch, and smell are all rewards of cooking experiences. Early positive encounters with food also help children gain the knowledge they will use to form lifelong eating habits. Just watch what infants and toddlers can do with a banana.

FIGURE 9-8
Food Guide Pyramid for Children.

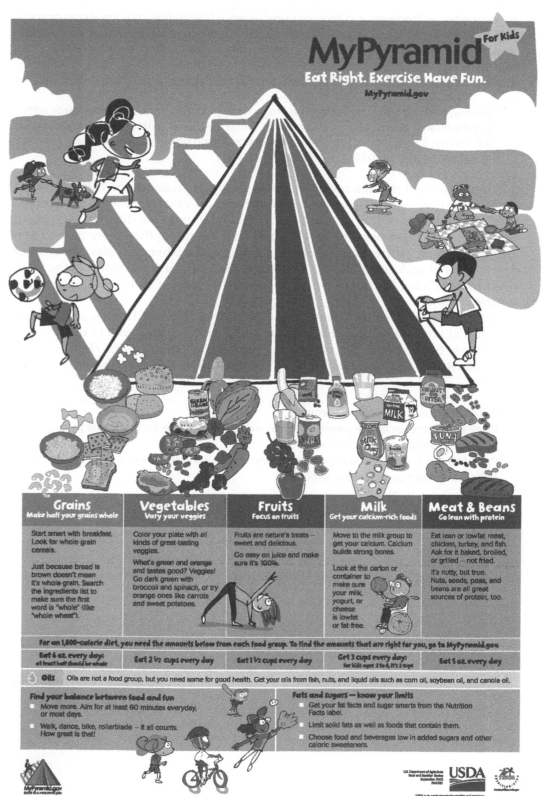

By including opportunities for children to cook, you offer additional times for them to practice math (comparing sizes, shapes, and measurements; one-to-one correspondence; fractions; and temperature), science (vegetables that are stems or roots, fruit that grows on trees, what happens to sugar on hot cereal), reading and writing (making lists and using recipes and rebus charts), social studies (learning more about their world and community resources), following directions, putting things in sequence, and learning to communicate and cooperate with each other.

> You may find that some children will need to go through a similar "messing about" stage with any significantly new type of cooking material, just as they do when they first encounter a new art material. So be prepared to allow this exploratory period before you introduce any new type of cooking experience to young children. (Colker, 2005)

It is important that the cooking projects are appropriate for the children's ages, interests, and understanding and that these experiences value cultural diversity. Foods from other cultures offer opportunities for children to taste the different ingredients and flavors. This also helps to develop their understanding that many of the foods they eat are both different *and* similar to those eaten in other countries. On an even deeper level of understanding, children can relate to the fact that many of the foods eaten in the United States are greatly influenced by all the cultures represented in America today.

Principles of developmentally appropriate practice can link cooking-related activities at home to school activities. You could meet with parents to discuss relationships between family and classroom goals of working together. Here are some suggestions for involving families from Marotz (2009) and other early childhood teachers:

● Ask them to assist in planning menus.
● Place weekly menus on the parent board, as well as suggestions for foods that provide nutritional additions to each menu.
● Provide a report on the food experiences done in class and ask the families for feedback on their child's reaction to these experiences.

Cooking activities give children the opportunity for firsthand experiences when they are involved in the entire process.

© Cengage Learning

- Invite families to attend a potluck (food sharing) dinner and bring special ethnic or traditional foods unique to their culture.
- Help in developing guidelines for acceptable foods that families could bring to the center/school to celebrate a birthday or other holiday.
- Help families understand how they can foster positive eating habits at home. Encourage good eating behaviors, such as always sitting down for snacks and meals.
- Discuss ways to prevent obesity and why it is important to do so.
- Remind families about ways to involve their child with food in the home, such as helping prepare food with age-appropriate, safe kitchen tasks and sharing in cleanup activities.

PURPOSES AND OBJECTIVES

When you include cooking activities in an early childhood environment, you will encourage children to

- feel responsible, independent, and successful.
- learn about nutrition, the food groups, and related food skills, such as how to plan a healthy meal.
- work independently or cooperatively in small groups (the younger the children, the smaller the group should be).
- complete tasks from preparation to cleanup.
- learn about new foods and become aware of recipes from cultures other than their own.
- learn about different careers that involve foods and cooking (farmers, truckers, grocers, bakers, and chefs, for example).
- introduce new vocabulary and concepts, such as *measure, melt, knead, shake, sift, spread, baste, peel, hull, grind, grate, chop, slice,* and *boil.*
- develop beginning reading skills with rebus charts and simple recipe cards.
- learn math and science concepts.
- observe how cooking changes the ingredients added to a recipe.
- develop small and large muscle control and eye-hand coordination.
- extend cooking into dramatic play, puppetry, art, and other centers.

(See Figure 9–9, Skill Development in the Kitchen.)

THE TEACHER'S ROLE

- Emphasize the positive aspects of healthy eating rather than the harmful effects of unhealthy eating.
- Give children many opportunities to taste foods that are low in fat, sodium, and added sugars. Taste foods high in vitamins, minerals and fiber.
- Plan cooking on days when you have another adult helping you, such as an assistant, a parent, or a volunteer. Supervision is critical to ensure safety for the children.
- Review the food allergies of the children. Provide alternative activities for those children who are allergic to certain foods.
- Be sensitive to the beliefs of the families in your program concerning foods. Some families may have restrictions on what foods they can eat.
- Integrate cooking opportunities into the theme and lesson plan. Cooking is a creative sensory activity and not necessarily a separate center. Plan appropriate transition activities into and out of each experience.
- Explain the limits and rules to the children, such as their hands should be washed with soap and water before and after they prepare foods, smocks or aprons (not those used for art projects) should be worn while cooking, and fingers and utensils should be kept out of their mouths while they are cooking. Let the children help you establish other rules.

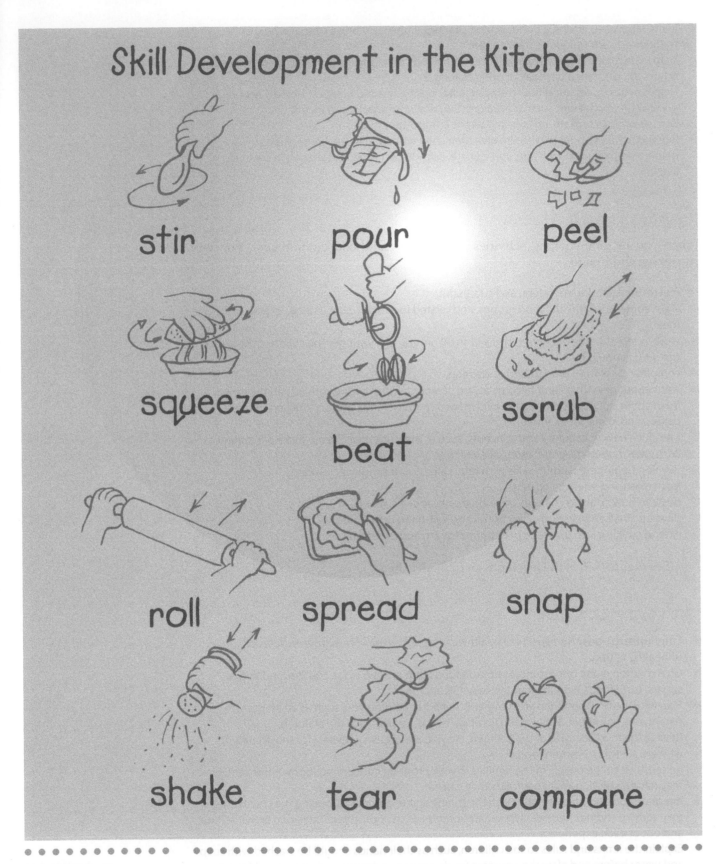

FIGURE 9–9
Rebus Chart: Skill Development in the Kitchen

- Take plenty of time to introduce foods to the children.
- Plan how to introduce the activities and how to plan appropriate transitions out of each activity.
- At first, and with younger children, attempt food activities that require no cooking. The children can mix ingredients together and feel successful when they taste the snack.
- Washing fruits and vegetables before they cut and eat them provides additional opportunities for beginning cooks. Remember, all cooks need practice and support to succeed.
- When interacting with the children, use correct terms for foods, measurements, equipment, and processes. Repeating and explaining terms will help extend language skills.
- Take the time to discuss foods with the children. Allow them to smell the food and ingredients, taste small portions at various stages of preparation, and experience the feel of textures.
- Ample time should be available for children to complete the recipe, permitting them to learn from the process as well as the product.
- With older children, take time to explain the sequence of how things are grown, harvested, packaged, transported, placed in stores and markets, sold, transported to homes, cooked, and served. Allow time for you to answer the children's questions. Repeat this information in different ways, such as lotto games, matching games, reading books, making books, and field trips.
- Remember to have the children wash their hands before and after each activity.

© Cengage Learning

Have the children wash their hands before and after each cooking activity.

EQUIPMENT AND SUPPLIES

Use real kitchen utensils and equipment. A list of suggested supplies follows:

- Unbreakable nesting bowls for mixing
- Individual bowls for children
- Measuring cups and spoons
- Wooden stirring spoons
- Slotted spoons
- Unbreakable pitchers
- Rubber spatula
- Vegetable peelers
- Plastic grater
- Pastry brushes
- Wire whisks
- Funnel
- Tongs
- Rolling pins
- Hand eggbeater
- Potato masher
- Colander
- Sifter
- Hand squeezing orange juicer
- Plastic serrated knives (for younger children)
- Serrated steel knives and kitchen shears (for older children)
- Plastic cutting boards or trays
- Cookie cutters and cookie sheets
- Muffin tins
- Bread loaf pans and cake pans

- Airtight containers with lids
- Hot plate or electric skillet
- Toaster oven
- Electric wok
- Electric blender and/or mixer
- Can opener
- Timer
- Smocks or aprons (not the ones used in the art center)
- Hot pads and mitts or holders
- Sponges used just for cooking activities
- Paper towels and paper napkins
- Waxed paper, foil, plastic wrap, and plastic bags

Basic ingredients to keep on hand include:

Flour	Salt	Oil
Milk	Baking soda	Vinegar
Sugar	Baking powder	Bread
Cornstarch	Peanut butter	Honey
Cornmeal		

SENSORY SNACKS

- Dried fruits: apples, raisins, apricots, and pitted prunes. (Let the children spoon out the portions.)
- Bananas sliced in orange juice. (Let the children slice the bananas and drop them in their own bowls of orange juice.)
- Melon chunks. (Let the children feel, hold, and cut the fruit and then remove and plant the seeds.)
- Finger foods (that children can help prepare): cinnamon toast, cheese toast, popcorn, raw or cooked vegetables, hard-boiled eggs (whole, half, quarters, slices), apple slices dipped in honey, tangerine wedges, pear sections, or plum pieces.

(See Figures 9–10, 9–11, 9–12 for Rebus Charts of Cooking Activities.)

Activities Suggested in the Five Senses Curriculum Web

Differing types of activities for the sensory centers are suggested in Figure 9–13, a curriculum-planning web using a children's favorite book as the theme (Aliki. [1991, Rev. ed.] *My five senses*. New York: HarperFestival; or Spanish edition: Aliki. [1995]. *Mis cinco sentidos*. New York: Rayo.) This web offers books, activities, and a special recipe.

The following activities involve all the senses. They are included in the curriculum web and are appropriate for young children to do. (Note: Refer to this text's student website for additional curriculum webs of "the senses.")

MAKING SANDPAPER.   Provide cardstock, watery glue, paintbrushes, and containers of sand of various grades. Children first paint on one side of the cardstock with watery glue. Then they choose a grade of sand and sprinkle it on the card. Allow to dry overnight. When dry, the cards can be examined and touched by the children to compare how the different types of sand feel.

BUTTERFLY SALAD

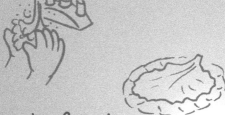

Wash hands.

Place one lettuce leaf onto a paper plate.

Slice 2 pineapple rings in 1/2 to use as an outline of

the butterfly's wings. Use one celery stick as the body.

Place a small amount of cottage cheese inside of

pineapple rings. Decorate the cottage cheese with

green and black olives.

FIGURE 9–10
Rebus Chart: Recipe for "Butterfly Salad." Source: Jackman, (2005) *Sing Me A Story! Tell Me A Song!*

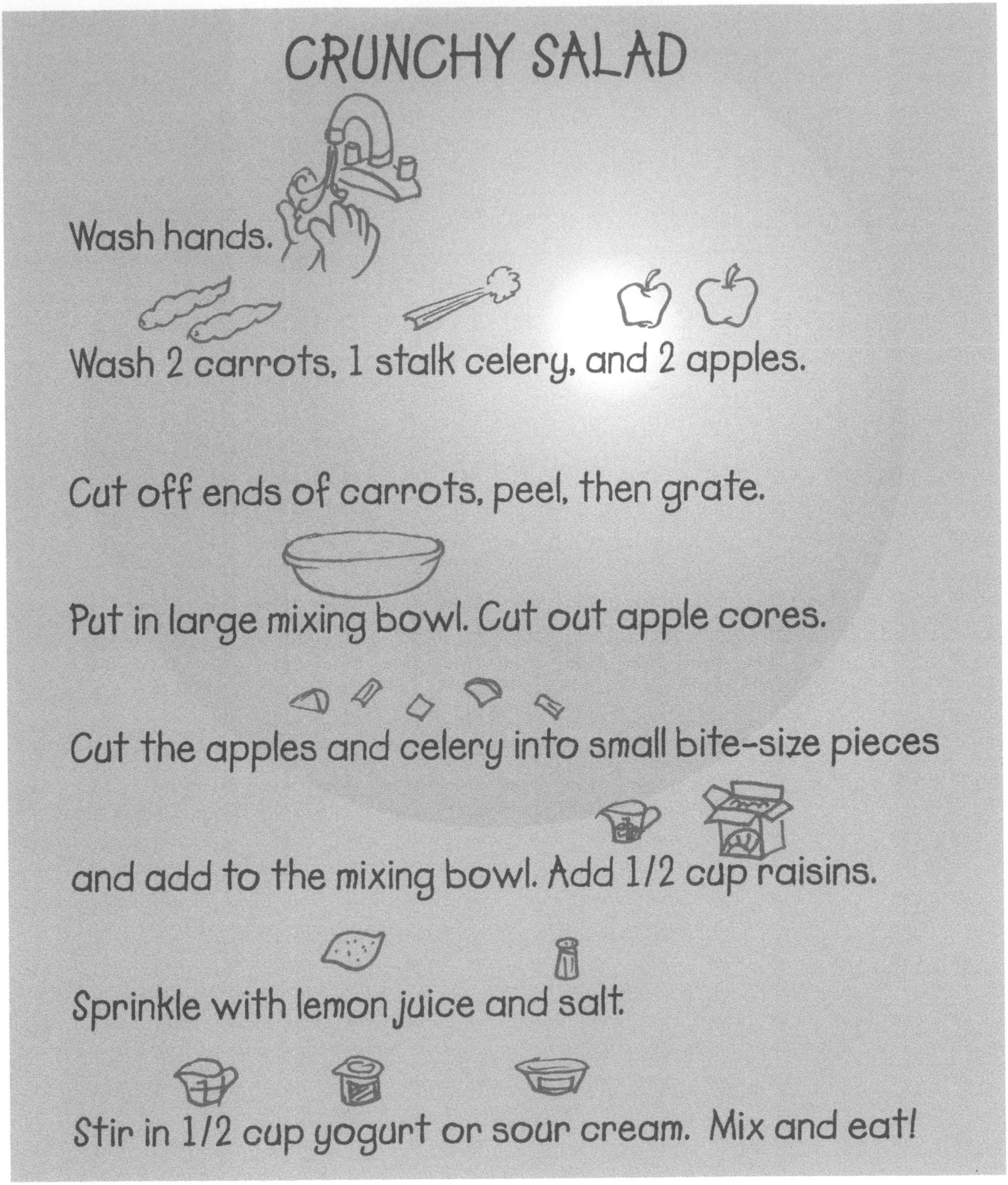

CRUNCHY SALAD

Wash hands.

Wash 2 carrots, 1 stalk celery, and 2 apples.

Cut off ends of carrots, peel, then grate.

Put in large mixing bowl. Cut out apple cores.

Cut the apples and celery into small bite-size pieces

and add to the mixing bowl. Add 1/2 cup raisins.

Sprinkle with lemon juice and salt.

Stir in 1/2 cup yogurt or sour cream. Mix and eat!

FIGURE 9–11
Rebus Chart: Recipe for "Crunchy
Salad." Source: Jackman, (2005)
Sing Me A Story! Tell Me A Song!

ANIMAL MERRY-GO-ROUNDS

Wash hands.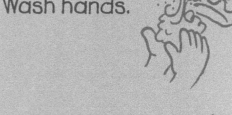

Cut one apple in half.

Spread peanut butter over each apple half.

Add animal crackers and pretzel sticks to make the

merry-go-round animals and poles.

Look at your creation and then eat! Yum!

FIGURE 9–12
Rebus Chart: Recipe for "Animal Merry-Go-Rounds." Source: Jackman, (2005) *Sing Me A Story! Tell Me A Song!*

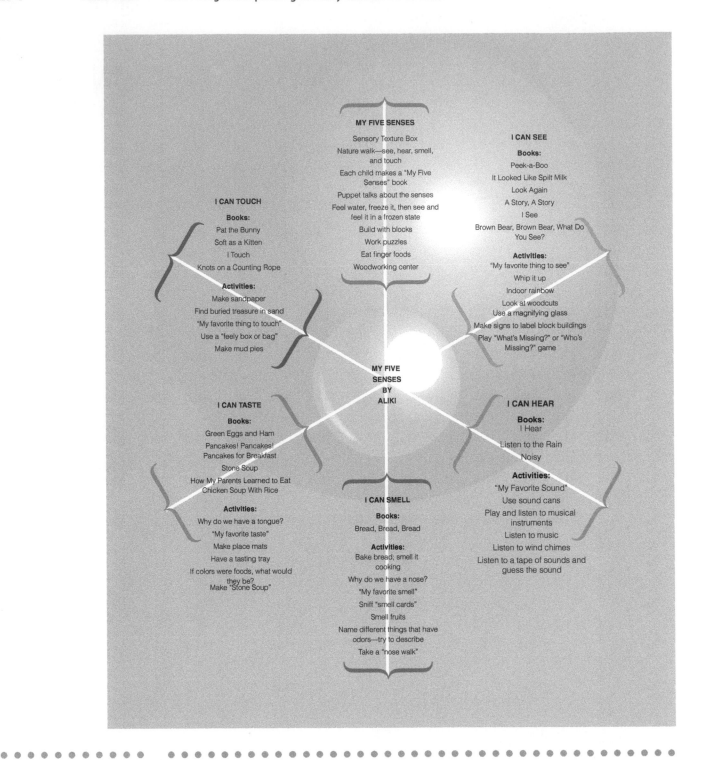

FIGURE 9–13
A curriculum planning web using the children's book *My Five Senses,* by Aliki.

WHIP IT UP.   Using a hand rotary eggbeater, dish pan, and liquid dishwashing detergent, children can turn the beaters and whip up bubbles in the individual dishpan or the sand and water table.

INDOOR RAINBOW.   Fill a clear glass jar with water and set on a windowsill in the bright sunlight. Place white paper on the floor to "capture the rainbow." The children can paint rainbows with watercolors.

LOOKING AT WOODCUTS. Woodcuts or woodblocks are among the oldest artistic media in both Western and Eastern cultures. Some of the earliest books for children were illustrated by black-and-white woodcuts.

> To create a woodcut, an artist draws an image on a block of wood and cuts away the areas around the design. After rolling ink onto this raised surface, the artist presses the woodblock against paper, transferring the image from the block to the paper. (Norton, 1999)

Color prints require a different woodblock for each color in the picture. G. Haley used woodcuts to illustrate her version of an African folktale, *A Story, A Story* (1988), New York: Aladdin.

Research local artists in your community to see if any of them have created woodcuts or woodblocks. Invite them to visit the class and demonstrate their art to the children. Perhaps the school-age children could make some of their own in the woodworking center.

SENSORY TEXTURE BOX. You can make this for the infants and toddlers *or* you and the older children can make one. Use an appliance box at least 3 feet square. Put several pounds of sand or gravel sacks in the bottom of the box to stabilize it. Close the box and tape down the flaps. Paint or decorate the box. Glue textured materials securely to the four sides of the box. Use sandpaper, cotton balls, egg cartons, kente cloth, silk flowers, foil, twigs, and other textured materials. This is a different kind of "texture board" for you and the children to enjoy in the classroom (adapted from Parks, 1994).

MAKE PLACE MATS. Make place mats for use at snack and meal time. Cut out colorful labels from food packaging, magazines, or construction paper. Glue these on a piece of paper and laminate. The children can share these, or each child can use the one he made.

LET'S USE ALL OUR SENSES. Set up a special "tasting tray" with foods that taste sweet, sour, salty, spicy, and bitter. Create "smell cards" using different spices and herbs secured to cards with white glue. (The glue does not have any odor.) Make "sound cans" by placing paper clips, beans, and so on in small, empty plastic containers. Make a "feely box" or "feely bag" filled with different items that emphasize shape and softness. Let the children feel an object and tell you what it feels like and what they think the items are without looking. Then they get to see if they guessed correctly or not.

RECIPE SUGGESTED IN THE CURRICULUM WEB

See the rebus chart in Figure 9–14, the recipe and visual directions for Stone Soup. (Review the rebus chart for applesauce in Chapter 3.)

Suggested books:
1. *Stone Soup* by M. Brown (1997), New York: Aladdin Picture (traditional story)
2. *Stone Soup* by J. Muth (2003), New York: Scholastic (revised story)

> **Stone Soup Recipe**
> (Read the story first. Have three clean rocks ready!)
> 3 stalks of celery, chopped
> 2 large carrots, chopped
> 2 medium onions, chopped
> 2 medium potatoes, chopped
> 3 medium tomatoes, chopped
> 1/2 teaspoon basil
> 1/2 cup fresh parsley
> 1 1/2 tablespoons salt
> 1/2 teaspoon pepper

Everyone can chop or measure something. Put all the ingredients into a big pan on the stove. (An electric crock pot will work, too.) Add water to cover. Cook using low heat 2 to 3 hours. You can add rice (1 to 2 cups) to thicken.

STONE SOUP

Wash hands,   Wash 3 clean rocks,

Chop and measure 3 stalks of celery, 2 large carrots,

2 medium onions, 2 medium potatoes, 3 medium tomatoes,

1/2 teaspoon basil, 1/2 cup fresh parsley,

1 1/2 tablespoon salt, and 1/2 teaspoon pepper.

Put all ingredients in a big pot and place on the stove.

Add water to cover the vegetables, Cook for 2 - 3 hours.

Add 1/2 cup rice to thicken the soup. ENJOY!

FIGURE 9–14

Rebus chart, the recipe and visual directions for "Stone Soup." Source: Jackman, (2005). *Sing Me A Story! Tell Me A Song!*

Afterview

Through sensory activities, a child

- has opportunities to develop taste, olfactory, tactile, auditory, and visual skills.
- develops perceptual discrimination by shape, size, color, detail, and design.
- experiments with concepts of balance, leverage, volume, weights, and measurements.
- learns that the parts make up the whole.
- explores spatial relationships.
- learns to solve problems.
- practices reading and writing readiness activities.
- develops strength and coordination of large and small muscles.
- practices eye-hand and hand-hand coordination.
- experiments with new materials and tools and learns to apply rules of safety.
- enjoys a sense of achievement and self-control.
- practices oral language by interaction with peers.
- learns to work independently as well as cooperatively with others.
- learns to complete a task and to be responsible for cleaning up after himself.
- has opportunities to make choices.
- expands his knowledge of the world.

Reflective Review Questions

1. What is meant by *sensory experiences* of young children? Why are these important in the growth and development of children? Explain.
2. What is the role of the teacher as young children engage in block play?
3. Discuss why sensory activities can offer problem-solving experiences to young children. Identify by sharing examples of at least two activities.
4. As a teacher in a preschool classroom, discuss how and when you can successfully integrate nutrition and cooking activities into your curriculum. What skills will these activities develop in young children? Create a list of essential equipment you would need.

Key Terms

hollow blocks	nutrition	unit blocks
obesity	sensory awareness	woodworking center
nutrients	sensory experiences	

Explorations

1. Select an early education classroom and observe for at least one hour. Describe, in writing, six sensory activities the children were involved in at the time you were observing. What did you learn from this observation? Did any of these activities explore diverse cultures?

2. Select and plan a cooking or creative food experience for young children. Specify which age group this activity is planned for: toddlers, preschoolers, kindergarteners, or primary-age children. What nutritional aspects will you include? In writing, list objectives, materials needed, step-by-step procedures for presenting this activity, follow-up activities, and evaluation guidelines. (A blank activity plan worksheet is available online at this text's premium website.) Create a rebus chart for the recipe you used.

3. Select an early education classroom and observe for one hour. Describe, in writing, what happened in the block center during your observation. How many children were in the center at one time? Were these the same children for the entire hour you observed? How many boys? How many girls? What were they building? Describe the developmental stages you saw. What did you learn from this observation? Explain. Were any props or additional materials added to the block activities? Did the nature of the activities change? Describe how the children used the added props and materials.

4. As a teacher in a preschool classroom, discuss how and when you can successfully incorporate woodworking into your curriculum. What skills will this activity area develop in young children? Create a list of essential equipment for a woodworking center, as well as a budget. (Consult early childhood supply catalogs for pricing.)

5. As stated in this chapter, young children are attracted to water. They enjoy pouring, measuring, splashing, and siphoning water. Observe children involved in water play. Describe the learning experiences taking place. To which curriculum do they relate? Math, science, social studies, language, art? List the supplies and materials used.

Additional Readings and Resources

Alexander, N. P. (2000, Winter). Blocks and basics. *Dimensions of Early Childhood, 28*(1), 29–30.

Anderson, C. (2010, March). Blocks: A versatile learning tool for yesterday, today, and tomorrow. *Young Children, 65*(2), 54–56.

Cohen, L., & Blagojevic, B. (2002, September). Observing the whole child. *Early Childhood Today, 17*(1), 38–47.

Da Ros-Voseles, D., & Baldwin, V. (2002, Summer). In praise of sandboxes. *Dimensions of Early Childhood, 30*(3), 21–24.

Direnfeld, G. (2008, Spring/Summer). Healthy eating for kids. *TAEYC's Early Years, 30*(1), 10-20.

Kalich, K. A., Bauer, D., & McPartlin, D. (2009, July). Early sprouts—Establishing healthy food choices for young children. *Young Children, 64*(4), 49–55.

Lasher, E., Abraham, C., & Joy, J. (2002, January–February). My five senses. *Early Childhood News, 14*(1), 28–31.

Matt, M. M. (2008, November). Plant parts—A way to family involvement, science learning, and nutrition. *Young Children, 63*(6), 98–99.

Papert, S. (1999). *Mindstorms: Children, computers, and powerful ideas* (2nd ed.). New York: Basic Books.

Rogers, L., & Steffan, D. (2009, May). Clay play. *Young Children, 64*(3), 78–81.

Simons, B. (2002, March). The sand tray. *Young Children, 57*(2), 8–9.

Zan, B., & Geiken, R. (2010, January). Ramps and pathways. *Young Children, 65*(1), 12–17.

Helpful Web Connections

Action for Healthy Kids
http://www.actionforhealthykids.org
American Academy of Pediatrics
http://www.aap.org
Better Kid Care
http://www.betterkidcare.psu.edu
(In the search box, type in "Block Play")
Childhood Obesity
http://www.cdc.gov

Fruit Pages
http://www.thefruitpages.com
Kids Health Organization
http://www.kidshealth.org
NAEYC
http://www.naeyc.org
United States Department of Agriculture (Food Guide Pyramid for Kids)
http://www.mypyramid.gov

References

Alexander, N. P. (2008). All about unit block play. *Early Child-hood News.* Online at: *http://www.earlychildhoodnews.com*

American Academy of Pediatrics. (2010). Online at *http://www.aap.org*

Beaty, J. J. (2009). *Preschool appropriate practices* (3rd ed.). Clifton Park, NY: Wadsworth Cengage Learning.

Colker, L. J. (2005). *The cooking book: Fostering young children's learning and delight.* Washington, DC: NAEYC.

Dodge, D. T., Colker, L. J., & Heroman, C. (2008). *The creative curriculum for preschool* (College edition). Washington, DC: Teaching Strategies, Inc.

Essa, E. (2011). *Introduction to early childhood education* (6th ed.). Clifton Park, NY: Wadsworth Cengage Learning.

Feeney, S., Moravcik, E., Nolte, S., & Christensen, D. (2010). *Who am I in the lives of children?* (8th ed.). Upper Saddle River, NJ: Merrill.

Gestwicki, C. (2011). *Developmentally appropriate practice: Curriculum and development in early education* (4th ed.). Clifton Park, NY: Wadsworth Cengage Learning.

Gordon, A. M., & Browne, K. W. (2011). *Beginnings and beyond: Foundations in early childhood education.* (8th ed.). Clifton Park, NY: Wadsworth Cengage Learning.

Hendrick, J. (2003). *Total learning—Developmental curriculum for the young child* (6th ed.). Upper Saddle River, NJ: Merrill.

Hill, D. M. (1977). *Mud, sand, and water.* Washington, DC: NAEYC.

Hirsch, E. S. (Ed.). (1993). *The block book* (Rev. ed.).Washington, DC: NAEYC.

Hunter, D. (2008, November). What happens when a child plays at a sensory table? *Young Children, 63*(6), 77–79.

Jackman, H. L. (2005). *Sing me a story! Tell me a song!* Clifton Park, NY: Delmar Cengage Learning.

Jensen, B. J., & Bullard, J. A. (2002, May). The mud center: Recapturing childhood. *Young Children, 57*(3), 16–19.

Koster, J. B. (2009). *Growing artists* (4th ed.). Clifton Park, NY: Wadsworth Cengage Learning.

Marotz, L. R. (2009). *Health, safety, and nutrition for the young child* (7th ed.). Clifton Park, NY: Wadsworth Cengage Learning.

Mayesky, M. (2006). *Creative activities for young children* (8th ed.). Clifton Park, NY: Delmar Cengage Learning.

Miller, D. F. (2010). *Positive child guidance* (6th ed.). Clifton Park, NY: Wadsworth Cengage Learning.

Miller, S. A. (1994, March). Sand and water around the room. *Early Childhood Today, 8*(6), 37–45.

Nielsen, D. M. (2006). *Teaching young children: Preschool-K* (2nd ed.). Thousand Oaks, CA: Corwin Press.

Nimmo, J., & Halett, B. (2008, January). Childhood in the garden: A place to encounter natural and social diversity. *Young Children, 63*(1), 32–38.

Norton, D. E. (1999). *Through the eyes of a child—An introduction to children's literature* (5th ed.). Upper Saddle River, NJ: Merrill.

Ogu, U., & Schmidt, S. R. (2009, March). Investigating rocks and sand. *Young Children, 64*(2), 12–18.

Parks, L. (1994, Fall). Make it with a box. *Texas Child Care, 18*(2), 22–28.

Petersen, E. A. (2003). *Early childhood planning, methods, and materials* (2nd ed.). Boston, MA: Allyn & Bacon.

Robertson, C. (2010). *Safety, nutrition, & health in education* (4th ed.). Clifton Park, NY: Wadsworth Cengage Learning.

Starns, L. (2002, Summer). Don't take the blocks away!—Block centers in preschool and primary classrooms. *The Early Years, 24*(2), 2–3.

Stephenson, A. (2001, May). What George taught me about toddlers and water. *Young Children, 57*(3), 10–14.

Tunks, K. W. (2009). Block play: Practical suggestions for common dilemmas. *Dimensions of Early Childhood, 37*(1), 3–8.

United States Department of Agriculture (USDA). (2010). Online at: *http://www.mypyramid.gov*

Wellhousen, K., & Kieff, J. (2001). *A constructivist approach to block play in early childhood.* Clifton Park, NY: Delmar Cengage Learning.

chapter 10

Music and Movement

Objectives

After Studying This Chapter, You Should Be Able To:

● Discuss why music and movement education is developmentally appropriate for young children.

● Examine motor development and physical fitness relating to music and movement in early childhood.

● Describe musical experiences that should be part of a music and movement curriculum for young children.

● List the types of musical instruments that children can make from materials collected from home.

● Discuss how to set up effective music and movement areas and identify types of activities that children, teachers, and parents can enjoy throughout the day.

● Describe how to connect music and movement with other areas of curriculum.

Overview

A developmentally appropriate and creative classroom for young children has music and movement experiences woven into the daily curriculum. In fact, if you stop and listen to an active early childhood classroom, you will discover that it has a rhythmic pattern and beat all its own.

Unplanned, spontaneous moments occur daily in an early education environment. Young children hum, sing, clap hands, and move their bodies as they play and complete activities. Music, sound, and movement continuously contribute to the learning processes of young children. Human bodies function to rhythms (e.g., heartbeat, breathing), and children respond by moving. Music comes out of rhythm. "Music is one of our greatest inheritances as human beings. So global is the human experience of music that it has often been called the universal language of humankind" (Moomaw, 1984).

All humans come into the world with an innate capability for music. At a very early age, this capability is shaped by the music system of the culture in which a child is raised. That culture affects the construction of instruments, the way people sound when they sing, and even the way they hear sound (Shelemay, 2001).

Music is a language, a means of communication. It is communicated through **tone**, **rhythm**, **volume**, range, **tempo**, and movement (Greenberg, 1979). Music can communicate feelings to children even when its cultural origin and language is foreign to them. Children are acquainted with music from birth. The tone of a mother's voice, the rhythm of a rocking chair, and the chanting of nonsense syllables are basic to a child's life. Before she knows words, an infant experiments with vocal sounds and understands tones and rhythms. "Early language learning is, in a sense, early music learning, since children learn both skills simultaneously" (Miche, 2002).

A child's involvement with music includes listening; creative activities related to singing, body movement, playing, and making instruments; and aesthetic examination.

> Where does all this squirming energy come from? From the billions of active neurons hungry for stimulation and experience. I have come to appreciate the marvelous opportunities music and movement offer children for rich and varied learning experiences. (Palmer, 2001)

Music and movement are intertwined. They reinforce and strengthen each other. A child hears music, and she moves in response. A child's physical maturation process motivates her to move naturally in response to internal and external stimuli. Griss (1994) emphasizes that "children exposed to creative movement as a language for learning are becoming more aware of their own natural resources. They are expanding their concepts of creativity and of how they can use their own bodies."

In this chapter, we explore the ways music and movement can introduce concepts, foster growth in motor skills, reinforce and develop language skills, nourish positive self-esteem, encourage self-expression, explore diversity, and connect to other curriculum areas and chapters of this book.

tone An individual musical sound.

rhythm A sense of movement and patterns in music created by beats, the duration and volume of sounds, and the silences between sounds.

volume The softness or loudness of sound.

tempo A sense of slowness or rapidity in music.

© Cengage Learning

A developmentally appropriate and creative classroom for young children has music and movement experiences woven into the daily curriculum.

Music and Movement Education for Young Children

● ●

Most young children are uninhibited, enthusiastic performers and lovers of music and movement, both of which enrich children's lives and learning in many ways. These should be a focused part of the day and also be integrated with other content areas. (Copple & Bredekamp, 2009)

Music makes children want to clap hands, tap toes, beat drums, and dance. *Children learn best through acting upon what they experience.* Moving can be fun for its own sake and a way to enjoy music even more. Children express the music's aesthetic qualities through the movement of their bodies as they listen to, perform, and create music. "By using the body the child expresses what he *perceives* in the music, how he *feels* about the music, and what he *understands* in it" (Greenberg, 1979). Smith (2002) expands this thought even more:

> Every child learns by moving, and every teacher can teach by moving with the children. In dance, children interpret ideas and feelings through the use of their bodies in an open-ended search for a unique movement vocabulary. Children are able to create their own dances just as they create their own stories.

For young children in early education settings, including infants and toddlers, music and movement activities nurture the development of minds, bodies, emotions, and language. As you plan developmentally appropriate goals and objectives to encourage music and movement experiences, consider the following:

1. Include *physical development* activities that can help children gain increasing control over their large and small muscles, experiment with the movement of their bodies, and experience success in movement. Play, as discussed in Chapter 1 of this book, is the most developmentally appropriate activity in which young children engage. Researchers have validated this again and again. Brown (2009) emphasizes "that the learning of emotional control, social competency, personal resiliency and continuing curiosity plus other life benefits accrue largely through rich developmentally appropriate play experiences. . . . Play is who we are."

2. Incorporate *intellectual growth* activities that can stimulate children to experiment with how sound is created through their voices or musical instruments, to recognize songs, and to explore melodies by varying tempo, rhythm, tone, and volume.

3. Include *listening* activities that make music a part of the daily environment by asking for a response, remembering a song or parts of a song, recognizing musical instruments, focusing on sound, and developing auditory discrimination. Every time a child engages in a music experience, she is listening.

4. Provide children with *socially and emotionally responsive* activities that energize, soothe, and enhance children's expression of feelings and sharpen their awareness of feelings for others. Music and movement experiences can also help children know and appreciate themselves and promote cultural identity and pride in themselves and others.

5. Include musical *language development* activities that encourage the acquisition and use of language to extend vocabulary, to learn word and sound patterns through singing and listening, and to describe musical happenings that can help children develop an appreciation for the music and language of diverse cultures. "The songs and music of childhood are a part of our cultural heritage. The folk songs and ballads that have survived to the present day and the regional tunes parents and teachers offer are part of each child's cultural literacy" (Machado, 2007).

6. Take advantage of music and movement opportunities that stimulate children's *creativity* and *uniqueness*. Give children musically creative group time by offering each child the opportunity to add to songs and finger plays and to create new movements for action songs. Each musical creation adds to the creativity of the whole group.

All children need the opportunity to use the creative process in discovering their own original ways to move and in using their bodies to communicate their emotions and ideas. However, as they grow they also need to learn how to control their bodies and match their movements to rhythms, music, and the movements of others by participating in simple dances from our own and other cultures. (Koster, 2009)

Motor Development and Physical Fitness

Developing physical skills can be compared to learning to read and write, or understanding principles of math and science. Each requires a manipulative of some type to best develop skills and knowledge. Developing skill in physical activity requires the manipulation of balls, bean bags, paddles, scarves, hoops, ropes, and other objects. Children cannot learn to write without a pencil; they cannot learn to throw without a ball. (Sanders, 2006)

© Cengage Learning

Manipulative movement, a gross motor skill, is seen when a young child attempts to catch a ball. The child often stands with eyes closed and arms rigidly outstretched.

Music and movement early education curriculum should include well-defined opportunities, both indoor and outdoor, for young children to develop motor skills. As discussed in previous chapters, setting up the environment and planning appropriate activities depends on the developmental skills, interests, and needs of the children.

Large muscle (gross motor) development usually precedes small muscle (fine motor) development. For this chapter, we will focus on motor development that includes locomotor skills, large muscle activities, and physical fitness. Underlying all of this is the understanding that possibilities for exploration, creativity, and self-expression are included as part of the motor skill planning process.

Small muscle development is discussed in other chapters and includes such activities as turning pages of a book, finger plays, scribbling, drawing, writing, tearing, cutting, pouring, stringing beads, inserting pegs, pounding nails, and building with blocks. Involvement with music and movement projects can be very effective in furthering the development of small muscles.

Basic types of movement in young children, identified by Greenberg (1979) and expanded by Pica (2010), are locomotor, nonlocomotor, combination, and manipulative. All these actions need practice, encouragement, and an adult's understanding of individual growth patterns.

Locomotor movement (fundamental movement) is the ability to move the whole body from one place to another. This is demonstrated by crawling, creeping, walking, running, jumping, hopping, skipping, and climbing. "The progression of crawling to creeping is somewhat variable from one child to the next, with any of several postures employed, depending on the child. . . . Infants become toddlers when they expand their repertoire of movement and begin running" (Gagen, Getchell, & Payne, cited in Essa & Burnham, 2009). Closely following in development are the rest of the locomotor skills mentioned above with a reminder that hopping on one foot is a difficult skill for young children to control. As with all motor skills, children need opportunities to practice developing their physical abilities.

locomotor movement The ability to move the whole body from one place to another.

Nonlocomotor movement (axial or body movement) occurs when the feet remain stationary (as in standing, kneeling, sitting, or lying) while other parts of the body move. Examples are stretching, reaching, bending, twisting, bouncing, shaking, and clapping.

A combination of the previous two types of movement involves various motions that enhance coordination while giving children movement and rhythm combinations that occur simultaneously. An example of this is walking and clapping at the same time or hopping and shaking (Greenberg, 1979).

Manipulative movement skills in the physical education field are described by Pica (2010) as "gross motor movements involving force imparted to or received from objects . . . [or] any gross motor skill in which an object is usually involved (manipulated)." This is demonstrated by pulling, pushing, lifting, striking, throwing, kicking, and ball catching. Catching is harder to master than throwing. When first attempting to do this, young children often stand with their eyes closed and their arms rigidly outstretched. This is part of the developing stage that children go through. As teachers we should continue to offer encouragement.

Isbell and Raines (2007) add another important factor: **kinesthetics**—the use of the body to learn about physical capabilities, develop body awareness, and gain understanding of the world. Howard Gardner's (1983) theories of multiple intelligences describe bodily-kinesthetic intelligence as the ability to unite the body and mind in physical performance.

For you, as a teacher of young children, this means planning and providing daily developmentally appropriate movement and exercise activities for the children in your care. This specifies allowing time for movement exploration. Start with slow stretches to get their bodies "warmed up." For example, the children can touch their toes, then make circles with their arms, and finally stretch their arms way above their heads. You should demonstrate the importance of health and fitness by encouraging and participating with your actions as well as your words. Gagen, Getchell, and Payne, cited in Essa & Burnham (2009) offer the following insight, "[C]hildren who become proficient movers are more likely to use those movement skills in activities that will enhance the state of their health and well-being over their entire lifespan."

Locomotor, large muscle, and fitness activities can easily be combined with creative movement and music activities. There are no limits on how to accomplish this. You and the children together can discover wonderful things through movement and music!

Plan and provide daily developmentally appropriate movement and exercise activities for the children.

© Cengage Learning

Types of Music

A music curriculum for young children should include many opportunities to explore sound through singing, moving, listening, and playing instruments, as well as introductory experiences with verbalization and visualization of musical ideas. The music literature included in the curriculum should be of high quality and lasting value, including traditional children's songs, folk songs, classical music, and music from a variety of cultures, styles, and time periods. (Music Educators National Conference [MENC], 1994)

The basic sources of music are the human voice, instruments, environmental sounds, and music from radio, television, DVDs, and CDs. As you use these sources to plan music experiences for young children, remember to connect them to their life experiences. See Figure 10–1 for basic terms.

SONGS AND SINGING

Young children love to sing. Beginning in infancy and continuing on throughout their childhood, they are experimenting with their voices and the sounds that they can make. Billhartz (2007) helps us understand this even more:

A young child will first attempt to sing by isolating parts of words or selected words from a larger song. If provided a rich array of singing experiences, children will begin with spoken and singsong inflection as toddlers, and then move to matching pitches and singing entire songs as older preschoolers. Although many children will not sing in a group setting or in front of another child or adult, they will sing during playtime. This is a perfectly developmental way for young children to respond. As children become more comfortable with their singing voices, they will begin to join in group singing activities.

Here are a few more musical items to think about:

● Singing can be experienced alone or shared with others.
● Songs encourage the children to make up new words and to move with the music.
● Singing with children throughout daily routines nurtures important learning connections.
● Singing is a developmentally appropriate practice.
● Enthusiastic teacher participation in singing encourages the development of children's innate musical ability.

There is a whole generation that doesn't know nursery rhymes or traditional tunes. You and I have the responsibility and privilege of passing on our musical heritage and putting music back into children's lives. . . . Just open your mouth and SING! (Feldman, 2002)

Beat—An accent of sound or a continuing series of accents.
Melody—A sequence of tones of varying pitches organized in a rhythmically meaningful way.
Pitch—The highness or lowness of a tone on a musical scale.
Rhythm—A sense of movement and patterns in music created by beats, the duration and volume of sounds, and the silences between sounds.
Tempo—A sense of slowness or rapidity in music.
Timbre (TAM-bur)—The unique tone quality of a voice or musical instrument.
Tone—An individual musical sound.
Volume—The softness or loudness of sound.

FIGURE 10–1
Basic musical terms.

© Cengage Learning

Children enjoy singing and movement activities outdoors. Be involved. Children pick up on your enthusiasm.

There are many delightful and fun-filled songs to sing, such as the ones included in the developmentally appropriate activities at the end of this chapter and the following ones:

● Songs that offer repetition and chorus, such as "Polly Put the Kettle On," "Mary Had a Little Lamb," and "Here We Go Round the Mulberry Bush."
● Songs with repeated words or phrases that can be treated like an echo, such as "Miss Mary Mack" and "She'll Be Comin' 'Round the Mountain."
● Songs that ask children to supply sound effects or animal noises, such as "If You're Happy and You Know It" and "Old MacDonald Had a Farm."
● Ballads or songs that tell a story, such as "Hush Little Baby," "Humpty Dumpty," and "Little Bo Peep."
● Question-and-answer songs or name games that help children make the transition from speaking to singing, such as "Do You Know the Muffin Man?"

Let us not forget how important a song can be to a young child—songs with words often give rise to spontaneous play as well as to wonderful moments of magic. When music is integral to a child's life, then it becomes central to a child's play. Play is a time when children are integrating new concepts and music may provide the anchor children need to remember and repeat what is being learned. (McGraw, 2002).

USING THE VOICE

The voices of children are expressive as they speak, chant, and sing. When young children experiment with their voices and tongues, they can sound like musical instruments, animals, and the wind. Encourage the children to make some of these sounds:

whisper very quietly	cluck
talk very softly, then loudly	buzz
whistle	growl
sneeze	bark
purr	snore
hum	cry

CHOOSING CLASSICAL SELECTIONS

Research tells us that classical music stimulates musical responses from young children. Whether they are "conducting," relaxing, listening, or moving creatively to these recorded musical works, children enjoy and can get caught up in them. "Because children's tastes are so variable, it is best if the teacher introduces a wide variety of orchestral and instrumental pieces and lets the children select those they particularly like" (Moomaw, 1984). CDs are available in libraries or stores under many different labels and performing artists. Here are a few children's favorites:

● Britten/*The Young Person's Guide to the Orchestra*
● Copland/*Rodeo*
● Dukas/*The Sorcerer's Apprentice*
● Grofé/*Grand Canyon Suite*
● Mozart/*Concerto for Flute, Harp, and Orchestra*
● Prokofiev/*Peter and the Wolf*

- Rimsky-Korsakov/*Flight of the Bumble Bee*
- Rossini/*William Tell Overture*
- Saint-Saëns/*Carnival of the Animals*
- Strauss, R./*Till Eulenspiegel's Merry Pranks*
- Stravinsky/*The Firebird*
- Tchaikovsky/*The Nutcracker Suite*
- Tchaikovsky/*The Sleeping Beauty*

For infants and toddlers, gradually introduce classical background music into the environment. As you plan your music curriculum for all the developmental stages, think about when and why you want to have music playing, and then choose it carefully. For all ages, research has shown that classical music has a significant effect on the brain. "Thoughtfully planned music experiences can support and nurture each of the domains of development—social-emotional, physical (motor), thinking (cognitive), and language and literacy" (Parlakin & Lerner, 2010).

> As with language, children should not be deprived of the whole musical picture because they are too young to understand it. Children learn and understand a great deal more than they can speak about during their first years, but we would never think of not speaking to infants and toddlers just because they cannot speak. . . . Music deserves the same natural assimilation. (Andress & Walker, 1992)

Musical Instruments

Instruments of all kinds have value in the musical environment of young children. They should be encouraged to listen to the instrument, touch it, and experiment with making sounds and music on it. Have instruments of good quality that are well cared for, such as tambourines, wooden maracas, woodblocks, rhythm sticks, drums, finger cymbals, bells, triangles, and rain sticks. Teacher- and child-made instruments should always be included, as well as wind chimes, gongs, and music boxes.

"Invite a musician to play an instrument for the children, tell about it, and pass it around to be touched most respectfully. The children should have many listening experiences and exposures to many kinds of music and musical instruments" (Andress & Walker, 1992).

TYPES OF INSTRUMENTS

Usually the first instrument sounds a child hears and experiments with are those created in the home, such as banging on pots and pans (drums), jingling two spoons together (castanets), shaking a ring of metal measuring spoons (tambourine), banging two wooden spoons together (rhythm sticks), and crashing two lids or metal pie pans together (cymbals).

It is important for early education programs to encourage young children to continue this exploration of sounds and to broaden their understanding of musical instruments and the sounds they make. Percussion instruments are the ones most widely used in an early childhood setting. See Figure 10–2 for a list of musical instruments.

> Musical instruments have many uses, actually. Everybody knows that music can be entertaining. But instruments can do more than please an audience. Around the world, they play a big role in religion, celebration, communication, and even politics and war. In fact, you can travel anywhere on earth and you'll find musical instruments in almost every culture along the way. (Corbett, 1995)

Drums are used in the music and dances of many cultures, including African, Native American, Korean, and Thai (hand drums, tom-toms, and long drums carried on one shoulder with a strap). Maracas and claves sticks (short, polished hardwood sticks) are part of the Mexican and Caribbean musical heritage.

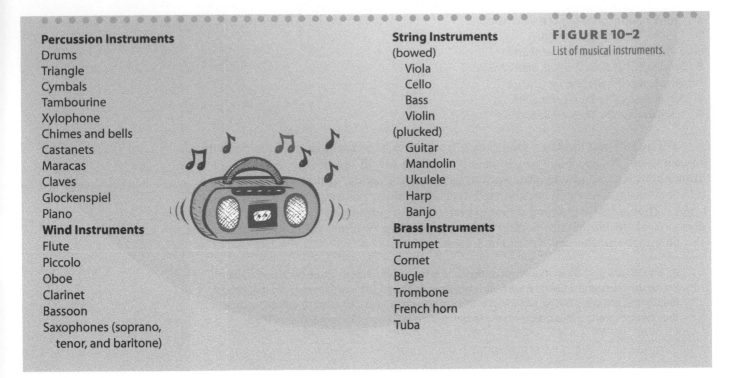

FIGURE 10–2
List of musical instruments.

Percussion Instruments
Drums
Triangle
Cymbals
Tambourine
Xylophone
Chimes and bells
Castanets
Maracas
Claves
Glockenspiel
Piano
Wind Instruments
Flute
Piccolo
Oboe
Clarinet
Bassoon
Saxophones (soprano,
    tenor, and baritone)

String Instruments
(bowed)
    Viola
    Cello
    Bass
    Violin
(plucked)
    Guitar
    Mandolin
    Ukulele
    Harp
    Banjo
Brass Instruments
Trumpet
Cornet
Bugle
Trombone
French horn
Tuba

The combination of personal experiences and hands-on involvement with instruments will enrich all children.

© Cengage Learning

Other instruments also have been a part of ethnic music for centuries, such as the flute from Native American and African cultures and the bamboo flute from Chinese, Japanese, and Korean cultures. Stringed instruments, such as the Japanese *samisen* and *koto* (a type of harp), and the Thai *so sam sai,* add beautiful sounds to music selections (Allen, McNeill, & Schmidt, 1992).

Ask parents and community musicians to visit your class and share their music and musical instruments with the children. The combination of personal experiences and hands-on involvement with percussion, string, woodwind, and brass instruments will enrich the children *now,* during their formative years.

INTRODUCING MUSICAL SOUNDS AND INSTRUMENTS

We know that music is a spontaneous and joyous part of young children's lives. They hear it in the world around them and they respond by cooing, babbling, singing, dancing, and interpreting it in their individual ways from infancy onward. How we gather and keep the energy and interest of the children depends on how we include music in our daily curriculum.

Bea Wolf, composer and performer of children's music, suggests the following activities for sharing musical experiences with young children:

● Introduce musical recordings that children can sway to. Have the children close their eyes and move their arms to the music. Ask them "What do you hear?" Listen to their responses. Suggest that they sway their bodies with the music. A waltz tempo is easy to begin with, by swaying on the beat of **1** (**1**–2–3, **1**–2–3, **1**–2–3, etc.).

● Select a favorite song and have the children clap to the rhythm of the music. They can clap their hands together, clap hands on knees, and clap hands on the floor. Often they will continue this activity on their own by humming, singing, and clapping to themselves throughout the day.

● Wind chimes offer a delightful way to have the children focus on soft sounds. Group time can be a special time for children to listen closely as you share the sounds of several different kinds of wind chimes. Have the children listen closely to what these sound like. Then let them play the chimes gently by themselves.

● Music boxes offer other unique sounds for children to listen to. Bring in several different sizes and types for the children to explore. Ask them to bring ones from home, too.

● It is helpful to introduce musical instruments one at a time before combining all the instruments in conjunction with musical recordings. The *triangle* extends listening skills and shapes awareness. Shaking the *maracas* (use only one at first) invites children to shake their own rhythm, as does shaking the *jingle bells,* tap-tap-tapping and then rub-rub-rubbing with wooden sticks, shake-shake-shaking the tambourine, and beat-beat-beating the drums. Try having the children play the instruments to this beat: *sshhh-sshhh/ssh-ssh-ssh/ sshhh-sshhh/ssh-ssh-ssh or 1–2/1–2–3/1–2/1–2–3.*

● It is fun to divide preschoolers and older children into two groups, facing each other with each child having an individual instrument. For example, one group has jingle bells, the other group has one maraca each. Play a recording of an instrumental musical selection. Explain to the children that you (or one of the children) will be the conductor and direct each group when to play individually or together. It is helpful to have the children sitting in groups at first. When the bells play, the maracas are placed gently on the floor; then when the maracas play, the bells are placed gently on the floor, so that the children can listen to their friends play. Then both groups can play together when the conductor directs them to do so.

● Jingle bell instruments are fun to play along with the song "Jingle Bells," even in the month of June. Other fun songs to play bells with are Stephen Foster's "Oh, Susanna" and lively folk songs such as "This Ole' Man" and "She'll Be Comin' 'Round the Mountain."

● Children five years and older enjoy discriminating between sounds and listening to the vibrations of various instruments. Introduce gongs and give the children time to experiment with them. Wooden sticks offer vibrations that sound differently. Place the serrated stick flat against the floor and rub it with the other stick. The floor becomes the amplifier. You can hear different sounds when you place sticks on a carpeted floor and then on a noncarpeted floor.

MAKING MUSICAL INSTRUMENTS

Young children enjoy making their own musical instruments with materials collected from home, including:

● rolls from bathroom tissue and paper towels
● aluminum pie plates
● paper plates
● salt, cereal, and oatmeal boxes
● large, round icecream cartons
● bottle caps
● spools
● embroidery hoops
● wooden blocks

The process of making musical instruments further extends the children's self-expression, their knowledge of how sounds can be made from their environment, and the possibilities for hands-on experiences. This activity also combines language, art, science, math, social studies, and sensory learning opportunities (younger children will need guidance and supervision from the teacher). Some easy-to-make instruments include:

DRUMS.   Children can make drums from salt or cereal boxes or from large icecream cartons. Glue the lid to the box or carton and decorate with markers and paint. Drums can be played by hitting or tapping with fingers or with soft drum sticks made from pencils covered at one end with felt. See Figure 10–3.

FIGURE 10–3
Drum.

TAMBOURINE.   Take an aluminum pie plate or a heavy paper plate, punch several holes on the rim, and tie small bells or bottle caps with thin wire, string, or pipe cleaners to the plate in such a way that the bells hang freely. Then, shake to the musical **beat**. See Figure 10–4.

WOOD-BLOCK TAMBOURINE.   The materials needed to make a wood-block tambourine are one block of wood (approximately ¾ inch by 1 1/2 inches by 6 inches), six or more bottle caps, and nails with wide heads. Hammer a nail through the bottle caps partway into the wood block (Figure 10–5). Be sure the hole in the bottle cap is wide enough so the cap will slide freely along the nail. Any number of nails and bottle caps can be used.

SANDPAPER BLOCKS.   Glue, staple, or thumbtack sandpaper to two wooden blocks (approximately 3 inches by 2 inches by 1 inch) on one 3-inch side of each block. On the opposite side, glue a spool or a small drawer handle. Try experimenting with sandpaper squares of different coarseness. Rub the sandpaper blocks together to make interesting sounds (when the squares wear out, replace them with fresh sandpaper). See Figure 10–6.

SHAKERS.   Young children can make shakers from small boxes or clean plastic milk jugs of various sizes (the handles are easy to hold onto). Place clothespins, small pieces of wood, pebbles, dried beans, or birdseed in the container. Another type of shaker is made with paper plates. Take two paper plates and decorate them with crayons, markers, or paint. Place pebbles, dried beans, or birdseed between the two paper plates. Staple the plates together or sew them together with brightly colored yarn. Then, shake and shake to the rhythm of the music! See Figure 10–7.

WIND CHIMES.   Wind chimes can be made from many different materials, such as various sizes of nails, scraps of metal, pieces of bamboo, or old silverware. Tie various lengths of string, evenly spaced, to a coat hanger or embroidery hoop. Tie nails to the strings, and adjust string lengths so that the nails strike each other when blown by the wind or gently swayed. For a variety of sounds, use items of several different sizes, and substitute silverware, pieces of bamboo, or scraps of metal for the nails. See Figure 10–8.

NAIL SCRAPER.   Materials needed to make the nail scraper are a block of wood about 2 inches by 2 inches by 8 inches and nails of different sizes. Hammer a few nails of the same size into a block of wood so that they are all the same height. Leave a large space and then hammer some other size nails into the wood, making these all the same height. Continue placing nails in the wood until there is no more room. To play this instrument, take a large nail and run it quickly along the row of nails. The different lengths of the nails will make different sounds. See Figure 10–9.

SHOE BOX GUITAR.   This instrument is made by taking a shoe box and cutting a 2-inch oval hole on the top of the box. Stretch strong rubber bands lengthwise around the box. Place a pencil at one end of the top of the box under the rubber bands. Move the pencil to get different tones as the shoe box guitar is strummed or plucked with the fingers. See Figure 10–10.

FLUTE.   The children can make their flutes from bathroom tissue, paper towel, or wrapping paper cardboard tubes. Cut a circle of tissue paper or waxed paper and place over one end of the tube. Attach with a rubber band. Cut several small holes on the side of the tube. The children can hum into their flutes while they place their fingers on the holes to change the sound. See Figure 10–11.

FIGURE 10–4
Tambourine.

FIGURE 10–5
Wood-block tambourine.

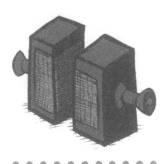
FIGURE 10–6
Sandpaper blocks.

FIGURE 10–7
Examples of two types of musical shakers.

STORING AND CARING FOR INSTRUMENTS

All instruments, including those made by the children, should be treated with care. Guide the children into understanding that each instrument is to be handled carefully and valued. *Musical instruments are not to be used as toys or weapons.*

Rules (limits) should be developed and explained when you introduce musical instruments to the children. For example, "treat the instruments gently," "be careful not to touch anyone else with the instrument, stretch both arms out until you don't touch anyone else—this is your personal space," and "be careful not to hit instruments on the floor or anything else."

Each type of instrument should be stored in a special storage place. According to Haines and Gerber (1996),

> Instruments should never be dumped indiscriminately into a cardboard carton or piled in a basket or on a shelf. This is not good for the instrument or for the attitudes of children toward them. Attractive, accessible storage that the children can use independently should be provided. Damaged instruments should be discarded.

FIGURE 10–8
Wind chimes.

WHY I TEACH YOUNG CHILDREN

This is short, but it says it all.
I asked a 4-year-old to smile during dance class. She said, "When I dance, my body smiles!"

—NANCY SEALE

FIGURE 10–9
Nail scraper.

Music and Movement Environments and Activities

"Play is the primary vehicle for young children's growth, and developmentally appropriate early music experiences should occur in child-initiated, child-directed, teacher-supported play environments" (MENC, 1994). We should provide numerous music and movement activities that invite and encourage children to move around, especially because many children live in confined spaces. Integral to the success of these activities is well-planned space that is adaptable to a number of uses. Consider sound levels that will not interfere with the simultaneous activities of other groups or individuals. These spaces should not be confined to the outdoors or a large motor room. Classrooms should be arranged (or rearranged) to accommodate music and movement activities.

FIGURE 10–10
Shoebox guitar.

"SIMON SAYS MOVE FINGERS, HANDS, AND ARMS" ACTIVITY

Start this activity by explaining to the children that they will play a game by moving a part of their body without music, such as their fingers, hands, or arms. Later add music. This can be played as a "Simon Says" type of game. Introduce the movements first, a few at a time, suggesting only the movement exercises that are applicable to the age and stage of development of the children in your classroom. Remind the children to stay in their "own space." Let one of the children take your place, inserting the child's name to replace "Simon" or "Teacher Says." Accept whatever movement each individual child makes, unless it is inappropriate. The following are some examples:

FIGURE 10–11
Flute.

- moving fingers and hands: bending, separating, stretching, curling, making fists
- moving arms: pushing, pulling, stretching, swinging
- moving feet and legs: stomping, kicking, crossing, and uncrossing
- moving elbows: touching, making circles
- moving head: bending, shaking, rolling, nodding
- moving eyes: opening; shutting; looking up, down, side to side, around
- nose: wiggling, breathing in and out
- mouth: opening wide, making shapes, shutting tight

FRIENDS GO MARCHING ACTIVITY

This is a variation of the traditional activity "The Ants Go Marching." It can be both a movement/music and a transition activity.

> *The friends go marching two by two,*
> *Hurrah, hurrah.*
> *The friends go marching two by two,*
> *Hurrah, hurrah.*
> *The friends go marching two by two,*
> *It's the greatest thing to do.*
> *As we all go marching,*
> *Marching around the room.*

Expand this activity by adding extra verses, such as: friends go jumping, stomping, skipping, tiptoeing, and walking. Add musical instruments to emphasize the beat.

POEM, MUSIC, AND MOVEMENT ACTIVITY

The following are several verses of a poem a kindergarten class helped me create. We tried to move like many animals and fly like a lot of birds before we decided on the ones included in the poem. The next day we tried to put the poem to music. Each child selected a part of the poem to sing and made up his or her own tune. This activity continued for several days as the children proceeded to think up new words and melodies. I recorded their wonderful songs and put the CD in the music center for them to listen to whenever they chose to do so. We also made a book of the poem, with the children drawing the illustrations. This went into the book center.

Here is the poem:

> *I can hop like a bunny.*
> *I can spin like a top.*
> *Hop, spin, hop, hop, hop!*
> *I can gallop like a horse.*
> *I can jump like a clown.*
> *Gallop, jump, up and down!*

Here is another verse the children created later:

> *I can bark like a dog. Arf ! Arf !*
> *I can moo like a cow. Moo! Moo!*
> *I can sound like a cat. Mee-ow!*
> *I can hoot like an owl. Whoo! Whoo!*

OBSTACLE COURSE ACTIVITY

Design an obstacle course (an arrangement of physical challenges or tasks) for older children by setting up a path that leads around chairs and boxes, over piles of pillows, and through tunnels made of tables covered with blankets (or commercially made tunnels of varying lengths). For the younger children, set up an obstacle course with fewer parts and hand or feet prints for the children to follow. Adapt and change the course to fit your location and abilities of the children. This activity can be set up indoors or outdoors. Emphasize that the obstacle course is not a race and they should not speed through the activities. Stress to the children that they should keep some space between them. If a "traffic jam" does occur, help the children wait until it is their turn (Krull, 2009).

BEANBAG ACTIVITY

Use beanbags for many lively activities. They are easier for some children to catch than a ball. Ask the older children to experiment with how many different ways they can catch a beanbag, such as with one hand, two hands, their feet, or their head.

Set up several baskets into which children can practice throwing beanbags. Mark a tossing line on the floor with masking tape (or a wide chalk line, if the activity is played outdoors).

The children can take turns tossing beanbags into the basket. A variation of this game can be two teams tossing beanbags at the same time or moving the toss line up closer or farther back to make the activity easier or more difficult.

Make beanbags from colorful fabric or felt. The children can help you by deciding if they want them to be circles, squares, rectangles, triangles, or ovals. Fill the beanbags with bird seed, Styrofoam "peanuts," or dried beans.

MOVE WITH SCARVES ACTIVITY

Moving with scarves (or any lightweight material) is another way for children to practice their creativity by moving and swaying to music. Take this activity outdoors for a change of pace. These scarves can encourage them to create stories through movement and act out stories using the scarves and other props. The children are also practicing manipulative movement skills. Krull (2009) offers the following ideas for getting the children started:

Children being active when they are young can influence them for a lifetime.

- Throw the scarf in the air with one hand and catch with the other.
- Toss and try clapping once or twice before catching the scarf.
- Hold the scarf together with a friend as you move together around the classroom.
- Toss the scarf in the air, spin around and catch it before it falls to the ground.
- Catch and toss with a partner.
- Dance with the scarf to music.
- Play "Follow the Leader" where the child at the head of the line does a movement with the scarf and all children will copy that movement. Do this activity until every child has a chance to be the leader. Use music or musical instruments to accent the beat of each action.

Connecting Music and Movement with Other Areas of the Curriculum

Many activities already mentioned in this chapter offer ways to connect music and movement experiences with other areas of the curriculum. It is important to think specifically about this when you select your theme and organize your lesson plan.

FIGURE 10–12
Suggested books and CDs about music and movement.

Books

Aliki. (2003). *Ah, music!* New York: HarperCollins.
Bassett C. (2003). *Walk like a bear, stand like a tree, run like the wind: Cool yoga stretching and aerobic activities.* New York: Nubod Concepts.
Krull, K. (2003). *M is for music.* Illustrated by S. Innerst. New York: Harcourt.
Kubler, A. (2002). *Head, shoulders, knees, and toes.* (Board Book). Auburn, ME: Child's Play International.
Kubler, A. (2005). *Sign and sing along: Itsy bitsy spider.* (Board Book). Auburn, ME: Child's Play International.
Moss, L. (2001). *Our marching band.* Illustrated by B. Bluthenthal. New York: Putnam.
Moss, L. (2003). *Music is.* Illustrated by P. Petit Roulet. New York: Putnam.
Schulman, J. (Adapter). (2004). *S. Prokofiev's Peter and the Wolf: With a fully-orchestrated and narrated CD.* Illustrated by P. Malone. New York: Knopf Books for Young Readers.
Turner, B. C. (2000). *Carnival of the animals: Classical music for kids.* Illustrated by S. Williams. New York: Henry Holt.
Wagrin K. (2004). *M is for melody: A music alphabet.* New York: Sleeping Bear Press.
Wenig, M. (2003). *Yoga kids: Educating the whole child through yoga.* Photographed by S. Andrews. New York: Stewart, Tabori, & Chang.

CDs

Disney. (2005). *Here come the ABCs.* New York: Disney Productions.
Eklof, J. (2000). *My favorite animal/Mi animal favorito; So many ways to say "good morning"* (CD with picture song book). Dallas, TX: Miss Jo Publications.
Palmer, H. (2000). *Early childhood classics: Old favorites with a new twist.* Freeport, NY: Educational Activities.
Seeger, P. (2000). *American folk, game, and activity songs.* New York: Folkway Records.
Sesame Workshop. (2003). *Songs from the Street: 35 years of music.* New York: Sony/Wonder.
Sesame Workshop. (2008). *Platinum all time favorites: Sesame Street.* New York: Koch Records.
Verve/Various Artists. (2004). *Jazz for kids.* New York: Verve Music Group.

One of the most effective tools to promote mathematical thinking is through the use of music and musical activities, according to Geist and Geist, 2009.

> The very first patterning activity that a child encounters is musical. When a parent or teacher comforts a crying child they may pat, rock, or bounce the child using a steady beat or a rhythmic pattern. They may even sing them a simple song when they do this. . . . The goal for using music to support mathematics should be to provide infants, toddlers, and preschoolers with a stimulating and interactive environment. Next time you are looking for a way to engage children's mathematical mind, try a song—any song, and then ask the children to talk about the beat, rhythm, tempo, or melody. We think the children will surprise you with what they know about mathematics through music.

Music and movement are vital components of an early education environment. They contribute to language curriculum by introducing vocabulary, sound patterns, and literacy skills. Simple songs, such as question-and-answer songs or name games, can help children make the transition from speaking to singing. Examples of this are included in the songs in this chapter, and in Figure 10–12, music and movement CDs and children's books.

Additionally, music and movement can support social studies by bringing into the classroom music, musical instruments, and dances from around the world and creating a vibrant early childhood setting. Use the suggestions discussed in this chapter to stimulate your curriculum.

Tips for Teachers

> Music gets the whole child involved in the process of learning. Music activities prepare the brain for more difficult tasks needed later by preparing the brain to work from both hemispheres. (Harman, 2007)

The following are some final suggestions to help you share and enjoy music and movement with children:

- Invite parents to participate in your music experiences. Ask them to think about songs that hold special cultural and family memories—songs they learned from their parents and grandparents when they were younger. Encourage them to bring musical instruments and music that are a part of their cultural heritage and share them with the children.
- Use a variety of approaches in introducing songs. Use flannelboard characters, puppets, books, or simple props. Know the songs well yourself and sing them to the children several times while they listen. New songs should be sung to the children in their entirety, not phrase by phrase. Children pick up the tune and words naturally without having to be taught them. Incorporate simple actions into the songs. This offers visual clues to help children remember the words.
- Ask children to provide sound effects for a story. The more music and rhythm is used and the more complex listening is experienced, the broader the foundation laid (Shore & Strasser, 2006).
- Observe and listen to the children. They will let you know what is working and what is not.
- Enjoy singing songs, playing musical instruments, and participating in movement activities. *Be involved! Be part of the activity!* The children pick up on your enthusiasm (or lack of it). Do not be concerned about your singing voice. Young children are not critical! They'll be so happy that you celebrate music with them.

© Cengage Learning

Indoors or outdoors, a parachute offers young children a unique experience in active body movement.

> Children need music every day and every year of their learning lives, and the more complex, the better! Continuing to listen to complex music throughout childhood and even adulthood is as important for brain development as learning to read letters and words. Music has much to offer our educational settings, even beyond simply touching our feelings. Music can touch our minds! (Shore & Strasser, 2006)

WHY I TEACH YOUNG CHILDREN

Having grown up in a family of teachers, this seemed to be my destiny. I love being around children and observing their natural curiosity and eagerness to know "why." After teaching for many years in different environments, these little people never cease to amaze me. I feel rewarded to provide them with learning experiences. Each day is special as they make me laugh and give me unconditional love in return.

—JULIE MUCHIN

The following two groups of songs by Bea Wolf and Jo Eklof are some of the favorites requested by young children in early childhood settings. Once they and their teachers know these songs, they sing them often. These songs and stories offer a multitude of opportunities for stimulating creativity and enjoyment of music and movement activities. (Wolf and Eklof songs are included in many other chapters throughout this book.)

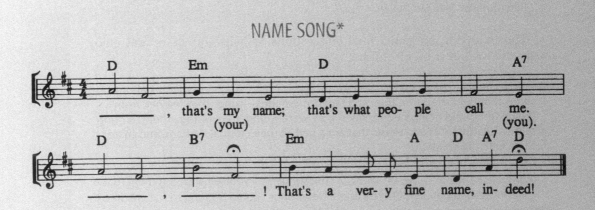

NAME SONG*

Reproduced by permission of B. Wolf—1995
Copyright B. Wolf—1993

PUPPY DOG STORY*

Once there was a puppy dog, as nice as he could be.
He thought he'd like a little playmate, just for company.
One day he saw a kitty who was playing in a tree.
He called to her, "Sweet kitty cat! Will you come play with me?"

And the puppy dog said, "Bow-wow!"
And the kitty cat said, "Meow!"
Then the puppy dog said, "Let's play!"
But the kitty cat said, "Go 'way!"

Then the puppy saw the kitty was afraid of him.
She thought that he would bite her,
so she climbed out on a limb!
But then the puppy told her he was gentle, good, and kind;
he'd be the nicest playmate anyone could ever find.
And the puppy dog said, "Bow-wow!"
And the kitty cat said, "Meow!"
Then the puppy dog said, "Let's play!"
And the kitty cat said, "Okay!"

The pup was very gentle, and the kitty wasn't rough,
and all the time they played
they never got into a huff!
Now the puppy and the kitty are the best of friends.
They play together every day,
and so our story ends,
with the puppy who says, "Bow-wow!"
and the kitty who says, "Meow!"
When the puppy dog says, "Let's play!"
then the kitty cat says, "Okay!"

Reproduced by permission of B. Wolf—1995
Copyright B. Wolf—1993

SONG TO ACCOMPANY PUPPY DOG STORY*

WINDSHIELD WIPERS
(activity song)
(Suitable for Two- to Five-Year-Olds—Entertainingly
Presents Concepts of Big/Little, Loud/Soft)

If children are old enough to understand, lead a short discussion about windshield wipers—when they are used and why. Then introduce the song and proceed to the following three activities:

Part 1: With children seated, explain that first we are going to be the windshield wipers on a very small car; therefore, we will use our small, soft voices to sing. As the song is sung, children use upraised index fingers and move hands in rhythm to simulate small windshield wipers.

Part 2: Explain that next we will be windshield wipers on a larger vehicle, such as a big car, or perhaps even a pickup truck. We will use medium voices for this, and we will make the windshield wipers by extending arms in front of us, bent at the elbows, with hands and fingers stretching up. Forearms, hands, and fingers then act as a unit to imitate wiper motions as song is sung. Children may perform this part of the activity either seated or standing.

Part 3: Now we are going to be windshield wipers on a *really* big vehicle, such as a bus. Children may wish to contribute their own examples of huge vehicles—fire trucks, eighteen wheelers, etc. We will become the largest windshield wipers we can be by standing, extending arms up as high as we can, and using our bodies from the waist up to simulate the wipers in motion. We will sing the song with our *very* loud voices!

SONG TO ACCOMPANY
WINDSHIELD WIPERS*

*Reproduced by permission of B. Wolf—1995
Copyright B. Wolf—1993

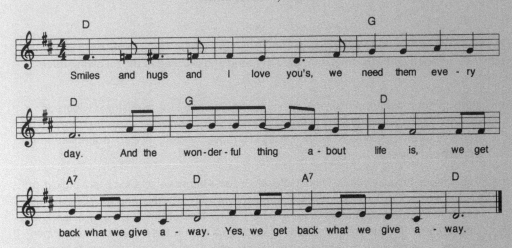

SMILES AND HUGS AND I LOVE YOU'S
Words and Music by Jo Eklof

I'M A SPECIAL PERSON AND SO ARE YOU

Words and Music by Jo Eklof

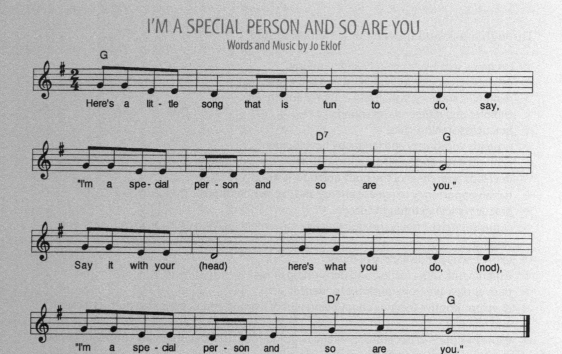

Additional verses:

Eyes - blink..........
Tongue - click.........,
Shoulders - hunch..........
Arms - flap..........
Hips - sway..........
Feet - jump..........
Now sit down - bump..........
Hands - clap..........
Now let's whisper - say (whisper)..........

From *Bringing Out The Best in Children Songbook*
Reprinted by permission of Miss Jo Publications
http://www.missjo.com

Afterview

Through music and movement activities, a child

● becomes sensitive to beauty and harmony.
● validates creativity, individuality, and self-expression.
● reinforces auditory, visual, and comprehension skills.
● explores and differentiates sounds.
● practices listening skills.
● expands vocabulary and language development.
● explores large and small muscle movement.
● develops awareness of the body and how it works and moves.
● has an opportunity to release energy and express emotions.
● practices moving through space.
● expresses herself freely through creative movement, playing musical instruments, and singing.
● experiences a wide variety of music.
● experiments with creating and performing music.
● derives pleasure from musical experiences.
● develops positive feelings about being part of a group and participates both as a leader and follower.
● expresses pride in her ethnic heritage by using songs, dances, musical instruments, and recordings from her culture.

Reflective Review Questions

1. What is the difference between locomotor movement, nonlocomotor movement, and manipulative movement? Identify four examples of each.
2. Name and describe five different ways to make musical instruments that young children could enjoy playing. How would you introduce these to the children? Explain.
3. Describe the types of opportunities that are available for children to use music or to be introduced to music in an early childhood environment. Give examples of how children can be encouraged to use music and/or movement creatively.
4. Choose a classical music selection from this chapter and plan how you would share it with a group of kindergarten children. Describe your plan in writing.

Key Terms

beat	manipulative movement	tempo
kinesthetics	nonlocomotor movement	tone
locomotor movement	rhythm	volume

Explorations

1. Select an early childhood classroom. Observe for at least one hour. In writing, describe any music and movement activities you observed. Did the children or the teacher initiate these activities? Describe some examples of how the children spontaneously approached these activities.

2. Describe a resource person and what that person might do on a visit to a classroom of young children that would enhance children's appreciation of movement and music. Indicate how you would prepare the children for the experience and what follow-up activities you would use.

3. In writing, discuss the ways musical instruments can be used in music activities with young children. Make one of the musical instruments suggested in this chapter. Introduce the use of the instrument to a group of children. Discuss why you chose this instrument. Did you achieve your objectives? What were the children's reactions? Were they stimulated to make this and other instruments? What would you do differently if you presented this activity again? Explain.

4. Select one of the songs in this chapter and create a flannelboard story to accompany this song. Present this song and story to a group of young children (toddlers or preschoolers). Evaluate the activity. What should be kept the same for the next time it is presented? What should be changed and why?

5. How useful are music and dance in developing multicultural awareness in young children? How could a teacher accomplish this? Give four examples of activities or experiences that would promote either or both.

Additional Readings and Resources

Armistead, M. E. (2007, November). Kaleidoscope: Creative arts enrichment program. *Young Children, 62*(6), 86–93.

Bernath, C., & Masi, W. (2005, Fall). Movin' and groovin': Integrating movement throughout the curriculum. *Dimensions of Early Childhood, 33*(3), 22–26.

Dow, C. B. (2010, March). Young children and movement: The power of creative dance. *Young Children, 65*(2), 30–35.

Humpal, M. E., & Wolf, J. (2003, March). Music in the inclusive environment. *Young Children, 58*(2), 103–107.

Kim, J., & Robinson, H. M. (2010, March). Four steps for becoming familiar with early music standards. *Young Children, 65*(2), 42–47.

Marcon, R. A. (2003, January). The physical side of development. *Young Children, 58*(1), 80–87.

Moore, T. (2002, July). If you teach children, you can sing! *Young Children, 57*(4), 84–85.

Moravcik, E. (2000, July). Music all the livelong day. *Young Children, 55*(4), 27–29.

Pica, R. (2003, March–April). But we don't have room. *Early Childhood News, 15*(2), 24–26.

Pica, R. (2007). *Moving and learning across the curriculum* (2nd ed.). Clifton Park, NY: Wadsworth Cengage Learning.

Ratey, J. (2008). *SPARK! The revolutionary new science of exercise and the brain.* New York: Little Brown.

Ringgenberg, S. (2003, September). Music as a teaching tool: Creating story songs. *Young Children, 58*(5), 76–79.

Schilling, T., & McOmber, K. A. (2006, May). Tots in action on and beyond the playground. *Young Children, 61*(3), 34–36.

Steies, A. (2003, March–April). Childhood obesity: A new epidemic. *Early Childhood News, 15*(2), 15–23.

Vagovic, J. C. (2008, May). Transformers: Movement experiences for early childhood classrooms. *Young Children, 63*(3), 26–32.

Wellhousen, K. (2002). *Outdoor play every day: Innovative play concepts for early childhood.* Clifton Park, NY: Delmar Cengage Learning.

White, J. (2009). Healthy heart. *Scholastic.* Online at: *http://www2.scholastic.com*

Helpful Web Connections

Children's Music Network
  http://www.cmnonline.org
Children's Music Web
  http://www.childrensmusic.org
Hap Palmer's Music & Movement
  http://www.happalmer.com
NAEYC
  http://www.naeyc.org

National Association of Music Education (MENC)
  http://www.menc.org
National Institute for Play
  http://www.nifplay.org
Zero to Three (type in search box: music or movement)
  http://www.zerotothree.org

References

Allen, J., McNeill, E., & Schmidt, V. (1992). *Cultural awareness for children.* Menlo Park, CA: Addison-Wesley.

Andress, B. L., & Walker, L. M. (Eds.). (1992). *Readings in early childhood music education.* Reston, VA: Music Educators National Conference.

Billhartz, P. (2007). Let's make music. *Early Childhood News.* Online at: *http://www.earlychildhoodnews.com*

Brown, S. (2009). *Play: How it shapes the brain, opens the imagination, and invigorates the soul.* New York: Penguin.

Copple, C., & Bredekamp, S. (Eds.). (2009). *Developmentally appropriate practice in early childhood programs* (3rd ed.). Washington, DC: NAEYC.

Corbett, S. (1995). *A world of difference: Shake, rattle, and strum.* Chicago: Children's Press.

Essa, E. L., & Burnham, M. M. (Eds.). (2009). *Informing our practice: Useful research on young children's development.* Washington, DC: NAEYC.

Feldman, J. (2002, Spring). Keep a song in your heart! *Early Years, 24*(1), 6–7.

Gardner, H. (1983). *Frames of mind: The theory of multiple intelligences.* New York: Basic Books.

Geist, E., & Geist, K. (2009, March). The beat goes on! Mathematics and music with young children. *Early Childhood Today.* Online at: *http://www.scholastic.com*

Greenberg, M. (1979). *Your children need music.* Englewood Cliffs, NJ: Prentice Hall.

Griss, S. (1994, February). Creative movement: A language for learning. *Educational Leadership, 51*(5), 78–80.

Haines, B. J. E., & Gerber, L. L. (1996). *Leading young children to music* (5th ed.). Upper Saddle River, NJ: Merrill.

Harman, M. (2007). Music and movement: Instrumental in language development. *Early Childhood News.* Online at: *http://www.earlychildhoodnews.com*

Isbell, R. T., & Raines, S. C. (2007). *Creativity and the arts with young children* (2nd ed.). Clifton Park, NY: Delmar Cengage Learning.

Koster, J. B. (2009). *Growing artists: Teaching the arts to young children* (4th ed.). Clifton Park, NY: Wadsworth Cengage Learning.

Krull, S. (2009). Obstacle courses. *Early Childhood News.* Online at: *http://www.earlychildhoodnews.com*

Machado, J. M. (2007). *Early childhood experiences in language arts* (8th ed.). Clifton Park, NY: Delmar Cengage Learning.

McGraw, G. (2002, Winter). Songs of childhood. *Early Childhood Connections,* Leadership Bulletin, *Vol. 8,* No.1. Greensboro, NC: Foundation for Music-Based Learning.

Miche, M. (2002). *Weaving music into young minds.* Clifton Park, NY: Delmar Cengage Learning.

Moomaw, S. (1984). *Discovering music in early childhood.* Boston, MA: Allyn & Bacon.

Music Educators National Conference (MENC). (1994). *The school music program: A new vision* (Position Statement). Reston, VA: Author.

Palmer, H. (2001, September). The music, movement, and learning connection. *Young Children, 56*(5), 13–17.

Parlakin, R., & Lerner, C. (2010, March). Beyond twinkle, twinkle: Using music with infants and toddlers. *Young Children, 65*(2), 14–19.

Pica, R. (2010). *Experiences in movement and music: Birth to age 8* (4th ed.). Clifton Park, NY: Wadsworth Cengage Learning.

Sanders, S. W. (2006, Winter). Physically active for life. *Dimensions of Early Childhood. 34*(1), 3–10.

Shelemay, K. (2001). *Music on the brain: Researchers explore the biology of music.* Online at: *http://www.news.harvard.edu/gazette/2001/03.22/04-music.html*

Shore, R., & Strasser, J. (2006, March). Music for their minds. *Young Children, 61*(2), 62–67.

Smith, K. L. (2002, March). Dancing in the forest. *Young Children, 57*(2), 90–94.

chapter 11

Puppets

Objectives

After Studying This Chapter, You Should Be Able To:

- Discuss the history of puppetry.

- Plan for puppets in an early education classroom.

- Describe and give examples of easy-to-make puppets that are developmentally appropriate for young children.

- List the types of materials needed for children to make puppets.

- Identify how to integrate puppets easily into an early childhood setting.

- Connect puppets into curriculum areas both indoors and outdoors.

- Identify how puppets on television have influenced teachers and children.

- Describe how to involve families in puppet play.

© Cengage Learning

Overview

Puppets have always been popular in the early childhood classroom, although in many class-rooms they are under-used. For a storyteller, they can be an important and effective tool in maintaining children's attention, involving listeners in the telling of the story, and providing a visual and kinesthetic experience to augment the aural one. (Richards, 2007)

Puppets can teach, entertain, and delight children and adults. Historically, puppetry has been described as a folk art, one produced by and for the people. Puppets have been around for thousands of years and are found virtually everywhere in the world, embedded in every continent and culture.

Raines and Isbell (1994) tell us,

Storytelling and puppetry are ancient forms of oral expression that developed historically in similar ways. The story told was passed from generation to generation and became a binding link for families and cultures. The puppeteer often augmented the storytelling by providing visualization and surprise elements to the story's presentation.

"Puppets delight children and touch the hearts of adults. Increasingly, it is recognized that puppetry is a unique and innovative way to reach out to people of all ages. Puppets can entertain, inform, persuade and appeal. They are part of the world's ancient history, and at the same time, they are also part of the world's modern imagination" (UNICEF, 2007).

Historical View of Puppetry

puppetry The art of making or operating puppets or producing puppet shows.

● ● ● ● ● ● ● ● ● ● ●
FIGURE 11-1
Indonesian puppet.

No one knows exactly when the art of **puppetry** began. Were the first puppeteers primitive people casting shadows on darkened cave walls? Were the early priests and shamans who used puppets to celebrate important life cycle events some of the first puppeteers? Did the Egyptians invent the first puppet, as some historians have suggested? According to the Center for Puppetry Arts in Atlanta, Georgia, written documentation of puppetry's beginnings can be traced back to Asia, where it developed simultaneously in India and China in the ninth century B.C. In *Indonesia*, flat, leather *shadow puppets* and *three- dimensional rod puppets*, introduced centuries ago, are still used in performances today. (See Figure 11–1.)

Vietnam is famous for its unique tradition of water puppetry which combines both rod and strings to manipulate the figures. The performance appears in a lake. The puppeteers are hidden in a structure resembling a Vietnamese communal house built in the middle of the lake. The puppets are attached to long bamboo rods and strings. When the audience views the show they see puppets acting on a watery stage with the puppeteer's house in the background. (Center for Puppetry Arts, 2010)

Contreras, cited in Jalongo (2003), continues, "In the case of *Vietnam's water puppetry*, it is an expression of traditional values, a source of national pride, and for those outside the culture, a way of promoting intercultural understanding."

Puppetry also has roots in *Africa*, dating back to the fifth century B.C. *Puppet pageants* are still performed there for the entire community to celebrate important events, such as planting and harvest time.

In *Japan*, *Bunraku* originated in the sixteenth century. This is a highly refined form of rod puppetry, using three puppeteers to perform a single character. One controls the head and one arm; another, the second arm; and the third, the feet. The puppeteers

FIGURE 11–2
Japanese Bunraku puppet.

usually dress in black, are visible behind each puppet, and possess great skill and coordination (Center for Puppetry Arts, 2010; Henson, 1994). (See Figure 11–2.)

Hand puppets began appearing in *Europe* and *colonial America* in the mid-1700s. The *English Punch and Judy*, the most popular characters, were descendants of an *Italian puppet* named *Pulcinella*. Punch and Judy appeared in marketplaces, at community fairs, on the street, in town halls, at circuses, and in schools. Similar *puppets*, with different names, were also performing in *Germany, France, Russia*, and *Turkey*. (See Figure 11–3.)

The *Mamulengo* tradition in puppetry can be found in *South America*. These puppeteers fuse the folk traditions of native populations and black culture, as well as draw from colonial Hispanic and Portuguese influences when they present street puppet theater (Center for Puppetry Arts, 2010).

As you continue through this chapter, you will find ways for you and the children to create, enjoy, and develop skills by using this ancient form of folk art. You will find that the use of puppetry can enrich all the curriculum areas in your early education program. Most importantly, using a puppet to mirror feelings, creativity, and learning processes can enhance a child's positive self-esteem. Puppets can also make a child's connection to the world exciting.

Planning for Puppets in Early Education

Children relate to puppets from their earliest years because they are used to making inanimate characters come to life. Children are puppeteers themselves from the first time they pick up a shoe, a squeezed-out half orange or a hairbrush and make it move and talk. Toys and dolls take an active role in children's play. They laugh and talk and argue. They put on personalities and take them off again. (UNICEF, 2007)

What exactly is a puppet? Cheryl Henson (1994), daughter of the late Jim Henson (the puppeteer who created the Muppets and the *Sesame Street* characters), explains,

FIGURE 11–3
Punch and Judy puppets.

"A puppet is an object that appears to be alive when it's manipulated by a human hand. Some puppets look like dolls; others look like stuffed animals. Still others look like pieces of sculpture or even like piles of junk!"

For children in an early education program, a puppet is *whatever they say it is!* For young children, the discovery of themselves as puppeteers can be a wonderful discovery of themselves. Their excitement, enthusiasm, and imagination in creating and sharing puppets will become contagious to others, adults and children alike.

"Isenberg and Jalongo encourage the use of puppets as a nonthreatening device for improvisation and social collaboration or as a vehicle for building self-esteem and taking risks" (Esch & Long, 2002). Children can also explore the values of other cultures by recounting legends, folktales, or myths from around the world using puppets as storytellers.

For young children, the discovery of themselves as puppeteers can be wonderful. You and the children, together, should plan for and decide when and how to use puppets in your classroom. Here are some suggestions for getting started:

● Begin by selecting a puppet for you, the teacher. Your first puppet, either one created by you or a ready-made commercial one, should become your special friend. Usually a hand puppet is the most comfortable; the more you use it, the more it fits like an old, favorite glove.

For young children, the discovery of themselves as puppeteers can be wonderful.

© Cengage Learning

- Identify why this particular puppet appeals to you. Does it remind you of a toy, doll, or puppet you had as a child? This discovery will help you decide on the puppet's name, personality, and voice. Remember, you do *not* have to be a ventriloquist.
- Practice with your puppet. Watching yourself in the mirror might be useful in helping you decide how to use the puppet.
- You do not need to use a stage or puppet theater. The personal interaction with a child or group of children is important.
- Reinforce your own creativity and enjoyment of teaching. Let the puppet do for you what it does for a child: Allow your imagination to flourish, your creative play to flow free, and your unique thoughts, feelings, and language to emerge.
- Use puppets on a regular basis. As with any new or special materials you bring into the classroom or playground, demonstrate the appropriate use of the puppets.
- Depending on the age of the children you teach, decide how often and how much you will use puppets. Usually, the younger the child, the more time you should take to make him feel comfortable with and trusting of the puppets. As with any toy or activity, use only safe materlals.
- For infants, having familiar stuffed toys and animals "talk to them" is a way of introducing puppets. Another way is to "walk" two of your fingers up a child's arm. Use a rhythmic, sing-song voice and say: "Here comes a little person walking up (child's name) arm. Now it's on your shoulder. Now it's on your neck. Tickle, tickle."
- Take lots of time with toddlers. Start with finger plays and hand puppets. Leaving plenty of space between the puppet and the child usually helps this age child feel more comfortable.
- Use puppets with your favorite finger plays, poems, songs, books, and flannelboard stories. Group time is a good opportunity to introduce puppets. When telling a familiar story, allow the children to hear the story several times. The retelling of the story allows you and the children to manipulate the puppets in a familiar setting. Children will eventually tell the story spontaneously and expand it in their own way *using puppets*.

Most young children do not truly see the actual puppet, but rather the imaginary being it becomes through their play. . . . Puppets can share secrets, read stories, and play with the children. They allow the adult to enter the child's world. (Koster, 2009)

● INTRODUCING PUPPET ACTIVITIES

The introduction of the puppet activities can be done in three stages:

1. Model the use of puppets during group time and in many curriculum areas. By doing this, you, as the teacher, affirm the use of puppets. By demonstrating *nonviolent* behavior with puppets, you are showing the children how to enjoy them appropriately. Introduce them one at a time. As with any new activity, doing too much at one time can overstimulate the children.

2. You and the children should create and use puppets together. Allow children plenty of opportunities to practice with a variety of puppets before they begin to create their own. The guidance techniques you use will demonstrate additional and appropriate ways to enjoy puppets. Keep puppet construction, props, and stages very simple. Allow children to improvise, using their own creativity.

3. Let individual children or a group of children make and interact with puppets through activities integrated into the lesson plan and the total curriculum. The activities should be open-ended and allow children opportunities to extend the activities. Remember to make puppets accessible to children and give them time to explore with them. Provide the materials, but remember not to make a model for the children to copy. (The illustrations in this chapter and those online at this textbook's premium website are designed to give teachers *ideas* for making puppets, *not* to be used as models for the children to make.)

SETTING UP THE ENVIRONMENT

By introducing children to different types of puppets, you can offer developmentally appropriate alternative learning experiences. These wonderful creations can tell a story, carry on a conversation, be good listeners, and entertain. While handling materials, manipulating, and organizing them, the *process*, as always, is the major focus.

> When adults realize the most important aspect of creativity is the process, not the product, they will support the child's desire to experiment and create in individual ways. They will understand that the thing "made" is not nearly so important as what is happening in the process. (Fortson & Reiff, 1995)

Young children can explore and stretch their abilities in all developmental areas through the process of creating and operating their puppets. They are:

● experiencing the sheer joy of playing and fantasizing
● developing positive self-images and independence
● using a safe and acceptable outlet for expressing themselves
● expanding vocabulary and communication skills
● improving social skills by sharing and cooperating and communicating ideas
● learning problem-solving skills and abstract thinking
● using fine motor skills
● practicing hand-eye coordination, hand-hand coordination, and muscle control

© Cengage Learning

By introducing children to different types of puppets, you can offer alternative learning experiences.

Easy-to-Make Puppets

There are three basic categories of puppets: hand puppets, rod puppets, and marionettes.

HAND PUPPETS

Hand puppets come in many types and varieties and are easy for young children to make and manipulate. Starting with finger puppets, the child gains ownership right away. It is fun to put two eyes, a nose, and a mouth on the child's thumb and fingers with a felt-tip pen. You will find some children do not want to wash their fingers after this activity. They like their puppets and want to keep them (see Figure 11–4).

Another kind of simple finger puppet can be made out of felt. Glue the two pieces together (as shown in the three-step illustration of Figure 11–5). Place eyes, a nose, and a mouth on the puppet. These can be easily manipulated by younger children and offer an unusual small muscle activity.

Other finger puppets can be made easily to illustrate shapes, numbers, nursery rhymes, or other concepts. You can first introduce them at group time and then put them in the manipulative center for the children to play with. By placing two fingers in one of these, the child can add "legs" to make the puppet walk and dance. (See the three-step illustration in Figure 11–6.)

DAP

FIGURE 11–4
Example of a finger puppet that is appropriate for young children.

FIGURE 11–5
Example of how to make finger puppets out of felt fabric.

STEP 1: Cut 2 finger puppet shapes out of felt.

STEP 2: Glue the 2 shapes together along outside edges. Be sure to leave bottom open for finger.

STEP 3: Decorate with marker, glitter, cut shapes of felt, etc.

FIGURE 11–6
Example of how to make finger puppets out of cardboard.

STEP 1: Cut puppet figure out of cardboard or paper .

STEP 2: Decorate with markers, paints, crayons, glitter, buttons, cut shapes of fabric, etc.

STEP 3: Play!

hand puppets Puppets that are put on the hand; come in many types and varieties and are easy for young children to make and manipulate.

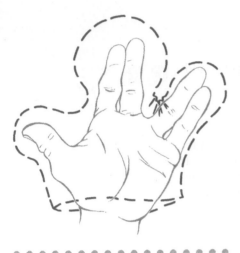

FIGURE 11–7

Placement of the hand in a hand puppet.

FIGURE 11–8

Example of a completed hand puppet.

Basic hand, glove, and mitt puppets provide a close link between the puppet and the puppeteer. Toddlers, especially, enjoy this type of puppet. There are many commercially made examples, but the ones the teacher and children make are the most fun.

Figures 11–7 and 11–8 illustrate the easy-to-make basic design. The hand can be the whole body, with two fingers as the arms and one or two fingers operating the head. This hand puppet can be made easily from two pieces of felt or other fabric glued or sewn together and cut to fit a child's or an adult's hand. Eyes, nose, mouth, ears, hands, and hair can be attached with Velcro, glued, or sewn to the fabric. Felt squares of tan, beige, cream, brown, peach, and black can be used so a child can make a puppet that has his skin tone. (See basic patterns and new puppet patterns added online at this textbook's website.)

Rubber household gloves, which have a smooth surface, and garden gloves, which are available in many colors and designs, can be used to make another kind of hand puppet. This variety allows you to move all five fingers, independently as separate characters. Use double-stick tape on the rubber glove or sew small pieces of Velcro to the fingertips of the garden glove. Place the same kind of material on matching story pieces. This gives you and the children flexibility in creating hand puppets (see Figure 11–9).

Ready-made mittens or household hot pad mitts can also be used to create another variety of hand puppets. Commercially crocheted puppets, usually representing animals, and sets of puppets are also available. Evaluate these carefully to be sure they are safe and appropriate for use with young children.

Think of all the finger plays, poems, songs, and stories you and the children can share with each other using sock puppets. These are probably the easiest puppets to make and use. Ask parents to donate unneeded children's socks in all sizes and colors. Once a child puts the sock on his hand, the puppet will "come to life." Add eyes made from buttons, commercial wiggly eyes, or anything you wish. Hair, made from yarn, string, steel wool, or cotton balls, and ears give extra personality to the character (see Figures 11–10 and 11–11).

FIGURE 11–9

Example of a rubber glove puppet with finger characters.

FIGURE 11–10

The hand position for a sock puppet.

Paper plate and paper bag puppets are some of the most fun to make and use. They are inexpensive, children can create more than one, and they are easily remade if they get torn. You and the children will design many kinds of paper puppets, but to get you started, a few examples follow.

Staple two paper plates together, leaving the bottom portion open for the puppeteer's hand. (You will find thin plates are easy for the children to handle.) Decorate this puppet, and it is ready to use!

For a paper-bag, floppy-mouth puppet, use a small- or medium-size bag. Draw a puppet face on the bag or cut and glue one from a magazine. Use crayons, markers, paints, glue, yarn, cotton balls, or other material to finish the puppet. It is easy to work by placing your fingers inside the flap of the bag and moving them up and down.

Other paper puppets can be made from products such as paper cups or pudding, oatmeal, or small cereal boxes. Add these to the other creative materials in your puppet center for the children's exploration and experimentation.

FIGURE 11–11
Example of a sock puppet.

STICK OR ROD PUPPETS

Stick or rod puppets are controlled by a single stick, such as a tongue depressor, dowel rod, paper towel roll, craft stick, or ice cream stick. An even smaller character might be placed on a paper straw. The figure itself can be cut from magazines, catalogs, and wrapping paper; traced from a pattern; or drawn by hand. Then it is glued to the stick or straw. Many card shops or toy stores have paper plates in the shape of animals. These make wonderful puppets when stapled to a dowel rod. These can be reinforced with tagboard and covered with contact paper or laminated.

A wooden spoon makes another delightful puppet. The bowl of the spoon makes a perfect head, and the handle becomes the body. Use felt-tip markers, crayons, or paint to make the face.

The "stick people puppet" (Figure 11–12) is made out of cardboard or tagboard and then attached to a stick or dowel rod. Encourage children to add eyes, a nose, a mouth, hair, clothes, and shoes. Multicultural or skin-toned paints, crayons, and construction paper should be available for the children to use. This promotes self-awareness and positive self-esteem. Another variation of the stick people puppet is one depicting a face (Figure 11–13). The children can cut out the eyes, then add a nose, a mouth, and hair. Attach a straw or craft stick to create a stick puppet or mask. Primary-grade children enjoy this activity.

> **stick or rod puppets** Puppets controlled by a single stick, such as a tongue depressor, dowel rod, paper towel roll, craft stick, or ice cream stick.

FIGURE 11–12
Making a stick people puppet.

STEP 1: Cut out people puppet shape from cardboard.

STEP 2: Decorate with paint, markers, crayons, cut shapes of paper, fabric, etc.

STEP 3: Glue stick to back of finished puppet.

FIGURE 11–13
Making a people mask puppet.

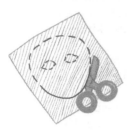   

STEP 1: Cut face shapes from cardboard or paper.

STEP 2: Decorate with paint, markers, crayons, cut shapes of paper, fabric, etc.

STEP 3: Glue stick to back of decorated face shape.

STEP 4: Let it dry and then play!

marionettes Puppets controlled by strings that offer an extra range of expression and full body movement.

shadow puppets Puppets held from rods against a translucent screen lit from behind. These puppets offer a visual dimension that other types do not.

MARIONETTES

Marionettes, controlled by strings, offer an extra range of expression and full body movement. As teachers, we should appreciate the sophisticated skills needed to make and operate a marionette. In encouraging a school-age child who wants to make this type of puppet, the first question a teacher should ask is, "What do you want it to do?" It is important to think through and plan each step in the creation of a marionette. The "airplane control" is the simplest design to manipulate, usually with one string to the head and a string to each of the hands (Figure 11–14). Children need time to experiment and to experience the frustration of the puppet not working the first time it is tried. It is important to support them through the frustration. The failure and success of making and manipulating a marionette is part of their *process*. Maintenance and care of the marionette is also part of the experience. To avoid tangling the strings, it should be hung after it is used. Hanging marionettes make a distinctive classroom decoration.

SHADOW PUPPETS

Shadow puppets offer a visual dimension to puppetry that other types do not. Shown in a darkened room, they are held from below by rods against a translucent screen lit from behind. Puppeteers manipulate flat, cut-out silhouettes that the audience can see on the other side of the screen as moving figures. One of the simplest shadow animal puppets, a flying bird, is described by Cheryl Henson (1994):

> All you need is a single light source—a standing lamp with the shade removed or a desk lamp tilted to the side. Interlock your thumbs and slowly flap your hands. When you pass them between the light source and a blank wall, the shadow they cast will look like a bird in flight.

Progression from this simple example to more complex shadow puppets will occur as older children discover creative ways to investigate and make these puppets (Figure 11–15).

Materials Needed

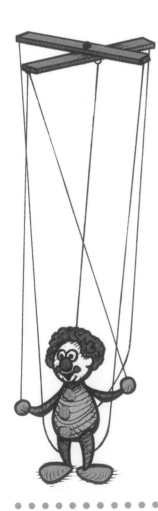

FIGURE 11–14
Example of a marionette.

All of the various types of puppets can be made from a wide variety of materials. (Puppet patterns for teachers can be found online at this textbook's website with new puppet patterns added.) An easy way to collect these is to place a box in the classroom

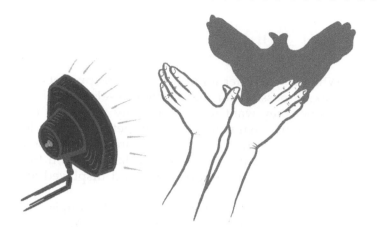

FIGURE 11–15
Example of a shadow hand puppet.

simply labeled, "Materials for Puppet Making." This keeps it visible for parents and children while reminding them that all kinds of things are needed. The following is a list of what needs to be gathered:

- boxes—especially small cereal and salt boxes
- buttons and wiggly eyes—especially the larger ones
- clothespins
- cloth scraps—felt, lace, cotton, towels, and washcloths in tan, beige, cream, brown, peach, and black
- cotton balls, steel wool, sponges, pipe cleaners, corks, hair curlers
- crayons, markers, pencils, pens, paints
- egg cartons
- feathers
- gloves—cloth, garden-type, and rubber
- leather scraps
- magazines, catalogs, and newspapers
- office supplies—scissors, envelopes, paper clips, glue, brads, rubber bands, gummed labels and stickers, stapler and staples, and rulers
- paper products—cardboard; sandpaper; all sizes of paper bags, plates, and cups; towel and bathroom paper rolls; crepe paper; wrapping paper; tissue paper; wall paper; waxed paper; foil; straws; and construction paper in all colors representing skin tones, including tan, beige, cream, brown, black, and peach
- socks—especially those that will fit a child's hand and soccer socks for making adult-size puppets
- spools
- sticks—tongue depressors, ice cream sticks, craft sticks, yardsticks, toothpicks, and dowel rods
- Styrofoam balls and scraps
- tape—clear, masking, and double-stick types
- wooden spoons
- wood scraps—preferably already sanded smooth
- yarn, string, ribbons, and shoelaces

Making a puppet should not be a one-time activity but something the child will return to again and again in order to create a character or persona with which to face the world. After introducing puppet-making supplies at the art center, they should be available on a regular basis for whenever a child wants or needs to create a puppet. (Koster, 2009)

Some children prefer to examine the puppets, try them on, and then play with the puppets while giving them personalities.

© Cengage Learning

Suggestions for Placement and Storage of Puppets

Whether you offer a puppet center or puppets in every center, make it possible for the children to select and interact with any puppet they want to make or play with. The children should feel the freedom to move the puppets to another location to best meet their needs. Children are more likely to use puppets if the guidelines for use are clearly explained and if the puppets and puppet materials are organized and displayed attractively and accessibly.

At first, some children prefer just to examine the puppets and try them on to see how they feel. Others enjoy making puppets, and still others just like to play with ready-made puppets. Allow for individual and developmental preferences.

For the creative and spontaneous use of puppets, a stage is not necessary. As mentioned earlier, you, as a teacher, do not need to use a stage, and neither do the children. If you feel you need a creative boost, Hunt and Renfro (1982) suggest a story apron.

> This is an ideal costume for you to wear as a puppeteller. It signals that Puppetime is about to begin, it provides a background for your story, poem, or song and it hides puppets and props until you are ready to use them. . . . A general all-purpose story apron can be made by adding pockets to a store-bought apron or by creating your own custom-apron from selected fabric.

If the children insist on needing a stage for their puppets, here are some easy ways to provide one:

● Construct a puppet stage from a large packing carton. Cut the center out of the box to form a "stage opening."
● Drape a cloth over a piece of rope suspended horizontally.

● Turn a small, sturdy table on its side so the children can "hide" behind it and show only the puppets, or use a table top draped in front with a sheet.
● Using a shower curtain rod, hang a piece of fabric low across an open doorway.
● Place two adult-size chairs back to back at a short distance. Drop a curtain or cloth over a yardstick placed between the chairs.
● Use a "gutted TV" (a television set from which the insides have been removed). This offers another dimension to a child's puppet play.

The following are ideas for puppet storage that many teachers use. They are suggested by Hunt and Renfro (1982), Raines and Isbell (1994), and the author's personal preferences:

● Hang a clothesline along a wall at child's eye and arm level, and use clothespins to clip the puppets to the line.

For younger children getting to know a puppet inspires curiosity and creativity.

© Cengage Learning

- Clip the puppets to a multiple-skirt hanger.
- Store finger puppets in egg cartons.
- Store puppets in tiered hanging baskets.
- Use a shoe bag or shoe rack to organize puppets.
- Place shoe boxes or clear plastic boxes on low shelves.

A child might like to make a home for his very special puppet. Select a box into which the puppet will fit. Have the child decorate the box any way he chooses, including adding windows and a door. A scrap of soft material inside the box makes a bed for the puppet friend. The box can be placed in or near the child's cubby.

Connecting Puppets to Curriculum Areas

It is helpful to brainstorm ideas with colleagues and classmates, but here are a few suggestions to stimulate your creativity:

- Puppets can speak in any language. This shows that all languages are valued. For example, Mister Number is a puppet that can count from 1 to 20 in many languages. Another puppet says only "yes and no" or "hello and goodbye," but does so in ten different languages. Multicultural puppets can also be used to introduce cultural celebrations.
- Expand the language arts center by adding puppets and props. A puppet with a microphone can encourage creative play. Puppets can even interview other puppets. Because the characters can be human, animal, or "Mr. and Ms. Anything," they can ask questions about families, feelings, favorite foods, where you come from, or where you live. For older children, the questions can also concern current events, nutrition, math, science, or ecology.
- *In the digital age, the need has never been greater for teaching tools that are high-touch— that foster a bond between young and adult, [as well as] emotive intelligence, creativity, freedom, and individuality. . . . [Puppets can help] teachers reach all kinds of learners in ways that: activate and employ the hands; create powerful experiences for learners to help them articulate, express, and remember what they learn; foster socialization and civic values; employ upbeat and imaginative group dynamics; and build upon innate learning skills and strengths. (Peyton, 2009)*
- Encourage storytelling with sock puppets representing "The Three Billy Goats Gruff" by P. C. Asbjørnsen and J. E. Moe, "The Little Red Hen" by P. Galdone, or characters from *Winnie the Pooh* by A. A. Milne and *The Velveteen Rabbit* by M. Williams. Use finger puppets or hand puppets to read the storybooks *Corduroy* by D. Freeman, *Leo the Late Bloomer* by R. Kraus, or *Horton Hatches the Egg* by Dr. Seuss (T. Geisel). Relating puppets to familiar stories can extend the retelling.
- Add a puppet holding a toy telephone to the dramatic play center. This presents an additional dimension to telephone talk.
- A puppet "helper of the day" can offer you a unique way to reinforce cooperation, cleanup rules, and problem solving. The puppet can ask the children questions, leading them to solve a problem themselves, instead of needing you to solve it. This puppet character can help defuse many disputes and difficulties that occur in an early childhood setting.
- Introducing a "listening puppet," one with big ears, can help you emphasize the importance of listening. One puppet might talk to or answer children only in song or verse. Perhaps

another only dances. A very shy puppet who will not talk can learn to do so with help from the children.

● Create some puppets for outdoor play. Have all types of clothing available for these puppet personalities. The children can select the appropriate clothes for the weather that day.

Sharing with Families: Taking Puppets Home

Getting families involved with and enthusiastic about puppetry will take time and patience on your part. You might find the following suggestions helpful:

● Send information home (via letters or email) to families about puppet presentations available in your community. It is important that children have opportunities to see live performances.

● Figure 11–16 on page 324 shows a letter to be sent home with the children in your program. The younger children can add illustrations to the letter. The older children can write their own letter to invite their families to a special evening at the center. If the parents speak a language other than English, ask someone to help you translate the letter into their native language. Send both copies home with children.

● Have an informal parents' meeting. After a light supper, including foods the children have made, the parents and children go to different learning centers in the room. This is a good time to introduce new or favorite activities. Set up the centers with materials and supplies for the families to make things together. One of the activities should be making puppets. Whatever the family group makes, they take home.

● Offer a puppet lending library to the children and families. Display durable, commercially made puppets available for the families to sign out. Encourage parents to enjoy the puppets with their children. Supply a bright-colored sack or large envelope in which the borrowed puppet can be returned.

Puppets and Television

Since the beginning of television, puppets have been a part of the daily viewing schedule. Local television stations usually began their day of live broadcasting with programs that featured puppets.

In the United States, eight great puppeteers introduced their creations to many children who had never before seen puppets:

● Edgar Bergen (1903–1978): a ventriloquist who entertained children and their parents with his wooden partners, Charlie McCarthy and Mortimer Snerd, on radio, stage, and television.

● Bil Baird (1904–1987): puppeteered marionettes for over 60 years and created more than 3,000 puppets seen on stage, television, and film.

● "Buffalo Bob" Smith (1917–1998): "Hey kids, what time is it?" "It's *Howdy Doody* time!" Hundreds of children, in the studio and at home, answered the question from 1947 to 1960 when "Buffalo Bob" and his marionette, Howdy Doody, a real-life but nontalking clown, Clarabell, and their friends entertained children during the early days of live television.

● Burr Tilstrom (1917–1985): best known during the 1950s on television for his hand puppets Kukla and Ollie, along with Fran, a human being who stood in front of the stage and interacted with the puppets.

- Jim Henson (1937–1990): created the Muppets and to this day inspires children and families all over the world to laugh and learn together while enjoying *Sesame Street* and the Muppet movies and home videos.
- Shari Lewis (1934–1998): innovative ventriloquist-puppeteer shared her endearing sock puppets Lamb Chop, Charlie Horse, and Hush Puppy with children and their parents for four decades in person and on television, her last being *Lamb Chop's Play-Along* and *The Charlie Horse Music Pizza.*
- Fred Rogers (1928–2003): believed everyone is special, and his use of puppets in the Neighborhood of Make-Believe (King Friday and his friends) dealt with things that are important to young children. Mister Rogers was there through good times and bad times. He was there for teachers and parents as well. Mister Rogers and his words will continue to inspire as we enjoy his videotaped television series and books. Visit the Family Communications website for information about the life and works of Fred Rogers, online at http://www.fci.org
- Bob Keeshan (1927–2004): known to children and adults the world over as *Captain Kangaroo.* His children's network television program, with puppets Mr. Moose and Rabbit, ran from 1955–1984, plus an additional six years following on PBS. Why he chose the persona of the old captain, Keeshan explained: "I was impressed with the potential positive relationship between grandparents and grandchildren, so I chose an elderly character."

All of the puppeteers mentioned hold special places in the development of television for children. Following in their creative footsteps are today's puppeteers, who have created characters such as those in PBS Kids *It's a Big, Big World* and *Between the Lions.* Many cable TV channels offer ensemble puppet characters to emphasize learning activities for young children and their families. *Sesame Street* offers the longest-running popular children's TV program featuring full-bodied and hand puppets—Jim Henson's Muppets. When I visited *Sesame Street* I spend a most enjoyable afternoon visiting with two of these enchanting puppets and their puppeteers.

WHY I TEACH YOUNG CHILDREN

"Mommy, mommy, come see. We have a surprise for you." My three-year-old son grabbed my hand and pulled me down the hall to his five-and-a-half-year-old brother's room. Both sons seated me in a chair facing them as they hid on one side of the bed. In a few seconds, up popped their hands, each holding a brightly colored rock. Then they proceeded to present a delightful "rock puppet show." Twenty-one years later, my three-year-old son was making Muppets for Jim Henson.

—HILDA JACKMAN

A CONVERSATION WITH BIG BIRD

For 41 years, and counting, *Sesame Street* has entertained and educated young children and their families. One of the most delightful and favorite puppet characters on television is Big Bird. Caroll Spinney is the talented and thoughtful puppeteer who, along with Jim Henson, created Big Bird and Oscar the Grouch. Spinney continues to give life to these two very special puppet individuals. The following is a conversation between the author (**HJ**), Caroll Spinney (**CS**), and Big Bird (**BB**).

HJ Why do you think puppets have become so successful for children's television?

CS There has been a change in the way puppets have been perceived. Jim Henson and his approach to puppets on television—this really isn't biased when I say it—was such a change. It just seems natural now. How else would you do it? Up to 1969 you couldn't sell puppets on television. It was cartoons and cartoons. TV saw puppets as "silly little things." Jim's approach was something that was more alive and more exciting. It succeeded in overwhelming cartooning. Cartoons are now enjoying the best age they've ever had. Every time you see puppets on TV now, they all look like something Jim made.

HJ Why do you think children respond so well to puppets, especially on TV? What is it about puppets that is better than cartoons?

CS My experience with "The Bird" is that he seems to live, talk, and include in his life those who are watching.

© 2010 Sesame Workshop/Colleen Douglass

Cartoons are celluloid. They don't relate to you. They have their own life and you just observe.

The Muppets on *Sesame Street* "stroke the camera" all the time. The children all feel they're involved. It's something you can't do with cartoons, and if they do it, it's not spontaneous. We have the advantage with television and its immediacy. The puppets communicate more directly. Children identify with us. After 41 years, I still admire *Sesame Street*.

HJ Why do you think Oscar the Grouch has been so successful? Why do you think showing his kind of personality through a puppet instead of through a person makes it more appealing to you?

CS That's a good question, because I've always said I wouldn't walk across the street to talk to a "creep" like Oscar the Grouch. I'm amazed that I can play a character like that, because I'm appalled at things he says. I've even talked to the producers of *Sesame Street* and told them that he's rude. I asked, what is he teaching? I've decided he's not evil, he does have a heart. Oscar is really a grouch, but he's moral. We are trying to teach. I sometimes act like a censor or critic. I edit Oscar myself, it's instinctual. Perhaps it's a lot like teaching.

HJ What makes Big Bird different? Why is he so loved and respected?

CS He doesn't change. He's constant. It's his longevity. Big Bird is like a "teddy bear."

He's a compassionate kid, as human as anyone on the show.

With *Sesame Street* there are elements of entertainment and teaching at the same time. We show the children that there's something worth looking at. We're not annoying. *Sesame Street* is a counterforce until the children are about seven years old. We're together until then.

HJ **Why do you think puppets are important in early childhood education? What can teachers do to introduce children to puppets?**

CS Introduce children to a good group of "live" puppeteers. Have them visit the classroom. It becomes more personal. Puppeteers of America [is] a good resource. [There are regional and community groups in most areas.]

Teachers should try puppets themselves. Give life to each puppet. There is a power of puppets to teach, to explore, and [to] learn. Have fun with puppets! Use puppets to get the children's attention. Have lots of puppets available. If I had been a teacher I would have had to use them all the time. Puppets give adults another way to relate to children. You can teach real humanity.

HJ **Now, I'd like for Big Bird to talk to the teachers. This is a question for you. You went to bird preschool, didn't you?**

BB Yes, I was with a bunch of sparrows.

HJ **What were some of your favorite things when you were in preschool?**

BB I built towers with blocks. Teacher had a big, yellow-and-white box full of wooden musical instruments like clackers and we asked the teacher when we could play with them. She always said "by-and-by," and we never did. I never did trust "by-and-by" as an answer anymore. The afternoon children she liked much better. They got to play with the instruments. It wasn't easy being only three years old and 5 feet 11 inches. Now I'm six years old and 8 feet 2 inches tall.

HJ **If you could talk to the teachers, what would you tell them to teach the children?**

BB I remember asking Gordon, on *Sesame Street*, because he is very wise. He's a teacher. I asked him why did he do that. He said, "It's important to raise the children in the way they should go." Wouldn't it be smart to teach them about the good, nice stuff, not just about the bad stuff?

HJ **Why do you think it's important to go to school and meet friends?**

BB Because friends are important. They're the ones who make up the rest of the world besides me.

HJ **Anything else you'd like to say?**

BB Yes. When I grow up, I'm going to be a Professor-Bird.

HJ **Thank you both so much. I've enjoyed being on *Sesame Street* and visiting with you.**

A CONVERSATION WITH ROSITA

Sesame Street is being broadcast on television in countries around the world. Some countries air the original American show, whereas others create new versions in their own languages. Sesame Workshop has coproductions from Bangladesh to Kosovo. For example, there are the Israeli/Palestinian coproduction *Rechov Sumsum/Shara's Simsim* and *Hu Hu Zhu* in China. Children in Mexico enjoy *Plaza Sesamo*, and *Galli Galli Sim Sim* appeals to children across India. The newly launched *Sesame Tree* fosters cooperation and sharing among Northern Ireland's Children (Sesame Workshop, 2010).

The charming Carmen Osbahr, who previously performed on *Plaza Sesamo*, is the puppeteer who gives voice and personality to Rosita on *Sesame Street*. Rosita, a delightful turquoise Muppet, speaks both English and Spanish, her native language. She's the first bilingual Muppet to ever appear on *Sesame Street*. The following is a conversation between the author (**HJ**), Carmen Osbahr (**CO**), and Rosita (**R**) when we met on *Sesame Street*.

HJ Carmen, why do you think puppets are so successful for children's television?

CO I grew up with puppets and television, *Sesame Street–Plaza Sesamo*. I think puppets have always been fun for children and grownups. With the introduction of puppets on television you are able to reach more people. Speaking as a puppeteer, you can be everything you want to be, go everywhere, and take the children watching along with you.

HJ You mentioned that you were always interested in puppets. What were the puppets in Mexico?

CO My parents used to take me to live shows. In kindergarten

© 2010 Sesame Workshop/Gil Vaknin

I remember my teachers, on Fridays at lunch, used to have these little theaters with puppets and little sets to go with the stories they told. I remember *Caperucita Roja* (*Little Red Riding Hood*) and *La Bella Durmiente* (*Sleeping Beauty*). They were very simple, little "Guignol" hand puppets. I think simple is best. I remember they changed the costumes with a little color and added different backgrounds. The teachers had fun too. I was just fascinated. Puppets were always around my life. I was 10 or 11 years old when *Plaza Sesamo* began. I was amazed.

HJ Did you make puppets? When did you get started?

CO I probably started in kindergarten. I remember doing the sock with the eyes glued on and making the puppet with the little ball head where we created our own little face. I'd go home and try to do more by myself.

HJ **Well, here's Rosita. Hi, Rosita.**

R HI! (Rosita uses a very big voice.)

HJ **Do you mind if I ask you some questions?**

R OKAY!

HJ **How old are you?**

R One, two, like this (holds up fingers). One, two, three, four, five, SIX! I just turned SIX! *Uno, dos, tres, quatro, cinco, seis.* I'm a six-year-old little monster. My whole name is Rosita, *La Monstrua de las Cuevas*—Rosita, the monster of the caves. See my wings? I can't fly. I don't know why I have them. I have my mommy, my daddy, my uncle Tito, my aunt Lola, and my cousin. I asked why do we all have wings and they don't know why because none of us can fly.

HJ **It's part of who you are.**

R YEAH! YEAH! (in a very big voice)

HJ **Do you go to school?**

R Yes, I do. I play. I have my friends. I run around, I sing a lot, and I learn my ABCs. I know how to count and I know all the colors, and I love my teacher, and that's it.

HJ **Do you help teach the other children about all those things in Spanish?**

R Yes, the ones that are curious, you know, but yeah, they like Mexican food, so I have to explain that that's an enchilada, and that's the mole, and of course to count in Spanish. Everybody knows how to count in Spanish.

HJ **Do you think you'll be a teacher when you grow up?**

R I never thought about it. Yeah, I will teach Spanish.

HJ **I think you'll be very good and you love to hug children . . .**

R Everybody, I love to hug everybody. I like to hug you.

HJ **Muchas gracias. How do you say my name Hilda in Spanish?**

R "Ilda" [whispering]. In Spanish the H is silent. "Ilda." I want to sing to you. My song is "Sing to the Sun."

Solecito que temprano,
Siempre me llenas de alegría
y calor mi vida.

In English, I said:
The sun that comes out really
early in the morning
Always brings me happiness
and warms my life.

There's about 200 verses, but I only know one.

Well, I'm going to go play with my dolly, so I'll be around. Bye.

HJ **Goodbye, Rosita. I really enjoyed talking to you. Thank you again for the hug.**

R *Muchas gracias.* That means "thank you"!

HJ *Muchas gracias.* **Thank you.**

R No, thank you!

HJ **Let me know if you ever fly.**

R OKAY! I'll have my mommy send you an email.

HJ **And *muchas gracias* to you too, Carmen.**

Tips for Teachers

The puppet can be whatever the puppeteer and the child make it. It can be the child's friend without demanding something in return. It can be a clown. It can be naughty and get into trouble without hurting anyone. It can say what the child thinks, feel what the child feels and share a child's sadness. It can show a child who knows poverty, hunger, war and loss that there can also be joy and love and a happy ending. A puppet can tell a child who rarely hears it that he is loved. A puppet can show a child that her father or mother can also be sad, and it can demonstrate the value of love, the futility of quarrel and the benefit of cooperation and support. (UNICEF, 2007)

Throughout this chapter, I have suggested guidance techniques and tips for introducing and using puppets. I have always used puppets in teaching young children and adults, on television, and in the classroom. Puppet creations will become a valuable teaching tool for you too. They can help you encourage appropriate behavior and speech. Once you feel comfortable in creating and using puppets yourself, you will discover that these wonderful characters can help you throughout the day. The more you use puppets, the more you will see for yourself how much children relate to and love puppets.

It is important for you to establish the following guidelines with the children in your classroom. These should affirm the children's creativity and promote puppetry. Explain to the children that they can

- take all the time needed to make a puppet.
- make the puppet their own way.
- be creative and imaginative.
- wait until *they* are ready.
- explore, experiment, and create.

Dear Family

[or whatever the child calls his parent using the language spoken at home],

Please come visit my school on [date and time]. We are cooking for you. We have planned some special things for you to do. One thing is to make puppets with me. We have been doing this and it's lots of fun. It will be lots of fun for you too. You can see my teacher and all my friends.

[Child's name]

FIGURE 11–16
An example of a letter to send home with the children.

ACTIVITY PLAN WORKSHEET

DEVELOPMENTALLY APPROPRIATE ACTIVITIES

Children's age group: appropriate for toddlers if the activity is simplified; otherwise, the activity is appropriate for preschool, prekindergarten, and kindergarten children.

NAME OF ACTIVITY AND BRIEF DESCRIPTION

"Sound game with puppets and props"

PURPOSE/OBJECTIVES OF ACTIVITY

- to listen to different sounds that promote auditory discrimination
- to recognize sounds in the environment
- to classify sounds
- to develop mental images of what is heard
- to recognize loud and soft sounds
- to recognize high and low sounds
- to listen to instructions

SPACE AND MATERIALS NEEDED

Depending on the number of children playing the game at one time, the area of floor space needed may be large or small. A puppet with attachable puppet ears is needed along with a cloth bag filled with objects having distinctive sounds, such as an eggbeater, a timer, a box of rice, some maracas, and a musical triangle.

PROCEDURE

1. Have the children sit on the floor in a circle.
2. Attach large ears to "Ms. I Listen" puppet. (You can use the basic hand puppet suggested in Figure 11–7. The pattern can be found online at this textbook's website. Ears can be attached easily with Velcro.)
3. Use the puppet to introduce the activity by singing "Put Your Finger in the Air." End with "Put your finger on your ear and tell me what you hear."
4. Use the puppet to lead a discussion on why we have ears.
5. After discussion, use "Ms. I Listen" puppet to introduce the sound bag. Have her choose one child to be "it."
6. Give "it" the sound bag."
7. Have children stand, join hands, and circle clockwise, while the child who is "it" remains stationary outside the circle holding the sound bag.

8. The children continue circling until they hear "it" call "Stop!"
9. The child who is "it" chooses something from the sound bag and makes a sound with it. The child who has stopped directly in front of "it" must guess what is making the sound.
10. If he guesses correctly, he becomes "it" and changes places.
11. If the guess is incorrect, the teacher, using the puppet, guides the child into making the correct choice, and then he changes places with "it."
12. Continue until all items in the sound bag have been identified.
13. Use the puppet to direct children into the next activity.

GUIDANCE

If possible, a small group of children should do this activity the first time it is presented. Once they know how the activity is played, they can then help the puppet, "Ms. I Listen," explain the game to the other children.

It is important to establish limits for behavior and boundaries of the activity.

It is helpful to anticipate problems that may develop during this activity and consider ways in which they may be handled. You know your group of children best. Therefore, use the guidance that will work best for your situation.

ASSESSMENT STRATEGIES AND FOLLOW-UP

Evaluate this activity to see whether the children were able to achieve the skills or understand the concepts presented. Consider how this activity could be changed to be more effective.

Follow-up activities could include attaching a large nose to the same puppet or big eyes or large hands with fingers. Put appropriate items in the cloth bag to correspond with the added body parts.

Another activity could use sound cans or jars filled with rice, beans, sand, large nails, paper clips, and metal washers. For the children to match sounds, use two cans or jars for each item. Children first match sounds—then identify sounds.

Develop your own list of activities, using the puppet, that can extend or give practice of the skills or concepts of this activity.

Afterview

Through puppets, a child

- builds self-esteem.
- develops independence.
- learns acceptable behavior.
- improves listening skills.
- learns new ways to express feelings.
- learns to share with others and to take turns.
- learns to make choices.
- develops large and small muscle skills.
- practices language skills.
- uses creative thinking and imagination.
- strengthens problem-solving skills and abstract thinking.
- reveals thoughts and attitudes through conversation.

Reflective Review Questions

1. What are the benefits to young children of creating and operating puppets? List at least six benefits.
2. Even some of the simplest puppets require developed motor movement and coordination. Think about finger puppets and sock puppets, to name just two. What kinds of motor skills would children have to have in order to be able to make their puppets move?
3. Describe ways in which puppets can connect with various curriculum areas. Cover at least four areas, and state specifically how the puppets might be used.
4. Discuss the experience of attending a puppet show. What was memorable about the experience? If you have never seen a puppet show during your adult life, find someone in your class or in your community that can recommend one for you to see. Make an effort to go and see it.

Key Terms

hand puppets   puppetry   stick or rod puppets
marionettes   shadow puppets

Explorations

1. Select a classmate or colleague as a partner. Share ideas on how a teacher can encourage social, emotional, and language development with puppets.
2. Review the types of puppets discussed in this chapter. Then create a puppet. Share this puppet with a group of children. Use any of the ideas found in this chapter.

3. As a group activity, select a children's book and make puppets to represent the characters in the book. Discuss the criteria for the book selection and carefully choose the materials to use in making the puppets. Upon completion, invite a group of children in to watch the presentation of the story with puppets. Later, discuss the children's reactions to the puppet story. How did the puppeteers feel about this activity? What will you change and why?

4. Some people can think of puppets only in terms of elaborate stages and complicated marionettes on strings. What are some basics that an early childhood education teacher can follow when introducing puppetry to young children? Does it have to be expensive?

5. Either through research or personal interviews, find out which community resources or agencies present puppet activities or puppet plays and which early education programs offer puppets as part of their learning environment. Share your findings with your classmates or colleagues.

Additional Readings and Resources

Baird, B. (1965). *The art of the puppet.* New York: Macmillan.

Contreras, G. (1995). Teaching about the Vietnamese culture: Water puppetry as the soul of the rice fields. *Social Studies, 86*(1), 25–28.

Crepeau, I. M., & Richards, M. A. (2008). *A Show of hands: Using puppets with young children.* St. Paul, MN: Redleaf Press.

Dolci, M. (1994, July/August). When the wolf both is and is not a wolf—The language of puppets. *Child Care Information Exchange, 98,* 43–46.

Finch, C. (Ed.). (1993). *Jim Henson: The works—The art, the magic, the imagination.* New York: Random House.

Isenberg, J., & Jalongo, M. J. (2001). *Creative expression and play in the early childhood curriculum* (3rd ed.). Upper Saddle River, NJ: Merrill.

Koralek, D. (2003, July). It's you we like: Remembering NAEYC's good friend, Fred M. "Mister" Rogers. *Young Children, 58*(4), 72–73.

Machado, J. M. (2010). *Early childhood experiences in language arts* (9th ed.). Clifton Park, NY: Wadsworth Cengage Learning.

Mayesky, M. (2006). *Creative activities for young children* (8th ed.). Clifton Park, NY: Delmar Cengage Learning.

Moses, A. M. (2009, March). Research in review: What television can (and can't do to promote early literacy development. *Young Children, 64*(2), 80–89.

Helpful Web Connections

Between the Lions
   http://pbskids.org/lions/
Caroll Spinney
   http://www.carollspinney.com
Center for Puppetry Arts
   http://www.puppet.org
Early Childhood News
   http://www.earlychildhoodnews.com

Folkmanis Puppets
   http://www.folkmanis.com
Legends and Lore
   http://www.legendsandlore.com
PBS Kids
   http://www.pbs.org/kids
Sesame Street Workshop
   http://www.ctw.org

References

Center for Puppetry Arts. (2010). *Museum guide.* Atlanta, GA: Author.

Esch, G., & Long, E. (2002, January). The fabulously fun finger puppet workshop. *Young Children, 57*(1), 90–91.

Fortson, L. R., & Reiff, J. C. (1995). *Early childhood curriculum.* Boston, MA: Allyn & Bacon.

Henson, C. (1994). *The Muppets make puppets.* New York: Workman Publishing.

Hunt, T., & Renfro, N. (1982). *Puppetry in early childhood education.* Austin, TX: Nancy Renfro Studios.

Jalongo, M. R. (2003, Summer). The child's right to creative thought and expression. *Childhood Education, 79*(4), 218–228.

Koster, J. B. (2009). *Growing artists: Teaching the arts to young children* (4th ed.). Clifton Park, NY: Wadsworth Cengage Learning.

Peyton, J. L. (2009). *Puppet art recast as language and technology.* Online at: *http://www.puppetools.com*

Raines, S., & Isbell, R. (1994). *Stories: Children's literature in early education.* Clifton Park, NY: Delmar Cengage Learning.

Richards, A. (2007). The story is just the start. *Early Childhood News.* Online at: *http://www.earlychildhoodnews.com*

Sesame Workshop. (2010). Online at: *http://www.sesameworkshop.org/aroundtheworld*

UNICEF in Action. (2007). Online at: *http://www.unicef.org/puppets*

Additional information and resources on early childhood curriculum can be found on the Education CourseMate website for this book. Go to **www.CengageBrain.com** to register your access code.

chapter 12

Dramatic Play

Objectives

After Studying This Chapter, You Should Be Able To:

● Define and give examples of dramatic play.

● Specify developmental stages of dramatic play.

● Discuss the teacher's role in planning and preparing the environment for dramatic play, including adaptations for children with special needs.

● Describe the purpose of making prop boxes for dramatic play activities, and how to involve families in the process.

● Discuss integrating developmentally appropriate dramatic play into all the curriculum areas.

● Understand the positive and negative aspects of young children imitating superheroes.

● Describe several developmentally appropriate dramatic play activities.

Overview

● ●

Play is the natural language of the child. It helps a child observe and respond to her relationship to others and to the world in which she lives. Play is at the core of developmentally appropriate practice. Dramatic play helps to expand this important self-motivated behavior that will serve each child throughout her life. (Review Chapter 1 for additional information on the importance of play.)

From pat-a-cake to peek-a-boo, a baby watches others and then copies them. "The infant year is spent in close and intense observation of the human species. The baby learns to *read* every expression and gesture of the important adults around her. Toward the end of that first year, imitation begins" (Miller, 2002). The more you can play such pretend games with an infant, the more the infant learns. As the baby coos and babbles, your smiles and hugs give encouragement. When you say a word over and over, the baby will try to say it too. An infant's awareness of human expression, gestures, and sounds is the beginning of creative thinking.

A young child enjoys imitating people and playing different roles. Having props available increases the learning experience.

Toddlers love the world of pretend. They will use dishes and pretend to eat and drink. "Toddlers have *object hunger.* They love objects of all kinds and use them in every conceivable way. This shows up in their early pretending. As long as the toy looks like an object they have seen, even if it is not exact, the child will use it in the intended way" (Miller, 2002). They enjoy pretend hellos and goodbyes. As you talk and enter such play, you are helping them learn about the real world. Children learn by repetition. Your willingness to do the same thing over and over is the key that opens the door to their learning. Although toddlers may pretend for short periods of time alone, they need other children and adults to give words and some direction to their play.

Dramatic play is one of the most valuable forms of play in children. "Early childhood educators know the value of dramatic play with preschoolers. Children learn empathy as they practice literally putting themselves in someone else's shoes. Language is enhanced as their play characters express themselves to their peers and social relationships are strengthened" (Miller, 2002). Preschool children love to have stories read to them. They will retell the stories as they play. A few props will get them going on the story. They may give their own twist to the story each time they "play the role." They're trying out new ways to solve problems as well as "trying on" being adults.

Children are fond of imitating people they have seen at the grocery store, the doctor's office, the service station, and the restaurant. Preschoolers like to emulate family members as well as define their own relationships with them. Home relationships are intense, and in dramatic play children graphically show their varying relationships to different family members. This creative play reveals children's pressing needs at the moment. They may seek in play the warmth and affection they fail to get at home. If they are consistently urged toward mature behavior at home, they may seek infantile roles in their role-playing.

Play also handles a child's uniqueness of being little in a world of big people. Through dramatic play, a young child can indicate confusion or misinterpretation of facts, as well as possible fears and attempts to master these fears. "Dramatic play can help children grow in social understanding and cooperation; it provides a controlled emotional outlet and a means of self-expression" (Deiner, 2010).

Primary-age children enjoy creating their own activities. They may make them up as they go along. You will see familiar stories in most of their dramatic play. Children's group play usually has "the bestest good guys" and "the baddest bad guys." The good guys will win and often invite the bad ones to be good and win with them.

Children will play out their ideas of death, marriage, parenting, daredevil escapades, superheroes, and everyday life. Although the plots may be complicated, the theme remains the same. That theme of "everything turns out right" adds to a child's feeling of security. The dramatic play area offers a safe haven for children to act out their fears and anger, knowing that the teacher will be there to respond to their individual needs.

As we continue through this chapter, we will explore how theorists, researchers, and educators explain the developmental stages of dramatic play. We will also appropriately plan and prepare the early childhood environment to integrate this fantasy play into the learning centers and curriculum, as we encourage the development of the children's cooperative interaction skills. Elkind (1994) explains, "When children are engaged in dramatic play, one of the things they are learning is how to transfer what they learned in one setting and apply it in another. One could hardly wish for a better learning activity than that!"

Dramatic play allows a child to explore and to imitate the people around her. Sometimes, even the teacher gets involved in the fun.

Dramatic Play Defined

dramatic play A type of creative, spontaneous play in which children use their imaginations to create and dramatize pretend characters, actions, or events.

McCaslin (1990) describes **dramatic play** as "the *free play* of the very young child in which he explores his universe, imitating the actions and character traits of those around him." Dramatic play is spontaneous and can be expanded or repeated over and over again just for the fun of it.

With **sociodramatic play**, the highest level of symbolic play, young children create their own happenings based on their experiences. They imitate the actions and people that they have experienced in their play. They repeat, solve problems, and relive these experiences (Isbell & Raines, 2007). Gordon and Browne (2011) provide an additional explanation:

sociodramatic play The highest level of symbolic play in which young children create their own happenings based on their experiences.

> Sociodramatic play happens when at least two children cooperate in dramatic play. Dramatic play provides the means for children to work out their difficulties by themselves. By doing so, they become free to pursue other tasks and more formal learning. [This] type of play involves two basic elements: imitation and make-believe.

Researchers believe the *fantasy* element of dramatic play is quite useful. It enables the child to discharge or accomplish through imagination what she is unable to do in reality. Fantasizing relieves tensions and offers a way to interpret and put together the pieces of the complex puzzle that is a child's world. For example, animal play releases aggression, but this is not the only function of this type of dramatic play. A child will often impersonate animals when feeling shy or insecure about verbalizing. I remember such a child, a three-year-old named Michael.

> He came into the classroom growling like an animal. His hands were in the position of paws. Michael entered freely into dramatic play with other children as a dragon, tiger, or wolf. Many times he got the attention of several children when he played the big bad wolf. Morning after morning, The Three Little Pigs was played out. The other children, laughing and chattering happily, hid under the tables to escape the wolf. Michael was capable of expressing himself verbally, but he didn't. Instead, he found peer acceptance in dramatic play. Later, when he was ready to talk and enter into other dramatic play activities, he did so.

A young child invites a teacher to join in his fantasy play.

Developmental Stages of Dramatic Play

Theorists, researchers, and educators emphasize the importance of *developmental stages* of dramatic play in varying ways. As discussed in Chapter 1, *Mildred Parten* (1932) categorizes six stages of social play: unoccupied behavior (infants), onlooker behavior, solitary play, parallel play (toddlers), associative play (young preschoolers), and cooperative play (older preschoolers, kindergartners, and primary-age children).

Jean Piaget's research (1962) has helped us understand play in terms of cognitive development by presenting play in three stages:

- **Practice play** takes place during the sensorimotor stage of development (infancy to two years), in which infants explore the sensory qualities of objects and practice motor skills. This is observable through a child's physical movements and interactions with objects in the environment.
- **Symbolic or dramatic play** takes place during the preoperational stage of development (two to seven years), when we see children transfer objects into symbols, things that represent something else. Symbolic thinking is observable during dramatic play when realistic objects such as pots and pans are used for "cooking soup," a block becomes a "real" telephone and the child "talks" into it, and older children, using gestures and actions, pantomime props when there are none.
- **Games with rules** takes place during the concrete operations stage of development (seven years and older), in which children's spontaneous play develops into games involved with perfecting physical skills and organizing games with rules that are both physical and cognitive. This type of play is observable when it demonstrates children making up their own rules for the games they play, their ability to accept and relate to another person's point of view, and their ability to understand rules to a game that cannot be changed.

Sara Smilansky (1968) divides play into four types of sociodramatic play:

- **Functional play** (infancy through early years) occurs when a child takes on a role and pretends to be someone else. This type of play embodies sensory and motor exploration of the environment and the people in the environment. This is observable when children play in "dress-up clothes" or use props to identify the person they are portraying.
- **Constructive play** (toddlers and preschoolers) helps children understand their experiences. This type of play can occur alone or with others as the child plans the manipulation of objects or people to create a specific experience. This is observable when a child puts keys in a pretend car, starts the motor, adds the sound effects ("Vroooom"), and lets others ride in the car with her.
- Dramatic play (toddlers through primary-age children) involves pretending and make-believe. This represents a higher level of play behavior and is observable when two or more children take on related roles and interact with one another. "Rules that children follow in make-believe play teach them to make choices, to think and plan about what they will do, to show willingness toward self-restraint, as children learn to follow the social rules of pretend play. This is important preparation for real-life situations" (Gordon & Browne, 2011).
- Games with rules (older preschoolers and primary-age children) require children to behave according to preexisting rules. This is observable when children play board games and many outdoor sports.

(Review Chapter 1 for other theories and discussions of play and young children.)

UNDERSTANDING FANTASY AND REALITY IN YOUNG CHILDREN

Dramatic play experiences help young children sort out what is make-believe and what is real. "Human beings have a gift for fantasy, which shows itself at a very

---

practice play During Piaget's sensorimotor stage (infancy to two years), infants explore the sensory qualities of objects and practice motor skills.

Symbolic or dramatic play A type of play that allows the child to transfer objects into symbols (things that represent something else) and images into people, places, and events within his experiences. Symbolic play occurs during Piaget's preoperational stage (two to seven years). Superhero fantasy play is considered a type of symbolic play for a young child.

games with rules Children's spontaneous physical and cognitive play that occurs during Piaget's concrete operations stage of development (seven years and older).

functional play Play that occurs when a child takes on a role and pretends to be someone else.

constructive play Play that helps children understand their experiences. Involves planning or manipulation of objects or people to create a specific experience.

eaily age and then continues to make all sorts of contributions to our intellectual and emotional life throughout the lifespan" (Harris, 2002). "Children need ample supplies of fantasy and reality. Gradually children learn to separate fantasy and reality, identify which is which, and travel between them purposefully" (Vail, 1999).

It is both appropriate and developmentally important that young children try out ways to differentiate fantasy from reality. The younger the child, the more dramatic play is rooted in fantasy. Children confuse fantasy with reality because they believe what they think is true, whether or not it is true in reality. Read, Gardner, and Mahler (1993) explain further: "Children need help and time to make the distinction between reality and fantasy without having to reject their fantasies. They have a right to imagine and to create fantasies as well as a need to learn to identify reality."

At age five or older, children understand when they are

Dramatic play produces sheer joy and delight.

pretending and when they are in the real world. Their understanding is sometimes very sophisticated. "Rather than try to force understanding, which is usually in place by the end of kindergarten, encourage children to use language as a tool to ask questions and explore their thinking. . . . 'Do you think that could really happen?'" (Vail, 1999).

Planning and Preparing the Environment

Dramatic play offers many opportunities for supporting a young child's growth and development. Dramatic play produces sheer joy and delight. A child's total being is involved in the activity. Her body, face, language, and emotions mirror enthusiasm for life. To support all of this, you should provide unstructured time, adequate space, flexible materials, and uninterrupted opportunity for the children to enjoy dramatic play. Most important, *let the children have input!* The environment should say, "Pretending is welcome here!"

If you see that a child is not ready to enter freely into dramatic play, your understanding is vitally important. This child needs sufficient time to watch and learn and proceed at her own pace. Perhaps if you pretend with the child at first and then gradually pull away, this will be all she needs.

> It takes time to conjure new ideas, and it takes a welcoming and accessible environment for children of all abilities to explore and express the content of their imaginations. . . . [W]hen children know they have an uninterrupted stretch of time, they are more likely to try new roles, take emotional risks, negotiate rich worlds and stories, build tall towers and learn about the properties and possibilities of materials and objects in their environment. (Haugen, 2002)

THE TEACHER'S ROLE IN CHILDREN'S DRAMATIC PLAY

The following guidelines should help to define the teacher's role in children's dramatic play. Here, as in other curriculum areas, the teacher's role is primarily that of facilitator, so that dramatic play remains a child-initiated activity:

● Provide stimulating props, unstructured time, and adequate space for dramatic play.
● Create curtains, windows, a fireplace, and real plants to make the area home-like, comfortable, and welcoming.
● Monitor the dramatic play area so all children have the opportunity to participate.

- Assist children in learning acceptable kinds of social interaction.
- Allow children to solve their own problems as often as possible.
- Encourage creativity in language and play.
- Keep in mind the children's developmental capabilities.
- Value this type of play.
- Allow children opportunities to "try on" adult roles, both male and female.
- Limit the number of children in the area at one time.
- Introduce props to small groups of children.
- Select props that are authentic and can be used naturally and safely.
- Change props frequently and include ones that reflect different cultures.
- Avoid props and activities that are sexist or racist.
- Serve as a facilitator rather than teacher so dramatic play remains a child-initiated activity.
- Select dress-up clothes and outfits that are simple, durable, and easy to get on and off.

Encourage creativity and value dramatic play.

Some teachers keep the home living (housekeeping) area intact as a permanent center and set up a second dramatic play area that expands the theme of the lesson plan or project in which the children are involved. Others, who are limited in classroom space, may choose to have a dramatic play center that changes periodically and sometimes will include the kitchen area or another room in the home. Still others take the dramatic play center outdoors to take advantage of the additional space available.

Change the scene occasionally. Put all the chairs away. Bring in large moving boxes. Hang sheets like a stage curtain, a maze, or a tent. Change rooms with another class. . . . Create discovery kits to take along when you explore new environments. Include a magnifying glass, collecting bags, cameras, and so on. (Haugen, 2002)

The basic equipment for the home living/dramatic play center should be: child-size furniture made of wood or sturdy plastic including tables; chairs; rocking chair; shelves; a "play" sink, stove, and refrigerator; and a full-length mirror. Dolls of both sexes representing differing features and skin coloring, a doll bed or cradle, and a sturdy, nonworking telephone should also be included.

Sometimes, the most creative and appropriate dramatic play area is one that has very little in it and does not have a specific theme. When a special "soft area" is created by adding some pillows, beanbag chairs, and a soft area rug, it becomes a totally child-directed dramatic play area. The children feel relaxed and safe, free to be creative and imaginative. The pillows become props, as needed, or the children can bring in props from around the room.

Adaptations for Special Needs Children

"All children, whatever their physical, cognitive, or emotional level of development, have individual interests and special capabilities" (Isbell & Raines, 2007). The following suggestions, from Deiner (2010), Isbell and Raines (2007), and Mayesky (2009), are intended to help teachers include children with special needs in dramatic play:

1. Apply only those rules that are really needed for the child to play safely.
2. Let the child take the lead. This may involve some patient waiting for the child to choose something to do.

3. To encourage the child to play with others, define the space where the children can play, and keep it small at first.

4. If a child wants to play with another child or a group of children but does not know how to join in, encourage her to gradually become involved, and then slowly lessen your own involvement.

5. Encourage verbalization during play by asking questions and encouraging communication with other children.

6. Offer dramatic play materials that are familiar and part of a child's daily life experiences.

7. Set up the dramatic play area in a variety of different ways. If children want to play through medical experiences, set it up as a doctor's or dentist's office.

8. Use puppets as a way for children to talk indirectly about experiences.

9. Provide some dress-up clothes that are simple to put on or take off.

10. Sharing ideas with peers helps children with developmental delays see how things work and how they are to be done.

11. Provide a lot of props. Be sure that at least some of them give obvious cues (tactile as well as visual) about the activity going on.

12. Some children with developmental delays fatigue very easily. Make sure that the child has supportive seating. Some children need chair inserts or standing aids.

Sharing with Families: Making Prop Boxes

A vital part of the planning and preparing process for dramatic play activities is the creation of prop boxes. A **prop box** is a collection of actual items related to the development and enrichment of dramatic play activities focused on a specific theme or lesson plan. These items should be collected for easy accessibility and placed in sturdy boxes that can be stacked for storage. Empty cardboard boxes with lids make great prop boxes.

Label each prop box clearly for identification. A picture or drawing on the outside can suggest what is inside. Cover the boxes with colored contact paper to give them an uncluttered and uniform appearance. (See Figure 12–1.)

The props selected for the dramatic play areas should stimulate interest, encourage creative expression, create opportunities for problem solving, relate to and expand the experiences of the children, and represent many cultures. These props can be found anywhere and everywhere: in the families' and staff's closets and garages; at surplus stores, thrift stores, and garage sales; and at local businesses and offices that have used and throwaway items. Invite the children to bring appropriate props from home that represent their interests, their hobbies, their lifestyles, or the current theme. Share with families the learning possibilities that prop boxes provide. Invite them to visit the classroom to see how the children use the different contents of the prop boxes. Guide them into making prop boxes at home *with* their children.

Hanvey (2010) offers other learning opportunities for children with an outdoor prop box:

> When I introduced the prop box to the children, we discussed how they were responsible for bringing the prop box outside with them each day, returning the props to the box at the end of play, and bringing it back to a designated area. . . . This outdoor prop box experience not only enabled children to practice and extend academic skills they were learning indoors, but also enhanced their social skills. We observed the children using conflict resolution techniques

prop box A collection of actual items related to dramatic play activities that focuses on a specific theme or lesson plan.

FIGURE 12–1
Prop boxes for dramatic play.

when trouble arose. The kindergarteners took turns with the materials and learned what it meant to be responsible as they restored the prop box each day and put it back where it belonged.

Fill a plastic tub or crate with many different items for the children to take outdoors—items that will encourage exploration outdoors. For example, you might include ping-pong balls, tennis balls, marbles, blocks, books, magnifying glasses, chalk, small buckets to be filled with water, brushes, measuring tape, bubbles, wind socks, and blankets. The outdoor boxes should be different from the indoor prop boxes. This will help keep the children interested and involved.

CLOTHES FOR THE DRAMATIC PLAY CENTER

Clothing that helps children "dress up" in various roles is an important part of dramatic play. The clothes should be easy for children to put on and take off, as well as being attractive, durable, and washable. Wash and dry donated clothing before sharing them with the children. Hem the garments to make sure the children can wear them comfortably and safely. Remove long rope belts, or stitch them into place so they cannot be used around children's necks. Replace back zippers with Velcro hook-and-loop fasteners. Teenager-size clothes are useful for young children, or (if you do not sew) perhaps there is a parent who will be willing to make some new "dress-up" clothes for the class.

There should be a special place where clothing is displayed or stored. A cardboard box "closet" with a rod placed across at the children's height can hold clothes on hangers. Clothing hooks or a shortened clothes or hat rack are also appropriate. Whatever you select will help the children understand that after they have used the article of clothing it should be placed back where they found it.

A variety of cultures should be represented by using clothing made of fabric that is tie-dyed and batiked and clothing made from madras prints and kente cloth. The clothing styles should include saris, kimonos, serapes, ponchos, grass skirts, and dashikis (Allen, McNeill, & Schmidt, 1992). You should research many cultures and consult with parents as you develop your dramatic play center.

Integrating Dramatic Play into the Curriculum

The following examples of dramatic play centers, and the prop boxes to accompany each, have proven to be successful in early education curriculum. They represent developmentally appropriate play areas and offer creative opportunities for individual or small groups of children.

In setting up areas for infants and toddlers, change very little from what they are used to. Add props or change the room arrangement very slowly. The children will guide you by what they will or will not play with. Older children will help you decide when to change areas, when to add additional props and materials, and what areas of the room need to be expanded for more dramatic play.

DRAMATIC PLAY FOR INFANTS

● *A doll corner:* Select sock or soft dolls (depicting many cultures) that are easy to launder and simple cardboard beds for the dolls. The clothing on the dolls should be washable and easy to take off and put on.
● *A home living area:* Choose washable household items that the infant can grasp, such as pots, pans, lids, boxes, plastic cups, bowls, and baskets. These will encourage the child to bang, stack, squeeze, and put the objects together.

- *An area (indoor and/or outdoor) for push-and-pull toys.* This should include doll buggies, wagons, wheelbarrows, and trucks.
- *An area for crawling and climbing:* Provide a rocking boat, short tunnel, and climbing steps.

DRAMATIC PLAY FOR TODDLERS

- *Home living area:* In addition to all types of dolls and child-size furniture, add empty food boxes of all sizes and shapes that represent what the children eat at home. This should include empty food boxes with print in different languages on them to represent foods from diverse cultures.
- *Dress-up clothes:* Include items that relate to community helpers (e.g. police officers, firefighters). Toddlers love sunglasses with plastic lenses, gloves, purses, and clothing that fits them.
- *Prop box:* Fill it with shopping bags, lunch boxes, toy telephones, keys, pots, pans, small cars, and trucks. (Miniature animals and people can be added to the block center prop box as well. This is discussed fully in Chapter 9.)
- *A corner for puppet and mask play:* This should offer glove puppets, finger puppets, and people puppets; as well as animal masks with eyes, mouth, and nose cut out and a handle under the chin for easy manipulation, as described in Chapter 11.
- *A beauty/barber shop:* Provide washable black, brown, blond, and red wigs, both male and female styles; curlers; empty plastic shampoo bottles; and old hair dryers with the plugs and cords cut off. (Note: Wash or spray wigs and hats often with diluted bleach—one-half teaspoon bleach to one quart of water.)

One prop, such as a red wig, can encourage a young child to act out her favorite fairytale or create a new character to add to the story.

One prop, such as a red wig, can encourage a young child to act out her favorite fairytale or create a new character to add to the story.

DRAMATIC PLAY FOR PRESCHOOLERS

The dramatic play center in the three-, four-, and five-year-old classroom can start with one specific theme. The concept can be expanded to include adjacent space as more children become involved.

- *Travel agency:* Set up a ticket counter and chairs. The prop box for this activity can include tickets, maps, brochures, posters, pens, pencils, flight schedules, boat schedules, and car and hotel information. The tickets, maps, schedules, and information sheets can also be made by the children.
- *Ship:* All it takes is a balance beam becoming the gangplank, cardboard boxes becoming the outer part of the ship, and "water" (painted by the children) surrounding the ship. Let the children help you add to this adventure by deciding where the ship will land. This is a wonderful opportunity to expand the dramatic play into various ports and countries, such as Hawaii, Africa, Mexico, Alaska, and the Caribbean. Set up prop boxes for each country. Selecting what goes in each is both creative and educational and helps children develop problem solving skills. Packing small suitcases or briefcases with clothing for warm climates (straw hats, beach toys, suntan lotion, sunglasses, and short-sleeved shirts) and clothing for colder areas (gloves, earmuffs, mufflers, stocking caps, and sweaters) helps start this dramatic play.
- *Train station and train, or airport and airplane:* This can expand the travel agency dramatic play or add to the lesson plan relating to transportation. As with the ship theme, develop a prop box for each, including appropriate clothing. Plan the destination with maps and brochures.
- *Supermarket/grocery store/farmer's market/mercado:* Fill the prop box with a toy cash register, calculator, play money (or money the children make), price tags, sales slip pad, empty food

containers (some with print in different languages on them to represent foods from diverse cultures), artificial fruit and vegetables, grocery boxes, shopping bags, small shopping carts, brown paper bags, telephone, coupons, and shopping lists. Make signs in several languages and with pictures to explain what is for sale.

● *Picnic:* This is fun for indoors or outdoors and is an excellent dramatic play activity to plan for snack or lunch time. The children decide what to take on the picnic and place the items in a picnic basket. They can wear "dress-up" clothes and use props from the prop box, such as plastic or paper cups, plates, tableware, tablecloth, napkins, eating utensils, aprons, and blankets.

● *Ants at a picnic:* Put several large picnic baskets in the dramatic play area. Add play food. Then, make a tunnel by taking the ends out of boxes. Line the boxes up, and tape them together to form a tunnel. You can use a cloth tunnel, if you already have one, to have more than one tunnel for the "ants." The children can pretend to be ants taking the "food" from the picnic basket to their home through the tunnels. Continue to add items that the children want to use.

Other suggestions for dramatic play centers are restaurant, florist shop, pet shop, post office, library, book store, music shop, musical instrument store, recording studio, health center, doctor or dentist office, gymnasium, campsite, shoe store, fix-it shop, and apartments in the loft and lower level of the dramatic play area.

DRAMATIC PLAY FOR PRIMARY-GRADE CHILDREN

Any of the dramatic play suggestions listed for the preschoolers can be expanded or adapted for older children. Give them the list of acceptable themes and allow them the freedom to make choices and select their own activities. For example, if they choose to visit another country as they play, the children may "discover the rain forest" or "go on a safari in Africa." This child-initiated form of dramatic play encourages the older child to take an interest in the wider world, and it is exciting to watch as it unfolds. Some children get involved with one aspect and tackle it as an independent project. Others make the theme a special event or a cooperative venture.

The following are a few examples of other dramatic play exercises and activities: that are appropriate for school-age children:

Young children enjoy dressing in costumes as part of dramatic play.

● *Rag doll, tin man, and marionette:* Have the children perform simple warm-up exercises by being as limp as a rag doll; they can bend from the waist and bob up and down and swing their shoulders. As stiffened tin men, let them discover how their movements change. Expand this activity and have the children choose a partner. One becomes a marionette and the other becomes the puppeteer. The puppeteer stands in front of the marionette and moves the strings attached to the various parts of the marionette's body. The marionette responds with the proper movement.

● *The imaginary machine:* First, one child will form a "machine-part shape" with her body and add a made-up sound to fit that shape. Each successive child connects to the shape last made with her own unique shape and sound until all of the children are involved in the imaginary machine. Slow the machine down and speed it up. To demonstrate the importance of the parts on the whole, "break" one of the parts. What happens to the machine?

● *Mirror images:* Each child chooses a partner. They face each other, always keeping each other in full view. One child becomes a mirror that reflects what she sees her partner doing. Perhaps the child puts on clown makeup, exercises, or puts on a tie. After a while, the partners change places, with the other partner becoming the mirror.

DRAMATIC PLAY AND OTHER LEARNING CENTERS

Dramatic play lends itself to every aspect of the curriculum. As an example, Beaty (2009) states, "Although it is not necessary to initiate dramatic play by reading a book, some teachers have found that it is a fine way to integrate dramatic play into other learning centers."

Language and literacy development, socialization, exploration of feelings and fears, and problem solving are ongoing components of these activities. Music and rhythmic movement become dramatic and creative when a child makes use of them to become someone or something other than herself.

Math and science concepts apply to many dramatic-play situations. Charlesworth and Lind (2010) offer some examples:

● One-to-one correspondence can be practiced by exchanging play money for goods or services.
● Sets and classifying are involved in organizing each dramatic play center in an orderly manner.
● Counting can be applied to figuring out how many items have been purchased and how much money must be exchanged.
● Comparing and measuring can be used to decide if clothing fits, or to determine the weight of fruits and vegetables purchased.
● Spatial relations and volume concepts are applied as items purchased are placed in bags, boxes, and/or baskets and as children discover how many passengers will fit in the space shuttle or can ride on the bus.
● Number symbols can be found throughout dramatic play props, such as on price tags, play money, telephones, cash registers, and scales.

As you select the theme, brainstorm using the curriculum planning web worksheet in Chapter 2. Develop your lesson plan, integrate the learning centers, and gather supplies and materials to discover how to meet your goals and objectives through the use of dramatic play.

WHY I TEACH YOUNG CHILDREN

The first year I taught preschool, a young child was very happy to tell me that his mother was going to have a baby. For most of the year the class got regular reports about how things were progressing: mother threw up breakfast, mother is sleepy, mother's feet hurt, and mother cannot sit on the floor anymore. Finally, the baby was born. I asked, "What did mother bring home from the hospital that she did not take with her?" The child thought for a few seconds, smiled, and answered "Flowers."

—Diane B. Ratner

Tips for Teachers

The appearance of television or movie heroes, such as Spiderman or Wonder Woman, may change children's dramatic play. When you hear these heroes' names, you will want to observe the children's play more closely. Sometimes the stunts on television and in movies are dangerous when children try to do them. Rough play may become too much a part of the play as they pretend to be superheroes. Your observation will give you an opportunity to teach better ways to solve problems without aggressiveness.

Beaty (2009) suggests there are both positive and negative aspects of children's imitation of superheroes:

The fantasy element of dramatic play enables each child to accomplish through imagination what she is unable to do in reality.

The superhero is a good character who is good-looking, strong, loyal, helpful, unselfish, ready to fight against evil, and always the winner. The bad character is evil-looking, strong, selfish, disloyal, underhanded, sneaky, always challenging the good character, and always the loser.... Children are going to attempt superhero play whether or not it is allowed.... [S]uperheroes are powerful symbols, indeed, to young children. When you understand that such symbols can represent positive values in our society, then you may want to consider allowing superhero dramatic play in the classroom if it can be controlled and directed into prosocial channels.

© Cengage Learning

Additionally, superhero play can offer children a way to deal with their real fears and anxieties and answer the "big questions about the world such as 'what is right and wrong, what is good and bad, what is fair and unfair, what is life and death, what is a boy and a girl, and what is real and fantasy'" (Hoffman, cited in Gordon & Browne, 2011).

Let us think about how we can deal effectively with the superhero characters in an early education setting. One of the first things to do is to become familiar with *what* is available for the children to watch on television, videos, and the movies. Second, think about *why* the children are imitating these characters. Ask questions of the children and talk to them about other, more appropriate, choices for play. It's important to establish limits ahead of time.

Slaby, Roedell, Arezzo, and Hendrix (1995) explain further:

> Because young children have relatively little real-world experience by which to evaluate the relation of media violence to real life, they stand to benefit greatly from discussing these connections with adults.... A teacher might say, "He wants to stop that man from doing bad things, but the only way he knows how to do that is to fight him. I'll bet you can think of other ways that he could stop him without fighting."

"Teachers sometimes think they have to solve these problems for children. In a classroom community, a better alternative is a group problem solving" (Dodge, Colker, & Heroman, 2008). Besides open discussions with the children, teach conflict resolution skills and invite real, healthier role models (such as community helpers and family members) to visit the classroom. Help children regain control of their play by changing it from imitative play to creative, imaginative play. And importantly, work with parents, other teachers, and the early childhood community to understand and support each other's efforts to deal with the marketing of violence to children.

The National Association for the Education of Young Children has these comments that are as appropriate today as they were when they were stated in 1997:

1. Show children that superheroes are not special just because they are physically powerful. Point out when superheroes show kindness and helpfulness to others, and show appreciation to the children when they do the same.
2. Talk about real heroes and heroines with children. Introduce them to people like Helen Keller and Martin Luther King, Jr., and discuss how everyday people can demonstrate acts of courage and goodness.
3. Help children build on their interests through superhero play. Watching *Star Wars* may lead to learning about space travel, whereas the *Spiderman* movie or comic book may lead to exploring the world of insects. Always keep your eyes open to learning opportunities for children.

Additional Developmentally Appropriate Activities

The following song and activities ("Humpty Dumpty" by Bea Wolf) show how a finger play activity that is developmentally appropriate for toddlers and three-year-olds can be expanded to a dramatic play activity appropriate for four- and five-year-olds. The "Humpty Dumpty Song" is provided in Figure 12–2.

The song and dramatic play activity "The Doughnut Shop" by Bea Wolf is appropriate for four- and five-year-olds. Think about how you could use it for other age groups. "The Doughnut Song" is provided in Figure 12–3.

Books and stories can be used to integrate all areas of the curriculum, including dramatic play. The selection of a familiar story such as "The Three Billy Goats Gruff" or "The Three Little Pigs" can be the first tale to be acted out. Then add another book, such as *Brown Bear, Brown Bear, What Do You See?* by Bill Martin, Jr. (1983), *Gilberto and the Wind* by Marie Hall Ets (1978), or *The Talking Vegetables* by Won-Ldy Paye and Margaret Lippert (2006). Put the book away once you and the children are familiar and comfortable with the story. This gives more freedom to add to or change the basic story as you go along. Simple props and settings can add to the dramatic play. Once the children experience the enjoyment of this kind of activity, they can then expand the activity.

HUMPTY DUMPTY*
(finger play activity with song)
(Suitable for Toddlers and Three-Year-Olds)

FIGURE 12–2
"Humpty Dumpty Song" and activity for young children.

Before attempting this activity, read or recite the rhyme to the children on several occasions so they become thoroughly familiar with it. If possible, find a colorful illustration to stimulate their interest. The teacher asks the children questions while pointing to various features of the illustration:

Teacher: Who is this?
Children: Humpty Dumpty!
Teacher: What is Humpty Dumpty sitting on?
Children: The wall!
     (If children are too young to answer, teacher supplies the answers.)
     Teacher guides the children in identifying articles of clothing worn by Humpty Dumpty, points out the horses and soldiers and anything else of visual interest. If children are old enough to understand, some discussion may take place about the fact that Humpty Dumpty is an egg and eggs can break. Children are prepared for the activity when they appear well acquainted with the rhyme.

Teacher: Now we're going to tell the story of Humpty Dumpty with our hands.
     First, make a wall, like this: *(Teacher holds forearm as though looking at a wristwatch.)*
     Now, make a fist with your other hand. This is Humpty Dumpty! Set him down on the wall. Is he happy there? Let him sway back and forth.
     (Sway fist as though rocking back and forth on forearm.)
Teacher: Now everyone sing (or say):
     Humpty Dumpty sat on a wall.
     Humpty Dumpty had a great fall—Boom!

(Bend wrist down so that Humpty Dumpty drops off wall. Establish a rhythm by beating hands on thighs to simulate horses galloping. Sing or chant the next lines to this rhythm:)

> All the king's horses and all the king's men
> Couldn't put Humpty together again—
> Couldn't put Humpty together again!
> Why? *(Extend hands outward in a large shrug.)*

(During the next phrase extended hands slowly rise to meet over head, simulating an egg shape. Fingers meet on the word egg.)

> Because he was an egg!

(This activity provides a good opportunity to point out that an egg is oval shaped and to practice shaping ovals using fingers, hands, and arms.)

Review the nursery rhyme. Conduct a group discussion based on the fact that, once broken, an egg can never be put together again. Many children will have their own experiences to relate regarding this subject.

Announce that we are about to dramatize Humpty Dumpty. Explain that the word dramatize means to act out.

Guide the children in "falling" safely from a seated position to a lying down position on the floor. For this practice, children should already be seated on the floor so there is very little distance to fall. Explain that this is a fake fall, that we are acting, and that everyone must fall softly so as not to be hurt. Allow a very short time for fake fall practice (two or three falls should do it). Then guide children in pretending to be soldiers or king's men on horseback. Let them pretend to hold reins and gallop about for a short time; then announce that everyone seems ready to dramatize the story.

Divide the class into two groups. Group 1 consists of Humpty Dumptys, and group 2 of king's men. Instruct the king's men to wait quietly in a designated area until they hear their cue, which is the galloping rhythm the teacher will clap at the appropriate time. Instruct the Humpty Dumptys to sit on their wall, which can be a line on the floor. When everyone is ready, start the Humpty Dumptys swaying back and forth as all sing or say the first two lines of the rhyme. On "had a great fall," all Humpty Dumptys fake-fall on the floor and lie still. The teacher then claps the gallop rhythm. All the king's men then gallop over to the fallen Humpty Dumptys, dismount, and pat them gently, trying to put them together. On "Why?" the Humpty Dumptys sit up and all the children shrug with hands out. On "Because he was an egg," all slowly form an oval shape with arms above heads, fingers meeting on the word egg.

Repeat the dramatization, with group 1 switching roles with group 2.

*Reproduced by permission of B. Wolf

HUMPTY DUMPTY SONG*

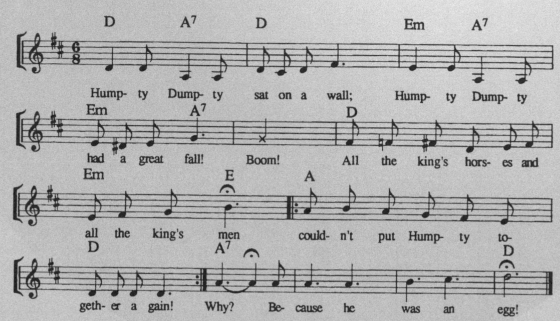

*Reproduced by permission of B. Wolf—1995
Copyright B. Wolf—1993

THE DOUGHNUT SHOP*
(dramatic play for four- and five-year olds)
(Entertainingly illustrates the concept of subtraction)

FIGURE 12–3
"The Doughnut Song" and activity for young children.

This activity requires the following cast:

1. A group of children who act as doughnuts.
2. A group of children who each purchase a doughnut.
3. A cashier or shopkeeper.

Begin by selecting the shopkeeper. The teacher can fill that role herself, delegate the role to a child who has earned a special privilege, or select the shopkeeper in some impartial way.

The children who act as doughnuts are seated in a row, on chairs or on the floor, in a designated area. The purchasers, each equipped with an imaginary or simulated coin, sit or stand in a different area. The shopkeeper sits near the doughnuts and operates an imaginary cash register.

The song is sung as many times as there are doughnuts lined up. Each time it is sung, a different child is named from the group of purchasers. That child walks over to the "shop," pays the shopkeeper, and selects a doughnut to take "home" (back to the purchaser area). Between each repetition of the song the teacher asks, "Now, how many doughnuts are left in the shop?"

After the last doughnut has been purchased, children usually wish to repeat the activity, with the groups switching roles.

*Reproduced by permission of B. Wolf

THE DOUGHNUT SONG*

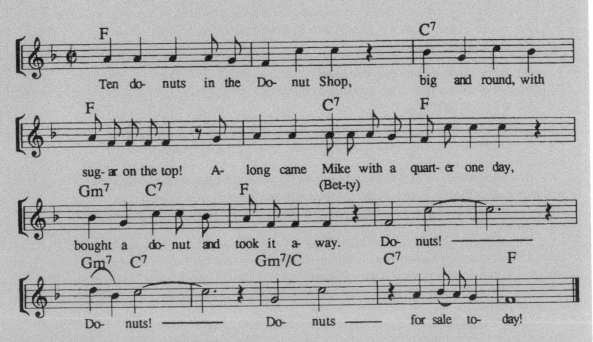

Reproduced by permission of B. Wolf—1995
Copyright B. Wolf—1993

Afterview

Through dramatic play, a child

- improves socialization skills.
- practices social skills through role negotiation and conflict resolution.
- develops external expressions of emotions.
- chooses safe outlets for aggression and creates a climate for nonviolence.
- identifies and empathizes with feelings of others.
- develops self-confidence through role-playing.
- acts out familiar situations, "tries on" family roles, works out problems and concerns, and experiments with solutions.
- distinguishes fantasy from reality.
- stimulates imagination and creativity.
- improves problem-solving skills.
- enhances sensorimotor skills.
- develops muscular coordination, listening and oral language skills, and math readiness.
- learns to make choices.

Reflective Review Questions

1. Reflect on the teacher's role in supporting children's dramatic play. Is the dramatic play theme part of the lesson plan? How much input should the children have in deciding what to play? What types of limits are placed on children during dramatic play?
2. Describe three themes for dramatic play that preschoolers enjoy engaging in, and identify items you would include in the center and how you would arrange them. What input might you receive from children before changing the center?
3. Why is it both appropriate and developmentally important that young children try out ways to differentiate fantasy from reality?
4. Relate dramatic play to four other learning centers. Be specific in the ways that dramatic play would help teach concepts in these other learning areas.

Key Terms

constructive play   games with rules   sociodramatic play
dramatic play   practice play   symbolic or dramatic play
functional play   prop box

Explorations

1. Select an early education classroom and observe for at least one hour. Describe, in writing, several dramatic play activities the children were involved with at the time of your observation. Describe the activities, which learning centers were part of the activities, how props were used, who initiated the play, and how many joined it.

2. Visit a child life center in a local hospital or health facility. Observe how children's dramatic play is the same or different from classroom play. Describe objectively (factually) what you saw. (For example, were the children giving shots to stuffed animals and placing bandages on the hurt places? Were dolls getting casts put on their arms or legs?) Discuss subjectively (opinion) what you felt and learned from this observation.

3. Discuss children's dramatic play on the playground. What are some of the activities that take place? What limits does the teacher place on outdoor activities? Are they different from indoor dramatic play activities? Explain.

4. Select and plan a dramatic play or creative dramatics activity for young children. Specify which age group this activity is planned for: infants, toddlers, preschoolers, or primary-age children. In writing, list objectives, materials needed, step-by-step procedures for presenting this activity, follow-up activities, and evaluation guidelines. (Use the activity plan worksheet in Chapter 2. A blank activity plan worksheet is available online at this textbook's website.) Prepare this activity and demonstrate it during class or with a group of children.

5. Based on the information in this chapter and on your observations of early education environments, select a partner and develop a dramatic play prop box appropriate for a group of young children. Describe the theme of the lesson plan and discuss how the prop box will be used within the context of the curriculum. Present this activity and demonstrate it during class or with a group of children.

Additional Readings and Resources

Alexander, N. P. (2001, Winter). Real learning: The joy of discovery. *The Dimensions of Early Childhood, 29*(1), 24.

Bergen, D. (2001, November). Pretend play and young children's development (*ERIC Digest* EDO-PS-01-10).

Berk, L. E. (1994, November). Vygotsky's theory: The importance of make-believe play. *Young Children, 50*(1), 30–39.

Chenfeld, M. B. (2010, March). The performing arts: Music, dance, and theater in the early years. *Young Children, 65*(2), 10–13.

Chudacoff, H. (2007). *Children at play: An American history.* New York: New York University Press.

Greenspan, S. I. (2006). When a child's play themes are violent. *Early Childhood Today.* Online at: *http://content. scholastic.com/browse/article.jsp?id=7759*

Lobman, C. (2003, May). The bugs are coming! Improvisation and early childhood teaching. *Young Children, 58*(3), 18–23.

Machado, J. M. (2010). *Early childhood experiences in language arts* (9th ed.). Clifton Park, NY: Wadsworth Cengage Learning.

Wanerman, T. (2010, March). Using story drama with young preschoolers. *Young Children, 65*(2), 20–28.

Helpful Web Connections

Early Childhood News
   http://www.earlychildhoodnews.com
International Play Association (USA)
   http://www.ipausa.org
Kids Source Online
   http://www.kidsource.com
NAEYC
   http://www.naeyc.org

PBS Teachers
   http://www.pbs.org/teachers
Scholastic
   http://www.scholastic.com
Strong National Museum of Play
   http://museumofplay.org

References

Allen, J., McNeill E., & Schmidt, V. (1992). *Cultural awareness for children*. Menlo Park, CA: Addison-Wesley Publishing Company.

Beaty, J. J. (2009). *Preschool appropriate practices* (3rd ed.). Clifton Park, NY: Wadsworth Cengage Learning.

Charlesworth, R., & Lind, K. K. (2010). *Math and science for young children* (6th ed.). Clifton Park, NY: Wadsworth Cengage Learning.

Deiner, P. L. (2010). *Inclusive early childhood education* (5th ed.). Clifton Park, NY: Wadsworth Cengage Learning.

Dodge, D. T., Colker, L. J., & Heroman, C. (2008). *Creative curriculum for preschool* (College ed.) Washington, DC: Teaching Strategies.

Elkind, D. (1994). *A sympathetic understanding of the child, birth to sixteen* (3rd ed.). Boston, MA: Allyn & Bacon.

Gordon, A. M., & Browne, K. W. (2011). *Beginnings and beyond: Foundations in early childhood education* (8th ed.). Clifton Park, NY: Wadsworth Cengage Learning.

Hanvey, C. E. (2010, January). Experiences with an outdoor prop box. *Young Children*, 65(10, 30–33.

Harris, P. (2002). Imagination is important for children's cognitive development. Online at: *http://www.researchmatters.harvard.edu*

Haugen, K. (2002, November–December). Time, trust, and tools: Opening doors to imagination for all children. *Child Care Information Exchange* (148), 36–40.

Isbell, R. T., & Raines, S. C. (2007). *Creativity and the arts with young children* (2nd ed.). Clifton Park, NY: Delmar Cengage Learning.

Mayesky, M. (2009). *Creative activities for young children* (9th ed.). Clifton Park, NY: Wadsworth Cengage Learning.

McCaslin, N. (1990). *Creative dramatics in the classroom* (5th ed.). New York: Longman.

Miller, K. (2002, November–December). The seeds of dramatic play: Enhanced by adults. *Child Care Information Exchange* (148), 25–26.

National Association for the Education of Young Children (NAEYC). (1997). Online at: *http://naeyc.org*

Parten, M. B. (1932). Social participation among preschool children. *Journal of Abnormal and Social Psychology, 27*, 243–269.

Piaget, J. (1962). *Play, dreams and imitation in childhood*. New York: W. W. Norton.

Read, K., Gardner, P., & Mahler, B. (1993). *Early childhood programs: Human relationships and learning* (9th ed.). New York: Harcourt.

Slaby, R. G., Roedell, W. C., Arezzo, D., & Hendrix, K. (1995). *Early violence prevention*. Washington, DC: NAEYC.

Smilansky, S. (1968). *The effects of sociodramatic play on disadvantaged preschool children*. New York: John Wiley & Sons.

Vail, P. L. (1999, January). Observing learning styles in the classroom. *Early Childhood Today, 13*(4), 20–27.

Additional information and resources on early childhood curriculum can be found on the Education CourseMate website for this book. Go to **www.CengageBrain.com** to register your access code.

Appendix A

My Self: Integrated Curriculum Theme with Activities

MY SELF

FEELINGS

Loving
Happy   Sad
Afraid
Surprised
Angry   Lonely
Friendly
Excited
Verbal   Nonverbal

SELF ESTEEM

Being special
Having ideas and thoughts
Being creative
Doing some things well
Having a special body
Having a family
and friends

SELF-CONTROL

Learning appropriate ways
to show and say
how I feel
Listening to others
Saying "no" to things
that will hurt me
or others

SELF-MOTIVATION

Learning how to
do new things
Learning by using my mind
and all my senses
Playing and doing things
by myself
or with friends

THEME GOALS

To provide opportunities for children to learn the following:

- I am special because I am **me**. There is no one else just like me.
- I am still discovering how to do new things.
- I can use my mind and my senses to accomplish many things.
- I can play and do things by myself or with friends and family.
- I can show my emotions and say how I feel without hurting others.
- I can say "no" to things that will hurt me or others.

Integrated Curriculum Theme with Activities

Children-Created Bulletin Board

This bulletin board gives children an opportunity to express how they feel about themselves. Throughout the theme, the bulletin board changes as the children learn more about feelings, self-esteem, self-motivation, and self-control.

- Cut poster board cards in various shapes, such as circles, squares, rectangles, and triangles.
- Have each child select one card in his favorite shape.
- Write or have the child write anything about himself on the card, including the suggestions that follow in the "Special Recipe."

"SPECIAL RECIPE FOR (CHILD'S NAME)"

Two big (color) eyes,

One great smile,

(Long, short—color) hair,

Smooth (color) skin,

One cup of niceness,

Two cups of laughter.

- Children add anything they want about themselves. Give a few examples to get them started: "Add one cup of books. Stir in puzzles. Mix together and discover (child's name)."
- You may find it easier to do this with each child individually.
- Put the finished recipes on the bulletin board.
- Have the children add photos of themselves or pictures they draw of themselves.
- As they learn to do more things during this theme, children can add to the original recipe.
- Drawings that express feelings also can be added.
- Adding new items will make this an interactive bulletin board.

Vocabulary Starters

Let the children add words.

creative—discovering new ways of doing things.

feelings—what you mean when you talk about or show being happy, sad, afraid, angry, or surprised.

learn—to know and understand something you did not know or understand before.

self—whatever is just about you and nobody else.

thoughts—what happens when you get ideas and decide to do things?

Language Experiences

BALL NAME GAME

All you need for this activity are the children and a large ball. This is a good transition activity. When a child's name is called, he can choose a learning center and go to it.

- Everyone sits on the floor in a circle.
- Talk about how special everyone's name is.
- Roll the ball to a child. Everyone says the child's first name.
- Ask the toddler to roll or bring the ball back to you. Continue rolling the ball and saying each child's name.

- The preschooler can roll the ball to someone else. Everyone says that child's name. The ball passes from one child to another until each child's name is called and repeated.
- Extend this activity by rolling the ball to a child and saying the child's last name.
- Continue until each child's last name has been called.

WHOSE VOICE IS THIS?

Use a tape recorder to tape each child's conversational voice, giggling, laughing, or singing.

- Record each child privately, away from the other children. If children do not know what to say, help them say something with you. This way you are recording your voice too.
- Next, play back what each child recorded and have the other children guess whose voice they hear.
- Talk about how each person's voice is unique.
- Place the tape recorder in the music center. The children can listen to the voices whenever they wish.

LET'S SHARE

- Read Hutchins's *The Doorbell Rang*, listed in the Children's Books section later in this appendix.
- Discuss the concept of sharing as a way of showing someone you care about him.
- Ask open-ended questions such as: "What have you shared?" "With whom did you share it?" "Why do you need to share?" "How do you feel when someone shares with you?" "What are some things we could share in the classroom?"
- *The Doorbell Rang* is about sharing cookies. Buy or bake a giant cookie, and let the children find ways to share.

Dramatic Play

I AM HAPPY

This activity can be done indoors or outdoors.

- Give the children opportunities to show emotions (happy, sad, angry, afraid, and surprised) by the way they run, walk, hop, throw a ball, or move their bodies.
- Role-play appropriate ways to handle situations.
- Ask children to share what makes them feel happy, sad, and so on.
- This could be repeated throughout the year to help children deal with their feelings.
- Puppets can also help children talk about how they feel.

PANTOMIME TIME

Read Carle's *The Mixed-Up Chameleon*. See the Children's Books section later in this appendix.

- Ask open-ended questions, such as: "Why do you think the chameleon was feeling unhappy?" "What feelings do you have about the chameleon?"
- Help the children decide which "chameleon character" they want to pantomime. Act without using words. One child can even be the sun and another the fly.
- Read the story again.
- The children pantomime their roles as the story unfolds.
- To extend this activity, have the children create paper costumes of the different "chameleon characters."
- The children also can draw their own chameleons.

Puppet Play

TENNIS BALL PUPPET FRIEND

Let the children name this puppet. For the purpose of describing this activity, we will call the tennis ball puppet "Happy." This activity promotes positive self-esteem, self-motivation, and self-control.

- To make Happy, an adult should cut a slit in the middle of a tennis ball, across from one seam to the next. (See the illustration for clarification.) **Caution:** Be careful when cutting. A tennis ball is difficult to cut. It is hard to hold without slipping.
- Use markers or "puff paint" to make eyes, eyebrows, nose, and mouth.
- To make Happy "talk," press the sides of the ball.
- Use a box to make a special home for the puppet.
- Let a different child take Happy home each day after school and bring him back the next day.
- Happy reports on his overnight (or weekend) adventure at the child's home.

- This gives the child an opportunity to develop a voice for the puppet and tell what happened.
- You and the children can write in a special book what happens to Happy. Where did he go? What did he eat? Whom did he see? Where did he sleep?
- The children also can illustrate their books.
- Children vote on who gets to take Happy home.
- Next, you and the children can make a calendar and count the days until Happy goes home with the next child.

FEELINGS PUPPET

Children of all ages enjoy this activity.

- Put tongue depressors, crayons, and markers out for the children to use.
- Encourage the children to make a set of "feelings" puppets.
- Children can draw faces on the tongue depressors that show happy, sad, fearful, angry, and surprised expressions.
- Give the children envelopes in which to put their "feelings." They place the envelopes in their individual cubbies. When the children want to express how they feel, they can pull out their "feelings" puppet.

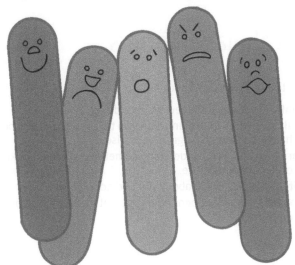

Music

SONG: "HELLO, HELLO"

The following song is a *musical beat* activity. It also can be chanted.

Hello, hello,

We sing in many ways.

Hello, hello,

Let's sing them now today.

In the following verses of this "Hello" chant, a simple method of indicating the beat is used. Though the chant is original, the system of indicating the beat is adapted from Sally Moomaw's *More Than Singing* (1997), published by Redleaf Press, St. Paul, MN.

Use a drum or other musical instrument to reinforce the beat. A vertical line (I) above a syllable means that it is accented. An asterisk (*) indicates a pause (or "rest," as in music) in the phrasing. In addition, phonetic pronunciations are provided under the foreign words.

ENGLISH

Hel-lo hel-lo **
*We sing in ma-ny ways **
*Hel-lo * hel-lo **
*Let's sing them now to-day **

SPANISH

*>Ho-la * ho-la **
(oh-la oh-la)
*We sing in ma-ny ways **
*Ho-la * ho-la **
*Let's sing them now to-day **

FRENCH

*Bon-jour * bon-jour **
(bone-zhoor bone-zhoor)
*We sing in ma-ny ways **
*Bon-jour * bon-jour **
*Let's sing them now to-day **

GERMAN

*Gu-ten tag * gu-ten tag **
(goo-ten tog goo-ten tog)

ITALIAN

*Ci-a-o * ci-a-o **
(chee-ah-oh chee-ah-oh)

JAPANESE

*Kon-ni-chi- wa * kon-ni-chi- wa **
(koh-nee-chee-wah koh-nee-chee-wah)

CHINESE

*Ni-hao * ni-hao **
(nee-how nee-how)

KOREAN

*An nung * an nung **
(ahn nyong ahn nyong)

VIETNAMESE

*Chao * chao **
(chow chow)

HEBREW

*Sha-lom * sha-lom **
(sha-lome sha-lome)

ARABIC

*Mar-h-ba * mar-h -ba**
(mar-hah-bah mar-hah-bah)

Movement

. . . .

EXERCISES FOR OLDER INFANTS AND TODDLERS

- **Push the chair,** to practice walking. Have the infant on his feet holding onto the back of a low, sturdy child's chair. Help him push the chair while practicing walking.
- **In and out of the box,** for coordination. Use a heavy cardboard box or tub, and place the baby inside. Encourage him to climb in and out.
- **The rocking chair,** for fun and to strengthen muscles. Have the infant sit on the floor next to you. Bring your knees up, and rock back and forth. Encourage the child to do the same.
- **Pop-up,** for upper body and stomach strength. Do this exercise together. Have the baby sit on the floor and bend over. Quickly have him straighten his legs while sitting upright and stretching his arms up high. Hold for two seconds, then quickly return to bent-over position. Repeat.

LET'S WAVE, WOBBLE, AND WIGGLE

Do this activity with or without recorded music, or try it using the traditional tune "The Bear Went over the Mountain."

My thumbs, my thumbs want to pop up.

My thumbs, my thumbs want to pop up.

My thumbs, my thumbs want to pop up.

That's what they like to do.

Continue the pattern with the following changes:

My hands, my hands want to shake …

My arms, my arms want to wave …

My head, my head wants to wobble …

(That's what *it* likes to do.)

My legs, my legs want to wiggle …

My feet, my feet want to dance …

Now all of me wants to jump …

(That's what *I* like to do.)

End with:

Oh, I am starting to giggle,

I am starting to giggle,

I am starting to giggle,

I think I'll just sit down!

I'M THE LEADER

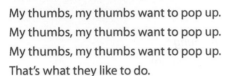

- Everyone forms a big circle. Select one of the children to be the leader.
- Suggest that he hop, jump, or crawl, and say, "Do it just like me."
- The other children then try to do what he does.
- Continue with the children taking turns.
- This is one of those quick activities that can be used anytime.

RIGHT, LEFT, RIGHT, STOP!

This movement activity helps with recognition of left and right.

- Let the children help you come up with other ideas.
- Older children like to combine several body movements at one time.
- Children like to do this at home with family members too.

March with feet	Sway with upper body
Left, right,	Right, left,
Left, right,	Right, left
Left, right,	Right, left,
Stop!	Stop!

Raise arms	Move head
Left, right,	Right, left,
Left, right,	Right, left,
Left, right,	Right, left,
Stop!	Stop!

Sensory Art

EXPRESSING FEELINGS

To ease the times a child may feel frustrated, angry, or full of energy (and "using his words" won't help), bring out the clay or play dough. Many types and textures are available. A recipe for play dough is provided in Chapter 8.

- Set up a special space for the child to have some alone time with the clay or play dough.
- For a toddler, a special place to pound, such as on a plastic pounding bench, can help defuse feelings.

MAKE AN "I'M SPECIAL" VEST

Do this project with each child individually, if possible.

- Take a large paper grocery sack and invert it.
- Cut straight up the center of one of the wide sides to where the bottom creases.
- Here, cut a large round circle out of the bottom of the sack.
- On each narrow side of the sack, cut a vertical oval that starts at the bottom crease and extends about eight inches.
- The child puts the vest on by placing his head through the large, round opening, with the long vertical slit to the front and arms through the two side ovals.

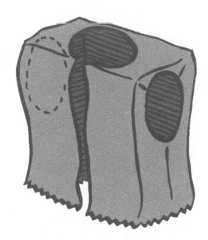

- Have each child decorate the "I'm Special" vest with crayons, markers, felt and fabric scraps, construction paper, feathers, cotton balls, and all kinds of shapes, stickers, and buttons.
- Put magazines and catalogs out as well, and suggest that children cut out pictures of what they like and glue these to the vest.

TWO-DIMENSIONAL ART GALLERY

In a school hallway, walkway, or entrance area, display some of the children's art along with posters or pictures of famous paintings.

- Mat and attractively exhibit all of the art, so that the children's creativity is treated the same as that of well-known artists.
- Let the children help you mount the exhibition.
- This is a good way to introduce the children to great works of art and the painters who created the works.
- Many children's books on art are available to share with the children, for example, *Getting to Know the World's Greatest Artists Series*, published by Children's Press, and *New York's Metropolitan Museum of Art Series*, published by Viking.

Creative Food Experiences

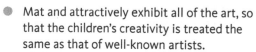

HAPPY FACES

You will need the following:

a loaf of bread
cream cheese
peanut butter
apple jelly
raisins
nuts

  HAPPY FACES!

Wash hands.

Cut circles from bread with a round cookie cutter.

Spread bread with cream cheese, peanut butter,

or apple jelly. Use raisins and nuts to make

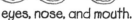

eyes, nose, and mouth.

ENJOY!

1. Let the children cut circles from bread with a round cookie cutter.
2. Spread bread with cream cheese, peanut butter, or apple jelly. Children sometimes use all three.
3. Use raisins and nuts to make eyes, nose, and mouth. Enjoy!

Note: Omit peanut butter and nuts for those children who are allergic.

LET'S MAKE A CAKE

This recipe is easy for the children to do and can give them a sense of accomplishment. It also is a fun one to pass on to families.

1. Wash hands.
2. Put one can of fruit, with the juice, into a buttered 9-by-13-inch metal or glass pan.
3. Dump one box of white or yellow cake mix over the fruit.
4. Cut one stick of butter or margarine into small pieces.
5. Dump butter or margarine pieces on top of the cake mix.
6. Bake at 350 degrees for 30 to 40 minutes.
7. Eat!

Math

THE LANGUAGES OF MATH

This activity encourages learning to count from one to five in many languages. It also helps build self-esteem for children of other cultures.

English	Spanish	French	German	Italian
One	Uno (ōō-no)	un (ŏon)	eins (īnes)	Uno (ōō-no)
Two	Dos (dose)	deux (dŏo)	zwei ([ts]vye)	Due (dŏō-eh)
Three	Tres (trais)	trois (t(r)wah)	drei (dry)	Tre (treh)
Four	Cuatro (kwáh-tro)	quatre (ká-tra)	vier (fear)	Quattro (kwáh-tro)
Five	Cinco (seén-ko)	cinq (sank)	funf (foonf)	Cinque (cheén-kay)

English	Chinese	Japanese	Hebrew	Arabic
One	Yi (yee)	ichi (ée-chee)	achat (a-(h)áht)	Wahid (wáh-hid)
Two	Er (uhr)	ni (nee)	shta'yim (shtah-yéem)	Ithinin (ith-nín)
Three	San (sahn)	san (sahn)	shalosh (shah-lōśh)	Thalatha (ta-lá-ta)
Four	Si (suh)	shi (shee)	arba (ar-báh)	arba'a (ar-báh)
Five	Wu (woo)	go (go)	hamesh ([h]ah-meśh)	Kamisa (k(h)aĥm-sa)

MATH COOKIES

Relate this activity to Hutchins's book *The Doorbell Rang*. See the language experience activity in this theme. This activity promotes problem solving, one-to-one correspondence, and cooperation.

- You and the children make three dozen "cardboard cookies." These can be made easily out of heavy cardboard or poster board cut into circles.
- Decorate the cookies with markers and crayons.
- Some of the cookies should be alike.
- Make up math games that can be played with the cardboard cookies.
- Younger children can sort the cookie circles by color or by the number of "chocolate chip" dots on the cookies. They also can practice making a straight line with the cookies.

- Older children can practice counting and sorting the cookies into pairs, as well as figuring out how many children are in the class, whether they can share the cookies equally, and what they have to do to share the cookies equally.

Science

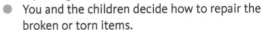

FIXING THINGS

- Collect broken toys, torn books, or anything that can be fixed with masking tape, clear tape, or glue.
- You and the children decide how to repair the broken or torn items.
- Children may work in pairs to figure out how the broken pieces might fit together again.

MY BODY IS MADE OF HINGES

This project has many levels. The beginning levels are appropriate and interesting for preschoolers. The entire procedure is fascinating for older children. To introduce this activity, have a variety of hinges in a box.

- Demonstrate how the hinges work, and allow the children to experiment with them for several days.
- Next, talk about hinges in the room, and then show how children's bodies have "hinges."
- Let children bend their fingers, wrists, knees, and so on to music.
- Introduce silhouette pieces, such as head, neck, trunk, arms, hands, legs, and feet. These can be made from black construction paper or shiny, lightweight black art paper.
- Have a prepared figure put together with brads to show how the body moves.
- Prepare the silhouette body parts for each child, and place the pieces in individual envelopes.
- Go through magazines and catalogs for action poses.
- Encourage each child to select one picture. Using glue sticks, glue it on half of an $8\frac{1}{2}$ by-11-inch piece of white paper.
- On the side of the page opposite the picture, have the child position the silhouette body parts in the same position. Children may need guidance to do this.
- When each child is satisfied with the pose, he glues the parts, one at a time, onto the paper.
- Place all of the finished silhouette pictures on the bulletin board.

Social Studies

CELEBRATING BIRTHDAYS AND SPECIAL MONTHS

Birthdays are special days for children. Help them celebrate by setting up a big classroom calendar that you and the children design.

PRESCHOOL–K

PRIMARY-GRADE

- Have each child write his name and birth date on the calendar.
- Since some cultures and religions do not emphasize birthdays, also include on the calendar special events that happen each month in your community or nationally.
- You can celebrate birthdays and other special days at the same time.
- Play special recorded music, eat a new snack, or read a new book to celebrate each child's birthday.

Here are some suggestions for special events to celebrate. You and the children can decide how you will observe the day.

September	Monarch Butterfly Migration Month
	Good Neighbor Day (fourth week)
October	Popcorn Month
	Apple Month
	Teddy Bear Day (Oct. 27)
November	National Children's Book Week (third week)
	Homemade Bread Day (Nov. 17)
December	Birds in the Snow Week (fourth week)
	Poinsettia Day (Dec. 12)
January	National Soup Month
	New Year's Day in 123 nations (Jan. 1)
February	Black History Month
	Presidents' Day (second week)
March	National Nutrition Month
	Children's Poetry Day (March 21)

April	Week of the Young Child (Consult the National Association for the Education of Young Children for specific dates: 1-800/424-2460.)
	Earth Day (April 22)
May	Be Kind to Animals Month
	National Safe Kids Week (second week)
June	Children's Day (second week)
	Flag Day (June 14)
July	Blueberry Month
	National Ice Cream Day (third week)
August	National Clown Week (first week)
	Family Day (second week)

Children's Books

Anderson, Peggy P. (2002). *Let's Clean Up!* Boston: Houghton Mifflin.

Carle, Eric. (1984). *The Mixed-Up Chameleon.* New York: HarperTrophy.

Carle, Eric. (1996). *The Grouchy Ladybug.* New York: Harper-Collins.

Catalanotto, Peter. (2002). *Matthew ABC....* New York: Atheneum.

Cowell, Cressida. (2003). *Super Sue.* Illustrated by Russell Ayto. Cambridge, MA: Candlewick Press.

French, Simon. (2002). *Guess the Baby.* Illustrated by Donna Rawlins. New York: Clarion.

Getting to Know the World's Greatest Artist Series. (1990). Chicago: Children's Press.

Got, Yves. (2003). *Sam's Busy Day.* (Boxed Board Books). San Francisco: Chronicle.

Hill, Elizabeth S. (2002). *Chang and the Bamboo Flute.* Illustrated by Lesley Liu. New York: Farrar, Straus &Giroux.

Hoffman, Mary. (2002). *The Color of Home.* Illustrated by Karin Littlewood. New York: Putnam.

Hutchins, Pat. (1989). *The Doorbell Rang.* New York: Mulberry Books.

Isadora, Rachel. (2003). *On Your Toes: A Ballet ABC.* New York: Greenwillow.

Lebrun, Claude. (1997). *Little Brown Bear Is Growing Up.* New York: Children's Press.

Lee, Suzy, (2009). *Wave.* New York: Chronicle.

MacCarone, Grace. (1995). *The Lunch Box Surprise.* New York: Cartwheel Books.

Mayer, Mercer. (1995). *I Am Sharing.* New York: Random House.

McGee, Marni. (2002). *Wake Up, Me!* Illustrated by Sam Williams. New York: Simon & Schuster.

McGhee, Alison. (2009). *Little Boy.* Illustrated by Peter H. Reynolds. New York: Atheneum.

New York's Metropolitan Museum of Art's Series. (1993). *What Makes...a...?* New York: Author and Viking.

Raposo, Joe. (2001). *Imagination Song*. Illustrated by Laurent Linn. New York: Random House.

Reiser, Lynn, Rebecca Hart, and Corazones Valientes Organization. (1998). *Tortillas and Lullabies/Tortillas y cancioncitas*. New York: Greenwillow.

Singer, Marilyn. (2003). *Boo Hoo Boo-Boo*. Illustrated by Elivia Savadier. New York: HarperCollins.

Stuve-Bodeen, Stephanie. (2002). *Elizabeti's School*. Illustrated by Christy Hale. New York: Lee & Low.

Waber, Bernard. (2002). *Courage*. Boston: Houghton Mifflin.

Walsh, Melanie. (2009). *10 Things I Can Do to Help My World: Fun and Easy Eco-Tips*. Cambridge, MA: Candlewick.

Wollman, Jessica. (2002). *Andrew's Bright Blue T-Shirt*. Illustrated by Anna L. Escriva. New York: Doubleday.

Zemach, Kaethe. (2003). *Just Enough and Not Too Much*. New York: Arthur A. Levine/Scholastic.

Zolotow, Charlotte. (1985). *William's Doll*. Illustrated by William Pene DeBois. New York: HarperTrophy.

Family Letter (Preschool)

Dear Family,

We are starting another theme this week, "My Self." We will provide opportunities for the children to learn the following:

- I am special because I am me. There is no one else like me.
- I am still discovering how to do new things.
- I can use my mind and my senses to accomplish many things.
- I can play and do things by myself or with friends and family.
- I can show emotions and say how I feel without hurting others.
- I can say "no" to things that will hurt me or others.

We will be talking about the following:

- feelings
- verbal expression
- nonverbal expression
- self-esteem
- self-motivation
- self-control

Things you can do at home with your preschool child include:

- Welcome "Happy" (the tennis ball puppet) when it comes home with your child. It will be in the box it "lives in," but "Happy" enjoys getting out sometimes. "Happy" should be included in family activities, such as going where your child goes and sleeping in the room with your child.
- Sing songs with your child, and record these on a tape recorder or video camera. This will give your family a special musical cassette or videotape.
- Make cookies or a cake with your child.
- Let your child help you repair things around the house.

Family participation opportunities at school will include:

- Help us make "I'm Special" vests.

  Date _____ Time _____
- Come visit the children's art gallery.
- Help us make silhouettes.

  Date _____ Time _____

Our wish list for this theme includes:

magazines and catalogs
posters of famous paintings
tennis balls
large paper sacks
heavy cardboard

Thanks!

Appendix B

Resources for Teachers, with Website Listings

The following online resources offer publications, educational and interactive materials, services, and other resources for teachers. They are listed in association with chapter content. See Helpful Web Connections sections listed in each chapter of this text for additional online resources.

INTERNET DISCLAIMER

The author and Wadsworth Cengage Learning make every effort to ensure that all resources are accurate at the time of printing. However, due to the fluid, time-sensitive nature of the Internet, Wadsworth Cengage Learning cannot guarantee that all URLs and website addresses will remain current for the duration of this edition.

Chapter 1

- Child Care Information Exchange
  (Professional magazine for early childhood administrators and teachers)
  http://www.ccie.com
- Council for Professional Recognition (CDA)
  Child Development Associate
  http://www.cdacouncil.org
- Especially for Parents
  http://www.ed.gov/parents
- National Association for the Education of Young Children (NAEYC)
  http://www.naeyc.org
- National Association for Family Child Care (NAFCC)
  http://www.nafcc.org
- National Association for Gifted Children
  http://www.nagc.org
- National Institute on Early Child Development and Education
  U.S. Department of Education
  http://www.ed.gov
- National Institute for Play
  (Emphasizes the importance of play)
  http://www.nifplay.org
- *Scholastic Early Childhood Today*
  (Professional magazine for early childhood teachers)
  Scholastic Inc.
  http://www.scholastic.com

- School-Age Notes
  (National resource organization for school-age care)
  http://www.schoolagenotes.com
- Society for Research in Child Development
  http://www.srcd.org
- ZERO TO THREE
  (Helping babies and toddlers grow and develop)
  http://www.zerotothree.org

Chapter 2

- American Academy of Pediatrics
  (Committed to the attainment of optimal physical, mental, and social health and well-being for all infants, children, adolescents, and young adults; this website has current and helpful information for teachers and parents)
  http://www.aap.org
- American Dental Association
  (Provides information on good dental health for children, parents, and teachers)
  http://www.ada.org
- American Montessori Society
  http://www.amshq.org

- Anti-Defamation League
  ADL Resources for Classroom and Community
  http://www.adl.org
  (Click on Behind the Homepage / Education / Children's
  Bibliography for anti-bias/multicultural curriculum
  materials for teacher resources and audiovisual materials.
  Many cities have a local office that also has these materials)
- Association Montessori Internationale/USA
  http://www.montessori-ami.org
- Bank Street College of Education
  http://www.bankstreet.edu
- Children and Computers
  http://www.childrenandcomputers.com
- Circle of Inclusion
  http://www.circleofinclusion.org
- Common Sense Media
  http://www.commonsensemedia.org
- Council for Exceptional Children
  (Offers comprehensive information and publications)
  http://www.cec.sped.org
- Culturally and Linguistically Appropriate Services
  http://www.clas.uiuc.edu
- Early Childhood Educators' and Family Web Corner (NAREA)
  (Lists teacher information programs on many subjects)
  http://www.users.sgi.net/~cokids/teacher.html
- Gryphon House Inc.
  http://www.ghbooks.com
- Head Start Information and Publication Center
  U.S. Department of Health and Human Services
  Administration for Children (Head Start/Early Start)
  http:www.acf.hhs.gov/programs/ohs
- High/Scope Educational Research Foundation
  http://www.highscope.org
- Individuals with Disabilities Education Act
  http://www.idea.ed.gov
- National Child Care Information Center, U.S.
  Department of Health & Human Services
  Administration for Children & Families
  (A national resource information link to ensure that
  all children and families have access to high-quality
  comprehensive services)
  http://nccic.org
- National Dissemination Center for Children with
  Disabilities (NICHCY)
  (Publications are free; includes *Parent Guide* and
  publication list)
  http://www.NICHCY.org
- National Program for Playground Safety (NPPS)
  University of Northern Iowa
  School for Health, Physical Education, and Leisure Services
  http://www.uni.edu/playground
- Project Approach (Katz & Chard)
  (Provides resources for project-based learning with young
  children)
  http://www.projectapproch.org

- Redleaf Press
  (Resources for early childhood professionals)
  http://www.redleafpress.org
- Reggio Emilia
  Website of North American Reggio Emilia Alliance
  (NAREA) provides information for educators.
  http://www.reggioalliance.org
  Official website for Reggio Children with information in
  both English and Italian
  http://www.reggiochildren.it
- Southern Poverty Law Center (Tolerance Organization)
  (A principal online destination for people interested in
  dismantling bigotry and creating communities that value
  diversity; helpful site for teachers who want to implement
  anti-bias practices in their classrooms)
  http://www.tolerance.org

Chapter 3

- American Foundation for the Blind
  http://www.afb.org
- Center for the Study of Books in Spanish for Children and
  Adolescents
  California State University San Marcos
  http://www.csusm.edu/csb
- The Children's Book Council (CBC)
  (A nonprofit trade organization dedicated to encouraging
  literacy and the use and enjoyment of books; CBC is
  the official sponsor of *Young People's Poetry Week* and
  Children's Book Week)
  http://www.cbcbooks.org
- Dragon Tales
  (Created especially for preschoolers, Dragon Tales is
  designed to nurture young children's curiosity and
  enthusiasm for learning)
  http://pbskids.org
- Get Ready to Read
  http://www.getreadytoread.org
- Internet Public Library
  (Offers references, reading zone, books and authors,
  teacher's and parent's information and activities on art,
  music, science, math, etc.)
  http://www.ipl.org
  (Click on "For Kids")
- National Children's Literacy
  (Part of The Soho Center's National Children's Literacy
  Information Project)
  http://www.child2000.org
  (Click on "Yes," then click on "National Children's Literacy
  Website")
- National Council of Teachers of English (NCTE)
  (Click on ECE Assembly of NCTE)
  http://www.ncte.org

- Reading Is Fundamental
  http://www.rif.org
- Reading Rockets
  http://www.readingrockets.org
- Society of Children's Book Writers and Illustrators
  (Helpful research links that offer literacy and literature websites for teachers and parents)
  http://www.scbwi.org/links/research.htm

Chapter 4

- Bank Street Children's Book Committee
  (Founded over 100 years ago to guide librarians, educators, and parents to the best books for children published each year)
  http://www.bankstreet.edu/bookcom
  (Publishes *The Best Children's Books of the Year* and *Books to Read Aloud for Children of All Ages*)
- Cricket Magazine Group
  Babybug for infants and toddlers
  Ladybug for young children
  Spider for beginning readers
  Cricket for young people
  Ask for young people
  http://www.cricketmag.com
- *Highlights for Children Magazine*
  http://www.highlights.com
- National Center for Family Literacy
  http://www.famlit.org
- National Children's Book Week (November)
  (Information and classroom "streamers" and posters available from the online catalog)
  Children's Book Council
  http://www.cbcbooks.org
- Reading Is Fundamental (RIF)
  (Information for teachers and parents)
  http://www.rif.org
- *Stone Soup: The Magazine by Children*
  http://www.stonesoup.com
- *Weekly Reader*
  http://www.weeklyreader.com

Chapter 5

- Activities Integrating Mathematics and Science (AIMS) Education Foundation
  http://www.aimsedu.org
- Helping Your Child Learn Math
  (Site for parents—what to do to help your child achieve in math)
  http://www.ed.gov/pubs/parents/Math/index.html

- The Math Forum @ Drexel University
  (Provides resources, materials, activities, person-to-person interactions, and educational products and services that enrich and support teaching and learning)
  http://mathforum.org
- National Council of Teachers of Mathematics
  http://www.nctm.org
- National Library of Virtual Manipulatives
  http://nlvm.usu.edu
- Webmath
  (Resource site for children, teachers, and parents—helps children with math problems they are working on right now; teachers can create a math test online)
  http://www.webmath.com

Chapter 6

- Arbor Day and Earth Day—Arbor Day Foundation's Nature Explore Program
  (For teachers and children)
  http://www.arborday.org/explore
- *Audubon* Magazine
  National Audubon Society
  http://www.audubon.org
  (Click on Education)
- Bring Birds to Your Backyard
  (A number of government-sponsored booklets are offered to children *free* for the asking: "Homes for Birds" describes the characteristics of various birds and tells the best housing for each; "Backyard Bird Feeding" tells how to attract different species to your house)
  http://www.pueblo.gsa.gov
  (In site Search box, type in the names of these publications and click on "Go" to download these and other booklets)
  http://www.earthsciweek.org
  (In the Search box, type in "Backyard Birds" and "Bring Birds to Your Backyard")
- EPA—United States Environmental Protection Agency
  (Provides information and services on teaching about the environment, especially designed for classroom use)
  http://epa.gov
- Friends of the Environment Foundation—Earth Day Canada
  http://www.ecokidsonline.com
- Green Teacher
  http://www.greenteacher.com
- National Science Teachers Association
  (Information focused on you and your teaching environment)
  http://www.nsta.org
- National Wildlife Federation
  (Offers several magazines and programs especially for young children)

Some of these are:
1. *Wild Animal Baby*—12 months to 3 years
2. *Your Big Backyard*—ages 3–6
3. *Ranger Rick Magazine*—ages 7–12
(Explore schoolyard habitat, backyard wildlife habitat, and National Wildlife Week online)
http://www.nwf.org
● Nature's Classroom (Environmental education programs)
http://www.naturesclassroom.org
● Space Day
(Generally held in May and designed to advance science, mathematics, and technology education)
http://www.spaceday.com
(Try the Space Puzzlers. Click on Games. The children will enjoy this site.)
● USDA Forest Service
http://www.fs.fed.us
(Under Forest Service Home, click on "Just for Kids")

Chapter 7

● Visit children's museums online. Here are some websites to get you started.
● Canadian Children's Museum
http://www.civilization.ca
● Children's Discovery Museum of San Jose
http://www.cdm.org
● Children's Museum of Boston
http://www.bostonkids.org
● Children's Museum of Houston
http://www.cmhouston.org
● Children's Museum of Manhattan
http://www.cmom.org
● The Eric Carle Museum of Picture Book Art
http://www.picturebookart.org
● Chicago Children's Museum
http://www.chichildrensmuseum.org
● Science Museum of Minnesota
http://www.smm.org
● Smithsonian Institution
http://www.si.edu
http://national/zoo.si.edu
(National Zoo from the Smithsonian)
● National Association for Bilingual Education
http://www.nabe.org
● National Council for the Social Studies
http://www.ncss.org
● National Geographic Society
(Source for materials about geography, environmental science, and global studies)
http://www.nationalgeographic.com
(In the Search box, type "for teachers")

● United States Committee for UNICEF
United Nations Children's Fund
http://www.unicefusa.org
(To receive their catalog of cards and gifts, type "catalog of cards and gifts" in the Search box, then click on the "Order a Catalog" link, and then enter your information.)

Chapter 8

● Aline D. Wolf 's "Mommy, It's a Renoir" and four volumes of accompanying art postcards titled "Child-Size Masterpieces"
Parent Child Press
http://www.parentchildpress.com
(Click on Art Education.)
● Artsedge
(Supports the place of arts education at the center of the curriculum through the creative and appropriate uses of technology)
The John F. Kennedy Center for the Performing Arts
http://www.artsedge.kennedy-center.org
● Artsplay
(An interactive resource from Wolf Trap Institute for Early Learning Through the Arts, an arts-in-education program for the early childhood community; a great resource for teachers)
http://www.wolftrap.org
(Click on Education)
● Crayola
(Explore this site—it's full of ideas and information for stimulating creativity)
http://www.crayola.com
Global Children's Art Gallery
http://www.naturalchild.com
(Click on Global Children's Art Gallery and view over 1,000 works of children's art from over 69 countries)
● The Kennedy Center Alliance for Art Education Network
(Includes 46 state alliance organizations operating in partnership with the Kennedy Center)
http://www.kennedy-center.org
(Click on Education, then type in National Networks in the Search box, and then click on Kennedy Center Alliance for Arts Education Network [state organizations])

Chapter 9

● Centers for Disease Control and Prevention—Childhood Obesity
(Offers information for parents and teachers on obesity and multiple children's health issues)
http://www.cdc.gov

- Cooking with Kids
  (Hands-on nutrition and food education curriculum guide)
  http//:www.cookingwithkids.net
- Farm to School
  (Offers contacts and programs listed state by state)
  http://www.farmtoschool.org
- Kids Food Cyber Club
  (Provides food and nutrition ideas for children)
  http://www.kidsfood.org
- National Association for the Education of Young Children
  http://www.naeyc.org
- Nutrition Explorations
  (This website is an excellent resource for children, educators, parents, and school food service personnel)
  http://www.nutritionexplorations.com
- USDA
  (Offers a copy of the *Food Guide Pyramid for Young Children* booklet and PDF posters online plus multimedia-interactive tools and print materials. This pyramid provides educational messages that focus on children's food preferences and nutrition requirements.)
  http://www.mypyramid.gov

- National Dance Association
  http://www.aah.perd.org/nda
- PE Central
  (Website for health and physical education teachers, parents, and students—their goal is to provide the latest information about developmentally appropriate physical education programs for children and youth)
  http://www.pecentral.org
  (Click on Preschool Physical Education)
- West Music
  http://www.westmusic.com
- Wolf Trap Institute for Early Learning Through the Arts
  (Offers workshops for teachers, parents, and administrators to introduce performing arts activities that will help early childhood educators teach a variety of physical, cognitive, social, and emotional skills to preschool children; these staff development workshops stress the importance of children creating their own stories, songs, and dances, and include material that is appropriate for children with special needs)
  http://www.wolf-trap.org
- ZERO TO THREE
  (Explains the powerful influence of music on a young child's development)
  http://www.zerotothree.org

Chapter 10

- Children's Music Network
  (Connecting people who celebrate the positive power of music in children's lives by exchanging ideas, visions, and music)
  http://www.cmnonline.org
- Children's Music Web
  http://www.childrensmusic.org
- Early Childhood Music and Movement Association
  http://www.ecmma.org
- Jo Eklof's "Miss Jo's Picture Book Learning Songs" (read-along and sing-along large print picture books, big books, and musical CDs)
  Jo Eklof is available to do appearances for child care centers, schools, and libraries.
  Miss Jo Publications
  http://www.missjo.com
- M.U.S.I.C.
  http://learningfromlyrics.org
- Music Together
  (Program for children, infant to kindergarten, and their adult primary caregivers)
  http://www.musictogether.com
  (Click on the videos, for example: preschool classes)
- National Association of Music Education (MENC)
  http://www.menc.org

Chapters 11 & 12

- Center for Puppetry Arts
  http://www.puppet.org
  (Information about the Center for Puppetry Arts Museum, featuring puppets from all over the world and their special "Create a Puppet" workshops)
- Folkmanis Puppets
  (Offers many play and creative activities plus a wonderful collection of puppets to see or buy)
  http://www.folkmanis.com
- Kathy Burks Theatre of Puppetry Art
  (Artist in residence at Dallas Children's Theater)
  http://www.kathyburkspuppets.com
- International Play Association (USA)
  http://www.ipausa.org
- Mister Rogers' Neighborhood
  (Information on training and curriculum materials)
  http://pbs.org
  (In the Search box, type in "Mister Rogers")
- PBS Teachers
  (Classroom resources for all ages and professional development online)
  http://www.pbs.org/teachers

- The Puppet Museum
  ("Hello, Hello, Hello!!! I'm Ping Pong, the Panda, and I'm your tour guide here at the museum." This begins a visit that takes you through the Olde World Puppet Theatre, Ping Pong's Puppet Workshop, puppet website links around the world, and many other places.)
  http://www.puppetmuseum.com
- The Puppeteers of America, Inc.
  http://www.puppeteers.org

- The Puppetry Home Page
  (A free resource for the puppetry community and dedicated to helping people connect to the world of puppetry)
  http://www.sagecraft.com/puppetry
- Sesame Street Workshop
  http://www.ctw.org
- UNICEF
  (Learn about puppets around the world)
  http://www.unicef.org/puppets

Appendix C

Professional Organizations

Alliance for Childhood
PO Box 444
College Park, MD 20741
http://www.allianceforchildhood.org
(Publishes multiple reports and policy briefs)

American Academy of Pediatrics
141 Northwest Point Blvd.
Elk Grove Village, IL 60007
(Publishes information for parents and teachers on children's health issues)

American Library Association (ALA)
50 E. Huron Street
Chicago, IL 60611
http://www.ala.org
(Publishes *American Libraries Booklist*)

American Speech-Language-Hearing Association
2200 Research Blvd.
Rockville, MD 20850
http://www.asha.org
(Offers online ASHA Leader Newspaper)

Association for Childhood Education International (ACEI)
17904 Georgia Avenue, Suite 215
Olney, MD 20832
http://www.acei.org
(Publishes *Childhood Education* and *Journal of Research in Childhood Education*)

Association for Supervision and Curriculum Development (ASCD)
1703 N. Beauregard Street
Alexandria, VA 22311
http://www.ascd.org
(Publishes *Educational Leadership* and *Journal of Curriculum and Supervision*)

Canadian Association for Young Children (CAYC)
http://www.cayc.ca
(Publishes *Canadian Children*)

Children's Defense Fund
25 E Street NW
Washington, DC 20001
http://www.childrensdefense.org
(Publishes Early Childhood and Child Care Research Data and Publications)

Council for Early Childhood Professional Recognition (CDA)
2460 16th Street NW
Washington, DC 20009
http://www.cdacouncil.org
(Publishes *Council Newsletter* and CDA Assessment and materials, training materials, and general early childhood resources)

Council for Environmental Education (CEE)
5555 Morningside, Suite 212
Houston, TX 77005
http://www.councilforee.org
(Publishes materials and provides programs, services, and training for conservation and environmental issues)

Council for Exceptional Children (CEC)
1110 North Globe Road, Suite 300
Arlington, VA 22201
http://www.cec.sped.org
(Publishes *Exceptional Children's Journal* and *Teaching Children*)

Early Childhood Music and Movement Association (ECMMA)
805 Mill Avenue
Snohomish, WA 98290
http://www.ecmma.org
(Publishes the journal *Perspectives*)

Families and Work Institute
267 Fifth Avenue, 2nd floor
New York, NY 10016
http://www.familiesandwork.org
(Publishes research and other materials)

International Reading Association Inc.
800 Barksdale Road
Box 8139
Newark, DE 19714
http://www.reading.org
(Publishes *Reading Today, The Reading Teacher*, and *Reading Research Quarterly* online)

Learning Disabilities Association of America
4156 Library Road
Pittsburgh, PA 15234
http://www.ldanatl.org
(Publishes *Learning Disabilities Journal*)

National Art Education Association (NAEA)
1916 Association Drive
Reston, VA 20191
http://www.naea-reston.org
(Publishes *NAEA Newsletter* and *Art Education*, a quarterly journal)

National Association for Bilingual Education (NABE)
1313 L Street NW, Suite 210
Washington, DC 20005
http://www.nabe.org
(Publishes *NABE News Magazine* and *Bilingual Research Journal*)

National Association of Early Childhood Teacher Educators
http://www.naecte.org
(Publishes *Journal of Early Childhood Teacher Education*)

National Association for the Education of Young Children (NAEYC)
1313 L Street NW, Suite 500
Washington, DC 20005
http://www.naeyc.org
(Publishes *Young Children* and *Teaching Young Children*)

National Association for Family Child Care (NAFCC)
1743 W. Alexander Street
Salt Lake City, UT 84119
http://www.nafcc.org
(Publishes NAFCC accreditation materials)

National Association for Gifted Children (NAGC)
1707 L Street, Suite 550
Washington, DC 20036
http://www.nagc.org
(Publishes *Gifted Children Quarterly*)

National Association of Music Education
1806 Robert Fulton Drive
Reston, VA 20191
http://www.menc.org
(Publishes *Music Educators Journal, Teaching Music*, and *General Music Today* online)

National Black Child Development Institute (NBCDI)
1313 L Street NW, Suite 110
Washington, DC 20005
http://www.nbcdi.org
(Publishes *Child Health Talk*)

National Council for the Social Studies
8555 16th Street, Suite 500
Silver Spring, MD 20910
http://www.ncss.org
(Publishes *Social Education* and *Social Studies Professional Newsletter*)

National Council of Teachers of Mathematics (NCTM)
1906 Association Drive
Reston, VA 20191
http://www.nctm.org
(Publishes *Teaching Children Mathematics*)

National Head Start Association
1651 Prince Street
Alexandria, VA 22314
http://www.nhsa.org

National Information Center for Children and Youth with Disabilities (NICHCY)
1825 Connecticut Ave. NW, Suite 700
Washington, DC 20009
http://www.nichcy.org

National Institute for Literacy
1775 1 Street NW, Suite 730
Washington, DC 20006
http://www.nifl.gov
(Publishes resources on literacy)

National Science Teachers Association (NSTA)
1840 Wilson Blvd.
Arlington, VA 22201
http://www.nsta.org
(Publishes *Science and Children* and E-newsletters)

Save the Children
54 Wilton Road
Westport, CT 06880
http://www.savethechildren.org

Southern Early Childhood Association (SECA)
1123 S. University Ave., Suite 255
Little Rock, AR 72204
http://www.SouthernEarlyChildhood.org
(Publishes *Dimensions of Early Childhood*)

Stand for Children
516 SE Morrison Street, Suite 410
Portland, OR 97214
http://www.stand.org
(Publishes an e-newsletter, *Stand Update*)

Zero to Three—National Center for Infants, Toddlers, and Families
2000 M Street NW, Suite 200
Washington, DC 20036
http://www.zerotothree.org
(Publishes *The Zero to Three Journal*)

Glossary

A

accommodation—Piaget's theory of modification of existing cognitive information. Cognitive schemes are changed to accommodate new experiences or information.

advocacy—An attitude that encourages professionals, parents, and other caring adults to work together on behalf of young children.

aesthetic environment—An environment that cultivates an appreciation for beauty and a feeling of wonder and excitement of the world in which we live.

alphabet books—Simple stories based on the alphabet that present letter identification and one-object picture association.

anecdotal record—A brief, informal narrative account describing an incident of a child's behavior that is important to the observer.

anthropology—The study of the way people live, such as their beliefs and customs.

anti-bias—An attitude that actively challenges prejudice, stereotyping, and unfair treatment of an individual or group of individuals.

art—Visual communication through the elements of color, line, shape, and texture instead of words.

assessment—Refers to the collection of information for the purpose of making educational decisions about children or a group of children or to evaluate a program's effectiveness.

assimilation—Piaget's process of cognitive development, which occurs when a child handles, sees, or otherwise experiences something.

associative play—An activity of a three- or four-year-old child playing with other children in a group; the child drops in and out of play with minimal organization of activity.

astronomy—The study of the universe beyond the earth's atmosphere, such as sun, moon, planets, and stars.

B

beat—An accent of sound or a continuing series of accents.

beginning-to-read books—Predictable books that are easy to read and present words that are simple and repetitive.

bias—Any attitude, belief, or feeling that results in unfair treatment of an individual or group of individuals.

bicultural—A term used to describe an individual from two distinct cultures.

big books—Oversized books that present extra-large text and illustrations.

board books—First books for infants and toddlers made of laminated heavy cardboard.

C

case study—A way of collecting and organizing all of the information gathered from various sources to provide insights into the behavior of the child studied.

checklist—A record of direct observation that involves selecting from a previously prepared list the statement that best describes the behavior observed, the conditions present, or the equipment, supplies, and materials available.

chemistry—The science dealing with the composition and transformations of substances.

classifying and sorting—Grouping objects by a common characteristic, such as size, shape, or color.

cognitive development—The mental process that focuses on how children's intelligence, thinking abilities, and language acquisition emerge through distinct ages; Piaget's study of children's thinking, involving creating their own mental images of the world, based on encounters with the environment.

collage—An art activity that involves making a picture containing glued-on objects on paper.

concept books—Books that present themes, ideas, or concepts with specific examples. They also identify and clarify abstractions, such as color or shape, and help with vocabulary development.

concept development—The construction of knowledge through solving problems and experiencing the results, while being actively involved with the environment.

constructive play—Play that helps children understand their experiences. Involves planning or manipulation of objects or people to create a specific experience.

cooperative play—A type of play organized for some purpose by the four-year-old and older child. It requires group membership and reflects a child's growing capacity to accept and respond to ideas and actions not originally his own.

counting books—Books that describe simple numeral and picture associations, and often tell a story. They show representations of numbers in more than one format and vary from simple to complex.

crayon resist—A type of art for older children that involves drawing a picture in light-colored crayons then covering the picture with watercolors or thin tempera paint. The paint will cover all but the crayon drawing.

crayon rubbings—Duplicating an object of texture by placing it under paper and rubbing over it with a crayon.

creativity—The process of doing, of bringing something new and imaginative into being.

culture—The sum total of a child's or family's ways of living: their values or beliefs, language, patterns of thinking, appearance, and behavior. These are passed or learned from one generation to the next.

curator—The person who decides what art to display and how to display it.

curriculum—A multileveled process that encompasses what happens in an early education classroom each day, reflecting the philosophy, goals, and objectives of the early childhood program.

curriculum web—A visual illustration or process that integrates various learning activities and curriculum areas.

D

development—Systematic and adaptive changes in the body and mind.

developmentally appropriate practice—The curriculum planning philosophy expressed by NAEYC defines and describes what is developmentally appropriate for young children in childhood programs serving children and families, birth through age eight.

developmental theories—Principles that examine children's growth, behavior, and process of learning.

dramatic play—A type of creative, spontaneous play in which children use their imaginations to create and dramatize pretend characters, actions, or events.

E

early mathematics— Refers to exposure to and interaction with materials that contribute to the acquisition of knowledge about the underlying concepts of mathematics.

earth and space science—The study of earth materials, objects in the sky, and changes in the earth and sky.

ecology—The study of living things in relation to their environment and to each other.

economics—The study of the production, distribution, and consumption of goods and services.

egocentric—A stage when individuals think about the world only in relation to themselves.

emergent curriculum—A curriculum that emerges out of the interests and experiences of the children.

emergent literacy—A process of developing awareness about reading and writing before young children can read or write.

environment—In an early childhood setting, the conditions and surroundings affecting children and adults.

equilibrium—A balance of one's cognitive schemes and information gathered from the environment; assimilation and accommodation.

evaluation—The process of determining whether the philosophy, goals, and objectives of the early childhood program have been met.

F

flannelboard—Used as a prop to tell or extend a story effectively.

folk literature—Tales that come from the oral tradition of storytelling that appeal to the child's sense of fantasy.

format—The overall arrangement of the way a book is put together, such as size, shape, paper quality, colors, and content of each page.

functional play—Play that occurs when a child takes on a role and pretends to be someone else.

G

games with rules—Children's spontaneous physical and cognitive play that occurs during Piaget's concrete operations stage of development (seven years and older).

genre—Category used to classify literary works, usually by form, technique, or content.

geography—The study of the earth's surface, resources, and the concepts of direction, location, and distance.

geology—The study of the earth, such as rocks and shells.

geometry—The area of mathematics that involves shape, size, space, position, direction, and movement.

goals—The general overall aims or overview of an early childhood program that consider what children should know and be able to do developmentally across the disciplines.

H

hand puppets—Puppets that are put on the hand; come in many types and varieties and are easy for young children to make and manipulate.

history—The study of what has happened in the life of a country or people.

hollow blocks—Wooden blocks larger than unit blocks and opened on the sides.

I

inclusion—Reflective of the blending of practices from early childhood education and early childhood special education.

inclusive curriculum—Underscores the importance of individual differences, special needs, and cultural and linguistic diversity among young children.

informational books—Books that offer nonfiction for emergent readers by providing accurate facts about people and subject matter.

inquiry—A questioning process that encourages curiosity and exploration. The opposite of rote learning.

integrated curriculum—Encourages young children to transfer knowledge and skills from one subject to another while using all aspects of their development.

interaction books—Books used to stimulate imagination by using some device for involving young readers, such as pop-ups, fold-outs, scratch and sniff, pasting, puzzle pictures, humor, and riddles.

K

kinesthetics—The use of the body to learn about physical capabilities and to develop body awareness.

L

language—Human speech, the written symbols for speech, or any means of communicating.

language development—Developmental process of a predictable sequence that includes both sending and receiving information. It is related, but not tied, to chronological age.

learning—Change in behavior or cognition that occurs as children construct knowledge through active exploration and discovery in their physical social environments.

learning centers—Curriculum centers (sometimes called interest centers, zones, clusters, or activity centers) where materials and supplies are combined around special groupings and common activities.

lesson plan—An outgrowth of theme selection, brainstorming/webbing, and selection of projects and activities. Involves making a series of choices based on the developmental stages, learning styles, and interests of the children; the goals and objectives of the program; and the availability of materials, supplies, and resources.

life science—The study of living things, people, plants, and animals.

literacy—The ability to read and write, which gives one the command of a native language for the purpose of communicating.

literacy development—A lifelong process that begins at birth and includes listening, speaking, reading, and writing.

literature—All the writings (prose and verse) of a people, country, or period, including those written especially for children.

locomotor movement—The ability to move the whole body from one place to another.

logico-mathematical knowledge—Includes relationships constructed in order to make sense out of the world and to organize information, such as counting and classification.

M

manipulative movement—Large (gross) motor movements demonstrated by pulling, lifting, throwing, or kicking an object.

manipulatives—Toys and materials that enable young children to gain the fine motor control they need to accomplish tasks important to their growth and development.

marionettes—Puppets controlled by strings that offer an extra range of expression and full body movement.

measurement—Finding the length, height, and weight of an object using units like inches, feet, and pounds.

melody—A sequence of tones of varying pitches organized in a rhythmically meaningful way.

meteorology—The science of weather and atmosphere.

Mother Goose and nursery rhyme books—Books passed from generation to generation and known by children all over the world. These are often a child's first introduction to literature.

multicultural books—Books that develop awareness of and sensitivity to other cultures. They also help to increase positive attitudes toward similarities and differences in people.

multiple intelligences—Gardner's theory, which proposes that one form of intelligence is not better than another; all eight are equally valuable and viable.

N

nonlocomotor movement—Occurs when the feet remain stationary (as in standing, kneeling, or sitting), while other parts of the body move.

number sense—A concept that develops over time as children think about, explore, and discuss mathematical ideas.

nutrients—Substances found in foods that provide for the growth, development, maintenance, and repair of the body.

nutrition—The study of food and how it is used in the body.

O

obesity—An excess percentage of bodyweight due to fat, which puts people at risk for health problems.

objectives—The specific purposes or teaching techniques that interpret the goals of planning, schedules, and routines, as well as meaningful descriptions of what children are expected to learn. These objectives are designed to meet the physical, intellectual, social, emotional, and creative development of young children.

object permanence—A mature state of perceptual development. According to Piaget's theory, a baby thinks that objects, including people, cease to exist the moment he stops seeing them. An older child starts to search for the missing object or person.

observation—The process of observation is taking in information and objectively interpreting it for meaning.

one-to-one correspondence—The pairing of one object to another object or one group of objects to another group of equal number.

onlooker play—The play of young children introduced to new situations that focuses on an activity rather than the environment.

P

parallel play—Observable play in the older toddler and young three-year-old that emphasizes being near another child while playing with an object rather than playing with a child.

pattern—A sequence of colors, objects, sounds, stories, or movements that repeats in the same order over and over again.

perceptual development—Type of development in which children use their senses to learn about the nature of objects, actions, and events.

philosophy—In an early childhood program, expresses the basic principles, attitudes, and beliefs of the center, school, or individual teacher.

phonemes—The smallest units of speech.

phonics—The relationship between the letters of the written language and the sounds of spoken language.

phonological or phonemic awareness—The ability to hear and identify individual sounds and spoken words.

physical development—Type of development involving children using large muscles, manipulating small muscles, developing eye-hand coordination, and acquiring self-help skills.

physical knowledge—Learning about objects in the environment and their characteristics, such as color, weight, and size.

physical sciences—The sciences (physics, chemistry, meteorology, and astronomy) that relate to nonliving materials.

picture books—Books written in a direct style that tell a simple story with illustrations complementing the text.

pitch—The highness or lowness of a tone on a musical scale.

play—A behavior that is self-motivated, freely chosen, process-oriented, and enjoyable.

poetry—A form of literature that contributes imaginative rhyme, rhythm, and sound.

portfolio—A collection of a child's work over time and a record of the child's process of learning.

portfolio assessment—An evaluation method based on a systematic collection of information about a child and the child's work, gathered by both the child and teacher over time from all available sources.

practice play or sensorimotor play—The stage in cognitive development during which the young child learns through repetitive sensory and motor play activities.

predictable books—Books that contain familiar and repetitive sequences.

prejudice—An attitude, opinion, or idea that is preconceived or decided, usually unfavorably.

process skills—The abilities to process new information through concrete experiences.

project—An in-depth investigation of a topic.

prop box—A collection of actual items related to dramatic play activities that focuses on a specific theme or lesson plan.

psychology—The study of the mind, emotions, and behavioral processes.

psychosocial—Erikson's eight stages that describe the interaction between an individual's social-emotional condition and the interpersonal environment.

puppetry—The art of making or operating puppets or producing puppet shows.

R

rational counting—Requires matching each numeral name, in order, to an object in a group.

realistic literature—A form of literature that helps children cope with common, actual experiences by offering positive solutions and insights.

rebus chart—Visual pictures, such as signs, illustrations, and directions, to help children make sense of any activity.

reference books—Books that emphasize individualized learning through special topic books, picture dictionaries, and encyclopedias.

reflective log or diary—A teacher or administrator's record of the most significant happenings, usually made at the end of the day or during an uninterrupted block of time.

rhyming—The ability to auditorily distinguish two words that end the same way.

rhythm—A sense of movement and patterns in music created by beats, the duration and volume of sounds, and the silences between sounds.

rote counting—The ability to recite names of numerals in order.

routines—The events that fit into the daily time frame of an early childhood program.

S

scaffolding—The adjustable support the teacher offers in response to the child's level of performance.

schedule—The basic daily timeline of an early childhood program.

schema—An integrated way of thinking or of forming mental images.

science as inquiry—Offers frequent opportunities to question, investigate, clarify, predict, and communicate with others.

science in personal and social perspectives—A developing understanding of personal health, changes in environments, and ways to conserve and recycle.

science and technology—The focus on establishing connections between natural and man-made items.

self-help skills—In early childhood, a child's ability to care for himself, such as dressing, feeding, and toileting.

self-regulation—A child's natural ability to exercise control over physical and emotional behavior in the face of changing circumstances.

sensory awareness—The use of the senses.

sensory experiences—Experiences that use the senses and offer opportunities for free exploration in a variety of curriculum areas.

seriation—Seriation or ordering of objects is based on the ability to place them in logical sequence, such as smallest to largest or shortest to tallest.

series books—Books written for primary-grade children and built around a single character or group of characters.

shadow puppets—Puppets held from rods against a translucent screen lit from behind. These puppets offer a visual dimension that other types do not.

social and emotional development—Type of development consisting of children developing positive images of themselves, expressing personality and individualism, representing imagination and fantasy, establishing enjoyable relationships with others, and expressing feelings.

social sciences—The core of social studies: anthropology, sociology, history, geography, economics, and psychology.

sociocultural theory—Vygotsky's theory that emphasizes that a child's learning development is affected by culture and family environment.

sociodramatic play—The highest level of symbolic play in which young children create their own happenings based on their experiences.

sociology—The study of group living, cooperation, and responsibilities.

software—A set of instructions used to direct a computer to perform some activity.

solitary play—Independent play behavior of a child without regard to what other children or adults are doing.

spatial sense—Comparisons that help children develop an awareness of themselves in relation to people and objects in space, such as exploration using blocks and boxes.

stereotype—An oversimplified generalization about a particular group, race, or sex, often with negative implications.

stick or rod puppets—Puppets controlled by a single stick, such as a tongue depressor, dowel rod, paper towel roll, craft stick, or ice cream stick.

string painting—A type of painting that involves moving string dipped in paint around on paper to make a design.

symbolic or dramatic play—A type of play that allows the child to transfer objects into symbols (things that represent something else) and images into people, places, and events within his experiences. Symbolic play occurs during Piaget's preoperational stage (two to seven years). Superhero fantasy play is considered a type of symbolic play for a young child.

symbolic thinking—The formation of symbols or mental representations, allowing children to solve problems by thinking before acting.

T

teacher- and child-made books—Books made by the teacher and child that encourage self-esteem, creativity, and the sharing of ideas. They also encourage children to articulate experiences.

tempo—A sense of slowness or rapidity in music.

theme—A broad concept or topic that enables the development of a lesson plan and the activities that fit within this curriculum plan.

theory—A systematic statement of principles and beliefs that is created to explain a group of facts that have been repeatedly tested or widely accepted.

three-dimensional art—Any art form that has three sides. Play dough and clay are examples of three-dimensional materials.

timbre—The unique tone quality of a voice or musical instrument.

tone—An individual musical sound.

transitions—Activities or learning experiences that move children from one activity to another.

U

unit—A section of the curriculum based on the unifying theme around which activities are planned.

unit blocks—Hardwood blocks used in early education environments, especially in block center play.

unoccupied behavior—Refers to a child (infant or toddler) who occupies himself by watching anything of momentary interest.

V

vocabulary—This refers to the words we must know to communicate.

volume—The softness or loudness of sound.

virtual manipulatives—Refers to interactive, web-based computer-generated images of objects that children can manipulate on the computer screen.

W

woodworking center—An activity center providing many different sensory and three-dimensional experiences.

wordless picture books—Books that tell a story with visually appealing illustrations. These books promote creativity by encouraging a child to talk about experiences and use his or her imagination.

word wall—An alphabetically arranged display or chart of words that children have experienced throughout the school year.

Z

zone of proximal development—The range of potential each child has for learning, with that learning being shaped by the social environment in which it takes place.

Index

A

Accident prevention, 50–51
Accommodation, 7, 8, 371
Active learning, 40
Activity plans, 67, 136
Activity plan worksheets
    example of, 68
    for literature activities, 137–143
    for math activities, 167–168
    for puppetry, 325
Adopt-a-tree or plant-a-tree activity, 183
Advocacy, 4, 371
Aesthetic environment, 233–234, 371
African Americans, 41
Alphabet books, 114, 371
American Academy of Pediatrics (AAP), 264
American Library Association, 120
Anecdotal records, 70, 165, 192, 371
Animals, in classroom, 187–189
Anthropology, 201, 371
Anti-bias, 19, 42, 371
Anti-bias curriculum, 44–45
Anti-Bias Curriculum (Derman-Sparks & A.B.C. Task
    Force), 43
Anti-bias environment, 51
Applesauce recipe, 101, 105
Art
    child development and, 223, 224
    explanation of, 223, 371
    family support for, 241–242
    for infants and toddlers, 224–225
    math concepts in, 161
    methods to display, 242
    observation and assessment strategies for, 244–245
    for preschoolers and kindergartners, 225–227
    for primary-grade students, 226–228
    as stimulus for other curriculum areas, 239–241
    three-dimensional, 238–239, 375
    use of grocery sacks and newspapers to make, 183
Art activities
    for children with special needs, 241–242
    developmentally appropriate multicultural
        and anti-bias, 243–244
    drawing as, 237–238
    involving children in, 234
    outdoor, 233
    painting as, 235–237
    sensory, 354–355
    tearing, cutting and gluing in, 234–235

    technology and, 243
    three-dimensional, 238–239
    use of food in, 232
Art curriculum
    creativity and experimentation in, 229–230
    environment for, 229–231, 233–234
    strategies for, 231–232
    teacher as facilitator and observer in, 228–229
Art kiosks, 242
Assessment
    art, 244–245
    explanation of, 72, 371
    of field trips, 213–214
    of math concepts and skills, 164–165
    play-based, 72
    portfolio, 70–72
    of science concepts and skills, 191–192
    to support literacy learning, 94–96
Assimilation, 7, 8, 371
Association, between sounds, 83
Association for Childhood Education International
        (ACEI), 23
Associations, professional, 367–369
Associative play, 20, 371
Astronomy, 177, 371
Auditory patterning, 154
Authors, children as, 127–129
Autonomy vs. shame and doubt stage
        (Erikson), 4, 7

B

Babbling, 83
Bank Street method, 39–40, 58, 85
Basic trust vs. mistrust stage (Erikson), 4
Batista, Barbara, 131, 254
Beanbag activity, 293
Beat, 285, 290, 371
Beginning-to-read books, 114, 371
Behavior modeling, 50
Bergen, Edgar, 318
Bias, 19, 371
Bicultural children, 43, 371
Big books, 114, 371
"Birds On the Rooftop" (Wolf), 170
Block play
    developmental stages of, 257–258
    guidance techniques for, 259
    purposes and objectives of, 259
    teachers role in, 260–261

An Educator's Guide to
Field-based Classroom Observation

Gary D. Borich
The University of Texas at Austin

James M. Cooper, Series Editor
University of Virginia

CONTENTS

PREFACE

Cengage Learning publishes outstanding education textbooks in the areas of foundations of education, introduction to education, educational psychology special education, and early childhood education. These textbooks introduce students to many concepts, policies, and research that undergird educational practice. However, as is the case for virtually all introductory texts, many topics are introduced but not covered in great depth. The Cengage Learning Teacher Education Guide Series is designed to provide more in-depth coverage of selected educational topics studied in the teacher education curriculum.

At the present time there are eleven guides in the series:

- Diversity in the Classroom
- Classroom Assessment
- Inclusion
- Technology Tools
- School-based Interventions
- Classroom Management
- Field-based Classroom Observation
- Differentiating Instruction
- Student Motivation
- Teacher Reflection
- Co-teaching

The topics for these guides were selected because they are addressed in virtually all teacher education programs, and contain vital information for beginning teachers if they are to be successful in the classroom. Instructors may use the guides either for required or enrichment reading.

Each of these guides provides pre-service teachers with greater in-depth knowledge, application suggestions, and additional resources on its particular topic. All the guides share a common format that includes an introduction to the topic, knowledge that the prospective teacher should possess about the topic, examples of and suggestions for how the knowledge can be applied, and resources for further exploration. Each guide also contains 10-15 questions designed to help the prospective teacher reflect on the concepts and ideas introduced in the guide, as well as a glossary of key terms.

Most teacher education programs now provide many opportunities for prospective teachers to observe in school classrooms and to partake in instructional activities. Integrating pedagogical training with experiences in schools allows teacher education students to merge theory with practice. In this guide, Gary Borich identifies key concepts and tools for helping teacher education students to focus their classroom observations so as to understand better the busy and complex interactions occurring in school classrooms. One researcher found that as many as 1000 interactions occur daily in elementary classrooms! Seeing and understanding what is happening in classrooms is not easy and requires considerable training and practice. Borich provides a number of different research-based lenses for viewing classroom behavior, and practice exercises to develop interpretative skill to make sense of the data collected. As prospective teachers take these tools into classrooms to collect and interpret information on classroom behavior, they will gain deeper understanding of the teaching and learning that occurs there.

PART I: INTRODUCTION*

Playing in the park, 3-year-old Jake looks up to see his mother approaching. He runs down the sidewalk to greet her. In his haste, he trips on an uneven stone and lands, unceremoniously, at his mother's feet.

For a moment, Jake looks stunned—about to cry. His mother wonders if he is hurt as he glances up at her face with a questioning look.

Laughing, Jake's mother scoops him into her arms. "Hi, honey!" she chuckles. "What fun to have you so excited to see me!"

The imminent clouds on Jake's face clear, and the toddler smiles.

How often have you observed a similar event—noting that split second when a child seems to decide how to respond to a given situation? Like Jake, each of us experiences many interactions with the world every day. As we try to make sense of these events, we create a personal framework or set of expectations about the nature of the world and our appropriate responses to events within it. This set of expectations influences what we see in a particular setting, as well as what we choose to ignore.

Many psychologists believe that professionals create frames for understanding within their chosen fields, just as individuals construct a frame for interpreting the events of daily life. Experts know what to look for and rapidly learn from what they see, and thereby rise to the top of their profession long before others who do not have a structure for sorting out the least relevant from the most relevant details. Sternberg (1995) believes that intelligent behavior may be marked more by the structure or frame one brings to a problem or task than by what one knows about the problem or task beforehand. Thus, developing a **professional frame** from which to evaluate and act objectively on events is a critical skill for becoming an expert.

From observing the actions and interactions of professionals, less experienced individuals gain a sense of what is valued in a particular discipline and how professionals working in that field typically respond to

---

* For further content on the field-based observation techniques in this booklet, see Borich, G. (2003). *Observation Skills for Effective Teaching,* (4th ed.). Upper Saddle River, NJ: Merrill/Prentice-Hall. The author thanks Debra Bayles Martin for contributions that appear in this booklet.

events. But, while observation seems as simple and commonplace as dressing, eating, or driving a car, it is important to remember that, like Jake, each of us interprets the world and responds to it according to our personal frame. Without some outside direction, it is possible that our classroom observations may serve to validate much of what we already "expect" to see—allowing us to overemphasize some things and overlook others. As a result, observations need to be focused if they are to be helpful in our professional life.

The field-based observation techniques for the training of teachers come from more than twenty-five years of research on effective teaching and from national standards for the teaching profession representing how students and teachers best learn. For decades, teaching reflected a direct instruction model, where teachers were expected to present or "transmit" knowledge to students—who were expected to receive, store, and return information upon request. Many researchers and educators have challenged this view, suggesting that learners do not simply "receive" knowledge; rather, they actively construct knowledge through interacting with the social, cultural, and linguistic context in which an experience occurs (Richardson, 1997). Effective teachers function as able facilitators, coaches, and guides for students' knowledge-building processes.

Reflecting this more interactive view of teaching, the **National Board for Professional Teaching Standards (NBPTS)** was formed in 1987 with three major goals:

1. To establish high and rigorous standards for what accomplished teachers should know and be able to do;

2. To develop and operate a national, voluntary system to assess and certify teachers who meet these standards;

3. To advance related education reforms for the purpose of improving student learning in American schools.

During that same year, the **Interstate New Teacher Assessment and Support Consortium (INTASC)** was formed to create "board-compatible" standards that could be reviewed by professional organizations and state agencies as a basis for licensing beginning teachers. The INTASC standards (Miller, 1992) are written as 10 principles, which are then further explained in terms of teacher knowledge, dispositions, and performance. In other words, they describe what a beginning teacher should know and be able to do. Listed below are these 10 principles, which were intended in part to be acquired through field-based observation.

Principle 1:

The teacher understands the central concepts, tools of inquiry, and structures of the discipline(s) he or she teaches and can create learning experiences that make these aspects of subject matter meaningful for students.

Principle 2:

The teacher understands how children learn and develop, and can provide learning opportunities that support their intellectual, social and personal development.

Principle 3:

The teacher understands how students differ in their approaches to learning and creates instructional opportunities that are adapted to diverse learners.

Principle 4:

The teacher understands and uses a variety of instructional strategies to encourage students' development of critical thinking, problem solving, and performance skills.

Principle 5:

The teacher uses an understanding of individual and group motivation and behavior to create a learning environment that encourages positive social interaction, active engagement in learning, and self-motivation.

Principle 6:

The teacher uses knowledge of effective verbal, nonverbal, and media communication techniques to foster active inquiry, collaboration, and supportive interaction in the classroom.

Principle 7:

The teacher plans instruction based upon knowledge of subject matter, students, the community, and curriculum goals.

Principle 8:

The teacher understands and uses formal and informal assessment strategies to evaluate and ensure the continuous intellectual, social and physical development of the learner.

Principle 9:

The teacher is a reflective practitioner who continually evaluates the effects of his/her choices and actions on others (students, parents, and other professionals in the learning community) and who actively seeks out opportunities to grow professionally.

Principle 10:

The teacher fosters relationships with school colleagues, parents, and agencies in the larger community to support students' learning and well-being.

Much of classroom observation focuses on ways you can observe other teachers to learn about the teaching profession. The information you gain from these observations will help you expand your professional framework to include insights about teaching which follow the INTASC and NBPTS standards. But, classroom observation also addresses ways to apply observation techniques and insights to your own teaching. Thus, while you are observing others to learn about their approaches to teaching, you will also be learning to observe yourself—and to be observed by others. These observations can provide important insights about your growth and development as a teacher.

PART II: KNOWLEDGE

GOALS FOR FOCUSED OBSERVATIONS

The ability to consciously consider your personal growth is called *reflection*. There are many goals you will want to work toward in order to reflect on your own behavior. But some of the most important for focused observations are to achieve empathy, establish cooperative relationships, become realistic, establish direction, attain confidence, express enthusiasm, become flexible, and become self-reliant. As you observe professionals working to achieve each of these goals, you will want to reflect on your own development—and then set some goals for yourself. Because a cycle of observation, reflection, and goal setting is so important to becoming a productive and successful professional, let's consider these eight goals for focused observation in more detail.

Goal 1: To Achieve Empathy

Effective teachers exhibit *empathy*—a willingness to see events from different points of view and to appreciate others' interpretations or reasons for acting the way they do. An empathic approach can help you to understand student behavior from the student's point of view—which often provides insights for effective ways of dealing with problems or challenges. Your ability to empathize during classroom observations will serve you well both as an observer and as a teacher. For example, when you observe a teacher implementing an unusual classroom rule, you may be tempted to pass judgment on the teacher's effectiveness or on the rule's appropriateness—from your point of view. While your own experiences are an important source of information in evaluating what you observe, you will also benefit from trying to understand events from the teacher's vantage point. You may ask yourself, "Is what I am seeing working within the context of this classroom? Why or why not?" As you consider these questions, you may discover that a seemingly ineffective strategy in one context may be effective in another. As a result, your observations will extend beyond your personal and textbook knowledge of teaching to include an awareness of the variety of social and learning contexts that can influence a teacher's decisions. Enhancing your ability to empathize will help you approach your own teaching with more flexibility—and with the instructional alternatives you need to be an effective teacher.

Goal 2: To Establish Cooperative Relationships

Early on, effective teachers identify people who can help them in their teaching. They understand that, in the hectic and stressful environment of the classroom, people need other people to offer ideas, support, and collegiality. As you become involved in student teaching, and later in your beginning years of teaching, you will find a need to develop cooperative relationships with your colleagues. Experienced teachers have a wealth of information about students, curriculum, textbooks, and media with which you will be working. As you observe in different classrooms, you can and should take the opportunity to discover how professionals create and maintain cooperative relationships and how you can become an active participant in these relationships. These experienced teachers can answer many questions you will have now—and later.

Goal 3: To Become Realistic

Most beginning teachers understandably have an idealistic view of schools and teaching. While idealism motivates us to renew and extend our efforts, it also creates pitfalls when we are unreasonable in our expectations of students or ourselves. For example, beginning teachers who believe that schools *should be* a certain way may spend a great deal of time and effort trying to change a particular setting—failing to see and accept the strengths of the context they are working with. From your classroom observations, you will learn that schools and classrooms vary widely—and that each context offers both advantages and challenges. As you observe and reflect upon different classrooms, you will become more realistic in evaluating both what is desirable and what is possible in different classrooms.

Goal 4: To Establish Direction

Another purpose of classroom observation is to establish the professional goals toward which you will want to work during your student teaching and first years of teaching. By observing others, you will identify characteristics and practices you will want to emulate in your own teaching. Recording these characteristics and practices during observation can form the basis of short- and long-term goals of self-improvement. One of the advantages of focused observation is the opportunity to identify particular patterns and sequences of teacher behavior and to evaluate their effectiveness in a variety of settings. Over time, you should be able to identify teaching strategies specific to particular purposes and contexts that you value and to integrate them into your own teaching.

Goal 5: To Attain Confidence

Most of us in the course of learning to become teachers make judgments about what we believe is effective teaching. In the course of teaching, we then make decisions that follow from these judgments. Many of these decisions about what and how to teach represent gut feelings, the exact source of which may not be known to us. Some writers refer to this way of knowing as *tacit or practical knowledge* (Canning, 1991). Tacit knowledge represents what we know by experience, but rarely, if ever, articulate. Just as in the example with Jake, each of us compiles vast amounts of tacit knowledge through everyday experiences. This knowledge often guides our actions as effectively as does the knowledge we gain from formal instruction. Our tacit knowledge is put to use by acting, sometimes unconsciously, on thoughts and feelings acquired from day-to-day experiences. Tacitly acquired knowledge often helps us distinguish what is right from wrong, appropriate from inappropriate, and effective from ineffective. Through observation, beginning teachers learn to test their judgments and to trust their instincts.

Goal 6: To Express Enthusiasm

Effective teachers demonstrate an enthusiasm for the subject matter they teach, and for the teaching profession. The ability to express enthusiasm stems from a belief that what we do matters. Having an image of a future self who is growing provides us with the courage to work hard and attain the goals we select. You can enhance your personal enthusiasm and learn to calm your fears by seeing others attain goals, perform activities, and produce results that you would like to accomplish. As you observe successful teachers, you will find yourself saying, "I want to be like that." From this, you will set goals such as, "I want to *try* that." As you try various techniques, you then discover that you *can* accomplish particular goals, and your enthusiasm for teaching grows. Focused observation of successful and enthusiastic teachers can help you dare to express the enthusiasm within you.

Goal 7: To Become Flexible

A part of setting and achieving any goal is being willing to take risks. Effective teachers most often achieve their goals in the context of trial and error. This means that to develop as a professional, you must try new things and risk occasional failure. We seldom succeed in attaining a goal, performing an activity, or achieving the desired results the first time we try something. The key to our improvement is to persevere long enough for success to occur. Since some struggle is inevitable in becoming an effective teacher, it is important to develop a flexible attitude. For example, you may practice a behavior exactly as you observed it in a particular classroom—and not achieve the desired results. This is the time to consider various aspects of the behavior that could be adapted or altered in some way. The fact that you have observed teachers in many different settings will likely suggest variations you can try to improve your strategy. In other words, as you observe teachers implementing a strategy in different ways, you, too, can gain the ability to see and act more flexibly in your own teaching.

Goal 8: To Become Self-reliant

Perhaps the most important goal of focused classroom observation is becoming self-reliant. As you observe across many educational contexts, you will be building a professional frame from which to interpret events and make decisions. The greater the detail and scope of your observations, the greater your sense of personal confidence, enthusiasm, and flexibility will be in achieving your goals. Focused observation in classrooms will reveal that teaching is a complex profession for which no amount of formal training can provide all the preparation needed. It will also underscore the fact that effective teachers exist because of the challenges of teaching and that, with careful reflection and effort you can be one of them.

PROFESSIONAL GOALS FOR IMPROVEMENT

As you prepare to observe in classrooms, it is important to consider what sort of "lens" you will observe through. All of us develop our own views of the world or ways of looking at life. Our view is influenced throughout our lives by the experiences we have, the emotions we feel, and the way we choose to interpret them. What are the characteristics of your world view? How might they affect the way you "see" particular teachers or classrooms? Let's try a little experiment to find out. Read the sentences below (from a study by Sanford & Garrod, 1981, p. 114) and create a mental picture from the words.

John was on his way to school.

What picture formed in your mind as you read the sentence? How old is John? What does he look like? What time of day is it? What is the weather like? Remember what you pictured and read on.

He was terribly worried about the math lesson.

Now what is the picture you see? Has it changed? Does being worried about a math lesson "fit" the picture you have already developed in your mind about what John is like? Keep reading.

He thought he might not be able to control the class again today.

Has anything in your mental picture changed? What? Why? Now keep reading.

It was not a normal part of a janitor's duties.

What do you see now in your mental picture? How old is John? What does he look like? Were you surprised at the information in the last sentence? Why?

Just as you formed mental images and expectations while reading about John, you have probably formed a number of mental images and expectations about schools and classrooms. To explore a few of these images, take a minute and make a list with the following headings:

The perfect classroom (how it looks, smells, feels, etc.)	The perfect teacher (his or her classroom management, instructional methods and presentation style, etc.)	The perfect lesson (subject, duration, type of activities, etc.)

Source: From Borich, G. (2003). *Observation Skills for Effective Teaching*, 4th edition. Upper Saddle River, NJ: Merrill/Prentice Hall. This and the following graphic reprinted with permission.

Now, take a minute to create a second list with these headings.

A terrible classroom (how it looks, smells, feels, etc.)	A terrible teacher (his or her classroom management, instructional methods and presentation style, etc.)	A terrible lesson (subject, duration, type of activities, etc.)

What do you notice about the two lists you have created? Can you think of any specific experiences that may have influenced each of your lists?

WHAT REAL CLASSROOMS ARE LIKE

As you make formal and informal observations on your way to becoming a teacher, it is important to realize that you are about to enter a complex and demanding profession—a profession that requires not only intelligence, physical stamina, and motivation, but also an acute sense of sight and sound. Your ability to perceive what is happening in a classroom will be critical to your success as a teacher. Because the teaching profession is complex, it is important for you to consider how your preconceived ideas about teaching and students may influence what you see and hear—and how you interpret that information. No doubt you have already formed, from your years as a student, a set of beliefs about good and poor teaching, teachers, students, and lessons. While these opinions and beliefs comprise an important part of your view of education, they can also act as "blinders," and even limit your teaching goals for particular students or settings (Walqui, 2000). In order to look beyond personal experience to obtain a more complete view of classrooms, let's consider four characteristics of classrooms that will affect what you see: *rapidity, immediacy, interruption,* and *social dynamics.*

Rapidity

One of the first things you will notice from observing in classrooms is that events move rapidly. In fact, some authors have estimated that there are up to one thousand teacher-student interchanges in most classrooms in a single day. These interchanges include asking questions, soliciting information, clarifying answers, probing for details, reciting facts, and responding to student requests. In other words, events do not move slowly in classrooms; they are constantly changing at a rapid rate from teacher question to student response, and from student question back to teacher response—creating a momentum of classroom activity that puts the teacher on the front lines practically every minute of the day. The teacher's ability to move the class along at a brisk pace, keep transitions between major instructional events short and orderly, and establish milestones toward which all students work contributes momentum and a sense of accomplishment to the classroom. Being able to see how rapidly changing events in a classroom can be used to establish momentum is an important observation skill.

Immediacy

Closely related to the rapidity of life in classrooms is the immediacy of the interactions that occur within them. Immediacy pertains to the need to respond quickly to rapidly occurring events. For example, teachers often do not have time to think about how they will respond to a student question, but rather must have an answer—some answer—ready for almost any question or situation that may occur. To delay or ponder for very long over what to say may create an awkward void in the flow of classroom events that can, and often does, result in a loss of momentum and problems in classroom management (Emmer, Evertson, & Worsham, 2003). But even more important, the momentum of the classroom must be maintained with responses and interactions that satisfy student needs and instructional goals. Few reactions or responses of the teacher can be put off until tomorrow, until the end of the period, or even for a minute. Most of the queries, questions, and solicitations made by students need immediate responses if they are to be effective in satisfying student needs. This makes practically every exchange a test of the teacher's responsiveness. It also tests the teacher's skill at keeping the flow going in ways that respond to, rather than put off, student needs for information, clarification, or further discussion.

Interruption

Think back to some of your experiences as a student. How often were classroom routines interrupted by an unexpected announcement from the office or someone at the door? A third characteristic of classroom life that you will notice is the number of times the natural flow of the classroom is interrupted. A source of frustration for most teachers, such events can so alter the momentum within a classroom that both student achievement and classroom discipline can be affected by them. Perhaps in no other profession are individuals interrupted so frequently in the course of delivering or providing a message than in teaching. Even unsolicited salespeople generally are allowed to complete their message—and who ever heard of a surgeon being interrupted during an operation by a messenger at the door! Messengers, public address bulletins, students straggling in late for class, changing course schedules, getting parent signatures, and making announcements are only some of the many interruptions that invade the instructional routine of daily classroom life. As even your earliest classroom observations will reveal, teachers do a lot more than teach, and sometimes are interrupted more than they teach. Being able to see the many types of interruptions that occur in classrooms and how effective and ineffective teachers manage these interruptions is another important skill for observation—and for teaching.

Social Dynamics

The fourth characteristic of a classroom is its social dynamics. Let's not forget: teaching is a group process. Even in one-on-one encounters, students are aware of other members of the group, and so rarely perceive themselves as individuals in the classroom. As a result, teachers confront many important instructional and management decisions related to group dynamics (Borich, 2004, chapters 9 & 10).

In order to capitalize on the positive aspects of group membership and encourage a sense of inclusion, many teachers implement discussion sessions, student teams, small groups, and the sharing of instructional materials to create opportunities for positive social interaction among their students. But learning in groups can also create opportunities for social distraction—which may dampen the learning process. Friends and enemies are often found in the same class, and excitement and expectations that often start outside class are easily carried into the classroom. There is, in other words, ample opportunity for groups in school to behave as groups do outside of school, with all the same characteristics: jealousies, competition, playfulness, laughter, and argument. Although common outside the classroom, these characteristics can create social distraction and off-task behavior within the classroom. Few professions require their members to work in such a confined space with so many individuals for so long a time during the day as does teaching. Add to this scene the fact that some individuals do not want to be there, and you have the perfect social setting for learners to become distracted by one another. The teacher's ability to plan and carry out activities that promote cooperative interaction and discourage social distraction can make the difference between an effective and an ineffective classroom. Observing the social dynamics of classrooms will help you discover what types of activities minimize social distraction and maximize cooperative interaction among students. It will also help you understand how and why teachers can sometimes be unaware of how their own behavior contributes to or detracts from establishing a cooperative and cohesive learning environment that includes rather than distances learners.

BECOMING AWARE OF CLASSROOM BEHAVIOR: LENSES FOR SELF-IMPROVEMENT

Given the rapidity, immediacy, interruption, and social dynamics of classrooms, it is easy to see why teachers are busy people. Few occupations could boast of having a thousand or more interactions with clients or customers in a single day, yet teachers customarily do this not just for one day, but for practically every day of the school year. Add to this the fact that the teacher's job is to facilitate the learning of subject matter content and to determine that what is taught is learned, and we have a particularly demanding job. The effect of this ambitious undertaking is that most of a teacher's attention is focused on the subject matter and the students rather than on him or herself. Within the busy schedule of a school day, teachers do not have many opportunities to reflect on the relative merits of the strategies and methods they use. To pause for contemplation during instruction could disrupt the rapidity of classroom events, and almost surely would result in a loss of momentum; to pause after class or at the end of the school day would require the ability to accurately recall events that may have occurred hours earlier. As a result, teachers frequently can be observed performing behaviors that are unintentional and that they are unaware of, such as dominating discussions and allowing too little response time for students to think through an answer, staying with or encouraging answers from high-ability students more than low-ability students, calling on members of one sex more than the other, giving preferential treatment to high-achieving students and more frequently criticizing the wrong answers from low-achieving students, and responding to students from various cultures and linguistic backgrounds differently than to those from the teacher's own background. These behaviors have been observed even among experienced teachers, suggesting that at least some teachers may be so involved in conveying their subject matter content that they are unconscious of many of their own patterns of interaction.

A second reason teachers may be unaware of their teaching behavior is that they are not always given specific signs that define "good" teaching.

Broad indexes of effectiveness, such as the number of students completing homework, high grades on classroom quizzes, accumulated points for work completed, and improvement from year to year on standardized tests, are often used to gauge progress within a classroom. Although these are convenient end products of individual student progress, their disadvantage for determining a teacher's effectiveness is that many factors other than the instruction being provided can contribute to them—student motivation, aptitude, past achievement, learning readiness, and home life, to name only a few. Also, since end products often result from many different instructional activities over an extended period of time, they rarely point explicitly to what should be changed to improve the quality of the outcome, and therefore provide little corrective value for changing teacher behavior.

Without clear signs of what to look for to evaluate their teaching, and without the time to consider and reflect on classroom events, many teachers fail to adequately consider their teaching behavior. Thus, focused observation activities and accompanying observation tools are needed to help you develop professional "lenses" for observing others, as well as for assessing your own development as a teacher. A detailed presentation of these professional lenses and tools for observation can be found in *Observation Skills for Effective Teaching,* 4th edition (Borich, 2003). Below we will present a brief introduction and synthesis of them.

As you learn to observe through these lenses, you will want to work toward four major goals: (1) to become aware of your own teaching behavior; (2) to discover alternative instructional practices and new solutions to instructional problems; (3) to learn your personal teaching strengths; and (4) to focus your reflections on important areas of teacher growth and effectiveness. Let's look at each of these goals for classroom observation.

To Become Aware of Your Own Behavior

Although teachers make many decisions each day about the instructional process (how to capture student attention, who they will call on, how they will structure the content, how to summarize the lesson, how misbehavior will be handled, what seatwork to assign, etc.), they sometimes make these decisions unconsciously in the course of meeting the demands of the classroom. They may become bound by routine, failing to recognize how easily decisions can be altered. Instead of being pulled along unconsciously by the stream of rapidly paced events in the classroom, teachers can and should be active decision makers who influence the quality and nature of events in the classroom. They should actively question their own assumptions, and seek input from parents and others on a regular basis (Compton-Lilly, 2000). As you observe in classrooms, you will become aware that the stream of events is not the same in every classroom, and that sometimes teachers make decisions simply out of habit. If your observations lead to questions such as "Should I be doing that?", "Could that work in my classroom?", or "Would I have done that?", your observations are beginning to make you more aware of your own teaching. That awareness can help you discover some of your own unconscious decisions and unchecked assumptions. Even after you complete your university preparation, taking the opportunity to observe others will help remind you of your own behaviors—and how they may appear to others.

To Discover Alternative Instructional Practices and New Solutions to Instructional Problems

Another goal for focused observation is to seek information and example behavior related to a specific area of interest. While each of us has experienced a number of instructional methods and practices as a student, there are many we did not experience—or that we experienced in a limited context. As you enter the teaching profession, it is natural to wonder about new instructional practices, methods, and strategies, and whether new and different educational ideas will help you become a more effective teacher. As you read textbooks, observe other teachers, and practice teach, you'll develop questions about the "how-to's" of teaching. Whether the basis of your curiosity stems from wondering about your own experiences as a student, from wanting to see some textbook procedure come alive in the classroom, or from having experienced a seemingly intractable problem in your own teaching, observation of other classrooms is often a practical solution for discovering and applying new ideas. For example, as you watch a teacher lead a class discussion, you may wonder how a teacher can successfully blend fact- and concept-type questions in the midst of the same discussion. Or you may encounter a problem with misbehavior in your own classroom and want to learn more about the variety of rules used by other teachers for keeping students from calling out without being acknowledged. Focused observations can be among the most rewarding, because they occur in response to an immediate need that has some sense of urgency for your thinking—and later, for your teaching.

To Determine Your Personal Teaching Strengths

Aside from helping you find solutions to instructional problems, focused observation helps put your personal teaching strengths in perspective. Teachers do not always see that a decision they have made, either consciously or unconsciously, could solve an instructional problem of another teacher. This may be due to the fact that many teachers rarely observe others and do not have sufficient opportunities to describe to others the positive achievements in their own classrooms. As you observe, you will discover areas where *your* knowledge and experience provide insights that can help other teachers address a particular challenge. Taking the opportunity to share insights about successes and challenges builds a healthy sense of competence and shared professionalism. This benefit alone is why so many career-ladder and professional development programs require peer observation.

To Focus Your Reflections on Important Areas of Teacher Effectiveness

Handbooks and reviews of classroom research, such as those by Banks and Banks (2001), Brophy (2002), and Richardson (2001) summarize the results of more than twenty-five years of research in classrooms. In these and related texts (Borich, 2004; 2003; Borich & Tombari, 2004, 1997; Cantrell, 1998/1999; Taylor, Pearson, Clark, & Walpole, 1999), the processes used by teachers to instruct students (for example, activity structures, questioning strategies, methods of organizing content) are related to student outcomes (such as engagement in the learning process and performance on classroom and standardized tests). This research has identified effective teaching behaviors related to: (a) the learning climate of a classroom; (b) classroom management; (c) lesson clarity; (d) instructional variety; (e) teacher's task orientation; (f) students' engagement in the learning process; (g) students' success; and (h) students' higher thought processes and performance outcomes.

PART III: APPLICATIONS

LENSES FOR VIEWING CLASSROOM BEHAVIOR

Because classrooms are busy and complex, observers often choose a particular professional frame-or lens-to gain insight regarding a particular aspect of classroom life. Over time, observations are completed using different lenses, resulting in a more comprehensive and detailed understanding of teaching and learning. While the lenses we will use are not the only ones that could guide observation in classrooms, each has been researched and has been found to influence the performance of learners. Other lenses for viewing classroom behavior are also available, and new lenses will undoubtedly emerge from classroom research in the future. For our purposes, the following lenses will serve as an introduction to acquiring classroom observation skills and beginning to teach effectively.

Area 1: Consider the Learning Climate

The **learning climate** of a classroom refers to its physical and emotional environment. Some observable features of the learning environment are (a) the warmth, concerns, and expectations conveyed to students by the teacher; (b) the organization of the physical aspects of the classroom, which promotes or precludes cohesion and interaction among students; and (c) the competitiveness, cooperation, or independence encouraged by the structure of activity within the classroom.

As you observe the learning climate of a classroom, you will want to note how students feel about themselves, about one another, and about their classroom, and the activities and materials that promote feelings most conducive to learning.

Area 2: Focus on Classroom Management

Classroom management involves how teachers organize the classroom and anticipate and respond to student behavior to provide an environment for efficient learning. Some observable features of classroom management are organizing the physical aspects of the classroom to match instructional goals; preestablishing and communicating classroom rules; developing and communicating instructional routines; establishing a system of incentives and consequences; and using techniques for low-profile classroom management. Because many beginning teachers find effective classroom management challenging, you'll want to pay close attention to how effective teachers orchestrate and facilitate learning with their classroom management skills.

Area 3: Look for Lesson Clarity

Lesson clarity refers to a teacher's ability to speak clearly and directly, and to organize and structure content at the students' current level of understanding. Some observable features of lesson clarity are informing learners of expected skills and understandings before a lesson; providing advance organizers that place the lesson content in the perspective of past and future learning; reviewing and summarizing; and using examples, illustrations, demonstrations and instructional media that can expand and clarify lesson content.

Area 4: Verify Variety

As you recall from your own experiences as a student, **instructional variety**, using different modes of learning (visual, oral, and tactile) maintains interest and attention. Effective teachers select an appropriate mix of instructional approaches to support particular learning objectives. Some observable features of instructional variety are the use of attention-gaining devices; variation in eye contact, voice, and gestures; use of alternate modes through which learning is to occur (seeing, listening, and doing); and using appropriate rewards and reinforcers to sustain student interest and engagement.

Area 5: Observe Task Orientation

Task orientation involves effective teaching practices that help the teacher maintain an instructional focus. It includes managing classroom activities efficiently; handling misbehavior with minimum disruption to the class; reducing instructional time devoted to clerical duties; and maximizing time devoted to content coverage. Some of the most observable features of task orientation are lesson plans that reflect the text and curriculum guide, use of rules and procedures that anticipate and thereby reduce misbehavior, and established milestones (for example, tests, reviews, and assignments) for maintaining instructional momentum.

Area 6: Examine Engagement

Students learn best when they become actively engaged in the learning process. Teachers promote **student engagement** by providing exercises, problem sets, and activities that allow students to think about, act on, and practice what they learn. Some observable features of teachers facilitating student engagement in the learning process are the provision of activities for guided practice; the use of feedback and correctives; the use of individualized and self-directed learning activities; the systematic use of meaningful verbal praise; and checking and monitoring of classroom assignments during seatwork.

Area 7: Measure Student Success

Students' learning is enhanced when they complete work at moderate to high levels of success. Some of the most observable features of teaching that promote **student success** are unit and lesson organization that reflects prior learning; immediate feedback and corrections; gradual transitions to new content; and a classroom pace and momentum that builds toward major milestones (for example, reviews, projects, practice exercises, and tests).

Area 8: Look for Higher Thought Processes and Performance Outcomes

Higher thought processes include decision-making, problem-solving, critical thinking, and valuing behaviors that alone cannot be measured by standardized tests of cognitive achievement. Some observable features of teaching for higher thought processes are using collaborative and group activities; demonstrating mental models and strategies for learning; arranging for student projects and demonstrations; engaging students in oral performance; providing opportunities for independent practice; and using performance assessments and student portfolios.

Although you will want to observe classrooms with specific questions or goals, your first few observations may be more general so that you can get a feel for particular grade levels or schools. These eight professional lenses can be used to help you consider the overall picture of a classroom. To see how all eight lenses can work together to inform your observation and suggest specific questions for further study, let's visit a fictional classroom taught by Ms. Koker. Before we begin, look over the eight professional lenses for focused observation below. Then, when you are finished reading about the events in Ms. Koker's classroom, complete the *General Observation Form* below to rate her classroom on each of our eight professional lenses.

General Observation Form

Instructions: On the blank for each lens place a check mark, closest to the word that best describes the classroom you are observing.

Learning Climate

Teacher Centered __ __ __ __ __ __ __ Student Centered

Classroom Management

Orderly __   __   __   __   __   __   __ Disorderly

Lesson Clarity

Clear __   __   __   __   __   __   __ Unclear

Instructional Variety

Varied __   __   __   __   __   __   __ Static

Teacher's Task Orientation

Focused __   __   __   __   __   __   __ Unfocused

	Students' Engagement in the Learning Process
	Students Students Involved __ __ __ __ __ __ __Uninvolved
	Students' Success in Basic Academic Skills High __ __ __ __ __ __ __ Low
	Higher Thought Processes & Performance Outcomes Many __ __ __ __ __ __ __ Few

Source: From Borich, G. (2003). *Observation Skills for Effective Teaching,* 4th edition.
Upper Saddle River, NJ: Merrill/Prentice Hall. Reprinted with permission.

A CLASSROOM DIALOGUE

The scene is a middle school social studies classroom. Ms. Koker is
beginning a unit on forms of government. It is early in the school year, so
the class is still new to her. The first several weeks of school were a bit
rough for Ms. Koker because she was somewhat unprepared for the
aggressive talking-out behavior of some of the students, and because of the
new textbook, which devotes less time to some of her favorite topics.
Things have calmed down somewhat now that Ms. Koker has established
some classroom rules and has decided to organize her lessons more tightly
with questions and recitation. Ms. Koker's goals for this lesson are to
introduce three types of government, and then begin to develop the
concept of democracy. Aside from a tendency to be loud and talkative, this
class is composed of mostly average-performing students, with a few who
are high-performing and a few who regularly challenge her authority.

Ms. Koker: Today we begin a unit on various forms of government. In
the next few days, we will study the concepts of monarchy, oligarchy, and
democracy, and how governments are formed using each of these three
concepts. In fact, we will cover these three forms of government so
thoroughly that at the end of the week, each of you will know how to

create a government of your own using each—but, please, don't start any revolutions with what you learn! [Class laughs.] Let's start by defining what a monarchy is. Does anybody know? [At this point, some class members turn to their neighbors to ask if they know the answer.]

Ms. Koker: Please, no talking. Bobby, do you know what a monarchy is?

Bobby: No.

Ms. Koker: Christina, do you have any idea?

Christina: No, I'm afraid I don't, Ms. Koker.

Ms. Koker: Tim, you're not in your seat, so I'll have to ask you. Do you know what a monarchy is?

Tim: Yep, it's a butterfly. [Class bursts out in laughter.]

Ms. Koker: That's an extra assignment for you tonight. Okay, I'll tell you. A monarchy is a government that is ruled or governed by a single person. It's a form of government in which a single person, a king or queen for example, is the supreme head of a state for his or her entire lifetime. Now, what other names besides "King" or "Queen" do we have for individuals who serve as head of a country for a lifetime? Let's go from left to right across the first row.

Mary: I'm not sure what you mean, Ms. Koker.

Ms. Koker: Next. Felipe?

Felipe : You mean, what do we call someone who is just like a king, but called something else?

Ms. Koker: You're on the right track. Next. Anna?

Anna: Well, I would call a king an emperor.

Tim: [Talking out] Yeah, like in "The Emperor's New Clothes!" [Class laughs.]

Ms. Koker: Okay, that's the second time you've spoken out of turn, Tim. You will answer two extra homework questions tonight if you don't want me to write up a detention slip. Now, go up and write your name on the board, so I won't forget to give you the assignment. [By now, talking has grown louder and a few students have left their seats waiting for Tim to return from the board.] Let's see now, where were we?

Student: [From somewhere in back of room] We were talking about emperors.

Ms. Koker: Yes, emperors, like kings, usually indicate a monarchy—or rule by a single person over a long time. Other names for heads of state that indicate a monarchy are *czar*, which was a title once used in Russia; *kaiser*, which was a term used in the early German empire; and *sultan*, which is a word still used today in the Middle East. These individuals, like kings and emperors throughout history, have often had absolute power over the people and lands they ruled. Traditionally, these rulers gained their power from the family they were born into, and not from any accomplishments of their own. In some cases today, a type of monarchy exists alongside some other form of government. Can anyone think of a country like our own that has a king or a queen? Let's go across the second row this time. Rashaun?

Rashaun: England. They have a queen and royal weddings and that kind of stuff that we don't have in this country.

Ms. Koker: Good, Rashaun. Some present-day monarchs, like the Queen of England, still exist. However, in England the queen possesses only minor authority and exists for mostly symbolic purposes, or as a way of showing the country's historical roots. Although kings and queens did at one time have absolute authority over England, today they serve mostly ceremonial functions. That was a good response, Rashaun. Now, before we move to another form of government, called an oligarchy, does everyone understand what a monarchy is? [No one responds.]

Ms. Koker: Okay, I guess we can go on. Let's see, where did we leave off in the second row? [Tricia meekly raises her hand.] Can you tell us what an oligarchy is, Tricia?

Tricia: I don't know.

Ms. Koker: Next. Raul?

Raul: Don't know.

Ms. Koker: Well, I guess I'll have to tell you—but it's in the chapter, which you should have read. An oligarchy is a form of government in which absolute power or authority is given to a few persons, instead of a single ruler as in a monarchy. These individuals usually come to power not through heredity or being born into the right families, but through some political struggle or compromise. Oligarchies, which were common in ancient times, are hard to find today, but some governments almost like an oligarchy still exist. Can anyone think of one? Jeff, Kathy, you're the last two in the second row. Any ideas?

Jeff : I'm not sure, but is it like a mother and father in a family?

Ms. Koker: What do you mean?

Jeff : Well, my parents have a kind of agreement—not written or anything like that—in which my mother is responsible for taking care of the house and my brothers and sisters, and my father is responsible for his job and doing repairs. That's a kind of sharing of responsibility, isn't it?

Ms. Koker: Yes, maybe. But it's not what we're talking about here. Kathy?

Kathy: I can't think of any examples.

Ms. Koker: Well, ancient Greece was ruled for a brief time by a group of persons called the Thirty Tyrants. This may have been the very first oligarchy. Also, we've been hearing a lot lately about a country called Yugoslavia. In that country power and authority used to be divided among individuals representing each of the states or regions. Now, let's compare the two forms of government we've been discussing—monarchy and oligarchy—with our own form of government. First, let's remind ourselves of what our form of government is called. Let's pick up with the first person in the third row. Quann?

Quann: I'm not ready.

Ms. Koker: Everyone should be ready when I call on them.

Quann: Well, I didn't get to read this yet. [Class begins to snicker at Quann getting in trouble.]

Ms. Koker: Okay, I'm going to make the rule that everyone must read the whole assignment before we begin a topic. That means that the reading for the entire week must be done by class on Monday. [Loud moans are heard.]

Tim: [Speaking without acknowledgment] But that means we'd have homework over the weekend, and no other teacher makes us do that.

Ms. Koker: [Ignoring Tim's comment] We still have one more form of government to discuss. Joan is next. [Class becomes noisy and restless at the thought of weekend homework.]

Joan: We live in a democracy.

Ms. Koker: What else can you tell us about a democracy?

Joan: Well . . . [Just as she is about to begin, the public address system clicks on.]

Principal: [On P.A.] I'm sorry to interrupt, but two lunchtime jobs are still available for any students who want to be paid for working in the cafeteria during the second half of their lunch. We need some workers for today, so, teachers, if anyone is interested, please write them a hall permit and send them to the office immediately. Thank you. [Roberto and Tim raise their hands, indicating their interest in the job. The teacher ignores Tim and writes a pass to the office for Roberto.]

Ms. Koker: Okay, we were discussing democracy. Time is short, so take out paper and pen and write down everything I say. Another rule we will start tomorrow, since you're not doing the reading, is to take notes on everything I say. The word *democracy* comes from the Greek word *demos*, which means "the people," and the Greek word *kratein*, spelled K-R-A-T-E-I-N, which means "to rule."

Brittany: [Calling out] How is that first word spelled?

Ms. Koker: [Responds by spelling the word.] D-E-M-O-S. So, who's next to be called on? [Rhonda raises her hand.] Okay. Rhonda, putting these two words together, what does the word *democracy* mean?

Rhonda: It means that the people rule.

Ms. Koker: Good. And who are the people in a democracy? Sam?

Sam I guess it's all of us—everyone that lives in a certain place.

Ms. Koker: Okay, a democracy differs from a monarchy and an oligarchy by who is given the authority to rule. As we have seen, in a monarchy, a single person, usually chosen through heredity, is given absolute authority, and in the case of an oligarchy, a small number of persons, representing only a fraction of all the people in the land, are given the authority to rule. In a democracy authority to rule rests in the hands of all the people. But how could such a system work when everyone has authority over everyone else? Next person. Diana?

Diana: We—or I should say all the people—elect persons to represent us. I guess that's what our senators and representatives do.

Ms. Koker: So when we say that all the people have the authority to rule in a democracy, we really mean . . . Next. That's you, Phil.

Phil: We elect persons—like Diana said—representatives and senators, and we give them the authority to rule.

Ms. Koker: Yes. So in a democracy like ours, the people have authority, but indirectly, through the election of individuals that represent their interests. In our form of democracy, called *representative democracy*, a legislature composed of senators and representatives is elected by the people. Does anyone know of any other kind of democracy? Mark, you're next.

Mark: Nope.

Ms. Koker: Did you take notes on the chapter?

Mark: I was going to do that tonight.

Ms. Koker: I will begin checking notes at the end of every class. Since some of you haven't read the assignment, we'll use the remaining time to read Chapter 7.

Reactions From Observing Ms. Koker's Classroom

Although this dialogue may not have been fair to Ms. Koker's everyday teaching, classroom exchanges such as this occur at almost all levels of schooling. They are, to be sure, uneven, rough, and sometimes even crude attempts to convey information in the midst of all sorts of competing forces—misbehaving and unprepared students, interruptions, quickly sketched lesson plans, and insufficient instructional time, to name only a few. The flow of events in a classroom, as shown in the dialogue, is not always a neatly packaged, smooth unit of instruction. Instead, teachers and students often struggle, sometimes with themselves and sometimes with each other, to complete the day's lesson. Although Ms. Koker's classroom may have had some problems, these problems are not uncommon for any teacher at one time or another.

Think back for a moment on the dialogue you have just read. In your opinion, was it an example of effective teaching or ineffective teaching, or did it contain some examples of each? What are your impressions of Ms. Koker as a person and as a teacher? What about her knowledge and use of instructional methods? Did she do the right things most of the time, even though not all the students conveniently cooperated, or did some of her decisions make it less likely that the goals of the lesson would be achieved? Do you believe the goals for this lesson, as stated before the dialogue, were met? If not, whose fault was it—Ms. Koker's, for not motivating the students; the students', for not reading the assignment; Tim's, for misbehaving; or the principal's, for creating a distraction at a crucial time?

Of course, all of these factors and others were instrumental in the way life in this classroom unfolded. But if we were to attempt to fully understand life in this classroom, each of the questions we asked ourselves would point us in equally narrow, and perhaps even biased, directions. A broader set of lenses than individual questions or idiosyncratic concerns that happen to gain our attention would be necessary to view classroom life. As you consider the interactions in Ms. Koker's classroom, look over the *General Observation Form* and complete your rating for each of our eight professional lenses for focused observation.

In what areas did you notice positive interactions? In what areas do you feel concern? Did seeing the observation form earlier help you "observe" Ms. Koker and her students more effectively?

The eight areas of effective teaching can help us achieve the breadth of vision we need to understand the events in Ms. Koker's classroom. Let's use each of these "professional frames" as a lens to achieve a more focused observation of life in Ms. Koker's classroom. After viewing the events through each of these lenses, we will bring all our data together to form some general impressions of the strengths and weaknesses of Ms. Koker's presentation. As you read the following discussion, add any notes to your *General Observation Form* that may help you remember key points about each of the eight lenses.

Consider the Learning Climate

Recall that the learning climate of a classroom involves the social and emotional environment in which learning takes place. Some of the most noticeable features of a learning climate are the warmth, concerns, and expectations conveyed to students by the teacher; the organization of the physical aspects of the classroom that promote or preclude cohesion and interaction among students; and the competitiveness, cooperation, or independence encouraged by the teacher's instructional routine. Using these aspects of the learning environment as our lens, let's look back at the dialogue to see how the learning climate may have influenced the achievement of Ms. Koker's goals for the lesson.

In many ways, the learning climate in Ms. Koker's classroom appears tense. On one hand, Ms. Koker seems genuinely committed to having students contribute their ideas to the development of the concepts she is teaching. But, on the other hand, few students seem to feel free or relaxed enough to share anything but the most obvious answers. As a result, very little genuine discussion takes place.

The manner in which Ms. Koker responds to students may also have increased the tension in the classroom. Rarely is an answer followed by another question to the same student. In the case of an inaccurate answer or no answer, the teacher quickly moves to the next student instead of staying with the student to correct a partially wrong answer, or drawing out a partially correct response that another student might build on. Even when opportunities present themselves to stay with a student and develop his or her response further, such as when Jeff equates the sharing of responsibilities among members of an oligarchy with the sharing of responsibilities between his mother and father, the teacher responds with a curt "But it's not what we're talking about here." These moves on the part of Ms. Koker enhance the competitive nature of this classroom by treating each individual student response as either all right or all wrong, thereby missing the opportunity to connect the discussion to the students' own experiences.

Another aspect of the tense learning climate results from Ms. Koker's desire to keep firm control of the events occurring in her classroom. Ms. Koker decided on a carefully controlled row-by-row recitation of answers instead of an open discussion. Perhaps in an effort to enhance classroom management, she restricts any interaction that is not a direct response to her questions. Consequently, she restricts the very type of response that her discussion-oriented agenda seems to call for. Without realizing it, Ms. Koker sets up a learning climate of opposing forces. The students resist being drawn into the discussion to avoid saying anything unacceptable; the teacher asks for student participation but responds with mostly unrewarding answers. Had the atmosphere of the classroom been less rigid, this class might have been more conducive to the cooperative interchanges being sought by the teacher. Now let's get a feel for some of the other lenses through which life in Ms. Koker's classroom can be observed.

Focus on Classroom Management

What did you notice about Ms. Koker's classroom management style? Did it appear to be more of a reaction to student behavior than a well-organized system of rules and procedures thought out in advance? At several points in the lesson, Ms. Koker seems to make up rules on the spot. Although sometimes necessary, this practice is risky. It can convey to students a sense of arbitrariness about the rule itself, making it seem less credible, and therefore less likely to be obeyed. Apparently, Ms. Koker failed to convey some basic rules earlier in the school year (for example, when to complete assigned reading and take notes). Without a well-organized system of rules and class procedures, Ms. Koker may continue to react defensively, at first tolerating a wide range of behavior, and later using valuable class time pulling back to respond to behaviors she didn't foresee.

Ms. Koker's classroom also exhibits problems with conduct. Talking out, for which presumably a rule was communicated earlier, seems to be a persistent problem. This comes as no surprise, because Ms. Koker's response to talking out, even in this short episode, was inconsistent. Notice that Ms. Koker is adamant at first about not speaking out. After reminding the class at the beginning of the lesson, "Please, no talking out," and reprimanding Tim for talking out, she accepts without reprimand a call out from an anonymous student. After which she switches unexpectedly to a nondirective style ("Let's see now, where were we?") more suited to an informal discussion session than the row-by-row recitation format she had pursued from the beginning of the lesson.

Did you also notice the amount of class time and resulting problems created by Ms. Koker's response to Tim's misbehavior? Although Tim's misbehavior might have been unpredictable, Ms. Koker's response to it may have created an even bigger problem. First, she responds by assigning extra homework, thereby equating homework with punishment. Second, during the time it took for Tim to leave his seat, go to the board to write his name, and return, the rest of the class waited without direction. The momentum, or pace, which previously kept the class moving forward and focused on the lesson, was lost. These momentary lapses, whether due to interruptions from misbehaving students, public address announcements, or visitors at the door, require special classroom management procedures to keep students engaged in the learning process. Ms. Koker's use of instructional time for discipline might have been avoided had she established and consistently reinforced an organized system of classroom rules and procedures from the start of the school year.

Looking for Lesson Clarity

Lesson clarity involves communicating clearly and directly, and presenting content at the students' current level of understanding. Clarity involves not only the visual and oral clarity of a teacher's delivery, but also the proper organization and structuring of the material to be taught. For example, to organize and structure the material to be taught, the teacher must know how much knowledge the students already have about the day's lesson. Notice that Ms. Koker begins the lesson by saying, "Let's start by defining what a monarchy is. Does anybody know?" The responses she receives, however, are not too encouraging. The first two students called on say no, after which Ms. Koker says, "I guess I'll have to tell you then" This beginning involves two aspects of clarity: checking for relevant prior knowledge, and summarizing or reviewing when it is discovered that the students do not have the knowledge necessary to understand the day's lesson. Had Ms. Koker not discovered early in the lesson that students had little or no knowledge of the day's topic, she might have gone on to more advanced concepts, never realizing her students did not have a basis for understanding the material she was presenting. As it was, most of the lesson seemed to cover the basics of what the students should have already learned from reading the text. Phrases such as "Okay, I'll tell you" and "It's in the chapter" are clues that not all of the class may have read the assignment, leading Ms. Koker to make explicit a rule that, in the future, all assigned reading be completed before a topic is discussed in class.

Some other aspects of clarity involve informing the students of the skills or understanding expected at the end of the lesson, and organizing the content for future lessons. Recall that, to some extent, Ms. Koker's opening remark reflects both these aspects of clarity. The students are informed of the three forms of government to be covered, and are told that they are expected to know how to form the three types of government at the end of the unit. Both of these ingredients of the day's lesson worked to make Ms. Koker's lesson more understandable.

Verifying Instructional Variety

Another lens through which to observe Ms. Koker's classroom is instructional variety. Instructional variety includes the varied use of rewards, reinforcements, and types of questions asked (for example, recall vs. application), as well as the teacher's use of instructional media to enhance student attention and engagement with the lesson. It also involves the flexibility of the teacher to change strategies or shift directions when needed. Variety can be enhanced by a teacher's animation (through variation in eye contact, voice, and gestures), as well as through the use of different instructional strategies and media within the same lesson. We did not see Ms. Koker teaching, but from what we read, there seems to have been little variety to her lesson. She persists with her questioning technique, even though she seems to have little success with it, until finally, out of necessity, she assumes a more direct lecture approach at the end of the lesson. Also, her questions call only for basic facts and definitions: "What is a monarchy?" and "Can you tell us what an oligarchy is?" instead of "What are its advantages and disadvantages?", "How is it formed?'', or "What lessons can we learn from these three forms of government for governing ourselves?" Focusing only on factual recall may fail to engage some students in the learning process.

Instructional variety is also achieved by choosing specific activity structures to convey lesson content. The term **activity structure** refers both to how the students are organized for learning and how the lesson is organized. Both categories of structure appear in Ms. Koker's classroom. For example, we note that Ms. Koker chooses to organize her instruction around student recitation in an almost drill-and-practice format. We noted previously the possible mismatch between such a format and what appears to be the discussion-oriented goal of her lesson. At that time, we suspected that this structure was selected more as a way to manage classroom talk than as an effective vehicle for achieving the goals of the lesson. The choice of a recitation format led Ms. Koker to call on students one by one in a predesignated order, as might be done if students were giving their answers orally to questions from a workbook. The results were factual responses that avoided any risk on the part of the students, rather than the type of responses that could result in more complex or integrated learning.

Observing the Teacher's Task Orientation

Teacher's task orientation is the percentage of time allocated to a lesson in which the teacher is actually teaching material related to the topic. In the dialogue, attention to the misbehavior of individual students, time spent introducing new rules about conduct and academic work, and interruption from the school administrator all took their toll on the time that could have been devoted to instruction. As a result of these interruptions, the time Ms. Koker actually spent teaching the content was limited. When teachers inefficiently handle misbehavior or spend large amounts of class time doing clerical chores (for example, passing out papers, stapling and collating, reprimanding misbehaving students) which may be done more efficiently in other ways or at other times, instructional time may be only a small percentage of the total amount of time allocated to the lesson. Although we have no way of knowing the exact amount of time Ms. Koker's instruction was interrupted by noninstructional demands, a simple count of the total number of lines of dialogue minus the number of lines containing dialogue *unrelated* to the goals of the lesson reveals that about 34 percent of Ms. Koker's teaching was off-task. If this continued throughout the school day, more than 18 minutes of every hour would be devoted to noninstructional events.

Noninstructional events that compete for instructional time include formulating classroom rules, giving directives, administering reprimands, dealing with interruptions, creating orderly transitions between subjects or activities, and engaging in activities that structure the learning environment. The amount of time actually devoted to instruction often depends on how efficiently noninstructional activities are managed. Poor classroom management can detract from time spent on instructional tasks, decreasing students' engagement in the learning process and, predictably, interfering with success in completing assignments correctly. Although we saw only a brief view of Ms. Koker's classroom, she made some important decisions about classroom rules, the use of reinforcement, and the handling of misbehavior that affected the amount of time devoted to instruction during this lesson.

Examining Students' Engagement in the Learning Process

A sixth lens through which to observe a lesson is student engagement in the learning process. Like the task orientation of a teacher, this behavior is often measured as a percentage of time. Student engagement in the learning process pertains to the percentage of time the teacher presents instructionally relevant content (is task oriented) *and* the students are acting on, thinking about, or otherwise using the content being taught. In contrast to a teacher's task orientation, a student's engagement in the learning process may be much more difficult to determine. A student may look attentive or appear to be working through the workbook, but her thoughts may be miles away. In the example, part of the time Ms. Koker was teaching, at least some of her students were not engaged in the learning process.

By relying on individual recitation, Ms. Koker does little to involve students in the lesson. Aside from her questions and a few attempts to reward a correct answer with praise, Ms. Koker seems to encourage only a passive or mechanical involvement in the lesson. Absent from Ms. Koker's lesson is a broad range of questions that might excite the imagination of students and encourage them to keep trying after a wrong answer or no answer. Perhaps most relevant to the apparent disengagement of some of the students was Ms. Koker's drill-and-practice style, which requires students to respond in order across rows. This ordered-turns approach is often recommended for content in which many discrete pieces of knowledge with clearly defined right and wrong answers is being recalled. But Ms. Koker's content seems concept-oriented. After a time, students in the back half of the room could pretty much guarantee that they would not get called on during the class, providing even more opportunity for these students to disengage from the learning process. This, together with Ms. Koker's sometimes critical responses to a wrong answer or no answer, may have provided a reason for those who had already responded to turn their attention elsewhere. If more complicated and time-consuming responses were being sought, it may have been better for Ms. Koker to call on students who volunteered and who, therefore, may have provided answers around which she could have built lesson content. Ms. Koker could also have implemented any of a number of cooperative group activities to encourage greater student participation.

Measuring Student Success

What signs of student success did you see in Ms. Koker's classroom? Student success pertains to the percentage of correct responses given to classroom questions, class exercises, and workbook assignments. When an expository or didactic approach (which seems to fit Ms. Koker's recitation format) to learning is used, the percentage of student success after the first time through the material should be about 60 to 80 percent to encourage further response and engagement in the learning process. When the success rate is, on the average, less than 60 percent, it may indicate that the lesson content is too difficult or that the exercises are inappropriate for the material being taught. Ultimately, homework and further assignments should work toward creating an average success rate of 90 percent or higher.

Ms. Koker's students seemed reluctant to participate, avoiding, rather than engaging in, the lesson. Students found it safer to say "I don't know" than to risk a wrong or partially wrong response and be criticized for it. Ms. Koker seemed to accept only a narrow definition of correct responses. As a result, the success of her students in answering questions was not very high. Most students avoided answering altogether, and others failed to provide the correct answer. These two student behaviors tell us a lot about Ms. Koker's classroom. Failure to actively involve students in the lesson and present instruction that most students can respond to correctly are indications that the level of the lesson may not have been properly matched to the students' current level of understanding.

As was the case with student engagement, there are certain teacher activities that encourage a moderate to high success rate. These include providing correctives immediately following a wrong or partially right answer, dividing lesson content into small segments at the learner's current level of understanding, planning transitions to new content in small, easy-to-grasp steps, and continually relating the parts of the lesson to larger objectives and goals. Seatwork assigned prior to the day's lesson is one way to check student success rate. If a low success rate is confirmed, Ms. Koker could provide more practice opportunities or cooperative learning activities to actively engage students in the learning process before embarking on the next lesson.

Looking for Higher Thought Processes and Performance Outcomes

The final lens through which to observe Ms. Koker's classroom takes the previous lens, student success, to a higher level. For this lens our focus turns from the recitation of correct responses to higher thought processes, which arise out of teaching and learning activities that promote critical thinking, reasoning, and problem solving. These processes cannot be measured by tests of cognitive achievement alone. The higher thought processes required for analyzing, synthesizing, and decision making in adult contexts are stimulated by interacting with peers and adults and by increasing awareness of one's own learning.

By requiring oral responses, Ms. Koker encourages students to exhibit higher thought processes. But, Ms. Koker fails to follow up on her students' responses and lift them to a higher level. Recall that most of her responses were short and noncorrective, often moving to another student if the response was right, or failing to probe more deeply with another question if the response was incorrect. Ms. Koker saw each answer as either correct or incorrect—not as an opportunity to make a wrong answer right or a good answer better. This left her students responding at the lowest level of behavioral complexity, even though her lesson seemed, at times, aimed at acquiring concepts, patterns of thinking, and judgments.

In other words, Ms. Koker's presentation lacks a plan for helping her students meaningfully learn the content. For example, alerting her students at the start of the lesson to look for some of the features that could distinguish a monarchy from an oligarchy from a democracy might have encouraged her students to analyze the differences between various forms of government, their purposes in history, and advantages or disadvantages in today's world. Although not every lesson need achieve these types of higher thought processes, teachers can and should capitalize on potential opportunities whenever possible.

Also, while student collaboration was not a lesson objective, students collaborating with one another or building on the responses of others could have created classroom interaction that engaged more students and improved student understanding of the concepts being presented. Ms. Koker could have shaped responses in small steps or allowed the thoughts and judgments of individual students to inform the group, so that larger concepts, patterns of thinking, and judgments could have accumulated gradually and cooperatively. By using student responses and collaborative learning activities to encourage problem-solving and judgment skills, routine recitation at the beginning of the class might have turned into higher thought processes by the end of the class.

If you thought our description of Ms. Koker's classroom seemed a bit unfair, you're probably right. A lot happened to Ms. Koker in less time than it generally takes to teach a single lesson. Although our picture of Ms. Koker was compressed for illustrative purposes, teachers at all levels of experience and training are confronted with, and must manage, similar events. Real teachers in real classrooms are never immune from these and similar problems, despite the extent of their training or years of experience.

As we conclude our discussion of Ms. Koker's class, it is important to note the interrelationship among all eight lenses through which we viewed these classroom events. Seldom is the behavior observed under one lens independent of that being observed under others. This reflects the interactive nature of life in classrooms. In other words, if we were to observe Ms. Koker's classroom with only one or even a few of our lenses, an incomplete and possibly distorted observation would result. This is especially obvious when we consider how the learning climate established by Ms. Koker, her classroom management techniques, and the presentation of content all work to influence student behavior. Remember, too, that Ms. Koker's behavior, classroom management style, and presentation were influenced by her students' behavior during the lesson. Thus, it would be futile to separate these interactive aspects of a classroom in real life. Your final goal as an experienced observer is to understand the overall patterns and rhythms of classrooms using all of our lenses.

PART IV: EXTENSIONS

Because systematic observation involves observing and then recording behavioral signs in a form that can be retrieved and studied at a later time, it usually involves a record, or instrument. The instruments used for recording classroom behavior can range from relatively unstructured (taking notes), to highly structured (involving explicit procedures for when and how long to observe specific behaviors). In this section we briefly summarize some of the most frequently used tools to systematically observe and record classroom observations arranged from least structured to most structured. These and other recording formats and observation instruments are described in greater detail and illustrated in *Observation Skills for Effective Teaching,* 4th edition (Borich, 2003).

NARRATIVE REPORTS

Narrative reports represent the least structured method of recording classroom observations. Narrative reports do not specify the exact behavioral signs to be observed, but instead simply describe events, in written form, as they occur. Little guidance is given to the observer about what to include or exclude from the observation. Thus, narrative reports are sometimes referred to as *open-ended,* meaning that considerable flexibility about what events to record is given to the observer. You may find it helpful to think of narrative reports as note-taking activities. While there are many ways to take notes, four methods are particularly helpful for classroom observations: anecdotal reports, ethnographic records, thematic notes, and visual maps.

Anecdotal Reports

An **anecdotal report** describes a critical or unusual incident that occurs in the classroom which may be related to an event of larger consequence. It takes the form of a written paragraph that describes what, how, when, and to whom the critical incident happened. Because of the special significance of separating fact from interpretation, anecdotal reports are divided into two distinct parts: (a) facts (for example: "John began reading and the teacher asked him to read louder, saying, 'speak up, or you'll never be good at public speaking'") and (b) an interpretation of the facts (for example: "The teacher's comment to John in front of the class may have reduced his confidence and discouraged others from volunteering").

Anecdotal reports are most useful when they occur over time. For example, after an observer makes an initial interpretation, she returns to the classroom at a later date (perhaps several times) to clarify that interpretation. The focus of later observations is to expand on the interpretation's usefulness and validity.

Ethnographic Records

Ethnographic records report events sequentially, as they occur, without selecting a specific focus or incident. Ethnographic records differ from anecdotal reports in that the observer records a continuous stream of events on a laptop computer, usually for the duration of an entire class period and occasionally longer, and records all the behavior occurring, not just selected incidents. For example:

8:30 Children have just been let into the classroom. Several boys are in the corner fighting and some girls are sitting on the floor playing a puzzle. Teacher and teacher aide are in the back of the room talking.

8:35 Teacher says, "Blue group, get your folders and go up to the front. Green group, come here."

8:38 Noise level drops and children begin to follow directions, etc.

As with anecdotal reports, it is important that the observer record only what is observed, and avoid judgments or interpretations unless they are clearly divided from the factual portion of the record.

Thematic Notes

Thematic notes are facts recorded in traditional outline form, according to predesignated categories of observation. Much like the detective at the scene of a crime who jots down predetermined categories of facts, such as suspects, motives, times, and places, you can use thematic notes to jot down relevant data. Thematic notes can be recorded using Roman numerals (I, II, III, and so on), representing the major areas to be observed, and letters of the alphabet (A, B, C, and so on), representing the factual information observed under each of the more general areas. For example:

I.   Learning Climate
    A.   Teacher's exchanges with kids are mostly businesslike.
    B.   Atmosphere is competitive as workbooks are being checked.
    C.   Teacher evaluates student workbooks orally by using phrases such as: "read over what you've written," "check your work," "follow directions."

To prepare thematic notes, first determine the precise themes or areas on which to focus the observation, and then jot down key facts corresponding to these areas as the action unfolds.

Visual Maps

Visual maps use pictures instead of words to serve much the same purpose as narratives. Visual maps portray the spatial relationships among physical objects—learning centers, reference libraries, groups at work—that may be important to fully understanding anecdotal reports, ethnographic records, or thematic notes. When you observe events that are clearly related to the spatial layout of a classroom, you'll want to construct a visual map to help you (and others) better understand your narrative record. Often, a visual map can help show how a particular instructional activity was implemented, or cooperative activities were organized (for example, how cooperative groups are spaced in the classroom to allow communication between the groups).

RATING SCALES

Narrative reports allow the observer a great deal of flexibility in choosing which behaviors will be observed. On the other hand, rating scales are more structured and offer you the opportunity to record not only what behaviors you observe, but also the degree of the behavior that you note. In order to use a rating scale, you identify, in advance, the behaviors you want to observe. Rating scales can be used individually or in conjunction with other observation tools such as narrative reports. Two common types of rating scale formats are checklists and summated rating scales.

Checklists

The simplest type of rating scale is a **checklist**. Checklists consist of a list of the behaviors to be observed alongside response boxes labeled yes/no or present/absent. Your job as an observer is simply to note the presence or absence of a particular behavior during an observation and mark it on the scale. (For example: Teacher asked higher order questions: Yes ☐ No ☐.) Simple checklists of this sort are most useful when you are observing behaviors that are difficult to evaluate in degree, but that can be identified as either occurring or not occurring.

Summated Rating Scales

Summated ratings differ from checklists in that more than two degrees of discrimination are possible. Summated rating scales help you focus more closely on the degree of behavior because they typically describe a behavior at its extremes and at selected intermediate points. As you observe a behavior, you compare what you observe with the scale and choose the degree or number that best matches your observation. When items represent a common underlying theme, scores across individual scales are summed and averaged, hence the name *summated ratings*. The most common summated rating scales offer five or seven degrees of discrimination. For example: This classroom is:

Teacher centered ___ ___ ___ ___ ___ ___ ___ Student centered

You used a summated rating scale when you completed the *General Observation Form* to assess Ms. Koker's classroom.

CLASSROOM CODING SYSTEMS

Observation systems that help you record the *frequency* with which various teacher and student behaviors occur are called **classroom coding systems**. They are sometimes referred to as low-inference observation systems because they require fewer judgments or inferences on the part of the observer than summated ratings. Unlike the general concepts measured by rating scales, coding systems measure the frequency of specific and distinct units of behavior, such as "Teacher asks questions" or "Teacher used example," that can be tallied during relatively brief intervals of time. One of the most popular observation coding system is called a *counting* system. With a counting system, the observer counts the number of time intervals in which various teacher and/or student behaviors occur. A time interval (such as every five seconds), represents a frame for the observation that is established before the observation begins. Every time the interval or frame elapses, a tally is made to indicate which behavior on the instrument occurred during that interval.

FOR REFLECTION

1. Describe in your own words what a "professional frame" is and give several examples.

2. Of the eight goals for focused observation, what would be two toward which you would work the hardest?

3. Identify four characteristics of classrooms that make them unlike most other work environments.

4. Identify eight professional lenses for observing in classrooms. Describe the behavioral indices you would want to observe for two of them.

5. Using the *General Observation Form* used to observe Ms Koker, what were her strongest and weakest areas?

6. What is the purpose of a narrative report?

7. What are four methods for making a narrative report? Describe how you would record what you see for one of them.

8. How does a checklist differ from a summated rating scale?

9. How is a classroom coding system different from a checklist or summated rating scale?

10. With the help of *Observation Skills for Effective Teaching*, 4th edition, construct an example of a checklist, summated rating scale or classroom coding system for measuring one or more of the eight professional frames for focused observation.

GLOSSARY

activity structure This term refers both to how students are organized for learning and how the lessons are organized.

anecdotal report A form of narrative reporting that describes a critical or unusual incident that occurs in a classroom which may be related to an event of larger consequence.

checklists A list of the behaviors to be observed alongside a yes/no or present/absent response scale.

classroom coding systems Observation systems that record the frequency with which various teacher and student behaviors occur.

classroom management How teachers organize the classroom and anticipate and respond to student behavior to provide an environment for efficient learning.

ethnographic records A form of narrative reporting in which events are recorded sequentially, as they occur, without selecting a specific focus or incident.

higher thought processes Critical thinking, reasoning and problem solving behaviors that alone cannot be measured by formal tests of cognitive achievement.

instructional variety The teacher's use of different modes of learning (visual, oral, and tactile) to maintain interest and attention and promote learning.

Interstate New Teacher Assessment and Support Consortium (INTASC) NBPTS (see below) board compatible standards reviewed by professional organizations and state agencies as a basis for licensing beginning teachers.

learning climate The physical and emotional environment of the classroom indicating its degree of warmth, cohesion, interaction and cooperation.

lesson clarity The teacher's ability to speak clearly and directly to the class, and to organize and structure content at the students' current level of understanding.

National Board for Professional Teaching Standards (NBPTS)   A set of standards prepared mostly by and for teachers indicating what teachers should be able to do along with a voluntary system to certify teachers who meet these standards.

professional frame An objective viewpoint from which to evaluate and act on events critical to becoming an expert.

student engagement The teacher's ability to actively get students to think about, act on, and practice what they learn.

student success Student success pertains to the percentage of correct responses given to classroom questions, class exercises, and workbook assignments. When an expository or didactic approach to learning is used, the percentage of student success after the first time through the material should be about 60 to 80. Ultimately, homework and further assignments should work toward creating an average success rate of 90 percent or higher.

summated rating scales A type of scale in which the observer compares what is observed with what is on the scale and chooses the degree (number) that best matches the observation and then sums and takes the average of all the comparisons made, for example, as in five-point scales.

task orientation The teacher's use of practices that help maintain an instructional focus by managing classroom activities efficiently, handling misbehavior with a minimum disruption to the class and reducing instructional time devoted to clerical duties to provide students the maximum opportunity to learn.

thematic notes A form of narrative reporting in which facts are recorded in traditional outline form, according to predesignated categories of observation, much like a detective at the scene of a crime who jots down facts about suspects, motives, times and places.

visual maps A form of reporting in which pictures portray the spatial relationships among physical objects in a classroom, such as learning centers, reference libraries, groups at work.

REFERENCES

Borich, G. (2004). *Effective teaching methods,* (5th ed.). Upper Saddle River, NJ: Prentice-Hall/Merrill.

Borich, G. (2003). *Observation Skills for Effective Teaching,* (4th ed.), Upper Saddle River, NJ: Prentice-Hall/Merrill.

Borich, G. and Tombari, M. (2004). *Educational assessment for the elementary and middle school classroom,* (2nd ed.). Upper Saddle River, NJ: Prentice-Hall/Merrill.

Borich, G., & Tombari, M. (1997). *Educational psychology: A contemporary approach, 2nd edition.* New York: Addison-Wesley Longman.

Canning, C. (1991). What teachers say about reflection. *Educational Leadership, 48*(6), 69–87.

Cantrell, S. C. (1998/1999). Effective teaching and literacy learning: A look inside primary classrooms. *The Reading Teacher, 52*(4), 370–378.

Compton-Lilly, C. (2000). "Staying on Children": Challenging stereotypes about urban parents. *Language Arts, 77*(5), 420–427.

Emmer, E., Evertson, C., & Worsham, M. (2003). *Classroom management for secondary teachers* (3rd ed.). Englewood Cliffs, NJ: Prentice-Hall.

Interstate New Teacher Assessment and Support Consortium (INTASC) (1992). *Model standards for beginning teacher licensing and development: A resource for state dialogue.* Retrieved July 30, 2003 from http://www.ccsso.org/intascst.html

Richardson, V. (1997). Constructivist teaching and teacher education: Theory and practice. In V. Richardson (Ed.), *Constructivist teacher education: Building new understandings* (pp. 3–14). Washington, DC: Falmer Press.

Sanford, A. J., & Garrod, S. C. (1981). *Understanding written language.* New York: John Wiley & Sons.

Sternberg, R. (1995). *The nature of insight.* Cambridge, MA: MIT Press.

Taylor, B. M., Pearson, P. D., Clark, K. F., & Walpole, S. (1999). Effective schools/accomplished teachers. *The Reading Teacher, 53*(2), 156–159.

Walqui, A. (2000). Access and engagement: Program design and instructional approaches for immigrant students in secondary school [Monograph]. *Language in Education: Theory and Practice 94*(Topics in Immigrant Education 4). Washington, DC: Center for Applied Linguistics.